MW00856814

"*God and Soul Care* is a bold and courageous book. In it, Eric Johnson argues that Christian faith is fundamentally 'therapeutic' and that it provides tools that contribute to healing that secular counselors cannot make use of. Those tools require a deep and powerful understanding of Christian faith itself, rooted in the trinitarian understanding of God that God's revelation in Christ makes possible. Johnson recognizes the value of the knowledge gained by modern psychology and the helpful tools found there and in secular counseling as gifts given by God's common grace. However, he argues that these tools would be put to better use if they were used in the context of a distinctively Christian approach to human flourishing that differs radically from the worldviews implicit in much psychology and counseling. This is a book that will benefit both psychologists and theologians."

C. Stephen Evans, university professor of philosophy and humanities, Baylor University

"Eric L. Johnson is one of the most thoughtful and thorough Christian scholars of our day. In *God and Soul Care*, Dr. Johnson once again demonstrates the profound continuity between Christian doctrine and Christian approaches to counseling, pastoral care, and psychotherapy. Each chapter of this text explores both the complex nuances of the Christian faith and why these nuances matter for those who care for souls. This volume will have both immediate value for the training of Christian counselors and longstanding value as a reference source as those counselors move through their careers."

Mark R. McMinn, professor of psychology, George Fox University, author of *The Science of Virtue*

"Exercising meticulous analysis and demonstrating thoughtful synthesis of the book of God's work (the sciences) and the book of God's Word (the Bible) while drawing from his own breadth of exceptional scholarship, Johnson offers an impressive and much-needed contribution to the disciplines of Christian counseling and psychology. As a biblical counselor and licensed practitioner who daily enters in with those suffering from the complexities associated with severe psychological disturbance, enslaving sin, and spiritual confusion, I will consult this insightful volume often and for many years to come."

Jeremy Lelek, president, Association of Biblical Counselors

"Augustine's *Soliloquies* includes a dialogue between himself and his Reason, who asks him what he wants to know: "'I want to know God and the soul.'" "Nothing more?" "Nothing at all."' Eric Johnson wants to know how God heals the soul. This book is his answer. It's a work of radical Christian scholarship that lets theology into the driver's seat of psychology from the start. The result is a salutary theology that features the psychological health-giving implications of various Christian doctrines, united by a common trinitarian framework. This is the main course for which Johnson's Foundations for Soul Care was the appetizer. Christianity as theo-therapy: Augustine would no doubt be pleased."

Kevin J. Vanhoozer, research professor of systematic theology, Trinity Evangelical Divinity School

"In our good but fallen world, few of us escape the need for counseling at some point in our journey. Caught amid the unexpected, we hope for wise counsel that will help us find our way in and through the darkness. Alas, too often we are faced with the dilemma of simplistic Christian counsel or secular psychology that refuses to take our deepest commitments seriously. This is one of many reasons that I am so grateful for Eric Johnson's work. He not only resists a false dichotomy between faith and the insights of psychology but has devoted his life's work to mapping the intricate networks between Scripture, faith, theology, and psychology. *God and Soul Care* is a gift, and if it is received as it should be, it will go a long way toward helping shape counseling and counselors so that when we need them they are well equipped to work alongside God in pointing us down the road of deep healing, to the glory of God and our personal well-being."

Craig G. Bartholomew, Redeemer University College

"*God and Soul Care* is a beautifully balanced book composed by one of the most generous hearts and capacious minds in Christian counseling. Eric Johnson is as much theologian as he is psychologist, and the result is a thoughtful and thorough application of the resources of the Christian faith (God, gospel, and church) to the broken stuff in our lives. There's nothing else like it in the Christian counseling compendium, and it therefore is a must-read for biblical and Christian counselors, pastors who take shepherding their people seriously, and thoughtful missionaries aiming to contextualize the gospel in any Western context."

Sam R. Williams, professor of counseling, coordinator of master's degrees in counseling, Southeastern Baptist Theological Seminary

"Deftly building on his *Foundations for Soul Care*, Johnson erects a framework of systematic theology for those who counsel as Christians. He draws from a dazzling diversity of sources to help the reader think through the theological dimensions and implications of counseling, and this is vital in an age when many who counsel even in the name of Christ have little training in the deeply biblical worldview needed to counsel well. Johnson knows both the psychological and biblical sides of the story and weaves them together in a wonderfully coherent book. A must-read for Christians who counsel professionally or in pastoral and ministry contexts!"

Timothy A. Sisemore, director of research, professor, Richmont Graduate University

"*God and Soul Care* shows how Christian theology characterizes human flourishing, and it alerts us to the cure of all ills and the cultivation of all facets of our human condition in and through Jesus Christ. We need counselors today—trained professionals, alert pastors, and wise laypersons—with deeper theological formation in the Catholic and Reformation traditions of doctrinal and exegetical reflection as well as a discerning engagement with the psychological field. Eric Johnson proves yet again to be a model and guide of the first order in summoning us to consider the ways in which knowing God reorients and renews our concern for faithful soul care."

Michael Allen, academic dean, associate professor of systematic and historical theology, Reformed Theological Seminary, Orlando

"*God and Soul Care* by Eric Johnson is another deep and substantial contribution to the further development of a truly Christian psychology and to Christian counseling and soul care. He describes the therapeutic resources of the Christian faith by clearly explicating the implications of fundamental biblical truths for Christian psychotherapy and counseling. I highly recommend this book as essential reading!"

Siang-Yang Tan, professor of psychology, Fuller Theological Seminary, author of *Counseling and Psychotherapy*

"When Eric Johnson's extraordinary magnum opus *Foundations for Soul Care* was published in 2007, I thought this would be the peak of his writing career, but as he says in the preface to this new volume, that was just 'a prolegomenon to the present work.' So now we have two weighty parts of a much-needed, wonderfully comprehensive Christian psychology that will stand for many years as the primary reference book on the relationship between Scripture, the character of God, the person of Christ, and insights from psychology. Johnson aims for 'the proper synthesis of all relevant biblical, theological, psychological, and philosophical forms of knowledge about human beings with the goal of understanding human beings as comprehensively as possible, that is, as much like God as we can.' His patient, diligent, and careful scholarship is an amazing gift to the church at a time when there are many significant advances in contemporary psychology and Christians need help to know how to think biblically about this area of life that affects us all—what he calls 'creation grace.' Johnson writes, 'Most of *God and Soul Care* . . . is focused on the use of *redemptive* grace resources that only Christian counselees can utilize.' Behind this work of scholarship is a man with a profound love for God, truth, people, and life who has poured all his resources into the task of developing Christian psychology. I will have no hesitation in recommending this valuable resource to my counseling and theology students."

Richard Winter, professor emeritus of applied theology and counseling, Covenant Theological Seminary, St. Louis

"Eric L. Johnson takes on the task of reimagining what we often think of as modern psychopathologies in the context of his larger thesis of a truly Christian psychology. Agree or disagree with his thesis, you will want to engage this work."

Mark A. Yarhouse, Rosemarie S. Hughes Endowed Chair of Psychology, Regent University, coauthor of *Modern Psychopathologies*

"We live in an age of academic overspecialization that too easily undercuts attempts at disciplinary integration. Thankfully, Eric Johnson resists that trend and seeks to bring his background in psychology into meaningful dialogue with theology and pastoral care. While not everyone in the different disciplines will agree with every move he makes, each can appreciate and learn from his noble attempt at a holistic approach. There is much to beneficially ponder in these packed pages."

Kelly M. Kapic, professor of theological studies, Covenant College

"*God and Soul Care* offers readers the fruit of Eric Johnson's lifelong passion to articulate a thoughtful and thoroughly Christian perspective on psychology. The body of Christ—the living church of Jesus Christ—is often depicted as an organic therapeutic community where relationships, discipleship, and worship nurture healing and growth. Johnson skillfully displays how the content of evangelical theology is itself therapeutic for the soul. This companion to *Foundations for Soul Care* is a comprehensive achievement. Johnson seamlessly weaves profound Christian teaching with a contemporary understanding of human beings as biopsychosocial as well as ethical and spiritual beings. For followers of Jesus Christ who counsel in mental health clinics, pastor in ministry settings, serve as chaplains to pluralistic communities, or offer spiritual direction, *God and Soul Care* is an accessible and relevant theological treatise for personal reflection, professional reference, and faith enhancement."

Stephen P. Greggo, professor of counseling, Trinity Evangelical Divinity School, coeditor of *Counseling and Christianity*

God & Soul Care

THE THERAPEUTIC RESOURCES

of

THE CHRISTIAN FAITH

ERIC L. JOHNSON

IVP Academic

An imprint of InterVarsity Press
Downers Grove, Illinois

InterVarsity Press
P.O. Box 1400, Downers Grove, IL 60515-1426
ivpress.com
email@ivpress.com

InterVarsity Press® is the book-publishing division of InterVarsity Christian Fellowship/USA®, a movement of students and faculty active on campus at hundreds of universities, colleges, and schools of nursing in the United States of America, and a member movement of the International Fellowship of Evangelical Students. For information about local and regional activities, visit intervarsity.org.

All Scripture quotations, unless otherwise indicated, are taken from the New American Standard Bible®, copyright 1960, 1962, 1963, 1968, 1971, 1972, 1973, 1975, 1977, 1995 by The Lockman Foundation. Used by permission.

Cover design: Faceout Studio
Interior design: Daniel van Loon
Images: © Piotr Zajda/Shutterstock

ISBN 978-0-8308-5159-1 (print)
ISBN 978-0-8308-9161-0 (digital)

Printed in the United States of America ∞

Library of Congress Cataloging-in-Publication Data
Names: Johnson, Eric L., 1956- author.
Title: God and soul care : the therapeutic resources of the Christian faith / Eric L. Johnson.
Description: Downers Grove : InterVarsity Press, 2017. | Includes bibliographical references and index.
Identifiers: LCCN 2017013117 (print) | LCCN 2017005123 (ebook) | ISBN 9780830891610 (eBook) | ISBN 9780830851591 (hardcover : alk. paper)
Subjects: LCSH: Christianity—Psychology. | Psychology, Religious. | Theology. | Psychotherapy.
Classification: LCC BR110 (print) | LCC BR110 .J5584 2007 (ebook) | DDC 261.5/61—dc23
LC record available at https://lccn.loc.gov/2017013117

P 23 22 21 20 19 18 17 16 15 14 13 12 11 10 9 8 7 6 5 4 3 2 1

Y 36 35 34 33 32 31 30 29 28 27 26 25 24 23 22 21 20 19 18 17

The Holy Scriptures

BY GEORGE HERBERT

Oh Book! Infinite sweetness! Let my heart
    Suck ev'ry letter, and a honey gain,
    Precious for any grief in any part;
To clear the breast, to mollify all pain.

Thou art all health, health thriving till it make
    A full eternity: thou art a mass
    Of strange delights, where we may wish & take.
Ladies, look there; this is the thankful glass,

That mends the looker's eyes: this is the well
    That washes what it shows. Who can endear
    Thy praise too much? Thou art heav'ns Ledger[1] here
Working against the states of death and hell.

    Thou art joy's handsell[2]: heav'n lies flat in thee,
    Subject to ev'ry mounter's bended knee.

Oh that I knew how all thy lights combine,
    And the configurations of their glory!
    Seeing not only how each verse doth shine,
But all the constellations of the story.

This verse marks that, and both do make a motion
    Unto a third, that ten leaves off doth lie;
    Then as dispersed herbs do watch a potion,
These three make up some Christian's destiny:

Such are thy secrets, which my life makes good,
    And comments on thee: for in ev'ry thing
    Thy words do find me out, & parallels bring,
And in another make me understood.

    Stars are poor books, & oftentimes do miss;
    This book of stars lights to eternal bliss.

---

[1] ambassador; also a pun on *ledger* as *register*
[2] first installment of payment; a gift

Contents

Preface

MANY CHRISTIANS TODAY are suspicious of therapy in any form, and there are good reasons for their suspicion. We live in an era and a culture in which a secular therapeutic orientation has replaced religion as the primary pathway to greater well-being (Browning & Cooper, 2004; Holifield, 1983; Rieff, 1966), particularly among Western intellectuals, and increasingly across the populace—and the church has not been unaffected (Smith & Denton, 2005).

A wholesale rejection of therapy by Christians, however, would be a tragic overreaction to this situation, for Christianity, from its beginning, has been a therapeutic religion. A significant theme of the Christian Scriptures—highlighted in the Gospels—is the portrayal of Jesus Christ, the Son of God, as the world's supreme soul physician, who came to earth from heaven to heal humankind of its worst maladies, spiritual and ethical in nature, through his teachings and activities and symbolized by the many physical healings he performed (see Mk 2:1-17; Jn 9; 11:25, 40; 17:22-26). Much of the rest of the New Testament explores, though more indirectly, the implications of this portrayal, and we learn there that Christian salvation involves a process of spiritual and psychological healing and transformation, analogous to physical healing (Rom 12:2; 1 Cor 1:18; 15:2; 2 Cor 3:18; Eph 2:4-10; 1 Tim 4:10; see also Ps 103:3; Is 53:5; Colijn, 2010; Reichenbach, 2006). The root meaning of *psychotherapy* is soul healing (*psychē* = soul; *therapeuō* = to heal), which is a pretty good descriptor for the Christian life.[1] Charry (2007) has suggested that

> Christianity is not simply therapeutic, but *theo*-therapeutic. Its foundation for constructing Christian psychology and its criterion for conversing with other fields are its vision of God. For classic Christianity, theology, psychology, ethics, and spirituality are indivisible, for they work together in the unified undertaking of helping us know, love, and enjoy God better—and use

ourselves better as a result. They all help us understand and come to terms with God and ourselves. (p. 12)

Viewed from this perspective, we might justly say that Christianity is a psychotherapeutic enterprise established by God himself.

Moreover, Christians should also reject the temptation to throw out the science of psychology (which includes research and theory on psychotherapy and counseling). In spite of the distorting spectacles of its dominant worldview (naturalism), modern psychology has discovered a tremendous amount of knowledge about human beings in its short history (since around 1879), and all knowledge of God's creation belongs to him and is a fruit of his creation grace. Consequently, Christians should be among the most eager to learn from the sciences, even the human sciences, rightly interpreted. No, the discomfort some Christians have regarding therapy in our day is not with science or therapy per se; it is with the particular configuration of the therapy framework that has come to dominate the West, much as Christianity did for many centuries. As the result of a secular revolution (Smith, 2003) that has been spreading for the past few centuries and is now almost complete, the God of Christianity has been deposed and, too ironically, the original beneficiary of God's therapeutic intentions, the human self, has assumed the throne, and this regime change has been extremely difficult for Christians to bear.

THE BACKGROUND TO THIS BOOK

Putting it this way is provocative but not really an exaggeration; and part of the prudence we need in this era of late modernism is to figure out the best way to respond, based on our particular calling, which will differ for different Christians. My own response, since before I went to Michigan State University to get a PhD in educational psychology, has been shaped by Augustine's two cities (1958) model of cultural analysis and Kuyper's (1898) two sciences model of the human sciences. According to Augustine, humanity can be divided fundamentally into two groups: the city of humanity, into which everyone is born, which loves self and despises God; and the City of God, into which one must be born again by grace and faith, which loves God and despises self—a contrast that sounds simplistic when stated that starkly but captures well their respective ultimate values and motivational orientations, that is, the religion of each city. Living when modern psychology was founded, Kuyper extended Augustine's analysis to the human sciences, which he similarly argued fell into two groups, on the basis of the divine regeneration of believers, resulting in fundamentally different understandings of human beings, reflecting their respective religious orientations (though Kuyper believed religious assumptions did not much affect the basic observations, measurement, and logic of the human sciences, a concession we now know was somewhat naive). Unfortunately, since first articulated, his approach to the human sciences has been largely neglected.

One might suppose that if Kuyper's model applies anywhere, psychotherapy and counseling would be good candidates, given that both religion and psychotherapy/counseling are social institutions and serve some of the same cultural functions: improving human well-being; shaping human thoughts, emotions, and activities for the social good; and forming positive social bonds, within a specific worldview context. Consequently, there would seem to be significant warrant, from a Kuyperian standpoint, to develop the therapeutic resources that God has provided in Christ and revealed in the Bible into advanced models of therapy that are as sophisticated and well investigated as those of modern psychology, while learning whatever we legitimately can from modern models.

Though trained to be a professor of academic psychology, my own interest in psychotherapy and counseling began while attending John Piper's church for ten years. Early in his ministry, he somewhat controversially labeled his approach to the Christian life "Christian hedonism" and coined a motto that has had great currency since—"God is most glorified in us as we are most satisfied in him"—and his teaching had a huge impact on me. While teaching psychology at a Christian liberal arts college in the Twin Cities (University of Northwestern), I got involved in the church, eventually doing some pastoral counseling and lay counseling training there, while the conviction grew in me that Christian hedonism strongly implied a model of Christian counseling that needed to be worked out. So, when a friend recommended that I apply for a position at Southern Baptist Theological Seminary in the counseling department, I did so. Shortly afterward I signed the contract for this book.

After a few years of writing, I began to realize that no one had ever tried to justify, at an academic level, the use of the Bible in the science of psychology and psychotherapy/counseling, and according to the assumptions of modern psychology, such use was quite objectionable. As a result, I took what I felt to be a necessary detour to complete in 2007 a prolegomenon to the present work, *Foundations for Soul Care: A Christian Psychology Proposal.* There I tried to describe the basic structure of a Christian psychology for soul care—to frame the house, as it were—as preparation for this book, which concerns the Christian *content* relevant to psychotherapy and counseling—the interior design of the house, perhaps. Both books were written as texts for graduate-level study in Christian psychotherapy and counseling.

"We know truth, not only by the reason, but also by the heart, and it is in this last way that we know first principles" (Pascal, 1680/1941, p. 95). Put in more contemporary terms, Pascal is saying that worldview assumptions cannot be demonstrated in the way that a formal logical argument can. "Every worldview demands faith in its foundational principles" (Poplin, 2008, p. 151). The following book is an exposition of the "first principles" of Christianity with regard to psychotherapy and counseling as they emerge from the Bible and the Christian tradition.[2] The project has been driven throughout by the question, What is the therapeutic benefit of this particular aspect of the Christian faith?

That might seem like too utilitarian of an agenda to lead to much Christian good. We cannot here get into much depth regarding the first principles of Christian psychotherapy and counseling (CPC) that we will be exploring. However, a few themes might be mentioned to show the book's trajectory. First, we will be assuming—with Piper, and Edwards before him (and Augustine and Aquinas before Edwards)—that God created humans to flourish best when he is the center of their life and his glory is their greatest motive. Second, a core feature of God's manifesting his glory is the revelation that he is triune—Father, Son, and Holy Spirit—so the model of CPC developed here is trinitarian. Finally, the Trinity's glory-agenda is refined further by its concentration on Jesus Christ, the Son of God and the Son of Man. Consequently, this project could also be labeled *christological* psychotherapy and counseling,[3] since Christ looms so large in the orientation, both in terms of its understanding of human beings and of how their healing is best facilitated. A theocentric orientation transforms everything within its orbit, showing how benefits to us serve the greater good of God's glory.

THE AUDIENCE FOR THIS BOOK

God and Soul Care was written with Christian mental health professionals (MHPs) in mind, both those with experience and those in training, who want to learn more about how the resources of the Christian faith can inform their work, especially when working with Christians. While contemporary systematic theologies cover the content of the faith, they are typically written at some distance from the work of therapy, so this book could be a textbook in required theology classes in Christian psychotherapy and counseling programs. It is also hoped that Christian ministers will find this book useful, especially those who counsel and desire a better understanding of the therapeutic implications of the Christian faith. There is a great need in our day for Christian ministers and MHPs to work more closely together, and this becomes more likely when they share a common understanding of the Christian care of souls. I would be happy if this book promoted more dialogue and collaboration between these two groups of the body of Christ, each with different gifts and callings.

CHRISTIAN PSYCHOTHERAPY AND COUNSELING ARE TRANSDISCIPLINARY PROJECTS

According to contemporary disciplinary boundaries, this book looks a lot like a theology book. However, as the name "Christian psychology" implies, the central task of this approach is the development of a distinctively Christian version of psychology. One of the problems of knowledge in the modern era, from a Christian standpoint, is that it has become fragmented and has no central set of texts or axioms that provide higher-order ethical and spiritual principles that can guide the interpretation of knowledge and the living of life. As a result, intellectual disciplines operate autonomously from one another, and Christians recognize the resultant knowledge is explicitly unrelated to God, its Creator, that is, it is *secular*.[4]

Many methodological advances helped modern psychology become the dominant approach in our day, yet most, if not all, of its methods can be used by members of *any* worldview community. Nevertheless, most worldview communities will also have their own methodological assumptions that guide their respective pursuit of knowledge, and therefore their approach to various disciplines. Christian psychology is distinguished from modern psychology by its expanded list of valid sources of knowledge. According to Christianity, the God of the Bible is the Creator of the universe, and he knows how all knowledge is interrelated, ultimately because it is all related to him. Moreover, he has revealed in the Bible the first principles of his understanding and evaluation of reality, from which can be deduced his basic design plan for human beings, what is most wrong with them, a broad outline of his unique therapeutic path for recovery, and the end of human life. In addition, Christian theologians and philosophers have reflected carefully on this revelation for centuries. Consequently, in addition to empirical research—the *only* official source of knowledge for modern psychology—the project of a Christian psychology will utilize biblical, theological, and philosophical knowledge for its content. Since biblical and theological knowledge has been separated from other forms of knowledge for many generations, it is especially needful in our day to engage in an exercise of retrieval and to reinvest significantly in these "metadisciplines" in order to develop a more thoroughly Christian framework for understanding reality among Christians, to strengthen their Christian identity in the academy, and to guide the formation of knowledge in all the disciplines. This will result in some necessary reorganization of the disciplines according to transcendent, revealed principles, highlighting their underlying unity in God, and will even add content, insofar as their subject matter legitimately bears on a particular discipline—*and with psychotherapy and counseling there is considerable overlap*. This reconceptualization of the academic enterprise is being called "radical Christian scholarship" or "Christian transdisciplinary scholarship" (see Johnson & Bartholomew, unpublished manuscript), and it probably goes without saying that our secular colleagues will disagree.

All that to say, from a Christian psychology perspective, this book is a psychology book that focuses especially on biblical and theological knowledge, along with some empirical and philosophical knowledge, to develop the first principles of Christian psychotherapy and counseling.

Many classic works could be cited as its inspirations, including Augustine's *Enchiridion*, Bonaventure's *Breviloquium*, Calvin's *Institutes of the Christian Religion*, Richard Baxter's *Christian Directory*, and Archibald Alexander's *Thoughts on Religious Experience*. This work obviously differs from them, however, in its engagement with the knowledge and therapeutic innovations of modern psychology.

In recent years, a number of books have been written with an agenda somewhat similar to this one: *Christ-Centered Biblical Counseling*, edited by MacDonald, Kellemen, and Viars (2013); Robert Kellemen's own *Gospel-Centered Counseling* (2014); and Heath Lambert's *A Theology of Biblical Counseling* (2016), from the biblical counseling side of the Christian counseling spectrum. On the integration side, Virginia Holeman has written *Theology for Better Counseling* (2012). Each has its strengths, and they overlap in some respects with the present work. However, biblical counseling and integration, in very different ways, often (though not necessarily!) have tended to assume the modern separation of theology from psychology (and psychotherapy and counseling). The aim of this book is a synthesis of all relevant biblical, theological, psychological, and philosophical forms of knowledge about human beings with the goal of understanding human beings as comprehensively as possible, that is, as much like God as we can.[5] It is obvious that this book is more biblical and theological than empirical. However, understood as a corrective and an exercise in retrieval, it is hoped that future works and generations will do a better job of synthesis.

PSYCHOTHERAPY AND COUNSELING *WITH CHRISTIANS*

From the standpoint of Christian psychology, the most important assessment in therapy is whether the counselee is a follower of Christ or not, as best as can be determined. Most of the time, that assessment is relatively easy to make—questions on an intake form or asked during the initial session reveal the counselee's self-understanding, or the counselee is a member in good standing of the church at which one counsels. At other times, the lines are blurred, because the person is either moving toward Christianity or away.

This diagnosis, though, is so important because, when working with Christian counselees, the Christian counselor can make use of all the therapeutic assets that Christ has procured for those who believe in him—what we might call "redemptive grace" resources. When working with non-Christians, there is still much that Christian counselors can do, but they have to work with what we might call "creation grace" resources, which are available to everyone regardless of their personal relationship with Christ. The latter resources are, of course, well developed in the field—and still given by Christ (Jn 1:9; Col 1:15-20; 1 Tim 4:10)—and include practices such as forming a therapeutic alliance, training to recognize one's automatic thoughts, exploring how early attachment patterns are affecting current relationships, and role-playing more effective social skills. Mainstream psychotherapy researchers have also found that certain "common factors" are correlated with good outcomes in therapy, regardless of the theoretical system of the therapist, for example, the quality of the therapeutic alliance, counselor empathy and transparency, sharing the same goals for therapy, and so on (Lambert, 2013; Norcross, 2011; Wampold, 2010). As a result, Christian counselors need training in creation-grace therapy resources and "common factors" skills.

However, even in these areas, a Christian interpretation will be distinctive. For instance, how one understands a common factor or what counts as a good outcome can differ in some respects, depending on one's worldview. Forming an empathic bond between counselor and counselee, to cite just one example, has been found to be one of the most valuable common factors in therapy. Yet Stephen Muse (2015), an Eastern Orthodox psychotherapist, calls the Christian experience of an empathic bond *dia-Logos*, because it mediates the presence and love of Christ, enabling counselor and counselee to share in the communion of the Trinity.

There are many, many books, Christian and secular, that address common factors and describe what we are calling creation-grace resources, and some of what follows will take this work into account, since all CPC utilizes common factors and creation-grace resources all the time. Most of *God and Soul Care*, however, is focused on the use of *redemptive*-grace resources, which only Christian counselees can utilize. What is needed today is more efficacy research on Christian-saturated models like the present one (Appleby & Ohlschlager, 2013; Garzon, 2008; Johnson, Worthington, Hook, & Aten, 2013; Knabb & Frederick, 2017; Tan, 2011, chap. 15; Wardle, 2005). A corollary step is the development of credentials for distinctly Christian psychotherapy and counseling with the highest standards for theological and psychological understanding, and advanced therapy skills.

A VIABLE CHRISTIAN ALTERNATIVE IN CONTEMPORARY PSYCHOTHERAPY AND COUNSELING

According to MacIntyre (1984), an intellectual community/tradition is viable only to the degree that it is actively engaged with its chief competitors, constructively contesting the alternative frameworks, and incorporating their advances and translating them into their own forms of thought and practice, while showing where the deficiencies of the other community/tradition lie, particularly when compared with one's own community/tradition. The same applies to a therapy community/tradition. In the current contentious cultural milieu, it is easy for Christians to be pushed toward one of two extremes: simply accommodate themselves to the dominant community/tradition— modern psychotherapy and counseling (MPC)—faithfully observing its discourse rules and therapy rules without question and negotiation; or isolate themselves, resist engaging with MPC, and stay out of public mental health. Without discussing the legitimate Christian reasons for both options, the goal of this book—and Christian psychology in general—is to develop a viable Christian alternative to modern psychotherapy and counseling, where our respective worldviews make a difference.

Admittedly, in the contemporary fields of psychotherapy and counseling, a Christian approach is hardly acknowledged. To even begin to be taken seriously by MPC, Christian psychotherapy and counseling (CPC) first has to deepen its own Christian psychological and therapeutic identity and understanding, by retrieving, reinvesting in, and rearticulating the distinct resources of its own community/tradition in light of the best work of MPC. For this to be successful, we first have to do this *within the borders of our own community/ tradition*—communicating among ourselves—otherwise our identity and understanding will likely be somewhat distorted by the dominant worldview values of MPC in ways that are hard to identify when one is intellectually embedded in another community/tradition. But second, our community/ tradition needs to communicate and collaborate with those in MPC, wherever possible, contesting where appropriate and incorporating/translating whatever is valid. Third, and functionally the most important, CPC has to develop research programs that systematically test its own hypotheses and proposals, according to its own standards for good research, to whatever degree possible, while conforming enough to the majority's standards to get published. There is a logical priority to begin with the first task, and that is the focus of this book. However, in actual fact, we have to bloom where we are planted and work toward greater Christian coherence on the tasks that are close at hand, given our location and calling, with the hope that a critical mass of Christian texts, research, and theory building will eventually emerge that demonstrates the viability of CPC. (For the record, I am also working on the latter two tasks, where I can; see Johnson, 2015a; 2015b; August, 2015.)

Some theologians, philosophers, and counselors (e.g., biblical counselors, healing prayer practitioners, and spiritual directors) have already done a good deal of helpful work in retrieval and reinvestment. I thank God for that. However, given their calling and training, few have been in a position to actively engage with the language and literature of MPC. By contrast, leaders in integration have been successful in participating in MPC and psychology, even influencing it in significant but subtle ways. I also thank God for that. However, at best, they can do no more integration than the rules of secular discourse and therapy currently allow. All members of the Christian community who have something to contribute are needed to participate in order for a viable alternative community/tradition to reemerge.

The problem, as we have already hinted at, is that contemporary psychology is a community/tradition that is largely *secular in conviction*, in spite of explicit claims of neutrality toward other ultimate perspectives and the recent openness toward spirituality and religion (for which I am also thankful). Consequently, most members of that community/tradition do not see the world the same way that Christians do. As a result, challenging current thinking in the field too much will result in some degree of rejection (for example, of articles submitted to journals for possible publication, which I know from personal experience). In the meantime, we have to create many more "locations" where Christians in the field can make believing reference to the triune God, Scripture, and salvation, *at least when dialoging among ourselves: in local churches, our own educational institutions, journals and books, research programs, conferences, and counseling sessions.* Gradually, as our identity and understanding as a distinct intellectual and therapeutic community/tradition grows, along with our scholarly literature and research on sophisticated psychological and "theo-therapeutic" models that are empirically validated and thoroughly consistent with a Christian worldview, the current dominance of secularism can be more vigorously contested. Before that, Christians working in mainstream psychology will need the support and encouragement of other Christians, and great discernment. How much Christian discourse gets shared with members of other worldview communities, and when, will depend on a host of communicative factors: the current cultural openness to genuine worldview diversity, its relevance to the subject at hand, one's credibility in the field, the quality and context of the relationship, and one's personal calling. There is some awareness in psychology, at least among its more philosophically minded members, that the positivist bias against metaphysics that has characterized modern psychology since its inception is itself beyond empirical proof (Richardson, Fowers, & Guignon, 1999; Slife, Reber, & Richardson, 2005; Toulmin & Leary, 1992). Christians can hope that eventually such an awareness will lead to a more pluralist understanding of psychology as necessarily consisting of a family of psychologies, based on different worldviews, shared by members of particular intellectual and therapeutic communities/traditions. This may be the best and most just discourse system we can attain in a fallen world, given all of our finite and sinful capacities—though Christians are warranted in believing a Christian understanding most accurately reflects reality (Plantinga, 2000).

To advance such an agenda, it will help to find fair-minded mainstream psychologists who are willing to dialogue. Duarte, Crawford, Stern, Haidt,

Jussim, and Tetlock (2015) have recently argued that social psychology would benefit from greater *political* diversity, suggesting it would help expose liberal biases that currently dominate the field, open up new areas of scientific exploration afforded by novel perspectives, and reduce the mischaracterization of underrepresented groups. To support their call for reform, they cite social psychology research on the problem of confirmation bias and the role minority influence can play in reducing the distorting effects of social cognitive processes such as groupthink, leading to deeper thought about controversial, disputed issues, higher-quality group decisions, and enhanced problem solving. It is just a matter of time until such awareness is extended to the need for *worldview* diversity. Of course, this may not happen. But in the meantime, all interested parties should hope and pray, and those whose location and calling make it possible to influence the fields of psychology, psychotherapy, and counseling to become more open to greater worldview diversity should do so. And we need to be ready for that day. Of course, there will be some who will say that working toward a pluralist psychology and public mental health system is hardly a goal worth pursuing, and these are undoubtedly complex matters about which good Christians will disagree. But along with some other Kuyperians (e.g., Skillen, 1994), a "principled pluralism" seems to me to be the best framework for negotiating the existence of multiple, viable worldviews in a culture. As some have said about democracy, it is not a perfect system, but it is the best system we can attain in this world. Similarly, a pluralistic psychology and public mental health system would not be perfect, but it would be better than the current system, which so favors naturalism, and so long as humans disagree about worldview assumptions, it may be the best cultural option there is.

Regardless of what happens in contemporary psychotherapy and counseling, the Christian community at large will benefit considerably from the development of the most sophisticated and comprehensive models of psychotherapy and counseling possible, fundamentally shaped by the triune God's agenda to glorify himself by promoting the most substantial soul healing possible in Christ, before we arrive home, perfectly holy and whole. Let's dive into one such attempt.

Acknowledgments

I AM GRATEFUL TO SO MANY PEOPLE who have improved this work. Many students over the years have read chapters of earlier versions and helped further my thinking through conversations in and outside class. I especially want to thank Lydia Kim, Ben Askins, Jonathan Badgett, Unhye Kwon, Sean Brooks, Michael Spalione, Chris Croley, Jordon Goings, Brett Vaden, Gene Burrus, Kyu Bo Kim, Kyunga Song, Todd Hardin, Natalie Pickering, David Svihel, Soon Park, Jinse Kim, Brandon Wright, and Aaron Kennedy. I also want to single out Kristine Johnson, Jenny Johnson, Ben Askins, Jordon Goings, Sean Brooks, and Brett Vaden for their help with the indexes.

In addition, some of my professional colleagues have given me helpful feedback on specific chapters, and they include Tom Schreiner, Shari Stewart, Philip Jamieson, Tyler Wittman, Jonathan Pennington, and Bruce Ware.

Some of my dialogue partners over the years on matters relating to this book have included Kathrin Halder, Werner and Agnes May, and other faculty at IGNIS: The Institute for Christian Psychology; P. J. Watson, Warren Kinghorn, Robert Roberts, Timothy Sisemore, C. Stephen Evans, Stephen Greggo, David Powlison, Richard Winter, Siang-Yang Tan, Michael Cook, Shannon Wolf, John Coe, Sam Williams, Todd and Elizabeth Hall, Mike Wilkerson, Chuck DeGroat, Jeremy Lelek, Robert Kellemen, Diane Langberg, Ed Welch, Jeremy Pierre, Heath Lambert, Mark McMinn, Peter Hill, Alan Padgett, Fred Sanders, and James Olthuis, and I'm sure many others whom I have sadly forgotten and am unfortunately leaving out.

I would like to also thank my editors, Joel Scandrett, Andy LePeau, and especially David Congdon, and my readers Phil Monroe and Gary Deddo. Gary, in particular, spent more time on this manuscript than anyone else besides me, helping to correct mistakes, omissions, and imbalances, and he helped alter my views on a number of matters. But I take responsibility for the final form of this book and its remaining limitations.

A portion of my writing was funded by a grant through the Lilly Theological Research Grants Program, which coincided with a sabbatical granted to me by President Mohler and the board of trustees of the Southern Baptist Theological Seminary, and then a few years later I received a second sabbatical from Southern, during which time I completed the manuscript. During the first sabbatical I was given office space and wonderful hospitality by the leaders and faculty of IGNIS: The Institute for Christian Psychology in Kitzingen, Germany. May God bless that small but mighty institution. In addition, I want to thank the Templeton Foundation, the Center for Christian Thought, and Biola University for a grant that permitted me to become a fellow of the center for a semester in fall 2014. I also want to thank the other fellows that semester who gave me great feedback on chapter one and the book in general. What a wonderful few months those were!

I would also like to express my appreciation to Mid-America Reformed Seminary, specifically its president, Cornelius Venema, faculty (particularly Alan Strange, Nelson Kloosterman, and Mark Beach), and students, as well as the visitors who attended lectures I delivered there in November 2009 that were based on four of the chapters in this book, a number of whom gave me specific, helpful feedback.

Analytical Outline

THE FOLLOWING IS AN ANALYTICAL OUTLINE of the book that provides its logical organizational structure. Each chapter begins with one of the statements from the outline and is an attempt to expound that statement. So the outline also serves as a summary of the therapeutic content of the Christian faith.

FIVE AXIOMS OF CHRISTIAN PSYCHOTHERAPY AND COUNSELING

AXIOMS 1-4: *The Triune God*, the Center of Christian Psychotherapy and Counseling

Axiom 1: The triune God is the center of his creation, and he made human beings in his image, so that reflecting and participating in his glory is their transcendent, final goal.
  Corollary: The proper flourishing of human beings is therefore an immanent, subordinate goal in God's design (chap. 1).

Axiom 2: God is a triune communion of persons, the archetype of the personal and social form of life of human beings.
  Corollary: The Father has determined that the Holy Spirit bring fallen humans through faith in the Son into their communion to be an ever clearer sign of the Trinity (chap. 2).

Axiom 3: The triune God is especially glorified in the communication of the Son, Jesus Christ, who, as God and a human, provides the ultimate unity of Christian psychotherapy and counseling.
  Corollary: The intrinsic goal of individual human development is conformity to the image of Christ.

Expansion of the corollary: The image of Christ consists of holiness, creational wholeness, and active receptivity (chap. 3).

Axiom 4: The Holy Spirit is the triune God's indwelling gift of himself to believers, uniting them to the Son, and the ultimate means of the proper well-being of humans.
Corollary: The Holy Spirit uses many secondary, creational means to promote the proper well-being of humans (chap. 4).

Axiom 5: *The Triune God's Word in Scripture,* the Primary Agenda Setter for Christian Psychotherapy and Counseling

Axiom 5: The triune God's word in Scripture singularly communicates his understanding, appraisal, and activity regarding human beings, particularly his redemptive mission for them in Jesus Christ, so that the Bible is the canon of Christian psychotherapy and counseling, the primary guide for its agenda, and provides its "first principles" (see Johnson, 2007).
Corollary: The triune God did not convey through Scripture his *entire* understanding of human beings, so the use of other, relevant sources of knowledge about human beings for Christian psychotherapy and counseling is legitimate and highly desirable, so long as they function subordinately to Scripture (see Johnson, 2007).
Expansion of Axiom 5: The fundamental organizing framework of God's word in Scripture is the drama of God's self-glorification in human history, summarized as the Christian metanarrative of creation, fall, redemption, and consummation, the climax of which is the story of Jesus Christ, into which the stories of believers are now being written (chap. 5).

TEN STRATEGIC PRINCIPLES OF CHRISTIAN PSYCHOTHERAPY AND COUNSELING

Principle 1: A worshipful, loving relationship with the triune God in all his perfections is supremely good for human beings (chap. 6).

Principle 2: The triune God created human beings to develop into participants in his glory, the grateful reception of which contributes to their fullest flourishing (chap. 7).

Principle 3: Psychopathology is most comprehensively understood from three perspectives: sin, suffering, and biopsychosocial damage (chaps. 8–11).

    Expansion 1: Biblical revelation focuses primarily on sin, because it is psychopathology fundamentally contrary to God's glory and human well-being (chap. 8).

    Expansion 2: Suffering and biopsychosocial damage are also significant aspects of psychopathology, because they can be Either hindrances or means to God's glory and human well-being (chaps. 9–10).

Principle 4: The Son of God became a human being and provided the concrete ideal of human life by fulfilling his Father's will, a perfection that is credited to believers through union with Christ and that they also realistically pursue by the Holy Spirit and faith (chap. 12).

Principle 5: Christ's atoning death overcame sin and its penalty, and, to some extent in this age, many of its soul-disordering consequences, through union with Christ by the Holy Spirit and faith (chap. 13).

Principle 6: The new creation begun in Christ's resurrection and through union with Christ is being realized in and among believers by the Holy Spirit and faith (chap. 14).

Principle 7: The spread of the new creation is being guided by the exalted Christ in and among those who are united to him by the Holy Spirit and faith (chap. 15).

Principle 8: The church is the body of Christ—the new creation becoming visible—its members being conformed to Christ individually and to the Trinity communally by the Holy Spirit and faith (chap. 16).

Principle 9: Conformity to Christ is the personal realization of the new creation through redemptive differentiation and integration in Christ by the Holy Spirit and faith (chaps. 17–19).

Principle 10: Already being a part of the new creation orients believers to an eternal future with God and radically reframes their lives on earth (chap. 20).

PART I

The Doxological/
Therapeutic Agenda
of the Trinity

ACCORDING TO MOST CHRISTIAN THINKERS, biblical teaching and human reasoning lead to the conclusion that God created the universe ultimately to manifest his glory (*doxa*), that is, the beauty of his perfections (Aquinas, 1947; Balthasar, 1982–1991; Barth, 1957a; Calvin, 1559/1960; Edwards, 1989; Piper, 1991; 1996). God must be his own highest motive and end, or else *that* would be God. Having been created in God's image (Gen 1:28-29), for his glory (Is 43:7; 1 Cor 10:31), and for a relationship of reverence and love with him (Eph 3:16-19), human beings flourish best the more his glory becomes genuinely their highest motive and end. God also constituted human life so that humans have created needs and desires—including a need for a relationship of reverence and love with him—the fulfillment of which are legitimate, secondary goods (Gen 1:26-31; 2:18; Ps 104; 1 Tim 4:3-5). However, Christianity also teaches that humans are fundamentally alienated from God, so that their reason for being has been thwarted and the matrix of their needs, desires, and loves has become fundamentally disordered. Consequently, their greatest need is to be restored to the way of life for which they were created—but that restoration is beyond their own abilities.

God's glory was further manifested through the revelation that God is a triune communion of persons, who have a unified set of missions to rescue humanity and restore it to the life for which humans were designed, culminating in the Son of God becoming a human being, suffering and dying for sin, rising from the dead, and ascending to heaven, so the Holy Spirit would come to bring about that restoration. As a result, God's glory is now being manifested through the healing, strengthening, and well-being of human beings in Christ's name, in which it is *their* glory to participate. Scripture is structured around this metanarrative and contains the story of the interrelationship between the manifestation of God's glory and human participation in it.

The dominant forms of psychotherapy and counseling today operate within a naturalistic worldview and naturalistic evolutionary metanarrative, where there is no God, and human well-being is pursued without his help. While Christian psychotherapy and counseling can be enriched by the knowledge modern psychology has discovered by God's creation grace, the doxological agenda of the triune God involves a radically different therapeutic orientation.

—1—

The Orbit of the Human Soul

Axiom 1: The triune God is the greatest Being there is, and he made humans in his image, so that reflecting and participating in his glory is their transcendent, final goal.

Corollary: The proper flourishing of humans is therefore an immanent, subordinate goal in God's design.

Lift up your heads, O gates, and lift them up, O ancient doors,
that the King of glory may come in! Who is this King of glory?
The LORD of hosts, he is the King of glory.

PSALM 24:9-10

Enjoy GOD, cheer when you see him!

PSALM 68:4 *THE MESSAGE*

WHAT WOULD IT HAVE BEEN LIKE to gaze up at the sun in the ancient world? At that time, nothing could have seemed more obvious than the sun's movement across the sky, from east to west, and nothing could have seemed more sure than the fixedness and immovability of the earth on which one stood. It is hard for us now to imagine how the earth and sun were perceived back when humans "knew" the sun and all the planets and stars revolved around the earth and that the earth was the center of the universe. How crazy it must have seemed at first, when certain astronomers began suggesting that it was the earth that was moving around the sun, rather than the reverse.

Even now, the sun does not look that big. From where we are, it is much larger than the stars, but compared to the earth, stretched out all around us, the sun seems relatively small. Yet we now know that the appearance of the sun and the earth is quite the reverse of the reality—over one million earths could fit inside the sun! For centuries we vastly underestimated the size of the sun and overestimated the size of the earth. One's perspective is so important.

But let us probe this a little deeper. Why might God have created the celestial system we find ourselves in to have an appearance so different from reality? Why would God create it this way, knowing how we would perceive it for thousands of years, and knowing that we would only "catch on" in the fifteenth to sixteenth centuries AD, after mathematics and astronomical observation had developed enough to discover the way things actually were? Of course, we can only speculate what God's reasons might have been, but at least one plausible explanation might be the following. Perhaps this arrangement is itself meaningful—perhaps it is a sign. Maybe God set it up to serve as a profound analogy—at the "center" of creation and of human cultural development—of the radical tendency that we humans have to view ourselves as the ultimate center of the universe, rather than God.[1]

It seems so natural for us to assume, while hardly being aware of it, that we are supremely important. Our own interests so easily loom larger than anyone else's (God, the rest of the creation, other humans). To break out of this basic way of life, more was needed than mathematics and careful empirical observation. God himself had to explain it to us directly in Christ and the Scriptures, and perhaps indirectly through his creation. From these sources we find out that he is the greatest being there is: transcendent and supremely majestic, perfectly loving and perfectly righteous, the unlimited, all-knowing, and all-powerful Creator and Redeemer, the unfathomable source of goodness, truth, beauty, and love. The corollary of this revelation is, of course, that we are not this being. We can look pretty important, compared to rocks, trees, and cows. But compared to the greatest being there is—and the source of all that is other than himself—we realize that we are actually profoundly insignificant, situated in one place and time, with extremely limited abilities and skills, and vulnerable to sickness, injury, and eventual death. Perspective is so important. So, perhaps God created the solar system the way he did as a sort of ironic metaphor, intending it to be an illustration of our eventual fallen perspective of ourselves and the rest of reality, which would only be brought to light to humanity in the unfolding of its cultural and scientific development in the 1400s and 1500s.[2]

In this chapter—and really in the whole book—we will explore the therapeutic significance of what lies at the center of one's heart and life, one's relational universe, and one's worldview. For there is tremendous psychological fallout from one's orientation with respect to this most important matter of all. Living from anything other than the true center of reality contributes to a great deal of the misery and strife we find in human society and the human heart, and moving toward that center leads toward a resolution of many of one's greatest psychospiritual problems and ultimately to one's enduring happiness. Christians believe that being drawn by grace into an orbit around God can bring about the best kind of human flourishing and that that is the best path to greater healing and strengthening and maturing of the human soul. This is the case, according to Christianity, because humans were made for just such an orbit. All our desires—both good and bad—signify, in one way or another, our fundamental need to be in a living, loving relationship with the greatest Good there is, in conscious dependence, worship, communion, and gratitude, and to desire him above all else. Consequently, human flourishing and the fulfillment of all human relationships and activities are found ultimately in their proper relation to God.

Human life itself offers a variety of subtle but compelling evidence of its fundamental, transcendental orientation. Religiousness is ubiquitous, religions have flourished for millennia, and religious people tend to be healthier and happier than less religious people (Masters & Hooker, 2013; Park & Slattery, 2013; Myers, 2000). Prayer and meditation can reduce stress and anxiety (Spilka & Ladd, 2013; Wachholtz & Austin, 2013). Most people believe that morality transcends cultural norms. Finding meaning in life is deeply satisfying (Baumeister & Vohs, 2002). Taking responsibility for ourselves, self-control, and virtue contributes to our well-being (Baumeister & Exline, 2000; Peterson & Seligman, 2004; Wong, 2014). Living beyond self-interest, with others in mind, is part of human nature (Batson, Ahmad, Lishner, & Tsang, 2002). Gratitude is correlated with well-being (Emmons & McCullough, 2004). A Christian account of reality makes the best sense of such findings, on the whole, but such an interpretation is based on the teachings of Scripture, which claims to reveal humanity's ultimate motivational context according to its Creator.

How is it, then, that religion for many people in the West is a rather peripheral affair? Most of us seem far more concerned with our lives on earth than focused on God. Families, jobs, homes, and entertainment consume far more of most people's attention and energy today than the quality of their relationship with God. Yet even here, hidden within the pursuit of these legitimate human goods, we can discern a quest for something far greater, underscored by the fact that our best earthly joys possess a fleeting temporality and core insufficiency that signifies there is something more. The satisfaction of our desires *and* their restlessness both signify a fulfillment to be found in an immeasurable happiness that knows no end.

At the same time, there is a dark side of human desire. In our search for greater happiness on earth, most of us become more or less frustrated when we don't get what we want. We can become so disappointed with ourselves and ashamed of our limitations. When disappointed by others, some of us get angry, others get hurt; and when we are mistreated, most of us hold nebulous grudges and sometimes become vengeful. And what explains the outright abuse, violence, and domination of others that occur so commonly throughout the world? Trace these problems back to their source, and we find confirmation of an insight on which both Christ and Buddha agree: most (if not all) human suffering (one's own and that of others around us) is caused by thwarted human desires that flow from a way of life organized around oneself—living as the center of one's universe is both universal and universally criticized.

The self-defeating nature of self-centeredness is brought out most clearly in those with narcissistic personality disorder (NPD). *Clinically* self-absorbed, they expect to be recognized as superior, seek the admiration of others, lack the ability to empathize with others, and can be painfully envious and arrogant. Christianity's teaching on universal fallenness, however, encourages us to not look down on such people but to see manifested the excesses of our own native tendencies, less restrained by self-awareness and social propriety. What if *all* humans possess a defective and inordinate self-regard, generally less overt than NPD—indeed, sometimes looking like its opposite—but nonetheless warped and liable to break out in times of duress, for example, with the loss of one's love, job, or attainments? As long as most things go our way, so long as we feel our desires are being basically satisfied—the world revolving around us, if you will—this tendency remains hidden. According to Christianity, an excessive and unnatural motive of self-centrality can be divined in all of us. Where does it come from?

Most Westerners consider the Bible to be a great religious and ethical text. Yet one of its main themes is the exposure of this excessive self-concern, which is labeled there *sin*. Indeed, the Bible's portrayal of humanity is overall so unflattering that much of it is difficult to read, if we are to be honest, without in some way distancing ourselves from it, whether through academic criticism of the Bible or criticizing those who rely on such criticism. But what if the Bible is right on both scores? That God is the true center of the universe, and we are all disposed to be our own center far more than we are aware.

After years of wandering, Augustine (trans. 1958) came to accept the biblical portrayal, and he concluded that fallen humanity is composed of but two basic communities. The first he called the city of humanity, since all humans are born into it. This city, he wrote, is motivated fundamentally by the love of self and the despising of God. The second he called the city of God, and one enters it only by being born of the Spirit (Jn 3:6). The members of the second city are being taught by the Spirit how to distrust themselves, in the right way, love God according to his worth, and find the fulfillment for which they were made. All human history, Augustine thought, can be read Christianly as a conflict between these two communities (and within everyone's heart) regarding the true spiritual center of the universe.

If Augustine is correct, we would expect each city to be busy working out the implications of its ultimate motives. One place where that would happen is in each city's soul-healing practices. Every religion and every system of counseling and psychotherapy has a set of assumptions regarding human nature and its flourishing, what's wrong with it, and how best to care for it and cure its disorders (Roberts, 1987; 1988). Whether well articulated or more implicit, such beliefs constitute its "edification framework" (Johnson & Sandage, 1999). From a Christian standpoint, the most important part of such a framework is what is considered central.

THE CENTER OF MODERN THERAPY

When I was young, I used to look forward every year to the annual television broadcast of *The Wizard of Oz*. What a great story: the excitement of a quest, the development of character, the joys of friendship, an intense conflict between good and evil, and even a little terror (those monkeys!). So it was quite a shock to watch it as an adult, after becoming a Christian, and realize it is a modernist parable. After the Wicked Witch is finally destroyed, Dorothy and her friends head back to the "wizard," who had told them earlier he would help them if they brought back the witch's broom. However, the "Great and Mighty Oz" (recognizable to adults as a blustery, threatening God-figure) is proved to be actually a charlatan who admits he is incapable of granting anyone's requests (prayers?). On the contrary, the wizard tells Dorothy and her friends that all along they had had within themselves all the capacities they needed to help themselves, anticipating person-centered therapy by fifty years.

Like Bunyan's *Pilgrim's Progress* and *The Holy War* over two centuries earlier, Frank Baum's tales of Oz were allegories that symbolized a distinct worldview and understanding of humanity. The original *Wizard of Oz* was published in 1900, eight years after the founding of the American Psychological Association, in the early days of modern psychology's ascendancy to becoming the dominant psychology of the West. Frank Baum and most of the early leaders of modern psychology shared some values about human beings and their improvement, and they were also participants in a broad-based transfer of worldviews from Christianity to late modernism that was occurring among the intellectual leadership of Western culture, in what has been called the secular revolution (Smith, 2003).

A worldview is a set of normative assumptions, including beliefs, goods, and practices, that orient, guide, and contextualize one's understanding of everything (Naugle, 2002; Koltko-Rivera, 2004).[3] Worldviews are maintained by communities, and people are generally socialized into the worldview of the community within which they were raised (though beginning in adolescence, one can convert to another). Worldview adherence is especially complicated in a highly communicative culture like the West, where different worldviews are held by many; information is variously interpreted and widely exchanged, so that most members of Western culture are influenced by more than one. I would suggest that late modernism[4] is the worldview shared by a majority of diverse intellectuals in the West, and among its normative assumptions are the following: (1) humans arose as the result of purely natural evolutionary processes; (2) human knowledge can only be derived from reason/mathematics, careful observation, and social discourse; therefore, (3) religious beliefs and metaphysical beliefs beyond the natural order cannot be known to be true; (4) in religion and metaphysics, the individual human (in community) is the highest authority; (5) the official stance of a democratic culture should be to be worldview neutral, that is, it should not promote any religious or metaphysical worldview, meaning, it should be secular; therefore, (6) society should protect the rights of all individuals to pursue their own understanding of well-being, limited only by the pursuits and well-being of others; and finally, (7) rules of discourse and practice are necessary to maintain the secularity of the public square (e.g., government, business, education, public media, and mental health). Something close to this set of assumptions, I think, nearly universally constrains the public square of contemporary America.

Late modernism has other assumptions, some of which are compatible with a Christian worldview (indeed, some of them were shaped by Christianity, such as the value of science).[5] However, these two worldviews obviously differ in a number of key respects. Perhaps the greatest difference, from a Christian standpoint, concerns what is considered central to human life. By "central" I mean one's highest value or greatest good (what Charles Taylor [1989] called a "hypergood"). That which functions as central touches on everything else in one's life and thought; it is what motivates a person most deeply, what is most important or most loved in one's life, what one is most devoted to, we might say. However, we must also distinguish one's center *ideal*—what one *consciously desires* to be central—from what is *actually* central in one's heart—one's *psychological* center. Determining what is psychologically central is obscured by one's conscious religious and ethical beliefs and norms, a lack of self-awareness, and the sheer opacity of these matters, as well as the many objects there are that compete for our affections and desires. But an important implication of Christianity is that being in God's image makes humans intrinsically religious in their hearts. Created for God, and in the absence of a relationship with God, normal adults will necessarily have something (or a plurality of things) that is ultimately central in their lives, whether they are aware of it or not.

Theistic worldviews, such as Christianity, almost by definition are explicit about their center ideal, for it is communally designated. By contrast, worldviews that are not explicitly religious, such as late modernism, have no official, publicly identified center ideal. As a result, many candidates vie unofficially for supremacy in Western culture—wealth, comfort, relationships, sex, achievement, sports, entertainment, music—shaped by cultural trends and personal taste. Nonetheless, a good case can be made that the primary, unofficial, implicit center of late modernism, both ideally and psychologically, is the individual human being, which we will term "the self."[6]

Needless to say, this is a contestable claim, and fully substantiating it is beyond the scope of this book,[7] but the case has been made repeatedly elsewhere (see Baumeister, 1993; Bellah, Madsen, Sullivan, Swidler, & Tipton, 1985; Giddens, 1991; Lasch, 1979; Taylor, 1989; Twenge & Campbell, 2010; Yankelovich, 1981). Given that Christians are persuaded that all humans have a psychological center (or centers), with the lack of a publicly agreed-upon center ideal, one must interpret cultural symbols, activities, and values to infer what the ideal and psychological centers are. Indirect support for the claim is found in the fact that high self-esteem, personal freedom and happiness, self-expression, self-realization, and self-fulfillment are currently among the West's most cherished values and, conversely, that low self-esteem and public criticism of the fulfillment of any of the self's desires (so long as no one else is harmed) are among the West's greatest evils. This is a value set very different from that of ancient China or thirteenth-century Europe, for example.[8]

Before going any further, it should be acknowledged that I am not a neutral observer of these cultural dynamics. I grew up in late-modern culture and drank deeply of its waters, causing innumerable problems for myself and those close to me, so I am neither unbiased nor able to cast stones. The point here is simply to highlight the obscure contemporary social influences that have intensified the obscure, unconscious dynamics that Christianity teaches are embedded in all human hearts. As Pascal (1941), a latter-day Augustinian, observed: "The Self has two qualities: it is unjust in itself since it makes itself the centre of everything; it is inconvenient to others since it would enslave them; for each Self is the enemy, and would like to be the tyrant of all others" (p. 151, no. 455). As early as Genesis 3, Judeo-Christian theism has taught that the human self wants to become its own god.

What does this have to do with psychotherapy and counseling? A great deal, actually, for late-modern psychiatry, psychology, and psychotherapy/counseling[9] have been major players in the cultural developments discussed above (Adams, 1971; Cushman, 1995; Holifield, 1983; Johnson & Sandage, 1999; Rieff, 1966; Vitz, 1994; Wallach & Wallach, 1983). In addition to investigating human beings with the powerful methods of the natural sciences, their task was to help an emerging secular intellectual leadership forge a "modern" way of understanding people and treating their psychological problems, unhindered by discredited religious and philosophical systems (see Thorndike, 1905; Watson, 1925). Though Carl Rogers (1951; 1961) was one of the most explicit and consistent regarding a client-centered/person-centered agenda, all late modern/secular forms of psychotherapy and counseling share an edification framework in which "the self" is at least implicitly the center ideal, and its realization and satisfaction are assumed to be the highest goals of life (within bounds that protect the pursuits of other selves).[10]

As a result, late-modern soul care (psychiatry, psychotherapy, and counseling) has difficulty identifying the more subtle types of pathology that result from living as one's ultimate center, beyond its most obvious forms (e.g., antisocial and narcissistic personality disorders). Research on secular therapy has convincingly demonstrated that it can improve human functioning. But Christians might argue it does so, to some extent, by its cultivation of an increasingly sophisticated and adaptive autocentrism, "civilizing" it, if you will, by training autonomous selves how to get along better with others and inhibit *excessively* self-serving behavior, while simultaneously normalizing it,[11] encouraging "self-reliance" and "self-determination" and, in the process, unwittingly undermining social bonds.[12] The cost of modern therapy to the contemporary family has been enormous (Cushman, 1995; Rieff, 1966; Twenge & Campbell, 2010; Wallerstein, Lewis, & Blakeslee, 2000).

At the same time, Christians should not overreact to this state of affairs by abandoning the contemporary field of mental health. On the contrary, Christianity supports many of the cultural goods it promotes, including the care for the mentally ill, the alleviation of suffering, research on therapy effectiveness, and others too numerous to mention. The human sciences and the field of mental health belong to God. Moreover, late-modern psychology has strengths that the Christian tradition has historically lacked: an emphasis on empirical research, comparative psychology, and a developmental orientation, to say nothing of the massive body of psychological knowledge discovered by the research and theory of this community's work! Indeed, a love for God leads Christians to relish and utilize the significant contributions of late-modern psychology, since they are due ultimately to God's creation grace. As Calvin (1559/1960) opined: "If we regard the Spirit of God as the sole foundation of truth, we shall neither reject the truth itself, nor despise it wherever it shall appear, unless we wish to dishonor the Spirit of God" (p. 273).

Furthermore, the value of Christian participation in the current fields of psychology and public mental health should be self-evident. Such involvement has already led to significant, strategic contributions (e.g., Jones, 1994; McMinn, 2006; Miller & Delaney, 2004) shaped by Christian values, especially in areas such as psychology of religion and spirituality, values in psychotherapy, forgiveness, gratitude, and other areas of positive psychology.[13]

Nevertheless, our appreciation for these goods ought not to obscure the significant differences that exist between the worldviews, thinking, and therapy goals of these two communities. Christians believe that an autocentric orientation cannot satisfy human beings for very long. As creatures—

insufficient in ourselves—we need a transcendent, personal ground for our lives, and as those made in God's image—relational, responsive, and dialogical—we need a personal God who loves us and we can love, with whom we can interact and for whom we can live. As this century (and research on distinctly Christian counseling and psychotherapy) proceeds, Christians would expect that the transcendent, tripersonal theism of Christianity will be shown to be a better center for human life and therapy than the center of secular modernity.

CHRISTIAN TEACHING REGARDING GOD'S CENTRALITY

Counselors seek to help people deal with reality. But what is reality? How are we best to conceive of it? Naturalism assumes reality consists of all the molecules in the universe. The social constructivist thinks it is the product of our cultural system. The subjectivist believes reality is simply one's beliefs, feelings, values, and interpretations. From a Christian perspective, "God is the supreme reality" (Danielou, 1996, p. 3). Before matter existed and humans developed cultures and began reflecting on the world, God was . . . and is and is to come. According to Scripture and the Christian tradition, the triune God is the only *necessary* being; he is the only being that *has* to exist. Everything else is *not necessary*; everything else that exists is *contingent*; it is derived from and dependent on God and his word.

So, in the beginning, God spoke and the creation appeared. He verbalized everything else into being and now holds it together by the word of his power (Heb 1:3). The creation is the expression of those ideas in God's mind (Edwards, 1994, no. 247; or in his infinitely fertile imagination), which he chose to *realize*, such that they are now real, but in a contingent, derivative way, compared with the necessary, eternal reality of God. To put it in a more trinitarian way, the creation is that which the Father meant to bring into being through the Son, the Word (or expressed meaning) of God (Jn 1:1-3; Heb 1:3), by means of the Spirit, the explanatory power of God.

The creation is real (in contrast to it being mere illusion, as Hinduism teaches), but it is a reality of a different order, one that is entirely dependent on the triune God for every moment of its existence. Since God is its origin, it is incomparably inferior to him (Gilson, 1936, chap. 4). To regard anything in the creation to be divine like God (again, as Hinduism teaches humans are at their core) is, according to Christianity, the worst of illusions. It is *idolatry.* On the contrary, all created things are to be interpreted as subordinate and subservient to the triune God. They revolve around him. O'Donovan (1986) calls this fact "the 'teleological relation' of the creation" (p. 33), that is, it is ordered to a *telos,* an end or goal, outside itself.[14]

According to Scripture, everything exists *for God* (Ps 148; Prov 16:4; Heb 2:10). He is the ultimate raison d'être of all of creation. "For from Him and through Him and to Him are all things. To Him be the glory forever. Amen" (Rom 11:36). The Scriptures declare that God is "the first and . . . the last," "the Alpha and the Omega" (Is 41:4; 48:12; Rev 1:8; 21:6). He is the source, the sustenance, and the supreme purpose of all his creation. God alone is self-existent and self-sufficient.

Paul applies this theme directly to humans. "For us there is but one God, the Father, from whom are all things, and we exist for Him" (1 Cor 8:6). Humans find the main reason for their existence in God, not within themselves. God is the true center of human life, infinitely more significant than anything merely human. The Scriptures put God's centrality in human life in various ways. Humans are to use their bodies for God's glory (1 Cor 6:20) and to do good works to glorify their Father (Mt 5:16; 1 Pet 2:12). They are to live to God's glory in all things, from the simplest animal-like functions (eating, drinking) to the exercise of their spiritual gifts (1 Cor 10:31; 1 Pet 4:11). It appears that the glory of God is a shorthand expression in Scripture for the highest goal of human life (see 1 Chron 16:28; Is 42:10; 60:21; Jer 13:11; Jn 15:8; Phil 1:10-11; 2:11; 2 Thess 1:10; Rev 4:9, 11; 11:13).

God's official centrality to human life is also uniquely underscored in the ancient biblical teaching that humans are made in God's image (Gen 1:27; 9:6). This implies at least two related themes. First, humans are not ultimate. Humans are "signs"[15] of something else, something transcendent to which they are ordered; they are replicas of the original. Second, to be God's image means humans are intrinsically and fundamentally relational. They therefore ought not to be understood solely on their own terms. They are necessarily related to Another, and in that relationship they find their meaning and fulfillment. From a Christian standpoint, nothing about humans is more significant than this. Therefore, to most fully realize their purpose or function, humans have to be rightly related to the triune communion of persons to whom they are made to fundamentally correspond. Humans are needy beings, and their greatest need is to have God at the center of their lives, for they need to love and be loved by that infinitely greatest being. Only that reality is enough to fully satisfy the human soul.

God's Glory Is His Chief End

Humans, then, are made to have God as their center ideal and their psychological center.[16] However, in order to pursue the implications of this for counseling and psychotherapy, we need to know what God's deepest reasons are for what he does (e.g., why did he create the world, and why did Christ die?), because that will help us understand what we are doing here. Some of the giants of the Christian tradition—Augustine, Aquinas, and Calvin—developed a Christian answer, and over the past fifty years some stellar lights have elaborated it (Balthasar, 1982–1991; Barth, 1957a; Hart, 2003). In addition, Reformed scholasticism tackled it in the 1600s and 1700s (Muller, 2003), and Jonathan Edwards (1765/1998) wrote the best essay in English on the topic, *The End for Which God Created the World* (with Piper 1991; 1996 popularizing this Edwardsian theme in our day). In the first half of the essay Edwards gives a philosophical explanation, and in the second half he organizes and discusses much of the relevant Scripture, showing that God does what he does for his own sake (Is 48:11), for his name's sake (Ex 9:16; Is 48:9), for his glory (Is 43:7; 61:3; Jn 13:31-32; Eph 1:5; Phil 2:6-11), and for his praise (Jer 13:11; Phil 1:11). The plethora of such expressions throughout the Old and New Testaments leaves little doubt regarding God's ultimate motivation for his actions. God loves himself supremely. He delights ultimately in himself and his activity; he does what he does ultimately for himself, that is, for his own glory.

What is glory? The Hebrew word for glory, *kābôd*, has the root meaning of "heaviness" or "weight," and it came to mean the "weightiness" or significance or greatness of a person, honor and prestige, and visible splendor (Bauckham, 2015; Oswalt, 1980b). The Greek word used to translate *kābôd* in the Septuagint is *doxa*, so that was used in the New Testament for honor/prestige, magnificence/praiseworthiness, as well as brightness, splendor,[17] and radiance; and especially for the radiance of God's greatness (Arndt & Gingrich, 1957; Bauckham, 2015; Kittel, 1964). Summarizing both Testaments, God's glory is the manifestation of his honor and greatness, the outshining of his intrinsic majesty, holiness, and goodness. Barth (1957a) defined God's glory as "the fullness, the totality, the sufficiency, the sum of the perfections of God in the irresistibility of its declaration and manifestation" (p. 645). Edwards characterized it in a number of ways: as God's intrinsic excellence—his virtuous character and all his perfections, that which makes God "infinitely the most beautiful and excellent" being (1765/1998, p. 550; see 1765/1998, pp. 429-33); and also as the awareness and celebration of that excellence; so, in the case of God, it consists of his knowledge of himself, love of himself, and joy in himself (1765/1998, p. 438).[18]

Christians have also distinguished between God's *internal* glory and his *external* glory. Edwards (1765/1998) considered God's internal glory to be the summation of his infinite knowledge, infinite virtue or holiness, and infinite joy and happiness (p. 244), all the goodness and beauty that God is in himself from all eternity. So his internal glory is his knowing, loving, and valuing himself absolutely, infinitely beyond anything else.

However, God decided to *display* his intrinsic greatness and grandeur, so he created this universe to be a "glorious theater" (Calvin, 1559/1960, p. 72). God's *external* glory consists of the *manifestation* of his internal glory "outward," in and through the creation and through his actions in it, in the Scriptures, and especially in the Son's life on earth (Jn 1:14, 18). Then, such is the triune God's goodness and love that he chose to create some beings with whom he could share that glory (that is, his knowledge and love of himself and happiness in himself), so that their happiness could become one with his own, by communicating his glory to them and gradually drawing them freely into the Trinity's communion (Edwards, 1765/1989, pp. 531-33). God's external glory includes his creatures in his ends (Edwards, 1765/1989, p. 454; Hart, 2003, p. 17). As a result, the chief manifestation of God's glory in the creation is that in which humans themselves personally *participate*.[19] God created humans so that we could join his celebration.

At the same time, we must admit that God's doxological (*doxa* = glory) agenda has a paradoxical quality, because God is obviously, for now, "keeping back" most of his glory. In his creation, his power and divine nature are usually manifested *indirectly*, mediated through his creation and his prophets (Ps 19:1-6; Rom 1:20), and they are even more obscured by natural calamities and the sin and evil of humanity. Even when the Son of God came to earth, most of his glory remained largely hidden. We might note that his capacity to become a baby and to suffer and die does not contradict his greatness, however, but illustrates it. His majesty and his hiddenness are both aspects of his glory, since together they disclose a humility of incomparably great degree.

Fittingness or Appropriateness

Thus, God created the world for his own sake, for the purpose of manifesting his internal glory. Before unpacking some of the implications of God's glory for counseling and psychotherapy, we should consider a common objection.

This *theocentric* orientation makes God sound selfish. He seems to want the adulation of humans and is using them for his own purposes. Doesn't this imply that God is the ultimate narcissist?

Edwards (1765/1998) recognized the problem and came up with a number of good explanations (Holmes, 2001), but the best one is surprisingly simple (pp. 142-44, 168-71). God is the greatest being there is. He is necessarily self-existent and self-sufficient, all-good, all-powerful, all-knowing, and holy. It is fitting that God should love himself supremely and should be his own end. It is appropriate that God should do what he does ultimately for his own sake and not for the sake of a lesser being. The regard one should have for someone or something should be proportional to that person's or thing's significance. So, if God is infinitely great, he should regard himself above all other things infinitely. It is fitting; it could be no other way. In fact, if God were *ultimately* motivated by anything outside himself, *that* would be *his* god; *that* would then be the most important being in all the universe. Therefore, were God to create or redeem for some other ultimate reason besides his own glory, God himself would be an idolater. Of course this cannot be. So God's perfection is revealed in his own loving of himself more than anything else. For God to act for his own sake is infinitely fitting and appropriate. He *has* to be the center of his own concerns.[20]

So, is this God selfish and narcissistic? Narcissism was considered a character flaw until Kohut (1971), derived from the story of Narcissus, who loved himself excessively, to the point of self-destruction. This ancient Greek insight comports well with Christianity. If we consider narcissism to be an *unwarranted* and *inappropriate* centering on oneself, God necessarily cannot be selfish and narcissistic. Our problem on his score, really going back to the Garden of Eden, is that there is an absolute, reciprocal asymmetry between God's nature and ours.[21] As God, he must love himself supremely and love his creation in a way absolutely subordinate to his love of himself. As his creatures, we are to love him supremely and love ourselves subordinate to our love for him, as an analogue to his perfect self-love. We are not to image God *exactly*, but *correspondingly*. Appropriate self-love for him is narcissism for us; appropriate self-love for us (loving another [God] more than ourselves) would be idolatry for God.

God's Glorious Love

Accepting that absolute, reciprocal asymmetry between God and ourselves is basic to all theism, rightly understood. However, *trinitarian* glory is intrinsically the opposite of what humans consider "selfish." God's eternal nature is love (1 Jn 4:10), because God is triune. God's self-love is essentially also the mutual love of the Father and the Son in the Spirit. God is, therefore, not ultimately individualistic (as must be the God of any mere monotheism), but eternally communal, interpersonal, and dialogical. Indeed, the love of the Trinity is a significant part of their mutual glory (see Jn 14–17, esp. Jn 17:5, 24; and the next chapter).

Second, Jesus Christ is the triune God's personal manifestation of his glory. He reveals the nature of God's glory (Jn 1:14; 14:1-11; 17:22), and he showed us a God who emptied himself of his divine prerogatives for our sake (Phil 2:7), who healed the sick and hung out with sinners, and who laid down his life for his friends (Jn 15:13). No, this God is anything but selfish. Central to God's glory is his love.

God Is Seeking Willing Participants in His Glory

Hence, God's (internal) glory includes his intratrinitarian love, which he purposed to manifest and share with his creatures (the greatest feature of his external glory). So God's glory is intrinsically relational (Kelsey, 2009). It is the cause of all things, including his design to create humans in his image, free them from sin, and draw them into his trinitarian communion. Part of being made in God's image means we can *participate* in his glory, and we can do so in at least three ways: first, through our *perception* of it, that is, our recognition and understanding of God's supremacy, beautiful character of holy love, and infinite perfections in our minds (we might call this cognitive participation)—including the conscious consent that God is our center ideal; second, through our *delight* in and *love* of God and his character and perfections in our hearts, expressed in adoration and the desire for greater, fitting union[22] with him, and sharing it with others (this is carditive participation—pertaining to the heart, *kardia*); and third, through our *dependent and partial (analogical) emulation* of his character and well-being ourselves, by the Spirit, as we pursue a differentiated union[23] with him in Christ and walk in God's holiness and happiness and love one another (this also is carditive). These last two kinds of participation pertain to the actuality of God as one's *psychological* center.[24]

Being *images of God*, humans were created both to desire God and to be active recipients of his goodness, responsive and dialogical, but necessarily (and more or less consciously) dependent on the Source. On the one hand, we contribute absolutely nothing "out of ourselves" (see Jn 5:19). God shares his glory, and we can do nothing other than receive and give it back to him in what might be called a "circle of glory." Edwards (1765/1989, pp. 530-31) likened the believer's participation in glory to the luster, beauty, and brightness of an object evident in the rays of the sun. "The beams of glory come from God, and are something of God, and are refunded back again to their original" (p. 531). Humans shine like the planets around the sun; they reflect the light that comes from another source.

At the same time, on the other hand, *our theocentric activity is intrinsic to God's glorification.* Participating in God's glory involves the *personal, generally conscious, active* return of his glory back to God in praise, love, differentiated union with him, happiness, obedience, loving others, and the healing of our souls. It is a covenantal and relational union rather than an ontological fusion of natures (Horton, 2005). This willing participation is something trees and buffalo cannot do. They glorify God in the same way software fulfills its programmer's intentions: automatically and without the self-conscious awareness, joy, and freedom possible for an image of God.[25] Mature believers are therefore uniquely capable of glorifying God through the developing gift of *freely and consciously* enjoying and replicating God, analogous[26] to how God freely and wholeheartedly loves himself and acts accordingly, sharing in God's eternal happiness in himself. Covenantal participation is summarized in Philippians 2:12-13: "Work out your salvation with fear and trembling; for it is God who is at work in you, both to will and to work for His good pleasure."

Human sin and brokenness have, of course, tragically disrupted this circle of glory. Yet from eternity God had incorporated these fatal conditions into his doxological agenda, since he permits them to demonstrate aspects of his virtuous character that would not have been displayed otherwise: fortitude, patience, mercy, compassion, forgiveness, and so on. Indeed, it was God's intention to display the glory of the Trinity precisely by their direct involvement in providing a comprehensive remedy for human fallenness, by the Son's becoming human and dying for our sin and the Holy Spirit's coming to dwell in those who believe, and thereby enabling them to participate personally, but dependently, in their recovery and share in God's happiness. Put differently, participation occurs through faith in Christ, as we learn how to die to our fallen ways of centering on other gods and how to become new selves who are increasingly centered on the triune God. Finally, God intended the church to image the trinitarian communion as its members help each other participate in this circle of glory, growing ever more in love with God and one another (Eph 4:12-16), and seek in turn to draw more people into this happy communion. Obviously these aims are only yet being partially realized.

Our Well-Being, His Glory

"God is glorified in making us happy, and we enjoying happiness, must glorify God" (Sibbes, 1635/1973, p. 247). One of the most beautiful aspects of this entire economy is how God has chosen to manifest his goodness throughout a radically asymmetrical, hierarchical union. God's love of himself shines on all that he has made (Edwards, 1765/1998, pp. 176-77). In fact, part of God's delight in us is due to the fact that he is sharing himself with those who are other than himself (see Piper, 1991, chaps. 3, 7-9). But God's glory is especially concentrated in the life, death, resurrection, and exaltation of the Son and the indwelling of the Holy Spirit and, further, in the healing and conformity of believers into the image of the Son, through union with Christ and the help of the Spirit, so that his joy and ours become increasingly, self-consciously one. As Piper has famously put it: "God is most glorified in us when we are most satisfied in him" (1996, p. 50). Or as Ireneaus reputedly wrote, long before Piper, "The glory of God is a living soul." This relation between God's glory and our happiness or well-being forms the bedrock of a theocentric therapy paradigm.[27]

Curved In on Ourselves

This all sounds wonderful, but to greatly increase the dramatic force (and glory), it occurs under conditions that would seem to be the most calculated to undermine the entire enterprise, since those appointed to glorify God are now thoroughly opposed to him being their center and are disposed to being their own. As Luther put it, we are curved in on ourselves (Bayer, 2008). Modernism is not our greatest problem—that is just a contemporary manifestation of the unconscious opposition/disposition all humans have that the Bible calls *sin*.

For God to be God, he must be absolutely opposed to our opposition of him. Anything less would indicate God himself is complicit in our sin and evil. His glory is further manifested by his holding humans accountable for their sin and evil and judging us accordingly. Consequently, the beginning of wisdom is the fear of God, and part of that wisdom is the true knowledge of ourselves (Calvin, 1559/1960, I.i.1), knowledge that leads us to Christ (Gal 3:24). Unfortunately, simply becoming a Christian does not destroy this psychological/relational disorder but only begins its diminishment, which is furthered through our deepening participation in God's glory, that is, through the therapeutic practices of faith and repentance in Christ.

Theologians of Glory and Theologians of the Cross

We finish this section with a caution about glory. A few years after his evangelical deepening, Luther (1518/2005) made a remarkable and provocative contrast between what he called a "theologian of glory" and a "theologian of the cross."[28] The former, he said, "calls evil good and good evil," while the latter "calls the thing what it actually is" (p. 49). Luther's love of paradox is in full display in this paper that summarized some of the self-understanding he gained from his arduous, decade-long quest for spiritual perfection (and made him the first Christian deconstructionist of religion, who both anticipated and influenced Kierkegaard).

A theologian of glory, he explained, "prefers works to suffering, glory to the cross, strength to weakness, wisdom to folly, and, in general, good to evil" (in Lull, p. 58); that is, he or she still desires worldly fame and success, just hidden under the cloak of religion. A theologian of the cross, by contrast, recognizes that "God can be found only in suffering and the cross" (p. 58). Luther knew from personal experience that sin's deceptiveness is such that it comes to take up residence in our best thoughts and deeds, *even in our pursuit of God and his glory*. Perhaps with the Pharisees in the Gospels in mind, he was reminding us that our unconscious tendency to be centered on ourselves is masked best by a conscious and very public God-centeredness. Luther's caution reminds us to handle topics such as God's glory with great care, being quick to examine our motives and listen to feedback, so we can grow in self-awareness. In addition, he was encouraging us to look for glory in surprising places—people such as the mentally impaired and those with personality disorders, schizophrenia, the anxious and the depressed, yes, and even sinners, who, like "jars of clay, . . . show that this all-surpassing power is from God and not from us" (2 Cor 4:7 NIV).

SOME THERAPEUTIC IMPLICATIONS

We have seen that God has more than a supportive role to play within a Christian therapeutic framework. God and God alone is humanity's greatest good (Bavinck, 1956, p. 17). As a result, human well-being is promoted through centering our lives on him and participating in his glory. How does the ideal of God's centrality affect Christian counseling and psychotherapy? "You have made us for yourself, and our heart is restless until it rests in You" (Augustine, 2009, p. 3). From a theocentric perspective, human life in adulthood is a search for God, whether conscious or not. Everyone who seeks counseling is looking for happiness of some sort, for some kind of satisfaction. Christians historically have understood such a search to be fundamentally an unconscious yearning for the perfection and communion that can only be found in God (Burnaby, 1938, p. 141). Our Creator has so constituted human life that all the legitimate joys of life, from infancy onward, have hidden within them a beckoning to something greater, a Someone who is the only soul-satisfying fulfillment of all creaturely joy. Only in the love of God can humans find a transcendent solace, forgiveness, and the reason for their being.

It is true that many people seem reasonably happy without God. Perhaps they are. But an Augustinian interpretation might suppose that maintaining that state requires the repression of a subtle, chronic sense of incompleteness or meaninglessness that others, for various reasons, cannot ignore. Many others are aware of great stress and frustration in their attempts to find satisfaction in this world that keep it out of reach. Perhaps this is because these unfulfilled longings are actually longings for an infinite Being and are impossible to fulfill in lesser things that last only for a time and leave one always wanting more.

But those who have consciously tasted the glory of God know that this is what they were made for. There is an unparalleled kind of fulfillment that humans experience in the worship and love of God. There is something so clean and good in the praising of God, something purer, higher, and greater than any other joy in this life, including the good of sex. Extolling his beauty makes us happy; receiving his love gives us peace; savoring his immensity, his holiness, his wisdom and compassion just feels good, and it feels good because it is good. Such feelings testify to the value of the object. Positive psychology has well documented that a positive orientation is good for the soul; what can be more positive than to direct our minds and hearts regularly on the infinite positivity of God's beauty and perfections? Getting lost in the greatness of God can provide a "glorious distraction" from the sorrows and abuse of this world, as well as our personal difficulties and sins, for a time at least, until we can learn how to address them more effectively in Christ. Worship itself is therapeutic, and it can move believers from having

God merely as their center ideal to being increasingly their psychological center, where his centrality can bring far more healing to the soul. Christian counseling and psychotherapy therefore promote spending time with God every day—praying and meditating, singing or journaling, and sharing it with others. Researchers have found that activities such as "elevation"[29] and awe are associated with human flourishing (Shiota, Thrash, Danvers, & Dombrowski, 2014). We need *Christian* positive psychology research on the benefits of participating in "the love of Christ which surpasses knowledge, that you may be filled up to all the fullness of God" (Eph 3:19).

Before moving on, however, we must also acknowledge that our sin and brokenness, and bad experiences in a sinful and broken world, inevitably hinder our capacity to experience consistently God's glory. Even mature believers report times of spiritual desertion and dark nights of the soul. As a result, we have to temper our expectations regarding God's glory in this life, realizing our experience of it seems to come and go. In fact, God actually seems to use such desertions to benefit our souls and increase our future participation in his glory (Voetius & Hoornbeeck, 2003; Exline, Hall, Pargament, & Harriott, 2016). Moreover, believers themselves differ in their capacity for God, depending on where they are on the journey. As a result, Christian counselors need great wisdom regarding how to help people into the happiness of God.

Having God at the Center of One's Relational World

Human life is characterized by social interaction—people relating to each other, talking and doing things together. Yet from a Christian standpoint, without a personal relationship with God, we are fundamentally, psychologically alone. As images of God, made for God, without God we are relationally compromised. Yes, we need other humans (a need created by God, be it noted; Gen 2:12), but without God to serve as our meaningful, relational center, we are inevitably motivated to be on top, to be admired, or to serve others selfishly and one way or another, to try to get them to meet our needs. At the same time, our significant faults suggest we are unworthy of such esteem. As a result, the typical human "devotes all his attention to hiding his faults both from others and from himself, and he cannot endure either that others should point them out to him, or that they should see them" (Pascal, 1941, pp. 38-39). This leads to a paradoxically precarious existence for us fallen humans, who desperately want the love and esteem of others but fear getting too close, lest they be "found out" and rejected.

Object relations therapists have discovered that humans develop psychosocial dynamic schemes in the course of their early social experiences: emotionally loaded units formed of a self-representation and an other-representation (called internal objects) through which they interpret their current relationships and relational experiences. If their early caregivers were poor images of God and repeatedly sinned against them, causing them a lot of pain, these structures become correspondingly distorted, and significant psychological defenses form to keep as much pain as possible out of consciousness. As a result, self- and other-representations can become split off from each other (the bad from the good), shifting emotionally in seesaw-like patterns with the self felt positively and the other negatively, and later, vice versa; shame and anxiety are infused throughout these processes, causing most of this internal activity to be kept out of awareness.

These are important discoveries. But what happens to such structures of believers as they open up their souls experientially to the psychological centrality of the infinite God in worship and meditative prayer? It seems likely that they could be significantly altered. The greatest difficulty for believers, perhaps, is the profound dissociation that can exist between the conscious knowledge that God is one's center-ideal and what is actually going on *psychologically* in the hiddenness of one's darkened and wounded heart, related to indwelling sin and poor early social experiences. This gap in self-awareness gives Christian counselors and their counselees much to work on and also makes the concrete presence of counselors essential as a healing agent, imaging something of the true God in sessions. This complexity requires a triangular model of relationship, with God at the top (signifying his supremacy or centrality) and "self" and "other" at the two bottom angles (see Johnson, 2007, chap. 9).

Decentering and Recentering the Self

"We live in a world of unreality and dreams. To give up our imaginary position as the center, to renounce it, not only intellectually but in the imaginative part of our soul, that means to awaken to what is real and eternal" (Weil, 1951, p. 159). *Decentering* is a verb form recently coined by postmodernists that makes good sense in a Christian vocabulary. This term, I think, can help us interpret some the "hard sayings" of Jesus regarding discipleship: "If anyone wishes to come after Me, he must deny himself, and take up his cross and follow Me" (Mk 8:34), and his encouragement to "hate" one's family members and even oneself (Lk 14:26). Paul took this theme further and encouraged his readers to consider themselves "crucified with Christ" (Gal 2:20) and "dead to sin" (Rom 6:11), teaching of "a *wrongly* centered self that needs to be de-centered by being nailed to a cross" (Volf, 1998, p. 69).

Having oneself as one's psychological center means that everything in one's life and soul—relationships, thoughts, desires, and way of life—is curved in on the self and organized excessively around one's own agenda. An important part of God's salvation/therapy, then, concerns the continual, deepening repositioning of the soul's center, from its default locus to a *re-centering* on God and his beauty, thoughts, desires, and commands.[30] Worshiping and loving God is the primary way one works this psychological recalibration. However, this process is advanced by an intentional realigning of more and more of one's internal world and relationships according to God's glory. This is a gradual, lifelong journey involving regular (ideally, daily) times of solitude that include prayer, self-examination, journaling, and meditative psychological reorganization and usually the help of others in periods of therapy.

Perfectionism—the desire to be or appear perfect—exists in all humans to some extent, both a sign of the self's "very good" image-bearing origin and an ironic symptom of the self's current imperfection (Winter, 2005). Decentering and recentering in Christ and the Spirit also involve the painful practices of coming to terms with our sins and weaknesses, learning to be honest about them with others, and resisting the tendency to pretend like we have it all together. As God is increasingly trusted and felt to be the psychological center of one's universe, pressure is lifted from feeling the need to always be right, or otherwise omnicompetent. One God in the universe is enough, freeing us to see the truth about ourselves: that we're actually finite creatures with many limitations, we sometimes do evil, and we have indwelling sin that taints all we do well. Growing in such realizations is good for counselees, for it aids the death of the old self, particularly what Merton (1961a; and Winnicott, 1965) called the *false* self, that part that believes and presents oneself as being better than one actually is. As counselees rest increasingly in God's absolute perfection, believe who they *really* are in Christ, and accept who they *actually* are now, they are able to modify their mostly unconscious desire to be perfect in themselves and become increasingly content with where they are in the journey.

Recognizing God's centrality also helps people develop appropriate boundaries with others. Without a strong sense that God is their psychological center, anxiety about disappointing others comes more easily, as well as being overly concerned with what others think and working hard just to please them (Cloud & Townsend, 1992; Welch, 1998), a tendency that reflects some degree of codependency. Strengthening one's soul by centering it on God—so that he is one's rock and shield (Ps 18:2)—better enables one to take others seriously without feeling one's identity being conformed to the preferences and attitudes of those ultimately as limited as oneself.

Toward a Theocentric Hierarchy of Values

Humans have many legitimate, created needs and desires: food, safety, love and belonging, and (as we become adults) meaning, a sense of competence, sexual enjoyment, and many others. Such needs and desires were created good by God, so generally speaking (unless twisted beyond their designated bounds), the satisfaction of these needs and desires are goods, established by God (1 Tim 4:4-5). The desire to avoid suffering is one of those created desires, given to us by God because suffering is a "mixed evil."[31] Consequently, all things being equal, it is good to avoid suffering and laudable to help others avoid it.

At the same time, recognizing that God is one's greatest good affects one's interpretation of one's lesser goods, including how one approaches suffering. Let us consider a couple of examples. Most marriages involve some suffering, and the Bible teaches that when the suffering reaches a certain threshold of severity, divorce is permitted, particularly when one spouse has functionally abandoned his or her vows (Mt 5:32; 1 Cor 7:15). However, most of the time, distressed couples should not consider divorce to be the best option. Why? Because of the conjunction of God's glory and their long-term well-being. First, persevering in the face of some marital suffering is a picture of Christ's love of his church, in spite of its shortcomings (Eph 5; 1 Pet 2:20-23)—so God is specially glorified.[32]

Second, it is easy for spouses to blame each another for their problems, especially in the early years of the marriage, so some perseverance (and often counseling) is necessary to break through the wall of one's defenses, in order to start seeing exactly how one is contributing to the marriage's difficulties, so that one can really work on oneself, in dependence on Christ. This process yields growth and virtue (and glory) that might never be attained when divorce is sought too readily.

Third, people in conflicted marriages were often initially attracted to their spouse, at least in part, because of unconscious, unresolved issues due to a poor relationship with their opposite-sex parent. There is probably no better way to promote their psychological healing and to face the wounds derived from their family of origin and work through them than in the context of their present marriage, and as a result of such gradual resolution, one's marriage will often improve. Consequently, God's glory and one's well-being can both be promoted by working through marital difficulties.

Medication, properly used, glorifies God, since it is a gift of creation grace and is sanctified by the word of God and prayer (1 Tim 4:4-5). Indeed, for severe psychopathology—psychotic episodes or severe depression or anxiety—psychotropic medication should usually be the first level of intervention. There are, however, at least three orders of human nature higher than the biological (from lower to higher): psychosocial, ethical, and spiritual (Johnson, 2007, chaps. 8-9, 15). With this framework in mind, I suggested the following two guidelines for therapy in *Foundations*: Christians should intervene at the highest levels possible and the lowest levels necessary. The lowest-level interventions, such as psychotropic medications, only ameliorate symptoms due to neurological malfunction; they do not change the patient's brain organization. So, if the biological symptoms are on the mild to moderate side of the spectrum, therapists should generally first try to promote more permanent change through higher-level interventions, such as the counseling relationship and the teaching of cognitive, affective, and spiritual strategies, all of which actually modify and form new neural networks, which will then help in the future. Second, while God gets glory from healing at all four levels, the effective use of strategies that rely explicitly on Christ's death and resurrection, for example (to be discussed in later chapters), would seem to advance God's doxological agenda the most, all things being equal, by bringing into the healing process those of his activities that most manifest his glory. (With more severe disorders, of course, medical and therapeutic interventions may need to be initiated simultaneously.)

By contrast, many modern therapists—assuming a framework in which the (immediate) well-being of the self is the highest value—tend to focus primarily on the reduction of all counselee suffering, without enough regard for other potential positive outcomes of mild to moderate suffering (as evidenced in studies of posttraumatic growth; Calhoun & Tedeschi, 2014). In such a context, solutions such as divorce or medication may be resorted to more quickly than is actually in the long-term best interests of the counselee. A theocentric orientation casts human needs and suffering in a different light, where the good of relieving suffering in the short term is relativized by the greater goods of greater long-term well-being conjoined with greater glory for God. Our *greatest* need is to be rightly related to the greatest Being in the universe and to be in communion with him. Indeed, "unless a person takes God as her deepest heart's desire, her heart will always have at its deepest core a yearning that is both inchoate and unsatisfied" (Stump, 2010, p. 440).

Of course, suffering per se will not be valorized by a Christianity true to Christ's mission and message. When he healed the sick and raised people from the dead, he was revealing God's heart and prefiguring God's eschatological agenda to eventually remove all suffering from our lives (Rev 21:4). So, love and glory will incline believers to alleviate as much suffering as possible. Nonetheless, the choice to endure avoidable suffering is a matter of Christian liberty. When done for the sake of others, it is a matter of Christian charity. When done for God's glory, as in the call to missions or martyrdom, it is an act of worship and image bearing, for all of *God's* suffering is freely chosen, since he could have created a possible world other than this one. When also done for the self's future happiness, whether in this age through one's psychospiritual growth or in the age to come in eternal bliss, the self's autocentric agenda is being undermined and transformed into a higher order that is both theocentric and therapeutic.

God Wants You to Flourish!

Perhaps if this book had the title *God Wants You to Flourish* it would sell better! To some Christian ears, that would sound too anthropocentric, and as we have seen, God's glory is vastly more important. But the great tradition of Christianity has concluded that the Bible teaches that God desires our proper flourishing precisely because God has chosen in this universe to join his glory to proper human flourishing (Charry, 2010; Edwards, 1765/1998; Piper, 1991; Sherwin, 2005). Through the course of that revelation, we learn that the glory of the triune God is love, and it is his nature to want to share that love and bring others into that glory. "Our Lord's great will is that [his love] should be kindled in the hearts of men. As God he wills nothing else, since his glory and our happiness—the two ends of all he does—are inseparably bound up with the Father's love" (Grou, 1796/1962, p. 2). Yes, it's all about him. God is the greatest being in the universe and so worthy of our praise. But one of the most amazing parts of his doxological agenda is his desire to bring us into his glory, love, and happiness. The Christian life is designed to be a journey into glory. "Ultimately, God is our happiness" (Sherwin, 2005, p. 81). Consequently, part of what makes Christian counseling so gratifying is its participation in God's glorious love for humanity and his desire to draw more people into that love. He accomplishes this by saving/healing people, so that they desire him supremely (Piper, 1991).

Yet this wondrous agenda is not well appreciated, even by many in the church. There are plenty of reasons for this—God's hiddenness, feeble Christian teaching, the problem of evil, our sinful resistance, overwhelming personal suffering, and growing up with angry or neglectful parents who were poor images of God. The main challenges, then, for theocentric counseling and psychotherapy are to help counselees, first, understand the correlation between having God as their center-ideal and their flourishing and fulfillment, and second, cultivate an increasingly God-centered orientation throughout their souls. According to a Christian positive psychology, that is how humans will flourish best. Hopefully, this book will help counselors learn how to do more of both.

RESOURCES FOR COUNSELORS AND COUNSELEES

Classical

Augustine. (2009). *Confessions*. (H. Chadwick, Trans.). New York: Oxford University Press. After the Bible, this is the place to begin reading to understand God's glorious soul-healing purposes.

Balthasar, H. U. von. *The glory of the Lord: A theological aesthetics* (7 vols.). San Francisco: Ignatius. ‡ A monumental work by a Catholic on the greatest subject of all.

Barth, K. (1957). *Church dogmatics* 2.1. (T. H. L. Parker, W. B. Johnston, H. Knight, & J. L. M. Hare, Trans.). Edinburgh: T&T Clark. ‡ See the section on God's glory on pp. 640-77.

Edwards, J. (1989). *The works of Jonathan Edwards, Vol. 8: Ethical writings* (P. Ramsey, Ed.). New Haven, CT: Yale University Press. ‡ This volume of the critical edition of Edwards's works has *The end for which God created the world* and *True virtue*.

———. (1998). The end for which God created the world. In *God's passion for his glory*. Wheaton, IL: Crossway. (Original work published 1765). ‡ Arguably the most important essay ever written in the English language, and this is the easiest way to purchase it.

Hopkins, G. M. (2003). Instructions. In J. F. Thornton & S. B. Varenne (Eds.), *Moral beauty, God's grace: Major poems and spiritual writings of Gerard Manley Hopkins* (pp. 180-84). New York: Random House. A sweet, succinct summary of God's glory.

Luther, M. (2005). Heidelberg Disputation. In T. F. Lull (Ed.), *Martin Luther's basic theological writings* (2nd ed., pp. 47-61). Minneapolis: Fortress. (Original work published 1518)

Tozer, A. W. (1992). *The knowledge of the holy.* New York: Harper. See particularly the chapters on God's self-existence and self-sufficiency.

Contemporary

Crabb, L. (2009). *66 love letters.* Nashville, TN: Thomas Nelson.

Forde, G. (1997). *On being a theologian of the cross: Reflections on Luther's Heidelberg Disputation, 1518.* Grand Rapids, MI: Eerdmans.

Hart, D. B. (2003). *The beauty of the infinite: The aesthetics of Christian truth.* Grand Rapids, MI: Eerdmans. ‡ A difficult but dazzling work by an Eastern Orthodox theologian.

Keller, T. (2009). *Counterfeit gods: The empty promises of money, sex, and power, and the only hope that matters.* New York: Dutton.

Piper, J. (1986). *Desiring God.* Sisters, OR: Multnomah. As is well known, Piper is the great contemporary popularizer of Edwards's theocentric vision of life.

———. (2000). *The pleasures of God* (2nd ed.). Sisters, OR: Multnomah.

———. (2001). *The dangerous duty of delight: The glorified God and the satisfied soul.* Sisters, OR: Multnomah. Only 82 pages, so it makes a good homework assignment.

Storm, S. (2004). *One thing: Developing a passion for the beauty of God.* Ross-shire, UK: Christian Focus.

Welch, E. (1997). *When people are big and God is small.* Phillipsburg, NJ: P&R.

‡ More intellectually demanding, so recommended more for counselors and pastors than for counselees

—2—

The Glorious Missions
of the Trinity

Axiom 2: God is a triune communion of persons, the archetype of the personal and social form of life of human beings.

Corollary: The Father has willed that the Holy Spirit bring fallen humans through faith in the Son Christ into their communion to be an ever clearer sign of the Trinity.

The grace of the Lord Jesus Christ, and the love of God,
and the fellowship of the Holy Spirit, be with you all.

2 CORINTHIANS 13:14

IN THE PREVIOUS CHAPTER, we focused on God's remarkable agenda to glorify himself through the flourishing of humanity. According to Augustine, that great trinitarian psychologist, the Trinity "is the supreme source of all things, and the most perfect beauty, and the most blessed delight" (1948, Vol. II, p. 770; *On the Trinity*). At the same time, the Trinity is the greatest of mysteries, transcending our capacities to fully comprehend it. So this exposition will move slowly, to take in as much as possible. Our tour will be conducted in three "stages." First, we will consider the glorious nature, acts, and communion of the Trinity. Second, we will focus on how the Trinity manifests its glory by making possible a restoration in humanity's relationship with God and one another: by the activity of the Son of God—both God and human and so the "bridge" between humans and the Trinity—and by the activity of the Holy Spirit, who indwells believers, drawing them into the trinitarian communion. Third, we will examine the role believers are to play in the glorification of the Trinity by means of their participation in and resemblance to that God in their lives together.[1]

CHRISTIAN TEACHING REGARDING THE TRINITY

Judaism and Islam are monotheistic religions. They assert there is one God; however, that God is absolutely and eternally solitary. Because no one is God's equal, there is no one to whom God can fully relate, and this may have led to an implicit assumption that God is fundamentally an isolated, solitary, and aloof sovereign. Perhaps building on this assumption, when thinking about why God created humans, some have simplistically supposed that a solitary God desired a relationship with *someone*—he was lonely. Christianity believes that God is one, but it is monotheism with a difference: it is *trinitarian*. Submitting to the revelation of the New Testament, Christianity affirms that the Creator God is three persons in one Being. Such a God is not solitary but exists eternally in a perfect, blessed communion of love and mutual delight. This God needs no one else, because his nature is fundamentally interpersonal and relational. Christianity teaches that "the whole basis of being is a community of persons," and the essence of their being is love (Danielou, 1969, p. 45; 1 Jn 4:12).

Orthodox Christians believe that the one Creator of the universe and Savior of the world is Father, Son, and Holy Spirit. Since the first centuries of the early church, Christians have commonly declared that God is a single being (or substance or essence) who consists of three persons (or subsistences or hypostases) (cf. Augustine, 1948; Bavinck, 2004; Barth, 1936; Emery & Levering, 2011; Holmes, 2012; Thompson, 1994). Yet Christians have long considered the Trinity to be a mystery—something beyond full human understanding, the Being of beings who has some paradoxical features that we need to understand as best as we can.

Based in Hebrew monotheism, Christianity has always affirmed that there is only one true God: "Hear, O Israel! The Lord is our God, the Lord is one!" (Deut 6:4). In the context of rampant polytheism, God began his self-revelation to humanity with the disclosure that there was only one divine being. Only after emphasizing that foundational truth for centuries did God take the next step to reveal more fully that this one being is also tripersonal, in the coming of the Son with his teaching about the Father and Spirit, and the coming of the Spirit. The apostles then gave us a preliminary inspired description of this complex being in the New Testament. Consider the following: the Father knows future historical events (Mk 13:32), chooses (Mt 11:27), loves (Jn 3:35), responds to prayer (Eph 3:14), and so on; the eternal Son of God upholds all things (Heb 1:3), speaks (Rev 2:18), sympathizes (Heb 4:15), gives understanding (1 Jn 5:20), and so on; and the Holy Spirit is listed along with other persons, such as the apostles (Acts 15:28), Christ (Jn 16:14), and the Father and the Son (Mt 28:19; 2 Cor 13:13), and he is self-conscious (Acts 13:2) and self-determining (Acts 16:7; 1 Cor 12:11), teaches (Jn 14:26), can be grieved (Eph 4:30), testifies of Christ (Jn 15:26; 16:13-14), can speak audibly to believers (Acts 13:2), and from within them prays (Rom 8:26) and cries out, "Abba! Father!" (Gal 4:6). The members of the Trinity also relate to and interact with each other. The Father sent the Son (Jn 5:37), and they both sent the Spirit (Jn 14:26); the Son obeys the Father (Jn 12:49-50); and both Son and Spirit pray to the Father (Mt 11:25; Jn 11:41; Rom 8:26) (see Bavinck, 2004; Frame, 2002; Horton, 2011).[2]

Reflecting on such apostolic teaching regarding the coming of the Son of God and the gift of the Spirit of God, and the essential trinitarian form of their worship, leaders in the early church hammered out a more elaborate doctrine of the Trinity between AD 300 and 700, in the context of distortions that had arisen. This process led to the composition of formal documents, called creeds, which summarized the early-church consensus and have continued to unify the church up to the present. The early church still affirmed that God was one, but they also concluded that this one God was Father, Son, and Spirit; that each one is fully God; and that the Trinity is not three gods. To help describe this God, the early church settled on the terms *substantia* in the Latin-speaking church and *ousia* in the Greek to refer to the nature and being of the one God, and *persona* (Lat.) and *hypostasis* (Gk.) to refer to the individual members of the Godhead[3] and communicate their distinct identity (Bavinck, 2004). It has long been customary, therefore, to refer to Father, Son, and Spirit in English as *persons*.

Relations Among the Triune Communion

Central to the biblical revelation about the Trinity are the relationships that exist between these persons. As a result of their reflections on the available data, theologians came to distinguish between two major perspectives on the trinitarian relationship: immanent and economic.[4] Their immanent (or intratrinitarian) relations have to do with the kind of relations Father, Son, and Holy Spirit have with each other in eternity. Their economic relations, in contrast, pertain to the "economy"[5] of God's works in time, external to their own respective relations, in creation, providence, and redemption (Bavinck, 2004; Frame, 2002), and have to do with their respective roles and responsibilities in those activities. Theologians assume that their relations in history are congruent with and flow from their relations in eternity, but they cannot be equated, because the latter refer to God as he is in himself, without respect to the creation, and the former involve the paradoxical conditions of the eternal Son remaining what he was, while also becoming a temporal human being, and the eternal Spirit coming to indwell believers in history.[6]

Immanent trinitarian relations. The Bible, understandably, tells us far more about their relationship in time than their relationship in eternity (Bavinck, 2004), and that will be our main focus. Nevertheless, because the former are dependent on the latter, some consideration must be given to the latter. The following summarizes the church's settled interpretation of and conclusions regarding the available evidence. The Father is the eternal *origin*-in-himself, the unbegotten source of all—including, in a special sense, the personhood of the other members of the Trinity; the Son is eternally *generated* or begotten or spoken by the Father; and the Spirit *proceeds* eternally from both Father and Son.[7] The nature of the Trinity is such that each person is eternally "constituted" in relationship to the others. The Son is the Son by virtue of his relationship of filial dependence on the Father; conversely, the Father is who he is as the source of the Son and the Spirit, and so on. The persons are noninterchangeable, and they are who and what they are by their relations. God would not be God, and the Persons would not be who and what they are, apart from their unique relations with each other. Their relations with each other are essential to the Being of the triune God. But this also implies that there is an *order* or *taxis* within the Trinity— correlated with their absolute equality, since the Father has a preeminence as the source of the others, and both Father and Son send the Spirit.[8]

The Father's eternally glorious love of the Son. So far, the Trinity's immanent relations sound rather abstract, but they are also characterized in Scripture by love. "God is love" (1 Jn 4:8, 16), and many Christian theologians have suggested that this could only be true of a God who is threefold. We are told the most, however, about the relation of the Father and the Son by the apostle John. In Christ's high-priestly prayer, he referred to the relationship he had with his Father in eternity: "Now, Father, glorify Me together with Yourself, with the glory which I had with You before the world was" (Jn 17:5); and he prayed that his disciples "may see My glory which You have given Me, for You loved Me before the foundation of the world" (Jn 17:24; see also Jn 1:1-2; Prov 8:22, 30-31). In chapter one, we noted that God's love is central to his glory. Here, we note that the internal glory of the Trinity is *their* love. In particular, in the Bible, "the relation between Father and Son is portrayed as a life of love" (Bavinck, 2004, p. 215), with a special focus on the Father's love for the Son (Jn 3:35; 5:20; 15:9; 17:23-24, 26).

The Father's eternal love for the Son is echoed in history in his public expressions of delight in his Son, now human. First at his baptism (the initiation of his ministry to humanity and the fulfillment of his Father's calling) and later at his transfiguration (the special, visible glorification of the Son to three disciples), the Father's ebullient praise of his Son sounded forth, "This is My beloved Son, in whom I am well-pleased" (Mt 3:17; cf. Mt 17:5). What do we hear in this cry?[9] "The original, the primal, the deepest, the foundational joy of God is the joy he has in his own perfections as he sees them reflected in the glory of his son" (Piper, 1991, p. 38). This would appear to be the love of appreciation or delight, the sheer joy of the Father in the virtuous beauty of his Son, the consummate replication of his own perfection, which the Son himself fully reciprocates.

The Father's eternal love for the Son is also characterized as sharing. "The Father loves the Son and has given all things into His hand" (Jn 3:35), and "The Father loves the Son and shows Him all things that He Himself is doing" (Jn 5:20). As a result, they share everything in common, as Christ prayed, "All things that are Mine are Yours, and Yours are Mine" (Jn 17:10), including his self-existence: "As the Father has life in Himself, even so He gave to the Son also to have life in Himself" (Jn 5:26). Consequently, their relationship is later described as *koinōnia* (1 Jn 1:3; indicating "commonness, communion, fellowship"). What does the Father share with his Son? His glory (Jn 17:5, 11, 22-24), that is, his perfections as well as his plans and accomplishments. And the Son eternally acts correspondingly, for "he is the act of giving himself to the Father as Son in the Spirit of love. The Son is the act of filial love, sonship fully in act" (Weinandy, 2011, p. 390). Though the Son is coequal with the Father, perhaps we could capture the nature of this act as "receptive emulation." Like Father, like Son, for all eternity.

One of the greatest mysteries of intratrinitarian relations is their mutual indwelling. "Know and understand that the Father is in me," Christ said, "and I in the Father" (Jn 10:38; cf. Jn 14:10-13; 17:21). The Greek Fathers termed this relationship *perichoresis*, and the Latin Fathers *circuminsessio*, concluding from the above passages that the Father and Son interpenetrate, cosaturate, and indwell one another (Frame, 2002). Roberts (1997b) calls this quality "permeability," and Volf (1998) says that the Father and the Son are "mutually internal" (to each other, p. 208); they live within each other, sharing absolute self-consciousness while remaining distinct persons, without confusion of identity.[10] Such interpersonal permeability is only possible in God, because Father and Son are both infinite, omniscient, and omnipathic, so they can personally fully share in each other's personhood and activities. They therefore necessarily experience perfect unity and harmony through infinitely coextensive intimacy and joint activity.

Much of the biblical teaching on the immanent Trinity thus puts a spotlight on the relation of the Father and the Son, portraying the former as the Lover and the latter as the Beloved (Eph 1:6). We learn in Scripture that the Father delights in his Son and shares everything of himself with him as he responds in receptive emulation, and they dwell together in each other. So, the *main* picture the Bible paints of the eternal Trinity is the Father-Son relationship and its resulting communion.

The Holy Spirit of love. Yet, as we noted above, the Holy Spirit is also portrayed as an active, communicative agent in Scripture, and completely God, just as the Father and the Son. So where is the Spirit in the Trinity's eternal relations? We are frankly not told much about that in Scripture. Perhaps we find a clue in the Spirit being twice called the Spirit of *koinōnia* by Paul (2 Cor 13:14; Phil 2:1), and John uses the same word to refer to the communion enjoyed by the Father and the Son (1 Jn 1:3). But Christian theologians from Augustine to Aquinas to Edwards and Barth have thought more can be said than that. We recall that "God is love" (1 Jn 4:8, 16), and since all three persons are God, all three must participate equally in divine love—it is not as if the Father and the Son are eternal love and the Spirit is off in the corner somewhere. If God the Father is the eternal Lover and the Son the eternal Beloved, then we can say the Holy Spirit is the eternal Love or communion they share.[11] The eternal procession of the Spirit from the Father and the Son can be understood as their mutual love. The Spirit, then, is the personal quality of their relationship, but is not an abstraction, for the Spirit is just as fully a person as the Father and Son. "The Spirit is love in person" (Emery, 2007, p. 225), the one whom the Father shares with the Son and the Son shares (back) with the Father. He is their mutual gift, the joy of their mutual appreciation, the movement of their mutual well-wishing, the fullness of their mutual indwelling. The Holy Spirit is the divine person who brings beauty, goodness, and meaningfulness from one to another. "The Spirit is the 'gift' of the Father and the Son inasmuch as the Spirit is what the Father and Son 'make common' to one another" (Vanhoozer, 2010, p. 258). Bolstering this model from another vantage point, Richard of St. Victor (1979, p. 391) conjectured that three persons are actually necessary for perfect love, because the love of two persons attains a transcendent fulfillment when shared with a third who delights in their love without self-interest. "As the third, who receives and returns the love of Father and Son, and so witnesses, enjoys, and perfects it, the Spirit is also the one in whom that love most manifestly opens out as sheer delight, generosity, and desire for the other" (Hart, 2003, p. 175).

From reflection on this relatively sparse revelation, Christians have concluded that God's eternal nature enjoys mutual, self-giving generosity, one to another in fitting union. "God in himself enjoys never-ending, fully realized interpersonal communication: communion" (Vanhoozer, 2010, p. 244). Each person loves himself in loving the other infinitely, so their self-love and love of the other are equally ultimate, enabling them to be "self-outpouring love" (Hart, 2003, p. 298). The eternal glory of the Trinity is a mutual love than which none greater can be conceived, that lies at the fount of the universe and permeates our existence.[12]

Economic trinitarian relations. The vast majority of our understanding of the Trinity, however, concerns their *economic* relations, that is, how Father, Son, and Holy Spirit relate to each other with respect to their activities in time, specifically creation, providence, and redemption. Calvin (1559/1960) is typical in the following distinctions: "To the Father is attributed the beginning of activity, and the fountain and wellspring of all things; to the Son, wisdom, counsel, and the ordered disposition of all things; but to the Spirit is assigned the power and efficacy of that activity" (pp. 142-43). With respect to this universe, and particularly the humans in it, the three have different roles in common activities to achieve the Trinity's agenda to manifest their glory in history.

We must preface the discussion that follows, however, with a consideration of sin, since much of what distinguishes the roles of the different persons in history has to do with what they do about it. God could have remained glorious in himself by simply leaving humans in their fallenness and justly condemning them. However, he instead turned the human tragedy of sin into the greatest manifestation of his glory in the universe—both the excellency of his character and the riches of his triune nature—much more than judgment alone would have done.[13] The unique role for

Father, Son, and Spirit that each plays in the divine economy is called their respective "missions" (Thompson, 1994).

The missions of God. As the generative source, the Father's mission was the impetus of the plan behind everything that happens in the creation (Eph 1:11), including the missions of the other persons and the establishment and maintenance of that plan, first by sending his Son and then, with his Son, the Spirit, on their interrelated missions to save and restore sinful and broken humanity (1 Jn 4:10; Jn 15:26). The Father's mission, therefore, included giving up his beloved Son to mistreatment and murder, for their glory and our well-being.[14]

The Son's mission was twofold: divine and human. As the eternal Word, he is the expressive means of the Father's agenda to create (Jn 1:3), to maintain and care for their creation (Col 1:15; Heb 1:3), and to save (2 Cor 1:20). As the Son of Man, he laid aside his divine rights and went to the "far country" (Barth, 1956b), assuming a human nature and so becoming human to make visible the invisible God. Imaging his Father also entailed obeying his Father (Jn 4:34; 5:19, 30; 6:38; 10:17; 17:4)—which humans were created to do—and this is how he continued to abide in his Father's love as a human (Jn 15:10). In his receptive emulation of the Father, now in human form, he became both the representative of humanity to the Father (its high priest) and the Father's representative servant-Son to humanity—its Lord, Messiah, prophet, sage, savior, husband, archetypal role model, and much more (Torrance, 2008).

The redemptive part of his mission climaxed in the laying down of his life for humanity (its judicial sacrifice), manifesting the radical extent of God's design to deliver humans from their sin and suffering.[15] His vicarious obedience was vindicated by his being raised from the dead—the beginning of the new creation—and his mission continues now in his intercession in heaven on behalf of his people, which will end after he returns to earth and then gives everything back to the Father (1 Cor 15:28). Yet it was the Father's intention to magnify his Son especially, by giving him the most prominent role among all three in the salvation and healing of sinners.

The Spirit has also been involved in the creation in the beginning and until now in providence (see Gen 1:2; Ps 104:32), and his mission has been to bring the Father's purposes to fruition in the creation and in redemption. The Spirit aided the Son throughout his earthly ministry, helping him obey and emulate his Father (Mt 3:16; 12:18, 28; Lk 2:27; 4:1; 10:21). Then, after Christ was glorified (Jn 7:39), the Spirit was sent on the primary phase of his mission to realize in human beings Christ's mission on their behalf: to lead persons to salvation (e.g., by convicting them of their sin, Jn 16:8-11), dwell in those who believe (Jn 14:17; 1 Cor 6:19), conform them to the image of the Son individually (Rom 8:29; 2 Cor 3:18), and resemble the Trinity corporately (Gen 1:26-27; Jn 17:22; 2 Cor 13:14).

In the previous chapter we saw that God's external glory is the manifestation of the beauty or excellence of his character. When thinking about the Trinity in terms of their works, we should think of their mutual external glory as the *manifestation of their communal love, revealed most clearly in history through the Father's public delight in his Son, the Son's perfect giving of himself to his Father in filial obedience and conformity, and the Spirit's realization of the Son's form in the minds, hearts, and lives of believers.*

Human Life Drawn into the Triune Communion

We have seen that "infinite sharing is the law of God's inner life" (Merton, 1955, p. 3). How does this disposition help to explain what God is up to in redemption (and therapy)? Humans need redemption, of course, because of their sin, which now alienates them from God (Eph 2:1-3). However, God's intention from the beginning was to glorify himself as Trinity *through their recovery*, and even more astounding, *to realize that recovery by drawing them into the trinitarian communion* (1 Jn 1:4; see also Jn 14:20; 17:21)! How could the infinite, holy God commune with creatures, particularly sinful ones? And why would he? To answer that, we need to recall that God has always had room for "the Other" within his own triune nature (McIntosh, 2008). So it is congruent with God's nature to have others "within him" who are like him. As the Father delights to commune with the Son who corresponds to him in knowledge and love by the Spirit, so the Son delights to commune with humans who correspond to him in knowledge and love by the Spirit (Edwards, 1994, p. 272). His willingness to bring little creatures into that communion of resemblance manifests his infinite humility. What the triune God, especially the Son, had to go through in order to bring this about because of our sin is especially remarkable.

The Son, the mediating bridge to the triune communion. The Father's plan included the glorification of his beloved Son, by sending him—the eternal representation of the Father—to earth to also become the perfect human image of the Father. Coming primarily out of love for the Father, he also came "because his great love to us caused him to desire familiar communion with us," by joining himself to our nature (Edwards, 1994, p. 285).

Christ provides a crucial bridge between God and fallen humanity, for "he is of the same reality as God as far as his deity is concerned and of the same reality as we ourselves as far as his humanness is concerned" (the Chalcedon Creed in Leith, 1963). In this amazing union of natures, Christ also shows the fundamental correspondence and similarity between the persons of the triune God and human persons in his image in relationship with God and with one another, constituting a fundamental "analogy of relationship" between God and humanity centered in Christ (Barth, 1960a).[16] This also means, wondrously, that our nature is forever united, without confusion, with God's nature and now actually participates in a mediated way in God's activity. Christ's humanity "draws human attention after him into the mystery of his union with the divine" (McIntosh, 2008, p. 157).

But, as Athanasius suggested, he also had to assume our nature if he was to redeem it. The Son reconciled sinful humanity to God by becoming the divine-human priest and mediator between God and humanity (1 Tim 2:5) as well as the propitiatory sacrifice (Rom 3:25; 1 Jn 2:2; 4:10), in whom God's righteous wrath against sin was absorbed and absolved, and who was vindicated by being raised from the dead (Torrance, 2009). In the process, a lot happened: he was made sin (2 Cor 5:21) in his body on the cross and conquered sin's power in his body through its resurrection; so he remade human nature from within (McIntosh, 2008), and he paved the way for sinful humans to become new creations in union with him and to join him in his return into the triune communion (1 Jn 1:4). "As he is for God, he is also for man" (Barth, 1960a, p. 222). As a result, Jesus Christ is the everlasting basis of this new life with God—its template, guide, and goal—and the one whom his followers, therefore, are especially to know and to love.

The Spirit, the gift of the triune communion. The Father's plan to glorify the Son also involved their sending the Holy Spirit to bring what Christ had accomplished into fruition or realization in this present age. The gift of this divine Helper (Jn 14:24) takes what belongs to the Son and shares it with those who believe (Jn 16:14), beginning with the second birth (Jn 3:6), teaching and guiding them (Jn 16:13) and transforming them (2 Cor 3:5-18) in ways that transcend human capacity on its own (1 Cor 2:10-14). By indwelling believers (Rom 8:9; 1 Jn 2:27), the Spirit washes and renews them, along with Christ's holy humanity (Titus 3:5), pours out divine love into their hearts (Rom 5:5), reproduces the divine virtues (Gal 5:22-23; Rom 14:17), enables them to resist sin (Rom 8:13) and pursue Christ's holiness (2 Thess 2:13), and builds unity among them (Eph 2:22; 4:3, 13; Phil 2:1-2). But the

Spirit does not draw attention to himself. Rather, he grants believers "a vision of the Father's depths in the beauty of the Son" (Hart, 2003, p. 185) while drawing them into *their* communion.

Brought into divine glory. Through the Spirit, Christ's followers are enabled to participate in God's glory. As Christ prayed, "the glory which You have given me I have given to them" (Jn 17:22); in fact, he was already being "glorified in them" (Jn 17:10). We, by the Spirit, share in the Son's glorified humanity. Believers participate in that glory by faith, that is, receptive emulation, whereby they appropriate and internalize Christ's word and work—in his humanity—first cognitively, then carditively, and then manifesting it in their lives, particularly in their love of God and their loving relationships with one another.

Brought into divine love. The Son is the mediator of the Trinity's love. "He who loves Me will be loved by My Father, and I will love him" (Jn 14:21; also Jn 14:23; 16:27), because believers are "in the Beloved" (Eph 1:6) and nothing can separate them from that love (Rom 8:39). Through Christ, believers "pass over into the very heart of God" (McIntosh, 2008, p. 77).[17] However, believers experience and participate in that love by its being "poured into our hearts through the Holy Spirit" (Rom 5:5). "We recognize the marvelous symmetry of love between the Father, Son, and the Spirit, yet not in a circle of exclusion but in an ecstatic, eccentric, extroverted movement of embrace, to include even enemies in a communion of peace" (Horton, 2007, p. 131).

Brought into divine communion. Through the Spirit, believers also enter into something analogous to the divine *perichoresis*. Christ told his disciples that he and the Father will make their home with those who love him and obey his words (Jn 14:23; see also Rev 3:20); and he prayed for his disciples "that . . . even as You, Father, are in Me and I in you, . . . they also may be in Us. . . . I in them and You in Me" and that "the love with which You loved Me may be in them" (Jn 17:21, 23, 26). Since the Spirit mutually indwells and coinheres Father and Son in their *perichoresis*, his indwelling of believers is the means by which the Father and Son are said to indwell them. But Christ also directed his disciples to "abide in Me, and I in you" (Jn 15:4). Believers then have a role to play in this quasi-mutual indwelling, for through faith and love, they are able to "enter into" God and abide in Christ and Christ in them (Rev 3:20). Even so, this indwelling is radically asymmetrical given God's omniscience and omnipresence and the limited capacities of believers to "abide" in God. However, Father, Son, and Holy Spirit are one being, while human beings, joined to Christ by the Spirit, do not become one in being with God—they simply share in Christ's glorified humanity.

Brought into divine sharing. We have seen that the Father shares everything with the Son, and the Son is like his Father, so through the Spirit they share everything with those who believe. In addition to creational blessings, distributed among all humans, and in addition to God's glory and love, believers are lavished with every spiritual blessing in the heavens in Christ (Eph 1:3; 1 Pet 1:4-5), including eternal life (Jn 5:21; 10:28; Rom 6:23), peace (Jn 14:27), grace (1 Pet 5:5), righteousness (Rom 5:17), wisdom (Jas 1:5), rest for the weary and heavy-laden (Mt 11:28), and whatever believers ask in Christ's name (Jn 16:23; Mt 7:11). Indeed, having already given believers his Son, the Father will eventually give them *all things* (Rom 8:32).

And here we reach the Mount Everest of God's glory with respect to us, for the triune God has shared *himself* with us—and that twice over. He has sent his Son to us, who died for us and now lives praying and rooting for us in heaven, and he has given the gift of his Spirit to us (Jn 16:14; 1 Thess 4:8), who lives in us so that we can flourish in the divine communion. What kind of a God is this that he would share so much with those who are so little? Words are inadequate, but we must say something, so perhaps we could echo Paul: "Thanks be to God for His indescribable gift!" (2 Cor 9:15).

The Divine Communion and the Human Community

For the most part, Christians are to consider Jesus Christ, the Son of God and Son of Man, as the primary archetype or pattern for human persons and their development (Muller, 2003; Tanner, 2010).[18] However, there is at least one broad sense in which the Trinity altogether also serves as an archetype for human persons and their development: as *persons in reciprocal relationship.*[19]

We noted above that the concept of person was developed in the early church to help us understand what God did in Christ and the Spirit and his explanation in Scripture. Over centuries of reflection, the concept has been refined and clarified, leading to a clearer grasp of the mysterious, differentiated nature of the Trinity and also contributing, indirectly, to a remarkable evolution in our understanding of human beings.[20] Today, for example, a person is broadly understood to be a rational-linguistic, self-aware, and self-evaluative subject with narrative continuity, capable of (relatively) free actions for which he or she is responsible, and engaged in loving relations with others.[21] This contemporary notion of person had many influences, but one was the centuries-long reception and internalization of the triune God's revelation of himself in human history and Scripture and the power of that revelation to foster personhood. Reading Scripture today, we find that God (in the Old Testament) and the Father, Son, and Spirit (in the New Testament) act, speak, are referred to, and are treated as *maximal* persons of that sort. That fact, most importantly, combined with the fact that that revelation helped to shape the contemporary concept of person, gives us warrant to use the term *person* today to refer to the Three.[22]

But the *telos* of the triune God's developmental design for humanity would seem to be both personal and social: an interdependent community of persons, as exemplified ideally in the body of Christ (Eph 4:11-16). Such a *telos*, however, could only have been grasped *after* the concept of persons had become well developed in the West, after centuries of Christian influence, and therefore the viability and plausibility of the final Christian ideal for human life necessarily took longer. Similarly, and for directly analogous reasons, a broad acceptance of the implications of Scriptural teaching regarding the persons of the Trinity and their relationality, though anticipated possibly in the Cappadocians and certainly in Richard of St. Victor and Jonathan Edwards, also took longer. It seems likely that a fuller understanding of the one God's communal nature and God's ideal of interdependent human community are intimately linked together sociohistorically and conceptually. Both had been there all along in Scripture. The church just could not see them as clearly as some can now (just like it could not as fully grasp Paul's doctrine of justification by faith until the 1500s). Building on the progressive illumination of Scripture (Orr, 1898) that has preceded us, perhaps we are now better able to recognize the equal ultimacy of the triune God's being and persons, his communality and trifold agency, discovering in the divine life of the Trinity the perfect communion of perfect persons, and so, the formal archetype of human life, understood as an interdependent community of persons.[23]

Beginning with scriptural revelation, then, and the assumption that the Trinity is the eternal origin and ineffable perfection of persons-in-relationship (Eph 3:14), Christians interested in the flourishing of human life (such as counselors) may legitimately formulate norms for human development and maturation based on the Trinity and develop corresponding criteria of personhood and community—informed by research and reflection on human life,[24] qualified by an analogical orientation.[25] So, what is this divine communion of persons like?

Persons *in communion in perfection.* Since Father, Son, and Holy Spirit are equally God, they each possess the strengths and virtues of perfect persons interacting eternally in perfect communion, being both persons and communal in superlative degree and infinite capacity. In light of all the fore-going, we may properly infer that each one is pure act and infinite dynamism (Hart, 2004, p. 167), and an eternally perfectly rational, omniscient, and evaluative speaker; exhaustively self-aware; thoroughly responsible for his own actions; a maximally virtuous, loving subject, in loving communion with one another. Elaborating further, each person is perfectly decisive, resolute, properly motivated, having the same goals, capable of initiating and accomplishing significant courses of action (always together and in proper relation to one another), able to overcome all obstacles, no matter how large, and persevering through whatever they encounter. Sharing identical goals, each has an eternal sense of his personal existence and identity in relation to the others; perfectly regulates his emotions; takes complete responsibility for himself and his actions; and loves himself completely. Put negatively,[26] the triune persons are not unconscious, "weak-willed," insecure, self-hating, purposeless, unmotivated, vicious, or lacking in self-control or personal power. Each one, being fully God, is therefore a maximal person: a perfectly integrated center of conscious intentionality, energy, and activity —identical in every way except in their unique relations with one another— together exemplifying vigorous personal agency perfectly, coexisting as one God. And humans are to be finite personal agents like that.

Persons in communion in perfection. With regard to the relationality of the Trinity, we have already seen that it is eternally a communion of love, but how are we to understand love? Edwards and Aquinas offer some help. According to Edwards (1765/1960), there are two kinds of love. The love of benevolence is the desire for the well-being or happiness of the beloved, along with the desire for consent and union of heart with the beloved. The love of complacence is a delight in the beauty of the beloved. Edwards's model of love probably relies on that of Aquinas (1945, Vol. 1, p. 217; Pruss, 2013; Stump, 2010), except that Edwards's description of union entails consent, which involves a stronger differentiation of persons.

Elaborating on Aquinas's model, Stump (2010) suggests that the desired union of love entails joint attentional focus (or at least a desire for the beloved's presence in his or her absence) and their mutual closeness. The latter involves mutual sharing of thoughts and feelings, a mutual desire to be close to (intimate with) the beloved, and the internal integration of both of them. This last feature refers to their being single-minded and wholehearted in love, that is, without ambivalence or internal conflict. In Aquinas's model, love can be nonreciprocated, but it is fulfilled in reciprocity, since only in such mutuality is the desire for the beloved's well-being and for union fully realized, as well-being and union are found supremely in perfect reciprocal love.

The triune God is love in all these ways, maximally: each person eternally delights in the other with unsurpassable joy; each eternally acts in goodness toward the other; and they live eternally in perichoretic union that includes a complete sharing of what they know, intend, value, and do—having all things in common—except their respective relation to one another. Their unity is their communion (Jn 16:14; 1 Jn 1:3), being altogether omnipresent, omniscient, omnipathic, and united in will; since they lack internal conflict, they enjoy a perfect, reciprocal union of love. Edwards (1994) added that "one alone cannot be excellent," because "there can be no consent" (p. 284). The persons of the Trinity mutually consent to what the other knows, intends, loves, and does—a single-minded, wholehearted affirmation of the glorious personhood of one another—their love for each other being perfectly reciprocated (Edwards, 2003). Sharing the same identity eternally as the one God, yet fully differentiated from one another in their relational identity as persons, they enjoy complete solidarity eternally in their purposes and activity, while honoring and affirming their respective personhood.

Put negatively, the persons of the Trinity are not needy of each other, envious, competitive, suffering from boundary issues, "codependent" or enmeshed among themselves, threatened by the agency of each other, or living in fear of what one another might think. In their personal agency, they are not solitary, detached, aloof, autonomous, selfish, or narcissistic, never acting regardless of the others, and never do two of them align themselves over against the third. Rather, they are the perfect "system" of interpersonal (and family?) relations. Their eternal unity is manifested economically in their mutual consent to the Father's creational and redemptive agendas in this universe, in which they affirm and consent to their distinctive and respective roles and tasks in the economy (as in the Father's affirmations of the Son and the Son's obedience to the Father's will).[27] And humans are to be finite lovers like that.

At the same time, we must acknowledge that the Trinity is a mystery to the human mind. So we may not suppose that we can fully understand the form of the Trinity or that models of human life can represent the Trinity's form adequately, since God infinitely transcends us and our ability to comprehend him. Our finite concepts of him are necessarily *analogical*; that is, they can represent him, but only imperfectly. Perhaps most important, human persons are ontologically distinct beings, whereas the divine persons are ontologically one being. So a perfect correspondence between the Trinity and our understanding of the Trinity is impossible for us as creatures, and a perfect correspondence between the divine communion and the human community will elude us so long as we are sinful creatures.

Nevertheless, we can legitimately assert there will be and there *ought* to be *some* analogy between the divine communion and the human community, particularly in the church. Minimally we can argue that the equal ultimacy of agency and communion in the Trinity is normative for human beings in community. The glory of the triune God is seen both in his vigorous threefold agency and his vigorous love. Christians therefore should avail themselves of God's revelation of himself as Trinity to help formulate their understanding of human flourishing and the goals of Christian therapy, to which we shall turn next. One qualification, however, needs to be made. Because *person* is also commonly used to refer to all human beings (including the unborn), the term *personal agent* will be used to refer specifically to human beings who possess the set of characteristics of mature relational personhood discussed above.

SOME THERAPEUTIC IMPLICATIONS

So far, the doctrine of the Trinity may still seem largely irrelevant to psychology. However, if humans are made in the image of the triune God, and those who believe are saved by Christ and the Holy Spirit, then it would seem that we cannot properly understand human beings, and especially believers, without this doctrine. Therefore, we will assume in what follows that teaching on the Trinity lies within the disciplinary boundaries of a Christian psychology just as much as neuropsychology and personality theory. Let us explore how these teachings might be relevant to Christian psychotherapy and counseling.

The Beauty of the Triune God Is the Heart of Christian Soul Care

We saw in the first chapter that God is the center of the universe, humans were made to orbit around him, and nothing is better for their souls than doing so. In this chapter we consider that God is triune. The beauty of the triune God's holy, self- and other-affirming, and self-giving love will delight believers for eternity. God's passion for their healing is grounded in his passion to glorify himself by communicating and extending his own intratrinitarian glory and love to include the participation of others—those made in his image for that very purpose. The triune God's nature is expressed in his entire therapeutic program to bring sinful and broken humans into his communion. "Redemption is rooted in the restoration of relationships that takes place as humankind is drawn into Jesus' relationship with the Father in their Spirit" (McIntosh, 2004, p. 33). Christian soul-care providers are to practice with that same passion, helping others learn how to receive and participate in it by faith. Christian psychotherapy and counseling, therefore, is part of the realization of the Trinity's doxological mission, as the healing and glorification of Christ's humanity is more fully manifested in human persons and their relations with one another.

An Intersubjective Relationship with the Triune God Heals the Soul
Upon conversion to Christ through faith, humans are brought into a fitting union with Christ, the Father becomes *their* Father, and they are given the gift of the indwelling Holy Spirit. We saw above that through the Holy Spirit, believers experience something analogous to *perichoresis* with God (Jn 14:23; 15:4; 17:21, 23, 26). However, our experience of God differs radically from trinitarian *perichoresis*, because we are so different from God and because even the capacities of believers to dwell in God by faith and love are so compromised by remaining sin.[28] Nevertheless, there is something thoroughly remarkable in the communion we can enjoy (1 Jn 1:3). To begin with, divine communion is vastly superior to simply living and moving and having our being in God—which is true of all humans (Acts 17:28). The triune God is especially present within believers and knows them lovingly as his children, which he communicates through the Spirit's pouring out the love of God in their hearts (Rom 5:5) and enabling them periodically to receive God's presence and knowledge and give that love back to God in a way massively poorer but vaguely resembling the reciprocal love, affirmation, and joy of the Trinity. Through faith and love—what John calls "abiding" (Jn 15:4)—believers and the Trinity participate in a communion of consciousnesses, a harmonizing of their subjectivities (a positive kind of "intersubjectivity"). Stump (2010) considers this an aspect of love: sharing joint attention focus; personal presence; and thoughts, emotions, and desires—a psychological union hampered only by the internal conflict that remains in the believer.

One would think this could lead to significant psychospiritual benefits for believers; in this way, they can taste the richest interpersonal experience possible with an immaterial and infinite tripersonal being: a mature, secure attachment bond, friendship (Jn 15:13-15), intimacy with God, and a sense of being wanted, cherished, and loved by a holy God of love, pervasively conditioned by a spirit of dependence, worship, and obedience. Yet such blessings are not communicated automatically. Apart from the comparatively rare miraculous disposal, in order to realize these blessings in their lives, believers must "abide in Christ" (Jn 15:4), which involves intentional, conscious appropriation—Edwards's "consent"—and is therefore limited by the believer's capacity to do so.

Such intersubjective experiences with God occur through the believer's faith and joy and in prayer, Bible meditation, and worship as believers share attention with the omnipresent, indwelling God in love, focusing especially on Christ, and integrating all their lives into him. By this means they make possible a significant kind of healing through the reorganization of their brains/souls around God and his glory, creating reparative relational experiences with God by the Spirit that promote internal integration and reduce their double-mindedness and the conflicts of a divided heart.

Hindrances to Soul Healing

Our greatest impediment to such healing is the internal resistance to God called sin that all humans have, the resolution of which God has accomplished in Christ. Further hindering the ability to abide in Christ for many is the fact that humans form cognitive-affective/neural structures through the course of their early socialization—called an "internal working model" (Bowlby, 1988)—that come to constitute their deep view of themselves and others and condition the quality of their relationships with God and others (Coe & Hall, 2010; Guntrip, 1957; Moriarity & Hoffman, 2007; Spero, 1992). Through earlier intersubjective experiences with chronically poor caregivers, one's internal working model can be rather severely distorted, and unless there is healing, its effects will continue throughout life to condition negatively one's perceptions of others and interactions with them, *including one's deep perceptions of God* (called one's God-image; Moriarity & Hoffman, 2007), *and therefore the quality of one's interactions with him.*

While a fundamental recentering of one's life occurs at conversion, most of the damaging effects of previous development are not immediately remediated. The cognitive-affective/neural dynamic structures that were formed earlier in life remain, and it takes a certain amount of maturation just to recognize these effects, let alone learn how to undermine them and develop new, healthier structures. *Significant* change in memory structures grounded in the brain that underlie one's self-representation and perceptions of others (including beliefs, emotions, mental images, and actions, woven into one's narrative through experience and discourse) takes months and years of daily doses of loving communion with God.[29] Through *new*, repeated, positive intersubjective experiences with the triune God—the deeper and more emotionally intense the better—new, healthier beliefs, feelings, mental images, actions, and narrative episodes can be stored in one's brain/memory that can gradually modify the counselee's damaged internal working model (such relational healing among humans has been called "earned secure attachment," Hesse, 2008). A merely intellectual relationship with God, based solely on conscious head knowledge (one's God-concept; Moriarity & Hoffman, 2007) is not enough to heal the unconscious regions of the soul (Coe & Hall, 2010).

Consider, for example, the experience of adults who have been raised by chronically critical, rejecting parents, who often have within themselves a condemning psychological dynamic structure, sometimes called the "inner critic." Usually connected to and triggered by one's conscience, this structure can be a source of frequent internal criticism that maintains excessive shame that is experienced as self-evidently valid and "ego-syntonic." A loving, intersubjective relationship with the triune God, guided by well-interpreted Scripture, can give believers an alternative, transcendent perspective by which to view themselves, enabling them to identify, objectify, and then undermine such a "voice." As they make progress in doing so, they can, in turn, draw even closer into communion with the triune God, a reciprocal pattern that can continue deepening indefinitely.

Relationships with Others Can Also Heal the Soul

Perhaps the biggest challenge facing theocentric psychotherapy and counseling is the fact that we cannot now have a concrete, tangible relationship with the invisible God. God is immaterial (except for Jesus Christ, and he is now in heaven), and the presence of the indwelling Spirit is often obscure—we are frequently unaware of him and neglect to focus our attention on him, and sometimes he just feels absent, regardless of what we do (e.g., Ps 22:1). Remarkably, God himself told Adam it was not good for him to be alone, while God was with him (Gen 2:18)! Human relationships, therefore, are essential to human flourishing, as well as soul healing, and they are intended by God to be complementary to and reflective of our relationship with him. Humans were designed to be concrete images of God to one another. While adult relationships can turn into idolatry (Welch, 1998) in sinful and damaged hearts, humans can also be instruments in the Redeemer's hands (Tripp, 2002) and therefore a means of grace to one another, analogous to the other means of grace God has given us, including prayer, Scripture reading and meditation, public worship, and so on. Caring human relationships model the triune communion so that in Christ by faith they can become a more tangible, creaturely medium for theocentric soul healing, as loving counselors serve as signs of the triune God. Let us consider how this works.

Human-human intersubjectivity: An analogue to trinitarian perichoresis. We have already considered the kind of intersubjectivity God and believers can share through the indwelling Holy Spirit and the believer's faith and love (consent), but there is another kind of intersubjectivity that precedes and therefore conditions it.[30] Intersubjectivity was defined above as a communion of consciousnesses (co-consciousness). It occurs when persons share joint attentional focus and experience the same meaning at the same time, usually by means of mutual communication, including facial expressions, body language, tone of voice, and especially discourse. The maturation of personal agents capable of love requires the investment of loving communicative energy of relatively mature personal agents into the less mature, mediated by repeated positive intersubjective experiences involving empathic listening, meaningful dialogue, and usually some bearing of the burdens of the less mature. Discourse and empathy—which Kohut (1984) defined as "the capacity to think and feel oneself into the inner life of another person" (p. 82)—are key to this process.

Such intersubjective investment is especially evident early in life in loving parenting, but it also occurs throughout life in healthy marriages, friendship, teaching, pastoring, and counseling. Usually through affectively toned conversations, the more mature person passes on, to some extent, his or her own psychological infrastructure (beliefs, attitudes, emotions) into the less mature person's subjectivity, supplementing his or her present capacities (consider the effect a happy, socially skilled person can have on another while together for just a few minutes). The more mature mentor "enters into" the soul of the mentee through their presence and discourse, and the mentee, to some extent, receives or internalizes aspects of the mentor into his or her soul in a way that contributes to the mentee's self- and relational dynamic structures, at least temporarily, and, over time, permanently (Johnson, 2007; Martin, 1994).[31]

Human-human intersubjectivity, then, may be the closest creaturely analogue to the *perichoresis* of the Trinity there is. Such formative communion in adulthood is all too rare, and because of the reduced plasticity of the brain, it has nothing like the impact in adulthood that such experiences had in childhood, when the brain was much more impressionable. Counselors, however, are supposed to be experts in facilitating it.

Among Christians, these natural processes are still operative, of course. However, they are used by the Holy Spirit to bring about healing along theocentric lines. It is especially God's intention that other believers represent God to one another and that local churches serve as images of the Trinity (Grenz, 2001; Volf, 1998), being sites of relational healing and strengthening in the Spirit. As Christians grow in the knowledge and love of God, they become more equipped to love, encourage, comfort, admonish, and support other Christians in the communion they share with the Father and the Son (1 Jn 1:3) and so contribute increasingly and reciprocally to the "growth of the body for the building up of itself in love" (Eph 4:16). For believers who are especially damaged, Christian relational specialists are often needed—professionals trained in how to promote positive intersubjective experiences in Christ by the Spirit with those who have complex relational disabilities. Ideally, in the course of a given week, healing intersubjective experiences with the triune God in meditative prayer and worship will oscillate with analogous experiences with other believers, reinforcing each other and consolidating the redemptive brain/soul changes that are one of the goals of the Spirit's activity.

Unfortunately, for those who did not experience "good-enough" parenting, positive intersubjective experiences in the present are much more difficult to benefit from, because their current malformed self- and relational dynamic structures are likely to be reactivated in ways that distort their perceptions and experiences even of those who love them. The greater the previous damage, the more resistance to change will occur. This is why it is important for therapists and counselors themselves to be relatively healthier than those with whom they work. Knowing the Bible is essential for Christian psychotherapy and counseling, but without love, it is not enough.

Becoming Images of the Triune God

While Jesus Christ is the model of the image of God for human individuals (see chap. 3), we have seen there are good reasons to believe that the triune God is also the model for humans in relationship. This may be hinted at in the earliest teaching about the image of God: "Then God said, 'Let Us make man in Our image, according to Our likeness.' . . . God created man in His own image, in the image of God He created him; male and female He created them" (Gen 1:26-27).

The reference of the divine plural here is disputed, but since the days of the early church, Christians have wondered whether this was an allusion to the Trinity, suggesting that the image of God was necessarily plural, reflected in the fundamental distinction of humanity as male and female, and more generally as self and other (Barth, 1960a; Bonhoeffer, 1959; Grenz, 2001).

The evidence is sufficient to warrant that the form of the Trinity shapes a Christian understanding of human flourishing and the goals of Christian psychotherapy and counseling. God's intention is to manifest his triune glory and share it with humans that they might participate in and manifest his glory themselves by becoming individual signs of Christ and communal signs of the triune God. The triune communion and the Christian community are radically distinct (Creator/Redeemer–creature/sinner/redeemed), but they are being made one (Jn 17:22). Believers, amazingly, can participate in both by faith and love (consent), and in this way gradually become persons-in-community "ektypes" corresponding analogically to their trinitarian archetype.

As we have noted, however, because of sin and growing up in a fallen social world, human communities are more or less distorted images of the Trinity. God's creation grace enables all humans—individually and corporately—to retain some resemblance to God. But so terrible is our condition, without the saving acts of the Trinity—themselves the most remarkable manifestations of God's glory—humans would have no hope of substantial recovery and no ability to participate in his glory communally. In Christ, however, believers are given grace to do just that.

Vigorous human agency and individuality. The persons of the Trinity serve as "individual" archetypes for individual believers, particularly the person of Jesus Christ, since he is both a member of the Trinity and a human being who lives in dependence on God.[32] Individual Christians, therefore, glorify the triune God by thinking and feeling truly and deeply; becoming more self-aware; planning, deliberating, and acting decisively with appropriate willpower, earnestness, and perseverance (Prov 12:24; Eccles 9:10); carefully regulating their thoughts, emotions, and actions (Gal 5:23); taking responsibility for themselves (1 Jn 1:9); imagining a virtuous future; developing the most beautiful ethico-spiritual character they can (1 Cor 13; Gal 5:22-23); fulfilling their new covenant obligations by loving God supremely and their neighbor as themselves (Mt 22:37-39); and giving themselves wholly to God and wisely to one another.

Because of human fallenness, believers face tremendous obstacles to this calling by sin and damage to their agency through poor socialization and being sinned against, and this shows up in passivity, weak motivation, aggression, workaholism, narcissism, arrogance, pride, and the frustration of unrealized goals. In Christ, however, believers can be healed gradually, so that they can image divine agency increasingly better in their human agency on earth.

Vigorous human relationality and communion. The triune God serves as the communal archetype for believing communities. As a result, believers glorify the triune God by affirming and consenting to one another and promoting unity in Christ—that is, delighting in each other's gifts and virtue; speaking truth into each other in love (Eph 4:15); carrying one another's burdens (Gal 6:2); empathizing with and challenging one another; "forgiving each other" (Col 3:13); respecting human authority but resisting injustice; "being of the same mind, maintaining the same love" (Phil 2:2); transparently confessing one's sins and weaknesses to one another (Jas 5:16); walking with others so that we all increasingly repent from our sin; sharing our faith; caring for sinners, the weak and broken, and those with physical, emotional, social, or spiritual needs; giving ourselves for others, both within and without the Christian community; all the while promoting "the unity of the Spirit in the bond of peace" (Eph 4:3).

Because of human fallenness, believers face tremendous obstacles to this calling as well. The effects of sin, poor socialization, and being sinned against show up in servility, codependence, and enabling others to abuse their agency, as well as domination of others, envy, competitiveness, aggression, divisiveness, and isolation. In Christ and by means of repeated, intersubjective experiences with other healthier humans, however, believers can be healed gradually and learn how to participate in the loving power of God, so that they can increasingly image the divine communion in their ecclesial communities.

The personal and social life of human beings finds its transcendent ground, pattern, and power in the Trinity and its missions. Among the many benefits of the revelation of the Trinity is the provision of a dialectic of relational "limiting concepts" (Van Til, 1969) that can regulate Christian ideals and practices, helping Christians recognize and resist excessive dependence and independence (at least in principle). While Jesus Christ serves as the primary archetype for Christian personhood before God, the Trinity provides another archetype for the proper relation between the personal and the social: personhood among equals. At the same time, the lack of detailed criteria, combined with the fact that the Bible itself contains some progressive variety in how the personal and social dimensions of human life are negotiated (compare Old and New Testament), signals that Christians have some legitimate individual and cultural latitude in their representation of the perfect balance of the Trinity. Even so, the Trinity offers a "modest" dialectical *telos* that should also guide humanity's image bearing.

RESOURCES FOR COUNSELORS AND COUNSELEES

Classic

Augustine. *On the Trinity*. Various versions. ‡

Danielou, J. (1969). *God's life in us*. New York: Dimension. A short devotional treasure on the Trinity that warrants republication.

Grou, J. N. (1962). *Meditations on the love of God*. Westminster, MD: Newman Press.

Julian of Norwich. (1998). *Revelations of divine love*. New York: Penguin. ‡

Owen, J. (2007). *Communion with the triune God*. Wheaton, IL: Crossway. (Original work published 1657). The greatest—and most challenging—devotional work on the Trinity ever written in English.

Richard of St. Victor. (1979). Book three of The Trinity. In *Richard of St. Victor, The classics of Western spirituality*. New York: Paulist Press. ‡

Contemporary

Clarke, W. N. (1993). *Person and being*. Milwaukee, WI: Marquette University Press. ‡ A brief classic on the nature of the Trinity that emphasizes the mutuality of personhood and relationality in God and humanity.

Cloud, H., & Townsend, J. (1992). *Boundaries*. Grand Rapids, MI: Zondervan.

Crabb, L. (2009). *66 love letters*. Nashville: Thomas Nelson. An amazing walk with God through the Bible as he explains book by book his loving communications.

Emery, G., & Levering, M. (2011). *The Oxford handbook of the Trinity*. Oxford: Oxford University Press. ‡ The definitive treatment of the classical view of the Trinity.

Frame, J. (2002). *The doctrine of God*. Phillipsburg, NJ: P&R. ‡ Frame relishes the rich implications of the Trinity for understanding human life.

Grenz, S. J. (2001). *The social God and the relational self: A trinitarian theology of the* Imago Dei. Louisville, KY: Westminster John Knox. ‡

Manning, B. (1993). *Abba's child*. Colorado Springs: NavPress. A contemporary devotional classic.

McIntosh, M. A. (2008). *Divine teaching: An introduction to Christian theology.* New York: Blackwell. A worshipful, classical/contemporary discussion of Christian theology, centered on God's trinitarian nature (though weak on sin and the atonement).

Wilson, S. (1998). *Into Abba's arms.* Downers Grove, IL: InterVarsity Press. Draws readers into their adoption, especially aimed at those who struggle with shame.

‡ Recommended more for counselors and pastors than for counselees

—3—

The Word of the Son

Axiom 3: The triune God is especially glorified in the communication of the Son, Jesus Christ, who, as God and a human, provides the ultimate unity of Christian psychotherapy and counseling.

Corollary: The intrinsic goal of individual human development is conformity to the image of Christ.

Expansion of the corollary: The image of Christ consists of holiness, creational wholeness, and active receptivity.

He who did not spare His own Son, but delivered Him over for us all, how will He not also with Him freely give us all things?

ROMANS 8:32

In Him you have been made complete.

COLOSSIANS 2:10

But we all, with unveiled face, beholding as in a mirror the glory of the Lord, are being transformed into the same image from glory to glory.

2 CORINTHIANS 3:18

I WAS IN THE BOY SCOUTS as a young teen, and on one of our camping trips, I remember feeling quite baffled when, after some brief training, each of us was taken out to a separate location in thick and unfamiliar woods, given a map and a compass, and we had to find our way back. The only help the leaders gave us was to show us where we were on the map and where our camp was. But the most important part of the task, we were told, was to keep connected where we were in our natural surroundings with where we were on the map. My first thought after being dropped off was how easy it would be to get lost. And without the map and the compass, I *would* have been lost. The map had an arrow pointing north and markings that represented some of the features of the surrounding terrain (such as hills and streams), and the compass provided a point of reference beyond both the surroundings and the map that could be linked to the arrow pointing north on the map. I had to locate landmarks in the distance, preferably ones that were also on the map, and with the compass and map I was able to work my way back to camp.

The craft (or set of skills) of coordinating map, surroundings, compass, and one's location in order to reach a destination is called *orienteering*, and it offers an interesting analogy to psychotherapy and counseling (Johnson & Sandage, 1999). Life is a journey, and we could say that all religions and therapy systems implicitly have their own map (a representation of the soul-healing journey and its surroundings) and compass (an ultimate point of reference or understanding of the Good) based on their respective meta-narrative and worldview. Though sharing the same human nature (so that all "orienteering" models have many features in common), their respective "edification frameworks" (Johnson & Sandage, 1999) are further distinguished by their understanding of where people are "located" (diagnosis), what their destination should be (a concept of maturity, health, or well-being), and how best to get there (therapy strategies and spiritual disciplines). As a result, psychotherapists, counselors, and religious guides can be considered "orienteers" of a sort, guiding their clients or disciples to some maturity *telos*—beliefs, values, and actions that constitute the end or goal toward which human life ought to be moving—however well or poorly understood and articulated (Browning & Cooper, 2004; Richardson, Fowers, & Guignon, 1999; Roberts, 1987; 1988; 1993).[1] Let us look at a few of the maturity ideals that modern psychology has posited over its 125 years.

SOME MATURITY IDEALS OF MODERN PSYCHOLOGY

We should acknowledge at the outset that the modern *telos* has not been much discussed in its literature or training. One of the reasons for this is modern psychology's (MP) reliance on natural science methods and strong empirical bent. Maturity ideals assume values the validity of which are difficult, if not impossible, to prove empirically (some philosophers [e.g., Moore] have argued that one cannot derive moral ideals from empirical research). Furthermore, as positive psychology has recently pointed out, MP has historically focused much more attention on average humanity (the *mean*) and on abnormality (the variance below the mean) than it has on excellence and the human ideal (Seligman & Csikszentmihalyi, 2000; Sheldon & King, 2001). For decades MP's vigorous commitment to empiricism put its practitioners in an awkward position. On the one hand, they were supposed to be guided solely by research, but they were helping people develop in certain value-laden directions. As a result, MP's maturity ideals have tended to operate implicitly. However, that began changing over thirty years ago, and now most modern therapists recognize they have to assume at least some values (Johnson & Sandage, 1999). Moreover, with the emergence of positive psychology, the existence and importance of states of excellence have become more widely appreciated in the field.

Building on the work of others, Carl Jung and Abraham Maslow posited the processes of individuation (or self-realization) and self-actualization, respectively. Individuation is the process by which a person integrates and harmonizes the disparate aspects of his or her conscious and unconscious life and becomes whole or a self (Jung, 1966, p. 173). Maslow (1954) investigated what he called "self-actualizing" people and concluded they were characterized by an accurate perception of reality, deep self-acceptance, joy in living, spontaneity, a need for privacy, autonomy from others, and simultaneously an unusual capacity for deep interpersonal relations and concern about the well-being of others, a sense of oneness with all of humanity, periodic peak experiences of a sense of humor, and creativity (pp. 203-28; see also Maslow, 1968, pp. 71-95). Such an individual, Maslow (1968) asserted, was "more truly himself, more perfectly actualizing his potentialities, closer to the core of his Being, more fully human" (p. 97).[2]

More recently, evolutionary psychologists have tried to describe well-adapted human life, based on their interpretations of the human genome that was naturally selected and so now guides the development of human life and culture. According to strict evolutionary considerations, humanity's "maturity ideal" would be a function of reproductive fitness and survivability, which includes physical beauty and health, gender differentiation, strong social and coping skills, and intelligence. However, self-deception, the deception of others, and even male adultery also have some survival value, so a consistent naturalist has few grounds to argue against activities that most people still believe are immoral. As a result, the maturity ideals described by hard-core evolutionary psychologists will likely never be widely embraced.

By far the best work addressing maturity ideals in MP has been the contributions of the positive psychology movement (PP). Research has been done on many aspects of a maturity ideal: happiness (Diener, Lucas, & Oishi, 2002); optimism (Carver & Scheier, 2002); self-determination (Deci & Ryan, 2004); wisdom, intelligence, and creativity (Baltes & Staudinger, 2000; Sternberg, 2000), and a host of virtues, including courage, justice, and gratitude (Peterson & Seligman, 2004). Nonetheless, in spite of a focus on many positive *traits* (strengths and virtues), there has been a relative paucity of literature on a general model of maturity, perhaps because of its empirical focus on discrete traits and strengths.

Christians have approached the burgeoning PP literature with excitement and gratitude, perhaps especially because of its interest in virtue, a topic of great interest within historic Christianity. Nevertheless, by and large, PP has tended to interpret positivity constrained by the naturalistic and humanistic assumptions of modernism and its aims for universality (Kinghorn, 2016).[3] As a result, so far PP has promoted a community-generic virtue ethic and eschewed more community-specific maturity discourse, a stance some Christian moral philosophers have called into question (MacIntyre, 1984; Taylor, 1989).

Most of the maturity ideals of modern psychology point to legitimate aspects of human nature. However, the Christian maturity ideals differ in some significant ways. To begin with, in stark contrast to the individualistic orientation of modernism, the Christian *telos* is profoundly relational. Most basically, this is because the ideal is a person—Jesus Christ—and others can only move closer to that ideal in union and relationship with him. Jesus himself invited people to follow him and his way of life (Mt 4:19; Lk 9:23; Jn 1:43; 8:12; 13:14-15, 34), and the early church did so, in part, by encouraging the same (1 Cor 11:1; 1 Thess 1:6; 1 Jn 2:6; 1 Pet 2:21). We have seen that Christianity has a theocentric orientation—even trinicentric—and now we add that it is also christocentric.

CHRISTIAN TEACHING REGARDING THE WORD OF THE SON

As we become more familiar with the triune God's doxological agenda, we realize that he especially wants us to attend to the Son. In Christ's transfiguration, the Father said to those present, "This is My beloved Son. . . .

Listen to Him" (Mt 17:5). Christ said that when the Spirit came he would "glorify Me, for He will take of Mine and will disclose it to you. All things that the Father has are Mine; therefore I said that He takes of Mine and will disclose it to you" (Jn 16:14-15). It is through the Son that we are taken to the Father and sent the Spirit. He mediates our relationship with both by means of his risen and exalted humanity. Therefore, the worship and life of Christianity revolves especially around Jesus Christ, the Word and Son of God, the eternal delight of the Father, who sent him to play the most visible role in the divine doxological drama by becoming a human being, innocent of sin; suffering greatly and dying for the sin of other humans to reconcile them to God; and being raised from the dead and ascending to heaven, where he continues to reign over humanity and lead and heal those who abide in him. Christians can now benefit from Christ's activities because of their union with him by the Spirit through faith in him, so that *every* aspect of their lives is specially mediated by him—every moment of their lives Christ is now for them and with them, and they are to become increasingly oriented toward him.

This glorifying of Christ is fitting. We recall from the previous chapter that the Father dearly loves his Son—he is his pride and joy—and from eternity, it has been the Father's intention to glorify his Son, that is, to celebrate and magnify the beauty of his Son's nature and character, creating a universe and a human race in which his Son's goodness could be richly displayed. The Father created everything in, through, and for his Son (Col 1:16), appointing him the "heir of all things" (Heb 1:2). He is "the firstborn of all creation" (Col 1:15) and "the firstborn from the dead" (Col 1:18). These two uses of "firstborn" (*prōtotokos*) indicate his preeminence in both the creation and the new creation (Grenz, 2001, pp. 215-16). After his time on earth, the Father then highly exalted him, giving him a name above every name (Phil 2:9-11), putting all created things in subjection under him (Eph 1:19-22). All of this was according to the Father's "plan for the fullness of time, to gather up all things in [Christ], things in heaven and things on earth" (Eph 1:10 NRSV).[4] As a result, his assuming our human nature involved its being crucified, resurrected, and exalted with him, and in the process he communicated to us true humanity in right relationship with God and neighbor. So the Father wants to make much of his Son, and he wants fallen, broken humans to find him to be the source of their healing and strengthening. Therefore, the Son will understandably be the primary focus of *Christian* psychotherapy and counseling.

Jesus Christ, the Word of God

The apostle John identified the Son of God as *ho logos*, the Word of God (Jn 1:1), likening the second person of the Trinity to the spoken expression of the Father. The eternal Son of God is the creative Word through whom, along with the Spirit, the Father brings the creation into being (Gen 1), brings about change within it (Ps 148:8), and holds it altogether (Col 1:17). However, this person assumed human nature (Jn 1:14) and became the Sign of the Father, the human who perfectly re-presented the Father to us—the manifestation in this world of the invisible Father's mind, heart, and life: "he who has seen Me has seen the Father" (Jn 14:9). "No one has seen God at any time; the only begotten Son who is in the bosom of the Father, He has explained Him" (Jn 1:18). In addition, he is the perfect human in our place and on our behalf—acting and re-presenting us to the Father. As the perfect image of God, Jesus is the epitome of human life and flourishing, the fulfillment of human nature and the embodiment of God's design plan for us.

So, Jesus Christ is the main message from the Father to the world; the Father's saving, healing Word, who says, "Come to Me, all who are weary and heavy-laden, and I will give you rest" (Mt 11:28). In him the Father's therapeutic wisdom is concentrated (Col 2:3) and communicated to those who are sick (Mt 9:12). As a result, on the journey of the divine healing of the soul, Christ is the way (Jn 14:7), as well as the destination. He is the divine side of a therapeutic conversation God has begun with his creatures made in his image. In addition, he is the very human and holy response, who takes us back to God. His mission made him the mediator between God and humanity, humanity and God, and between humanity and ourselves. "Not only do we know God by Jesus Christ alone, but we know ourselves only by Jesus Christ" (Pascal, 1941, p. 173). Therefore, Christian psychotherapy and counseling will speak of him.

Jesus Christ, the Explanation of the Image of God

There are many aspects of Christ's person and work worthy of the attention of Christian therapists and counselors, many of which we shall examine in subsequent chapters. In this chapter we will focus primarily on four. The first concerns the nature of the image of God (the *imago Dei*), arguably the central concept about humans in the Bible (Cortez, 2010). Many explanations have been offered for what the *imago Dei* is, based on biblical exegesis and Christian reflection, and we will consider some of them below. However, the best explanation, according to the New Testament, has been given in Christ, "the most perfect image of God" (Calvin, 1559/1960, p. 190).

To begin with, being both God and human Jesus Christ shows the profound relational analogy between human beings and the triune God (Barth, 1960a). As we saw in the previous chapter, humans and God must share some kind of formal resemblance—divine and human personhood and relationality must correspond to each other to some extent—if the Son of God could become the Son of Man. Then, the coming of the Son led the New Testament authors to fundamentally reinterpret the concept of the image of God in relation to Christ (Grenz, 2001). He *is* "the image of God" (2 Cor 4:4); "the image of the invisible God" (Col 1:15); "the exact representation of [God's] nature" (Heb 1:3). This is also implied in Hebrews 2:6-8, where the author quotes Psalm 8: "What is man, that You remember him? Or the son of man, that You are concerned about him? You have made him for a little while lower than the angels; You have crowned him with glory and honor, and have appointed him over the works of Your hands; you have put all things in subjection under his feet." Alluding to Genesis 1, the original intent of the psalmist was most likely to marvel at the dignity God had bestowed on human beings in general. In applying this passage to Christ, the author of Hebrews was suggesting that Christ was the fulfillment and perfection of human nature, having been "because of the suffering of death crowned with glory and honor" (Heb 2:9).

Christ's preeminence in the creation is due, in large part, to his being a divine image of God, through whom was manifested the densest expression of God's internal glory. "The Word became flesh, and dwelt among us, and we saw His glory, glory as of the only begotten from the Father" (Jn 1:14). He was "the radiance of [God's] glory" (Heb 1:3), so his human nature was saturated with glory. As *the* image of God, the human Jesus was the greatest concentration of the glory of God ever manifested in this creation, both from God to us and from us to God (Jn 12:23; 13:31-32)![5]

The apostle Paul, in particular, believed that Jesus Christ was the key to understanding the concept of the *imago Dei* (Rom 8:29; 2 Cor 3:18; 4:4; Eph 4:24; Col 1:15; 3:10). What is the significance of this revolutionary insight for psychology and therapy? Christians understand Christ to be the perfect example of humanity. Thinking of this developmentally, he was raised by "good enough" human parents so that his neurological, cognitive, emotional, and created personal agentic and relational capacities developed according to God's design plan for human beings, as he grew in loving obedience to his heavenly Father (Lk 2:49, 52). Being without sin (2 Cor 5:21), he changed in his human nature from the immaturity of a holy child to the mature holiness of one "made perfect" through his suffering (Heb 5:9). Consequently, throughout his earthly life, Jesus Christ was able to manifest his Father's glory, constrained only by his human nature, faithfully and obediently doing and saying only what his Father did and said (Jn 5:19; 12:49; 17:1, 5, 22). He lived a dependent, receptive life, which he gave back to the Father in free, responsive, filial love. "For humanity," the life of Christ "is the fulfillment and consummation of its very being: imaging brought to the very fullest likeness" (McIntosh, 2008, p. 83). Jesus Christ, then, is the best explanation of the nature of the *imago Dei* that we have.

In light of the foregoing, some Christians have concluded that the Son of God is the original, eternal pattern or template on which the human form was based (Kline, 1986;[6] Barth, 1960). The eternal relationship between the Son and the Father forms the archetype of the human relation to God and the basis for the *imago Dei*. The Son of God himself is a primary *reason* for the human-God relationship, which is analogous to the Son's relationship to the Father, so it was fitting that he become a human, the perfect image of God, in order, in part, to manifest his eternal Son of God glory as a human being, in his life, death, resurrection, and ascension, becoming the "last Adam" (1 Cor 15:45), the "new Adam" (Gregory of Nazianzus, trans. 2002, p. 93), and the Son of God in power (Rom 1:4), in the process redeeming a race of fallen images, fulfilling God's intentions for humanity, and showing what it means to be in the image of God. "In his quality of Image, the Son is the author and the model of creation and re-creation" (Emery, 2011, p. 131). The Father's design to magnify his Son is proceeding as planned.

Jesus Christ, therefore, is humanity's "Archimedean point," the perspective by which humanity and its flourishing can best be comprehended. Because human nature is now corrupted and damaged, a psychology cannot rely exclusively on the empirical study of human beings in order to understand human nature properly, particularly its *telos*. Psychology needs also to study humanity in Scripture, especially the Christ revealed to us in Scripture. Similarly, he is of central importance to Christian psychotherapy and counseling. *He* is the one *ultimately* to whom we are to direct our counselees—not to ourselves, themselves, medications, counseling techniques, or the spiritual disciplines, though all of these have their proper place.

The Word of Immediate, Perfect Image Bearing: Christ as Guarantor

To summarize: Jesus Christ—*the* image of God—is the ultimate human exemplar. However, for broken sinners, this message from God could simply underscore their fallenness, since, in their present state, humans are incapable of emulating the holy pattern of Christ adequately. Fortunately, Christ came to save, not to condemn (Jn 3:17). Upon believing in Christ, humans are united to him by the Father and immediately granted a host of corollary benefits—everything necessary to be considered perfect and complete images of God themselves in the eyes of God. These benefits will be discussed in more detail in chapter fourteen. For now we will simply acknowledge Christ as the believer's comprehensive *goodness-guarantor* (see Heb 7:22, 28). In our culture, a guarantor is a person who agrees to be responsible for another's debt or performance if the other fails to repay or perform. Being creatures made for their Creator's glory, all humans are obligated to live a life devoted to God. Being sinners who have lived fundamentally for themselves, all humans have incurred a catastrophic debt, so great that they cannot repay it. However, the Father appointed Christ to become the guarantor of all who believe in him. As a result, the moment one embraces Christ by faith, one is joined to Christ and all he has accomplished and so is immediately released from all of one's debts to God (Col 2:13-14) and is credited with a perfect performance and complete fulfillment of one's obligations before God (Rom 4:24-25), having been made a fellow heir with Christ (Rom 8:17), given by the Father all the rights and privileges of a holy, perfectly obedient, loving image of God.

Christ's perfect image bearing, then, is imputed or donated immediately and fully to those who believe (Bavinck, 2008, p. 214). This comprehensive donation of ethicospiritual goodness is labeled in the New Testament in various ways, each highlighting a different feature: forgiveness (Acts 10:43), the gift of righteousness (Rom 5:17), "being justified as a gift" (Rom 3:24), adoption into the family of God (Jn 1:12), wisdom, holiness, and freedom (1 Cor 1:30), and access to the communion of the Trinity (Jn 14:23; 1 Jn 1:3) are just some of the most important. Consequently, believers are now already perfect or complete in Christ (Col 1:28; 2:10), and this immediate perfection becomes the basis of all further Christian healing of the soul and the ground of all future imitation. One of great challenges in Christian psychotherapy and counseling is to help believers internalize this word of perfection through union and communion with him, in spite of their remaining, unresolved sin, shame, guilt, and brokenness, so that their self-understanding is gradually revolutionized.

The Word of Destination: Christ as Goal

Once united to the perfect image of God, believers embark on a tremendous journey with him into the communion he shares with the Father and the Spirit and an increasing incorporation into their doxological agenda. Paradoxically, because he is the God-man, Christ is also an exposition of the goal of this journey. "As God he is the destination to which we move; as man, the path by which we go. Both are found in Christ alone" (Calvin, 1559/1960, p. 544). Since he is *the* image of God—both the original pattern for human beings and, in his earthly life, the realization of that pattern—*his* image has now become the goal of human development, flourishing, and spiritual maturation. As a result, we will take some time to understand the "multifaceted" aspects of the *imago Dei* that have been identified in church history (Cortez, 2010) and how they have been fulfilled in Christ.[7]

The imago Dei *as resemblance to God.* Historically, Christians have most commonly understood the *imago Dei* to refer to ways in which humans resemble God. Two major types of resemblance have been identified: formal resemblance and godliness.

The imago Dei *as formal resemblance: Embodied agency in communion or biopsychosocial wholeness.* According to Genesis 9:6 and James 3:6, all human beings—in spite of their sin—are still in the image of God. Consequently, along with most Christians in church history, we will begin this discussion of the *imago Dei* by considering those features of humanity that mature human beings have that are similar to characteristics of God, and I will group them in three categories that reflect historic Christian thinking.

1. *Dynamic-structural resemblance.* Probably the most well-known understanding of the *imago Dei* over the centuries has been termed by some the "structural" position. This model locates the *imago Dei* in one or more psychological *structures* that mature human beings would seem to share with God, including reason, memory, will, emotions, language ability, an immaterial spirit, creativity and freedom, personality, relationality, self-consciousness, joy, and morality, culminating in the emergence of personal agency with good character (Bavinck, 2004; Berkhof, 1939; Erickson, 1983–1985). However, because these so-called structures are actually constantly changing in one way or another, we shall refer to them as *dynamic* structures.[8]

Today, Christians can take this to a finer level of analysis. Research psychologists over the last hundred years have uncovered an enormous amount of detail in the intellectual, emotional, social, action, and moral processes that compose the dynamic structures of a mature personal agent. Christians can be grateful that modern psychology has focused a good deal of its energy on the investigation of these aspects of the *imago Dei*.[9]

The body, also, has a role to play in this model. While the eternal God is spirit (Jn 4:24), *images* are visible. In a creation like ours, imaging God entails a body as the material "site" of such imaging. Moreover, we now understand that all the psychological dynamic structures historically associated with the *imago Dei* are themselves grounded on neural structures (Johnson, 2007, chap. 10). All this confirms Calvin's (1559/1960) intuition that the *imago Dei* is embodied (pp. 186-87).

In recent years, the "structural" model of the *imago Dei* has fallen out of favor, with some suggesting it has been thoroughly discredited (Cortez, 2010; Grenz, 2001; Lints, 2006). That has to be an overreaction, however. The dynamic structures that mature humans share (analogically) with God, and that are largely lacking in other created organisms, constitute human life as we know it; without them, the other kinds of likeness to God would not arise in creatures. The multiple facets of the *imago Dei* are unsurprisingly thoroughly interrelated.

2. *Relational resemblance.* Relationality was included in the list of dynamic structures above. However, in the twentieth century, relationality came to be considered by some the *core* of the *imago Dei* (Shults, 2003). Barth (1960a) has been credited with developing this interpretation (though it was originated by Bonhoeffer, 1937/1959), based on Genesis 1:26-27: "Then God said, 'Let Us make man in Our image, according to Our likeness. . . .' God created man in His own image, in the image of God He created him; male and female He created them." In the earliest text in the Bible on the *imago Dei*, the concept is cryptically described as consisting of male and female, perhaps implying that human relationality—an *I* and *Thou*—is a picture of God's relationality (particularly in the Trinity, perhaps even suggested in the passage: "Let *Us* . . . according to *Our* likeness"). As a result, this understanding of the *imago Dei* is now often called "the relational model" (see Balswick, King, & Reimer, 2005; Grenz, 2001; Lints, 2006; McMinn & Campbell, 2007). Its proponents rightly point out that the mutual love, trust, enjoyment, intimacy, dialogue, and cooperation of humans portray in creaturely ways the vigorous communion of the triune God, who is love (1 Jn 4:8, 16). Yet in humans these relational capacities themselves depend on, emerge from, and build on underlying biopsychosocial dynamic structures shaped by genetics and attachment and later social experiences (forming what Bowlby called an "internal working

model"). Consequently, while this model warrants special attention because of its value in picturing the Trinity, there is no warrant in elevating it above the other formal resemblance models of the *imago Dei*.[10]

We must also add that individual human beings alone can never image God adequately. The Trinity is one reason; the *differences* of the persons of the triune God are the foundation for all the individual differences there are in human creatures. However, another reason is God's infinity. An infinite God can only be very meagerly imaged by many, many different human persons, with the full range of all of their personalities, gifts, and capacities (Hart, 2003). So there is a sense in which the entire body of Christ is needed for the fullest expression of the *imago Dei*.[11] Kuyper (1998) and Bavinck (2004) took this a step further, suggesting that a *corporate imago Dei* is being formed over the course of human history.

3. Functional resemblance. Another model of the *imago Dei*, promoted more by those in biblical studies, has been termed the "functional" approach. Based on the immediate context of Genesis 1:26-27 (particularly Gen 1:28: "Be fruitful and multiply, and fill the earth, and subdue it; and rule over the fish of the sea and over the birds of the sky and over every living thing that moves on the earth"), as well as research on ancient Near East cultures, where rulers often put statues (images) of themselves around the regions under their control, it has been argued that God similarly placed humans as representations of himself on earth in their exercising dominion over the earth, analogous to God's dominion (von Rad, 1962; 1972). This "creation mandate" is said by some to be part of the original covenantal relationship that God established with the human race from the beginning (Horton, 2005).

In the context, imaging divine dominion obviously includes raising children and agriculture, but perhaps all human cultural activity is embedded in the commands of Genesis 1:28, including manufacturing, business, science, art, medicine, and so on. In all legitimate work, humans resemble God, for they picture something of his agency and resourcefulness. In addition, personal competence and a sense of fulfillment would seem to be encompassed within this model, expressed in personal and social accomplishments that result from skilled human activity and one's ability to manage one's life well, often a focus of psychotherapy (see McMinn & Campbell, 2007). We might say that the functional aspect of the *imago Dei* is its embodied concretization in life on earth.[12]

Integrating the models of formal resemblance. Such dominion is itself only possible because of the dynamic-structural capacities with which humanity has been endowed—reason, creativity, personal agency, and so on—and culture formation is only possible through living and working cooperatively in relationships. So we note again the deep interrelatedness between these different models. Taken together they give us a comprehensive framework for understanding the features of the *imago Dei* that all mature human beings have in common, characteristics of well-developed personal agency in relationship with others, or what we might also call "biopsychosocial wholeness."[13]

Reformed theologians have called these formal aspects the "broad view" of the image. This likeness is accounted for in the doctrine of creation grace (what most theologians call common grace), which is due to God's goodness given to all humans (see Ps 104:15; Mt 5:44-45; Jn 1:9; Acts 14:17). As a result, humans in secular and non-Christian religious cultures can grow up resembling God, in terms of their dynamic structures, relationality, and overall competence, often more than many Christians. Such development glorifies God to some extent, first, because the beauty of every human manifests God's beauty; second, because it demonstrates God's love of all humans, even those who disregard him, and it is meant to lead them back to the Giver of such gifts (Rom 2:4); and finally, because such wholeness provides the creational "infrastructure" that makes possible the explicit, self-conscious glorifying of God for which humans were made. The greater one's biopsychosocial wholeness or personal agency—that is, the better one's brain, reasoning, self-awareness, empathic compassion, and overall flourishing—the better one is able *personally* or *self-consciously* to recognize, participate in, and celebrate the glory of God. At the same time, without redemptive grace, such creational capacities are a bit of a scandal, because the partial divine resemblance makes possible an existential-motivational independence from God that subverts his doxological design for full human flourishing.

How did/does Jesus Christ—*the* image of God—*formally* resemble God? We can reasonably suppose that, while on earth, Christ had well-developed and balanced dynamic structures and relationality, resulting in vigorous personal agency and the capacity to love and care for others, so that he functioned at a very high level, exemplifying a flourishing, responsible person who exercised proper dominion, in the fullest sense. Conformity to Christ, then, includes these facets, and Christian psychotherapy and counseling therefore is interested in promoting the healing of these capacities. Their importance is enhanced because they provide the "creational platform" for the other features of the *imago Dei*, which we will examine next.

Contemporary counseling and psychotherapy have tended to concentrate on the remediation of biopsychosocial characteristics of the "common" *imago Dei* in order to enhance the well-being of counselees (e.g., helping them to think more rationally, understand themselves better, and exercise more personal control in their lives) (a fact that McMinn & Campbell [2007] capitalize on in their model of integrative psychotherapy). But believers can image God in ways that those outside the faith cannot.

The imago Dei *as teleological resemblance: Godly character or ethicospiritual holiness.* Another perspective on the *imago Dei* has been termed the "narrow view" by Reformed theologians, because it was lost when humans became sinners, so its realization now requires a restored relationship with God. Calvin (1559/1960, pp. 189-90) pointed in this direction by focusing on the apostle Paul's teaching on the *renewal* of the image of God in Christ: "Put on the new self who is being renewed to a true knowledge according to the image of the One who created him" (Col 3:10); and "put on the new self, which in the likeness of God has been created in righteousness and holiness of the truth" (Eph 4:24). Christians are to become a *new self* that bears a greater resemblance to God than fallen humanity can, consisting of true knowledge, righteousness, and holiness of the truth. A comprehensive understanding of the *imago Dei,* therefore, includes an ethicospiritual, characterological aspect.

Holiness could be considered the central feature of this approach to the *imago Dei.* A complex concept, holiness encompasses God's absolute otherness and separateness (Bavinck, 1956; Harrison, 1982; von Rad, 1962), his total moral purity (Bavinck, 1951; Vos, 1948, p. 267), and his utter devotedness to himself and his purposes (Edwards, 1746/1959; 1765/1998; Gentry & Wellum, 2012), including the manifestation of his glory. From the beginning, God designed humans to image his holiness: they are to be holy as he is holy (Lev 1:2; 1 Pet 1:16). So, perhaps we could characterize human holiness as the qualitative degree of one's God-centeredness from the heart, and the *imago Dei* as characterized by the degree humans resemble God's regard for himself supremely. Humans are holy, then, as they are oriented supremely to God, and the more centered on God they are, the more like God they become. Since sin is the opposite of holiness, the human race lost this aspect of the *imago Dei* when it became sinful.

According to Edwards (1994), holiness is the greatest imaginable good,

> the highest beauty and amiableness, vastly above all other beauties. 'Tis a
> divine beauty, that makes the soul heavenly and far purer than anything here

on earth. 'Tis of a sweet, pleasant, charming, lovely, amiable, delightful, serene, calm and still nature. . . . It makes the soul a little sweet and delightful image of the blessed Jehovah. . . . What a sweet calmness, what calm ecstasies, doth it bring to the soul. How doth it make the soul love itself. (p. 163)

This is a stunning description of what was likely a recent (and frequent) experience of the young Edwards. As we saw in the first chapter, he believed that human happiness and fulfillment are found ultimately in God through participation in the holy happiness of the triune God. With echoes of Bernard's fourth stage of love, Edwards understood that, rather than being antithetical to self-love, holiness can actually be its cause, when self-love and the self's flourishing are transposed through redemption into a theocentric orientation where God's majesty and beauty are recognized to be the life-giving goods they are.

This perspective on the *imago Dei* adds two features not addressed in the models that apply "commonly" to all human beings: the properly functioning *imago Dei* is directed to God at its core; and it is based in *rectitude*. Bavinck (2004) defines rectitude as "the normal state, the harmony, the health of a human being; that without it a human cannot be true, complete, or normal." If this is lost, he writes, a human "becomes an abnormal, a sick, a spiritually dead human being, a sinner" (p. 551). From a Christian standpoint, human well-being cannot be properly understood apart from righteousness and holiness, that is, from godliness. The virtues of righteousness and holiness are the way that the more foundational aspects of the *imago Dei*—making possible human agency in communion—are to be oriented and realized. So, while non-Christians can certainly resemble the *form* of God in these foundational ways (in their psychological structures, relationships, and functioning), and therefore even glorify him implicitly (perhaps unknowingly or beneath conscious awareness), God is especially glorified through the emulation of God and his beauty in its depth or *splendor*, which is only made possible in Christ.

In terms of *this* model, Jesus Christ also exemplified in perfection the human capacity for righteousness and holiness. As "the Holy One of God" (Jn 6:69; Mk 1:24; Acts 2:27; Rev 3:7), he was completely devoted to God throughout his life. He was the faithful Son who obeyed his Father without sin—even in Gethsemane, where he experienced enormous internal conflict, given his strong, natural desires to avoid the terrible suffering he was about to experience, which, as Messiah, he was called to endure. Nevertheless, he still entrusted himself to God (1 Pet 2:23).

The imago Dei *as intentional reflection: Active receptivity and participation.* There is one more aspect of the *imago Dei*, which contrasts fundamentally with the ways in which humans positively resemble God. Given everything we have looked at so far about the *imago Dei*, one might suppose that imaging God is something humans do on their own. Having received Christ, Christians are now simply to look to Christ as their role model and then apply themselves to the task of imitation. But that is far from the truth. The entire notion of the *imago Dei* is based on its being derived from and responsive to its Creator. God is the archetype of which the image is a replica. In addition, God is the source of all good (Jas 1:17), and humans are dependent on him for everything (Hart, 2013). As a result, our emulation of God requires its empowerment from the archetype.

The apostle Paul used a metaphor that points toward this aspect of the image: "beholding as in a mirror the glory of the Lord, [believers] are being transformed into the same image from glory to glory" (2 Cor 3:18). Calvin (1559/1960) picked up on this metaphor and argued that we do not have a "full definition" of the *imago Dei* with a consideration of "those faculties in which man excels, and in which he ought to be thought the reflection of God's glory" (p. 189). The metaphor of a mirror reminds us that humans can contribute nothing "out of themselves" (see Jn 5:19), but their being an image includes receiving and reflecting back to God *his* goodness, beauty, and love.[14] Even if they were without sin, they could not emulate God on their own. Faith is so important in the Christian framework in part because it is the virtue of reception (Eph 2:8).

Some Christian "quietists" have concluded from this line of teaching that the Christian life is one of absolute passivity. Yet this participation model of the *imago Dei* paradoxically underscores that the image of God is dynamic. Aquinas recognized that, since God is pure act, the *imago Dei* necessarily involves activity (Merriell, 2005). Humans are dialogical agents who are response-able (Anderson, 1982) or respondable to God (Berkhof, 1979b), that is, able to hear him in his word, receive it, consent to it, and respond by living it out. Human responsibility and responsiveness to God's word are mysteriously realized in the divine gifts of human freedom and creativity. Humans are not robots like the rest of God's creation, dutifully and mindlessly carrying out God's word, "Fire and hail, snow and clouds" (Ps 148:8). Mature humans—to the extent they have been freed from the bondage of sin by Christ—are enabled to respond *freely* to God's word, even improvising new ways to love God and neighbor within the narrative context of their lives, with imaginations permeated and empowered by receptive faith.

However, human freedom does not arise ex nihilo, but—though conditioned by creatureliness and human limitations and compromised by sin—it too is dependent on God. This is true for all creatures, of course, but only humans can practice *active receptivity*, being conscious of their absolute dependence and receptively participating in God's gifts in love (Pinckaers, 2001, p. 88). To image God, then, is to be open to God, in radical dependence and gratitude, consciously living out of his glorious bounty. God gives and we receive, and so we become more like him, but in a way corresponding to our uniquely creaturely nature. The *imago Dei* "reflects God's life precisely by being ceaselessly called out of itself and into a joyous sharing in another; thus of course it echoes the Trinitarian self-sharing which is the creature's own cause" (McIntosh, 2008, p. 158). For this, humans need the Holy Spirit, who is the subject of our next chapter.

Christ was also the perfect exemplification of this aspect of the *imago Dei*. This is perhaps most clearly taught in the Gospel of John, where we read that Jesus did or said nothing "from Himself" (Jn 5:19; *aph heautou*; translated in NASB as "on [his] own initiative" in Jn 5:30; see also Jn 8:28; 14:10; 12:49). His exemplary human agency was the reflection of the Father's and empowered in his humanity by the Holy Spirit (Mt 3:16; 12:18, 28; Lk 2:27; 4:1; 10:21).

ASPECTS OF THE *IMAGO DEI*		FEATURES OF THE ASPECTS		RELATION TO OTHER ASPECTS	PERSONAL FAITH REQUIRED?
Resemblance	Formal	*Dynamic-structural*		Ground	No
		Relational	Functional		
	Godly character	*Love of God*		Core	Yes
		Holiness	Righteousness		
Receptivity		*Openness to God and his grace*		Core	Yes
		Dependence	Gratitude		

Figure 3.1. Three major aspects of the *imago Dei*

The realization of the* imago Dei *in Jesus Christ. A diagram of the three major aspects of the *imago Dei* can be found in figure 3.1: formal resemblance to God biopsychosocially (dynamic structures, relationality, and dominion/competence), holy resemblance to God ethicospiritually, and reflective participation. According to God's design plan, these three aspects are organically interrelated. On the one hand, the formal features of the *imago* (that all mature humans have in common) provide the creational "platform" or ground for the higher features, since a properly functioning mind, emotion system, and relationality (and so on) make it possible to reflect God's glory and holiness through dependent participation. At the same time, those aspects of the *imago Dei* that all mature humans have in common were intended by God to flourish in holiness and dependent participation on God's glory. Since the fall, humans have been natively unholy and unable to depend properly on God, so they are not images of God in the fullest sense. God's creation grace enables humans to resemble God formally (though there is, of course, a marked variety in these capacities in the human race), but without holiness and a proper sense of conscious dependence on God, this formal likeness is a superficial simulacra of flourishing, since it is not rightly directed to its true End. (This was why Luther taught that the *imago Dei* is absent in nonbelievers and Calvin considered it at best a remnant or vestige.) There is, therefore, a paradox intrinsic to the *imago Dei* teaching of Christianity. On the one hand, all humans exist essentially in the *imago Dei*, and on the other, all humans are now failures at the core in *living* as the *imago Dei*. From a theocentric standpoint, this disconnection between the formal and the more central aspects of the *imago Dei* is one of the most terrible outcomes of the fall.[15]

The Father sent the Son to earth to become human in part to repair this egregious breach in the *imago Dei*, so that God's design for human image bearing could be realized in its fullness. Jesus Christ himself, as we have seen, is the perfect union of all three aspects: as the Son of God he was eternally the infinite representation of the Father, whereas in his assumption of human nature, he developed into a mature human image of his Father, in which his formal resemblance to God flourished in holy receptivity and dependence on his Father in the Spirit, so that in him all three aspects of the *imago Dei* are indissolubly one. *The* image of God is revealed to us, then, primarily in his life, death, resurrection, and ascension, as interpreted within the entire context of Scripture. Future chapters will explore the therapeutic value of this material.

The **imago Christi** *as the fulfillment of the* **imago Dei** *in humans.* The only way the rest of us can overcome the dissociation of the formal and the "core" aspects of the *imago Dei* is through union with *the* image by faith. Having received the word of ethicospiritual perfection in Christ upon faith in him, believers participate in the receptive process of being changed into his way of life. "Whom [God] foreknew, He also predestined to become conformed to the image of His Son" (Rom 8:29), a goal that will be attained only in eternity but that is being realized to some extent in the present; believers "with unveiled face, beholding as in a mirror the glory of the Lord, are being transformed into the same image from glory to glory" (2 Cor 3:18; Grenz, 2001; Lints, 2006), suggesting that their conformity to Christ is fostered through experiential ("face-to-face") communion with the living Christ through the Spirit. As believers experience and practice their union with Christ through their communion with God, the formal and core aspects are gradually remediated and unified: they become more holy and more whole as their minds, emotions, wills, and relationality are increasingly healed by means of their growing love relationship with Christ, along with maturing relations with others.

Consequently, the Christian maturity ideal ought to be termed "the image of Christ" or *imago Christi* (Grenz, 2001). For Christians, Jesus Christ is the *telos* of human development. A major part of the doxological mission of the triune God, therefore, is the gradual increase in believers' conformity to the form and splendor (depth) of Christ, so that more and more they too are enabled to participate in the glory of the Trinity in their lives (Jn 17:5-22). Their capacity to manifest and participate in that glory is tied directly to their becoming like Christ, signs that increasingly resemble and reflect the life, holiness, and love of the triune God.

So, Jesus Christ is the beginning and the end of our reflection on the *imago Dei*. The template of the *imago Dei* that is inscribed on human nature was based on the form and splendor of the Son of God. In this life, it can only be properly realized, to some extent, through faith in Jesus Christ. As a result, the ultimate goal of human life has been reconstituted by redemption and union with Christ and is now called the *imago Christi*. This maturity ideal has the practical advantage over the *imago Dei* of being less abstract (structure, relationship, function, and so on), since its concrete portrayal is found in the Gospel narratives. Christ thoroughly exemplified the original *imago* ideal, so that in the accounts of the life of Christ in the New Testament we obtain the best fourfold description of the destination or flourishing of human life available to us.

The Word of Our Lord and Friend: Christ as Guide

Jesus Christ is the Word of God for Christian psychotherapy and counseling in another important sense: he has become the believer's primary guide and companion on the journey into the healing and flourishing of the soul. With the patriarchs, God *first* represented himself as a mysterious sovereign, who called people out of paganism to travel in the desert (Gen 12:1), initiated a royal covenant (Gen 15:18), and periodically spoke with and appeared to them (Gen 18:1-21; 22:1; 26:2; 32:30; 35:9). Later, through Moses, God represented himself even more impressively as the Creator of the heavens and the earth, an awe-inspiring lawgiver and judge at Sinai (Ex 19–20), a guide who accompanied them in the desert and into the Promised Land and a miracle-working protector. As salvation history progressed, his portrayal grew more complicated as he revealed himself as a shepherd (Ps 23) and a jealous husband (Hosea), as well as the king of Israel and the Lord of Hosts.

In the New Testament, all the previous representations still stand. God is forever a majestic sovereign (as the book of Revelation makes clear). However, the Word of God, Jesus Christ, communicates much more of the remarkable splendor and excellency of this God (Edwards, 1974). As the Son of God, he is still the King of kings (Rev 19:16), but the Son of David is also the "good shepherd" of believers, who knows his sheep and leads and feeds and protects and challenges them (Jn 10:14). He is their Lord and Messiah, but he is also their friend, who has laid down his life for them (Jn 15:13-15). He promised to be with his disciples forever: "Lo, I am with you always" (Mt 28:20), and now says, "I stand at the door and knock; if anyone hears My voice and opens the door, I will come in to him and will dine with him, and he with Me" (Rev 3:20). On the one hand, in the immediate context, opening the door is linked to repentance, with the Holy One advocating continuously for greater purity for his people. But the picture is also suggestive of one pursuing ever greater union and communion with them. "In Oriental lands the sharing of a common meal indicated a strong bond of affection and companionship" (Mounce, 1977, p. 129) and was a "symbol of enduring friendship" (Ford, 1975, p. 422). This passage is also supported by Jesus' teaching in John: "Abide in Me, and I in you" (Jn 15:4), an imperative/invitation to his disciples to commune with him, challenging believers to "open up" to his loving (omni) presence (Stump, 2010) and enter into reciprocal friendship with him (Jn 15:12-15; Torrell, 2003), with the ultimate goal of becoming a band of reciprocal friends that resembles and glorifies the Trinity: "that they may all be one; even as You, Father, are in Me and I in You, that they also may be in Us, so that the world may believe that You sent Me" (Jn 17:21).

SOME THERAPEUTIC IMPLICATIONS

Much of the rest of this book will be spent unpacking this chapter (we have a chapter on each stage of Christ's life, death, resurrection, and ascension), so we will finish this chapter on the implications that are best dealt with here.

The Word That Is New Every Morning

We have seen that Jesus Christ is the Christian's maturity ideal, but we first learned that he is a maturity ideal *that we have already attained in him!* This is the most important key to Christian soul healing,[16] for it alone provides an invulnerable basis on which we can walk with him into his communion with the Father, so as to partake in it and realize it in this life in some measure. Paul taught (and Luther rediscovered) the paradoxical truth that Christian transformation is built on the word of ethicospiritual perfection already accomplished in Christ. Only such a transcendent word can really undermine the shame, guilt, and anxiety that come from an awareness (mostly unconscious) of God's eternal perfection and keep fallen humans in denial, pretending they are themselves perfect and afraid to admit their sins and shortcomings. The humanist psychotherapist Carl Rogers (1961) recognized that humans develop best in an atmosphere of total acceptance he called unconditional positive regard, because it creates a safe place within which one can risk honesty and change. This is a monumental insight; but what Rogers himself rejected was that such safety could be given only by God. The difficult and often painful work of Christian psychotherapy and counseling proceeds from within the safe place of God's divine communion and its ethicospiritual perfection given through faith in Christ.

Orienteering in Therapy According to Christ

We began this chapter thinking about orienteering, a craft and set of skills that was likened to the therapy journey. Interpreting the metaphor Christianly, we could say that the journey consists of the realization of our individual and communal nature (understood biopsychosocially and ethicospiritually), Scripture provides the map, our compass points to the glory of God, our primary guide is Christ (as we noted) and secondarily other spiritual friends, and Christ is also the destination.

All humans by nature resemble the triune God formally, to some extent, the more they are personal agents in communion. Only in Christ, however, can such "preliminary images" become holy and actively responsive to God in love and worship—over time, more deeply—and so fulfill God's full design for his created images. Yet the fact that the formal/creational and holy/participatory/redemptive dimensions of the *imago Dei* can be distinguished should not lead us to treat them dualistically and separate them in our practice, as though they were ontologically independent of each other. Most fundamentally this is so because Christ—*the* image of God—is one person, and in him these two dimensions (collapsing holiness and receptivity into one) are thoroughly united and equiprimordial, implying and reinforcing each other. Second, and correspondingly, God's original design was that human persons be a unity of biopsychosocial and ethicospiritual well-being. Humans are a special kind of material creature, capable of living consciously dependent on God and participating in his glory. So the well-being of biopsychosocial wholeness is only brought to its proper fulfillment in the holiness of communion with the triune God. Third, though our common, created imaging capacities are now fallen, they are recoverable and flourish most fully in the redemptive blessings available through union with Christ. Fourth, social relationships and one's relationship with God are coextensive and interdependent (Coe & Hall, 2010), and since the triune God is love, loving neighbor and God together image him and glorify him the most fully (Jas 3:9-10; 1 Jn 2:5; 4:7-11). As a result, within a Christian framework (and other explicitly religious frameworks), psychological and spiritual well-being are two sides of the same coin.

Christlikeness then is the greatest happiness of which a human being is capable (Charry, 2010). Therefore, comprehensive Christian psychotherapy, counseling, and spiritual direction will consciously, if not always explicitly, promote the unified christocentric aim of fostering biopsychosocial wholeness and ethicospiritual holiness and participation, and will strive to avoid promoting one at the cost of the other. Although ethical and spiritual matters are the most important issues of life (see Johnson, 2007, chaps. 8-9), sometimes the counselee's condition will dictate focusing more on biopsychosocial issues (e.g., chronically low levels of serotonin production, family structural dynamics, lack of emotional awareness, or social skills). At other times, attention can be directed immediately to specifically Godward issues (e.g., repentance of a particular sin, experience of justification by faith, or opening up to God's love). Figure 3.2 represents different approaches to these two interdependent dimensions of Christian psychotherapy and counseling.

Our Creator/Redeemer God values both holiness/receptivity and wholeness. However, following the emphases of the Bible, human holiness/receptivity would seem to be of relatively greater importance to God than human wholeness, and the promotion of holiness/receptivity on earth would seem to be the church's greatest calling, particularly since it is the only social institution dedicated to that end. Arrow 1 in figure 3.2 represents a soul-care orientation that aims primarily at the promotion of holiness/receptivity. We could label this "*core* or *redemptive* psychotherapy and counseling," since it addresses the central issues of life—one's ultimate relationship with God in Christ, permeating all of life and flowing from redemptive grace, participated in through faith in Christ alone. Yet the generally Godward arrow is tilted to the right because the pursuit of holiness/receptivity necessarily fosters some degree of wholeness: better relationships, better coping with suffering, greater ability to fight bitterness, and so on. This is the general focus of biblical counselors and spiritual directors, and helping people move in this direction is the high calling of Christian ministers.

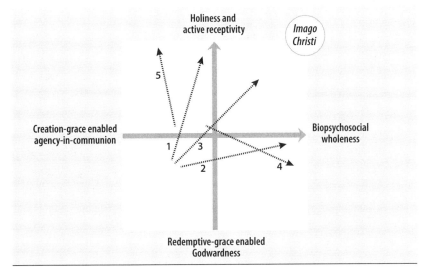

Figure 3.2

Arrow 2 represents therapeutic practice that concentrates on enhancing counselees' biopsychosocial functioning without necessarily making reference to holiness/receptivity—for example, in vocational assessment, training the mentally impaired, resolving marriage conflict, alleviating severe depression with medication, and helping at-risk youth. These types of activities could be labeled "*common* or *creational* psychotherapy and counseling," and in principle such "ministries of mercy" activities (Keller, 1997) are no different from helping a "low-resource community" build a better well for drinking water. When such efforts by Christians are done consciously in Christ, even implicitly, God gets glory and people get help. Common psychotherapy and counseling works with creation-grace resources to promote the common dimension of the *imago Dei*—the development of communal agency—and deals with psychopathology involving one's brain, behavior, thinking, and relationships the remediation of which does not bear directly on core issues. "When we reduce substance abuse or alleviate the clinical depression that causes a woman to neglect her children, we are reducing the evil impact of sin in a person's life even when we do not bring that person to Christ" (Jones, 2001, p. 72).

This orientation is prevalent among Christians who work in public mental health and seek to promote the biopsychosocial well-being of non-Christians as well as Christians. The arrow is tilted upward a bit, because such activity done consciously in Christ's name manifests the holiness/receptivity of God, particularly when periodically "tagged" with explicit reference to Christian beliefs in the course of a conversation or in the informed consent.

Arrow 3 aims at a comprehensive quality of psychotherapy or counseling that over time promotes biopsychosocial wholeness and ethicospiritual holiness/receptivity and works with both creation grace and redemptive grace resources. Holy and holistic care of this kind is rarer than it needs to be, largely because it requires both relatively sophisticated biblical/theological training and psychological training, and few programs currently train students how to work equally well with creational resources and redemptive resources. Integration programs more typically specialize in common/creation-grace training, and biblical counseling programs focus on core/redemptive-grace training.

All Christians would presumably want everyone to experience the greatest approximation to the full image of Christ possible. Different Christians, however, may legitimately focus on different therapeutic tasks, depending on their own calling and training, their location (e.g., public mental health or a local church), and where their counselees are and what their most pressing difficulties are. Arrows 1, 2, and 3 are all legitimate from a Christian standpoint, since each furthers at least one dimension of the complete image of Christ, with one qualification: so long as the other dimension is not undermined. Christian charity and liberty will lead Christians to respect the callings of other Christians and not condemn them simply because their calling differs from their own. The fullest understanding of Christian charity (Merton, 1955), however, will also lead Christians to pursue the doxological agenda of the kingdom, which aims at the eternal well-being of one's neighbor consciously and, where possible, explicitly, since the greatest well-being of counselees is coterminous with the greatest manifested glory of God. This will lead Christian therapists and counselors to look for opportunities to appropriately share their faith. Such practice is admittedly denounced within the field of public mental health. However, from a Christian standpoint, all therapists share their worldview assumptions at least implicitly with their clients in every session, based on what is and what is not talked about, including the role of God in the process. Being in the majority, modern psychotherapists and counselors are usually less aware of their assumptions since they are so widely accepted in the field than typically are minority Christians (Johnson, 2011b; 2012). The subtle genius of modern psychotherapy and counseling has been its implicit promotion of a faith in oneself alone, which is simply taken for granted by most modern therapists.

So, let us consider arrow 4, which indicates a path of increased biopsychosocial wholeness while the person is moving away from God. There is plenty of empirical evidence that this happens in secular psychotherapy and non-Christian religions, where people's personal agency and psychological well-being are relatively enhanced apart from Christ. While concentrating on the fostering of biopsychosocial wholeness, much secular psychotherapy and counseling, implicitly and usually unwittingly, addresses some "core" issues along the way, for example, by promoting healing without reference to God, through greater autonomy, self-reliance, and self-determination (see Johnson & Sandage, 1999; Vitz, 1994). Thankfully, it is gradually becoming more widely acknowledged that modern thought is distinguished not by the *absence* of what are fundamentally religious and axiological dynamics but by their repression and submersion into implicitness (Clouser, 2005; Taylor, 1989; 2007).

The positive outcomes of secular therapy should not surprise Christians; God has so constituted human life in this age that the love and wisdom of mature humans (given by creation grace) promote biopsychosocial wholeness, whatever the worldview of origin. Of greater concern is when *Christians* unwittingly foster such improvement. While Christians, of course, ought to deeply respect the free faith choices of others, they ought not to promote their ultimate well-being in ways that explicitly lead them away from Christ.[17] In such cases the Christian therapist is working as a guide within another religious system, promoting a different maturity ideal.[18]

Also of concern is the trajectory of arrow 5, where we see a Christian model of counseling that unwittingly undermines the current biopsychosocial wholeness of adherents, perhaps requiring extraordinary religious duties or compliance with severe ethical and social norms, maybe by blaming all problems on demons or isolating members from outsiders. Such an orientation is more common among fundamentalist Christians, but "spiritually abusive" practice may be the most inglorious because it distorts the *imago Dei* in the name of Christ.

Christ and the Journey

Christ has declared his desires and those of his Father toward those made in his image: "He who loves Me will be loved by My Father, and I will love him and will disclose Myself to him. . . . If anyone loves Me, he will keep My word; and My Father will love him, and We will come to him and make Our abode with him" (Jn 14:21, 23). Using the trail map of Scripture, Christ bids us to journey *with* him *toward* him, in prayerful meditation, dialoging with him audibly, and with our minds, hearts, and imaginations, and along with others on the way as we grow in intimacy, commitment, and sometimes passion. He is omniscient, so he already knows everything about us. By Scripture reading and other devotional reading (*lectio divina*) and prayer we get to know him, and in this way he "gets" to know us *interpersonally*. The interaction of loving, "face-to-face" dialogue (see 2 Cor 3:18) is not the same as mere factual knowledge,[19] and we get to know ourselves better and better—who we are as his gifted but damaged creatures, as sinners, and as saints united to him. He is leading us to himself through this deepening dialogue. Could the love poem of Song of Songs be analogous to such conversational, meditative prayer, where Christ tells his bride how beautiful she is to him, and we respond by extolling his beauty ("As the bridegroom rejoices over the bride, so your God will rejoice over you," Is 62:5)? And the Psalms, where we learn how to praise him and share our joys and sorrows with him. And Proverbs, where our folly gets exposed and throughout we discover Christ is the true Sage, who celebrates his wife in Proverbs 31. In our reading we seek to receive his guiding, loving words as deeply and healingly as we can.

An important part of helping others on the Christian therapy journey involves training them how to spend time with Christ, ideally every day: conversationally, in worship and prayer, opening up to him and sharing their hearts, repenting, letting him speak into them, and allowing themselves to be loved and purified by him, with increasing confidence that nothing can separate them from his love (Rom 8:39). In their Guide, Christian counselees have a companion with them who loves them like the Father loves Christ, in spite of their sin and weakness, and who challenges them to become more holy and whole. Looking to Jesus, believers see in him the practice of communion with the Father and themselves as ethically and spiritually perfect, released from all their shame, guilt, and sin by the transcendent love and declarations of their Maker and Savior. In a real sense (eschatological), believers have already arrived at their destination, and this word can foster the courage now to risk greater transparency to find their true selves in Christ.

RESOURCES FOR COUNSELORS AND COUNSELEES

Classic

Bernard of Clairvaux. (1983). *The love of God.* J. Houston (Ed.). Portland, OR: Multnomah.

Owen, J. (1965). Meditations and discourses on the glory of Christ. In Volume 1 of *The works of John Owen* (pp. 273-461). Edinburgh: Banner of Truth Trust. ‡

———. (2007). *Communion with the triune God.* Wheaton, IL: Crossway. ‡ (Specifically the lengthy section on communion with the Son.)

Rutherford, S. (1984). *Letters of Samuel Rutherford.* Edinburgh: Banner of Truth Trust.

Contemporary

Cortez, M. (2016). *Christological anthropology in historical perspective: Ancient and contemporary approaches to theological anthropology.* Grand Rapids, MI: Zondervan. ‡

Fitzpatrick, E. (2013). *Found in him: The joy of incarnation and our union with Christ.* Wheaton, IL: Crossway.

Grenz, S. (2001). *The social God and the relational self.* Louisville, KY: Westminster John Knox. ‡

Kapic, K. M. (2007). *Communion with God: The divine and the human in the theology of John Owen.* Grand Rapids, MI: Baker. ‡

———. (2010). *God so loved, he gave: Entering the movement of divine generosity.* Grand Rapids: Zondervan.

Smith, S. (2001). *Objects of his affection: Coming alive to the compelling love of God.* West Monroe, LA: Howard.

‡ Recommended more for counselors and pastors than for counselees

—4—

The Gift of the Spirit

Axiom 4: The Holy Spirit is the triune God's indwelling gift of himself to believers, uniting them to the Son and the ultimate means of the proper well-being of humans.

Corollary: The Holy Spirit also uses many secondary creational means to promote the proper well-being of humans.

I will ask the Father, and He will give you another Helper, that He may be with you forever.

JOHN 14:16

Work out your salvation with fear and trembling; for it is God who is at work in you, both to will and to work for His good pleasure.

PHILIPPIANS 2:12-13

What better thing could [God] give us than himself?

BERNARD OF CLAIRVAUX

IT SEEMS LIKE THE ONE CONSTANT in the contemporary world is change. Millions of streams of information are exchanged through the Internet every minute; scientific findings are unveiled every week, while the pace of technological progress seems to be reaching warp speed. Popular culture is in continual transformation—new movies, new music, new blogs, new buzz every day. As a result, at least the more economically advantaged around the world are coming to expect change to a far greater degree than ever before in human history.

These cultural influences have to affect the way we think about ourselves. A spirit of optimism pervades the wealthier half of the world community, leading to the impression that everything in our lives is improving, much of it requiring little effort on our part; we only have to click on something, and we are changed—by a new possession, a new experience, a new look—creating an ever-renewing sense of better. This zeitgeist undoubtedly contributes to a sense of hope regarding change in our selves—in our psyche—yet lasting psychological change generally proves difficult to sustain, leading to a vague awareness, only partially conscious, of unfulfilled aspirations and unresolved shortcomings, usually masked by the more superficial changes around us, but likely fueling a sense of despair among the most damaged.

PSYCHOLOGICAL CHANGE AND WORLDVIEW

Soul care—psychotherapy, counseling, and spiritual direction—is an interpersonal activity that promotes change in individuals, families, and groups. People who come for help want things to improve in their lives—a reduction in fear or an increase in happiness, enhanced relational skills, deeper experiences of God. However, their seeking help also implies they feel some limitation in their ability to change on their own. One of the most important agendas of soul care, therefore, is helping people change in their self-understanding regarding how they change. As we have seen, the relational assumptions of Christianity mean that Christian soul care involves a more accurate understanding of the respective roles of God and the believer in the change-making process, which itself constitutes an important part of the journey. By way of contrast, we will begin with an examination of the framework for change assumed by secular psychology and psychotherapy.

Modern Models of Psychological Change

We recall that modern psychology is the version of psychology that developed in the late 1800s based on the worldview of naturalism and the application of natural-science methods to the study of human beings. Consequently, the dominant framework for understanding human beings in modern psychology has been determinism, the belief that human action is completely the effect of natural causes, specifically biological and social.

Throughout most of the twentieth century, therefore, personal agency (or the will) was not considered a legitimate topic of study within mainstream psychology, and researchers concentrated their investigations on the biological and social (or environmental) factors that shaped human behavior, thinking, and experience. By the end of the twentieth century, we had a rich body of research on the many ways in which human life was indeed conditioned by such deterministic forces. Within such a framework, therapeutic change, at least theoretically, is seen as largely promoted by extrapersonal factors that shape the individual, either through medical therapy (psychiatry), the therapeutic relationship (psychoanalysis), teaching (cognitive therapy), or modification of the environment (behavioral therapy). Yet, there is a paradox at the heart of such therapy, since those involved *act as if* the counselee can influence the change process, whether through compliance in taking medication, homework practice, or self-reinforcement (as in operant therapy).

In the latter half of the mid-twentieth century, a significant libertarian voice arose in modern psychology—unsurprisingly dominated by psychotherapists, for example, Carl Rogers and Rollo May—that argued in favor of personal agency and sought to describe it scientifically, using human science methods (interviews of subjects to gain first-person accounts of human experience), as well as natural-science methods. In addition, mainstream social psychologists began to discover that humans often *believed* they had control over their actions and that such beliefs were often related to positive outcomes.

What nonetheless still united the naturalists and the humanists in modern psychology was the assumption of secularism—the belief that *only* natural forces are operative in the world, whether deterministic or personal. Consequently, the vast majority of modern psychology has only considered causal factors within the natural order. Even the modern versions of psychology of religion and positive psychology have so far only investigated *perceived* supernatural influences in human life, without considering them as actual causal factors in their own right.[1] In the following section we will survey some of the relevant literature to document these observations.

Beliefs of human causation in a natural world. As just mentioned, modern social psychologists have studied people's beliefs about the causes of people's actions. Rotter (1966), for example, investigated what he called *locus of control* beliefs regarding the source of rewards available in the environment, either internal (through one's effort and ability) or external (in others, chance, or situations themselves). Bandura (1977; 1999) later explored what he called *self-efficacy*, beliefs that one is capable of performing a behavior that leads to a desired outcome in certain conditions.

Modern attribution theory (Heider, 1958; Weiner & Graham, 1999) offered a more purely cognitive focus on beliefs about the perceived causes of various occurrences. Of particular interest were people's successes and failures. Attributions (i.e., causal explanations of events or actions) are made along a number of dimensions, but when making attributions regarding humans the most basic is *internal-external*, that is, the cause lies either within the individual (one's ability or effort) or outside (other people or special circumstances or luck). Attributions can also vary with regard to their *globality* (applied to all situations the individual encounters or only to particular situations) and temporal *stability* (with respect to the individual's actions all of the time or only on unique occasions) (Abramson, Seligman, & Teasdale, 1978). Further explorations of internal causal beliefs found they can vary in terms of *controllability* (Weiner, 1995). For example, intellectual ability is internal but is considered by many people to be largely uncontrollable (biological causation is commonly believed to be uncontrollable), whereas effort is internal and by definition highly controllable. Studies have shown that, generally speaking, believing that one has greater control over one's actions is beneficial.

Researchers have also discovered that people tend to form different *patterns* of attributions, called an attribution or explanatory *style* (Buchanan & Seligman, 1995). They have concluded further that an *optimistic* explanatory style (taking responsibility for good outcomes related to one's actions while blaming others and situations for bad outcomes) is generally related to greater psychological well-being than a *pessimistic* style (taking responsibility for bad outcomes related to one's actions while attributing to others and situations good outcomes).[2]

Self-determination theory (SDT) has integrated and extended the above research into an exemplary modern model of human motivation and action (Deci & Ryan, 2004). It assumes that humans have needs to feel autonomous, make choices, and engage in activities that are intrinsically rewarding. According to SDT, humans ideally move from the external regulation of their behavior in childhood to an increasingly internal orientation, in which they act in order to achieve self-chosen goals based on self-chosen values.

In spite of the large body of evidence that the belief that one causes one's own actions promotes human well-being, most modern psychology researchers continue to hold a naturalistic worldview and so refer only to persons' *beliefs* of causation and avoid making claims about whether humans can actually cause their own actions (with some asserting that free will is an illusion; see, e.g., Wegner, 2002). However, the number of researchers arguing in favor of genuine human causation has been growing (see Baumeister, Mele, & Vohs, 2010; Martin, Sugarman, & Thompson, 2003).

Modern psychotherapy assumptions. Attribution researchers have also recognized that psychotherapy assumes and addresses attributions (Brickman, Rabinowitz, Karuza, Coates, Cohn, & Kidder, 1982; Forsterling, 1986), as illustrated in the following quotes of some modern psychotherapists. Carl Rogers (1961) stated that therapy should promote "self-direction," which involves helping the client move "toward being autonomous. By this I mean that gradually he chooses the goals toward which *he* wants to move" (pp. 170-71). In a classic text on psychotherapy, Singer (1970) wrote with unusual worldview transparency that "man is capable of change and capable of bringing this change about himself, provided he is aided [by other humans] in his search for such change. Were it not for this inherent optimism, this fundamental confidence in man's ultimate capacity to find his way, psychotherapy as a discipline could not exist, salvation could come about only through divine grace" (p. 16). More recently, in a widely used counseling textbook, Egan (2002) states that one "goal of helping . . . deals with empowerment—that is, helping counselees identify, develop, and use resources that will make them more effective agents of change both within the helping sessions themselves and in their everyday lives" (p. 55). All three reflect humanistic assumptions and implicitly reject a strong naturalistic determinism with their explicit advocacy of greater internal and controllable attributions for one's actions as an important goal of therapy.

Religious questions. Modern psychologists have discovered many aspects of human beliefs about human actions. Notably absent from the social psychology literature, however, is consideration of God's role in human action. One only finds such investigations in the psychology of religion. In much of this "religious attribution" research, the respective activity of God and humans has been viewed as discrete and mutually exclusive, and God has been considered as an external cause (e.g., Degelman & Lynn, 1995; Ritzema & Young, 1983). A small number of studies, though, have examined beliefs about how God can be directly involved in individual human actions (e.g., Welton, Adkins, Ingle, & Dixon, 1996), and how God and humans might collaborate in human problem solving (Pargament, 1997). A few researchers have distinguished between *proximal* attributions (pertaining to human causal influence) and *distal* attributions (pertaining to divine causal influence), and found that Christian subjects may make both kinds of attributions regarding the same human action (Miner & McKnight, 1999; Weeks & Lupfer, 2000). Much more research in this area is needed.

A Christian Explanatory Framework

The evidence regarding biological and social influences on human action and the value of internal and controllable attributions for human actions is compelling and can be harmonized with a Christian view of humans as conditioned creatures made in God's image. Yet when we turn to the Christian Scriptures, we discover a much more complex explanatory framework regarding human actions than is found in modern psychology.[3] Most distinctive is the inclusion of an ultimate, supernatural causal dimension in which God is providentially involved in all human activity (Eph 1:11), is the ultimate source of all good in human activity (Jas 1:17), and is specially involved in the good actions of believers (Eph 2:10). In addition, the repeated appeals to human initiative to do good and the assumption that humans are generally responsible for their evil actions would seem to rule out the strong determinism of naturalism, while the autonomous self-determination of secular humanism would seem to be explicitly denounced: "Cursed is the man who trusts in mankind and makes flesh his strength, and whose heart turns away from the LORD" (Jer 17:5).[4] In this chapter we are especially interested in God's role in the good actions of believers. Consider the implications of the following biblical teaching for Christian psychology and psychotherapy/counseling.

"The salvation of the righteous is from the LORD; He is their strength in times of trouble" (Ps 37:39). "The LORD is my rock and my fortress and my deliverer, my God, my rock, in whom I take refuge; my shield and the horn of my salvation, my stronghold" (Ps 18:2). "Cast your burden upon the LORD and he will sustain you" (Ps 55:22). "Heal me, O LORD, and I will be healed; save me and I will be saved" (Jer 17:14). God "restores my soul" (Ps 23:3). So God is seen as the ultimate source of the believer's strength, protection, happiness, and soul healing. At the same time, as alluded to above, the innumerable commandments and directives throughout the Bible signify that humans are agents who themselves are responsible to act. Consequently, according to the

Bible, God's activity and the believer's genuinely good activity (competent, virtuous, healing, or otherwise flourishing) are mysteriously interrelated.

Nonetheless, while biblical authors recognized the legitimacy of human causation or agency, they often drew a sharp contrast between it and the empowering agency of God in positive human endeavors to emphasize the preeminence of the latter. For example, "The horse is prepared for the day of battle, but victory belongs to the LORD" (Prov 21:31). In the midst of a series of visions regarding sweeping events that were to happen to Israel, a Jewish leader in the postexilic period, Zerubbabel, was told, "'Not by might nor by power, but by My Spirit,' says the LORD of hosts" (Zech 4:6); and Asa, a king of Judah, was once criticized for seeking help from his physicians rather than God for a severe foot disease (2 Chron 16:12).

The biblical theme of boasting casts an interesting light on attribution issues. "Thus says the LORD, 'Let not a wise man boast of his wisdom, and let not the mighty man boast of his might, let not a rich man boast of his riches; but let him who boasts boast of this, that he understands and knows Me'" (Jer 9:23-24). Two different explanatory frameworks are being contrasted here: secular/autocentric and theocentric. Ideally, believers are to make their "boast in the LORD; the humble will hear it and rejoice" (Ps 34:2). Paul built on this theme and gave it a clearer trinitarian context (1 Cor 1:31). Christians, he wrote, "worship in the Spirit of God and glory in Christ Jesus and put no confidence in the flesh" (Phil 3:3). According to Ridderbos (1975), for Paul, faith is the "relinquishing of every human achievement, it is the exclusion of all 'boasting' or moral self-confidence" (p. 246). That is because the *ultimate* cause of all good in the Christian life is divine *grace*, not autonomous human effort. "For by grace you have been saved through faith; and that not of yourselves, it is the gift of God; not as a result of works, so that no one may boast. For we are His workmanship, created in Christ Jesus for good works, which God prepared beforehand so that we would walk in them" (Eph 2:8-10).

Yet human agency is constantly appealed to, for example, when commanding certain human actions, but it is assumed that these commands can only be obeyed when empowered by God's grace, in union with Christ by faith. Jesus himself taught this to his disciples, "Abide in Me . . . for apart from Me you can do nothing" (Jn 15:4-5), and they embraced this paradoxical attributional framework. John later wrote, "If we love one another, God abides in us, and His love is perfected in us" (1 Jn 4:12). The author of Hebrews blessed his readers, wishing that God would "equip you in every good thing to do His will, working in us that which is pleasing in His sight, through Jesus Christ" (Heb 13:21). Paul claimed that he "labored even more than all of [the other apostles], yet not I, but the *grace of God* with me" (1 Cor 15:10). The *locus classicus* of this attributional framework is found in Philippians: "Work out your salvation with fear and trembling; for it is God who is at work in you, both to will and to work for His good pleasure" (Phil 2:12-13). Commenting on this passage, Ridderbos (1975) wrote that whatever good deeds the Christian does, "he works by the strength of God, out of the power of the Spirit and by virtue of belonging to Christ" (p. 255). In chapter three I described this reliance on God as an aspect of the *imago Dei* termed *active receptivity* (Pinckaers, 2001, p. 88); here we note it also has attributional implications.

"Happiness is neither without us nor within us. It is in God, both without us and within us" (Pascal, 1941, p. 154). The Christian explanatory framework—particularly with regard to the genuinely good activity of Christians—cannot be fit into an either-or, internal-external attributional framework. It is simultaneously both internal and external—God's activity is expressed in and through the human activity, with the human activity being necessary but entirely dependent on that of God. According to biblical revelation, God in Christ is the *ultimate personal source* of good in the good activity of believers, who are nonetheless understood to be the actual, distinct, personal agents of their good activity.[5]

In contrast to the comparatively simple attribution framework of secular/modern psychology, the Christian explanatory framework has a number of unique features that reflect a different view of human beings. Grounded in the "God-*imago Dei* distinction,"[6] it is fundamentally interpersonal rather than individualistic. God is the eternal triune Creator who makes possible and empowers the lives of all human creatures, who are entirely dependent on him for all their good. As images of God, all human creatures were made to develop within families in order to become mature but finite personal agents, conditioned by biology and socialization, living in loving, devoted dependence on God. Their fallenness, however, has compromised their development into whole personal agents and absolutely prevents them from doing so in holy dependence on God. Consequently, the triune God devised a plan to restore them to whole, holy, and receptive images of God in Christ, by means of his own empowering dwelling within them in the person of the Holy Spirit.

CHRISTIAN TEACHINGS REGARDING
THE GIFT OF THE SPIRIT

In chapter two, we gave some consideration to the Spirit's place and role within the Trinity and within the Trinity's economy of salvation. Here, we will go into a little more detail to help us understand the Spirit's role within an explanatory framework for Christians.

The Holy Spirit Within the Trinity

We recall that the Holy Spirit is as fully and eternally God and as fully a divine person as are the other two members of the Trinity. Yet, as we have seen, Western interpretation of biblical revelation considers the Spirit to proceed eternally from both Father and Son. The Father and Son's eternal love and mutual glorification bring forth eternally the joy of the Spirit, and all together they celebrate their limitless plenitude of overflowing goodness and delight (McIntosh, 2008). The expression "Two's company, three's a crowd" denotes the human experience that the fallen love of two people can be exclusive, a zero-sum game, where the competition for finite affection leaves others out. The inexhaustible quality of God's love is seen in the Spirit's wholehearted rejoicing in the beauty of the love of the Father and the Son, without envy or resentment (Richard of St. Victor, 1979).[7] How is that possible? Because also being fully God, the Spirit is not diminished or threatened by their love but is likewise filled to overflowing with infinite and eternal joy in God (that is, in the Father and the Son, and in himself). So the Godhead is fully—within itself—infinite, interpersonal love. This is why their love can never be overturned or defeated, even in the face of resolute resistance, which is eventually judged.

The Holy Spirit Within the Triune God's Economy

We also noted in chapter two that the Spirit is the actualizer of God's works in this universe. He brings into creaturely being the Father's good plans and purposes regarding nature and culture, as well as the redemption of sinners, by means of the Son's mediating wisdom and work on earth and in heaven. The Spirit accomplishes the latter by revealing in Scripture the substance of the triune God's redemptive agenda to human beings and then bringing it to new creation realization received through the gift of their faith.

We should note that when the Son of God became a human creature, he lived in constant dependence on the Holy Spirit: Jesus Christ was conceived by the Spirit (Mt 1:18); while he was praying, the Spirit came to rest on him, as a dove, signifying his need for spiritual empowerment at the start of his ministry (Lk 1:22), and then leading him up into the wilderness (Mt 4:1), where he overcame the devil's temptations to become autonomous from God and his mission. He ministered thereafter "in the power of the Spirit" (Lk 4:14) and so fulfilled the prophecies about the Spirit-endowed Messiah (Is 42:1; 61:1; Lk 4:18), manifesting the Spirit's power in his works (Mk 3:29). After his death, he was raised by the Spirit (Rom 8:11; 1 Pet 3:18), who established him as the redeeming Son of God (Rom 1:4). The help given by the Spirit to the human Jesus Christ—though, in his divine nature, he needed no help—demonstrated Jesus' full human nature. As the *imago Dei* he was entirely dependent on the agency of the Spirit in his human activity.

At the resurrection, however, their (economic) relationship to us was altered: the Son became "life-giving spirit" (1 Cor 15:45)—the Lord who with the Father sends the Spirit (Jn 15:26; 2 Cor 3:17-18)—so that the Spirit is now the Spirit of Christ (Rom 8:9; 1 Pet 1:11), and having the Spirit is the same as having Christ (Rom 8:10; 2 Cor 13:5; Eph 3:17) (because of their mutual indwelling or *perichoresis*). Then, the risen, exalted Christ—the *beginning* of the new creation (Col 1:15)—sent the Spirit from heaven at Pentecost, a truly revolutionary event in human history (Jn 7:37), which furthered the Father's doxological agenda by extending the new creation to other human beings through union with Christ by means of the Spirit so that, just like the original creation, the new creation is the work of the Word and the Spirit (Bavinck, 2008, p. 33).

As a result, the redemptive mission of the Spirit that began at Pentecost centers on Christ. "He will glorify Me, for He will take of Mine and will disclose it to you" (Jn 16:14). Throughout creation, revelation, and redemption, the Holy Spirit is supremely humble, celebrating with humanity the special relationship of the Father and the Son and pointing especially to the Son, not to himself, *though the Spirit is no less God*. This manifests what has been called the Spirit's self-effacing quality (Thompson, 1994), the divine archetype of humility. The other-orientation of the Spirit reveals an astonishing excellence to the magnanimity and superlative greatness of the triune God given the preeminence and praise directed to the Father and the Son throughout Scripture and in the age of come (Rev 4–5). Yet the Spirit is still God and worthy of corresponding honor and respect, so that the Son of God warned that whosoever discredits the Spirit's work is guilty of the only unpardonable sin (Mk 3:29) (a warning given perhaps to prevent any misapprehensions among sinners regarding the nature of divine humility).

The Supreme Gift of the New Covenant

The Spirit is continuously but secretly active in the creation (Ps 104:30) and was manifestly but sporadically active in the history of Israel. However, at Pentecost the Holy Spirit was finally given as God's supreme gift to human beings (Acts 2:38; 8:20; 10:45; 11:17; 15:8; 1 Thess 4:8; Lk 11:1), the preeminent blessing of the new covenant (Ezek 36:26-27), restoring humans to their original communion with God (Bavinck, 2004, p. 559), filling their fallen emptiness, and pointing back to the mission and mediation of Christ. The Spirit also points ahead to the consummate fulfillment of the Father's redemptive purposes in heaven, when humans will experience perfect communion with the Trinity, giving humans much more than they lost in the fall (O'Donovan, 1986).[8] The (illocutionary) meaning of the new creation word is spoken in Christ (2 Cor 4:4) and gradually transforms believers by means of the (perlocutionary) effects of the Spirit's work in them and their relationships through their deepening faith (Johnson, 2007; 2011a; Vanhoozer, 2000), whereby the Spirit renders the Son's word subjectively real (Webster, 2003).

As a result of the Spirit's coming, a new era in human history has dawned, which only those who believe in Christ have yet entered (Rom 8:4; 2 Cor 3; Gal 6:15; Vos, 1952), derived from their union with Christ's resurrection, beginning a "new way" (see 2 Cor 3:6) of radical inner and relational renewal (Titus 3:5; Rom 12:1-2) that fosters repentance from the old way of the law of sin and death (Rom 7:6; 8:2) and undermines all the *imago Dei* distortions of their psychopathology. Along with Christ, believers are part of the new creation (2 Cor 5:17), in which now the entire cosmos is seen in a different, always new, eschatological light (Gal 6:15; Vos, 1952), so that life now in the new creation is also called being "filled with the Spirit" (Eph 5:18) and "walk[ing] in the Spirit" (Gal 5:16, 25) or "according to the Spirit" (Rom 8:4). In preparation for the age to come, the Spirit is in this age healing believers, in part, by teaching them how to set their minds and hearts on spiritual things (Rom 8:5; the above things, Col 3:2; Owen, Vol. 7, 1965), that is, how to do "soul work."

The Indwelling God

From the believer's standpoint, easily the most wondrous aspect of the Spirit's coming is his indwelling. "Do you not know that you are a temple of God and that the Spirit of God dwells in you?" (1 Cor 3:16; see Rom 8:9). Christianity (and most theistic religions) posits an absolute difference between God and his creation (in sharp contrast to the pantheism of Hindu [and New Age thought], which asserts that the human soul [*atman*] is part of absolute divinity [*Brahman*], thus obscuring the God/*imago Dei* relation). So it is unfathomably glorious that God would choose such an intimate and personal way to commune and communicate with believers. How does the Spirit's active presence within the bodies of believers differ from his infinite presence permeating and holding together and empowering the entire universe (including *every* human's body and soul)? To grasp the radical incongruity here we must remind ourselves that compared with the almighty God, humans are a mere breath (Ps 39:5) and, worse, unholy sinners (Is 6:6; Jn 3:36). In light of God's revulsion at the vileness of sin (Hab 1:13), the gift of the indwelling Holy Spirit is unspeakably merciful and provides concrete evidence for believers that they have been cleansed from their sin by Christ.[9]

At the sites of his special indwelling, God communicates and reveals far more of himself than anywhere else in the universe (analogous to his dwelling in the Old Testament tabernacle or temple, and an extension of his indwelling in "the temple" of Jesus Christ; see Jn 1:14; 2:19). The Spirit's immediate presence within provides the embodied ontological ground for our union with Christ and is the personal medium of its benefits (Calvin, 1559/1960; Ferguson, 1996). Having the Spirit of Christ in our bodies and in our hearts enables us to meet with Christ intimately, as it were, face-to-face (2 Cor 3). When announcing the Spirit's coming, Christ said, "I will not leave you as orphans; I will come to you," and "I will love [the one who keeps my commandments and loves me] and disclose Myself to him" (Jn 14:18, 21). Perhaps we could liken this to having personal access to the king in one's home, only better, for the triune King comes to make his home *within us* (Jn 14:23). "Behold, I stand at the door and knock; if anyone hears My voice and opens the door, I will come in to him and dine with him, and he with Me" (Rev 3:20). "By this we know that we abide in Him and He in us, because He has given us of His Spirit" (1 Jn 4:13; see Jn 14:20). By bringing the Trinity into believers (through the Trinity's *perichoresis* or mutual indwelling; see chap. 2), the indwelling Spirit brings believers into their communion.[10] So remarkable and mysterious is this union that the apostle Paul at times variously referred to the believer's actions and identity as the Holy Spirit's, Christ's, and God's (e.g., "It is no longer I who live, but Christ lives in me," see Gal 2:20; see also Gal 4:26; 5:16-18; Eph 2:10; Rom 8:15-16). Coe (1999) argues that Christian psychotherapy and counseling should be *pneumadynamic*,[11] as well as psychodynamic, since having the Holy Spirit within should make a significant impact on the experience and healing of believers.

The Glorious Spirit of the Reconciliation of Opposites

The coming of the Holy Spirit creates new possibilities for finite, fallen, and fragmented human beings: restored communion of sinners with God; love, joy, and peace in conflicted societies; thinking, feeling, acting, and loving that is gradually integrated into lives becoming increasingly whole, holy, and centered on God, causing a degree of unity and harmony to emerge out of conflict, competition, and opposition, impossible by ourselves. Unifying human souls, relationships, and cultures, overcoming chaos and rebellion, and transforming sinners into new selves in Christ are aspects of the special glory manifested by the Spirit's work. The greater the contrasts, oppositions, and evil in the source material the Spirit has to work with, the greater the excellence the Spirit manifests in the world.

The Spirit of empowering Christlikeness. The Word of God first expressed objectively in Jesus Christ the central themes of the Father's character and redemptive plan, and now the Holy Spirit re-sounds that divine meaningfulness by bringing it into created being through ongoing, partial realizations of the conformity of individual believers into Christ's image together. This entails the new-creation re-formation of images of God who learn how to actively receive the meaning/glory of God through faith and participate as creatures in God's theocentric agenda, love, and holiness.

In chapter three, Christlikeness was summarized as biopsychosocial wholeness and ethicospiritual holiness in active receptivity, exemplified primarily in Christ's life, death, resurrection, and exaltation, as interpreted within the context of the entire canon. As the member of the Trinity who realizes the Father's agenda in creation, the Holy Spirit brings about the Christlike union of these dimensions of the *imago Dei* in believers. The Holy Spirit is the only and ultimate cause of ethicospiritual holiness (Phil 3:3; Acts 4:13; 9:31; Rom 14:17; 15:13; Gal 5:22-23; 1 Thess 1:6; 1 Pet 1:2; 2 Thess 2:13), which can be displayed in many different forms of human beings, from children to adults and from severely damaged to the most whole. Nevertheless, according to the Father's design plan for the *imago Dei* as expressed in Christ, greater biopsychosocial wholeness is a secondary good, toward which all humans normatively move.[12] As a result, the mission of the Holy Spirit also involves the healing of brain function, cognition, emotion, relational patterns, and so on; just consider how such creational dynamic structures are related to the fruit of the Spirit: love, joy, peace, patience, kindness, goodness, faithfulness, gentleness, and self-control, as exemplified perfectly in Jesus Christ. The Spirit therefore is the ultimate power who makes possible the comprehensive *telos* of *all* Christlike change.

Christ told his disciples at his ascension that they would "receive power when the Holy Spirit has come upon you" (Acts 1:8). Stephen and Barnabas were exemplary post-Pentecost disciples: "full of faith and of the Holy Spirit" (Acts 6:5; 11:24[13]). The Spirit now strengthens believers with power (Eph 3:16), producing spirits of "power and love and discipline" (2 Tim 1:7), enabling the willpower necessary to become more holy, receptive, and whole images of God. The Spirit therefore is the ultimate agent of a new kind of human agency, mysteriously involving the coagency of the indwelling Spirit and individual believers.

Earlier we examined Christianity's unique explanatory framework, particularly focusing on its model of the good activity of believers, which we need now to connect to the presence and activity of the Holy Spirit within believers. As we have seen, Christians have another person living within them—an infinite, divine person—who is the ultimate source of their goodness. So, the activity of the believer's new self (Eph 4:24; Col 3:10) is actually the cooperation of two, radically asymmetrically related personal agents, constituting two differentiated loci of internal attribution: the ultimate, originating activity of God's gift of power through the Spirit and the subordinate, receptive activity of the believer's willpower, bringing the gift to its realization through participation in the power of God and manifested in increasing godliness and loving practice. Growth in understanding and receiving this two-personed explanatory framework is a key component of Christian psychospiritual development and identity formation.

The Spirit of truth and love. The redemptive mission of the Holy Spirit includes the drawing of all people to Jesus Christ (Jn 15:26) and his teaching (Jn 14:26). The Spirit of truth (Jn 14:17; 16:13) guides believers "into all the truth" (Jn 16:13). Consequently, the Spirit revealed to the prophets and apostles his healing salvation, even the mind of Christ (1 Cor 2:7-16), which was given a fixed textual form by the Spirit in Scripture (2 Pet 1:21).

Yet spiritual knowledge is more than linguistic, logical, or intellectual knowledge (2 Cor 3:6), but encompasses one's emotions and desires as well—and not only positive emotions such as love, joy, and peace (Gal 5:22-23) but also the darker emotions of conviction regarding sin, righteousness, and judgment (Jn 15:26; 16:13; Carson, 1991; see Edwards, 1746/1959; Johnson, 2007, chap. 9). The word of God is the "sword of the Spirit" (Eph 6:17; Heb 4:12), who turns believers into embodied letters of God as he writes that word on human hearts (2 Cor 3:3). Believers gradually learn by the Spirit how to put to death old ways of thinking, feeling, choosing, and relating, and how to put on the thinking, feeling, choosing, and relating of Christ (Rom 8:13; 2 Cor 3:18; Eph 4:22-24; Col 3:9-10).

Christian truth, therefore, is not less than propositional, but so much more. The person of Jesus Christ is the truth (Jn 14:7) that promotes "relational fidelity" to the triune God (Köstenberger, 2009, p. 398). According to Edwards (1971), the Holy Spirit—whom he equated with divine love—is "the main thing that [Christ] purchased" (p. 89). So the believer's love of God and neighbor is simply a creaturely participation in the the love of the Spirit (Rom 15:13) "poured out within our hearts" (Rom 5:5), given Christian form by Christian truth.

Christ called the Spirit "another Helper" or Advocate (*paraklētos*; Jn 14:16, 26; 15:26; 16:7-11, 12-15). In context, the word suggests the Spirit strengthens, empowers, educates, and encourages believers to live Christ-centered lives (Carson, 1991; Köstenberger, 2009), enabling them to participate through faith in the communal love of the triune God (Jn 15:9-10; Eph 3:16-19). On the basis of Christ's incarnate life and work, the Spirit is simply bringing created persons into his own celebration of the love of the Father and the Son and facilitating the reproduction of that love in the community of God's people, who speak the truth in love (Eph 4:15) and love one another in the truth (2 Jn 1-2).

The Spirit of unity/harmony and diversity/disruption. By drawing believers into the life and communion of the triune God, the Holy Spirit brings unity and harmony, internally and relationally. The ethicospiritual orientation of being "led by the Spirit" (Rom 8:14; Gal 5:18; see also Eph 5:18; Gal 5:16) creates top-down effects throughout one's soul, leading to the brain's reorganization and integration, and corresponding psychosocial dynamics— thinking, feeling, memories, and relational capacities—in accordance with God's design plan (Johnson, 2007; see Siegel, 2012; Thompson, 2011).

The communion or *koinōnia* of believers is "with the Father, and with His Son Jesus Christ" (1 Jn 1:3), but we participate in it through the *koinōnia* of the Spirit (2 Cor 13:14; Phil 2:1). Christ's ministry to sinners and the poor—in body and soul—is now being extended throughout the world by the Spirit (Jn 16:14-15) as sinners and the poor come to share the "same mind" and "same love" (Phil 2:2), experience "unity . . . in the bond of peace" (Eph 4:3), and different people groups are built "into a dwelling of God" (Eph 2:22).

The Spirit first anointed Christ to proclaim good news to the poor and liberty to the captives and oppressed (Lk 4:18), and later came upon the church at Pentecost to give prophecy and visions to young men as well as old, and to women as well as men (Acts 2:17). The Spirit also builds and unifies the body of Christ by distinguishing individuals with spiritual gifts (1 Cor 12:4-11; Eph 4:1-16), sometimes disturbing the established creational order and overturning traditions and cultural norms. The Spirit's disruption was so significant in Corinth (see 1 Corinthians), for example, that additional apostolic (and scriptural) guidance was needed, including the harmony-producing theme that everything should be regulated by love (1 Cor 13).

The Spirit works glory in Christ's church much like the glory he worked in Christ's life. As we have seen, Edwards (1974) considered Christ's excellence to be the conjunction of extremely diverse characteristics, for example, infinite greatness and infinite humility. Analogously, God's glory is wondrously displayed through the prism of the church as the Spirit enables very different people—some with significant strengths, others with significant weaknesses, and all born in sin's opposition—to love one another with the Trinity's love (Eph 4:12-16; see Hart, 2003), the infinite beauty and power of God being best displayed in the most diverse community, with greater brokenness and more sinful stories simply providing greater doxological opportunities. Conversely, we inhibit the display of his infinitely rich glory by minimizing creational differences, hiding our struggles and sin, and requiring bland uniformity and conventional conformity.

The book of Acts, the history of revival, and contemporary Pentecostal and charismatic churches should lead us to seek surprising narratives and unpredictable encounters and breakthroughs that the Spirit can accomplish where he wishes (Jn 3:8; Appleby & Ohlschlager, 2013). The new creation is *new*, after all, so walking with the Spirit involves risk taking and improvisation (Vanhoozer, 2005). The same history, however, also reveals the need to test the spirits (1 Jn 4:1); and try as we might, we cannot schedule the Spirit's miraculous interventions. So while we should pray for therapeutic signs and wonders, we must also be content to rely on his normal, usually much slower, change-making processes, in which the Spirit develops new neural networks and rewires brain regions through new thinking, feeling, acting, and relating, through his word in Scripture and relationships with his people (and sometimes anyone made in his image), as well as with himself over the course of individual lifespans on earth.[14]

SOME THERAPEUTIC IMPLICATIONS

How does the foregoing shine light on Christian psychotherapy, counseling, and spiritual direction?

Soul Care and God's Gift of the Spirit

God has given himself to humans in the person of the Holy Spirit to promote the restoration and flourishing of their well-being in Christ. God is resolutely committed to helping each counselee, and he works within believing counselors and counselees to better their lives and relationships. The same God who is the sovereign center of the universe is at the center of our individual embodied being, making himself continuously available to us. He is too great a God to be thwarted by our sin, brokenness, and repeated setbacks, and in his transcendent glory patiently (and usually gently) helps us, challenges us, and encourages us, ever new, never exhausted, and ever resourceful.

All therapy involves at least two human persons. *Christian* therapy is distinguished by the explicit involvement of at least *three* persons—two human and one divine, who indwells the humans, if they are Christians. Discussion in session of this profound, mysterious, interpersonal resource is warranted. This is not a merely human enterprise. At the same time, it is also a thoroughly human enterprise, since the Father's primary soul-healing intervention occurred through the very human Jesus Christ, and on that basis, the Spirit now works through the humans present, in spite of their limitations and sin, guaranteeing that progress will be typically slow and halting.

Promoting Christ in Christian Soul Care

The Spirit is ultimately responsible for all good experienced by people, including all therapeutic good (Kim, 2012; e.g., gladness of heart, Acts 14:17). However, the Spirit's primary mission on earth is to magnify Christ, so his passion in psychotherapy and counseling is to bring people to healing in Christ. Walking with the Spirit in Christian counseling, then, means that Christ is central to the counseling endeavor, so that counselors are consciously reliant on him and seek to emulate his ways through the course of their counseling, regardless of their counselee. When working with Christians that means explicitly promoting Christ's centrality in the healing process and utilizing him and his work on behalf of the counselee, optimally. When working with those who are not followers of Christ, it means a conscious but mostly implicit Christian witness (Tan, 1996), while addressing the counselee's psychosocial needs using creation-grace resources (empirically based counseling strategies, common-sense principles, ethical precepts, and so on), but maintaining a readiness to introduce Christ to the counselee's healing journey, sensitive to where the counselee is on the journey.

The Place of Prayer in Christian Psychotherapy and Counseling

Secular psychotherapy provides unique cultural and social support for the illusion that humans can remedy all their psychosocial problems with solely human resources. By contrast, the Christian counselor's task is to promote "the movement from illusion to prayer" (Nouwen, 1986, p. 114), and from autocentrism to an active dependence on God for all good, including all therapeutic good. Yet the secular pressures of the field can lead Christian counselors to be extremely hesitant to incorporate prayer into sessions.

> Clients and therapists should probably pray together only when three circumstances converge: (a) The client requests in-session prayer; (b) a thorough spiritual and religious assessment and psychological assessment have convinced the therapist that engaging in such explicitly spiritual and religious activities would not lead to the confusion of therapeutic role boundaries; and (c) competent psychological care is being delivered. Obviously, in-session prayer is no substitute for competent psychological practice. (McCullough & Larson, 1999, p. 101)

One can hold this view and still pray before a session or silently during. But such reticence to pray with clients is the norm in a secular-dominated mental health field. However, if a therapist believes that God is necessarily the source of all good, it would seem appropriate for that therapist to request to pray, unless there was some therapeutic reason not to or, of course, if the client was opposed. This would seem especially to be the case, under normal circumstances, when working with Christians. According to a Christian explanatory framework, God is the ultimate cause of the healing process, and both counselor and counselee need the Spirit's help. Christian therapy is essentially a trialogue (Johnson, 2007; Kellemen, 2014). In addition, part of the Christian counselor's job is to model this framework, and prayer is perhaps the most basic and fitting way to do so. Pastors and pastoral counselors are expected to pray. "No pastoral conversation is possible without constant prayer. Other people must know that I stand before God as I stand before them" (Bonhoeffer, 1985, p. 35). However, the same reasoning would seem to apply to the practice of Christian psychotherapy and professional counseling, so long as the therapists do good religious and spiritual assessment and counselees are agreeable and have given their consent.

The Comforter Within

"I have God within me!" What immeasureable dignity and honor is bestowed on believers by having the infinitely majestic God dwelling within their bodies and at the deepest part of their souls. The greatest imaginable gift to his people—God's gift of himself as *comforter*—is intended to be their utmost encouragement, and consequently, it has great therapeutic value. To begin with, the Spirit's indwelling would seem to have profound implications for one's self-understanding. The Holy Spirit can only dwell in those who have been definitively sanctified and declared "saints" (1 Cor 1:2) and holy (Col 3:12) by the Father through the Son. Reflecting and meditating on this truth introduces and elaborates a remarkable, positive cognitive scheme in one's self-representation.

"God is in my body." Believing that God is especially present within one's body, and opening up to his presence affectively, might help counselees anticipate and foster constructive emotion change. God is omniscient and knows everything that goes on inside each of his children—all one's negative thoughts, feelings, body states, and motives—and yet he is not put off or discouraged by any of that. The Spirit's indwelling presence signifies that God's infinite, omniscient enthusiasm for his beloved children is unrelenting—*in spite of their felt shame, guilt, anxiety, and pain*—and nothing can separate them from his love (Rom 8:39). In addition, focusing attention on the Spirit's immediate bodily proximity to those negative emotions may help to facilitate greater emotion awareness and acceptance of those emotions, for the sake of their being resolved, and then their therapeutic modification by the introduction of redemptive information *into* those emotions, for example, a fresh cleansing of shame by the blood of Christ. After all, the Spirit is *right there.*

"God is in my soul." Meditating on the Spirit's presence deep within one's internal world may also contribute to a sense of intimacy with God. Believers would seem to be able to share their thoughts and feelings with the Spirit rather easily, since he is omniscient and lives within them. Therefore, he listens with infinite concern (sympathetically and empathically) to their cognitive and emotional conflicts and is their eternal, internal companion, able to serve as emotion coach and guide. Reflecting deeply on this can draw Christians to open up to the Spirit's presence and acknowledge their unwanted negative emotions and then yield them to him, mindful of Christ, so that the Spirit "carries them away." Recognizing God's presence within can also help believers stand together with the Holy Spirit over against the affectively loaded representations of their old self, their sins, painful memories, and the sins of others against them. Since the Spirit is in their hearts, he is immediately present in the midst of all their psychological and relational experiences, and therefore can be focused on to comfort them, challenge them, or encourage them to speak up or to act (Mt 10:20). One might hypothesize that repeatedly engaging in such imaginative practices would promote less reliance on oneself alone or the therapist and instead greater reliance on God empowering the self's activity.

The "Spirit of truth" (Jn 16:13) is the believer's "inner teacher" (Calvin, 1559/1960, Vol. 1, p. 279), so he is the ultimate agent who communicates the mind of Christ (1 Cor 2:16) and growth in self-awareness in relation to God (therefore also promoting the closely correlated knowledge of God and self; Calvin, 1559/1960). An important part of this process involves enabling believers to bear the pain of conviction for sin, righteousness, and judgment (Jn 16:7-11) for the sake of their deepening and healing. The wise Spirit who knows the infinite depths of God (1 Cor 2:10) dwells deep in believers' hearts (Rom 8:26), underneath the darkness of their anxieties and sins (Mt 15:19). As a result, when they feel confused or overwhelmed by strong negative emotions, they can imagine the truth of the infinite Holy Spirit dwelling even deeper and so being able to cast out the confusion or lift the overwhelming emotion out of the soul. Counselors can pray on behalf of counselees who get suddenly confused in session and ask for the Spirit to give both of them greater clarity regarding what is going on in the counselee's internal world.

The Spirit of love (Rom 5:8) also aids believers (Jn 14:18; 15:14) by drawing them into experiences of and participation with the communion of the Father and the Son. Another person lives inside believers who is on their side and seeks their good (Rom 8:26) and resists the self-destructive tendencies of their flesh (Gal 5:17). The best friend imaginable lies within the internal world of believers, with all his benevolent and holy dispositions constantly poised toward their well-being. The long-term goal for the believer is the development of a disposition of active receptivity to this transcendent but very interpersonal acceptance in Christ. This is just what Paul called faith—extended to the therapeutic task.

If Christian therapy and soul-work practice at home are consistently *pneumadynamic* (Coe, 1999), a significant alteration would seem eventually to occur in the "internal structure" of Christian counselees—that is, in their emotionally tinged self- and other-representations by which they interpret and relate with themselves and others (St. Clair, 2000). Long-term, affectively rich awareness of, meditation on, and openness to the Spirit's indwelling would seem, over time, to result in a *psychological sense* of his personal presence that could help offset the psychological presence of antagonistic parts of the souls of counselees (self-destructive impulses, the "inner critic," false selves, and so on), and so better enable them to recognize and undermine those parts as well as the related defenses. Simply knowing intellectually that the Spirit is present within oneself is a starting point, but one needs also to regularly *experience* the Holy Spirit's help in one's heart if one is to become a significant *psychological presence* within that actually comes to affect one's self-representation and one's relational experiences with God and others.

All Christians have to admit that, because of their remaining sin and brokenness, they can easily forget the Spirit's indwelling presence—for days and weeks and even months at a time! Therefore, counselors might consider taking time periodically in session to focus on the Holy Spirit within to help remind counselees of his presence. Of course, some counselees will have greater internal hindrances to such activities than others, perhaps because of early abuse or neglect, including spiritual abuse, that results in a strongly negative self-representation and its accompanying distorted beliefs about self and others, and in this case, the Holy Spirit's dispositions to help. If a counselor discerns that a Christian counselee seems to lack the present capacity to open up to the Spirit directly, it may be desirable to focus predominantly on psychosocial dynamics for a while, by exploring current challenges in life or having the counselee tell more of his or her story. Relationally oriented Christian therapists understand that time spent strengthening the therapeutic alliance can also reconfigure the person's internal world, thus paving the way for the counselee to better trust and imagine similar empathic support by the Spirit.

Christian Reattribution Training

Secular cognitive therapists have advocated the use of reattribution techniques to help their clients take greater responsibility for their recovery (see, e.g., Beck et al., 1979, pp. 157-59). This can also be a part of Christian psychotherapy and counseling, especially when working with Christians, but using the radically different and more complex Christian attribution framework expressed in the following encouragement of Rutherford (1664/1984): "O created strength, be amazed to stand before your strong Lord of hosts!" (p. 582).

The challenge, of course, is to develop a *dipolar* attribution scheme in which the Holy Spirit is acknowledged as the ultimate source of one's inner strength and energy *while one is acting* (Coakley, 2013, p. 113). One way to facilitate this in session is to have the counselee imagine herself receiving the Spirit's power and then enabling her to engage in some desired activity, for example, talking to a stranger (and thus overcoming anxiety) or standing up for herself with an aggressive coworker. Most counselees tend automatically to activate old-self attributional patterns, in which they are alone and left to their own limited and fallen resources, when they enter certain settings that resemble psychologically those in which they first developed. Counselors can help them identify such activation, surrender the old-self attributional scheme to Christ, and replace it with its new-self alternative, in which the Spirit is accepted as the indwelling source of empowerment who is forever on the believer's side.

Primary and secondary control. Researchers have distinguished between two kinds of control and coping that people engage in: *primary* control (focused on external change, in which one seeks to alter people and things in the external world); and *secondary* (focused on internal change, in which one seeks to alter one's perceptions of the world, values,[15] or internal dynamics) (Hood, Hill, & Spilka, 2009; Rothbaum, Weisz, & Snyder, 1982). Depending on the nature of the problem, it is sometimes best to exercise primary control and at other times best to engage in secondary control (and one also needs the wisdom to discern the difference!). While a Christian understanding of these two kinds of control differs substantially from a naturalistic one, the distinction is valid in both. However, for Christians, both kinds of control are dipolar, entailing active receptivity and prayer. Christian therapy, moreover, will generally tend to favor secondary control more than secular models, given Christianity's prioritizing of internal change over external (Mt 5–7) and trust in divine providence (Rom 8:28).

In some cases, divorce is a legitimate type of primary control (e.g., Mt 5:32; 1 Cor 7:15). However, most of the time Christian marriage counseling will help couples recognize that their struggles are normal and that God designed marriage in part to promote the healing of the soul (Thomas, 2002; Hendrix, Hunt, Hannah, & Luquet, 2005). This involves learning to reframe one's marriage struggles as opportunities for learning secondary/internal control in the Spirit: "What am I doing to contribute to this struggle, O Lord? Please help me and heal me."

Promoting coagency understanding. Because of its paradoxical nature, grasping the dipolar nature of Christian action—receiving God's power in order to act freely—is a process and is itself part of Christian maturation. After their conversion, believers will typically shift back and forth from the divine locus to the human locus, looking to God to miraculously solve problems one moment and acting independently the next. Growing in the faith involves slowly coming to understand the nature of Christian receptive activity, so that it becomes a more habitual frame of mind (resulting from cognitive change), and eventually a more settled frame of heart (involving carditive change). Grasping this understanding, therefore, takes time and depends on a host of other precipitating factors, including exposure to childhood abuse and its consequent belief distortions that in adulthood have often become so automatic they are often not even recognized. Believing in an almighty God who has the ability to change people's internal world miraculously, but who most of the time works indirectly through secondary means, can create special challenges for some counselees.[16]

Freedom. One of the most important products of the Spirit's work is the freedom to love God and pursue him and his healing in Christ, a freedom lost when humans became sinful. Jesus said, "If you continue in My word, then you are truly disciples of Mine; and you will know the truth, and the truth will make you free" (Jn 8:31-32). Paul expanded on this theme: "The law of the Spirit of life in Christ Jesus has set you free from the law of sin and of death" (Rom 8:2), and believers will eventually experience the "freedom of the glory of the children of God." Until the complete redemption of their bodies and adoption that occurs in eternity (Rom 8:23), the new creation has already begun in their bodies and brains through faith, so that believers by the Spirit can now, little by little, break free from their autocentrism by receiving Christ and his ways more thoroughly, gradually practicing more of the fruit of the Spirit (Gal 5:22-23), leading over time to a new-creation character (Christlike habits of thought, imagining, feeling, and action). The God-intended destiny of believers is to overcome their deterministic tendencies—the continual repetition of fallen ways of relating and acting internalized earlier in their story—and live more and more in the new creation. The Spirit's freedom enables them increasingly to resist old-self patterns of behavior, shaped by biology and prior socialization, and imagine new, God-dependent ways of living and responding to stress, disability, and mistreatment, and even how to improvise actions that correspond more and more to the patterns of Christ's life, death, and resurrection (Vanhoozer,

2005) and participate in the emergence of the new creation *now*. This spiritual transformation, however, is generally an arduously slow process, in large part because it involves new habit formation and neural reorganization.

The Ultimate Cause and Secondary Means

The believer's dipolar self-understanding is one of the most practical implications of a basic assumption of a Christian worldview: God is the ultimate cause of all good (Jas 1:17), and the created order is simultaneously a causal network that is necessarily contingent and dependent on God (and therefore always open to his novel activity, usually called miracles). Humans are unique in the creation, because they are *consciously* dependent. Such an orientation teaches Christians to take very seriously creaturely causation ("a godly man will not overlook the secondary causes," Calvin, 1559/1960, p. 221) but to understand it *theocentrically*.

In the highly secular environment within which Westerners live and work (dominated by the worldview of naturalism but also influenced by humanism and postmodernism), it is perhaps understandable that some Christians have overreacted and reject the contemporary fields of psychology and psychiatry and their research on secondary causation in human development and therapy (genetics and neurology, socialization and family dynamics, human agency, medication, and therapy strategies that work with creational dynamics and not redemption), because it is almost entirely secular. A more subtle God-centeredness (complex theocentrism), however, seeks the glory, given by the Holy Spirit in creation grace (Bacote, 2005), found even in secular scientific research—the glory of the creational findings themselves and the glory of God's giving good to those who ignore him—while seeking to separate the *knowledge* from the distorting secular therapeutic framework within which it is embedded and "translate" it into a Christian therapeutic framework (Johnson, 2007). The Christian psychologist seeks to understand human beings, as much as possible, the way God does, and this means understanding that human creation, fallenness, and redemption cannot be understood independently of one another.

As a result, Christian psychotherapy and counseling recognize with gratitude and work with all creational and redemptive good that comes ultimately from God (Jas 1:17), and therefore give due consideration to relevant creational dynamics involved in therapy, including secondary causes (that could be called *means of creation grace*) such as physiology and genetics; diet, exercise, and sleep; human development dynamics; the role of other humans in childhood formation and adult reformation; cultural influences; body work; walks in nature; and the use of books, technology, and media; psychological tests; and legitimate biopsychosocial strategies (not discussed explicitly in Scripture and that do not necessarily flow from redemption, e.g., common sense, logical reasoning, acupuncture, the body work of yoga, systematic desensitization, transference, emotional processing, the therapeutic relationship, and exploration of one's past). In addition, when working with Christians, Christian psychotherapy and counseling will use secondary means that relate directly to God and his redemption in Christ (what we might call *means of redemptive grace*), such as faith, prayer, Bible reading and meditation, Christian music, fellowship with other believers, preaching, small groups, church involvement, baptism and the Lord's Supper, and so on.

Christians trained and socialized within a modern counseling and psychotherapy framework will have to be careful not to "forget" the Spirit's ultimate role in all human good, as well as God's primary doxological design to heal people in Christ. Otherwise, the therapy practice of Christians will be substantially naturalistic and humanistic, unwittingly reinforcing the autocentrism of Christian clients as well as non-Christian, and amounting to a kind of modern-day Pelagianism.[17]

"God, of his goodness, has ordained many lovely means to help us" (Julian of Norwich, 1998, p. 90). Therefore, holistic and holy Christian counseling and psychotherapy is free to use all that "God has created to be gratefully shared in by those who believe and know the truth. For everything created by God is good, and nothing is to be rejected if it is received with gratitude; for it is sanctified by means of the word of God and prayer" (1 Tim 4:4-6).

As a result, Christians should not use secondary means as if they were primary or as if they functioned independently from God. Instead, using doxological criteria, let us seek the most glory for God we can, working at the highest levels possible (the ethicospiritual), but the lowest levels necessary (the biopsychosocial) (Johnson, 2007).

As we saw above, the Holy Spirit has been commonly understood to be the bond of love between the Father and Son. Consequently, an important part of the Spirit's mission is to draw humans into *their* communion (*koinōnia*; 1 Jn 1:3), which in turn transforms believers into the creaturely communion called the church. The effusive, other-focused orientation of the Spirit within the Trinity and with respect to Christ on earth makes the Spirit the perfect helper to undermine our native sinful autocentrism; to heal us, to some degree, from the exacerbated narcissism and self-absorption of those who grow up in especially dysfunctional families; and to teach us how to become increasingly other-centered and love others authentically and in strength (rather than out of codependence).

According to God's design plan for fallen humanity, one of most important secondary means that the Spirit uses to accomplish the above goals is the communion of the church. Of special value in this part of his mission is the development of safe, trustworthy, empathic relationships with others who image God better than one's parents did, including psychospiritually mature pastors, counselors, or spiritual directors who participate in and practice to some degree the self-giving, other-oriented love of the Spirit. In a dynamic interaction of healing causation, the Holy Spirit gradually reshapes the believer's internal dynamic structures immediately and directly (through faith), as well as by means of the love of mature others who mediate God's love concretely, which in turn helps to reconfigure and establish new neural structures and enables ever-greater openness to and trust in God, others, and oneself (integrated with an increasingly realistic awareness of the fallenness of oneself and others). God's sovereign, creation grace is also evident when he even uses the love of well-formed non-Christians to bring about creaturely healing. The slow transformation in one's neurological/internal-relational world, in turn, increasingly facilitates freedom from one's old-self relational pathology, so that over time, believers come to act more and more freely in the love of God and his glory and in love of their neighbor. (More on the church in chap. 16.)

RESOURCES FOR COUNSELORS AND COUNSELEES

Classical

Basil the Great. (2011). *On the Holy Spirit.* Yonkers, NY: St. Vladimir's Seminary Press.

Edwards, J. (1959). *Religious affections.* New Haven, CT: Yale University Press. (Original work published 1746) ‡

Kuyper, A. (1900). *The work of the Holy Spirit.* New York: Funk & Wagnalls. Reprint, Grand Rapids, MI: 1975.

Owen, J. (2007). *Communion with the triune God.* Wheaton, IL: Crossway. (Original work published 1657) ‡ The section on the Spirit.

Winslow, O. (1961). *The work of the Holy Spirit.* London: Banner of Truth Trust. (Original work published 1840)

Contemporary

Apply, D. W., & Ohlschlager, G. (2013). *Transformative encounters: The intervention of God in Christian counseling and pastoral care.* Downers Grove, IL: InterVarsity Press. ‡

Billings, J. T. (2007). *Calvin, participation, and the gift: The activity of believers in union with Christ.* New York: Oxford University Press. ‡

Coe, J. H., & Hall, T. W. (2010). *Psychology in the Spirit: Contours of a transformational psychology.* Downers Grove, IL: InterVarsity Press. ‡

Packer, J. I. (2005). *Keep in step with the Spirit* (2nd ed.). Grand Rapids, MI: Baker. ‡

Payne, L. (1995). *The healing presence: Curing the soul through union with Christ.* Grand Rapids, MI: Baker.

Tan, S.-Y., & Gregg, D. H. (1997). *Disciplines of the Holy Spirit: How to connect to the Spirit's power and presence.* Grand Rapids, MI: Zondervan.

Zeiders, C. L. (2004). *The clinical Christ.* Birdsboro, PA: Julian's House. ‡

‡ Recommended more for counselors and pastors than for counselees

—5—

Stories of Glory

Axiom 5: The triune God's word in Scripture singularly communicates his understanding, appraisal, and activity regarding human beings, particularly his redemptive mission for them in Jesus Christ, so that the Bible is the canon of Christian psychotherapy and counseling, the primary guide for its agenda, and provides its "first principles."

Corollary: The triune God did not convey through Scripture his *entire* understanding of human beings, so the use of other, relevant sources of knowledge about human beings for Christian psychotherapy and counseling is legitimate and highly desirable, so long as they function subordinately to Scripture.

Expansion of Axiom 5: The fundamental organizing framework of God's word in Scripture is the drama of God's self-glorification in human history—summarized as the Christian ground-motive of creation, fall, redemption, and consummation, the climax of which is the story of Jesus Christ, into which the stories of believers are now being written.

But when the fullness of the time came, God sent forth His Son, born of a woman, born under the Law, so that He might redeem those who were under the Law, that we might receive the adoption as sons.

GALATIANS 4:4-5

WHEN WE *REALLY* WANT TO GET TO KNOW SOMEONE, we want to hear the person's *story*. We are usually not so interested in a list of facts: "I am 5′10″. I play piano. I was the second child in my family." We are more interested in the person's story line, perhaps how some of those facts fit together, but not so much the facts themselves. This is because in a fundamental sense a person really *is* their story. Narrative is basic to our humanity.

This narrative orientation is also central to the psychotherapy enterprise. Therapists need to get some basic facts in intake. What is your marital status? Are you on medication? But the main focus of the first few sessions is getting to know the person, and this involves hearing the person's story. What happened to you to bring you in here? What was it like growing up in your family? This is because the person's presenting problems are woven together in the person's story. So, all therapy is necessarily narrative therapy, to some extent. Narrative therapists take this insight a step further and believe that narrative is central to a person's healing.

Christianity, many have suggested, is first and foremost a story, based on historical events recorded in the history of the Bible. Many important truths are revealed about God and human beings in Scripture, but they are all embedded within the epic narrative/dramatic framework that constitutes its superstructure. But before we discuss the therapeutic implications of Christianity's narrative/dramatic structure we will consider the narrative structure of Christian psychology's main rival in the West.

THE METANARRATIVE OF MODERN PSYCHOLOGY

Over the past fifty years, some thinkers have suggested that human knowing occurs *necessarily* within a narrative context. All cultures of any complexity have a narrative of the origins of the universe and the story of humankind. Lyotard (1979) called such ultimate stories "metanarratives," noting that they are embedded with humanity-constituting beliefs and assumptions. The narrative structure of Christianity is easy to identify. However, according to Lyotard, modernism too has a narrative structure, though somewhat more complex and more difficult to discern.

A number of intellectual currents led to the founding of modern psychology, but one of the most important has to be the theory of naturalistic evolution. Virtually all the founders of modern psychology considered it to be central to their project, including Galton, James, the functionalists, the behaviorists, as well as Freud, and it profoundly influenced modern psychology's development. But naturalistic evolutionary theory (NET) also offers a story, and it would seem to qualify as a metanarrative, since within its narrative the existence of all contemporary life forms, including human beings, is accounted for solely with reference to natural forces. It is a story of creation without a Creator, at least the way it is usually told.

The early impact of NET on modern psychology was pervasive and led to important discoveries in individual differences, comparative animal research, and eventually human behavior (for the purpose of studying the simplest psychological structures on which higher-order human functioning was presumably based). Nonetheless, the full implications of NET for psychological science were not fully appreciated until its radicalization in recent decades in what has become known as evolutionary psychology. In what is still a minority orientation, the metanarrative of evolution is pressed into service to provide the primary explanatory justification for *all* psychological structures—not just those that pertain to reproduction and survival (respective body sizes of the sexes; physical attractiveness; achievement), but psychological phenomena much harder to account for by natural selection and genetic mutation, such as complex mathematics, altruism, and religion.[1] At the same time, one has to admire the thoroughness of evolutionary psychologists, for they recognize that, to be consistent, naturalistic evolution has to explain everything.

This matters to Western psychology and psychotherapy because of the deep nihilistic and skeptical assumptions regarding human life implicit in the story of naturalistic evolution. Though human beings designed by a virtuous Creator will never cease to be moral and epistemological realists (at least unconsciously), naturalistic assumptions have surely played some role in contemporary skepticism regarding consciousness, human agency, personal responsibility, and the existence of God so common today among Western intellectuals, as well as the broad acceptance of sexual libertinism, the multifaceted decline of the traditional family, and the marked preference for medical solutions to psychospiritual problems across Western culture. And because there is no author of the story of naturalistic evolution, the metanarrative can bestow no transcendent meaning on the stories of individual persons or cultures. All these matters are of profound psychological and therapeutic significance.

CHRISTIAN TEACHING REGARDING ITS METANARRATIVE

Christianity recognizes the triune God to be the ultimate author of human history (and the universe), who has used a variety of means to bring about the present form of the creation and "write the story." Moreover, this author has given us an authorized account of the story in the Bible. A drama, we might say, is an *enacted* narrative (Johnson, 2007, chap. 9) in which embodied persons actually perform their roles, so human history is both a narrative and a drama. Given that the triune God is both its ultimate author as well as the primary protagonist(s), Balthasar (1988–1998) designated the story a *theodrama*. Understood within this frame, the main plot of human history concerns the triune God's rescue of his image-bearing enemies at notable personal cost, bringing them into his family and gradually turning them into loving family members in the heart, "working in perfect communion for an even greater communion" (Vanhoozer, 2010, p. 259).

A typical drama is propelled by the protagonist's progress in resolving some problem that emerges near its beginning. We have noted repeatedly that God's chief end in creating human beings was the manifestation of his triune glory. However, humanity's primal sin created a fundamental obstacle to the realization of God's doxological agenda, since humans were supposed to play a primary role in God's glorification but became distrustful of him and antagonistic to this agenda. As if that were not problematic enough, humans also came to experience various kinds of suffering—which they are naturally motivated to avoid, raising questions about God's love and goodwill—as well as biopsychosocial damage, which further compromises some of their image-bearing capacities. Altogether these impediments to God's original goal would seem to be insurmountable. We see here the conditions necessary to mount a momentous and monumental drama, the significance of which is maintained over time by its unrepeatable, temporal unfolding, making every moment (and action) count (Johnson, 2007).

The other "end" of the story is the eschaton, in which God will bring about the end of history as we know it and inaugurate a radical new era of human flourishing—initiated, however, by a judgment toward which all the events of history and choices of human beings are now heading, most importantly, their interactions with God (O'Donovan, 1986). In that day, God's glory and final purposes will no longer be as obscure as they are now, and those who have believed in Christ will find their total fulfillment in the consummation of God's design plan in their love of God and enjoyment of him forevermore, the end of the theodrama that will finally make meaningful all that has happened and that therefore gives hope to believers now that the events and choices of their lives really matter (Kelsey, 2009).

The Major Events of the Christian Theodrama

The Christian philosopher Dooyeweerd (1960) labeled the major events, or epochs, of the Christian metanarrative—creation, fall, redemption, and consummation—as the Christian ground-motive.[2] The following is a brief exposition of that framework, as revealed in Scripture,[3] focusing on the details most relevant to psychotherapy and counseling. Further elaboration will appear in subsequent chapters of the book.

Eternal program notes: Before creation. To get the full picture of human history and its significance, we need to begin with the faint light shed on the triune God's activities and relations before history began. Paul taught in Ephesians that God "works all things after the counsel of His will" (Eph 1:11), that his salvation of human beings in Christ, in particular, was the result of the "kind intention of His will" (Eph 1:5; see Eph 1:4, 9, 11) from before the foundation of the world (Eph 1:4), and that its proclamation occurs "in accordance with the eternal purpose which He carried out in Christ Jesus our Lord" (Eph 3:11). Though shrouded in mystery, these teachings suggest that the meaning of every detail of the story is found in relation to the mind and heart of the Author and that the entire plot line is related to the salvation and healing of human beings through Jesus Christ.

Act one: Creation. God began the story of his self-glorification by creating two places—the earth, the primary setting of the theodrama and the dwelling place of humans, and "the heavens," the dwelling place of God and his angels and the source of all earthly significance. The stage and scenery is built in the first five days, and on the sixth, creaturely actors make their appearance. Many aspects of the creation set up the dramatic context of the rest of the story, including God's centrality to the action—everything else that exists comes from him: the verbal nature of his mighty, creative acts (Gen 1; Jn 1:1-3; Heb 11:3); humans being made in the image of God (the *imago Dei*) to be creaturely actors along with God (Gen 1:26-30; 9:6); the binary, complementary nature of humans as male and female (Gen 1:27; 2:18-25); the climactic evaluation of the creation as "very good" (Gen 1:31); God's continuing maintenance and care for the creation, termed "providence" (Ps 33; 104; 139; Heb 1:3); and the unique calling and purpose of the human actors to live so as to glorify their Creator (Gen 1:28-30; see also Ps 8; Is 43:7). Though creation is not much discussed through the rest of biblical revelation, it is assumed; there is no theodrama without the good creation (Kelsey, 2009).

Act two: The fall into sin and the divine judgment. Whereas God is the primary actor in act one, the deeds of humans are the main focus of act two. It begins with the surprising appearance of a reptilian tempter in paradise (Gen 3:1) who offers the humans an alternative interpretation of God and his purposes (Gen 3:1-5), and they respond by distrusting God and disobeying the test command of the Creator (Gen 3:6). We find out that sin and an experiential knowledge of good and evil have immediate, deadly consequences: shame and guilt (Gen 3:7-8), signified by the awareness of their naked sexuality and their attempt to hide from God's gaze (Gen 3:9-10); their awkward excuses and blame shifting (Gen 3:12-13); the suffering they would face (Gen 3:16-19); their expulsion from God's presence in paradise (Gen 3:23-24); and the murderous, competitive enmity that now mars human relationships (Gen 4). God is revealed to be a righteous judge in this act, and his actions expose human sin and declare just punishments. We also see that the drama of God's self-glorification in his creation was immeasurably complicated by the transformation into rebels of those he created to glorify him, "anti-images" opposed to him from the heart. Sin is so awful precisely because it distrusts and disvalues the Source of all goodness. If God were not absolutely antagonistic to sin, he would be a co-conspirator and himself an idolater. The dramatic tension could not be greater. As Carson (2008b) remarks, "the drama of the entire story line of the Bible turns on our persistent alienation from God" (p. 47).

As the story unfolds, we learn much more about human fallenness, including its corruption of the entire human race (Gen 6:5), thoroughly pervading all the capacities of its members (Rom 3:10-20); its "power" to oppose God's law (Rom 7:5-23); the revelation of eternal punishment for unrepentant sin as the expression of God's righteousness and fundamental opposition to sin; and the strength of humanity's overall resistance to the word and will of God—especially illustrated in the Israelites' waywardness in spite of God's covenant with them—issuing eventually in the crucifixion of the Son of God. The course of this doxological drama takes some shocking turns, through which we discover more of the splendor of God's character. We also find out that humanity is unknowingly under the degrading and enslaving influence of Satan (1 Jn 5:19), along with the "powers and principalities" (Eph 6:12), and the earth is now the site of a spiritual battle going on between Satan and his forces and God and his, ultimately limited by God's power and plan. Nevertheless, this warfare theme forms a significant part of the backstory for the theodrama (Aulen, 1931; Boyd, 1997).

At the same time, the goodness of God's creation and his ongoing providential care did not end with the human fall into sin, and they continue because of God's powerful (creation) grace. As a result, though corrupted by sin, culture is enabled to flourish in many respects (the good and the corruption both evident in the slow development of human culture).

Calvin wrote that the "knowledge of ourselves is twofold: namely, to know what we were like when we were first created and what our condition became after the fall of Adam" (Calvin, 1559/1960, p. 183). The creation and the fall provide perspectival lenses through which we can view all human beings, and their effects continue throughout the next act and persist until the last.

Act three: Redemption. After two comparatively brief acts (at least according to what is described in Genesis), we come to the epoch that spans essentially all of recorded human history, organized around the divine therapeutic initiative that constitutes its central plot. The first phase of the story is the manifestation of the glorious form of God: he is the Creator and Lord of the universe and the Judge of humankind. This characterization dominates the Old Testament. As the story unfolds, however, we see that what looked like a tragedy is actually an epic/romance set in a time of war. Edwards (1989) considered it fundamentally a romance: "The work of redemption . . . was the most glorious and wonderful work of love ever seen or thought of" (p. 143). However, it is also an epic drama, since the lead actor, the triune God, works over centuries in the pursuit of Christ's bride to bring about the most radical transformation in humankind ever: the gradual undermining (in this age) and eventual overturning (in the age to come) of the effects of its fallen transformation into anti-images of God, in the process overcoming three enormous obstacles to his purposes for humanity: a "worldly system" of cultures that exist in various levels of ignorance, indifference, and hostility to him; an alien, oppositional force that indwells all humanity, including those he has already rescued; and the fallen creature Satan and his spiritual army.

Scene one: Redemption promised and prefigured. In the Hebrew Testament we discover that God is planning a major initiative to resolve the tragic predicament of his image bearers and be reconciled to them, in which he is directly involved but which does not happen by the end of that Testament.

A. *Hope for Adam and Eve:* After declaring the punishment that would come upon his human creatures for their sin, God uttered indirectly a monumental promise to them and their descendents in his curse on the serpent: "I will put enmity between you and the woman, and between your seed and her seed; he shall bruise you on the head, and you shall bruise him on the heel" (Gen 3:15). In this obscure prophecy God foretold of humanity's coming Messiah. Too holy to minimize their sin and too august to be indulgent, God nonetheless subtly indicates his intention to restore his fallen creatures.

B. *The earthly redemptions of the Hebrew people:* The first step in God's therapeutic program was the establishment of a covenant with Abraham and (implicitly) his wife, whom he called to be the progenitors of a race that will bless all the families of the earth (Gen 12:3). Eventually, Abraham's descendants were subjugated to the Egyptians, and God called a leader-servant, Moses, to deliver them because he "remembered his covenant with Abraham" (Ex 2:24). After their astonishing rescue, God expanded his covenant with

Abraham by establishing another covenant with the entire community of Abraham's descendants through Isaac and Jacob, which entailed their adherence to "the law"—a massive set of religious, civil, and ethical norms, with animal sacrifice at the center—obedience to which would glorify God and signify restoration to his original plan for humanity.

C. *The rise and fall of the Hebrew kingdom:* Beginning with a divinely directed war for the Promised Land, the Hebrews entered into a protracted struggle with people groups that lived for other gods. Generations after settling down in the region of Canaan, the Hebrews sought an earthly king and chose one based on appearance, Saul, whose heart was not so devoted to God. Eventually, he was judged by God and killed in battle, and David ascended to the throne, a redeemer-king, a man after God's own heart (1 Sam 13:14). God promised David that one of his descendants would rule an everlasting kingdom (2 Sam 7:13-16), and "I will be a father to him and he will be a son to Me" (2 Sam 7:14). David and one of his sons, the wise Solomon, amassed a significant empire that pictured the glory of a future, spiritual kingdom. However, *even they* committed shocking sins of adultery, murder, and idolatry. God judged them also, their kingdom was divided into two, and both kingdoms pursued a path into sinful/idolatrous self-destruction, the northern part, Israel, more rapidly than Judah, the southern part. God raised up prophets to expose Israel's sin and bring the people back, with sporadic and marginal success. Eventually God judged both kingdoms, and the Hebrews were returned to a subjugation similar to what they were first delivered from.

Through the course of this long, sad, drawn-out account of covenantal pursuit and betrayal, we learn that the Hebrews, chosen representatives of humanity, are incapable of trusting God and fulfilling their covenantal responsibilities through obeying his law. Overall, God's plan for restoration and reconciliation appeared to be thwarted; human beings seem to be irredeemable. Yet along the way there were many anticipatory stories of concrete and material redemption—pertaining to deliverance from human oppressors and the acquisition of land—while the spiritual oppression and bondage of sin retained its hold on the human heart. But we learn in this Testament that humanity's divine ruler and suitor would not give up, and throughout this story he gave clues about what he would eventually do.

Scene two: Redemption accomplished in Christ. And then the Son of God assumed human nature himself and walked onto the stage! It was fitting that in the first phase of the display of God's glory he revealed himself as the monarch and judge of humanity. This provides the essential backdrop for the dramatic unveiling of God's remarkable splendor and excellence: the Lord of the universe became a human being, even a baby! What kind of God is this?

Through the seed of the woman, of Abraham, and of David, a son was born who would save humanity from their sin, suffering, and weakness. "When the fullness of the time came, God sent forth His Son, born of a woman, born under the Law, so that He might redeem those who were under the Law, that we might receive the adoption as sons" (Gal 4:4-5). Jesus Christ is clearly the hero in the act of redemption. *The* image of God (Col 1:15), the servant of the Lord (Is 42:1-4; Mt 12:18-21), he lived the life of a faithful son within the Hebrew covenant, obedient to its laws, fulfilling the calling of God on humanity, becoming the ultimate prophet, priest, king, and sage. He taught and he healed and he ruled in love, and he refused to collude with Satan and the powers of sin that ruled in the land. In response, those who assumed they were followers of Yahweh turned against Yahweh's servant in Yahweh's name, and this hero of heroes was betrayed, mocked, and murdered. Then came the greatest surprise in all history—this martyr was raised from the dead. Over forty days he appeared in various ways to his followers, until he was transported to heaven, "and a cloud received Him out of their sight" (Acts 1:9)!

But more was going on in these events than human eye could see. Unbeknown to the human actors, while the Son hung on the cross, his Father was simultaneously judging sin in him on behalf of Israel (Is 53) and all the sinners of the world (Acts 2:23). God's plan all along had been to come to earth *himself* to rescue humanity from their alienated selves. And we discover, obscurely at first, a stunning revelation: that the one God is actually more than one person. The crucified servant of the Lord was actually God the Son, and God the Father had sent him on this rescue mission, which would overturn humanity's death by means of his own (Heb 2:14-15). So the Son, in loving obedience to his Father, drank that cup to the bottom. At the cross, God "displays his own covenant faithfulness, his love and his justice" (Vanhoozer, 2005, p. 52). As a result, in the raising of Christ from the dead, the eternal life of the triune God, forever united to humanity, burst forth from and conquered death. Human rebellion against God and its worst consequences—death, suffering, brokenness, and godforsakenness—were ultimately overcome by the transcendently indefatigable love of the Father and the Son. In Christ's life, death, and resurrection are concentrated the greatest manifestation of God's glory ever seen in this creation. Then, the Son returned to his Father in heaven to reign at his right hand (Ps 110:1; Mk 16:19), physically separated from his followers while interceding on their behalf (Rom 8:34). In the story of Christ we learn something of the greatest therapeutic significance: *this* world, and all its problems (sin, suffering, and the shame of brokenness), is passing away, and a new world of unimaginable happiness is coming, and already is.

Scene three: Redemption offered and bestowed. The new creation begins as new life in Christ is received by sick and needy humans and spreads around the globe. Before going back to heaven, the Son of God co-missioned his disciples to share the news of what the triune God was now offering to humanity, based on what Christ had accomplished: a new covenant union with Christ, in which God forgives the sins of those who repent and believe this offer and shares with them some of the rights and privileges that belong ultimately to the Son, for example, unsullied righteousness and holiness and a fabulous inheritance (Eph 1:14; 1 Pet 1:4). Most significant, the Father and the Son sent another person, just like them—this God is *three!* So forty days after Christ's ascension, the Holy Spirit came to earth to carry out this next phase of God's mission and began to accomplish *in and among them* what Christ had accomplished *for* them. "Pentecost—the forming of the church—is thus part of Christ's work, part of the climactic action of the theodrama" (Vanhoozer, 2005, p. 55).

With the Holy Spirit, courage and boldness, humility and love began to characterize the early believers. Now like Jesus, they taught profoundly and healed diseases and delivered from demons. They shared with others what they had received from God, and many more came to believe. Even persecuting Pharisees, such as Saul of Tarsus, were changed by Jesus and his Spirit. A new era in human history had dawned.

Nonetheless, there was still sin in the camp (see Jn 7:18-24). A husband and wife lie to the Spirit and die by the Spirit (Acts 5:1-11). Though he has brought sinners into his family, the God of the new covenant remains as holy as ever, and on this occasion he underscored that his goal is the purity of heart of his followers, beginning with their consciousness. More drama continues throughout the final scene of this act: turmoil, disagreement, conflicts, and betrayal; some people even leave the faith (Acts 15:2-22, 39; 1 Cor 3:1-8; Gal 2:11-21; 2 Tim 4:10; Heb 6:1-6). As the early years of the church turn into decades, it becomes clear that this is just the beginning of the "last days" (Acts 2:17; Heb 1:2). Salvation has *already* begun but *not yet* been completed

(Dunn, 1998; Hoekema, 1994; Ladd, 1974; Ridderbos, 1975). Christians are being changed for the good, but not automatically, quickly, or uniformly. Rather, the coming of the new creation seems to be a very gradual affair (Is 66:22; 2 Cor 5:17). How much change can individual believers experience in this age in light of their finitude and remaining fallenness? Perhaps that is the greatest theodramatic question of the last days.

So the new creation begun in Christ's resurrection is now being realized by the Holy Spirit in the hearts and lives of God's people (2 Cor 4:6), though hindered by their residual sin, suffering, and biopsychosocial damage. The Christian life is a *journey* of faith and repentance, as Christians learn how to enter into Christ's dramatic activity on their behalf, renarrating themselves accordingly and grounding their new identity on the "above things" (Col 3:1-4), more and more deeply, but in light of the unique features of one's cultural and family context and personal calling. So the journey is necessarily similar and different for everyone.

Act four: The consummation. Jesus Christ, the Son of God, will come to earth again to judge all humankind and usher in another phase of human life and human and divine relationship that will last forever.

Much of what we know of the coming age has been communicated through symbol, so we cannot be entirely sure what it will be like, but a few things are fairly clear. The consummation, we might say, is a second climax in the theodrama, its dénouement. It is a wrapping up of the history of this creation in its present form. It begins with divine judgment—a holy reckoning of all that everyone has done regarding God and one's neighbor. Believers will see with a clarity that will finally undermine their remaining sin and (unconscious) self-boasting, and those who resisted their Creator throughout their lives (whether consciously or unconsciously) will finally obtain the consequences of what they have sought. This will be the ultimate courtroom drama, involving everyone and hinging entirely on whether one was joined by faith to the perfect Son who died for everyone (1 Jn 2:2). This beginning of the end of the story bestows on every human story a maximal momentousness.

Bakhtin pointed out the impossibility of discerning the meaningfulness of the life of a character in a novel while in the middle of it. Only at the end of a story, when one knows the completed whole of the character's life, can that be determined, an assessment Bakhtin called "consummation" (Vanhoozer, 2010, p. 326). Authors, of course, are supremely able to make such an assessment. Being the omniscient author of human history, God is the only one who can consummate the lives of those in the theodrama, and this constitutes the final judgment. In the meantime, he has given us some advance notice about such matters in Scripture. So, for example, because of union with Christ, believers already know that their lives will be consummated with the beauty and meaningfulness of Christ.

This future orientation of Christianity is called "eschatological" by theologians, because it looks way ahead, to the *eschaton* (from the Greek *eschatos*: the "last"), the everlasting age. Knowing about the judgment with which that age begins is supposed to engender in believers now a contented realism regarding their problems on earth. Sin, suffering, injustice, and weakness will somehow then be rectified, a process that begins in this age. There will be a cosmic resolution to all that has gone wrong down here, and God himself will comfort his people (Eph 1:9-10; Rev 7:17; 21:4).

However, an enormous caveat must be made at this point, because Christ's resurrection was actually the beginning of the age of come, and the gift of the Spirit to the church was the next step in its realization, so that the "last days" have already started (Heb 1:2), and the church through the Spirit becomes the one and only accomplishment of this first day of the new creation (2 Cor 5:17; Gal 6:15). Here and now, redemption and the consummation overlap (Vos, 1952).

After the final judgment, God will put in place a new order of things, a new way of life that has continuity with what has gone on before but will be transcendently improved. Little has been revealed about that age. What we know for sure is that believers will be ethically and spiritually perfect, they will not suffer, and they will be happy beyond their wildest dreams, possessing intimate, everlasting bliss because they will live together with God in mutual love forever (Jn 17:23-26; Rev 21:3). God will also bring in a new heavens and a new earth (Rev 21:1) in the "period of restoration of all things" (Acts 3:21). So there will likely still be cultural activity, such as work, invention, and vacations, as there will likely still be forests, seas, and animals. "The eschatological transformation of the world is neither the mere repetition of the created world nor its negation. It is its fulfillment, its *telos* or end. It is the historical *telos* of the origin, that which creation is intended *for*, and that which it points and strives *towards*" (O'Donovan, 1986, p. 55). So the creation mandate may still need to be realized, but it will be pursued without the curse. Humans there will have resurrected bodies, and they will still be active, personal agents, finally freed from sin and psychological damage, so that their biopsychosocial capacities can finally be used fully for the way in which they were designed and to the end for which they were created. All this will issue in the consummate glorification and happiness of God himself and the absolute (and growing?) fulfillment of his followers. Looking ahead to this future helps believers now.

The Christian Ground-Motive as a Set of Interpretative Lenses
The foregoing summarizes the biblical metanarrative. We might note that the thrust of three of the four periods (if we only consider heaven in the consummation) is positive and funded by God's immeasurable goodness to all who will receive it. There is so much, however, to consider. The major events of redemptive history, as Dooyeweerd (1960) recognized, are more than just some notable happenings in human history; they consist of four "meaning-perspectives," or interpretative frameworks—four distinct yet holistic viewpoints on human beings.

Calvin (1559/1960) likened the Scriptures to a set of spectacles. If the Christian metanarrative is a valid summary of scriptural teaching, then perhaps its four major epochs could be considered four lenses—quadfocal reading glasses, if you will—that psychologists, counselors, ministers, and laypersons need in order to "read" human beings (including themselves) aright.

Such a rich set of perspectives on human life allows Christian psychologists to do better justice to the biopsychosocial and ethicospiritual complexity and potential of human nature than either the univocal framework of naturalism or the dualistic fall-redemption framework of fundamentalism. The Christian metanarrative draws us "both backwards and forwards, to the origin and to the end of the created order. It respects the natural structures of life in the world, while looking forward to their transformation" (O'Donovan, 1986, p. 58).

Perhaps the most complicated aspect of this quadfocal orientation is the historically overlapping nature of the epochs, which "cannot be distinguished completely from one another, as one might do by separating physical elements through the use of chemicals" (Bayer, 2008, p. 155). Most of the aspects of human beings that are due to creation (and providence) continue to be true of humans after they have become sinners, and the nature of human beings due to the fall continues to be true about those who become believers. As a result, though these perspectives must be distinguished in our understanding of human beings, they are conceptually and temporally interrelated.

Wolters (2005) points out that reference to creation pertains to *structure*, whereas the fall and redemption pertain to *direction*, that is, the deep ethicospiritual motives (that arose from the fall) that draw humans away from God or move humans toward him (as a result of redemption). Things are even more complex than that, however, since the created structures of human life are not static but temporal and developing. So in this book they will be referred to as *dynamic* structures. Nonetheless, their postfall development proceeds inexorably away from God, unless and to the extent that that trajectory is undermined and overcome by creation or redemptive grace.

Since the human creation is now fallen and under judgment, its continued existence and remaining goodness is due to what Reformed Christians have termed God's "common grace" (common to all humans, irrespective of their personal relation to God). However, I use the term *creation grace* to underscore its relation to God's activity in creation (and providence) and the continuity there is between human goodness and the goodness of the rest of creation. All goodness comes to humans from the Father (Jas 1:17), mediated by the Son and dispensed by the Spirit. However, the special blessings of redemption are given by the Spirit only through personal faith in Christ. Most of the formal and material goods of human life in this age are benefits of creation grace, whereas redemptive grace provides efficient and teleological goods, rightly ordering and regulating creation grace and bringing it to its proper end in Christ.

Of special importance for psychology and therapy is the relation between creation and redemption (that is, the partial realization of the new creation in this age). Through creation/providence God provides the materials with which redemption works, whereas redemption is the fulfillment of the human creation. Put another way, the creation (especially the human creation) is the platform or stage (glorious in its own right) for the manifestation of God's glory through redemption. The natural world and human culture make the realization of redemption possible. At the same time, redemption restores the primordially good creation; it undoes the distortion and damage of the creation due to the fall and allows humans to better fulfill their design plan. Most importantly, redemption gave humanity a different kind of significance than it had by virtue of creation alone: God's children are now forgiven sinners, broken but beloved.

Fallenness, also, cannot be understood properly apart from the other lenses. To begin with, sin is a parasite on God's good creation. Moreover, only in the cross of Christ can sin be seen accurately as the evil that it really is. The consummation is also necessary to interpret sin, because only then will it finally be fully addressed by God. Reflecting on sin apart from Christ hardens our hearts, increases sin's power, and furthers our self-deception.

We should also consider their relative importance. As suggested above, creation/providence provides the setting and context for the rest of the metanarrative. However, sin would seem to be ultimately more significant than creational goodness in God's eyes, since God judges those who never repent and are not united to Christ according to their sin, even though they are still created in God's image. Redemption, in turn, appears to be more significant than sin, since the former releases believers from eternal judgment and reverses the effects of the fall. Finally, the consummation begins with the final evaluation, when the respective implications of the fall and redemption will be forever realized. With regard to self-understanding (and counseling), the foregoing suggests that Christians should focus most on who they are in Christ (redemption), since that is what is now most significant about them, second on their sin, and third on their created goodness. For believers, justification (or redemption) is God's *final* word.

The Christian Theodrama and
Modern Psychology and Psychotherapy

Next, let us consider how these lenses also help us "read" and interpret modern psychology and psychotherapy. We might say, in light of the foregoing, that modern psychology and psychotherapy mostly focus on the creational features of human beings. Indeed, here modern psychology excels, though it is not beyond criticism (e.g., for most of the twentieth century, naturalistic reductionism prevented most modern psychologists from recognizing the distinctive human features of personal agency and ethical activity). Modern psychology has also considered the effects of fallenness on created dynamic structures—for example, psychopathology, poor child rearing, and even some recent work on the psychology of evil; however, greater distortions are evident here than in the study of creation, because naturalism simply lacks the conceptual resources to understand properly the nature of evil, to say nothing of sin. This is especially clear in a modern resource such as the *DSM* (Johnson, 2007). Modern psychology and psychotherapy, however, are most handicapped by their complete disregard of redemption and the consummation. As a result, Christians cannot limit their understanding of human beings and their treatment to what is provided by modern psychology and psychotherapy. Moreover, this version of psychology and psychotherapy is fundamentally an expression of human fallenness, offering no more than a caricature of divine redemption.

The First Climax of the Theodrama: The Story of Christ

We have already recognized the unique place of Jesus Christ within the Christian metanarrative as the hero in the act of redemption. However, Christ's role is even more important than that; his earthly story was the "epitome" of the entire drama (Sayers, 1941/1987, p. 128), for in it he was the recapitulation of humanity (Irenaeus, 1990).

In chapter three, I noted that Psalm 8 is cited in Hebrews with reference to Christ: "What is man, that You remember him? Or the son of man, that You are concerned about him? You have made him for a little while lower than the angels; You have crowned him with glory and honor, and have appointed him over the works of Your hands; You have put all things in subjection under his feet" (Heb 2:6-8). In this New Testament reading, with implications for Genesis, Christ is identified as "the vindication and perfect manifestation of the created order which was always there but never fully expressed" (O'Donovan, 1986, p. 53). In Christ "we see man as he was made to be, . . . able for the first time to take his place in the cosmos as its lord" (p. 54). Paul also recognized a profound relationship between Adam and Christ. Adam may have been the "first man," but Christ was the "second man" (1 Cor 15:47) and the "last Adam" (1 Cor 15:45). Adam was a "*type* of Him who was to come" (Rom 5:14), because as the head of the human race, he pointed ahead to Christ, who in his life, death, resurrection, and exaltation became the head of a redeemed human race, and accomplished what Adam—and Israel—failed to accomplish: human life wholly devoted to God.

The eternal Son of God was sent into history in "the fullness of time" (Gal 4:4; Eph 1:10), and his death was the "consummation [*synteleia*[4]] of the ages" (Heb 9:26; rendered "the climax of history" in the New English Bible). The Father had planned from all eternity that, at the right time, Christ *in his story* would unite (*anakephalaioō*) all things in heaven and earth (Eph 1:10), that is, "that the goal of history should be embodied in Christ as he sums up and restores to harmony everything in heaven and on earth and this redounds to the glory of the one who created it all" (Lincoln, 1981, p. 189).

I noted previously that the Latin church father Irenaeus (1990) early recognized Christ's centrality for understanding humanity. Picking up on Paul's teaching in Ephesians 1:10 that all things are united or headed up in Christ (Eph 1:10; the Greek term *anakephalaioō* is translated *recapitulatio* in Latin, both having "head" as their root), Irenaeus believed that as the "head" of the human race, Christ "brought together" God, humanity, and humanity's redemption from sin *in his human life.* In contrast to the failed human life of

Adam, Christ *recapitulated* the history of humanity *in himself* by going through the stages of human development en route to conquering our sin in his death and obtaining eternal life for us.[5] In his incarnation, he assumed created humanity; throughout his ministry, climaxing in the crucifixion, he was identified with sinful humanity (Mt 3:14-15; Lk 23:32-33; 2 Cor 5:21); and in his resurrection and ascension he brought humanity into the new creation through redemption. When he comes again, he will bring in the consummation and bring about everyone's eternal destiny. In Christ's story we find the encapsulation of the entire metanarrative.

Christ's centrality to the proper understanding of humanity is now widely recognized by Christian theologians (see, e.g., Turner, 2010). Barth, in particular, made this the cornerstone of his anthropology. "Who and what man is, is manifest in its fullest significance in the fact that the Son of God has become man in Jesus, and that man is placed so wholly at the disposal of God in him" (Barth, 1960a, p. 64).[6] Bonhoeffer (1955; 1966) argued similarly that in Christ's incarnation we discover the essence and purpose of the creation, for he is the *real human*; in his crucifixion we discover the essence and end of the human fall into sin, for Christ is the *condemned human*; and in his resurrection, we see the radical deliverance accomplished for humanity, for he is the *new human*.[7]

In his classic five-volume work, Balthasar (1988–1998) has labeled the supreme dramatic significance of Christ's first coming within the overall context of human history as theodrama. The action of Christ in his life, death, resurrection, and exaltation at once portrays the "dramatic movement within the Trinity to us" (Murphy, 1995, p. 146), provides the greatest example of narrative tension in human history, and undoes the rebellion of humanity against God, drawing humans into the trinitarian love and life.

Vanhoozer (2005; 2014) has even more recently directed attention to the dramatic role Christ's first coming—as canonically understood—should play in Christian doctrine and life, suggesting that in order to know God and human beings, we need to know "a particular human history, the sum total of the incarnate Son's words, acts, and sufferings" (Vanhoozer, 2010, p. 357). Christ's action also constitutes the form that is to shape the nature and improvisatory practice of the church.

Christ became the head of a new race of humanity, reversing Adam's fall and eliminating the enormous obstacles that had prevented humanity from fulfilling its doxological calling by overcoming sin's opposition with his glory; identifying fully with human suffering, even godforsakenness, and infusing it with divine meaning; and turning human weakness into an excellent site for unique manifestations of glory. In the process he tied together strands of earlier stories, being the seed of the woman and the Lamb of God; the messianic Son of David; the true priest, prophet, sage, and king of Israel; as well as *the* image of God, the perfected recapitulation of individual human development. Consequently, the story of Christ is far and away the most important episode in human history. It is the defining, archetypal story of humanity and the climax of the theodrama, shining transcendent light on all other human stories.[8]

The main reason for its supreme importance, of course, is that Christ is the one human being who is also divine.[9] His divinity makes him an absolutely singular human being, while his humanity nonetheless makes him "one of us"; and only by assuming human nature was he able to redeem it. Consequently, he is the ultimate hero of human history, the carpenter's son who accomplished the saving action at the heart of the Trinity's self-glorification mission. And now, God invites all humans to reinterpret and understand their own stories in light of the story of Christ, beginning with the surrender of one's life (and story) utterly to this Christ and his doxological agenda.[10]

The Stories of Believers Within the Theodrama

I noted earlier in the chapter that God is the author of human history. However, God is a dialogical author rather than monological, having made humans partners in the authoring, answer-able to him and therefore response-able, but able also to write their stories in freedom along with God (see Vanhoozer [2010], following Bakhtin; also Anderson, 1982). Since the fall, humans have been answering not ultimately to God but to other voices—including their own. Redemption is the regenerative "calling" of the Father through the Word to fallen humanity, rendered internally (and socially) persuasive by the Spirit, which issues in increasing conformity and correspondence through personal and communal consent.

At the same time, united to the Son according to the Father's will, the stories of believers have been—and are being—divinely incorporated into Christ's story. As in Augustine's *Confessions*, they are now to renarrate their own story in the light of Christ's by faith. *Everything* in their stories now has to do with the story of Christ—their relationships, their sufferings, their victories, and their defeats. Believers, according to Paul, are crucified with him (Rom 6:6) and raised with him (Col 2:12; 3:1; Eph 2:6), so they now live with Christ (Rom 6:8; 2 Cor 7:3), suffer with him (Rom 8:17), and reign with him (2 Tim 2:12).

To be in Christ is to share or participate in Jesus' death and resurrection so that events that happened to him now become part of the narrative of our own lives. [Christian] doctrine does more than confer a role on us, then; [it] describes one's deepest self, one's truest identity, one's life "hidden with Christ in God" (Col. 3:3). Doctrine prepares us for fitting participation in the drama of redemption by telling us who we really are. (Vanhoozer, 2005, p. 393)

Consequently, the stories of believers are increasingly to take on the form of Christ's life, death, resurrection, and life in heaven (Horton, 2007, p. 183). Believers become, in effect, "little Christs" (Lewis, 1952) as they recapitulate his story in theirs. They "are being drawn in into the form of Jesus Christ, . . . as *conformation* with the unique form of Him who was made man, was crucified, and rose again" (Bonhoeffer, 1955, p. 80).[11] How does this happen? "God authors/elects creatures to be dialogical agents in covenantal relation through whom his Word sounds (and resounds)" (Vanhoozer, 2010, p. 331). God's goal is that we "correspond to the Author's own voice-idea for humanity revealed, and incarnated, in Jesus Christ" (p. 337). God is glorified in my story "by telling the story of my life as taken up into the perfect life of Jesus Christ" (p. 329).[12] Practically, this means Christians are to celebrate their created goodness in thanks to Christ, to die daily to their remaining sin in Christ, to be raised from the dead of their sin to walk with Christ in their daily lives, and to live mindful of their future perfection and so learn to accept their inevitable shortcomings in this life.

The hero of a story is simply a person "about whom a story could be told" (Arendt, 1958, p. 186). Everyone, therefore, is a hero, in this sense. But in the Christian metanarrative, with Christ at the center of the action, Christians are made *overcoming* heroes (Rom 8:37) through his redemption, learning to collaborate and participate with him in his glory manifestation as they gradually overcome sin—their own and that of others—persevere through and perhaps even become ennobled by the suffering allotted to them, and obtain some measure of healing for their biopsychosocial damage.

Each story, however, is unrepeatable. Humans are individually connected to Christ's story one at a time, by personal faith. Moreover, the precise unfolding of the events of everyone's story is utterly unique. Then, believers are called to personally identify their own stories with Christ's story—realizing one is playing a part in his story—so that their interior life, actions, and relational patterns are increasingly to become a series of "novel reenactments" of the drama of Christ (Vanhoozer, 2005). Christ's story is the Christian's focal narrative for realizing the trinitarian goal of becoming better developed, vigorous, and virtuous personal agents in communion with God and others (chap. 2); and the christoformic goal of becoming more biopsychosocially whole and ethicospiritually holy and receptive (chap. 3).

Yet each person's story is also being woven together with that of others. As members of local congregations together learn to live in Christ, they learn better how to bear one another's burdens, to visit and care for the troubled and broken, to challenge their own remaining sin and that of their siblings in love, all of whom are in various stages of disrepair and healing, doing so by the grace of Christ. By sharing their conflicted and redemptive stories with each other, in all their ironic complexity, believers learn how to love each other better, becoming more open to each other and honest with themselves, more empathic, more flexible, and more united. "The Spirit's mission is to be the love that unites and by uniting, transforms all that it unites" (Vanhoozer, 2005, p. 69, quoting Gaybba). When lived well, this story of complex communal edification makes their lives and discourse increasingly persuasive to those who have not yet been drawn into it.

SOME THERAPEUTIC IMPLICATIONS

Secular narrative therapy works with the narratives of counselees to promote their healing. However, it has little to work with compared to the rich, theodramatic resources available to Christian therapists. The Christian story offers a remarkable narrative framework for the healing retelling of the stories of believers.

Union with Christ's Story

The Father and the Spirit have established an indissoluble relation between the story of Christ and the story of the believer through faith in Christ. Yet, its impact on believers and their story is experientially dependent on their internalization by faith of that divinely spoken relation, beginning with a cognitive or identity appropriation. Christian counselors are to help their counselees make conscious connections between Christ's story and theirs so that they increasingly identify with him, a process that continues throughout life. As a result, the believer's identity comes to be characterized more and more centrally by their union with Christ rather than their past, their abuse, their family of origin, their sexual orientation, or their creational strengths or disabilities. Their core sense of self comes progressively to be shaped by the knowledge that, more than anything else, they are a "follower of Christ."

In addition, believers are to take Christ's story by faith more and more deeply into their hearts. We might call this a carditive appropriation of the relation, as believers take time to relate Christ's story intentionally to aspects of their internal world: their beliefs, feelings, attitudes, memories, and motives. Historically, this internalization process has been divided into two parts—mortification and vivification—and they will be discussed in greater detail in chapters seventeen to nineteen.

Finally, believers have the opportunity to practice Christlikeness by looking for opportunities to be an analogue to Christ on earth, serving others (Jn 13:14), bearing unjust suffering (1 Pet 2), sacrificing for others (Jn 15:12-13; Eph 5:23), and so on. This could be called active or imitative appropriation. Let us examine these appropriations in more detail.

Promoting Christian Metanarrative Self-Awareness

One goal of Christian soul care (and the Christian life) is the development of the ability to view oneself and others comprehensively in light of all four Christian metanarrative perspectives. With regard to oneself, this means developing an increasingly grateful sense for all of one's created goodness and an awareness of one's remaining sin and the damage one possesses due to the fall; a thankful recognition of who one is in Christ and the work of the Holy Spirit in one's life by faith; and a resting on one's future perfection, alongside a realism regarding the limits on one's growth, given one's story, in light of the consummation.[13]

Christians should also grow in viewing one another in this integrated, fourfold fashion. Similarly, Christians are to view non-Christians in terms of creation and the fall, mindful of their current tragic destiny apart from God as well as their possible redemption in Christ. Christian maturation involves learning to integrate deeply all four perspectives. Such metanarrative integration occurs at the neurological as well as psychosocial levels (Siegel, 2010; Thompson, 2011).

Changing One's Fallen Inner Narrative

By the time persons reach adulthood, they have formed a deep sense of the plot line of their lives: "I can do most anything I put my mind to." "I'll always be a failure." "People don't like me." Though largely originating from the events they actually experienced, especially through their interactions with early caregivers (McAdams, 1993), this carditive plot line becomes *their* story through the internalization of the perceived and communicated meaning of these events, resulting in the appropriation of certain narrative themes, distortions, and sometimes lies. We might call this an individual's *basal inner drama* that becomes the narrative frame within which all future episodes are interpreted, usually as confirmations of their earlier story. Well-taught Christians may know many truths about God's ways and their standing before God, but their basal inner drama is what *really* shapes their life, actions, and relational style.

Work with the narrative modality in Christian therapy (Johnson, 2007) seeks the gradual transformation of this deep plot line, so that it corresponds increasingly to the death-resurrection plot line of Christ's story, establishing a base of hope objectively, and subjectively enabling one to replace the negative narrative themes that may have been internalized earlier in life.

Counselors promote such change by using therapeutically relevant biblical and Christian stories. Christianity's central therapeutic story, of course, is Christ's death and resurrection, so meditation on one's union with him in those events is transformative (see Rom 6:1-11), along with the incorporation of one's own sin, suffering, and struggles into those events. One can also imaginatively rehearse better ways of handling ongoing challenges (e.g., a difficult coworker, the stress of child rearing, or a regular temptation) mindful of one's union with Christ. For example, knowing that one is beloved by God in Christ can empower believers to picture themselves responding humbly to harsh criticism by a chronically dissatisfied supervisor. Counselees can also be encouraged to read historical and fictional stories of those who have overcome adversity, and then take some time to make constructive linkages in Christ to their own story.

Counselees will need to be cautioned that when engaging in such work felt evidence of the basal inner drama will undoubtedly surface, especially at first. Such experiences need to be normalized. Indeed, these experiences are actually to be sought since one can only rewrite one's basal inner drama when it is "on line" and being experienced. Counselees will need to be instructed that, when it happens, they need to remind themselves of their union with Christ, then surrender to Christ the negative feelings aroused by their basal inner drama, and finally, bring in a positive emotion shift based on their union with Christ's resurrection and communion with God. We will discuss such procedures more toward the end of the book.

Christian psychodrama creates a setting where subjects, one at a time, reenact some aspect of their basal inner drama with the help of a skilled therapist and other participants playing roles of persons in the subject's story or of the subject's own internal "parts" that replicate and activate a negative narrative theme "right before their eyes," as it were. The therapeutic climax of a Christian psychodrama exercise involves the facilitation of some kind of redemptive narrative transformation, which allows the subject to experience a story of overcoming, in an embodied, effortful way, with the help of Christ (perhaps also portrayed by one of the participants) and other believers. (I have personally benefitted from this kind of work, thanks to Bob Hudson and others involved in the ministry Men at the Cross.)

Traveling to the City of God

Augustine suggested that humanity is composed of two basic communities: the city of humanity (that all humans are born into) and the city of God (that believers are born again into), which is fully realized only in heaven. Both communities on earth have the self at the center of their lives, but those in the second have discovered that God is the true center of the universe and wants to be the psychological center of their souls. We might consider the Christian life, then, a story of the journey from the city of humanity to the city of God, at which one does not arrive until death or this age is wrapped up.

The journey metaphor can help counselees understand that the Christian life and Christian counseling are a process. It reminds them that repentance, faith, healing, and maturation are ongoing processes and never finished in this life. An important part of the journey, therefore, is simply accepting where we are. We can do so remembering that we are now already perfect in Christ and will be perfect forever in heaven, so we do not have to be perfect now in ourselves. As a result, it can be helpful to regularly remind our counselees that "we are all on a journey!"

The Christian's "Fitting" Improvisation of the Theodrama

We saw in chapter three that Christ leads his followers into conformity with himself, which they already possess by virtue of their union with him. One way he does this is through his narrative, for the pattern of Christ's story of death and resurrection is to be reenacted by believers "in *new* ways" (Vanhoozer, 2005, p. 235), which requires the use of our imaginations.[14] "The most important habit that doctrine forms is neither linguistic nor conceptual but *imaginative*" (p. 377). As counselees envision new narrative possibilities during session and in meditative prayer, during their "soul-work" time, they make it more likely that they will instigate novel actions in daily life when the opportunity arises. Vanhoozer calls this creative activity "improvisation," the biggest challenge of which is figuring out what is most "fitting," in accordance with both the story of Christ and the present situation. "Fittingness," then, is "a matter of *dramatic* consistency" (p. 257).[15] Because of the strong tendency of one's prior story to repeat itself (Fenichel, 1945), counselees (and their spouses!) need to know that developing new dramatic patterns is very slow, involving the formation of countless intentions, imaginative rehearsals, and *in vivo* practice, in various relationships and settings, in order to gradually overcome one's basal internalized story of sin, damage, and suffering by folding Christ's death and resurrection into it by faith.

How might this work with a husband who carries a basal narrative of self-hatred and incompetence, and so typically withdraws from his often angry wife, who resembles his parents when she regularly shames him for his sins and failings? During his daily "soul-work" time, with emotions still fresh from last night's reactivation, he can bring those emotions and experiences imaginatively into the story of Christ, who died for his sins and failings and suffered himself unjustly, until he experiences an "emotion shift." Before finishing up, he can imagine how he'll respond tonight, should the same pattern happen again, and that night, he can improvise a new ending to their repeated story together.

Sometimes counselors will also have to see imaginatively beyond their counselees' past trauma and current disability and introduce some resurrection improvisation into a session, enabling their counselees to see themselves from another narrative perspective, and in the process providing scaffolding for their counselees' imaginations.

Christ's Story Validates Everyone's Story

Everyone's story is utterly unique. Many Christians have noted that the biblical stories of God's dealings with particular persons in history—especially Abraham and his descendants, culminating in the radical particularity of the life, death, resurrection, and exaltation of Jesus Christ—divinely underscore the special significance and dignity of each human's exceptional life. They would also seem to cast a shadow on psychologies that are concerned exclusively with the general, the abstract, and the universal. Similar to the story of the incarnate Son of God, everyone's story is unrepeatable and unsubstitutable, and therefore is, in its own way, momentous.

This may help those with stories of terrible suffering, much of it seeming, from our perspective, pointless and futile. Arguing from the greater to the lesser, if the human suffering of the infinite Son of God could be turned to good, perhaps ours can too. Or consider those who are prone to self-loathing because they have greatly sinned. Through faith and repentance, the sins of our story become occasions for the manifestation of Christ's glory. As a result, his "divine play invites us to see our play in its light. It offers a vision, one that is attractive to behold, that can heighten and dignify the broken dreams, fragmented goals, and failures of our finite existence by showing them to be not manifestations of a 'pitiless destiny' but creaturely realities embraced in the divine drama by 'grace and forgiveness'" (Steck, 2001, p. 57). For believers, everything in their story can be redemptively reversed, since it all proclaims his excellencies.

A Theodramatic Orientation Undermines Autocentrism

One of the tragic paradoxes facing secular narrative therapy is the need to free those who are narcissistically preoccupied with themselves by encouraging them to reinterpret their story in ways that affirm their own supremacy. This can easily foster a period of "self-expression" and "self-realization" in which marital bonds come to be interpreted as bondage and the well-being of one's children is hardly considered.

Christianity's focus on the biblical stories of God with others, concentrating on the story of Christ (in four Gospels!), helps believers to interpret themselves and their story in a larger relational context. Ultimately, it is not about me and my story, but him and his story! Yet, at the same time, his story profoundly communicates the relative importance of my story, since my story is woven into his and uniquely expresses his glory, enabling Christians legitimately to break out of the solipsistic impasse of our fallen, autocentric predicament.

Pilgrims/Heroes on a Momentous Journey into Glory

The healing journey in Christ is hard, and there are many obstacles along the way. The challenges are reframed, however, knowing that while Jesus Christ is the main hero of God's doxological drama, his followers play essential roles, while within the narrative they gradually change from pilgrims into heroes in their own right. Their story is written as they tackle and overcome those obstacles—their sinful dispositions and sins, trauma, damage, and suffering—and become increasingly integrated personal agents in communion, acting in faith, hope, and love, accomplishing good in this world for God, laying down their lives for others, and all of this uniquely recapitulating the divine glory as they become more like Christ. In union with his, our stories "complete" the greatest story ever told.

RESOURCES FOR COUNSELORS AND COUNSELEES

Classical

Augustine. (1950). *City of God* (G. G. Walsh, D. B. Zema, G. Monahan, & D. J. Honan, Trans.). (Abridged ed.). New York: Doubleday. ‡

———. (2009). *Confessions* (Henry Chadwick, Trans.). New York: Oxford University Press.

Bonhoeffer, D. (1966). *Christ the center.* New York: Harper & Row. ‡

Boston, T. (n.d.). *Human nature in its fourfold state.* Grand Rapids, MI: Associated Publishers and Authors. (Original work published 1729)

Calvin, J. (1960). *The Institutes of the Christian Religion.* Louisville, KY: Westminster John Knox. (Original work published 1559) ‡

Contemporary

Bartholomew, C., & Goheen, M. (2004). *The drama of Scripture: Finding our place in the biblical story.* Grand Rapids, MI: Baker.

Crabb, L. (2009). *66 love letters.* Nashville, TN: Thomas Nelson.

Emlet, M. (2009). *Crosstalk.* Greensboro, NC: New Growth Press. Shows how the narrative structure of Scripture relates directly to the Christian healing of the soul.

Hauerwas, S., & Jones, L. G. (Eds.). (1989). *Why narrative? Readings in narrative theology.* Grand Rapid, MI: Eerdmans. ‡ The definitive collection.

Horton, M. S. (2002). *Covenant and eschatology: The divine drama.* Louisville, KY: Westminster John Knox. ‡

Kellemen, R. (2015). *Gospel-centered counseling.* Grand Rapids, MI: Zondervan. A practical survey of the relevance of the Christian story to counseling.

Madigan, S. (2010). *Narrative therapy.* Washington, DC: American Psychological Association. A good summary of secular narrative therapy.

Plantinga, C. (2002). *Engaging God's world: A Christian vision of faith, learning, and living.* Grand Rapids, MI: Eerdmans.

Sittser, J. L. (2012). *A grace revealed: How God redeems the story of your life.* Grand Rapids, MI: Zondervan. Wonderful for Christian bibliotherapy.

Tripp, P. (2004). *Instruments in the Redeemer's hand.* Phillipsburg, NJ: P&R.

Vanhoozer, K. (2014). *Faith speaking understanding: Performing the drama of doctrine.* Louisville, KY: Westminster John Knox. ‡ A more accessible summary of the theodrama than *The Drama of Doctrine*, though the latter book is a classic.

Wolters, A. M., & Goheen, M. (2005). *Creation regained: Biblical basics for a reformational worldview* (2nd ed.). Grand Rapids, MI: Eerdmans. ‡

‡ Recommended more for counselors and pastors than for counselees.

PART II

The Goodness
of God and the
Human Creation

ACCORDING TO MOST THEISTS, God is a perfect being with infinite strengths and superlative virtues, or perfections, the source of all that is good in the universe and the opponent of all evil, and whose character is the ultimate ground of human morality and ethics. Informed by the Old and New Testaments, we might group his perfections around three themes: sovereign majesty, righteousness, and love. They are united in God's simple being, constitute the greatest beauty there is, and draw forth wonder, worship, love, and celebration in healthy human beings.

God's singular perfections mean that reality is fundamentally personal and positive, in contrast to worldviews where good and evil are in absolute and eternal conflict, or naturalistic worldviews, where the good is reduced to the most effective, enjoyable survival possible. Theists also tend to agree that God's creation is primordially good, signaling that human life in all its original, divinely intended, manifold complexity—human bodies, relationships, cultures, labor and leisure, psychological and spiritual functions, the arts and sciences—are good and should not be despised, and that human evil and sin are not intrinsic to human life. Christianity teaches further that human goodness was epitomized and realized in perfection only once: in the person of Jesus Christ. This framework provides a fundamentally positive ground for human well-being and psychotherapy and counseling.

—6—

The Beauty of God
and Human Flourishing

Principle 1: A worshipful, loving relationship
with the triune God in all his perfections is supremely good for human beings.

One thing I have asked from the LORD, that I shall seek:
That I may dwell in the house of the LORD all the days of my life,
to behold the beauty of the LORD and to meditate in His temple.

PSALM 27:4

JOHN CALVIN'S *INSTITUTES OF THE CHRISTIAN RELIGION* is widely recognized as the most important and influential systematic treatment of
Christian doctrine written between Aquinas's *Summa Theologica* in the 1200s
and Barth's *Church Dogmatics* in the twentieth century. Its strengths are many,
but perhaps its most surprising feature is how it begins. In one of the most
consistently theocentric works ever written, Calvin did not begin with a discussion of God or revelation or proofs for God's existence. He wrote instead
of the most basic, dipolar dialectic of human life: "Nearly all the wisdom we
possess, that is to say, true and sound wisdom, consists of two parts: the
knowledge of God and of ourselves. But while joined by many bonds, which
one precedes and brings forth the other is not easy to discern." Such an
opening often surprises Calvinists when they first learn of it.[1] Self-knowledge,
of course, had been extolled in ancient Greece as the preeminent mark of
wisdom. Refuting the human autonomy of fallen wisdom, Calvin was arguing

that self-knowledge is intrinsically relational, for it is fundamentally related to one's knowledge of God. In a person's life, God knowledge and self-knowledge belong together and are strangely reciprocal. We cannot understand ourselves aright as "dependent, derived, imperfect, and responsible" (Warfield, 1956, p. 31) apart from both a knowledge of God's perfections and an accurate knowledge of our sinfulness and limitations—and such knowledge, according to Calvin, is supposed to lead us toward God.

Calvin's relational insight is not an optional add-on to our understanding of ourselves or humanity, perhaps applying only to religious people. It reveals a fundamental difference between the psychology of the Christian community and that of the secular. "It is certain that man never achieves a clear knowledge of himself unless he has first looked upon God's face, and then descends from contemplating him to scrutinize himself" (p. 37). He continues: "As long as we do not look beyond the earth, being quite content with our own righteousness, wisdom, and virtue, we flatter ourselves most sweetly, and fancy ourselves all but demigods" (p. 38). Back in the 1500s Calvin laid a critical footing in the foundation of a Christian psychology.[2] What is the significance of this "true and sound wisdom" for Christian well-being and the care of human souls?

THE RELATION BETWEEN GLORY, BEAUTY, LOVE, AND WELL-BEING

Concerned to make clear the dependence of our being and well-being on God, this book began, more simply, with a focus on God and his glory. Readers will recall that his glory is the sum of his triune perfections. Edwards (1765/1960; 1998) believed that God's glory and beauty were identical, and one finds this theme in Augustine, Anselm, Aquinas, Bernard, Bonaventure, Barth, and Balthasar, with Calvin, the ABC's of Christian theology. These Christians recognized that God is the most beautiful being that exists—greater than which none can be conceived—and that therefore he is the very essence and standard of beauty.[3] God, according to Edwards (1765/1960), is "infinitely the most beautiful and excellent" being (p. 14), "the foundation and fountain of all being and beauty" (p. 15). Edwards believed that moral or spiritual virtue is the highest kind of beauty or excellency,[4] vastly transcending physical beauty in worth. Since God possesses the highest imaginable moral perfection, he is the most beautiful being that could be. In addition, the infinite greatness of his being means his beauty and virtue have inexhaustible and unsurpassable intensity, depth, and power.

Edwards (1765/1960) also defined true virtue as "benevolent love to being in general" (p. 3; that is, the love of all individual beings in proportion to their actual worth), and since God is the greatest being there is, he necessarily loves himself supremely. Put a little differently, "God is infinitely happy in the enjoyment of himself" (2003, p. 113). Key to Edwards's multilayered understanding of God's happiness in the love of his beauty was its trinitarian basis. According to Edwards, beauty, at the simplest level, is the harmony or "agreement" among various elements (e.g., shapes and colors in a painting) or, at a higher level, the harmony or concord that can exist among persons. The beauty of God is supreme because it is the harmony, concord, or agreement that exists among the three infinitely great persons of the Trinity. Each member of the Trinity infinitely affirms, rejoices in, and consents to the perfect loveliness of the others, so that they love one another, together, in infinite degree. Mutual love, then, is at the center of their trinitarian glory, beauty, and virtue, and is the essence of their happiness. So their beauty, happiness, and mutual love (or consent) are thoroughly related, coextensive, and boundless. Indeed, according to Edwards, only a triune God can be perfectly happy, since perfect happiness entails rejoicing in the joy of the other. Aquinas (1945) had already suggested that perfect happiness (beatitude) is possible only for a willing intelligence conscious of possessing perfect good, something that only God possesses necessarily. Edwards agreed but added that God's happiness is realized (cubed?) in the eternal mutual consent of the personal agents of the Trinity delighting in one another's beauty, as well as their own.

What does all this have to do with soul care? Influenced by Calvin, Edwards recognized that humans have a central role to play in God's agenda to manifest his glory/beauty/love/happiness in this universe, since the agenda itself includes having created us for it, overcoming our dullness and resistance to it, drawing us into it, and sharing it with us comparatively insignificant and sinful creatures. As a result, we obtain our ultimate happiness by joining the Trinity in their mutual consent, something called communion with God—and all of this communicates God's glory.

Today we might translate the classic meaning of happiness as *well-being*. In this chapter, therefore, I will consider how consenting to God's beauty contributes to human well-being and therefore to true and sound wisdom (and soul healing). What is the focus of all the celebration recorded in the Psalms? It is the beauty of the Lord. "One thing I have asked from the LORD, that I shall seek: that I may dwell in the house of the LORD all the days of my life, to behold the beauty of the LORD" (Ps 27:4). In the latter days, Isaiah said, the eyes of God's people "will see the King in His beauty" (Is 33:17). Christ has ushered in those latter days (Heb 1:1), so that the most basic prescription in Christian soul care is to help people "behold the beauty of the Lord Jesus Christ" and, by that means, become "transformed into the same image from glory to glory" (2 Cor 3:18).

FOUR HINDRANCES TO CONSENTING TO DIVINE BEAUTY

Humans unfortunately face a number of obstacles to the appreciation, enjoyment, and reception of God's beauty.

Original Sin

Humans are born in a condition of spiritual blindness, so that our ability to perceive God at all, to say nothing of his beauty, is severely compromised. Our perception of God is biased by a native autocentrism that warps our capacity to see.

The Objective Ambiguity of the Evidence

To complicate matters further, the infinite God is far beyond our creaturely capacity to perceive and understand him in himself. He is, in a word, *incomprehensible* (Frame, 2002). He is also invisible, so his beauty (aside from theophanies and Christ's incarnation) can only be indirectly perceived through the signs he has spoken (both material and verbal). Add to that the suffering of this world (the so-called problem of evil) and our alienation from him (reflected in his apparent absence from people's experience), and we are faced with what some have termed God's "hiddenness."

The Social Context of Our Development

Further complications result from being reared, socialized, and formed by parents (or others) whom God designed to picture himself but who, because of their own sin and brokenness, portray God through a glass darkly, in some cases very darkly—for example, along with verbal, emotional, physical, and sexual abuse. These early social experiences profoundly shape one's relational capacities, including one's beliefs about, and perceptions and experiences of, God. Also, families and subcultures vary in how much they participate in what biblical authors call "the world" and how much they have been exposed to the corrective lenses of Scripture, leading to different kinds of religious influences.

Our Subjective Perception of God

Everyone is born with a moral sense—a conscience (the law of God written on the heart, Rom 2:12-13), and what Calvin called a "sense of divinity." However, the foregoing influences have profoundly damaged both of these senses. As a result, humans tend strongly to believe that they are basically good and that everything rightly revolves around them.

This complexity has led to great variance in people's understanding, perception, and experience of God, and in what some psychologists have labeled people's "God-concept"—what one consciously believes and affirms about God—and their "God-image"—how one perceives and feels about God in the heart, whether or not one is aware of it (Moriarity & Hoffman, 2007). One's God-concept is shaped primarily by religious teachings, and, second, by experiences with God congruent with those teachings, whereas one's God-image tends to be shaped primarily by early social experiences and, later, by religious teachings and actual encounters with God, which may facilitate changes in one's God-image (see below).

As a result of these factors, humans are severely aesthetically challenged with regard to God, and fundamentally unable to discern true beauty, which, according to Edwards, significantly hampers our happiness or well-being and, conversely, contributes to our psychopathology.

CHRISTIAN TEACHING REGARDING GOD'S BEAUTY

Given the interdependence of knowing God and knowing ourselves in Christianity, knowing God better ought to contribute to our well-being. In fact, knowing God, Jesus said, is eternal life (Jn 17:3). Knowing the beautiful God, however, necessarily entails loving him, for one cannot know God aright without being moved to love and worship (Edwards, 1746/1959). As the Puritan Henry Scougal (1677/1976) wrote, "The true way to improve and ennoble our souls is by fixing our love on the divine perfections that we may have them always before us and derive an impression of them on ourselves" (p. 49). We become that which we love (Smith, 2009; 2016). Christian soul caregiving, then, involves helping people know and love God better.

God reveals himself through his communicative acts—both his speech and deeds, the most important of which he recorded in a fixed form in Scripture (2 Tim 3:16-17)—which we cannot understand aright without the

Holy Spirit (Jn 14:17, 26; 16:13; 1 Jn 2:27). Historically, God's characteristics have been called his perfections or attributes.

Theologians have identified many perfections of God (see Barth, 1957a; Bavinck, 2004; Frame, 2002), and unfortunately, we do not have the space to deal adequately with any of them here. So we will only touch on a few of those most relevant to soul care and will do so under three headings: God's sovereign majesty, righteousness, and love.

God's Sovereign Majesty

We open with God's sovereign majesty or greatness, underscoring that all of our considerations of him are conditioned by the radical difference between God and us. To begin with, God is infinite, and so the greatest being imaginable, superlative in every laudable way. He is self-existent and self-sufficient. He has life in himself (Jn 5:26) and exists necessarily and eternally. He therefore has no genuine limitations or imperfections, needs nothing from anything outside himself, and so is unimprovable. God is the never-ending source of his own love, power, sustenance, and goodness. By contrast, we are contingent and dependent on him for everything. "In Him we live and move and exist" (Acts 17:28). God is pure act and infinite energy, omnipotent and perfectly free, according to his virtuous nature. There is no power greater than his; he is the perfect and eternal realization of all reasonable and moral potentiality, the effulgence of truth and goodness, so there is nothing he cannot do (Jer 32:17; Dan 4:35). He is omniscient and knows all things, real and possible (Ps 139). And he is omnipresent, so he fills and transcends the creation in which he is everywhere in his entirety (also Ps 139). Christians have also understood the perfect God to be unalterably happy, contented, and existing in perfect bliss (see Jn 14:27; 17:13; Aquinas, 1945; Bavinck, 1951, p. 247). As a result,

> God is never irritable or edgy. He is never fatigued or depressed or blue or moody or stressed out. His anger never has a short fuse. He is not easily annoyed. He is above any possibility of being touchy or cranky or temperamental. Instead he is infinitely energetic with absolutely unbounded and unending enthusiasm for the fulfillment of his delights. (Piper, 1991, p. 192)

Out of his joyful nature, God "gives pleasure, creates desires and rewards with enjoyment, because He is pleasant, desirable, and full of enjoyment" (Barth, 1957a, p. 651). God is therefore the ruler of the universe; we might say the omnicompetent, joyful manager of all human affairs. All of this means that God is more different from us than we are alike—and we must never forget that.

The fitting response to this set of perfections is awe, worship, humility, and fear (Prov 1:7). Perceiving his sovereign majesty provides a crucial check on our native autocentrism and narcissism, and it can contribute to a deep sense of comfort and security. Each specific perfection offers its own psychospiritual consolation. Being in a loving relationship with a self-sufficient, contented God provides a solid psychological foundation for needy, insecure, neurotic creatures. His sufficiency more than meets the needs of our insufficiency. His omnipotence assures believers that no ultimate harm will come to them; God is their always-victorious protector (though we must redefine victory according to the gospel). Being omniscient, God knows the future and will not be surprised by anything that happens in the world or to us. He also knows all that is in our hearts. There is no point, therefore, in hiding from him (or from ourselves). Tozer (1961) wrote that God's omniscience is sweet because

> no talebearer can inform on us, no enemy can make an accusation stick; no forgotten skeleton can come tumbling out of some hidden closet to bash us and expose our past; no unsuspected weakness in our characters can come to light to turn God away from us, since He knew us utterly before we knew Him and called us to Himself in the full knowledge of everything that was against us. (p. 57)

His omniscience also means that he is exhaustively self-aware, which serves as an unattainable ideal for those made in his image. God's omnipresence tells us that no matter where individual believers are, God is there with them and will be there to support them through whatever happens. "Do not fear, for I am with you; do not anxiously look about you, for I am your God" (Is 41:10). So much in life is outside our control, so it helps believers to know their God is in ultimate control of every situation (though this does not mean things will be easy); he is always present in love, working all things together for their good (Rom 8:28); and is immovably contented, in spite of all in the creation that is contrary to his will. Deeply believing in God's absolute greatness gives God's beliefs and values greater weight in our souls, enough to transcend the opinions of anyone else (including our own): "We . . . will assure our heart before Him in whatever our heart condemns us; for God is greater than our heart and knows all things" (1 Jn 3:19-20; Welch, 1998). Knowing this great God better would surely reduce our stress and likely ease many of our other psychological difficulties, perhaps particularly perfectionism, grief, a sense of meaninglessness or insignificance, inferiority, anxiety, phobia, obsessive-compulsive disorder, depression, and feelings of personal incompetence. Edwards (1994) understood the psychological benefits of clear perceptions of God's majesty.

> The terribleness of God is part of his glory; and that a sense of it should be kept in the minds of creatures is needful in order to their right and just apprehensions of his greatness and gloriousness, and that perfect and becoming and answerable joy and happiness, in the spiritual sight and knowledge of him. That awful and reverential dread of God's majesty that arises from such a sense, is needful in order to the proper respect of the creature to God, and the more complete happiness in a sense of his love. (p. 469)[5]

Of course our spiritual sickness—being the broken sinners we are—means that we do not always find heart consolation in these truths. The fact is the knowledge of God's sovereign majesty can terrify even believers, particularly in light of the enormous evil there is in our hearts and in the world. Some have tried to find a solution in a smaller deity than the one revealed in the Bible, for example, one who created a world in which he has limited himself for love, so he cannot prevent the evil deeds of his free creatures; in fact, logically, he cannot even know them. This strategy may seem superficially to help sufferers (Boyd, 2003), since the deity does not exercise control over everything that comes to pass, so God is in no way implicated. But in the long run, it takes away far more comfort than it gives by removing the security of a sovereign God who renders meaningful everything that happens to us, even evil (Gen 50:20); who protects us from absolute destruction; and who will judge and overthrow evil in the end. The most therapeutic solution is not to come up with a novel model of God but to learn how to accept the unity of all of God's perfections (see below). On the other hand, counselors can do terrible harm if they deal with sufferers and such awesome truths glibly. Job's friends were at their best when they said nothing.

God's Righteousness

Religions outside the Western theistic traditions are more or less projections of humanity's own internal ethical conflict. In these schemes, the divine order is composed either of a pantheon of good and evil gods, with even the best being still flawed like us (as in Greek, Roman, Norse, and Hindu polytheism), or a monistic synthesis of evil as well as the good (as in Taoism and philosophical Hinduism). In contrast, the God of Scripture is impeccably virtuous. He is "Light, and in Him there is no darkness at all" (1 Jn 1:5). This God is of absolute moral purity, necessarily just and good in his actions and attitudes, utterly and resolutely opposed to evil and injustice. The giver of the law, his very character is the universe's standard of right and wrong. God's righteousness means he is "true to himself" (Thiselton, 2007, p. 344). "Your eyes are too pure to approve evil, and You cannot look on wickedness with favor" (Hab 1:13). This means, in addition, that God is the preserver and defender of justice in the universe. "He will by no means leave the guilty unpunished" (Ex 34:7). Without such a righteous, omnicompetent Judge, most evil in the world would never get addressed. His moral perfection guarantees perfect justice. The fitting response to this set of perfections is worship, admiration, relief, and (for sinners) guilt, shame, and fear.

An ethical system is most compelling and valuable psychologically when it is grounded in the transcendent (in contrast to its just being viewed as merely adaptive or existing to serve the state or the self). Human ethics make the most sense if they derive from our Origin, so there is a deeply satisfying congruence when one's worldview tethers one's ethical intuitions and the standards of one's conscience to the nature of God. According to Kierkegaard, a mature self is formed by commitment to a moral order that transcends one's own desires (Evans, 2009). Humans need to choose to adhere to righteousness in the face of conflicting inner desires if they are to realize their full created nature, part of which is God's law written on their hearts (Rom 2:12-13). As we will see in the next chapter, a divine law-based desire for wholeness and perfection pervades human life. In addition, humans' conscience (imperfectly) gives them an internal witness of God's righteousness and justice, an inner guide and self-evaluator that promotes prosocial behavior, integrity, and maturation. Who can estimate how much mental health is preserved and mental illness prevented simply by people living according to their conscience?[6]

Accepting and recognizing God's righteousness and justice can also help us overcome the shame, bitterness, and self-hatred that can arise from maltreatment at the hands of others. God's righteousness guarantees that everything wrong in this life will somehow be made right in the end. Children are tragically inclined to take responsibility for their mistreatment, so it can help recovering adults to know they have a divine advocate who knows the exact truth of what happened and who hated that sin—to whom they can lament and cry out to for justice—and that at some point he will address it in all of his glory.

Sin, however, has damaged our conscience and our perception of God's righteousness. Growing up in shame-prone families can crush children's spirits, who then can grow up with excessive shame and guilt, much of it false, who, without adequate healing, may go on to raise their children with the same pressures and abuse. In addition, sin can blind comparatively healthier people (including Christians) to their own pride, fueling more covert forms of psychopathology such as perfectionism, judgmentalism, divisiveness, and defenses such as projection. The worst evils are usually committed for putatively good causes (Baumeister, 1997).

Something should probably also be said here about God's anger, because of the variety of psychologically complex responses it engenders in humans. From Genesis to Revelation, God is portrayed as a deity who gets angry about sin and is committed to punishing it, eventually consigning to hell those who finally reject him and his offer of rescue in Christ (see 1 Kings 14:9; Jn 3:36; Eph 2:2; Revelation). This revelation communicates that retributive justice is a transcendent value in the universe. Some theists, for example, liberal Christians, are offended by and reject such notions (Lotufo, 2012), but since "there is no exegetically responsible way to dissolve the personal nature of God's wrath throughout the canonical Scriptures" (Carson, 2008b, p. 45), we must take another tack.

In this book we are asking the question, what is the therapeutic benefit of biblical teaching? Let us consider the psychological benefits of "working through" and consenting to the biblical portrayal of God's anger. To begin with, it shows he is resolutely opposed to sin and cares enormously about human evil. If the God of the universe were not to care so much, it would indicate to us his complicity. God's intense opposition to sin also communicates a concern for *our* well-being, since he values justice for those who have been sinned against while seeking to save everyone from the self-destructiveness that all sin entails (Prov 1:32; Mt 1:21; 1 Tim 2:4). Whatever our Creator calls unrighteous is bad for us, so his anger simultaneously signifies his love (a relation especially evident in God's jealousy for the worship and love of his people; see, e.g., Hosea). God's anger is not a sign of capriciousness or instability; in the Bible it is consistently, resolutely manifest only in the face of sin. The main difficulty humans have with God's wrath is the deep, largely unconscious sense of unresolved shame and guilt that everyone carries to some degree. As we become more deeply convinced that God is God—altogether of another order of being than us and absolutely righteous, even in his anger—and our shame and guilt get resolved in the cross, our intellectual opposition will increasingly acquiesce in grateful reverence.

However, another problem on this score is the unconscious projection onto God of our experiences of human wrath, which necessarily fall short of God's righteousness (Jas 1:20). This perceptual disorder may be especially pronounced if we grew up with a parent who was chronically angry, a tragically common problem in a fallen world. Consequently, part of Christian healing and maturation entails differentiating the various sources of our discomfort with divine wrath, confessing our sin and lamenting our suffering and the consequent damage to our perceptual and relational capacities. Sinful human anger is a distorted parody of God's—narcissistic and unconcerned for the welfare of the other, unfitting for God's children. At the same time, God's wrath reveals that there is a legitimate anger against sin and evil, which humans made in God's image ought to experience and which can be promoted and cultivated in analogically appropriate and virtuous ways. This is of particular value to those who have been emotionally and physically abused, as they will likely need to experience and work through such anger for a time—perhaps even praying imprecatory prayers to God about their perpetrators (such as Ps 35; 69; 70; 109) as a healthy, preliminary step toward authentic Christian forgiveness (Carson, 2008b, p. 62; Worthington, 2009).

Finally, and most importantly, we recall from earlier discussions that God's infinite worth means he must love himself supremely and defend his honor in the face of sin. "Sin invites divine wrath because our sin offends God personally" (Cole, 2009, p. 71). Anger against sin is absolutely fitting for a God of such infinite worth and dignity and a sign of utterly appropriate self-regard; anything less would mean he is not God. The revelation of God's anger against sin is therapeutic first and foremost, because it is a frontal attack on our own native autocentrism. So, when reading about God's anger and being tempted to judge him according to human canons and experiences, the healthiest response is to listen to our hearts and question our reaction. Perhaps it is due to our sinful resistance to God; perhaps we have been biased in our perception by previous exposure to sinful anger and aggression. Contrary to some contemporary sentiments, a deep trust in biblical revelation, allowed to shape our therapeutic convictions, leads to the insight that the virtuous anger of a sovereign, righteous, and preeminently loving God provides a context that best enables one to distinguish legitimate from illegitimate anger, and to work through and resolve anger that was unfairly deposited into one's bones by evil suffered in childhood, and repent of one's sinful anger against God more and more deeply.

God's Love

We have seen that love is an eternal characteristic of a triune God who lives forever in perfect love and communion within himself (Jn 17:23-24; 1 Jn 4:10, 16), manifested in time in the Father's ebullient pleasure taken in his Son (Mt 3:17; 17:5). So the God of Christianity *is* love, essentially, in a way that other monotheistic deities cannot be. But what does it mean to say that God is love?

Because of the notorious ambiguity of *love* in human usage, it is necessary to reason hard and biblically about the nature of divine love. Retrieving our model of love from chapter two, helped with insights from Aquinas, Edwards, and Stump, we recall that love has three aspects that have to do with the lover's bond to the beloved, and one that pertains to the lover. According to this model, love is a delight in the beloved (what some have termed a love of complacency), a desire for the beloved's ultimate well-being, and a desire for communion with the beloved, which consists of joint attention, sharing of thoughts and feelings, and a desire to be close, all of which require the lover's internal integration, that is, some degree of singlemindedness and undivided will.

As we noted earlier, God's being in himself and as Trinity is the perfect realization of love in these ways, given their unity, simplicity, and joyous intensity. However, sin constitutes a massive offense to God in his sovereign majesty and righteousness, making the divine love of humans incongruent, if not scandalous. Yet the excessiveness of his love—according to the standards of divine righteousness—manifests itself in its superseding those standards in his desire for the well-being of images of God and his desire to commune with them—in spite of their sin (Rom 5:8). And these desires are now being realized because of the redemption God himself has provided in his Son (1 Jn 4:9-10, 19), by which he now delights in sinners who through faith are in Christ (a love that some have termed benevolent), issuing in "union and nearness" (Owen, 1965, Vol. 2, p. 24). God's compassionate splendor is further demonstrated in the many created goods that he continuously shares with his friends (Jn 15:14-15), as well as those who live in opposition to him (Mt 5:45). Finally, the excellent nature of his love is shown in the regard the sovereignly majestic God has for those who suffer and who, compared to the majority, are especially troubled: the poor, the weak, the stranger, the handicapped, the oppressed, and even the sinful—all together, the poor in spirit (Mt 5:3). This should be of special encouragement to those with the greatest psychospiritual problems. "With his grace and his help we may stand and gaze at him in the spirit with unending amazement at this high, surpassing, inestimable love that almighty God has for us in his goodness" (Julian of Norwich, 1998, p. 49).

The fitting response to this divine initiative is to love God (since his love is greater than our fear, 1 Jn 4:18), and his love compels and inspires love in those who have been freed from their sin (2 Cor 5:14) and therefore are becoming internally integrated around God. Who would not want to know a person like this better? Knowing and experiencing God's love of delight in believers in Christ is to find the ultimate fulfillment that all humans are looking for, at least unconsciously, and the happiness for which we were created.

"The LORD your God is in your midst, a victorious warrior. He will exult over you with joy, He will be quiet in his love, He will rejoice over you with shouts of joy" (Zeph 3:17). According to Owen (1965, Vol. 2, p. 25), this verse indicates that God will find no fault with his saints, and his love will never be removed from them. Christ sees believers as beautiful. "My beloved is mine, and I am his" (Song 2:16; see Owen, 1965, pt. 2). When receiving God's love *personally*, "the heart is opened and enlarged to expect all good, and nothing but good from him" (Sibbes, 1635/1973, Vol. 2, p. 246). The more frequently and deeply believers experience God's love, the more their internal working models will be activated in relation to God, leading to their modification by God in adulthood, something called "earned attachment security" or "earned secure status" (Hesse, 2008; Granqvist & Kirkpatrick, 2008). This, in turn, can have an effect throughout their psychosocial system, contributing to the undermining of motives for sin and the fostering of greater self-care; the resolution of traits and specific episodes of shame, anxiety, sadness, and anger; and greater fortitude and kindness in the face of difficult relationships. As such healing spreads internally, believers who have lived with a sense of loneliness or incompetence will start to find it being gradually undermined; maybe God really *is* with them and their life really *is* worthwhile (Groeschel, 1993).

There are many aspects of divine love worthy of clinical attention and meditation: his kindness, patience, and superabundant generosity; his willingness to share himself, empathize, and interact; his conjugal passion, bliss, and indwelling in the Spirit; and his paternal discipline, coaching, and challenge. However, grace, mercy, and forgiveness are of special value for psychotherapy. Believers need to feast "their souls in the view of what is without them, viz. the innate, sweet, refreshing amiableness of the things exhibited in the gospel" (Edwards, 1746/1959, p. 251). This need is especially great for those who experience significant shame and guilt. "The way to diminish and even overcome those terrors which arise from partial and false apprehensions of God is to attain spiritual, clear, and enlarged views of Him as a God whose glory it is to be merciful and gracious even to the chief of sinners" (Colquhoun, 1814/1998, p. 164). As one accepts that the greatest Being in the universe delights in oneself and desires communion and one's ultimate well-being in Christ in spite of one's sin and dysfunction, a transcendent basis grows for resolving well-routinized patterns of shame and self-abhorrence. Secular therapy can provide significant human-to-human encouragement, which can certainly contribute to various kinds of recovery, but it has nothing specific to offer counselees who feel unlovable from a source outside this creation. Humans need the love of their Maker. That is why Owen (1965, Vol. 2) believed that God's love provides "the only rest of the soul" (p. 23).

Summary: The Simplicity of God and the Splendor and Unity of His Perfections

Being in God's image, humans can only become whole by being known and loved by God, and knowing and loving him receptively. Though we have only looked briefly at a few of God's perfections, perhaps it was enough to appreciate that every distressing or dysfunctional state humans can have has a corresponding therapeutic remedy in some aspect of God's beauty. Time spent with God gradually replaces meaninglessness with meaningfulness, shame with dignity, loneliness with the presence of Another. Our narcissism shrinks in the presence of God's fatherly affection. Meditating on his watchful sovereignty soothes our anxieties and fears. His righteousness, now given to us in Christ, increasingly frees us from the need to perform and fills us with humility, and knowing his justice enables us to reframe our mal-treatment at the hands of others. Whatever one's psychospiritual difficulties, opening up one's heart to this God can contribute to a fundamental recon-figuration of one's emotions and desires, relational schemes, narrative, ability to cope, and sense of one's place in the universe.

But we will be baffled by this God. He is beyond our comprehension (Rom 11:33-36) and presents our minds with the paradox of paradoxes. Some have tried to reduce the mystery by favoring some of his perfections over others and reinterpreting the rest accordingly, perhaps his sovereign majesty and righteousness over his love (too often in Calvinism) or his love over his righteousness (typical of liberalism and postliberalism). The three sets of God's perfections we have examined—sovereign majesty, righteousness, and love—provide a useful, if limited, way to "summarize" and safeguard the biblical portrayal of God. Each of these three perspectives would appear to be equally ultimate and irreducible to the other, forming a three-legged stool on which we may worship God; without any one of them, we fall over and our understanding becomes significantly distorted. Yet, there is no contradiction between them in God; the depth (or splendor) of his beauty consists precisely in their consonance. Classical theologians have argued that the infinite God is not composed of parts but is fundamentally one and therefore "simple." His perfections are not to be considered different, separable aspects of God, but are all necessarily interrelated and imply each other. "God is the perfect completeness of what he is; the boundaries of bounty, power, life, wisdom, goodness are set only where their contraries are encountered, but God is without opposition, as he is beyond nonbeing or negation, transcendent of all composition or antinomy; it is in this sense of utter fullness, principally, that God is called simple" (Hart, 2003, pp. 192-93). His righteousness is sovereignly majestic and loving, his sovereign majesty is loving and righteous, his love is righteous and majestic; and each in maximal degree.[7]

At the same time, we must admit that, to our finite reason, their conjunction presents tensions that are difficult, if not impossible, to fully resolve. His thoughts and ways are higher than ours (Is 55:8-9). Because no human can know God fully, we are deceiving ourselves if we think we have arrived at a complete knowledge of God. In counseling, moreover, we will often work with those who, for one reason or another, have gravitated toward one set of perfections and have a hard time with another set. Perhaps a sign of Christian healing and maturation is the depth to which one is able to accept the underlying unity of God's diverse perfections, in spite of the difficulty that unity presents to our finite, fallen, and, in some cases, damaged sensibilities, simply on the basis of biblical revelation and loving devotion. This may involve consenting to what seems to our minds at the time as contradictory perfections but which in God are thoroughly harmonious, and then our doing the best we can, with God's help, to trace their inner consonance by faith. Such receptivity promotes our happiness. "It is the greatest joy possible, as I see it, that he who is highest and mightiest, noblest and worthiest, becomes lowest and meekest, friendliest and most courteous" (Julian of Norwich, 1998, p. 51).

Christian counselors, however, will have to work compassionately with those who have experienced so much trauma, abuse, or personal sin that they find the experience and comfort of God's simple beauty to be outside their immediate psychological reach. Those better able to appreciate a fuller portrait of God's beauty have to be careful not to compound the difficulties of such folks by treating them without regard for their story or where they are on their journey. A stern-minded perfectionism lacks its own kind of aesthetic sensibilities—and is rarely successful. Like shepherds, Christian counselors need to guide counselees to the true rest, but they do so best by also being patient signs of God's approbation, building an incarnational/relational bridge to the counselee, regardless of the internal struggle, so that more direct, conscious, and explicit work with God can be done in the future.

SOME THERAPEUTIC IMPLICATIONS

People flock to the Grand Canyon, appreciate an attractive face, and enjoy great works of art because they are designed by God to experience happiness in the presence of many kinds of beauty. However, creaturely beauty is necessarily wanting; we can never get enough to satisfy us forever. So the beauty of the creation points us to a greater beauty, an infinite and eternal beauty most fully revealed in Christ, the enjoyment of which is the fullest kind of human flourishing (Pieper, 1998).

As we have seen, God's self-glorification agenda is remarkably correlated with his agenda to advance human well-being. God is seeking people to "proclaim the excellencies of Him who called you out of darkness into His marvelous light" (1 Pet 2:9), in part because that makes us happy. Promoting this correlation, therefore, is a chief goal of Christian counseling. "Labour thou by faith to set out God in his colours, infinite in mercy and lovingkindness. Here lies the arts of a Christian; it is divine rhetoric thus to persuade and set down the soul" (Sibbes, 1635/1973, p. 229).

A great deal of psychological research in modern psychology has been done on what we could call creational happiness (Diener, Lucas, & Oishi, 2002). Over the past fifteen years, modern psychologists have begun to consider the psychological benefits of attending to that which is greater than or beyond humanity, but which, given modern assumptions, has understandably been given generic, nontheistic labels such as "transcendence" or "elevation" (Peterson & Seligman, 2004; Haidt, 2003). In coming years, Christian researchers will likely focus more specifically on the benefits of the worship of the triune God. Let us consider what they may find.

Worship and Psychotherapy

Worship glorifies God while simultaneously fulfilling our deepest created needs for awe, wonder, significance, purpose, and love. So "when we neglect the praising of God, we lose both the comfort of God's love and our own too" (Sibbes, 1635/1973, p. 253). What might be some of the psychological benefits of worship? First, it changes worshipers by conforming them, little by little, into that which they most esteem. "The worth and excellency of a soul is to be measured by the object of its love. He who loveth mean and sordid things doth thereby become base and vile, but a noble and well-placed affection doth advance and improve the spirit into a conformity with the perfection which it loves" (Scougal, 1677/1976, p. 49). "Beholding," says Piper (1991), is "a way of becoming" (p. 15). This supposition can be traced back to Augustine (1956, p. 518):

> Our souls, brothers, are ugly because of their wrong-doing: by loving God they become beautiful. What sort of a love is it that makes the lover beautiful? But God is always beautiful, never deformed, never liable to change. He, the beautiful one, first loved us, and what were we like when he loved us? Ugly, deformed. And it was not to leave us ugly, but to transform us and turn us from ugly creatures to beautiful ones. But how do we become beautiful? By loving him back, him who is eternally beautiful. The more love grows in you, the more beauty grows, since love is itself the beauty of the soul.[8]

How does worship accomplish this? For one thing, "hearty" worship re-orders our hearts by putting everything else in perspective. It suggests implicitly the relative vanity of life in this world and the comparatively lesser importance of many of our wants and desires. It undermines narcissism and softens our self-protective defenses at the same time that it strengthens our created self-structures by contributing to a sense of significance and purpose. Worship gives believers hope by redirecting their attention off their problems and onto someone infinitely greater, who loves them everlastingly, and who is in no way put off by their sin or in despair about their life story or their limitations, like they might be.

God ought to be "the ravishing object of [the believer's] contemplation" (Edwards, 1746/1959, p. 253). However, we cannot manufacture this experience within ourselves. Rather, God's beauty "seizes and enraptures" (Scola, 1995, p. 2), but without coercion; it is internally persuasive, by means of his word and Spirit (Vanhoozer, 2010). On catching sight of God's singular beauty, humans are *compelled* to confess it *freely*, like a hiker in the mountains who utters a spontaneous cry of wonder on seeing a great vista. Yet humans are by no means passive in this process. "Adoration means to awaken ourselves to the wonders of God, . . . and to let them astonish and delight us" (Danielou, 1996, p. 9). To foster this, Smith (2009; 2016) recommends engaging in Christian liturgical practices that reorient our hearts and our identity to our ultimate concern: participation in public worship and celebrations of the Lord's Supper, regular times of Bible reading, meditation, and prayer.

The challenges, however, are compounded for Christians who come from dysfunctional families and have relational difficulties, for these create additional obstacles to communion with God, beyond the original sin that hinders all human beings. As a result, we may consider Christian therapists and counselors analogous to physical therapists, but working with *psychological* damage and disabilities rather than physical. So while they have the same goals as spiritual directors, they are always adapting their counsel to the particular mental, emotional, volitional, and relational deficits that their counselees possess.

Communion with a Simple God

For God's sake and the sake of truth, as well as our own sake, it is important to worship God according to his nature rather than according to our preferences. To the extent we misperceive God's nature, even just by emphasizing one set of perfections over another, our recovery will be correspondingly compromised. As we noted earlier in the chapter, there are two ways humans perceive God: God-concept (one's conscious, doctrinal understanding of God) and our God-image (one's emotional, largely unconscious perception of God, which is shaped more by one's relational experiences). Depending on one's family and ecclesial histories, God's sovereign majesty and righteousness may be far more salient than God's love, to the extent that the latter is obscured. For others, the love of God so dominates their perception of God that they cannot accept and perceive God's sovereign majesty or righteous anger. Christian therapy, therefore, will sometimes be directed to helping people overcome dissociated sets of perfections and accept God as he has revealed himself in Scripture, eventually learning how to perceive the deep harmony of all his perfections. Some may need to focus prayerfully on one set of perfections for a season to compensate for and heal deficits in their past knowledge or experience, eventually bringing those perceptions together with more of God's revealed character. Those who suffered severe abuse, for example, may need to concentrate prayerfully for months (or even years) on God's love (especially manifest in Christ on the cross) before they are able to interpret and accept in a healthy way his sovereign majesty (e.g., that he allowed terrible suffering to happen to them when they were children). When counselees feel ready to approach the difficult-to-accept (DTA) set of God's perfections, they could begin their prayerful considerations by spending time focusing their hearts on the set they find easier to accept (ETA), and then focus briefly on the DTA set, seeking to regulate the distress activated, before finishing up with the ETA set. We could call this psycho-spiritual process of faith "pendulation," since it is similar to other therapeutic change processes that undermine dissociation, but here one's knowledge and perceptions of God are being modified and integrated, leading to the development of a more comprehensive God-image, that corresponds better to one's (hopefully more accurate) God-concept. This warrants research.

Promoting a Better Aesthetic

"Though [praise] be God's due and our duty, and itself a delightful thing, yet it is not so easy a matter to praise God, as many imagine" (Sibbes, 1635/1973, p. 252). Perhaps we could say humanity's greatest problem is a sort of "spiritual philistinism," since our appreciation for beauty is so materialistic and, therefore, unrefined. Our spiritual senses dulled by original sin, we natively lack the ability to recognize the very best beauty. Even the most intelligent humans are transfixed by the beauty of creatures, far preferring it over the beauty of our Creator—a tendency hindered, but not destroyed, by our conversion. Perhaps we could call this fallen tendency an aesthetic psychological disorder.

Complicating matters, genetic factors can predispose people toward certain personality limitations, overly labile emotions, and impaired thinking that impact religiousness (Bradshaw & Ellison, 2008). Even more influential are psychosocial factors. Every culture presents its members with a particular set of preferred idols, each one having a certain modicum of beauty. Family socialization narrows the field some, inclining individuals toward some gods rather than others (sports or music; work or play; self or others). Finally, since the beginning of human experience, one of Satan's primary missions has been the distortion of human understanding of God through deception and disinformation (Gen 3:4-5; 1 Tim 4:1-3).

Idolatry is a variable of human life. The worst idols are those that are explicitly religious. They are fostered through inaccurate teachings about the divine to which one adheres—which form one's "God-concept"—and one's relational experiences with the images of God by whom one was raised, with whom one formed one's earliest attachments, and who therefore most shaped one's deep perceptions of others. These experiences eventually form one's deep perception of God—resulting in one's "God-image," what one actually feels about God, whether or not one is aware of it. Nonbiblical religions teach God-concepts that are inaccurate in some degree, resulting in a deity of lesser beauty than the true God. However, even well-taught believers necessarily have remaining distortions in their perceptions and experience of God, not realizing the gap that exists between their biblically based knowledge about God—of which they are consciously aware—and their more or less unconscious perception of God, a gap maintained by a lack of awareness of its existence. One of the most dangerous idols imaginable is one composed of perfectly orthodox propositions but without personhood—the formal deity of the philosophers, consisting of impersonal truth but "One" with whom the Christian has no real relationship. Regardless, distortions in one's God-concept and God-image constitute the greatest obstacles to one's ultimate aesthetic sense and therefore to one's worship as well as psychological well-being. Original sin is the ultimate source of idolatry. However, distortions in one's God-image are also mediated by the abuse or neglect of one's caregivers, which, in the extreme, can convey negative emotionally charged "evidence" that God does not exist or that he is one's enemy—even believers—which, together with one's original sin, can deeply persuade such persons that they are fundamentally unlovable and abandoned by God.

Of special difficulty are the experiences of the spiritually abused, those who grew up in theologically orthodox families and churches that little resembled the communion of the triune God. Such people find it especially hard to discriminate between the true God (revealed in Scripture) and their distorted God-image, because their religious concepts and experiences were severely contaminated by intense, toxic relationships with people who talked about the God of the Bible but whose lives to some extent more represented the antichrist. Such aesthetic experiences often lead to religious cynicism and even atheism (Vitz, 1999).[9] The silver lining of poor Christian family experiences is the grist they can provide for therapy and self-exploration, a better understanding of true Christianity, and eventually the glory manifested through overcoming such hindrances by means of Christ, who overcame his own spiritual abuse in the resurrection.

As a result of sin and the other fallen influences we have considered, humans are by nature severely aesthetically handicapped, "worshipping not God but a figment and a dream of their own heart" (Calvin, 1559/1960,

p. 47). Treatment for such a disorder requires God's Spirit, the light of the gospel and Scripture, the cultivation of active receptivity and prayer, and working with others. Christian counseling can help in many ways by sharing an orthodox God-concept, promoting meditative internalization of Scripture and related Christian writings, highlighting the gap between God-concept and God-image, advocating emotional engagement with the true God, guiding the exploration of the distorting effects of one's family-of-origin experiences, and providing meaningful experiences with relatively more accurate representations of God in session and in personal devotions on one's own. The greater the gap between the counselee's orthodox God-concept and distorted God-image, the more necessary it will be to discuss the family background of the counselee, especially memories of the parents, to help counselees, first, understand better how their childhood experiences may be influencing their current experiences of God and others and, second, disidentify with the distorted features of their God-image and replace them with more accurate perceptions.

God-image distortions cannot be altered by God-concept teaching alone, because emotion memories can only be modified through new emotional experiences. However, biblical teaching on God's nature provides divinely inspired cognitive guides for this healing process, given in part to help structure our emotionally charged experiences of God, so that we engage increasingly with the true God and decreasingly with idols. As a result, counselees should be encouraged to pursue emotionally significant, doctrinally faithful experiences of God's perfections through public worship, Scripture reading and meditative prayer, and indirectly through loving relationships with relatively healthy Christians. This may help undermine the false beliefs and defenses that past relationships and spiritual abuse have left, and heal distorted emotion and relational schemes associated with God. Coming to know and love the true God, who differs from the distant or chronically critical images of God one has grown up with, can in turn foster the relinquishing of pathological self- and other-representations and the incorporation of healthy relational and new-self schemes within one's God-self-other relational universe.

At the same time, counselees have to be reminded that deep neurological and psychological changes in one's "working model" are very gradual, analogous to the ease of learning one's first language and the difficulty of learning a second in adulthood. The seed of divine relational healing begins small (like a mustard seed?) and slowly builds on itself as Christian truth and divine love are increasingly experienced, internalized, and integrated, until some kind of threshold is crossed, at which point earlier accumulated anxiety and inner turmoil start receding and get replaced by a growing sense of God's favor and inner peace (Groeschel, 1993; Newton, 1960). Research documenting this deepening lifelong "conversion" would be invaluable.

Resolving a Sense of God's Animosity Toward Oneself

The most significant part of the human tendency to perceive God as one's enemy is due, according to Christian teaching, to humanity's primordial sense of shame and guilt (see chap. 8). God is perfectly righteous and opposed to our opposition to him, that is, our sin, and at some level of consciousness, all humans are aware of this (Rom 1:18-19; Kierkegaard, 1849/1980). Only the personal appropriation of the benefits of Christ's redemption can actually remedy *this* problem (see chaps. 12-15), because there God demonstrated "His own love toward us, in that while we were yet sinners, Christ died for us" (Rom 5:8). For those who believe in Christ, God's love wins.

So, when Christian believers feel fundamentally that God is opposed to them, they are experiencing in their relationship with God what has been called "psychic equivalence" in human relations (Fonagy, Gergely, Jurist, & Target, 2002); in this case, they are mistaking a distorted God-image for the true God. This is a kind of ultimate "negative transference," the projection onto their heavenly Father hostile beliefs and attitudes actually derived from earlier experiences with fallen humans. Because the Bible (and especially the cross) teach that God has been reconciled to his children, the therapy goal in such situations is to help counselees learn how to (1) "mentalize" or "objectify" or "disidentify" with their distorted God-image, (2) take it to the cross and surrender it there, and (3) replace it with fresh perceptions/experiences of their God as loving, in spite of their "old self" perceptions of God as their enemy.

Such work will probably be the most difficult for those from Christian homes where the images of God with which they grew up were chronically hostile and antagonistic, thereby contaminating their understanding and experience of God. In such cases, it may be desireable to help them distinguish sharply—in the heart—the true God and Jesus from the false. Counselees who are becoming aware of the extreme spiritual abuse and traumatization they experienced earlier in life may find it psychologically impossible, for a few months (or even years), to address directly their God-concept or

God-image. During this time, Christian counselors can work with them on other issues, including other relational distortions, for example, by allowing the counseling relationship itself to serve as a corrective to the counselee's subjective relational world and possibly bring about indirectly some remediation in a distorted God-image. Those without such abuse may have difficulty understanding what these persons go through.

Splitting God and Satan

The healthiest believers, having an accurate and integrated perception of God, are able to agree from the heart with Job's epiphany in the midst of his great struggle with God (and Satan): "Though He slay me, I will hope in Him" (Job 13:15). However, Job himself did not perceive God consistently in this way as he sorted through his suffering, in light of his faith and the theology of his friends. And Job, of course, is an archetypal believer, for the difficulties of human life raise questions about God and his love. When something bad happens, in addition to experiencing the negative emotions that are typically activated, religious people reflect on God's involvement, usually in accord with their God-concept. From a biblical standpoint, this is appropriate and even desirable, since God is sovereign over all that happens. However, because he is also righteous and loving, the Bible's portrayal of his involvement with evil (whether natural or personal) is very complex and multifaceted (Carson, 1990). As a result, thoughts about God, combined with the negative emotions that often come with sin and suffering, will usually also activate one's God-image and related self-representations, and if there are distortions because of poor socialization or teaching, strong negative emotions associated with one's God-image may be triggered.

The full biblical account regarding evil that happens to humans, however, also includes the involvement of Satan. The name Satan originally meant "adversary" (Heb.), and "devil" (*diabolos*, Gk.) meant "slanderer" or "accuser." Though we are told little about Satan's origins, he is portrayed as a created supernatural agent who is implacably opposed to God and the well-being of his image bearers and works to increase human sin and suffering, with the ultimate aim of turning humans away from God and preventing any improvement in their relationship (Gen 3; Job 1–2; Zec 3:1-2; Mt 4:1-11; 2 Cor 12:7). Yet he also ironically (and fiendishly) "echoes" the law of God by accusing God's people of sin, much like a prosecuting attorney (Zech 3:1-2; Rev 12:10). In this role Satan sounds very similar to and closely allied with the condemning mental force with which some people contend—namely, the "internal saboteur" (Guntrip, 1957) or "inner critic." Yet, the biblical authors also portray Satan as God's "servant" (Page, 2007), who can accomplish nothing without God's permission (Job 1–2; 2 Cor 12:7).

To help us understand how we might approach such problems, we will examine a psychologically intriguing theme in the work of Martin Luther. According to Bayer (2008), Luther's view of God verged on, but fell short of, being dualistic. On the one hand, Luther referred to the "hidden God" (*Deus absconditus*), the sovereign ruler of the universe, whom we meet in suffering, evil, and death, whose actions seem arbitrary and therefore incomprehensible, and who as a result comes across sometimes as an almost sinister opponent. Luther contrasted this perspective with that of the "crucified God" (*Deus crucifixus*), the loving, self-sacrificing Savior, revealed especially in Jesus Christ on the cross, who is "present in a saving way" (p. 198). Both are aspects of the one true God, exemplifying his sovereign majesty and love respectively. However, the "dark side of God," according to Bayer's reading of Luther, bears a terrifying resemblance to Satan. In fact, Bayer says that Luther sometimes referred to Satan as a "mask of the almighty God in his terrifying hiddenness. The deepest temptation is that in which God himself becomes my enemy and in which I can no longer distinguish God and the devil, so that I, as Luther says, 'do not know whether God is the devil or the devil is God'" (p. 205). Yet Luther adamantly held to the unity of God and rejected views of God that would deny either his sovereignty or his love.

Many Christians will feel uncomfortable with this interpretation of God, and it seems highly likely that it emerged out of Luther's engagement with the true God revealed in Scripture by means of a dichotomous God-image he had (perhaps shaped by poor and inconsistent parenting). But before we reject Luther's distinction out of hand, we should note that his perception of the hidden God resembles Job's perceptions of God in the midst of his suffering (see Job 7:20; 9:16-20; 13:24; 16:7-14). There are also many passages in the prophets where God's judgment of his people for their sin and his everlasting love for his people lie side by side, with little attempt at harmonization. What if Luther's dichotomous God-image enabled him to distinguish sharply features of God's simple character, which sometimes do seem to be in opposition from our standpoint? Let us remind ourselves again of God's transcendent incomprehensibility due to our finitude. We have to expect that the infinite God will exceed our capacities to grasp him in the unity of his being, leading to what sometimes feels like dichotomies between different attributes— such as his sovereign majesty and his love.[10] God is not split, but we may perceive him that way because of our sin, cognitive limitations, and in some cases creational damage. The challenge for believers is to receive and integrate *all* that has been revealed about God in Scripture, as best they can, by his Spirit, and interpret everything in life, including him, accordingly.

How might we use such considerations therapeutically? When counselees perceive that God is their enemy, it is especially important that therapists take time to gently forge an empathic, trusting relationship and not try to argue them into a more balanced position, because that will likely be experienced as similarly aggressive. Eventually, we will want to raise the possibility that such perceptions might be related to the malfunctioning of their perceptual equipment for perceiving God (what Calvin called their *sensus divinitatis*) due to our fallen condition, that is, our sin and, for some, perhaps growing up with less-than-perfect parents. (I have never known any person with such perceptions who grew up in a kind and loving family.) At the right time, we should discuss the revelation of God's love in Christ and what we might deduce about God in light of Christ's sacrifice of himself on the cross, and encourage the integration of God as love and sovereign majesty (much as Luther himself recommended, Kolb, 2002). Then we can encourage them to make a sharp distinction between *that* God and Satan and to allow themselves to open up to the possibility that God in Christ loves them, while perceiving Satan as their enemy, and suggest to them that *he* is the malevolent cause of the evil they have experienced, so they would be right to direct their animosity toward him (Ps 139:21-22). He truly is our ultimate enemy, so it is valid and therapeutically helpful to hate Satan! He is to be designated forever as our "bad object." Regarding the suffering counselees have experienced, we might encourage them to adapt a saying from Joseph and apply it to themselves, "[Satan] meant evil against me, but God meant it for good" (Gen 50:20). Repeated reflection, meditation, and perception along these lines, seeking to split apart in one's heart one's distorted God-image into the perception of Satan and the perception of the *true* God (according to biblical revelation) may facilitate one's ability to relate to God, and indirectly to oneself and others.

We can see from the foregoing that experiencing negative transference and projection with the perfect God is not all bad, because it can bring to one's awareness unresolved shame and guilt and psychospiritual material from when one grew up with imperfect images of God—for example, memories and feelings—which can then be identified as such, objectified, and "worked through." This religious therapeutic use of transference with God, of course, turns Freudian theory on its head by treating God as a real person—indeed, as the most real person there is—who can be psychologically alive in the believer's heart and relational universe, and involving him directly in the healing process, ideally facilitating additional changes in one's experience of oneself and others (see Spero, 1992, for a Jewish approach with similar theistic assumptions).

Participating in God's Beautification Program

To summarize the chapter thus far: part of Christian therapy involves learning how to know, worship, and love God in his diverse perfections. The triune God is a single, simple being whose perfections constitute a harmonious unity. While we cannot comprehend God in his totality, there are things we can do with the Spirit's help to promote the healing of our sinful and damaged equipment for perceiving God (the *sensus divinitatis*). The therapeutic challenge for all Christians is to learn how to open up, by the Spirit, our more or less damaged hearts to God in Christ as he is revealed in Scripture. In his presence, he enables us gradually to know, worship, and love him better and integrate his diverse perfections in our minds and hearts and lives (and brains). By this means our thinking and deep perceptions of him can get corrected, expanded, and remolded intellectually and experientially, and this will indirectly affect our perceptions of others and ourselves. To facilitate this, believers play a necessary role by spending adequate time with him. For various reasons, many Christians are unconvinced (at least unconsciously) that meeting with God will produce any psychospiritual benefits, so they need encouragement by pastors and counselors to continue to seek him in order to find him (Mt 7:7), as well as teaching about God and salvation and training in how to cultivate the frame of heart necessary to perceive and participate in God's beauty so they too can better flourish.

Thompson (2011) reminds us that this begins by *being known* by God, that is, by realizing that God already knows everything going on inside of us and by opening up, consciously, to his knowing and loving us in Christ. On our side, this involves enhancing our divinely restored relationship with him. The spiritual disciplines are relevant here. Prayer figures most prominently in the process. However, for transformation to occur there must be more than restless supplication. Praise, thanks, and love are essential. *Listening* prayer (a more dialogical kind than most people practice) can help to move believers in their prayer practice from mental prayer (in the head) to affective prayer (in the heart) to contemplative prayer (whole-souled happiness in God; see

Johnson, 2007, chap. 16; Pieper, 1998). Closely related to prayer is meditation on God, especially through Scripture reading, as well as other Christian devotional literature, so that we can engage with God increasingly as he really is, apart from our misperceptions. Just like other aspects of deep soul change, it takes months and even years to learn how to pray and meditate in ways that best promote the soul's flourishing through new perceptions and experiences of God, others, and oneself that allow his perfections (his form and splendor) to penetrate the mind, then the heart, and onward, throughout one's memories, imagination, action tendencies, and relational practices, along with the corresponding parts of the brain (e.g., the amygdala, hippocampus, and prefrontal cortex), leading to significant turns in one's story.

One way this occurs, as Brother Lawrence wrote, is through practicing his presence throughout the day, for example, going to the store with him, walking or exercising with him, working on our computers with him, digging in the garden with him, watching television with him, and talking with others with him. Of special value are nature walks, hikes, or camping trips in which some time is spent opening up to God's peaceful dignity, contentment, power, and wisdom, which are always being expressed through his creation, where such traits seem almost tangible.

Finally, we recall that counselors, as well as others, have an important role to play in portraying God to the counselee, for mature believers themselves manifest the form and splendor of God through the course of their reciprocal actions with others, providing visible, tangible experiences of the dignity, righteousness, and love of the invisible God. They are intended by God to complement, reinforce, and solidify the internalization of Scripture and the benefits of our relationship with God in the healing of our souls.

RESOURCES FOR COUNSELORS AND COUNSELEES

Classic

Augustine. (2009). *Confessions* (H. Chadwick, Trans.). New York: Oxford University Press.

Bennett, A. (1975). *The valley of vision: A collection of Puritan prayers and devotions.* Edinburgh: Banner of Truth Trust. A selection that promotes both the fear and the love of God.

Julian of Norwich. (1998). *Revelations of divine love.* (A. C. Spearing, Trans.). New York: Penguin.

Owen, J. (2007). *Communion with the triune God*. Wheaton, IL: Crossway. ‡ Weighty theology with a lover's heart.

Tozer, A. W. (1961). *The knowledge of the holy*. San Francisco: HarperCollins.

Watson, T. (1966). *A body of divinity*. Edinburgh: Banner of Truth.

Contemporary

Boyer, S. D., & Hall, C. A. (2012). *The mystery of God: Theology for knowing the unknowable*. Grand Rapids, MI: Baker Academic. ‡

Clinton, T., & Straub, J. (2014). *God attachment: Why you believe, act, and feel the way you do about God*. New York: Howard Books.

Crabb, L. (1993). *Finding God*. Grand Rapids, MI: Zondervan.

—— (2013). *66 love letters*. Nashville, TN: Thomas Nelson.

Hart, D. B. (2003). *The beauty of the infinite: The aesthetics of Christian truth*. Grand Rapids, MI: Eerdmans. ‡ A terribly difficult but wondrous book.

Moriarity, G. L., & Hoffman, L. (Eds.). (2007). *God image handbook: For spiritual counseling and psychotherapy*. Binghamton, NY: Haworth. ‡

Packer, J. I. (1973). *Knowing God*. Downers Grove, IL: InterVarsity Press. A contemporary classic.

Peterson, E. (2015). *Holy luck*. Grand Rapids, MI: Eerdmans. A slim treasury of poems that will make you laugh with wonder at the beauty of God.

Piper, J. (1991). *The pleasures of God*. Sisters, OR: Multnomah. Perhaps Piper's finest book.

—— (2005). *God is the gospel*. Wheaton, IL: Crossway. A slim volume, good for counseling homework.

Smith, J. B. (2009). *The good and beautiful God*. Downers Grove, IL: InterVarsity Press.

Smith, S. (2001). *Objects of his affection: Coming alive to the compelling love of God*. West Monroe, LA: Howard.

Tan, S.-Y., & Gregg, D. H. (1997). *The disciplines of the Holy Spirit*. Grand Rapids, MI: Zondervan.

Thompson, C. (2011). *Anatomy of the soul: Surprising connections between neuroscience and spiritual practices that can transform your life and relationships*. Wheaton, IL: Tyndale House. Explains how God can heal our attachment damage.

Welch, E. (1998). *When people are big and God is small*. Phillipsburg, NJ: P&R.

‡ Recommended more for pastors and counselors than counselees

—7—

The Way It's Supposed to Be

Principle 2: The triune God created human beings to develop into participants in his glory, the grateful reception of which contributes to their fullest flourishing.

God saw all that He had made, and behold, it was very good.

Genesis 1:31

Every good thing given and every perfect gift is from above, coming down from the Father of lights.

James 1:17

Everything created by God is good, and nothing is to be rejected if it is received with gratitude; for it is sanctified by means of the word of God and prayer.

1 Timothy 4:4-5

The glory of God is a living soul.

Irenaeus

THE PLOT LINE OF SCRIPTURE is heavily concentrated on the scandal of human rebellion and evil and the remarkable lengths to which humanity's Creator has gone to reverse the mutiny and bring humans into his triune communion. Scripture, consequently, focuses the attention of its readers especially on the correlated themes of sin and redemption. Those seeking to base their therapy on the "first principles" of Scripture, however, must not be so caught up in the main action of the theodrama that they fail to take note of its essential backdrop: the good creation that provides its staging, infrastructure, and context. Though the biblical story obviously begins with creation, its implications for the undergirding of human life, history, and culture are rarely made explicit in Scripture. As a result, Christians have sometimes reduced everything in human life to the opposition between God and sin, thereby overlooking creation and God's glory manifested there. While sin must be given due heed, a more deeply theocentric orientation will regard God's good works in creation and especially redemption to be vastly more worthy of our attention.

Those who grasp Christianity's essence have always recognized it offers a "creation-based worldview" (Bavinck, 2004, p. 435) that gives it a high view of the creation. Consider Aquinas (1945, Vol. 1), who believed that God loves all that he has created, because his "love is the cause of goodness in things" (p. 219). Or Calvin (1559/1960), who argued that the knowledge of ourselves is necessarily twofold: "namely, to know what we were like when we were first created" as well as what our condition became after the fall (p. 183). A robust Christianity is always founded on a hearty appreciation for the goodness of God's creation that exists in, through, and for Jesus Christ.

CHRISTIAN TEACHING REGARDING CREATION

Christians will obviously begin their study of the biblical doctrine of creation in the first three chapters of Genesis. However, additional teaching on creation is scattered throughout the Bible. The following is a summary of some of the chief lines of creational thought relevant for soul care.

Creation and Providence

We begin by noting that the good creation has continued since its creation, its continuation being due to what theologians have termed God's *providence*. To speak of creation *simpliciter* refers to God's original authoring of the created order ex nihilo (out of nothing), by which the heavens and the earth came into being. Providence points to God's ongoing authorial up-holding of the created order by the word of his power (Heb 1:3; see also Ps 148:6, 8; Col 1:17). Creation and providence imply each other, so that providence has been rightly considered by some to be a "continuous or progressive creation" (Bavinck, 1956, p. 179).

Created for God

From within the frame of reference of this universe alone we might conclude, along with many in our day, that we are merely highly evolved organisms who have no higher ideals than reproduction and resourceful survival. A secular society at its best can develop additional worthwhile values such as working hard, care for the disadvantaged, and the pursuit of many temporal forms of happiness. Noble naturalistic orientations such as classical Buddhism and mainstream positive psychology posit even higher values that can give a greater sense of purpose, for example, wisdom, compassion, and even transcendence (Peterson & Seligman, 2004). But because none of these values can address the deepest questions and needs of human life, there remains a mostly unconscious, unsatisfied longing in the human heart. Christians believe that the fullest sense of human meaningfulness and purpose is found beyond the natural order in communion with our triune Creator.

Basic to a Christian understanding of human life and identity is the Creator-creature distinction, the recognition that humans are of a completely different order of being from God and live in absolute dependence on him for everything and owe him complete fealty (O'Donovan, 1986, p. 33). This relation is infinitely asymmetrical, since their existence is totally contingent on the freedom of God. "Our very being is nothing but subsistence in the one God" (Calvin, 1559/1960, p. 35). This truth distinguishes a theistic psychology from a secular psychology across the entire subject matter of the discipline.

The Gifts of Life

We have already noted the expressive and generous nature of the triune God in the word of the Son and the gift of the Spirit toward humanity in salvation. The goods of creation provide further evidence of his communicative liberality. To begin with, existence itself is an amazing gift. God "gives to all people life and breath and all things" (Acts 17:25). Each human life, therefore, is a great good. "All existing things, in so far as they exist, are good, since the being of a thing is itself a good; as is likewise whatever perfection it possesses" (Aquinas, 1945, Vol. 1, p. 217). So it *is* better to be than not to be. Taking this a step further (by twisting another saying), it is better to have lived and suffered than never to have lived at all.

But God gives all humans more than mere life. Though the particular gifts vary considerably in this world, humans generally find themselves the beneficiaries of innumerable blessings: a dazzlingly beautiful world; specific bodies; and nourishment, care, and affection from caregivers (usually families), who (within cultures) pass on a language, knowledge, skills, and cultural resources, including technology. Each human life, therefore, consists of countless gifts, freely shared, that testify something of its Giver. "The world is charged with the grandeur of God" (Hopkins, 1985, p. 27), such that a current of transcendent goodness radiates throughout the created order, leaving its mark in every human heart, no matter how burdened, and a longing for more. "No drop will be found [in the creation] either of wisdom and light, or of righteousness or power or rectitude, or of genuine truth, which does not flow from [God], and of which he is not the cause. Thus we may learn to await and seek all these things from him, and thankfully to ascribe them, once received, to him" (Calvin, 1559/1960, p. 41).

At the same time, humans were not created to be passive observers. They are complex actors, made with many good desires, operating at different "levels"—biological, psychosocial, ethical, and spiritual—which they must organize as they develop into a matrix of desire hierarchies. At the top of this matrix is to be the love of God—the greatest Good—so that *he* becomes their heart's greatest desire. This is central to God's design plan. It is not, however, a "simple theocentrism," which minimizes the rest of creation. "Rather, it is the other way around. . . . The deepest desire of the heart for God gives an added value to every other heart's desire, because it turns into gifts other things on which a person has set his heart" (Stump, 2010, p. 444). And gifts, Stump reminds us, are "second-personal in character" (p. 445); they are relational and "part of a story"—signs, therefore, of God's love for individual persons with whom he seeks communion.

The Triune God Speaks the Creation, Including Humans, into Being

In the beginning the Trinity created the heavens and the earth by a communal speech act (Gen 1:3, 6, 9, 11, 14-15, 20, 22, 24, 26): the Father spoke, the Son was the Word or expression of what the Father meant (Jn 1:1-4; Col 1:16-17), and the Spirit accomplished the Father's intended meaning (hinted at in Gen 1:2) (see Bavinck, 2004, pp. 420-26). When creating humanity, the triune God said, "Let Us make man in Our image" (Gen 1:26), and he formed a triune family: first male and female, and (eventually) children (whose psychological form gets constituted in childhood through the speech acts of their parents!).

I might add that in the beginning human souls were formless and void, and God began giving them form by means of spoken directives: "Be fruitful and multiply, and fill the earth, and subdue it; and rule" over the rest of creation (Gen 1:28); and "from the tree of the knowledge of good and evil you shall not eat, for . . . you will surely die" (Gen 2:16-17). Like the speaking God, and in contrast to the rest of creation, humans are dialogical beings whose inner being is to be constituted in conversation with God. His initial communications established the basic parameters and patterns of human life on earth, conveying implicitly the message that humans will find their fulfillment by consenting to and carrying out his word. As dialogical-material creatures, they have unique capacities to *grasp* his word, *answer*, and *embody* it in their activity within the creation.[1]

So, while the rest of creation is formed immediately by God's word, humans are formed gradually by God's word as they internalize and correspond to it (Anderson, 1982; Johnson, 2007). Dialogue is intrinsic to human formation, for through it humans realize their *calling* (their vocation) to image God aright. Consequently, wherever we look, around us or within, we will find signs of our triune God's *meaning-making discourse*, the most important of which is expressed in human language (i.e., the Bible), though most of God's discourse in the creation is not so expressed.[2] God designed humans to become a certain kind of personal agent in communion by consenting to the meaningfulness that the triune God has and is communicating to us.

Created good and for good. On the sixth day, after the creation of humans, "God saw all that He had made, and behold, it was very good" (Gen 1:31). We ought to conclude from this declaration that all earthly creatures have a primordial and divinely established goodness, *especially human beings.* This declarative speech-act most importantly reveals "a loving and immensely strong commitment on God's part to his creation" (Goldsworthy, 1991, p. 94). A second implication is that while humans are necessarily finite and limited in various ways, they were not created by God with evil. According to biblical revelation (and implicit in natural law theory), though desecrated by humanity's sinful alienation from God, the goodness of human nature nonetheless remains providentially sustained by God's creation grace (goodness he continues to give sinful humans irrespective of their relation to him, in contrast to redemptive grace, which is given only to those in union with Christ; Barth, 1956b, pp. 8-9; König, 1989). Let us consider the relevance of this truth for Christian psychology and soul care.

Normativity. Central to the goodness of the created order are the laws or norms that give it its dynamic form. "One of the most significant parallels between the natural sciences and Christian theology is a fundamental conviction that the world is characterized by regularity and intelligibility" (McGrath, 2001, p. 218). The same can be said of the human sciences, for human life too is thoroughly normed (Johnson, 2007, chap. 8), a phenomenon maintained by God's creation grace and sometimes termed "natural law." Human life is regulated throughout by lawful biological processes; human development occurs in an orderly fashion; children are born with physical, social, and intellectual needs that have to be met or they will be damaged; there are optimal ways to raise children; as children develop, they appropriate social and cultural norms that regulate their lives; human faces, bodies, and abilities are evaluated according to ideal standards, so that humans begin in elementary school to compare themselves with one another and rank themselves accordingly; in adolescence and early adulthood humans typically form a mature conscience that regulates their ethical and spiritual life—evidence of God's law written on the heart (Rom 2:14). Jesus summarized the law of God with the commands to love God and love neighbor as yourself (Mt 22:37-39), and we should note the second command makes reference to a created norm of self-love as a criterion for evaluating one's neighbor love. Human life is thoroughly saturated with norms of many kinds, which give it a dynamic structure and shape human self-understanding (O'Donovan, 1986). According to Turner (2013), this natural law means our true, creational desires, ultimately for God, "are normative not as imposed by decree externally, but arising from their being constitutive of what it is to be human" (citing Aquinas, pp. 181-82). Sin corrupts and distorts this law, but it cannot be obliterated from human nature. Having so many creational norms leads inevitably to inner conflict, but in a perfect creation they would be regulated by their being subordinated to the greatest command, to love God supremely (Mt 22:37).

The law of God written on the human heart helps to explain the remarkable consonance in common sense, intuitive wisdom, and a deep respect for law found throughout the world (Lewis, 1947). This natural law[3] also has tremendous clinical significance, for it tells a severely abused child that what is being done to her is bad and can later guide her into greater self-awareness and healing as she sorts through what happened and reclaims her soul and her story. Unfortunately, our ethical intuition is now fallen, which can lead to some curious contradictions that nonetheless manifest its remaining force: relativists criticizing realists, a convicted murderer beating to death a pedophile in prison, an adulterous politician brought down by an otherwise sexually permissive media system. However, aided by the Holy Spirit and the light of Scripture (Ps 119:105), ethical intuition can become more trustworthy and with training turn into Christian prudence, which can help counselors and counselees navigate the inner workings of often murky souls. The greatest problem for humans now regarding the law of God written on the heart is that its requirements are absolute. One is either morally perfect or one is not. As a result, the good law creates enormous psychological pressures for human beings after the fall.

Many natural, human, and cultural norms seem to be fairly strictly determined by God's word in creation (e.g., rules of neural firing; the working memory module; thou shalt not murder my kin). Like the norms of the rest of the biological world, they are likely significantly controlled by genetics, emerging universally through normal individual development, and therefore are relatively resistant to human modification, except negatively. Other human and cultural norms are much more "open" or plastic, allowing for greater input from family, culture, and even personal taste. Among this more flexible category are norms are that are almost entirely taught or legitimated by culture (e.g., vocabulary, style), whereas others are guided by a more divinely circumscribed *telos*, in spite of significant personal and cultural diversity in a fallen world (e.g., sexual relations and gender). Determining the degree of normative flexibility is a task of prudence, cultivated by the Holy Spirit, Scripture, the Christian tradition, reason, and common sense.

Norms themselves can also be distinguished in terms of their universality and particularity. Universal norms apply to all persons at all times (e.g., to love God). Particular norms apply only to certain persons at certain times (to love this person specially, e.g., one's spouse). Moreover, God providentially situates each human uniquely. Humans are free personal agents who nonetheless are embodied and embedded (in specific physical, historical, social, narrative, and cultural contexts). Part of God's address to each individual is a call to accept and realize the distinctive determinations and opportunities of one's life in the best way possible (Kierkegaard, 1849/1980), more or less actively transforming possibilities into specific actualities before God.[4] As a result, there is an irreducible particularity to each human life, rendered momentous in each action (at least in normal adulthood). "What can be accomplished by me cannot ever be accomplished by anyone else." As a result, "I am—actually, irreplaceably—and therefore am obliged to realize my uniqueness" (Bakhtin, quoted in Coates, 1998, p. 28). One's uniqueness, then, in body, location, story, relationships, strengths, weaknesses, and calling is God-given.

In light of the pervasive lawfulness of human life, embracing bounded personal and cultural freedom and variability, and encompassing even the call to realize one's uniqueness, we might suppose that God has a variously specified design plan for individual human beings so that human goodness and flourishing corresponds both to one's proper functioning according to a general design plan for all[5] and the fulfillment of one's personalized divine calling. Indeed, since, according to Scripture (Eph 1:11) the sovereign God sets the laws and their parameters, as well as the particular details for his human creatures, we might consider his divine authority over one's life to be demonstrated supremely by one's consent to it all (Johnson, 2007, chap. 16). How better to manifest the infinite worth of God over the finite worth of his self-conscious creatures than to have them freely (and happily) affirm it?

Created for receptive communion with the triune God. Human goodness is especially tied to humanity's responsive, dependent relationship with God. On earth only humans are God's dialogue partners and conscious, active participants in his glorification. For this, humans always needed God's empowering, even before they became sinners. Loving God is necessarily the fruit of God's love. According to Bavinck (2004), even "before the fall, a human being was the dwelling place of the entire holy Trinity, a most splendid temple of the Holy Spirit" (p. 559). Consequently, the created goodness of humans entails, most importantly, the capacity for dependent, indwelling communion with God.

Created for interdependent human community. Humans are not individuals first, but *socials*. From conception on, we are dependent on others, as well as God, for our well-being and growth. Woman was created, God said, because "it is *not good* for the man to be alone; I will make a helper suitable for him" (Gen 2:18). Human goodness is a social kind, and humans are created with good needs for one another. Over the past one hundred years, the human sciences have disclosed just how thorough is our social being: humans are *intersubjective* before they become conscious, answerable, interdependent subjects (Siegel, 2012), and they are necessarily embedded in a variety of social contexts (Bronfenbrenner, 2006), including various power relations, friendships, and cooperative ventures, so that humans become individual personal agents by means of and always in relation to their social world.

Sexed and gendered. The first exposition of the *imago Dei* in the Bible is the sex/gender polarity of male-female (Gen 1:27), suggesting that this dichotomy is basic to God's design plan for humanity. Humanity was created in two ideal embodied/psychosocial forms, which together form a *whole* image of God, so that there are two fundamental ways of being a personal agent in community (Anderson, 1982; Grenz, 2001).[6] This view is affirmed and reinforced in Jesus' life and teaching (Mt 19:4-6) and throughout the New Testament (1 Cor 6:12-20; 7:1-40; Eph 5:22-33). In a fallen world, sexual and gender differentiation is somewhat open or plastic, and therefore it can be thwarted by a host of obstacles—biological, familial, cultural, and demonic—yet orthodox Christians believe the original creation norms remain inviolable, guiding the church's—and individual Christians'—approach to gender identity and sexual orientation. Contemporary culture tends to interpret their malleability as demonstrating that sex and gender are normless (ignoring the normative implications of evolutionary theory!). Endorsing a natural-law approach, however, does not make Christian recovery in these areas quick or easy or even inevitable (see Jones & Yarhouse, 2007). Similar to personality disorders, healing is often painfully slow and for some may be limited to learning to accept and manage virtuously the internal conflict.

Families. God originally designed that human beings would originate out of embodied heterosexual unions established by lifelong covenant and entailing parental authority over and responsibility for the care, development, and individuation of children, to prepare them for union and communion with God, the love of others, productive work, and leisure. In addition to providing good nutrition and loving physical contact, we now understand that healthy social relationships are prerequisite to the formation of healthy personhood, including moral awareness (Bowlby, 1988; Eisenberg, 1998; Cassidy & Shaver, 2008; Harmon-Jones & Winkielman, 2007).

For example, infants need responsive, attuned interaction with their caregivers, which signals an affirmation of their inner being, and healthy attachment, which fosters a sense of security and safety. As already suggested, families are intended by God to be finite representations of the eternal love of the Trinity (Ouellet, 2006). Parents in particular, being the first images of God to which children are exposed, are supposed to exemplify the perfect affirmation among the Trinity and, as the children develop, his righteousness as well. These experiences anticipate and prepare children to enter into the "circle of love" with God, self, and others that is supposed to constitute the dynamic, reciprocal relational world of mature adulthood (Halder, 2003). Empirical evidence for this can be seen in the causal influence of early childhood attachments on later attachment experiences with God and others (Hall, Fujikawa, Halcrow, Hill, & Delaney, 2009). So, humans become lovers in adulthood by being beloved in childhood, and this is another creational norm.

There are many other social processes that God established as norms to guide proper human development. We will consider only three that are of special importance to later discussions in the book: admiration, introjection, and identification. Admiration is the process of honoring someone because of her praiseworthy qualities. According to Kohut (1971, 1977), children typically begin in late infancy to admire their parents and derive a sense of their own goodness from them, since their sense of self is originally experienced socially.[7] Turned into a statement, this primitive process would be, "Because you are good, I am good." Introjection is the process, beginning in infancy, when infants take into themselves aspects of the other (attitudes, affects) that come to form part of their developing self (Hinshelwood, 1991; St. Clair, 2000). For example, when the infant feels loved and fed, the child introjects a positively valenced sense of self. We could turn this process into a statement: "I am what you think and feel about me." We might mention here that good-enough parenting involves the proper affirmation of the child's creational goodness. When such affirmation is seriously deficient, as too often happens in a fallen world, the child grows up more or less dissociated. In adulthood, the person may become alternately obsessed with proving (and insisting on) his or her goodness and depressed because of a felt lack of goodness; both extremes are tied to natural law.

Children were also created with a tendency to identify themselves with those they admire (Cooley, 1902; Erikson, 1950). Identification involves taking on the characteristics of the admired person (Tyson & Tyson, 1990) and has two components: it assumes a similarity between the self and the other (hence the sense of *identity*) that flows out of, but moves beyond, admiration; and consists of conscious and unconscious activities of imitation and appropriation of the other's attributes. Turning identification into a statement, we might say, "Because you are special, I would like to become more like you."

These mostly unconscious processes are foundational to childhood formation. "The traces of past [parent] relationships remain in the child's personality and cause the child to resemble his or her parents" (St. Clair, 2000,

p. 25). Such lawful regularities constitute some of the major building blocks of one's self, identity, and style of personal agency and communion (Cramer, 1991; Erikson, 1968) and prepare one for meeting God.

Cultures. Families are themselves situated within discursive communities and cultures with histories. Cultural psychology has found many modest but significant differences in personality, cognition, and relational style that are due to influences from culture (Kitiyama & Cohen, 2010). Such diversity makes it possible for humanity to image better an infinite God and therefore is also part of God's design plan for the human creation (Bavinck, 2004, p. 577; Hart, 2003; Kuyper, 1998, p. 175).

Created to become personal agents in communion. Created in the image of the triune God, humans are fundamentally characterized by agency and communion, created to live in dependence on the triune God, of whom they are dynamic representations. Divine agency or freedom and power is imaged in the conditioned agency, finite freedom, and created energy of humans, which are necessary to love God and one another, to imagine, and to enact projects in the world. According to empirical research on human agency, its mature form emerges out of the "good enough" early social experiences touched on above. However, Christians also recognize that their agency in communion is uniquely affected by their relationship with their God (Kelsey, 2009).

The following are some of the various good, created components that constitute healthy personal agency in communion.

Dynamic structures of personal agency and communion. God has mysteriously constituted humans as the conjunction of a material body and an immaterial soul. Such is their intimate interrelation that the soul is the life and psychological form of the body, yet the functioning of the soul on earth is dependent on the functioning of the body (particularly the brain, the rest of the nervous system, and the endocrine system), so that the soul's amazing capacities emerge as the brain develops through engagement with the world (Aquinas, 1945, Vol. I, pp. 682-718; Johnson, 2007, chap. 10; Piaget, 1977a; Siegel, 2010).[8]

The physiological and embodied basis of human life begins with the unique genome of each human person, formed at conception, which regulates all subsequent biological and psychological processes, making possible the phenotypic development of the form of the body (including an individual's physiognomy); organismic motives of hunger, thirst, sexual expression, reproduction, avoidance of pain, and pursuit of simple well-being; sensation and perception; positive and negative emotion systems (including moods and desires); emotion schemes (emotions stored with beliefs and attitudes); more socially constructed desires (e.g., self-regard, curiosity, "flow," different loves [*eros*, attachment, *philia*, and *agapē*]); gender and sexual identity; memory (including mental imagery, semantic and episodic memory, self-schemas); language/discourse, reason, beliefs, theories of mind, judgment, and imagination in all its richness (use of mental imagery, planning ahead, projecting possible futures); goals, intentions, volition, dispositions, and actions; self-regulation abilities (metacognition, emotion regulation, and action regulation); *habitus*; a unique configuration of personality traits, competences, and multiple intelligences; relational capacities (internal working model, attachment style, empathy, affection for others, understanding of social norms); the conscience (the module responsible for ethical perception); and the *sensus divinitatis* (the module for perceiving, desiring, and loving God).[9] Though most of these dynamic structures are not explicitly mentioned in Scripture, they are part of the infrastructure of God's good human creation, and their proper functioning is part of his design plan for human life.

Of special importance for therapy are the emotions—signs consisting of created energy that move humans toward God and goodness with him, either directly (positive emotions[10]) or indirectly (negative emotions[11]). Discrete emotions are therefore also motivating signs of evaluative meaning regarding one's relation to God and the good, and because emotions can be stored in memory, they also are a record of one's relation to God and the good.

Each human being, then, is an absolutely unique configuration of the created and developmentally conditioned phenotypic qualities that make that person—body and soul—the individual he or she is.[12] We focus next on a profound but subtle distinction that marks human experience.

Cognitive and carditive dynamics. Human beings are created body/souls constituted with two systems for understanding, interpreting, and living, which have great relevance for therapy. These two systems are consciousness or mind or "head"—where explicit or intentional psychological processing occurs—and the soul's deeper, less accessible regions: the unconscious or experiential part, sometimes called the heart or "gut," where a good deal of implicit or automatic processing goes on, most of which we are only marginally aware. These systems were designed to operate in a balanced and coordinated fashion, but in a fallen world they have become more or less disconnected.

Our consciousness, inclusive of our attention and working memory, refers to the psychological "site" where we remember, think, deliberate, form intentions and plans, imagine, love, and initiate activity.[13] Consciousness is the "site where humans are presently aware, grounded neurologically mostly in the prefrontal cortex" (Siegel, 2012). To use a computer metaphor, it is that part of the brain/soul that is currently online or on the screen. Consciousness "comes to us in a unified form" (Searle, 1998, p. 74) in that we experience it as a whole (e.g., we only feel one mood at a time), and it conveys a sense of personal continuity over time (i.e., each person is aware they have a story uniquely theirs). Generally speaking, consciousness also includes all that is relatively easily accessible to it, like what I am aware I believe (about God, myself, important others, the Bible, and the world) and what I am aware I love and hate (in unfallen persons there is no contradiction between awareness and actuality). Consciousness therefore refers to psychological phenomena that are *explicit* (Gawronski & Payne, 2010) and articulable, and are processed at the "head level" (Coe & Hall, 2010).

The experiential and less conscious dimension of the soul—the heart—includes layers of automatic psychological processes that are not easily accessible, if at all. They comprise carditive, characterological, relational dynamics (emotions, desires, and motives) that move and motivate us, mostly outside our awareness, for example, attachment memories, emotion schemes, and scripts, based in the brain stem, limbic system, and throughout the cerebral cortex (Bucci, 1997; Siegel, 2012). Yet in fallen persons significant obstacles are erected, making this realm even more difficult to access: sin, self-deception, defenses, and repressed memories. As a result, this experiential dimension of the soul now also includes psychological material that we want to avoid, such as what I may *actually* believe (about God, myself, important others, the Bible, and the world) and what I *actually* love and hate, in contrast to what I *think* I believe, love, and hate. All of this together now constitutes the human heart, which refers to psychological phenomena that are largely *implicit* (Gawronski & Payne, 2010) and that are processed at the "gut level" (Coe & Hall, 2010).

Humans were created with two major psychological systems—cognitive and carditive—grounded in distinct brain regions. Consciousness is obviously important to human life because that is where we actively engage with the world, think, and dialogue with God and others. This is where we focus our attention and take in and modify information and act. It feels like the center of our personhood and is the "place" where we internalize and process meaning (or glory), so it was designed to play a major role in the soul's development (and now in therapy). We should also note that consciousness is where images of God actively reflect or return the glory of God in worship. The maturation of one's consciousness (and its component skills), then, is key to one's active participation in God's glory. At the same time, the unconscious or experiential part of the soul, the heart, is especially important in Christianity, because it is the orienting center of the individual, that which most deeply guides one's actions, whether or not the individual is aware of it. It is the religious core of one's being (Dooyeweerd, 1960).

Tragically, human fallenness has turned a created difference between two aspects of human biological and psychological functioning into a severe "split," leading to some degree of dissociation between them. Therapy in a fallen world, therefore, seeks to repair the split as much as is possible in this age. One of the primary goals (and challenges) of psychotherapy is helping counselees bring up troubling material from the heart (e.g., implicit emotion schemes and "unconscious sources of personality disturbance"; Guntrip, 1957, p. 189) into their consciousness, so they can work on it, process it, and work through it without shutting down or getting overwhelmed by it. We will consider such activities in more detail in chapters eighteen and nineteen.

The triune God is (an) eternal "being-in-act" (Vanhoozer, 2010), more event than stasis (Kerr, 2002). Those who image him likewise are characterized by activity, energy, or power. Personal agency as designed is energy directed to God and the good; love is energy shared. As images of God, mature human beings have been endowed with their own created causal powers (or energy) that are concurrently dependent on God's transcendent causal powers that make them possible. So, always dependent on God, humans were created with energy to work (Gen 1:28; 2:15), marry and raise children (Gen 1:28), rest (which is also an act; Gen 2:3; Ex 20:8-11; Heb 4:11), celebrate (the Psalms; Jn 2), and love (1 Cor 13). Not being eternal, the activity of God's image bearers is necessarily temporal and storied. Human stories consist of the actions and interactions of personal agents in communion, designed to share their powers with each other to promote each other's well-being, to enhance the created order, and to display the glory of God (Gen 1:28-31; Johnson, 2007, chap. 9).

Empirical evidence of a "good-creation orientation." Given their primordial goodness, we would expect human beings even now to be characterized by a strong orientation toward the good, and that is what we find. In fact, a whole movement has arisen within the field of psychology called "positive psychology" that is investigating this fundamental human disposition. Evidence of a "good-creation orientation" (GCO), in spite of human fallenness (and sometimes carried to excess by human fallenness), includes the following.

1. Humans (along with all animals) are motivated by hedonic dynamics (Kahneman, Diener, & Schwarz, 1999); that is, they seek pleasure (satisfaction, fulfillment, happiness) and avoid pain, all things being equal. Similarly, humans generally possess a self-preservation or self-regard motive (though this is now disordered by sin).[14]

2. Humans prefer physical wholeness or soundness to brokenness. For example, when small children see a doll that is broken or a person missing an arm, they become alarmed. People are initially repulsed by physical disfigurements, and those with them often have difficulty accepting their lack of physical wholeness.

3. Regardless of their circumstances, most people tend toward a degree of satisfaction or hedonic well-being, which Diener, Lucas, and Oishi (2002) have (inaptly) called happiness.

4. Individuals are inclined to see themselves as better than they actually are. A majority of adults rate themselves better than average (especially on traits hard to evaluate objectively, such as friendliness); are more optimistic about their success; and are more confident that they will recover from cancer, be promoted, win the lottery, and so on, than the evidence warrants (Alicke & Govorun, 2005). Furthermore, optimistic people are happier and generally more successful than pessimistic people, and people prefer partners who are more optimistic (Carver & Scheier, 2002).

5. Humans tend to justify their behavior to themselves and others, even when they engage in wrongdoing, in order to maintain a positive view of themselves or a positive image before others (Aronson, 1988; Taylor, 1989). While a feature of fallen humanity, it also indicates a deep desire for self-perfection.

6. Children benefit from affirmation for their effort and are harmed by severe and chronic criticism, which can have devastating effects on their self-understanding, sense of competence and agency, and relational style (Harter, 2012). These negative outcomes suggest that the GCO is not strongly determined and can be compromised by destructive social experiences.

198 PART II—The Goodness of God and the Human Creation

7. Most people strive for some level of competence in what they do.

8. Some people are extreme perfectionists "who want to be perfect in all aspects of their lives" (Flett & Hewitt, 2002, p. 5), which causes distress to themselves and others. At the other extreme, failed perfectionism can lead to depression and underachievement. Such excesses would seem to reflect a distorted GCO.

9. Most people hold to the "just world hypothesis," the assumption that things usually work out fairly and justly, so that when something bad happens to someone, others assume that it must be deserved (Lerner, 1980).

10. Most people who believe in God also believe that he views them favorably.

11. When evil is done, it is usually perpetrated consciously in order to bring about "justice" or to promote some ideal (Baumeister, 1997).[15] Again, this signifies the existence of a deep sense of natural law, as well as the sin that uses it for its own purposes in fallen creatures.

12. Gazzaniga (2008) reports that lying requires a kind of "masking" that is detected as an abnormality in brain scans, suggesting that humans are hardwired for truth telling.

And this is just a fraction of the evidence. Such a variegated trend in so many diverse contexts offers solid empirical support for the Judeo-Christian belief that humans are created good and for the good. Naturalists will obviously interpret such findings according to their worldview, but they would seem to fit best with a metanarrative of a very good creation that precedes human fallenness than one that is propelled solely by natural selection in a meaningless universe.[16]

Augustine (1958) understood that every creature's "joy is in the goodness of God" (p. 233). According to Christianity, humans have a positive orientation because they were made for God, the source of all joy. But this also means that this positive orientation cannot be completely fulfilled apart from communion with God in heaven, except in an illusory fashion, through some measure of denial. Not surprisingly, some secular psychologists have actually advocated cultivating "positive illusions" as a way of coping (Taylor, 1991). But even such denial provides additional evidence of a GCO. Indeed, all human psychopathology, including sin, is paradoxically bound up with our primordial goodness in one way or another. Everyone, including Christians, demonstrates a distorted GCO to the degree one seeks to present to others an image of oneself as all good without sin and brokenness.

"Very good" does not mean fully realized. Finally, we ought not think that God's declaration of "very good" at the end of the first creation account meant that the creation was in its ultimately intended form. God built capacities into the human creation that would have to unfold and develop in order to be realized. It is necessary to distinguish between the absolute perfection of the infinite God and the relative, finite, temporal goodness of God's creation, the potentialities of which would have to become actualized over time and through the working of various created powers, processes, and activity. The original creation was a good project that had just begun (Gunton, 1998, p. 202).

In addition, we learn from Genesis 3 that humans were tempted in a good creation. Yet presumably being tempted to distrust God and reject his command was stressful. So some degree of suffering was compatible with this good creation.

Finally, contemporary research on happiness has found that humans around the world on average appear to have mildly positive emotions (Diener, Lucas, & Oishi, 2002). It seems likely that human emotional experience now would tend more to the negative side of the spectrum than in a creation without sin. However, though we must speculate, it also seems quite possible that God designed the human emotion system on earth to be set on "mildly positive" and that one of the ways in which human experience on earth is distinguished from that in heaven is that life on earth from the beginning is generally only mildly enjoyable, in contrast to the immense joy believers will experience when they are with God forever in heaven.

Created to Develop into the *Imago Dei* to Participate in Glory

We have already examined the notion of the *imago Dei* in chapter three with reference to Jesus Christ, who, as the Son of God, was the form or archetype according to which all humans were created, and who, as the Son of Man, became *the* human image of God. To summarize that discussion: a comprehensive account of the *imago Dei* includes (1) dynamic structural resemblance (e.g., rational-linguistic abilities, emotions, volition, creativity), relational resemblance, and functional resemblance (responsible ruling over God's creation), all of which was termed *embodied agency in communion* or *biopsychosocial wholeness.* This provides the creational platform for (2) the love and worship of God, the love of neighbor, and holy living, which was termed *godly character* or *ethicospiritual holiness.* Finally, the *imago* as mirror was termed (3) *active receptivity* with respect to God. The fulfillment of the image of God is the capacity of humans to receive, reflect, and participate in God's glory implicitly and explicitly and thereby exemplify him in his virtuous character, which can happen to the fullest extent only in Christ.

In this section, we will consider the *development* of these image-bearing/doxological capacities made possible by God's creation grace (given to all human beings, to some extent) and redemptive grace (available only through faith in Christ).[17] All humans are made in God's image (Gen 1:26-27; 9:6; Jas 3:9). However, its various aspects are not present (fully formed) at conception; they take time to emerge (ultimately by God's grace). Calvin (1559/1960) alluded to the development of the *imago Dei*: "The closer any man comes to the likeness of God, the more the image of God shines in him" (p. 601). However, most theological reflection on the *imago Dei* historically has been "adultist" in orientation. That is, the concept is discussed only with reference to its "adult form," so that surprisingly little attention has been devoted to its development. Consider, however, that our biopsychosocial wholeness normally increases throughout the lifespan, particularly during childhood, and it is obvious that well-functioning, normal adults image God in these ways more fully than infants or even adolescents. With regard to ethicospiritual holiness, seasoned, mature believers generally image God more fully than new, immature believers.[18] Recall that even though he was *the* image of God throughout his human life, Jesus Christ increased in wisdom in childhood (Lk 2:40, 52) and was being perfected in his human nature through his suffering (Heb 2:10; 5:8-9). We may conclude from these few comments that even *he* experienced *imago Dei* development as a human being.[19]

Such considerations simply follow from taking seriously human temporality. The image bearing of temporal creatures that start out as zygotes would *have* to involve a developing set of capacities that increases the correspondence of the finite human form and splendor to the infinite form and splendor of God, making possible an increase in one's capacity to manifest God's glory over time. Normal humans are in the process of *becoming* far more intensively than any other creature on earth, simply because they have the most extensive and complex capacities to develop. When functioning properly, humans are intended to grow in emotional complexity and increase massively in language ability, memory, and knowledge of others, self, and the world around them, and eventually of God. They become more aware of and "take in" (internalize) more and more of reality into their minds and hearts, and gradually integrate everything, relating it all together. And if they are believers, this occurs through actively receptive faith and love of God, becoming ingressed more pervasively, first in their consciousness and then more gradually in their heart, influencing their lives and relationships. Ideally, this process of increasing glory capacity should continue throughout the believer's life. By these means, finite humans to one degree or another become more like God, very limited approximations of his omniscient and omnipathic awareness, knowledge, understanding, and love, and so better able to glorify God. "Participation in the divine good is such that . . . it makes the participant ever greater and more spacious than before. . . . Everything that flows in produces an increase in capacity" (Gregory of Nyssa, quoted by Danielou, 1997, pp. 62-63). This is the end for which God created human development.[20]

While a more thorough discussion of the *redemptive* implications of these considerations will have to wait, two points ought to be made here. First, redemptive *imago* development is grounded in/supervenes on creational *imago* development. Without a cerebral cortex and memory development, for example, no redemptive change could become permanent. More importantly, the very kinds of change that lie at the heart of the *imago Dei*—holy, active receptivity with respect to God—are dependent on the creational capacities of personal agency (i.e., biopsychosocial wholeness). We need to become a self in order to be able to participate with God in this project, and this means "accepting the self I am as a gift and the self I should become as a task God has set for me" (Evans, 2009, p. 68). The actively receptive participation of believers in their own *imago Dei* development, therefore, is intrinsic to God's self-glorification project.[21]

The Relation Between Gratitude and Self-Love

The sheer abundance of life on earth is a sign that God is by nature a generous being without limit. Every moment the infinite fountain of limitless good is pouring out immeasurable blessing on every human around the globe. Our lives and all their good are gifts from God, as well as his personal invitations to enter more consciously into his exuberant celebration of his glory.

Yet God's gifts are fundamentally different from gifts given by humans, for God necessarily owns all that he has made, so his gifts cannot be transferred to creatures like property rights, so that they no longer belong to God. Instead, we should understand his gifts (and they are called gifts in the Bible, Jas 1:17) as his sharing his goodness with us, as a benefactor continuously wanting to have us live on his estate, at his largesse. As a result, while we own property and "possessions" with respect to other humans, with respect to God they still belong to him.

The way humans enjoy God's shared goodness is called gratitude. For theists, gratitude is necessarily a relational virtue. It is our delight in the Giver for that which he has given. So the enjoyment of God for his gifts is returned to God in thanksgiving. God's design is that humans consciously receive his goodness, and it leads to thanks, worship, love, and the emulation of God by sharing his gifts with others. Christians would therefore expect that gratitude would be good for the soul, a hypothesis strongly confirmed (Emmons & McCullough, 2004). It is basic to the life of the *imago Dei*.

Self-love *as designed* is closely tied to gratitude. Contrary to what simple theocentrism might conclude, self-love also is basic to the *imago Dei*, closely related to self-confidence and healthy pride in one's accomplishments. As we have seen, God loves himself supremely. Human self-love, then, is supposed to be the inverse, creational image of the divine self-love: we too love God supremely and ourselves in dependent relation to him, proportionate to our respective worth and corresponding to his love for us (see Edwards, 1852/1969).[22] Sin, of course, corrupted this natural self-love (see 1 Tim 4:3; O'Donovan, 1980), for without God at our psychological center, the self-love motive becomes gravely disordered. Unregulated by gratitude, it takes over the soul and changes into narcissism. On the other hand, in some, created self-love can become thoroughly repressed, perhaps because of the severe criticism of early caregivers, leading children to hate themselves, in some cases even to death. Nevertheless, created self-love cannot be destroyed, so that even when repressed, it may still shine through in a distorted way, for example, in defensiveness, hostility when treated unfairly, or overeating. Consequently, self-love now requires careful, ongoing self-examination, and in Christ it can be increasingly restored to God's original design. Indeed, a properly ordered self-love draws the self to God (Charry, 2010). As Augustine understood, "This indeed is how we love ourselves, by loving God" (O'Donovan, 1980, p. 37), which is reflected in Bernard of Clairvaux's (1987) final stage of spiritual development: the love of self for God's sake. Gratitude and self-love, therefore, are both intrinsic to the *imago Dei* and reciprocally related to each other, connecting together God and one's well-being.

Jesus Christ and the *New* Creation

For all the good that God invested in the creation, it has to be judged so far a failed investment because its pinnacle, the images of God, turned away from their Creator/King—he whom they were to signify in love, worship, obedience, and active receptivity. Yet the all-wise God was not taken by surprise. As Calvin wrote, God designed the creation to be a theater for his glory, but the glory he intended to manifest was far greater than what would have been manifest if the original creation had remained pristine. From eternity the triune God had intended to turn the tragic events of humanity's fall into an even more astounding display of his glory by taking on himself the judgment of sin in the person of the Son (1 Pet 1:20). So, we learn in the New Testament that—lo and behold—all things were created for the Son, who is now called "the firstborn of all creation" (Col 1:15-16). The Father's goal all along was to reconcile to himself all things through the Son (Col 1:20) and to sum up "all things in Christ, things in the heavens and things on the earth" (Eph 1:10). As a result, all the good of the first creation, as good as it is, has to be reinterpreted in light of the new creation, that is, *in Christ*. The glory and honor with which humans are crowned by the Creator God (Ps 8:5) was strangely brought to its proper fulfillment in the suffering of Jesus (Heb 2:8-9) and his resurrection.

So the apostle Paul wrote we are no longer to live for ourselves but for him who died and rose again on our behalf. "From now on we recognize no one according to the flesh. . . . Therefore if anyone is in Christ, he is a new creature; the old things passed away; behold, new things have come" (2 Cor 5:16-17). Based on Paul's teachings, Vos (1952) concluded that in Christ "there has been created a totally new environment, or, more accurately speaking, a totally new world, in which the person spoken of is an inhabitant and participator" (p. 47). Christians live within *both* creations— the old and the new—but by faith they are to revision and transpose everything in the first creation into the higher order of the new creation, including themselves. This eschatological agenda, we could say, is a primary task of Christian therapy.

SOME THERAPEUTIC IMPLICATIONS

Some might suppose there is little point in reflecting on humans solely as created, apart from their fallenness and Christ's redemption, since we now have no access to our primordial perfection. This would be a false conclusion to draw from biblical teaching, however, because God's good creation was not destroyed by sin, even if it was corrupted and damaged. On the contrary, the doctrine of God's good creation provides an essential safeguard against overly pessimistic, stern-minded versions of Christianity— more influenced by sin than its champions are aware—that underestimate the remaining goodness in human nature gone bad. Christian therapists have to practice within a creation/sinfulness dialectic, always looking for the presence of God's created goodness along with evidence of sin's pervasive contamination in those with whom they work, to say nothing of the additional blessings of redemption that Christians may enjoy.

At the same time, the kernel of truth in the stern-minded regarding creation is the fact that sin has thoroughly contaminated its good. Therefore, Christians constantly have to practice revisioning the old creation in light of the new—in effect raising it from the dead by faith.

Loving Images of God

The term *imago Dei* will not often be mentioned in a typical Christian counseling session, but its implications pervade everything we do (see McMinn & Campbell, 2007, as one helpful example of its relevance to therapy). Minimally, meeting with those made in God's image means they are worthy of our love and the greatest respect. It reminds us as well that everyone we meet is made for relationship with God and needs God more than anything else. People who seek counseling may have a range of issues to address, but they all pale in comparison with their relationship with God.

Christian counselors themselves are images of the love of the Trinity as they appreciate and affirm the images of God with whom they work. Encouraging others is a trialogical task: we celebrate God's gifts as we delight in them in others. In a secular culture, God rarely gets the praise he deserves. However, a stern "theocentrism" that would only praise God for goodness in the other—"Praise God for your good job!"—borders on the misanthropic and misses the opportunity to glorify God through the love of neighbor, perhaps out of an excessive fear of promoting pride. (This can be a special problem in authoritarian Christian child rearing.) Knowing every good gift is from above (Jas 1:17), a complex, mature theocentrism can praise God consciously and implicitly while explicitly praising one's neighbor. The affirmation of the other, as a result, comes across as a genuine celebration of the other within the context of the counselor's overall theocentric orientation.

Affirming others is just a part of being a Christian and connecting. Affirming counselees is even more important, because their created self constitutes the ontological "infrastructure" with which the therapy works. Christ-centered therapy makes much use of redemptive resources, especially the benefits of union with Christ, but "redemption suggests the recovery of something given and lost" (O'Donovan, 1986, p. 54). Most people come to counseling with damage to their created natures. Many have been *under-affirmed*, and they don't know how to receive and enjoy God's goodness within them. As a result, they can find it difficult to unlearn present patterns of self-hatred and defensiveness. Christian therapists notice their counselees' created goodness and affirm it to increase it and build on it, in the process promoting (and consolidating) healthy change in their brains, knowledge, memories, thinking, emotions, and relational patterns. Eventually this can lead to the emergence of stronger new selves, based on the synthesis of God's word in creation and redemption that is occurring in their hearts.

No matter how disturbed or sinful counselees may be, there is always something praiseworthy there, more basic than their disturbance or sin. Christian counselors have to become experts in looking beyond the sin and damage to identify and highlight the created and redemptive glory of their counselees—skillfully and sincerely. Otherwise, they will trigger discomfort or cynicism, either way hindering a heartfelt appropriation of the affirmation. Christian counselors are "glory hunters," always on the lookout for evidence of God's goodness. Salvation opens the eyes of believers to see better God's creation glory, and part of Christian counseling is training counselees how to see.

Gratitude as Therapy

"Only as he thanks God does man fulfil his true being" (Barth, 1960a, p. 170). The Psalms teach implicitly that God's design plan for humans includes thankfulness for his goodness (e.g., Ps 103–105), and as we noted above, research on gratitude has documented its psychological benefits (Emmons & McCullough, 2004). Christian therapists can promote growth in gratitude by exemplifying it, relishing counselee successes, periodically focusing on God's goodness in session, and assigning gratitude exercises as homework (e.g., at the end of each day, write down three things you are thankful for today; Emmons, 2007).

Some counselees will find sincere gratitude especially difficult. For example, shame-prone personalities raised in chronically critical families often find it very hard to identify blessings in their life, particularly personal strengths, and thank God for them. Perhaps most difficult is the task of sitting still in one's devotions and *enjoying* them! Time in session can be spent asking counselees to talk about some of the blessings of their lives, perhaps offering suggestions as needed, sometimes playfully, acknowledging the problem of internal resistance. On some occasions, the counselor can walk counselees through a guided imagery exercise in which they picture one or more of their gifts from God and imagine seeing and hearing Christ's expressions of delight in their created goodness. Over time, the affirmations of others like the counselor, experiences of God's approbation of them in Christ through guided imagery and their worship and meditative prayer, and grateful reception of their own created goodness from God may start to reinforce one another enough to begin contributing to a shift in the ratio of positive versus negative evaluations of their life with respect to God, others, themselves, and their future.

Interpreting Created Goodness Mindful of Human Fallenness

At the same time, Christians somehow have to learn how to affirm the primordial goodness of human nature without ignoring its contamination by human sinfulness. There is now a "natural" drift away from the glory of God in human created good toward autonomy, idolatry, and an often-implicit rejection of his authority. Created self-love has turned to self-worship; created diversity often leads to bigotry or envy; we use God's law to boast in ourselves and judge others; by nature we are "lovers of pleasure rather than lovers of God" (2 Tim 3:4).

So humans now are complex beings—created-good sinner-saints—and psychospiritual healing and maturation is reflected in part by a more comprehensive understanding of ourselves and others, including the ability to distinguish carefully our goodness and badness (a skill we will consider in future chapters). Knowing God is always giving us gifts while we still sin can lead believers to love God more and to the practice of ongoing and gradually deepening confession and repentance. We die in Christ while we are being raised in Christ from the dead, sometimes plucking out the good eye or cutting off the good hand when it becomes an obstacle to our journey to God.

Creation as Basic to One's Particular Identity

Well-taught Christians rightly focus much of their attention on the blessings they have received through salvation in Christ. However, the created realities of one's life and personality help to ground one's self-development in ways that Christian therapy should highlight. People's bodies, their strengths and weaknesses, their relationships, and the details of their stories give each person a specific identity that distinguishes them from other people. Humans are not just bearers of species characteristics, but each person is characterized by an incommunicability and a necessary unrepeatability, as we noted above. Every human is utterly unique and has a story that is truly one of a kind.

Similarly, believers are not nameless, faceless bearers of eternal blessings. The concrete, personal, and particular details of their stories and personalities have made them who they are in a fundamental, irreducible sense. The gift of salvation is the same for all, but it is not a generic salvation because it is given by an infinite, tripersonal God to Mary, Tom, Todd, and Joan, and it is realized, in each case, only in the particularity of their lives, in light of their personal story, personality, gifts, accomplishments, and weaknesses, all that makes them who they are. Therefore, a deeper appropriation of one's redemption is dependent on one's acceptance of the uniqueness of one's created particularity. *That* is how salvation works—spreading throughout the details of one's embodied being through the consolidation of one's unique self in Christ. To summarize: Christian soul healing is realized through the deep integration of one's unique createdness with the blessings all Christians share in common in Christ. Counselors can advance this process by assessing the personality traits of their counselees and celebrating the good, created features of their counselees' lives and then helping them tie their redemptive blessings into their individuality, their gifts, their weaknesses, the specific events of their lives (good and bad), and to own it all in union with Christ. At the same time, the blessings of redemption make individual believers more truly themselves as they fulfill better God's general design plan and individual calling for their lives.

I Am Dust

Might there be some soul-care implications from being made from dust? This humbling truth regarding our actual, ontological worth in ourselves, especially when compared with the infinite God, adds a very helpful piece to the puzzle of human self-understanding. "You are just a vapor that appears for a little while and then vanishes away" (Jas 4:14). "Every man at his best is a mere breath" (Ps 39:5).[23] Part of our healing now involves a retrieval of this ancient wisdom that helps us to see through the positive illusions and self-glory of this world and come to terms with our limitations and smallness before God and the universe, so that we can learn to see ourselves more from God's perspective. Such realizations release us from the implicit perfectionistic pressures that often compound our pathology and enable us to reevaluate and reframe the limitations, foibles, and weaknesses that make us who we are. Balthasar called such realizations the "positivity of the finite" (Steck, 2001, p. 52). As Bakhtin argued, "To accept our situation of need is the healthiest way to exist" (Coates, 1998, p. 44).

As a result, Christian therapy also invites people to come to terms with being finite creatures with limitations. Everybody has finite mental capacities and limits on their time and resources, along with their own peculiar weaknesses. Everyone makes mistakes; some people are damaged in various ways—some far more than others—and no one on earth will ever "arrive" at a state of completion. Kierkegaard (1849/1980) believed that humans experience a deep, mostly unconscious despair over these limitations, and that much human suffering is due to the pathological ways people address (or hide from) that despair. He suggested that Christian growth consists in part in facing the despair and *believing*, which he described as learning to accept one's limitations by means of resting in God and God's will for us (p. 82). We might add that this is based on our union with Christ.

Creation Meditation

"On the glorious splendor of Your majesty and on Your wonderful works, I will meditate" (Ps 145:5). In a chapter on creation mention should be made of the therapeutic benefits of meditating on aspects of God's creation. Calvin (1559/1960) offered some sound advice regarding this practice. "The Lord would have us uninterruptedly occupied in this holy meditation; that, while we contemplate in all creatures, as in mirrors, those immense riches of his wisdom, justice, goodness, and power, we should not merely run over them cursorily, and, so to speak, with a fleeting glance; but we should ponder them at length, turn them over in our minds seriously and faithfully, and recollect them repeatedly" (p. 180), and learn to apply this to ourselves, so that our "very hearts are touched" (p. 181). Therapists might sometimes, therefore, assign as homework "creation walks" that involve a leisurely gate and periodic stops where one opens oneself up to the divine glory manifested through the flora, fauna, and scenery.

God's Goodness Toward Us Is Continual

Much of this chapter pertains to creation grace, the divine source of all the physical and psychosocial blessings that counselees enjoy, regardless of their personal relationship with God.[24] As terrible as sin is and as important as it is in understanding human life from a Christian standpoint, there is always some good in every aspect of creation, including every aspect of human life. Even in the worst action of the worst characters, God's creation grace courses through their beings. Those whose parents chronically criticized and mistreated them typically have difficulty seeing the creation grace they are the beneficiaries of, so it bears repeating that one of the greatest blessings a counselor can give is to notice and make subtle mention of it along the journey of therapy. Really all counselors work with creation grace, whether aware of it or not. Research on secular psychotherapy, for example, has identified a number of what are called "common factors," aspects of therapy practice and experience that contribute to the success of the therapy, regardless of one's theoretical orientation, for example, the sense of a working alliance, therapist empathy, and the psychological mindedness of the counselee. Christians recognize that God's creation grace ultimately serves the higher purposes of the new creation: do you not know "that the kindness of God leads you to repentance?" (Rom 2:4). God's desire for everyone's salvation and healing is being continually manifested.

RESOURCES FOR COUNSELORS AND COUNSELEES

Classic

Aquinas, T. (1945). *Basic writings of Saint Thomas Aquinas.* New York: Random House. ‡

Bavinck, H. (2004). *Reformed dogmatics.* Vol. 2: *God and creation* (J. Vriend, Trans.). Grand Rapids, MI: Baker. ‡

Calvin, J. (1960). *Institutes of the Christian Religion.* Philadelphia: Westminster Press. ‡ (Much of book 1 is focused on creation.)

Kuyper, A. (1998). *Abraham Kuyper: A centennial reader.* Grand Rapids, MI: Eerdmans. ‡

Contemporary

Anderson, H. (2014). *Made for more: An invitation to live in God's image.* Chicago: Moody Press.

Baars, C. W., & Terruwe, A. A. (2002). *Healing the unaffirmed: Recognizing emotional deprivation disorder.* New York: Alba House. ‡

Chase, S. (2011). *Nature as spiritual practice.* Grand Rapids, MI: Eerdmans.

Emmons, R. A. (2013). *Gratitude works! A 21-day program for creating emotional prosperity.* San Francisco: Jossey-Bass. Some will wince at the title, but this is a pop-psych book that implicitly points people to God.

Emmons, R. A., & McCullough, M. E. (Eds.). (2004). *The psychology of gratitude.* New York: Oxford University Press. ‡

Grenz, S. J. (2001). *The social God and the relational self: A trinitarian theology of the imago Dei.* Louisville, KY: Westminster John Knox. ‡

Kelsey, D. H. (2009). *Eccentric existence: A theological anthropology.* Louisville, KY: Westminster John Knox. ‡ Extremely demanding but worth the effort though weak on the atonement.

Leithart, P. J. (2014). *Gratitude: An intellectual history.* Waco, TX: Baylor University Press. ‡

Levering, M. (2008). *Biblical natural law: A theocentric and teleological approach.* New York: Oxford University Press. ‡ There's no book quite like this.

Lopez, A. (2013). *Gift and the unity of being.* Eugene, OR: Cascade. ‡ A wonderful meditation on God's generosity.

McMinn, M. R., & Campbell, C. D. (2007). *Integrative psychotherapy: Towards a comprehensive Christian approach.* Downers Grove, IL: InterVarsity Press. ‡

Mouw, R. J. (2001). *He shines in all that's fair.* Grand Rapids, MI: Eerdmans. ‡

Shaw, L. (1998). *Water my soul: Cultivating the interior life.* Grand Rapids, MI: Zondervan.

Voskamp, A. (2011). *One thousand gifts: A dare to live fully right where you are.* Grand Rapids, MI: Zondervan. A Christian book that encourages gratitude to God.

Webster, J. (2016). The dignity of creatures. In *God without measure: Working papers in Christian theology.* Vol. 2: *Virtue and intellect* (pp. 29-48). London: Bloomsbury T&T Clark. ‡

‡ Recommended more for counselors

PART III

The Divine
Diagnosis

PSYCHOPATHOLOGY LITERALLY MEANS "soul disorder." Through the Bible's narratives and teachings, God reveals that humans have become disordered ethically and spiritually, a relational malady called sin. Theologians have further distinguished between an endogenous condition termed "original sin," common to all humans; sinful desires; sinful actions (or sins); and vices or habitual patterns of sinful actions. Contemporary psychiatry and psychology have developed a sophisticated diagnostic system for the identification of another class of soul disorders: syndromes characterized by a set of symptoms and usually various kinds of biopsychosocial damage. That system, however, is currently based exclusively on naturalistic worldview assumptions, so it leaves out ethical and spiritual considerations. Finally, while not a disorder per se, suffering can contribute to the development of a disorder—especially when experienced chronically in childhood together with some genetic vulnerability—and suffering is often a symptom of disorder.

God's understanding of psychopathology includes all relevant knowledge. These three perspectives together provide a more complex and comprehensive approach to psychopathology than any one by itself. The challenge for the Christian community is to develop a unified framework of discourse and diagnosis based on Christian worldview assumptions that recognizes the unique features of biopsychosocial and ethicospiritual disorders and suffering and seeks to understand how they interact in human life. What follows is one attempt at such a framework, in light of the knowledge currently available.

—8—

Sin and Psychopathology

Principle 3: Psychopathology is most compre- | **Expansion 1:** Biblical revelation focuses primarily
hensively understood from three perspectives: sin, | on sin because it is psychopathology fundamentally
suffering, and biopsychosocial damage. | contrary to God's glory and human well-being.

But from the tree of the knowledge of good and evil you shall not
eat, for in the day that you eat from it you will surely die.

GENESIS 2:17

God knows that in the day you eat from it your eyes will be
opened, and you will be like God, knowing good and evil.

GENESIS 3:5

The hearts of the sons of men are full of evil and insanity
is in their hearts throughout their lives.

ECCLESIASTES 9:3

To SUMMARIZE OUR CONSIDERATIONS thus far: God is good and made
us good in order to share in the Trinity's glory, agency, and communion,
loving him supremely and each other as ourselves, joyfully and gratefully.
The *telos* of our design is to be like God's Son, realized through a developmental journey made possible by God's Spirit.

However, that goal was rendered immeasurably more difficult than it might have been by human sin, suffering, and biopsychosocial damage. Each of these problems constitutes a major obstacle to the realization of God's doxological agenda through our participation. Sin is a mysterious dynamic within that predisposes us to oppose God and subvert his glory; suffering creates an inner conflict between our created desire for self-preservation and our calling to glorify God (Job 1:11); and physical and psychological damage compromises human functioning and so can affect our ability to glorify him. Humans, therefore, have three serious impediments to the ends for which they were created, and therefore three interrelated conditions of human psychopathology. As a result, in spite of God's goodness and ours, derived from his, there is a profoundly tragic dimension to human life (Schafer, 1975, p. 35). What might have been a pleasant holiday journey into adulthood with God (in a perfect, temporal creation) has become an epic drama of ultimate significance and, for some more than others, arduous and agonizing.

Pathology is the medical subspecialty that studies disorders of the body, especially diseases. Psychopathology, then, is the study of the disorders of the soul (*psyche*) or, more commonly today, *mental* disorders. Christians have only recently begun to develop biblically and scientifically informed models of psychopathology (for state of the art, see Coe & Hall, 2010; Flanagan & Hall, 2014; Yarhouse, Butman, & McRay, 2005), so four chapters will be used to survey the relevant literature. We begin with a chapter on sin, since so much of the Bible is focused on it.

THE HUMAN STAIN

According to international surveys, most people in the world report a positive sense of subjective well-being (Deiner, 2000). At the same time, there is plenty of evidence that human beings sense deep down that there's something wrong with them. To begin with, indigenous religions around the world universally recognize a state of contamination that humans can contract after violating a cosmic norm, a belief anthropologists have called a *taboo*. Usually one becomes contaminated by physical contact with something associated with badness, such as something dead, or by breaking a social norm, as with incest. If the impurity is not removed, the "cosmic order" will bring about "disastrous results" (Young, 1995, p. 44), indicating minimally a sense of an innate susceptibility to transcendent contamination and blameworthiness.

The world's major religions generally have a more sophisticated understanding of the awareness that "something is wrong," and they typically address it through a more elaborate and systematic set of procedures, using various "cleansing rites"—perhaps washing rituals; sacrifices of rice, flowers, or animals; or prayers—which are necessary to "purify" the worshipers and placate the gods. Why do humans from different cultures around the world experience themselves, at least at times, as unclean and desecrated and therefore needing cleansing? After reviewing the classical evidence of this in the West, Ricoeur suggested that it "points toward a quasi-moral unworthiness" (Ricoeur, 1967, p. 35), reflecting a primordial sense of ontological shame and guilt.

The cultic religion revealed by God through Moses (found in the Torah, the first five books of the Old Testament) assumed this sense of defilement, and seems intended to make it more salient and to shape and refine it in its stories and rules, especially in the detailed rituals of the Levitical sacrificial system (Vos, 1948). God was teaching the Jews that humans really *are* unclean before God; the corresponding negative emotions are not mere subjective feelings but, at their root, are valid signs that something is objectively wrong with us, ethically and spiritually, indicating that God himself is offended. The Torah teaches, further, that humans cannot have a positive relationship with their Creator apart from a system of restoration that he has initiated, involving the bloody death of an animal substitute in which the objective shame and guilt is transferred from the shameful/guilty one (or people) to a sacrificial animal (sometimes signified by laying hands on it), which was then either killed and burned or sent away, symbolizing the divinely sanctioned destruction or carrying away of "the badness" (cf. Lev 16:15-22; 17:11; Dempster, 2003; Vos, 1949). Christians realized that these cultic practices were a divine preparation for a much more radical and personal therapeutic intervention: the sacrificial death of God's Son. "Behold, the Lamb of God who takes away the sin of the world" (Jn 1:29; see 1 Pet 1:18-19).

THE MODERN "ABSENCE" OF DEFILEMENT

Of course, things are more complicated in our post-Christian, increasingly secular culture. As we have seen, absent a sacred Creator who is the source of a transcendent moral order, the self has become the implicit, religious center of a majority our culture. So, depending on the particular version of naturalism assumed, humans are believed to be either morally neutral or innately good—in either case, without evil or alienation from God[1]—and this has led, in turn, to the relative absence of a conscious awareness of a sense of defilement. Most Western intellectuals, therefore, understand shame and guilt feelings to be the result of ancient evolutionary dynamics and contemporary socialization, and therefore they have no ontological truth value other than promoting healthy social relations.

At the same time, in spite of decades of promoting an autocentric orientation in schools and media, a significant number of Westerners remain haunted by a sense of "badness." Millions are diagnosed with clinical depression (which usually includes feelings of shame and guilt) or anxiety (which often includes a foreboding that something bad will happen to them). Some people have disorders that would seem to symbolize self-punishment, most obviously cutting but also eating disorders and aspects of some personality disorders. Some think OCD may be related to "a perceived violation of moral standards, guilt, and inflated responsibility" (Doron, Sar-El, Mikulincer, & Kyrios, 2012, p. 293). Substance abuse can reduce shame and guilt feelings, whereas aggressive behavior, violence, prejudice, and even an undue interest in the failings of others may indicate the projection of repressed feelings of shame and guilt.

Yet such individuals are admittedly exceptional, and the extent of their sense of badness is often due, at least in part, to high levels of shame they internalized in their families of origin. More universal is the automatic reaction of even relatively healthy people to valid criticism, perhaps more subtly indicating the repressed remnants of a primordial, unresolved shame and signifying simultaneously the inner conflict between a sense of original goodness and the shame of alienation from one's Creator, lying on the boundaries of human awareness. One also wonders about the underlying significance of our culture's interest in evildoers who are different from us: "monsters" such as pedophiles, serial killers, and mothers who murder their children. Even so, much like its scientific eradication of many diseases, modern culture has done a fairly effective job of undermining and minimizing conscious experience of shame and guilt.

The Implicit Religious Agenda of Modern Psychiatry and Psychology

Modern psychiatry and psychology have played a critical role in this reduction by radically reconceptualizing what is wrong with human beings. In the premodern West, the soul's worst problems were understood to be ethical and spiritual. However, the replacement of theism with naturalism as the worldview underlying the care of souls in the West necessitated that psychic problems be understood solely in terms of natural dynamics (i.e., biological and psychosocial). Consequently, as a secular version of psycho-pathology developed, its practitioners very consciously restricted themselves to the observation of natural events and processes and observable symptoms, voided of their ethicospiritual significance. Relevant ethical terms—such as *envy, hatred, bitterness, adultery,* and *pride*—were studiously avoided. Similarly, the religious and spiritual significance and remediation of shame and guilt, as well as self-hatred, loneliness, meaninglessness, and unforgiveness, were rarely considered—except their influence on psycho-pathology (though thankfully that has changed remarkably in recent years). As a result, the sense of defilement manifest in shame and guilt came to be considered as either the tragic legacy of maladaptive upbringing or the socially adaptive effects of evolutionary selection. Consequently, secular treatment for these negative self-conscious emotions, when needed, is usually medication or talk therapy, in which counselees are encouraged to reinterpret their shame and guilt feelings as merely subjective experiences that are either basically false (Rogers, 1961) or, better, useful guides in one's social relations (Dearing & Tangney, 2011; Harter, 2012), but in neither case do they bear transcendent ethical or spiritual meaning.

TOWARD A MORE COMPREHENSIVE PSYCHOPATHOLOGY

Nonetheless, the way forward for Christians in psychopathology is quite complex. The church and its universities ought to avail themselves of the wealth of knowledge obtained by modern psychiatry and psychology through the deliverances of creation grace; their diagnostic systems alone are an enormous advance on the extremely limited understanding of psychological disorders in the premodern era. This will involve learning how to translate their contributions into a Christian model of psychopathology, in conjunction with a retrieval and rearticulation of relevant Christian resources. Such a synthetic task, while fraught with many challenges, will provide the most holistic, comprehensive psychopathology possible, one that takes seriously abnormality at the biological, psychosocial, ethical, and spiritual levels (see Johnson, 2007, chap. 15).

Driven by the emphases of Scripture, the church's great strength historically has been its understanding of the latter two levels of dysfunction, and given Christian values, they are ultimately more important. "The Christian faith goes mainly to establish these two facts: the corruption of [human] nature, and redemption by Jesus Christ" (Pascal, 1680/1941, p. 69). The key to a Christian psychopathology is the fundamental recontextualization and revisioning of all psychological problems with reference to Christ (O'Donovan, 1986). In that process, psychopathology gets redeemed—both the disorders and the subdiscipline.

Our goal, then, in the limited space we have, will be to understand psychopathology as Christianly and as comprehensively as possible, constructed from the relevant texts of God's revelation in Scripture, the Christian traditions, and contemporary psychology and psychiatry. And now on to a consideration of sin.

CHRISTIAN TEACHING REGARDING SIN

We noted in the previous chapter that all created things are expressions of God's word (Gen 1; Ps 148; Jn 1:1). As a result, they are embedded with meaning and goodness (Gen 1:31), that is, with *glory*. By contrast, God did not speak human sin into existence. It had other origins, beginning with the serpent's word, and was implemented by humans. Consequently, though bounded by God's word, sin is not a part of God's creation. It is not a genuine ontological thing like God or anything created by God, but is more like a relational and personal deviancy that has no God-given reason for its existence. Struggling to do justice to its baffling presence within the created order, Christians have referred to sin as a "privation of being," a "wound," or a "nothingness" (Barth, 1960b), which nonetheless destroys (Bavinck, 2006); a perverse riddle at the heart of human life; a contradiction to God and his creation; an inexplicable human parasite (see Plantinga, 1995, chap. 5) that feeds on human nature but is not intrinsic to it (Barth, 1956b, p. 187; Bavinck, 2006; Berkouwer, 1971). Its essence is meaninglessness, and it works as an antiglory acid, in some measure dissolving the created order and spreading chaos, destruction, and damage. Nevertheless, we can talk about sin—God's Word in Scripture does—and talking about it can help us identify and label it, describe it, and resist it, even if sin itself makes no sense.[2]

Sin as the Ultimate Relational Disorder

The greatest deviation of sin pertains to humanity's relation to its Creator. I noted in *Foundations* that humans are fundamentally relational beings, existing in relationship with God, other humans, themselves, and the rest of creation. Most people tend to think of sin only moralistically—as the bad things humans do—but this is far too superficial. As both Calvin (1559/1960) and Kierkegaard (1849/1980) recognized, sin only exists *in relation to God.* "As it was the spiritual life of Adam to remain united and bound to his Maker, so estrangement from him was the death of his soul" (Calvin, 1559/1960, p. 246). Sin is best understood as fundamentally a relational problem, pertaining primarily to *my* ultimate relationship with the one who made me.

This theme is found throughout Scripture. The first temptation encouraged Eve to distrust God and his motives and to consider his agenda to be antagonistic to her own (Gen 3:3-4). The first sin was an act of disobedience to the Creator's express command (Gen 2:16-17; 3:6), and after sinning, Adam and Eve hid from God in the garden (Gen 3:8). The apostle John later defined sin as *lawlessness* (*anomia*; 1 Jn 3:4), conveying our Author's rightful authority over us, our primordial obligation to live for him, and sin as the disavowal of that relationship (Vanhoozer, 2010).[3] "Sin is man's act of defiance" (Barth, 1956b, p. 143). Though rarely consciously, sin mocks God and his sovereignty; it seeks "to ungod God, and is by some of the ancients called *Deicidium*, God-murder or God-killing" (Venning, 1669/1965, p. 30). The Bible astoundingly declares that human creatures now are "haters of God" (Rom 1:30), and the human mind now is "hostile toward God" (Rom 8:7), an antagonistic dynamic illustrated most tragically in the murder of the Son of God.

How can all this be true when we humans, by and large, are quite religious and generally concerned to do the right thing? The Bible is a disturbing book, particularly because of its divinely revealed psychodynamic interpretation of humanity. Though created for God and good—which helps explain why most humans are consciously committed to both—we learn from the Bible that we are now *unconsciously* hostile to God and repress that knowledge (Rom 1:18). The Bible, therefore, is part of God's talk therapy for treating my psychopathology. It offers an interpretation of humanity that gives me insight into my unconscious religious dynamics, which resonates with my sense of defilement—though it contradicts my conscious self-understanding—saying to me: "You are not all you think you are. Your basically all-good self-appraisal is a distortion. You are actually, at the core, fallen from your primordial goodness in relation to God, and your 'remaining goodness' is in deep conflict with dark, destructive motives of which you are hardly aware." The Bible reveals to me that I am a divided self, in fundamental conflict with God and others, and calls me to greater self-awareness.

At its deepest level, this conflict is *rebellion* against our Creator (1 Tim 1:13; Adams, 1999, p. 103), a mostly unconscious rejection of God's lordship over our lives and of his word, law, and will for us, including, in some cases, his providential ordering of our story. But this is the level of which most humans are least aware. (Only Satan, Kierkegaard [1849/1980] thought, is fully aware of his rebellion.) Closer to everyday consciousness is the experience of *resistance* to God, evident in the lukewarmness and lethargy we often feel in our religious activities, our subliminal desire for distractions, and the sins we commit, all of which, again, we are just barely aware. At the most superficial level, this opposition to God, self, and others is paradoxically manifested in conscious overidentification with God. Here, we might say, sin cloaks itself under the guise of one's religiosity, where one is consciously "on God's side" and opposed to sin. Yet this reaction formation is the most dangerous side of our opposition, supremely displayed in the murder of Christ in the name of God and righteousness.[4]

Stump (2012) calls sin "willed loneliness," for it leads us to reject our greatest good: our loving God. Avoiding his presence results in transcendent loneliness, shame, and anxiety. Created for the most profound attachment relationship with God, humans are now radically alone in the universe—this is not human life as God designed. As a result, some fundamental forms of psychopathology characterize all humans in some degree—shame, guilt, defenses, anxiety, internal conflict, idolatry, envy, and an inability to love well—all of which, from a Christian standpoint, stem from the ultimate disorder of sin.

God's response to sin. So far we have been focusing on the human side of our broken relationship with God, but we must also consider his response (Vanhoozer, 2010). Because he is righteous, he is absolutely opposed to sin, an opposition reflected in judgment on agents of sin. This is evident in God's breaking fellowship with Adam and Eve and their exclusion from Eden immediately after they sinned (Gen 3:8). From then on, throughout the Bible, God is portrayed as the righteous opponent of sin and the judge of sinners, even as he seeks their repentance and restoration.

We discussed God's righteousness and opposition to sin in chapter six, so there is no need repeat all that here. A few points, however, bear underscoring. Since God is of infinite glory and value, sin against him is of infinite import. Sin is an affront to his holiness, power, and love. So God must be perfectly opposed to sin and his justice requires that he punish it, one way or another; otherwise he would be complicit. So the biblical portrayal of God's emotion of anger against sin simply signifies his holy, resolute response to its fundamental incompatibility with his nature. In addition, sin is self-destructive and contrary to our well-being, so his vehement opposition to it is correlated to his love for us. God "is hostile toward the corruption of his work rather than toward the work itself" (Calvin, 1559/1960, p. 254). Therefore, in a theocentric universe, it makes sense to consider sin the worst kind of psychopathology there is, because as bad as the other forms are, sin is the only kind that separates us from our greatest good.

The role of Satan in human sin. Sin is a puzzle; another puzzle is the presence of a tempter and trickster in the biblical account of the fall, fundamentally antagonistic to God, in an otherwise good creation. There we read of a speaking, personal agent (later called Satan and the devil) whose goal seems to be to thwart God's design plan for humanity and its flourishing, and who won a kind of victory in humanity's sin.[5] As a result, he became, in some way, "the ruler of this world" (Jn 12:31; also 2 Cor 4:4; Eph 2:2), so he was apparently given some authority over human beings with power to influence for evil: he blinds their minds (2 Cor 4:4), and he is somehow involved with the biopsychosocial havoc and tragedy of this world (Job; Eph 2:2), most terribly in demonic oppression and possession (Mk 5:1-20). Even the powers and principalities of the created order appear to be under his sway (Eph 6:12), so that the whole world now lies within his power (1 Jn 5:19), including cultural institutions such as governments, economies, churches, and psychological associations. Satan's role in human affairs creates for Christians a legitimate external attributional explanation for evil. If the devil doesn't *make* us do it, he somehow at least aids and abets us when we sin. Nevertheless, in Genesis 3 we learn that the woman's seed will crush the serpent's head, and in the New Testament, we find out that that is a prophecy about Christ, who slays "the dragon" at the cross (Rev 12; Heb 2:14). As a result, the days of Satan's "reign" are numbered, and an important theme of the theodrama is the enlisting of humans through faith in Christ to participate in the final realization of his victory over Satan's tyranny and collaborate with him in the restoration of God's comprehensive reign over human affairs (Boyd, 1997). Given the ultimate folly of Satan's agenda, signified by his conscious opposition to his sovereign Creator, we might consider Satan to be absolutely insane.

The deception of autocentric discourse. In the garden the serpent offered a perverse interpretation of God's one prohibition, suggesting that God was hiding something from them because of his own insecurities and therefore he could not be trusted as the source of their well-being: "God knows that in the day you eat from [the tree of the knowledge of good and evil] your eyes will be opened, and you will be like God, knowing good and evil" (Gen

3:5). To paraphrase: "God is not interested in your well-being. To obtain your *true* good, do not trust him or his word, and live autonomously."

Satan argued that God's well-being and ours constitute a zero-sum game, so that God's interests are ultimately opposed to ours. But this line of reasoning assumes that God's happiness has limits. We find out much later, in Christ's temptation, that Satan's agenda was rooted in his own autocentrism: he wants to be worshiped himself (Mt 4:9) and therefore wants to remold humans into his own image. Sin is necessarily religious; it is essentially self-worship, and it promises a better happiness than loving receptivity with God. Satan, then, is the paradigm of self-determination and self-actualization, and sin is an autonomous kind of personal agency and individuation, "freed" from dependence on God. As Eve (and Adam) listened, Satan's rationale for autonomy from God became plausible, and afterward, it became a pervasive, unconscious dynamic that influences all human action, including the religions and therapies of the world (and Christians are not immune).

Recognizing the discursive means of Satan's influence on humanity helps us understand the ultimate role that other religions and therapies play in the cosmic conflict between God and Satan. The devil initiated a "new hermeneutic," an anti-Logos,[6] a fallen system of discourse that articulates human autonomy and self-sufficiency and so makes plausible the possibility of humans "living for themselves," apart from conscious dependence on their Maker and his authoritative understanding of human life and his design plan for their flourishing.[7]

The spread and breadth of self-deception: defenses and dissociation. A Christian framework locates the fundamental origin of psychopathology in the falsehood of our alienation from our true Good and everything else in relation to him. Jesus called the devil the "father of lies" (Jn 8:44), and "lies bring to speech thoughts that fail to correspond to anything in the world" (Vanhoozer, 2010, p. 343). Satan's allegation of God's untrustworthiness should be interpreted as the beginning of all human falsehood, including that which runs like a thread through so much human psychopathology, from conscious deception, to overgeneralizations, catastrophization, false core beliefs, false selves, body dysmorphia, gender dysphoria, same-sex attraction, false shame and guilt, defenses and defensiveness, dissociation, the misinterpretations and misrepresentations of others, and the hallucinations and delusions of psychosis.[8] Satan has indeed blinded our minds (2 Cor 4:4), a blindness that mitigates human responsibility—we do not sin consciously like Satan—but does not absolve normal adults of blameworthiness. We still need forgiveness: "Father, forgive them, for they know not what they do" (Lk 23:34 ESV) (Johnson & Burroughs, 2000).

Falsehood is parasitic on the truth. Bakhtin said fallen humans are "pretenders" or "imposters" (Coates, 1998, p. 30); today we might say "posers." To the degree I resist my Maker's meaning, I'm tempted to fabricate my own, though always based on some partial truth and goodness, just "elaborated," pretending to be a bit better than I am and obscuring my limitations and sin. "My false and private self is the one who wants to exist outside the reach of God's will and God's love—outside of reality and outside of life. . . . A life devoted to the cult of this shadow is what is called a life of sin" (Merton, 1961b, p. 34). Kierkegaard (1849/1980) called the evasion of who we really are our "sickness unto death." Sin's power lies precisely in its deception and dissociation, for it hides in the noblest of causes (Baumeister, 1997).

Temptation from the creation. The presence of a tempter in an otherwise good garden might be a surprise, but it indicates first, that temptation would seem to be a fundamental feature of human life in this creation, and second, that being tempted is not itself sinful. Temptation creates a dramatically charged, character-forming fork in the road, requiring action leading to the development either of good character (like Christ) or of evil (e.g., King Saul). By labeling something temptation we highlight its potential to lead us to sin.

Also noteworthy is the fact that it is one of God's creatures—the serpent—that voices the temptation. This points to what is now a commonplace truth: God's, and our, enemy uses God's good creation to separate us from our Creator and the union of our wills. Much of our sinfulness reflects this pattern—envy of others, pride in one's gifts, bitterness from a thwarted desire to get married.

Sin and Human Relationships

One reason the Bible has been so esteemed over the centuries is its profound psychological insight. Significantly, the early chapters of Genesis draw a direct line between the disruption in our relation with God and the enmity that exists between humans. After disobeying God together, Adam and Eve were ashamed together and covered and hid themselves together (Gen 3:7-8). Then Adam blamed Eve for his transgression, even as he blamed God, who gave her to him (Gen 3:12). Collaborative hiding and human scapegoating were the immediate psychodynamic consequences of sin against God (Girard, 1996).

In Genesis 4 we find that human alienation from God has led to the emergence in the human heart of internal conflicts that resulted in a disastrous social conflict issuing in murder. Abel was favored by God,[9] which would not be threatening to a God-centered brother, but Cain became envious and bitter, the first example of narcissistic rage. Sin was "crouching at the door," God told him, "and its desire is for you" (Gen 4:7—a stunning early personification of sin), and in due time, it won him over, so that he got rid of his "competitor." We learn here that "sin is social: although it is first and foremost defiance of God, there is no sin that does not touch the lives of others" (Carson, 2008a, p. 48). Sin also unconsciously "constricts and restricts human beings from the abundance and plenitude of being-in-relation which is proper to them; [it] dissipates, blocks, disorients or counters the dynamics of genuine and full mutuality" (McFadyen, 2000, chap. 8).

Ethical evil flows from spiritual sin (Johnson, 2007, chap. 15). This is because without God's supremacy and love, humans look to the closest analogue—human relationships—to fill the void that mere creatures cannot fill. Nevertheless, whether with narcissistic tyranny (pride) or codependent conformity (sloth), we manipulate others in a doomed attempt to repair our transcendent loneliness (McFadyen, 2000). As a result, Pascal (1680/1941), that early Christian psychodynamic theorist, concluded darkly that "all men naturally hate one another. They employ lust as far as possible in the service of the public weal. But this is only a [pretence] and a false image of love; for at bottom it is only hate" (p. 150). This primordial opposition can come in many forms: Cain hated his brother because he was preferred; the Pharisees hated their brothers because they were sinners. Neither was their brother's keeper.

Sin and the Self

The third consequence of the relational disorder of sin is death, the reflexive destruction and alienation of oneself. God told Adam that disobedience would lead to death, but the death of which he spoke was first and foremost psychospiritual, that is, becoming a self-without-God (Eph 2:1, 12), severed from communion with the living, life-giving God. The subsequent physical death was simply the symbolic fulfillment of the vastly more significant spiritual death. This death established a fallen personality structure and self-understanding in which created self-love, unregulated by the uncreated love of God, becomes narcissistic to the point of self-descruction, and our gifts, strengths, and blessings are unconsciously "stolen" from God, being misattributed as originating (mostly) from our autonomous self.[10] We are all like squatters, living in flats and wearing clothes that belong to someone else. "Radically and basically all sin is simply ingratitude" (Barth, 1956b, p. 41).

Sin as the inversion of the imago Dei. We saw in previous chapters that the core of the *imago Dei* construct is a loving receptivity of God that comes to resemble the character of the triune God, as seen in Christ, who lived a fully receptive life in dependence on his Father (Jn 5:19) and the Holy Spirit (Mt 4:1; 12:28). Sin radically inverts human image bearing. It makes humans resemble God (which Satan suggested, Gen 3:5), but in ways inappropriate for a creature—for example, loving oneself supremely as God loves himself supremely. "The man who has become like God has forgotten how he was at his origin and has made himself his own creator and judge" (Bonhoeffer, 1955, p. 18). No longer centered on God, the human self is now curved in on itself (Bayer, 2008). "In becoming like God, he has become a god against God" (Bonhoeffer, 1955, p. 19).

God's images, then, have become active inversions of themselves (Anderson, 1982), shallow imitations (Mouw, 1990), poser gods, autonomous in the heart, in contrast to the rest of the creation, which obeys God's word automatically. Through an all-new kind of quasi-autonomous "freedom,"[11] humans willingly give sin its deceptive "being," so we could say that sin is the only human creation not based in God's enabling word. Sin, instead, is ultimately a "self-construction" (*selbstherstellung*, Halder, 2004) that results, ironically, in "voluntary servitude" to things other than God (Calvin, 1559/1960, p. 296).

Contrary to all human goodness, sin warrants an absolutely novel, internal causal attribution. "I alone have done it," underscoring why God holds adults ultimately responsible for their sin (while taking into account all extenuating circumstances), and why the best confessions involve blaming no one else, with no excuses. At the same time, God mysteriously remains sovereign over his sinful images. Sin itself "is not an autonomous reality. As the No which opposes the divine Yes, it is only a reality related to and contradicting that Yes . . . and the gracious will and act of God in Jesus Christ are superior to it and overcome it" (Barth, 1956b, p. 144). The sovereign God is able to regulate this quasi-independence, undermine it through grace, or if it persists in unrepentance, finally, judge it and punish those responsible for it.

Sin as internal fragmentation. Fallenness entails the loss of the center for which we were created, and the search for another. Without that center, humans are characterized by internal conflict and a lack of internal unity. In the previous chapter, we noted that created, unfallen humans would have natural internal conflicts stemming from having multiple desires, but they would naturally be resolved in their subordination to a supreme love for God. Without the self-regulatory unification provided by union with Christ and communion with God, human desires are disordered and in conflict, with weaker desires simply being subordinated to the stronger, shaped solely by self-interest and creaturely dynamics (nature, nurture, affordances, and free will), the conflicts themselves exacerbated by biological abnormalities, poor socialization, and bad choices.

According to Stump (2012; and Aquinas), sin is "a latent disease of the will" (p. 155) that is characterized by "double-mindedness" and "inner fragmentation" (p. 152),[12] and results in persons being divided against themselves. "An agent who is divided against herself will not be doing what *she* wants to do no matter what side of her divided self she acts on. That is because, when an internally divided agent acts in accordance with some desire of her divided will, the other part of her divided self will not want to do *that*" (p. 132). "Her lack of internal integration is just her unwillingness to unify herself in will. She is not internally integrated in will because she does not *want* to be" (p. 158). Being rooted in our wills, sin can only be undermined by intentional resistance to its dynamics (Owen, 1965, Vol. 6), as the will becomes unified *in Christ* by grace.

For many of us, the fragmentation is most evident in the dissociation between conscious awareness (one's "head") and one's underlying, unconscious motives (one's "heart"). Some non-Christian psychologists have studied aspects of this unconscious conflict fairly well from a secular standpoint (e.g., Freud, Horney, and object relations theorists), but they miss its fundamentally religious origin.

Sin as the knowledge of good and evil. Self-deception and internal fragmentation both contribute to the primary fruit of sin, according to Genesis 2–3: the knowledge of good and evil (Gen 2:17). Prior to the fall, we can surmise, humans had purity of heart and knew and willed only one thing— God's good will (Bonhoeffer, 1955; Kierkegaard, 1847/1938). One might have supposed that sinning would lead to the knowledge merely of evil. However, afterward, humans came to know and will two things—good as well as evil— so that, ironically, because of their primordial goodness, sinful humans became double-minded and divided against themselves *ethicospiritually*.

The strong tendency of most fallen humans to maintain their absolute goodness in their self-perception and their self-presentation to others is evidence of sin's tragic infection of our created goodness (utilizing here the law of God within; Rom 2:14-15), which in turn leads to the development of "false selves." As a result, though we actually prefer darkness over light (Jn 3:20), most humans consciously believe the opposite of themselves and tend to project their own darkness onto others.

At its core, the postfall dividedness against oneself is a complex, dissociated defense, in which whole-hearted dependence on God is gone, and one usually unconsciously identifies oneself with the good (and "God") and rejects the evil as other than oneself. This causes the "good side" to take up against "the evil," which, because evil is also within, leads to irresolvable unconscious conflict (which the law, by itself, only exacerbates; Rom 7:7-25). Sin therefore uses human created goodness to obscure its presence. According to this interpretation, human "knowledge of good and evil" is an inverse and negative image from divine, for it consists in the belief in one's autonomous goodness and a corollary denial and externalization of evil, whether conscious or unconscious.

At this point, building on the created distinction between the conscious and unconscious aspects of the soul noted in chapter seven, we should here distinguish between two dimensions of sin: explicit and implicit. Explicit sin is antagonism to God, self, and others that is relatively easily identified, for example, overt disobedience to God's commands. Implicit sin, by contrast, is antagonism masked by created goodness one believes to originate in oneself. Whereas explicit sin differs widely among humans, based on biology, socialization, and choice, implicit sin is common to all human beings in our "autonomous" goodness. The publican typifies one compromised by explicit sin, whereas the Pharisee is guilty of implicit (Lk 18:9-14).

Sin as a destructive wound. As we noted above, sin is a riddle. Not created by God, it has no comprehensible nature like God's creatures do; yet in the Bible sin is referred to as "an active corrupting principle, a dissolving, destructive power" (Bavinck, 2006, p. 137), "a compulsion or constraint which humans generally experience within themselves or in their social context, a compulsion towards attitudes and actions not always of their own willing or approving" (Dunn, 1998, p. 112). Somehow, sin is a power within humans that is contrary to their nature and its powers. At the same time, Augustine likened sin to a wound or a lack of physical wholeness or well-being, a "privation" of created goodness. As an ethicospiritual wound sin is manifested in ceaseless internal conflict and "restlessness" (Augustine, 1942, p. 3).

Sin as the avoidance of God's calling to be oneself. We have seen that all human beings are called by God to realize their own created uniqueness in relation to God. Everyone's existence is utterly novel and therefore utterly momentous, and everyone's story and the configuration of their strengths and weaknesses are utterly unrepeatable. Sin, by contrast, is the denial of one's "obligation-imposing uniqueness" (Bakhtin, quoted by Coates, 1998, p. 29). As a result, sin makes it impossible to accept oneself as one is before God, self, and others (Kierkegaard, 1849/1980).

Summary. Humans were created to be in harmonious relationship with God, others, and themselves. As a relational disorder, sin has three aspects: rebellion against God, enmity with one's neighbor, and sin against oneself (Barth, 1956b, p. 398), and each is characterized by falsehood: idolatry, the misinterpretation and misuse of others, self-deception, defenses, and false selves. Our next task is to examine the different forms sin takes.

Four Aspects of Sin

Original sin. Thus far we have been considering humanity's sinful *condition.* But when most people think about sin, they think of personal sins (sometimes called *actual* sins) or vices. This is natural, because they are the empirical manifestations of our sinful condition. Yet one of the most remarkable truths about sin, revealed with special clarity after Christ's death (Rom 1:18-32; 8:7; Eph 2:1-3; 1 Jn 1:7-10), is that humanity's greatest ethicospiritual problem is what Augustine called *original sin.*[13] The term harks back to the origin of human sinfulness in the primal sin of Adam and Eve and reminds us that in some mysterious way humanity continuously participates in that original sin.[14]

The vast majority of Scripture, admittedly, focuses on *personal sins* (discussed below). However, undergirding this explicit ethical orientation throughout the Bible is the implicit assumption that humanity's evil is due to a pervasive state of fallenness, rather than something occasional and merely volitional. The entire Levitical sacrificial system assumed a universal and chronic sin problem that manifested itself in the personal sins it was established to address. As a result, we find a few key biblical texts—more in the New Testament than in the Old Testament—that refer to a sin *condition,* what above was called implicit sin, which is the *source* of one's personal sins. While confessing his personal sin, David acknowledged the radical nature of his dilemma: "I was brought forth in iniquity, and in sin my mother conceived me" (Ps 51:5). Humanity's greatest problem is a deceitful, wicked heart that is difficult to know (Jer 17:9). Much of Christ's ministry zeroed in on the heart (Mt 15:19), and in their confrontation with Christ, the Pharisees ironically revealed just how radical and universal humanity's sin problem was. Only after Christ's crucifixion, and in light of its implications for human and religious self-deception, could humanity begin to understand how desperate was its predicament. Paul, the former Pharisee, was given the task of outlining in biblical revelation just how bad we are: "dead in your trespasses and sins" (Eph 2:1); "there is none righteous, . . . none who seeks for God" (Rom 3:10-11); he quoted Old Testament criticism of "the wicked" and applied it to all of humankind (Rom 3:13-18); he personified sin as an indwelling force with malevolent intentions (it "deceived me" and "killed me," Rom 7:11; see also Rom 7:8-9, 13, 17, 20), a *law*, principle, or dynamic (*nomos hamartias*; "law of sin," Rom 7:23, 25) that prevents humans now from living for God apart from divine salvation.

As a result, Christian thinkers have concluded that humans are born with an endogenous[15] condition called original sin that is "a wandering course of being, a more radical *mode of being* than any individual act" (Ricoeur, 1974, p. 282, italics in original). Perhaps the greatest work on original sin is Kierkegaard's (1849/1980) *The Sickness unto Death*, where he wrote in the final section that "the state of sin is a worse sin than the particular sins; it is *the* sin" (p. 106, italics mine).[16] Humans are continuously immersed in and motivated by sin, whether or not they *commit* a sin and whether or not they are aware of it.[17] One of Kierkegaard's chief concerns was that we not understand original sin as an abstract doctrine of universal human sinfulness. To know that "humans are sinners" or even that "I am a sinner" is not enough. One recognizes one's "original sinfulness" best as an ongoing corrupting influence currently compromising everything one does—mostly unconsciously—only revealed to consciousness by a transparent faith *before God*. Indeed, true Christianity, he believed, *begins* with this recognition (p. 120) and grows through the dialectic of a deepening realization of our sinful predicament and a deepening reception of who we are as established by God (pp. 14, 82).

We end with an attempt at a comprehensive definition: *original sin is a universal, continuous, mostly unconscious disposition that pervasively inclines humans to mistrust God and resist his glory, supremacy, and love, and so—apart from Christ—humans are at enmity with him, others, and themselves, contrary to their own ultimate well-being and that of others, subverting and corrupting their created goodness, and leading to idolatries of all kinds* (see Bavinck, 2006; Kierkegaard, 1849/1980; McFadyen, 2000; Owen, 1965, Vol. 6).[18]

Sinful desires, attitudes, and determined dispositions. As noted above, those with original sin necessarily experience concomitantly mostly unconscious conditions of shame and guilt, defenses, anxiety, internal conflict, idolatry, envy, and an inability to love well. As a result, they will experience sinful desires as a matter of course. "That which proceeds out of the man, that is what defiles the man. For from within, out of the heart of men, proceed the evil thoughts, fornications, thefts, murders, adulteries, deeds of coveting and wickedness, as well as deceit, sensuality, envy, slander, pride and foolishness. All these evil things proceed from within and defile the man" (Mk 7:20-23). Humans now have motives, desires, and goals that incline them to seek their happiness without God at the center. James argued that "each person is tempted when he is lured and enticed by his own desire [*epithymia*]. Then desire when it has conceived gives birth to sin, and sin when it is fully grown brings forth death" (Jas 1:14-15 ESV),[19] notably distinguishing mere desire from sinful acts.

In the New Testament the *epithymia* word group can be used for good created desires (Lk 15:16; discussed in the previous chapter), as well as godly desires (Phil 1:23), but it generally refers to sinful desires (Büchsel, 1965)— sometimes translated "lusts" in English—that are contrary to the word and will of God. These include sexually immoral desires, whether heterosexual (Mt 5:28) or homosexual (Rom 1:27; Jude 7), as well as covetousness (Col 3:5), envy (Gal 5:26), love of money (1 Tim 6:9-10), laziness (Prov 21:25), and selfishness (1 Cor 13:5; 2 Tim 3:2; Jas 2:8), to name a few—all of which have cognitive as well as affective components. Finally, fallen humans apparently can be born with or develop physiological dispositions toward certain kinds of sinful desires, including alcoholism, aggression, passivity, same-sex attraction, pedophilia, and opposite-sex gender identity without any originating personal intention or effort on their part.

Personal sins. Because mature humans are personal agents made in God's image, they are responsible for their actions. But this noble characteristic distinguishing them from lower animals has tragic consequences for sinful humans. Personal (or actual) sins occur when one adds *consent* to one's sinful desire and so engages in an action (whether internal or behavioral) that at its root is antagonistic to God's glory and violates his law[20] (that is, his design plan for human flourishing), for which one is responsible.

While many sins are easily identified—speech intended to hurt, sexual abuse, genocide—accurately assessing a deed's sinfulness can be complicated, because evil motive is intrinsic to sin's structure. Consequently, entire disciplines have been dedicated to identifying them (casuistry, moral philosophy, jurisprudence). Unconscious opposition to God and his will, narcissistic self-promotion, and a desire to hurt another are defining motives of sins, and helpful distinctions have also been made between sins of commission and omission, as well as behavioral and internal sins (Berkouwer, 1971; Owen, 1965, Vol. 6; Shuster, 2004). Much of Scripture, therefore, is focused on them, to help train humanity in their identification, epitomized by the Ten Commandments and aggregated in lists of sins and vices in the New Testament (see Rom 1:29-31; 1 Cor 6:9-10; Gal 5:19-21; Eph 4:19, 25-31; Col 3:5-9; 2 Tim 3:2-4; Titus 3:3).

Ultimately, however, personal sins are important because they provide a concrete manifestation and measure of our alienation from God. *Personal sins are signs of original sin*, and they unleash its destructiveness in the world. They also indicate the degree of one's dispositional disparity from God's design plan for humanity. Personal sins often have relational consequences: they can hurt others, one way or another, and they are necessarily hurtful to oneself and compromise one's well-being, regardless of their apparent short-term gain. The revelation of biblical law does a great service to humankind, then, by providing a set of propositional criteria that something is wrong with one's soul, as if God has drawn a circle around a class of human actions and said, "Watch out! Avoid these, for they indicate the worst soul disorder there is!" At the same time, the archetype of the Pharisee—who had comparatively few personal sins but nevertheless despised and killed Jesus—reminds us not to overemphasize personal sins nor ignore the self-deception that issues from *everyone's* original sin.

Vices. According to virtue ethicists, vices are bad traits (Adams, 2006) or "corruptive or destructive habits" (DeYoung, 2009, p. 14). A single personal sin is an isolated, relatively free action. The more frequently one commits the same personal sin, however, the more a disposition to commit that action again is laid down in one's brain/soul, a tendency for which one also is responsible (Adams, 2006). As suggested above, many of the lists of sins in the Bible can be considered lists of vices. In fact, the "seven deadly sins" of the Christian tradition (greed, sloth, pride, envy, gluttony, lust, and wrath) are better understood as vices. Because one can keep oneself from committing an isolated personal sin much more easily than one can undermine and change a vicious disposition, and because their ingrained character, in turn, increases the likelihood of future personal sins, vices are more serious ethicospiritual problems. A Christian DSM that includes ethicospiritual disorders as well as biopsychosocial damage will include various kinds of vices.

Summary. For many reasons, Christians are to address their personal sins and vices: they publically compromise God's glory; often harm others; are self-destructive; for they increase increases the influence of original sin, as well as the likelihood of them reoccurring (Owen, 1965, Vol. 6). Nevertheless, original sin is their origin and basis and corrupts all of humanity, including so-called good people, who may commit less frequent and less serious personal sins but who live in self-righteous autonomy and therefore in (usually unconscious) enmity with their Creator. Consequently, *implicit* sin is the more fundamental problem (Owen; Shuster, 2004), and personal sins and vices are best understood as symptoms. Symptoms need treatment, but a wise physician is most interested in treating the disease. Without the doctrine of original sin, we end up with moralism and legalism and a superficial diagnosis of ethico-spiritual pathology. According to Owen, therefore, Christianity's primary treatment goal is to reduce the frequency and duration of sins and the practice of vices *by weakening the power of original sin in the heart through Christ.*

The Embodiment of Sin

When we refer to indwelling sin, we allude to its embodied nature. One of the curious outcomes of Adam and Eve's sin was the awareness that they were naked (Gen 3:7). This suggests that their bodies registered and signified their sin, resulting in a sense of a defilement of their psycho-somatic being, activating an emotion called shame, and centering symbolically in their sexual organs. Perhaps this is intended to teach us that human life has been thoroughly desecrated and that desecration will be passed on generationally.

But there are other linkages made in the Bible between sin and human embodiment. We know that many personal sins involve the body directly, some more than others, and the apostle Paul highlighted this relationship: "Do not let sin reign in your mortal body so that you obey its lusts, and do not go on presenting the members of your body to sin as instruments of unrighteousness" (Rom 6:12-13; see Rom 7:5, 23), and he also referred to the "body [sōma] of sin" (Rom 6:6) and the "body of . . . death" (Rom 7:24).[21] Of special significance is Paul's unusual use of *sarx* (flesh) to refer to human fallenness (Gal 5:16-17, 19-21, 24; Rom 8:3-9; 1 Cor 3:1-3), as well as the connections he made between sin, flesh, death, and the body: "The mind set on the flesh is death" (Rom 8:6); the sinful passions at work in the body "bear fruit for death" (Rom 7:5); and the wages of sin is death (Rom 6:23; see also Rom 5:12; 7:9-10). In light of this teaching, and likely his own experience, Calvin (1559/1960) wrote, "We are besieged by many vices and much weakness so long as we are encumbered with our body" (p. 607).

Controversies have raged for centuries over how to understand the body from a Christian standpoint. Without retracing this history, we need to avoid the error that the body is intrinsically bad, since it too is part of God's good creation. However, Paul's teaching on the embodied nature of sin teaches us that the body now is also fallen and therefore is neither entirely good nor neutral, but rather is spiritually contaminated; its native desires—unregulated by God's centrality—now express sin's opposition to God.

This inspired network of associations may also be alluding to a biological basis for many particular expressions of sin, which contemporary research has well documented. In addition, the embodied shame highlighted in Genesis 3 would seem to suggest that sexuality in particular was affected by the fall. We now know that genetic and physiological abnormalities can lead to disorders such as same-sex attraction, gender dysphoria, and pedophilia; and repeated actions can strengthen these dispositions until they become habituated through reinforced and elaborated neural networks. Naturalists and Christians will differ sharply in their interpretation of some of these conditions, including their moral significance, but both communities can agree that knowing their biological influences should promote compassion and not hatred and rejection.

Human Beings: Paradoxically Good and Evil

Optimal self-awareness for created sinners involves an awareness of one's sin and also one's "remaining created goodness," in spite of remaining sin. We might say that all humans are *simul bona creatura et peccator* (simultaneously good creature and sinner), and both "sides" of the whole truth are necessary to understand human beings properly (dialectically). Humans were created good by God and are still in God's image, so for all of sin's baneful influence, it cannot annul or destroy the primordial goodness that characterizes God's images—both body and soul. Indeed, one's created goodness provides the ontological infrastructure on which sin (and redemption) works. "This twofold nature of man is so evident that some have thought that we had two souls" (Pascal, 1680/1941, p. 132).[22]

Created goodness and remaining sin are "limiting concepts" (Van Til, 1972) that have to be kept together as we work with sinful images of God (such as ourselves). On the one hand, God's grace and glory is present, in some degree, in all images of God, and there is always at least a trace of God's goodness in every human action and experience, no matter how terrible. Stalin was apparently a brilliant dictator. No human is without some of

God's goodness, no matter how much they have sinned. So the doctrine of created goodness should limit how much we emphasize sin in our counseling. Weary counselors will sometimes have to work hard to see the created goodness of their counselees when working day after day with seemingly hopeless marriages, long-term addiction, or rejection due to transference (especially as they are mindful of their own remaining sin).

On the other hand, the doctrine of sin also limits the emphasis we place on people's created goodness; otherwise, we can overestimate it and underestimate sin's effects. Paul's gloomy descriptions of fallen humanity (as in Rom 3:9-18; Eph 2:1-3; Titus 3:3)[23] led the Reformers to formulate the doctrine of *universal, total (or pervasive) depravity*. Humans are not as bad as they could be, but sin's oppositional dynamic thoroughly permeates the good created structures that constitute our individual and relational being: our mind (memories, beliefs, and thinking), our affective system (feelings, desires, and motives), our relational structures, the unconscious, will, and brain (what we might call the notional or cognitive, affective, psychodynamic, relational, volitional, and physiological effects of sin), so that they are now "bent" contrary to their created design, since they are being used for the autonomous purposes of sinners. Paul wrote that all humans have fallen short of the glory of God (Rom 3:23), but this does not mean there is no glory in fallen humans at all, simply that it does not shine as God intended through any part of our being or relationships.

According to Christianity, therefore, sin is the great equalizer among humans (Jacobs, 2009). There is great variety among people regarding their psychological well-being (or lack thereof), and only some are afflicted with serious problems such as schizophrenia and personality disorders. However, according to the Bible, all humans before God "are infected with the disease of sin" (Calvin, 1559/1960, p. 248), the most serious kind of psychopathology there is. This realization therefore relativizes all other forms of psychopathology. As bad as those conditions are, they are not as bad as the sin we all possess, and for which God has provided all with a divine cure.

Learning About Sin from Christ

Which brings us back to Christ. In our study of sin, we have followed the redemptive-historical trajectory of the Bible, examining sin as found in the canon, focusing on the fall narrative in Genesis 3 as well as other places in Scripture where sin is dealt with as a subject in its own right. However, Barth (1956b) cautioned against this traditional approach to sin, insisting that we understand it properly only in relation to Christ and arguing that any other knowledge of sin reinforces human autonomy and the presumption that we are capable of some good apart from Christ (in this case, the knowledge of sin), and this insight is of momentous importance.[24]

"Only when we know Jesus Christ do we really know that man is the man of sin, and what sin is, and what it means for man" (Barth, 1956b, p. 389). So Bromiley (1979) summarizes Barth as teaching that we see sin in the crucified Christ as "deicide, fratricide, and suicide" (p. 185), and how utterly terrible it is—if our redemption necessitated God's judgment of the Son.[25] We see sin with greater clarity in the Gospels than anywhere else in the canon. For example, we learn that the greatest sinners are actually the most religious, those who strove the hardest to obey the law, since they instigated the crucifixion of the perfect God when he came to earth. This is an astounding revelation of sin and a sort of paradoxical upheaval, if not reversal, of traditional ethical approaches to sin. In the story of Christ, in the fullness of time, we learn profound matters regarding religious self-deception, the remarkable depths of our depravity, and humanity's true views of God and the self. Most troubling, we realize there that we are contemporaneous accomplices in his murder, since he died for my sin and my ongoing sin continues to add to his crucifixion.

A christocentric approach to sin is valuable therapeutically because we discover there both the depths of our sin and the depths of our forgiveness, the heart of God toward us, and the ultimate remedy. This christocentric approach to sin brings us face to face with Christ, our Lord and friend and lover who is pursuing us in spite of our sin. What better way to produce healthy shame and guilt, contrition, confession, repentance, and the fearless reception of forgiveness, from glory to glory (2 Cor 3:18). This is something the law and theoretical treatments of sin by themselves cannot do.

As a result, Christianity is the only religion (and therapy) that truly exposes sin's essence. Unfortunately, Christians are still sinners and therefore are only partially cognizant of sin's true nature, but as they are drawn more and more into Christ and his cross, they are enabled to grasp with greater clarity the depth of sin's pervasive destructiveness. "We see Him, and in this mirror we see ourselves, ourselves as those who commit sin and are sinners" (Barth, 1956b, p. 390). A christocentric approach to sin is essential for our healing, for only in Christ can our worst disorder be treated.

SOME THERAPEUTIC IMPLICATIONS

Much later in the book (chaps. 17-19) I will focus in more detail on specific therapy with sin in light of the gospel. So in this chapter I will just reflect on the relevance of Christian teachings about sin to therapy.

Why Is There Sin?

If sin is so terrible, why would a good and loving God allow it in his good creation? Augustine (1947) supposed that God "deemed it better to bring good out of evil than not to permit any evil to exist at all" (p. 35). I will not attempt a fuller answer here, but we remind ourselves that sin presents the greatest obstacle to God's doxological agenda imaginable, creating the absolute height of dramatic tension, and at the same time providing a remarkable opportunity for the display of his glorious graces, as he triumphantly overcomes that which is intrinsically opposite to him. In addition, a fallen human creation permits the manifestation of certain excellences of God's character that would not be displayed in a sinless world (some not at all, some not as fully), for example, his patience, mercy, compassion, humility, love, forbearance (ability to suffer), and so on. Furthermore, the supreme manifestation of God's beauty is shown through the redeeming story of God's human Son, Jesus Christ, who *became* sin for us on the cross (2 Cor 5:21). What does it mean that he became that which is completely antagonistic to himself? We cannot know fully. But if God can deal with something as contrary to his being as sin, then maybe, with his help, I can deal with the sin and baggage in my life, and perhaps so can my counselees.

The Good News of Christian Teaching on Sin

What therapeutic value can there be in focusing attention on the Christian doctrine of sin? It seems counterintuitive, especially because it has so often been used for evil ends and resulted in so much spiritual abuse. Nevertheless, Christian teaching on sin is intended by God to contribute to human flourishing. We recall that Christian wisdom, according to Calvin, consists of knowing God and ourselves, and the latter knowledge requires in part a knowledge of our sin. "Whoever is utterly cast down and overwhelmed by the awareness of his calamity, poverty, nakedness, and disgrace has thus advanced farthest in knowledge of himself" (Calvin, 1559/1960, p. 267).[26] These Christian intuitions have recently been documented empirically. Watson, Morris, Loy, and Hamrick (2007) found that a mature awareness of sin (reflected in taking responsibility for oneself, humility, perfectionism avoidance, and realistic self-assessment) was positively correlated with positive self-esteem, moderately negatively correlated with depression and narcissism, and weakly with anxiety. There are many reasons why this ought not to surprise Christians.

1. If God has designed us to flourish in holiness and love with himself, that which alienates us from him cannot be good for us. Consequently, everything God has revealed to us about sin promotes our well-being. Sin therefore is a label for the opposite of human happiness, well-being, and flourishing. In his teaching about sin, God has identified the worst class of psychological abnormalities and is saying to us, as the ultimate counselor: "As your Creator I know what is most destructive to you and most contrary to your well-being. Trust me, and seek to undermine sin and its ways in your life, according to my treatment program in Christ, and your healing will increase and you will become better."

2. Fighting and undermining sin brings believers closer to God, our greatest good. "There is something in the very greatness of sin that may encourage us to go to God, for the greater our sins are, the greater the glory of his powerful mercy pardoning, and his powerful grace in healing will appear" (Sibbes, 1635/1973, p. 228).

3. Sin relativizes all other kinds of psychopathology, because if God has provided an adequate therapeutic intervention in Christ for our worst soul problem—a clear-cut divine resolution that vastly transcends our sinfulness and limitations and does not ultimately depend on our capacities—believers can be encouraged that all of their lesser forms of psychopathology are less threatening and more manageable.

4. The doctrine of sin promotes self-awareness. Research has shown the value of opening up one's soul and articulating the difficulties one has experienced or is going through, either through journaling or talking (Pennebaker, 1997). Because God is omniscient, he already knows the worst secrets about everyone, and in light of the gospel, Christians know that they will be accepted just as they are; they do not have to be afraid of God regarding that which they are most ashamed, so they can open up to him without fear (as well as to ourselves and to others) (McMinn, 2008). *Confession* is the biblical word for opening up our souls to God about our sins, and healthy confession is healing (1 Jn 1:9). "The possibility of [the sickness of sin] is man's superiority over the animal; to be aware of this sickness is

the Christian's superiority over the natural man; to be cured of this sickness is the Christian's blessedness" (Kierkegaard, 1849/1980, p. 15).

5. By holding adults responsible for their personal sins, Christianity promotes a high view of human beings: they are personal agents and not just biologically and socially determined organisms. Ultimately, this gives them a degree of hope incompatible with determinism (Adams, 1973). In the long run, this emphasis on their personal agency can help believers take more responsibility for their lives as they mature.

6. It follows, then, that by directing the attention of believers to that for which *they* are responsible, they will be less likely to blame others for their problems. Making this turn is especially important in marital counseling.

7. The religious self-deception central to the story of Jesus' murder casts a shadow over all human religiousness and righteousness and promotes the disposition of Christians to question their motives. May I confess here that much of my Christian life has been characterized by this kind of dissociation, so I know this problem very well.

8. Shame and guilt are painful emotions, and chronic shame in particular is deleterious. Since sin is the basis of our objective shame and guilt, and all three were taken away from believers on the cross (Col 2:14), the gospel provides a theocentric way to resolve the corresponding feelings of shame and guilt.

   Secular approaches to shame face an inherent self-undermining problem: people with severe shame feel they are severely deficient and unworthy of good, so why should they care to change the way they think and feel about themselves, since they are so unworthy? Christianity, by contrast, affirms their experience of shame by teaching that everyone is a shameful sinner, but also that everyone made in God's image matters to God, and he has provided a transcendent source of shame resolution in Christ—that comes outside the shameful self and takes away its shame.[27] "Shame can be overcome only when the original unity is restored, when man is once again clothed by God in [Christ]. . . . This is accomplished in confession before God and before other men. Man's being clothed with the forgiveness of God, with the 'new man' that he puts on" (Bonhoeffer, 1955, p. 23).

9. There is a kind of wisdom in grieving over our sinful condition. "The greatness of man is great in that he knows himself to be miserable. A tree

does not know itself to be miserable. It is then being miserable to know oneself to be miserable; but it is also being great to know that one is miserable" (Pascal, 1680/1941, p. 127). People who are depressed are not crazy; they are to some extent aptly but agonizingly captivated by a profound spiritual truth that most of us sinners do not face. Affirming this wisdom in therapy reframes depressive pathology, turning a liability into a strength.

10. Helping people address and overcome their personal sins is extremely valuable because of the turmoil, violence, and distress they cause human beings (think of the harm caused to children by the violence, adultery, or deception of a parent).

11. The Christian doctrine of sin provides a theological perspective on psychopathology left out of all secular approaches to the topic (McFadyen, 2000). Without this transcendent, sacred perspective, one cannot grasp the complexity of any form of psychopathology comprehensively.

12. Unresolved sin causes everlasting judgment in the age to come, so addressing people's sin through the gospel is ultimately the most therapeutic activity imaginable, for its positive effects are not just temporal but everlasting.

For all these reasons, Christian teaching on sin is fundamentally therapeutic.

The Subtle Danger of Spiritual Abuse

There can be a seductive sinfulness present in denouncing and exposing sin, and because of the strong negative emotions of shame and guilt evoked by such activity, a stern, legalistic approach to sin can be extremely damaging (Johnson & Van Vonderen, 2005). Christians responsible for the care of others—pastors and ministers, parents, and counselors—must be careful in how they handle the topic. A harsh, overbearing use of the doctrine of sin in the hands of broken sinners (who have less healing from sin than they imagine) can do terrible harm, promoting false shame and guilt and causing serious soul damage to children in the name of Christ. I know because of the hurt I have caused others, particularly my family, especially in early adulthood when my healing was mostly cognitive rather than carditive. Spiritual abuse is most difficult to combat in churches (and leaders) convinced that their current understanding of Christianity and the Christian life is unsullied by sin (including their teaching against perfectionism!), resulting in little genuine openness to God to increase their self-understanding.

RESOURCES FOR COUNSELORS AND COUNSELEES

Classic

Barth, K. (1956b). *Church dogmatics: 4.1.* (G. W. Bromiley, Trans.). Edinburgh: T&T Clark. ‡

Calvin, J. (1960). *Institutes of the Christian religion.* Philadelphia: Westminster Press. Book 2, chapters 1-4. ‡

Kierkegaard, S. (1980). *A sickness unto death.* (H. V. Hong, Trans.). Princeton, NJ: Princeton University Press. (Original work published 1849) ‡ The most important exposition of the Christian doctrine of sin ever. The church has still not caught up with Kierkegaard on this topic.

Owen, J. (2006). *Overcoming sin and temptation.* Wheaton, IL: Crossway. The definitive treatment of sin from the Puritan era.

Venning, R. (1965). *The plague of plagues.* Edinburgh: Banner of Truth Trust. (Original work published 1669)

Contemporary

Adams, J. (1979). *More than redemption.* Phillipsburg, NJ: Presbyterian & Reformed.

Beck, R. (2011). *Unclean: Meditations on purity, hospitality, and mortality.* Eugene, OR: Wipf & Stock. ‡

Blocher, H. (1997). *Original sin: Illuminating the riddle.* Grand Rapids, MI: Eerdmans. ‡

Coe, J. H. (2010). A transformational approach to psychopathology, sin and the demonic. In J. H. Coe & T. W. Hall (Eds.), *Psychology in the Spirit: Contours of a transformational psychology* (chap. 14). Downers Grove, IL: InterVarsity Press. ‡

DeYoung, R. K. (2009). *Glittering vices: A new look at the seven deadly sins and their remedies.* Grand Rapids, MI: Brazos.

Jacobs, A. (2009). *Original sin: A cultural history.* New York: HarperOne.

Lundgaard, K. (1998). *The enemy within: Straight talk about the power and defeat of sin.* Phillipsburg, NJ: P&R.

Mangis, M. (2008). *Signature sins.* Downers Grove, IL: InterVarsity Press. Written by a therapist and spiritual director.

McFadyen, A. (2000). *Bound in sin: Abuse, holocaust, and the Christian doctrine of sin.* Cambridge: Cambridge University Press. ‡ A profoundly therapeutic theology of sin, which includes a remarkably sophisticated theological analysis of how the sin of abuse wreaks havoc in the souls of children.

McMinn, M. C. (2007). *Grace and sin in Christian counseling.* Downers Grove, IL: InterVarsity Press. ‡

Plantinga, C., Jr. (1995). *Not the way it's supposed to be: A breviary of sin.* Grand Rapids, MI: Eerdmans.

Powlison, D. (1995). Idols of the heart and "Vanity Fair." *Journal of Biblical Counseling, 13,* 35-50.

Shuster, M. (2003). *The fall and sin: What we have become as sinners.* Grand Rapids, MI: Eerdmans. ‡

‡ Recommended more for counselors and pastors than counselees

—9—

Suffering and Psychopathology

Principle 3: Psychopathology is most comprehensively understood from three perspectives: sin, suffering, and biopsychosocial damage.

Expansion 2: Suffering and biopsychosocial damage are significant aspects of psychopathology because they can be either hindrances or means to God's glory and human well-being.

The LORD was sorry that He had made man
on the earth, and He was grieved in His heart.

GENESIS 6:6

He is the radiance of [God's] glory and
the exact representation of His nature.

HEBREWS 1:3

He was . . . a man of sorrows and acquainted with grief.

ISAIAH 53:3

In the world you have tribulation, but take courage;
I have overcome the world.

JOHN 16:33

ADVERSITY IS COMMONPLACE IN HUMAN LIFE. As a result, everyone suffers eventually, and some people suffer a lot. George Orwell reportedly observed, "Most people get a fair amount of fun out of their lives, but on balance life is suffering, and only the very young or the very foolish imagine otherwise." Indeed, some thinkers have concluded that the abundance of pointless suffering and inhumane evil in the world prove that a loving, righteous, and all-powerful God does not exist. So, why *would* God allow his good creation to become a place of such vast suffering and, in the process, seemingly threaten his doxological agenda? To answer that question, we need first to define what suffering is.

Suffering is commonly understood to be a state of conscious pain or distress, usually involving negative emotion, stemming from adversity.[1] However, suffering varies considerably in a number of ways. It exists on a continuum from mild to severe; when severe enough to damage the individual, it is called *trauma*;[2] when long term, it is called *chronic*; when severe but episodic, it could be called *catastrophic*. People also vary considerably regarding the resources they have to cope with and address suffering well (i.e., so that they are protected from damage and able to process the suffering productively and virtuously). Resources include biological, psychological, social, ethical, and spiritual capacities and skills that enable the management and resolution of suffering and adversity (Folkman & Moskowitz, 2004; Pargament, Falb, Ano, & Wachholtz, 2013). Children, by definition, have limited resources, which they typically develop with age. Meanwhile, children need the support of others to help them cope with adversity and resolve their suffering, as well as to train them in such resources. When children experience significant trauma without sufficient resilience or emotional scaffolding, they will be damaged, and the greater the chronicity, the more likely they will grow into adulthood with compromised coping skills and agency. Moreover, the patterns they developed to cope with their suffering usually make it difficult to learn more mature ways to protect themselves from suffering and cope with it well in adulthood.

As a result, we might interpret suffering as a biopsychosocial evil, since it is closely related to psychopathology in at least four ways.[3] First, in chapter six we noted that among the biopsychosocial motives with which humans were created are the avoidance of pain and the pursuit of well-being. According to the God-designed program of the avoidance-of-pain motive, suffering is absolutely negative. So when humans experience significant suffering, this good motive produces significant psychological pressure to avoid the pain, which can lead to inner conflict with other motives, such as loving God more than anything else in adulthood, as well as dynamic structural changes that systematically avoid pain (such as defenses and dissociation), which were adaptive at the time they were formed but later can constrict one's ability to flourish. Second, numerous studies have shown that severe suffering, whether episodic or chronic, can be deleterious to human functioning and psychological well-being, indicated by the negative physiological and psychological responses that can occur when we experience it (Everly & Lating, 2002; Van der Hart, Nijenhuis, & Steele, 2006). Third, severe suffering in childhood can create biopsychosocial damage that can significantly compromise psychological functioning in various ways, including the quality of one's adult agency and relationality (Kendler & Prescott, 2006; PDM Task Force, 2006). Finally, psychological pain or distress is a component of many kinds of psychopathology (American Psychiatric Association, 2013). Consequently, Christian counselors need to be experts in addressing and processing "the problem of human suffering."

At the same time, we should not conclude that suffering is itself intrinsically psychopathological. To begin with, negative emotions and emotional pain are thoroughly appropriate responses to adversity of various kinds. Indeed, people *not* feeling this way in such situations would itself signify a problem. Such emotions are meaningful, and they can indicate both the kinds and the degree of adversity to which one is (or has been) exposed. Therefore, rather than being intrinsically psychopathological, suffering actually indicates good functioning in response to the evil of a fallen world according to God's design plan (Wolterstorff, 2005). Nevertheless, because of the effects of chronic suffering on human beings, especially in childhood, it must be addressed in any comprehensive Christian account of psychopathology.

CHRISTIAN TEACHINGS REGARDING SUFFERING

There are many places to begin our discussion, but given our theocentric orientation, I will open up with a consideration of God. This is actually not uncommon in Christian treatments of suffering, since providence and God's involvement are important and relevant themes. However, having discussed God's sovereignty over human life in chapter six, we will begin with an even more controversial topic.

The Suffering of God

Until relatively recently, the notion that God suffers was viewed skeptically in the church. There are good reasons for this, which we cannot explore in detail.[4] Two of the most important are that divine suffering seems to imply (1) a deficit in God and (2) a change in God, which would mean that God were not ontologically and eternally perfect, respectively. Any orthodox treatment of the topic, therefore, will have to avoid those implications. There is, however, compelling evidence that raises questions about the traditional position that God cannot suffer: Scripture's repeated portrayals and declarations of a God pained by human activity and experience (e.g., Gen 6:6; Ex 32:10; Hos 11:8; Eph 4:30). The challenge, then, is to do justice to such texts, *as well as* those that teach God's sovereign majesty (including his control over all creaturely events and his blissful unchangeableness or immutability). Though affirming both God's suffering and his sovereign majesty might appear contradictory, God's simplicity (see chap. 6) assures us that all of his revealed attributes are unified and harmonious in him, and his incomprehensibility (see chap. 6) leads us to expect that we may not completely grasp how (Johnson, 2002).

God's sovereign majesty—his infinity, eternality, power, and perfection—guarantees that his happiness cannot be disrupted; he cannot increase in knowledge or experience (since he already possesses all good), and he can and will endure and overcome anything that resists him. In addition, his sovereign involvement in the details of our lives—whether good or bad—means that our stories are ultimately meaningful (Gen 50:20; Johnson, 2007, chap. 9).[5] Yet God's righteousness and love also necessitate that he is angry toward sin and compassionate toward suffering within his creation. Indeed, were his bliss to entail not caring about his creatures' sin and suffering, he would not be morally perfect. So, when Scripture reveals God's anger or sorrow about a human activity or experience, this indicates no change in God, but rather an occasion in time in which an aspect of his eternal nature was revealed.

God's sorrow and judgment for humanity's sinfulness. Within a few chapters of the opening of the Bible, one comes across what may be the saddest verses in the Bible. As the sin of the earliest humans spread, "the LORD saw that the wickedness of man was great on the earth, and that every intent of the thoughts of his heart was only evil continually. The LORD was sorry that He had made man on the earth, and He was grieved in His heart" (Gen 6:5-6). The extremity of human sin is repeatedly stressed—*great, every,* *only, continually*—and it led God to feel sorry or terrible,[6] and his "heart was filled with pain"[7] (Aalders, 1981, p. 158). Why? Being perfect, he necessarily feels fittingly[8] and virtuously, so the sin of humans *pained* their Creator,[9] pain due to the adversity of his intentions for his images being so tragically reversed, leading to a punishing flood.

Far from being an aloof and distant deity, untouched by human life and activity, God was deeply grieved in the face of the chronic evil of his image bearers and the thwarting of his desires to manifest his glory through their Godward flourishing. In this early episode in redemptive history, his next response was judgment, forcefully expressing his sovereign majesty and his holy revulsion toward sin. Other divinely fitting responses (such as laying down his life for his enemies)—at that point in time—would have been likely misconstrued as evidence of weakness or unrighteousness. Even so, we should note that in this account, painful grief preceded righteous judgment. Furthermore, the flood and God's deliverance of Noah and his family are both types that point ahead to the judgment of the sin of the world eventually laid on Christ, the Ark rescuing all who believe on him and pointing further to the final judgment and deliverance through faith in Christ at the end of time.

God's anger and sorrow regarding Israel. God later chose Abraham and his descendants intending that they would exemplify his design for humanity, and he blessed them with his personal involvement and guided them with his law. Nevertheless, the subsequent history of his dealings with the Israelites is mostly a slow, sad story of their grumbling, moral failure, and idolatry, ending with God's silence from the close of the Old Testament until the arrival of John the Baptist, who signaled the coming of the Son of God. Again and again, the Old Testament narratives and prophetic books recount the perennial Israelite resistance to God and God's perennial disappointment and judgment, as well as his persevering patience and love. Though God's electing, covenantal lovingkindness undergirds all their interactions, the divine pedagogy in the Old Testaments highlights God's anger against their sin (beginning with the golden calf; Ex 32:10) rather than his everlasting love (or his sorrow, for that matter), in order to underscore his sovereign majesty and righteousness, since understanding the latter features is developmentally prerequisite to understanding properly his love, which would be displayed so profoundly in the coming of the Son. The Old Testament record of God's experience with the Israelites shows that they gave him far more grief than joy. So why did God choose Israel knowing this people would cause him such grief?

Divine empathy: A partial answer. God loves those on whom he has set his affections (Ex 33:19). According to Aquinas, that entails their joys and sorrows becoming his own (Dodds, 2008). Human parents suffer when their children suffer, and God is perfectly virtuous. So we read of God toward Israel, "In all their affliction He was afflicted" (Is 63:9), and then we see this demonstrated in the life of Christ.[10]

The excellence of the God-man of sorrows. The early church faced a real conundrum regarding the obvious suffering of Jesus Christ, since he was both divine and human. After much reflection, it concluded that Christ must have suffered only in his human nature, since the divine nature cannot suffer—a conclusion we can now see was influenced more by Greek metaphysics than biblical revelation.[11] However, in the twentieth century Barth (1957b; 1956b) reminded the church that Jesus Christ being the Word of God communicates something more radical about God than was perhaps as fully appreciated before, for "the *crucified* Jesus is the 'image of the invisible God'" (1957b, p. 123, emphasis in original; see Oliphant, 2012, for a similar understanding of Christ from a more classical Reformed position). With regard to the present subject, the emotions and suffering of Christ reveal to us something analogous in the heart of the eternal God.

In Isaiah 53 we learn that the coming Messiah will be a "man of sorrows" and "acquainted with grief" (Is 53:3). He will bear our griefs, carry our sorrows, be wounded for our transgressions and crushed for our iniquities (Is 53:4-5). God (the Father) will "crush him, putting him to grief" (Is 53:10). As a result of "the anguish of his soul," God will be satisfied, because "he poured out his soul to death" (Is 53:11-12 ESV).

The Gospels fill out the details of Isaiah's prophecy. Though not told much about Christ's sorrows, we know he lost his human father earlier than most, he repeatedly experienced distress and anguish during his ministry (see Warfield, 1970), and he frequently ministered to the suffering—the sick, the grieving, and the sinful—perhaps most poignantly weeping with those who wept at Lazarus' grave. All this climaxed in the greatest affliction any human ever suffered, during the twenty-four hours before he died. In Gethsemane, he said his soul was "deeply grieved [*perilypos*], to the point of death" (Mt 26:38) as he contemplated with stark clarity what being forsaken (in some sense) by his Father for our sin would entail. During that time he felt an agony (*agōnia*; Lk 22:44) so extreme that he had a bizarre physiological-bodily reaction, signifying perhaps that his unfathomable turmoil had overwhelmed his finite human resources.[12] Even so, he remained the paragon of emotion regulation, expressing his fitting negative emotions in fervent prayer (Lk 22:44) and repeatedly surrendering his anticipation of the abandonment of hell to his Father.

On the next day Christ's suffering increased to the greatest proportions. The physical and emotional pain of being whipped, beaten, mocked, betrayed, and tempted by those he created for his glory (Is 43:7) was extreme by human standards but was rendered immeasurable by his being the august, eternal Son of God, now subjected to such degradation—having his majestic authority challenged by dust and his resolute love rejected by a representation of all humanity—though this was symbolic of what the triune God had endured throughout human history. And, finally, he experienced the divine judgment for our sin on the cross (Is 53). No human will ever fully comprehend his cry of dereliction: "My God, my God, why have You forsaken me?" To quote David's anguished words in Psalm 22:1 indicated, first and foremost, his assumption of our deserved alienation from the Father, because of our sin, as the sacrificial lamb of God. However, it also signified his identification with what was expressed in David's suffering—and as the one mediator between God and humanity (1 Tim 2:5), representatively also ours. At the same time, we must not suppose his cry indicated any fundamental break in the unity of the Father and the Son, for they remained united with the Spirit in their mission of reconciliation (2 Cor 5:18-19).

On the cross the incarnate Son of God overcame both our sin and our suffering, a holistic victory symbolized by his being raised from the dead. Years later, the apostle Paul uttered the pregnant phrase "the church of God which He purchased with His own blood" (Acts 20:28). This and other biblical passages led the early church eventually to recognize that Christ's divine personhood brought his divine and human natures into union without confusion. The early church, however, could not extend this understanding of Christ to support the conclusion that God had suffered on the cross.[13] Far removed from the reigning philosophical assumptions of Greece and Rome, it is easier for us today to see that "the picture of God that is given to us by the cross is that of a deserted, bruised, bleeding, and dying God, who gave new meaning and dignity to human suffering by passing through its shadow himself" (McGrath, 1994, p. 81).

"Was ever grief like mine?" Christ repeatedly asks in Herbert's poem "The Sacrifice." "No" is the implicit answer, of course, for the Son's experience of suffering was the greatest suffering in history. "The God on whom we rely knows what suffering is about, not merely in the way that God knows everything, but by experience" (Carson, 1990, p. 179). In addition, being also divine, Christ's suffering transcends and encompasses all the sufferings of his sinful, finite followers—"tempted in all things as we are, yet"—remaining faithful in his suffering—"without sin" (Heb 4:15)—for a greater than Job had come. Mysteriously, in Jesus Christ the sovereign, righteous love of the triune God assumed the worst of human suffering— godforsakenness—and overcame it in his divine nature.

What happened to Christ that day necessarily outstrips our comprehension. But whatever we do, we must not reduce the complexity so that our limited reason can fully grasp it, either by redefining the divine nature accordingly (as in process theism) or arguing that it tells us nothing of the divine nature (as many classical theists have done). Biblical revelation guides us between the Scylla of a classical God beyond emotion and the Charybdis of a God made in our own image (Horton, 2011).[14]

Perhaps a passageway can be found again in Edwards's (1974) notion of "the excellency of Christ," that is, the "admirable conjunction of diverse excellences" found in him (Vol. 1, p. 680). The beauty of Christ is seen precisely in his being a personal union of sovereign majesty and humble condescension, which is nothing other than the image and incarnate realization of the beauty of the divine nature. Christ's suffering was not *new*, in the sense that there was nothing in the divine nature to which it corresponded or with which it was compatible. If there were absolutely no corollary to suffering in the divine nature, perhaps one could argue that Christ's sufferings were *unnatural*, in the sense that they were fundamentally contrary to his divine nature, but that applies only to *sin*. Emotions are signs of value, and Christ's emotional responses to all that happened that day were *true* and were exactly what God would—and *did*—feel in that place. The Word of God, Jesus Christ, therefore, communicated to us the nature of our simple, excellent God: sovereign, righteous, and loving, and eternally acquainted with whatever is divine that is analogous to human compassion and grief.[15]

Mindful of the emphasis in Old Testament revelation on God's majestic sovereignty and righteousness, we find in the cross a shocking resolution of our sinful, suffering predicament, so different from what he did in Genesis 6–7, when he judged the humanity of that time. This time God *graciously* and *lovingly overcame* the world in Christ (Jn 16:33) by "integrating" his pain, regret, and righteous wrath with his love and mercy, and transferring the sin of the world to the Son, "metabolizing" and dissolving it in the infinite depths of his righteous, all-powerful love. Our God is an excellent God who has triumphed over the adversity of our sin and suffering by suffering for us and with us in the Son.

Conclusion. So why would God create a world in which there is so much suffering, both divine and human? As the Lord of the universe, he could regularly dramatically intervene and prevent evil and suffering, but he chooses to limit such unusual displays of his power, for the most part, to display aspects of his character not manifested in a perfect world, such as his capacity to suffer well. Rather than construing suffering, therefore, as an unmitigated evil, indicating a deficiency and degree of distress incompatible with God's sovereign majesty, Scripture compels us to radically reconceive it in his case. Suffering well in the face of adversity and empathically on behalf of others are two of God's *excellences*, manifested historically in Christ. Instead of being a sign of weakness or limitation, divine suffering signifies some of the splendor of his glory. His longsuffering in the face of humanity's ongoing evil manifests his superlative self-control and persevering patience as he resolutely works out his doxological, righteous, and therapeutic purposes in his own time. The willingness of the sovereign Lord of the universe to suffer, in his eternal nature, as he comprehends omnisciently and omnipathically[16] the evil and suffering of the world for all time, combined with its expression in his willingness to suffer as a human to redeem sinners, is easily the most excellent conjunction of fortitude, courage, humility, compassion, and forgiving love imaginable.

From the Son/the Word we learn that the *imago Dei* includes the capacity to suffer well—including suffering empathically for and with others. In *Foundations* I considered how emotions are meaningful signs that correspond to our perception of value. The biblical portrayal of an emotional God is far more than an exercise in anthropomorphism, because he is the source of all value, and whatever there is in God that corresponds analogically to human emotions is their standard (Edwards, 1746/1959). Christians rather should suppose that God is maximally virtuous in his empathic engagement with human activity and suffering,[17] while simultaneously perfectly content and incapable of being disturbed or overwhelmed. There is no better (or more excellent) parent or counselor to have with us in our suffering.

The Suffering of Humanity

Understanding something of God's excellent, majestic suffering casts a very different light on human suffering than that afforded by a stoic view of God as unaffected by the plight of his creatures. We consider next the main lines of biblical thought regarding human suffering. Bypassing many relevant narratives in the Old Testament, such as the wilderness wanderings of the Israelites, we begin with the wisdom book of Job, which deals with the problem of suffering more fully than any other book in the Bible (see Stump, 2012, for a remarkable interpretation).

Lessons from the book of Job. In the first chapters, we read of a wealthy, upright believer named Job, who experiences catastrophic suffering instigated by Satan, but allowed by God, to demonstrate the genuineness of his God-centeredness. Satan unsurprisingly intended Job's suffering for evil, to draw him away from God—another example of his tempting humans to sin using good, created motives to pry Job's heart away from loving God supremely. God, on the other hand, permitted the suffering for good: first of all to demonstrate his supreme value by Job's denying himself (i.e., his good, created motive to avoid pain) for God's sake by consenting to God's permissive will for his life, even when it includes suffering, and second, to promote Job's greater happiness and flourishing.[18]

Most of the book consists of a conversation between Job and his three "friends." At first, all four agree with the "just-world hypothesis" (Lerner, 1980) that suffering only comes on those who deserve it as punishment for their personal sin. Job, however, argues that his catastrophic suffering is therefore patently unfair, since he is innocent of wrongdoing. According to Stump (2012), "Job takes his stand with the goodness of God, rather than with the office of God as ruler of the universe" (p. 217), and takes God to task for allowing this injustice to occur. Having read, however, the heavenly backstory, the reader knows the great irony of the narrative: God allowed Job to suffer not because of his sin but because of his *virtue*. So, we learn from this subversive wisdom book that moralists like Job's friends are actually fools who can do great harm.

We also hear an exemplary believer complaining to God about his suffering, whom God ultimately vindicates when he says to Job's "friends," "You have not spoken of Me what is right as My servant Job has" (Job 42:7). So God must have indirectly approved of "Job's uttering these accusations because something about giving voice to the accusations is good even if the accusations are not true" (Stump, 2012, p. 195). At the same time, given God's previous rebuke, Job's accusations must also have reflected implicitly what Christians call "original sin," for over the course of Job's defense, his great sorrow turned into a self-righteous judgment of God. Anticipating New Testament teaching, we learn here that even the best believers are not free of original sin, which suffering can bring to light when sufficient to overwhelm their good capacities so that they sin. When God finally appears to his accuser (Job 38–41), he puts Job firmly in his place, making clear that humans have no right to judge their Maker, lacking the requisite omniscience necessary to comprehend what God is up to in the goings-on of this world. He is God, and we are not. Job met here with Luther's "hidden God" (*Deus absconditus*), an imposing sovereign, free to do what he wants, whom we are rightly to fear, and who here apparently has little empathy for sufferers. Yet Job responds in newly obtained wisdom to the divine reprimand, confessing the sin brought to light through his ordeal: "I have heard of You by the hearing of the ear; but now my eye sees You; therefore I retract, and I repent in dust and ashes" (Job 42:5-6).

One important inference to draw from the narrative is that the ultimate reasons for the suffering of individuals are fundamentally inscrutable. Another is that human suffering is designed to contribute to human flourishing while glorifying God. So long as Job's created motive to avoid pain was not activated, the genuineness of his fidelity to God was unconfirmed. "Until prosperity and goodness are pulled apart, it may not be a determinate matter whether Job loves the good for its own sake, or whether what he loves is mingled with good and wealth" (Stump, 2012, p. 207). Suffering therefore provides a singular opportunity for humans to display the supremacy of God above all things, as well as promote their ultimate wellbeing. Job faltered, as Satan had hoped. However, in his brokenness, Job took his suffering to God so that, in the end, his virtue increased, and in Job's greater flourishing, God got greater glory.

This is the Bible's foundational book of suffering. Yet Christians ought not to read it isolated from the entire canon,[19] for it was written early in revelation history, centuries before God came to earth in the flesh to reveal his excellence. The hidden God's encounter with Job can only properly be interpreted in light of the fuller revelation of God at the cross. There we find the transcendently ironic fulfillment of Job's suffering in the Son of God taking Job's place before God, bearing Job's sin, echoing the validity of his protest, and in the process, becoming his perfect uprightness (1 Cor 1:31).

According to wisdom, then, as difficult as suffering is for us, sin is vastly worse, because it separates us from our greatest good, which suffering does not (Powlison, 1995). Suffering is merely a biopsychosocial evil, whereas sin is ethicospiritual. If the only values in the universe were biopsychosocial, avoiding pain might be our greatest good. And without an explicit commitment to ethicospiritual values beyond the self, we can understand why secular therapy generally works so hard to help counselees avoid all suffering. Christianity also seeks to relieve suffering as much as possible, but it assumes not only that suffering and flourishing are compatible but that suffering can actually be a means of flourishing. This ultimately positive reframing of suffering—without glossing over its evil—is a distinguishing feature of Christian therapy.

Divine encouragement to lament. Job spoke "right" (Job 42:7) in his lament, and we find lament expressed repeatedly in the Psalms and the prophets, and perhaps most importantly by Christ on the cross. Lament is a special kind of biblical genre (Brueggeman, 2002) that has immense therapeutic value. First, biblical lament is active and dialogical rather than passive and private. Lament is doing something about our struggles— sharing them with our God and friend, the source of our well-being. Second, lament puts one's emotional turmoil into words, without repression, enabling one to objectify or mentalize it while feeling it (without dissociation), so that one can work through it in light of the Christian faith. So it enhances one's distress tolerance and emotion-regulation abilities (Pennebaker, 1997; Zvolensky, Bernstein, & Vujanovic, 2011). Third, in contrast to complaining and rumination, lament focuses one's attention on a powerful, loving God rather than the suffering itself. Finally, as believers passionately express their hearts' desires and sorrows to God, they come more and more to realize that their just and loving God knows, hears, and empathizes with them in their suffering, and this gives them psychological leverage to relativize and modify the suffering so that, eventually, it can be accepted and surrendered into the hands of God.[20] Its frequent occurrence in the Scriptures suggests that it should serve as a guide for dealing with suffering and that God desires us to pour out our hearts to him (Ps 62:8; Lam 2:19).

The paradoxical promotion of flourishing through suffering. Part of Christ's mission was to reveal divine suffering. Another aspect was to reveal its soul-building potential. We are told in Hebrews that it was fitting for God "to perfect [*teleiōsai*] the author of . . . salvation through sufferings" (Heb 2:10), which was both a kind of temptation (Heb 2:18) and the cause of his being "crowned with glory and honor" (Heb 2:9). A few chapters later, the apostle added,

> In the days of His flesh, He offered up both prayers and supplications with loud crying and tears to the One able to save Him from death, and He was

heard because of His piety. Although He was a Son, He learned obedience from the things which He suffered. And having been made perfect [*teleiōtheis*], He became to all those who obey Him the source of eternal salvation. (Heb 5:7-9)

The English word *perfect* can be confusing, because its meaning as a transitive verb (to perfect) is opposite to its meaning as a predicate adjective (to be perfect).[21] As a result, in the above passages it might be clearer if *teleioō* was translated "to complete," "to bring to its goal," or "to bring to full measure" (Arndt & Gingrich, 1957) than "to perfect," since the Son of God was already in a state of ethical and spiritual perfection. In light of our previous considerations, Christ's extraordinary sufferings were temptations to sin, because of the internal conflict he experienced as a human between the good avoidance-of-pain motive and his fidelity to God and his agenda. However, instead of leading to sin, his sufferings deepened his already perfect virtue—so that he increased in fortitude, patience, and wisdom—through the heartfelt resolution of his internal conflict in favor of God's agenda.[22] This teaching about Christ also suggests that suffering is part of God's design plan for the fulfillment of the human *telos* in this world.

So, Christ exemplified something implicit in the book of Job: God intends for suffering to increase virtuous character. The author of Hebrews went on to encourage believers to interpret their suffering *relationally*, within a familial context, as the discipline (*paideia*) of a caring Father (fulfilling the picture that God conveyed to Job), who intends for it to help his children share in his holiness (Heb 12:3-10). "All discipline for the moment seems not to be joyful, but sorrowful; yet to those who have been trained by it, afterwards it yields the peaceful fruit of righteousness" (Heb 12:11). Consequently, we suffer like Christ suffered so that we become more conformed to his image: more patient, more empathic and compassionate, better able to endure and suffer well.

In the soul-building reframing of suffering in Hebrews, its sorrow is still acknowledged. Paul and James raise the bar considerably in their reframing. "We also *exult* in our tribulations, knowing that tribulation brings about perseverance; and perseverance, proven character; and proven character, hope" (Rom 5:3-4), and "*Count it all joy*, my brothers, when you meet trials of various kinds, for you know that the testing of your faith produces steadfastness. And let steadfastness have its full effect, that you may be perfect and complete, lacking in nothing" (Jas 1:2-4 ESV).[23] The apostles challenged believers to frame adversity as a "trial"—as an event with potential to foster one's flourishing—and therefore to welcome it *gladly*. This presents a very lofty affective goal, given that it entails transcending the inclinations of our good created nature (as well as the autocentrism of our fallenness). But rather than promoting the denial and repression of the pain of suffering (and our natural aversion to it), the apostles advocate a cognitive reappraisal strategy to reflect on the transforming benefits of suffering by faith, leaving us to develop a fuller model of how to work toward that goal in Christ in the heart without repressing the inner conflict suffering creates. Christ in Gethsemane demonstrates both sides of that soul-building conflict: "If possible, take this cup from me. . . . Nevertheless, I accept your will." According to Moser (2013), Gethsemane provides an Archimedean point for human conformity to Christ (pp. 93-97).

Finally, building on biblical and Thomistic thought, Stump (2012) argues that the ultimate soul-building purpose of suffering is relational: communion with God. The character formation for which God uses suffering consists primarily in the integration of our souls in relation to God, our chief good. As a result, Christians historically have believed that pain has spiritual meaning, and "it is part of the life of those bent on Christian sanctity" (Coakley, 2005).

Positive outcomes from suffering have been documented in research on posttraumatic growth (Tan, 2013). Seventy percent of people report positive life changes following adversity (Linley & Joseph, 2004). Strong faith provides resources for addressing trauma (Smith, McCullough, & Poll, 2003), and how one interprets trauma (e.g., religious appraisal) has a significant impact on posttraumatic stress and growth (Schaefer, Blazer, & Koenig, 2008). How can suffering contribute to flourishing? By deepening one's faith and altering one's self-understanding (Schaefer, Blazer, & Koenig, 2008; Schaefer, 2014), perhaps by promoting the decentering and recentering of our self around God. "Suffering is the sole cause of consciousness" (Dostoevsky, 2009, p. 32). The inner conflict caused by suffering leads to self-examination and an ordering of one's desires, helping us become a self (Evans, 2009). Suffering also awakens us out of our immersion in routine, everyday life and "alienates us from ourselves" (Hauerwas, 1986, p. 25). Physical and psychological pain make a purely creational self-fulfillment impossible, requiring the self to look outside itself for the fulfillment for which it was designed, in God and his blessings in Christ, reserved in heaven (Col 3:1-4; 1 Pet 1:4).[24] As we gradually internalize our transcendent and eschatological happiness in Christ, we can become more honest about ourselves and our pain down here, better able to suffer and tolerate distress, and more compassionate toward and empathic with other sufferers. This process, in turn, fosters "the ability to make the suffering mine that is crucial if I am to be an integral self" (Hauerwas, 1986, p. 25), so that we can say, "My story has made me who I am." All of this contributes to our inward deepening and therefore our capacity for splendor, helping to make us "great-souled" people. "Depth of sorrow is the sign of a healthy soul, not a sick soul" (Sittser, 1995, p. 73).

Christians of various traditions have long recognized the soul-building value of suffering. Catholics call it a "dark night of the soul," Lutherans *tentatio* ("agonizing struggle") (Bayer, 2008), and the Reformed "spiritual desertion." Whatever tradition, obtaining the good in this life requires an active reinterpretation, a transposition by faith of the suffering into the spiritual order of our relationship with Christ, where the experience of suffering as a natural evil is modified by the knowledge that God "mean[s] it for good" (Gen 50:20), that is, the good of our flourishing and the manifestation of his glory. "Those who consider sickness as coming from the hand of God, as the effect of His mercy, and the means which He employs for their salvation—commonly find in it great sweetness and sensible consolation" (Brother Lawrence, 1895, p. 39).

The suffering of sin. There is also a close linkage established between sin and suffering in the Scriptures, especially in the Old Testament: the curse of suffering on our first parents as a consequence of their primal sin; the suffering of Israel and many of its leaders due to sins against God (for example, Samson; see Stump, 2012, chap. 10); and the teachings of the Deuteronomic law and the book of Proverbs that draw a direct correlation between sin and suffering (a pattern also identified by other religions, e.g., the Hindu principle of karma). Christians will interpret this judicial context for suffering as part of the pedagogical function of the law (Gal 3:24), reminding God's children through their suffering of humanity's native alienation from God and warning them of the negative consequences of sin to oneself and others. Indeed, perhaps the most painful kind of suffering is that caused by one's own personal sin. In addition to whatever physical or psychological distress one experiences, there is the pain of a violated conscience, the related emotions of guilt and shame, felt distance from God, and often its painful effects on others (consider the wide swath of harm adultery often causes). Personal sin almost surely brings about the bulk of human suffering.

Nevertheless, the total picture of suffering in Scripture limits how much a judicial perspective on suffering is warranted, at least regarding the sufferer. Remember Job's friends! Jesus himself taught that congenital blindness was not caused by anyone's personal sin, "but it was so that the works of God might be displayed in him" (Jn 9:3). Consequently, we must resist the tendency to assume people's sufferings are deserved, unless actually justified, and even then Christ showed us that such considerations should not prevent loving and caring for them, for example, in our counseling.

Future benefits of present suffering. Suffering is distributed massively unevenly across the human race. As Job knew, the Creator has the right to allocate blessings and sufferings however he sees fit (see also Rom 9:20-21). We belong to him, and he owes us nothing. But then we read Christ's words: "Blessed are the poor in spirit, for theirs is the kingdom of heaven. Blessed are those who mourn, for they shall be comforted" (Mt 5:3-4). In their context, this probably refers mostly to the blessedness of those in heaven. Paul later wrote, "I consider that the sufferings of this present time are not worthy to be compared with the glory that is to be revealed to us" (Rom 8:18). The heavenly joy of believers will apparently be so great that it will extinguish the pain of past suffering. Even more astounding, he taught, "Momentary, light affliction is producing for us an eternal weight of glory far beyond all comparison" (2 Cor 4:17). Similar to Romans 8:18, he says that suffering down here will appear "momentary" and "light" in contrast to the joy of eternal blessedness. Even more encouraging, he seems to suggest that God will compensate believers who suffer more on earth with greater happiness in heaven. The degree of their present affliction is producing or obtaining (*katergazomai*) for them a corresponding capacity for glory. This may also be implied in Christ's saying "the last shall be first" (Mt 20:16). God's justice and love unite to rectify the uneven distribution of the suffering of believers in this life by giving to those who suffered more on earth a proportionately greater share of eternal glory in heaven. Such knowledge is intended to console sufferers and modify the negative emotions associated with their suffering, without minimizing it.

Union with Christ and the fellowship of his sufferings. Perhaps the most astounding teaching on suffering in the New Testament is the suggestion that the suffering of believers is somehow identified with and a sharing in the sufferings or death of Christ. Paul said he sought to know Christ "and the power of His resurrection and *the fellowship of His sufferings*, being conformed to His death" (Phil 3:10). Wanting to know the power of Christ's resurrection is easy to understand, but the second phrase is surprising. He wishes to know or personally experience the fellowship or communion (*koinōnia*) of Christ's sufferings! In that way his union with Christ's death is being realized.

> We are afflicted in every way, but not crushed; perplexed, but not despairing; persecuted, but not forsaken; struck down, but not destroyed; always carrying about in the body the dying of Jesus, so that the life of Jesus also may be manifested in our body. For we who live are constantly being delivered over to death for Jesus' sake, so that the life of Jesus also may be manifested in our mortal flesh. (2 Cor 4:8-11; see also 2 Cor 1:5-6)

From God's standpoint, believers are mystically identified with Christ's death (Rom 6:4-6), and in their suffering enter experientially into a sharing in his crucifixion (see also Rom 8:17; 2 Cor 1:5; Phil 1:29; 1 Pet 2:21; 4:12-19). Paul actually coined a compound word for this reality: believers are "co-sufferers" with Christ (*sympaschomen*, Rom 8:17); as a process it has been termed *cruciformity* (Gorman, 2001).

Alluding to this union, George Herbert (1995) wrote,

> If all men's tears were let
> Into one common sewer, sea, and brine;
> What were they all, compar'd to thine?
> Thou art my grief alone,
> Thou Lord conceal it not: and as thou art
> All my delight, so all my smart:
> Thy crosse took up in one,
> By way of imprest, all my future moan.[25]

Paul took such an insight a remarkable step further: "Now I rejoice in my sufferings for your sake, and in my flesh I do my share on behalf of His body, which is the church, in filling up what is lacking [*hysterēmata*] in Christ's afflictions" (Col 1:24). If anyone but an apostle had said this, we might call it heresy. Given the infinite value of Christ's death for salvation, Paul could not have meant that there was anything deficient in its power to save. What then did he mean?

Contemporary New Testament scholarship argues that Paul is assuming a broad redemptive-historical framework—based on the Old Testament and the Gospels—that the Messiah's coming, along with the bringing in of the new creation, was associated with a period of persecution and suffering for all who follow after him (Beale, 2002; Moo, 2008; O'Brien, 2000). Paul believed that suffering was "integral to his apostolic ministry," since it provided evidence of his solidarity with the crucified Christ (O'Brien, 2000, p. 76). He thought the sufferings of believers were themselves harbingers of the age to come (Rom 8:17), because there is a "definite measure of affliction to be endured in the last days" (O'Brien, 2000, p. 80). Consequently, Paul's suffering and, by extension, the suffering of all God's people in this age participates in and brings to a completion the afflictions of Christ and points ahead to eventual resurrection.

Some might want to restrict this association to suffering that is explicitly Christian, for example, persecution *because* one is a Christian. Such suffering is special, because of its doxological intensity (Acts 5:41). However, there is no reason to exclude suffering that we might call *implicitly* Christian whatever its cause. Because of their union with Christ, *all* the suffering of believers is Christian and is sanctified by being brought to Christ and consciously folded into his redemptive agenda by faith (Stump, 2012, pp. 448-50). This is one way that each believer's story is being woven into the story of Christ (Vanhoozer, 2005).

Perhaps the worst thing about suffering is the sense that we are all alone in it. Communing with Christ in one's suffering and knowing that one is sharing in Christ's sufferings, therefore, has significant potential to alter the believer's experience of suffering and make the distress more tolerable while working through it toward resurrection.

Conclusion

God's theater of glory includes suffering, and part of his glory is being able to suffer well, particularly when being sinned against, a character trait exemplified supremely in the life and death of Jesus. The Father created humans in part so he could commune with more children like his Son. Suffering well for Christians means suffering *with Christ* with a transforming hope (Rom 5:3-5).

SOME THERAPEUTIC IMPLICATIONS

While Christian and modern therapies are both motivated by a desire to alleviate suffering, they differ in their interpretation of just how bad it is. According to modern assumptions, the supreme goal in life is individual happiness—often understood as subjective well-being, the opposite of suffering. As a result, for many (though not all) of our secular contemporaries, suffering is thoroughly bad, and its quickest reduction is of the highest priority, evident in trends such as the preference of divorce over working on a difficult marriage, a sex-change operation over coming to terms with one's body when there is internal conflict about one's sex, taking medication to reduce any distress (a lesser good) over the slower work of therapy and spirituality that would also reduce distress but lead to more substantial change (a greater good), and so on.

Within a Christian framework, suffering is complex, for it is a "mixed evil" (Chisholm, 1986), fundamentally bad and generally to be avoided but also capable of producing substantial good. As a result, its reduction is one important priority among others. To be sure, getting the balance right here is crucial and itself part of Christian wisdom. Those who oppose all psychotropic medication, for example, because they believe it will reduce suffering God uses to sanctify people tragically misunderstand (and misrepresent) God's intentions and heart.[26] Supposedly justified by the cross, a thread of misanthropy can be found throughout the Christian tradition on this score, illustrated in the extreme of self-flagellation. The best remedy for such "stern-minded Christianity" (Stump, 2012) is to become saturated with the fundamentally positive nature of God's doxological agenda through falling more in love with a supremely happy God who is discreetly but relentlessly pursuing our well-being in Christ. Let us consider how to promote his intentions in the face of suffering as we counsel.

Reinterpreting One's Suffering Within the Christian Story

We saw in chapter five the importance of narrative in Christian therapy and learned that union with Christ joins believers to his death and resurrection, by which they are to reinterpret their stories. Humanity's innate narrative sense includes a special love of stories in which people overcome great obstacles in order to accomplish some goal. Severe suffering sets the stage for such stories (Johnson, 2007, pp. 554-55). Relying on Bakhtin's understanding of the significance of "heroes" in novels, Vanhoozer (2010) argues that we can only grasp the meaning of someone's life from outside the story itself, after its consummation: "The completed whole—the meaning—of the hero's life is not something the hero experiences" (p. 325). "Only someone outside us and the story of our lives can see us, and our story, as a unified meaningful whole" (p. 324). In a novel, that person is the author,[27] and in real life, that person is God, the ultimate author of the story of history.[28] God establishes the glorious consummation of each believer's story—and the meaningfulness of even its suffering gets eschatologically recontextualized accordingly. While still in this vale of tears, God invites us to begin the process of reinterpretation beforehand, based on revelation concerning what is to come and its concrete, proleptic anticipation in Christ's now-consummated life, death, and resurrection. Suffering believers become new-covenant heroes through their identification with Christ, the consummate hero of history, as they endure, work through, and are transformed by their suffering in and with him. As a result, the meaning of a difficult marriage, a moral failure, even childhood abuse can be fundamentally altered by its being consciously folded into the higher purposes of a loving God (Stump, 2012). The utter unrepeatability of one's story makes one's suffering incomparable and uniquely significant.

The great challenge down here, of course, is that suffering activates negative emotions that make it very difficult to interpret adversity in any positive sense, particularly when chronic trauma has established a deep, negative interpretation of one's life, predisposing one to approach current suffering as a continual confirmation of the past.

Suffering in adulthood. Normal, relatively healthy adults have become personal agents with the capacities to cope with a good deal of adversity and suffering. Psychologists have distinguished between many kinds of coping (Folkman & Moskowitz, 2004). Two of special importance are problem-focused coping, which seeks to reduce the suffering by changing the environment, and inner-focused coping, which seeks to address the suffering through emotion regulation, finding meaning in the suffering, or obtaining social support. Both approaches are agentic, involving action to bring about change. Determining which focus is best in a particular situation requires wisdom. Sometimes the adversity itself has to be dealt with (e.g., stopping current sexual abuse), and some counselees need to learn how to stand up for themselves in their environment. Yet, most everyone is helped by therapy that teaches inner-focused coping strategies, and religion has been found to offer many, including conversion, spiritual support from God, forgiveness of those who have sinned against us, and religious reframing of the suffering (Pargament, 1997), some of which we have already noted. We might further distinguish between cognitive strategies, which lessen negative emotions engendered by suffering through changing how it is interpreted—many of which are taught in the Bible—and emotion strategies, which directly engage negative emotions by expressing them and down-regulating them (Folkman & Moskowitz, 2004); these are more often demonstrated in the Bible through personal example, as in lament. Either way, Christian counselors have a rich fund of coping strategies to offer adults for addressing their current suffering.

We must add, however, that everyone has limits (of intensity or duration) to how much suffering their physical organism can endure, after which it turns into trauma (or what Weil [1951] called affliction). Job seemed to handle well the loss of his children and many possessions, until the contraction of a horrible sickness pushed him over a threshold into overwhelming negative emotion and depression (Job 3). For the most part, crises like these call immediately for loving empathy and support and just enough problem solving to restore them to some kind of equilibrium (which sometimes may involve medication), at which time a long-term therapy plan can be developed.

Dealing with childhood suffering. The Bible was written mostly to adults and therefore addresses adult suffering but does not directly address the unique challenges of the impact of suffering on people before they become adults. Job's catastrophic suffering occurred when he was a mature personal agent and strong believer, with the corresponding adult capacities to cope with it, which he did very well for a while (Job 1:21-22; 2:10). But what about children who experience catastrophic suffering or, worse, chronic trauma, since they lack the agentic abilities to protect themselves and address properly either the problem or their suffering while their metacognitive and emotion regulation skills—and their faith—are still developing?

Children can suffer in many ways: the death of a parent, parental divorce, the distress of poverty, bullying or teasing, chronic illness, or frequent moves. Perhaps the worst form is long-lasting emotional trauma, whether due to chronic anger, aggression, anxiety, shame, neglect, or sexual abuse. The severe suffering of children activates strong negative emotional reactions, whether sadness, shame, anxiety, anger, or just pain. However, being children, and lacking the ability to regulate these emotions, they usually express them and may find out their reactions are not wanted and cannot be expressed, so in fear they will learn to shut down and hide their emotions automatically, which in turn will compromise the development of emotion-regulation abilities. At the same time, their increasingly concealed, strong negative-emotion experiences are exceeding the limits of their developing psychological capacities, leaving them with an underlying sense of being overwhelmed or out of control. As a result of these various contradictory, internal pressures, they gradually lose touch with their actual emotional and visceral experience—and their self.

Thus, the intense, chronic suffering of children takes its toll, causing long-term damage to their biopsychosocial natures, predisposing them to disordered desires and negative moods, expectations, and reactions regarding others, themselves, the world, and their suffering, and leading them to actions, spouses, and the formation of families also characterized by such distress. All this also compromises the development of the very personal agency abilities they could use in adulthood to actively, reflexively foster their healing. As a result, their suffering, if not their trauma, remains more or less chronic throughout their lives—at least until some healing can be effected in therapeutic relationships with God and others.

Christ has shown us that he loves children (Mt 10:42; 18:5, 10, 14; 19:14) and hates childhood suffering (Mt 18:6).[29] At the same time, as we have seen, God allows it. There are many things we do not understand in life, and this is surely one of the most difficult. However, we have also seen that the cross teaches us a deeper truth. So, in light of this mystery, when we read Christ say to those around him, "Come to Me, all who are weary and heavy-laden, and I will give you rest" (Mt 11:28), we should understand this invitation extends to adults who need healing from their childhood suffering, especially those who were traumatized, as well as to adults who are burdened and burned out. Now that those who suffered chronically in childhood are personal agents and able to work on the improvement of their souls, God desires very much to draw them into his communion so they can finally get the soul healing he has wanted for them since they were children. Whatever their previous suffering, now, in adulthood, it can be identified with the cross, surrendered to God, and given new meaning from its consummation in Christ. In addition, survivors of trauma usually need strong social support as well as skilled guidance in how to facilitate such internal change. Consequently, Christ also intends that these processes occur with the help of his body (Eph 4:12-16), perhaps in the form of a therapist, and ideally a circle of understanding friends and an emotionally healthy church (Scazzero, 2003). However, recovery from past suffering is a slow process, sometimes taking years, to work through past trauma and present damage, again and again and again, until one's story has been renarrated frequently enough that one deeply believes it is more heroic than tragic.

In light of the difference between coping with adult suffering and recovery from childhood suffering, perhaps we should distinguish between two kinds of cruciformity—our identification and sharing with Christ's sufferings—each requiring its own kind of remedy. The first, for believers undergoing present suffering, involves its reframing through consciously folding it into Christ's life, death, and resurrection. Believers who suffered in the past require a more complex "archaeological" and reconstructive identification with Christ's story, by which it is appropriated retroactively, in order to engage and release the pent-up suffering stored up for years in strongly negatively charged emotion schemes. Both kinds glorify Christ.

Reexperiencing and "working through" one's suffering. How does one go about facilitating healing of past trauma? Research from many theoretical orientations shows that it requires the reexperiencing of the negative emotions associated with the memory and then "working through" them, for example, by introducing other considerations into them (Greenberg & Paivio, 1997; Foa, Huppert, & Cahill, 2006). With therapeutic vision, Marcel Proust reportedly said, "We are healed of a suffering only by experiencing it to the full." Emotion schemes and emotionally charged episodic memories can only be modified when they are actively engaged in consciousness—online, as it were. Consequently, to promote healing of past suffering, one cannot engage in a mere intellectual description or rehearsal, which does not engage the troubling emotions. It has been said that the goal of psychodynamic therapy is "re-experiencing the old, unsettled conflict but with a new ending" (Alexander & French, 1946, p. 338). The story of Christ and our stories give Christians rich material to use in the application of this great therapy adage, for example, vividly recalling a painful event in one's life and walking with its associated emotions "through" the cross of Christ and into his resurrection, so that the emotions get modified.

Present suffering can be processed similarly. For example, a current, emotionally troubling event can be reframed in light of God's soul-building purposes or transformed by imagining Christ's loving presence with us in its midst. This too involves consciously engaging the relevant negative emotion associated with the suffering and resolving it into a positive emotion or modifying it into a more complex emotion, based on other, more positive meanings, so it becomes a healthier mixture of negative and positive emotions. To illustrate, while stinging from severe and mostly unfair criticism by one's spouse, one can withdraw for fifteen minutes to meditate on how this is analogous to Christ's suffering, until a new emotion-state emerges, made up of an honest but softened sense of sorrow that can be transposed into a higher purpose of *agapē* love, which enables one to explore the partial validity of the criticism and return later to one's spouse, recommitted to loving engagement and perhaps a fitting apology.

Working with Perceptions of God's Apparent Passivity in the Face of Abuse or Neglect

Like Job, many Christians have had times in which God allowed physical, emotional, or relational harm to happen to them, times when it felt like he was absent (Job 23:3-9), he did not answer prayers for rescue (Job 30:20), or he even felt like an opponent, rather than an advocate (Job 7:20; 9:16-20; 13:24; 16:7-14). Such people may ask, what does it mean that God allowed that to happen to me? How could he love me? Did he even care? Did he abandon me? As Sibbes (1635/1973) remarked, "God seems to walk sometimes contrary to himself; he seems to discourage, when secretly he doth encourage, as the woman of Canaan" (p. 124). Such experiences are especially problematic for survivors of physical, emotional, or sexual abuse, sometimes in Christian homes, who may have prayed daily for years that God would deliver them from the abuse. The prayer was eventually answered, but only after untold pain, and the all-knowing God appeared to them to be apathetic or even complicit regarding the abuse. This may be the most disturbing kind of suffering in all the earth.

One way to appreciate their adult apprehensions about God is to consider it a matter of evidence. Their abuse by one or more of the primary images of God to which they were exposed came to permeate their perceptions of others, including God, so that the human antagonism they have experienced gradually changes into "evidence" of God's antagonism. Such individuals often recoil at the portrayal of God in the Bible as majestic, righteous, and angry about sin, since it unconsciously reactivates the negative side of their self-other "relational filter" formed, in part, during those earlier hostile experiences. Consequently, they may need to avoid those portions of Scripture for a time while they learn more about God from other parts of Scripture, and some may have to stay away from the Bible altogether for a while. However, it would be a mistake to reject such portrayals entirely (see Lotufo, 2012). Aside from their being part of Holy Scripture, such liberal antipathy is also extremely shortsighted therapeutically. At the right time, reading about the righteous, sovereign God, for example at the end of Job, can activate one's distorted relational structures so they can be healingly corrected through communion with the one, simple God, who we learn in other Scripture passages is also loving and kind. Thus, working through the transference at the divine level can be facilitated by integrating Scripture's various portrayals. (Some aspects of these challenges were discussed in chap. 6.)

Another reason why the cross is so important in Christian psychotherapy is that there God completed and fulfilled the revelation of himself in the Old Testament, where he displayed the integration of his sovereign majesty, righteousness, and love by laying down his life for his friends, showing himself to be also the excellent, self-giving, healing God he has always been. On the cross, the Son was forsaken by the Father for us—to rescue us from our having forsaken God and to identify himself with those who have been forsaken in various ways by others. There is the only place on earth that survivors of abuse will find the concrete signs of infinite love that they need to undermine the heavy concentration of evil and "godforsakenness" they experienced and that was woven into their inner being. On the cross, the Son entered into the silence, abandonment, and unimaginable darkness of hell for our sakes, providing the ultimate contrary testimonial evidence of God's everlasting compassion for them that alone is great enough to overturn the empirical evidence of their suffering.

How Christian counselors communicate this part of the gospel to the abused—especially if the abuse came from religious caregivers—is critically important. Just sharing Bible verses with those who have been tortured by the Bible can unwittingly continue the torture by disregarding their story and their feelings about their story—perhaps vaguely resembling their abusers. Of course biblical teaching is relevant and can eventually be a source of healing for such people, but it must be carefully integrated at the right time into the reality of counselees' lives, the stories of their adversity, and their consequent suffering.[30] This requires dialogical communion, not lecture.

The Christian counselor, therefore, has to be wise—listening, taking seriously the suffering, and accepting everything that is said without reproach, even when there is hatred and bitterness mixed in, because this is how love sometimes has to begin. Later, counselees can be taught to discriminate between their suffering and their own sin, between lament and confession. Earnest listening without condemnation communicates that counselees are valued and safe, regardless of their performance, and trains them for lament (and confession) before a God who always accepts them in Christ.

"Coming to Terms" with One's Suffering

There are ultimately only two ways to relieve one's suffering, past or present: keep it out of consciousness (in various ways) or "come to terms" with it. Christians do the latter by reinterpreting it in the heart as part of God's ultimate good for life. We recall that consent (with-sentiment) for

Edwards (1989) refers to the conscious, heartfelt acceptance/reception of God and his will. Consent with regard to suffering, however, differs significantly from consent to God's wholly good gifts, whether from creation (e.g., personality strengths) or redemption, since suffering is a mixed evil and we were created with a motive to avoid it. As a result, we consent to God and the good in the suffering, but not to the evil. The key is the conscious transformation of our created aversion to suffering by trusting in a greater good than that of avoiding suffering. Stump (2012) argues that suffering is always intended by God to draw us into his communion. So, when suffering is contrary to the desires of our hearts—as it usually seems—our task is to refold those desires into God's love for us, and when we are successful, we both win, as God happily draws us more into our greatest good. Kierkegaard's (1849/1980) definition of faith is also useful here: "that the self in being itself and in willing to be itself rests transparently in God" (p. 82). This reminds us that faith (consent) entails being honest about all that is going on in us, including our aversion to suffering, the suffering itself, and our seemingly thwarted heart's desires, as we fold them all into God's empathy, love, and goodness. Such soul work is, of course, complex and challenging. However, the antithesis to consent— resistance to God's will, manifested in such traits as bitterness, despair, apathy, unforgiveness of others, and mistrust of God—is by all accounts not good for us. So God calls our resistance to his will sin.

Those who have suffered a lot will usually have to persevere in the therapy journey a long while to undermine a strong, automatic avoidant response to emotional pain in order to maintain negative emotion schemes and memories in consciousness, so they can work on them and bring about some resolution. Exposure therapy trains people to allow themselves to feel and endure their negative emotions, until they get used to them (Foa, Huppert, & Cahill, 2006), an ability called distress tolerance (Zvolenky, Bernstein, & Vujanovic, 2011).

"Coming to terms" with our suffering, then, summarizes an important means for realizing God's doxological agenda for us: drawing us into greater communion with him and toward Christlikeness, evident in an increasing hardiness, patience, resilience, and courage; empathy for others; and transparency about our suffering and our ambivalence toward it. As a result, perhaps those who have not experienced much suffering are, from a divine standpoint, the truly poor in spirit.

Helping Those Who Have Suffered Less

When life has been easy, faith and gratitude may come easily. So perhaps those who have suffered much have a responsibility to help those who have suffered less to understand God and suffering better and become more authentic in their faith. This may entail gently challenging a well-meaning but facile Christian positivity (whether charismatic ["Just say 'Praisallujah!'"] or Reformed ["Remember, 'All things work together for good!'"])[31] by daring to share one's suffering heart with others—the bad and the ugly as well as the good. This is risky, of course, because the motivation to avoid suffering is so strong that otherwise nice Christians can unwittingly speak cruelly to suffering brothers and sisters, thinking they're being spiritual but actually shutting down the sufferer to maintain their own comfort. Many who have suffered catastrophic or chronic loss have had to endure the impatience of others regarding their often slow recovery, because of the latter's simple inability to grasp the depth of the suffering. Nevertheless, by courageously "going public" with their sorrow—wisely, discerning their own readiness and that of the other—great sufferers encourage others who have suffered greatly, and they just may help those with less experience to be less critical and more open to it, in themselves as well as in others.[32]

Weeping with Those Who Weep

Counselors have a special role to play in this process by validating the reality of the suffering of their counselees, whether past or present. This is hard work, because empathy ("feeling with") involves feeling the same negative emotions of suffering that the counselee is feeling, and counselors have the same created motive to avoid suffering as everyone else. This aversion is seen in those who criticize the unrelenting strong negative emotions of some chronic sufferers as "wallowing" or engaging in "self-pity." Such an interpretation does not yet recognize the narrative significance of the emotion and the fact that there are probably good, historical reasons for so much negativity, requiring a long-term investment of others in this soul. Of course, some *are* oppressed by unproductive patterns of emotional experience and expression that are reflective of their fallenness—rumination or high levels of anxious arousal by which counselees are held captive. But we help them out not by exhorting them from the top of the hole, but by jumping in with them. Ideally, in-session emotion experience will lead to some measure of resurrection in Christ. But the sad truth is that there is no resurrection without the cross, and the healing journey requires reexperiencing the suffering in a new way, with others and ultimately with Christ. The skilled counselor plays a critical role here by acknowledging the meaningfulness of the suffering through attentiveness, concern, and a corresponding suffering, if only for an hour. Such confirmation helps the counselee come to terms with their pain and pictures to them the heart of Christ (Jn 11:35).

RESOURCES FOR COUNSELORS AND COUNSELEES

Classic

Julian of Norwich (1998). *Revelations of divine love*. London: Penguin.

Lewis, C. S. (1962). *The problem of pain*. New York: Macmillan.

—— (1961). *A grief observed*. New York: Harper & Row.

Schilder, K. (1945). *Christ in his suffering* (H. Zylstra, Trans.). Grand Rapids, MI: Eerdmans.

Sibbes, R. (1998). *The bruised reed*. Edinburgh: Banner of Truth Trust.

Warfield, B. B. (1970). The emotional life of our Lord. In S. G. Craig (Ed.), *The person and work of Christ* (pp. 93-148). Philadelphia: Presbyterian & Reformed.

Weil, S. (2009). The love of God and affliction. In *Waiting for God* (pp. 67-82). New York: Harper.

Contemporary

Billings, J. T. (2013). *Rejoicing in lament: Wrestling with incurable cancer and life in Christ*. Grand Rapids, MI: Brazos.

Brand, P., & Yancey, P. (1997). *The gift of pain*. Grand Rapids, MI: Zondervan.

Coakley, S., & Shelemay, K. K. (2005). *Pain and its transformations: The interface of biology and culture*. Cambridge, MA: Harvard University Press. ‡

Folkman, S. (2011). *The Oxford handbook of stress, health, and coping*. New York: Oxford University Press. ‡

Moser, P. K. (2013). *The severity of God: Religion and philosophy reconceived*. New York: Cambridge University Press. A little too creative at points, but a remarkable defense of the lengths a loving God will go to promote righteousness in persons.

Mouw, R. J., & Sweeney, D. A. (2013). *The suffering and victorious Christ: Toward a more compassionate Christology*. Grand Rapids, MI: Baker Academic. ‡

Payne, L. (1995). *The healing presence: Curing the soul through union with Christ*. Grand Rapids, MI: Baker. Includes an excellent discussion of the need to work through past suffering in the present in order to overcome it, a process she calls "remedial suffering."

Powlison, D. (2006). God's grace and your suffering. In J. Piper & J. Taylor (Eds.), *Suffering and the sovereignty of God* (pp. 145-75). Wheaton, IL: Crossway. Shows practically how God's sovereignty and love are integrated in Christian suffering.

Sittser, G. (2011). *A grace disguised: How the soul grows through loss.* Grand Rapids, MI: Zondervan. A luminous book that shares the story of a man who lost his mother, wife, and youngest daughter in a car accident. Stunning wisdom and hope amid pathos.

Stump, E. (2010). *Wandering in darkness: Narrative and the problem of suffering.* New York: Oxford University Press. ‡ Perhaps the most thorough Christian treatment of suffering ever written and a surprisingly accessible philosophy tome.

Tada, J. E. (2000). *When God weeps.* Grand Rapids, MI: Zondervan.

Tan, S.-Y. (2013). Resilience and posttraumatic growth: Empirical evidence and clinical applications from a Christian perspective. *Journal of Psychology and Christianity, 32,* 358-64. ‡

Thomas, G. (2002). *Sacred marriage.* Grand Rapids, MI: Zondervan.

——— (2005). *Sacred parenting.* Grand Rapids, MI: Zondervan.

Wolterstorff, N. (1987). *Lament for a son.* Grand Rapids, MI: Eerdmans.

‡ Recommended more for counselors and pastors than counselees

—10—

Biopsychosocial Damage and Psychopathology

Principle 3: Psychopathology is most comprehensively understood from three perspectives: sin, suffering, and biopsychosocial damage.

Expansion 2: Suffering and biopsychosocial damage are significant aspects of psychopathology because they can be either hindrances or means to God's glory and human well-being.

But we have this treasure [of the light
of the gospel of the glory of Christ] in earthen vessels,
so that the surpassing greatness of the power
will be of God and not from ourselves.

2 Corinthians 4:7

For when I am weak, then I am strong.

2 Corinthians 12:10

A stigma, according to Erving Goffman (1963), refers to "an attribute that is deeply discrediting, . . . a failing, a shortcoming, a handicap" (p. 3). Stigmas are identified by a majority group of "normals" who lack the attribute and perceive those with it as "not quite human" (p. 5). This disapprobation gets subtly communicated in various ways, typically leaving the stigmatized feeling shame about the odious trait, so they either avoid the "normals" or attempt to hide the stigma, if possible. Consequently, Goffman argues that a stigma has less to do with the feature in question than with the disapproving evaluation that makes it so.

Where does this social dynamic come from? To some extent, stigmas are due to humanity's normative orientation, activated in a fallen world. Created good, humans naturally interpret deficiencies in themselves and others negatively. Children stare at persons with a physical disability and get agitated when they first meet someone who is severely mentally impaired. As we get older, we learn to restrain such reactions, but a profound awareness of normalcy, excellence, and deficiency pervades human life that is tragically twisted by sin. Girard (1996), for example, has argued that humans need scapegoats in their communities to reduce the violence to which their competitive rivalry leads. As a result, humans experience some kind of discomfort in the presence of those identified with a stigma and often try to avoid them, and if they are aware they have one, they are naturally ashamed.

Unfortunately, the current human condition entails the potential for many kinds of stigmas, including biological and psychosocial damage. People can have genetic defects; their bodies and brains can malfunction; they can experience catastrophic or chronic trauma, which can alter brain function; their thinking and emotions can be consistently distorted; they can have difficulties connecting with others. And as with suffering, such biopsychosocial damage is massively unevenly distributed.

People have been aware of such damage in the West at least since Hippocrates (460–377 BC), who referred to madness and delirium and believed they were caused by problems in the brain (Segal & Coolidge, 2001). Over the past 150 years, our understanding of biopsychosocial deficits has exploded due to the work of modern psychiatrists and psychologists, and the Christian counseling community can benefit immensely from their contributions, for the God of the Bible cares greatly about those who are so disadvantaged and stigmatized. Consequently, a *comprehensive* Christian model of psychopathology has to take into account biopsychosocial damage, as well as sin and suffering. At the same time, we cannot ignore the fundamental worldview distortions of modern psychiatry and psychology. Our challenge is to translate this literature according to the discursive practices of Christianity, saturated with relevant biblical teaching, if we are ever to develop a distinctly Christian model of psychopathology, a project that has only just begun (see Coe & Hall, 2010; Flanagan & Hall, 2014; Johnson, 2007; Yarhouse, Butman, & McRay, 2005). What follows constitutes another contribution toward such a project.

UNDERSTANDING BIOPSYCHOSOCIAL DAMAGE

There are many ways to look at biopsychosocial damage, and given its complexity and differences in assumptions and training, a lack of unanimity is to be expected in contemporary psychopathology and psychiatry—and within the church—regarding how they are to be interpreted and classified. Moreover, the secular literature is too vast to even begin to summarize in this chapter. As a result, we begin with a mere outline of current knowledge, interpreted Christianity.

Orders of Causation

When considering etiology (the study of the causes of illness), modern developmental psychopathology restricts its study to biological and social causation, commonly referred to as nature and nurture. Nature, or biological causation includes the role of genetics, in utero experience, and neurological development, as well as the activity of the hormonal and neural systems. Heritability measures "the degree to which vulnerability to develop a disorder is influenced by genes" (Faraone, Tsuang, & Tsuang, 1999, p. 32). For example, in one important twin study, researchers found heritability estimates for disorders ranging from 16% for conduct disorder to 55% for bulimia (in between were anxiety [28%], depression [36%], substance use [39–61%], and phobia [27%]) (Kendler & Prescott, 2006). Genes order and organize and can alter neuron development and communication throughout life (Pennington, 2002). During in utero development, neurons proliferate and migrate to form distinct regions of the brain. They communicate with each other by electrochemical events (called an action potential or neural "firing") that release molecules, known as neurotransmitters, which bind to receptors on adjacent neurons, making them more or less likely to "fire." After birth, neurons get organized through experience into neural networks (patterns of neural firing) that communicate through neural pathways. All human activity, whether healthy or maladaptive, appears to be grounded in such patterns of neural communication. Biopsychosocial disorders develop when patterns of neural firing that ground human functioning depart from God's design plan and become routinized through repetition.

Within weeks of birth, nurture, or social experiences, begin to organize the brain and its psychosocial processes (memory, emotions, thinking), primarily within one's family of origin, especially in childhood, as well as secondarily through peer influences and other social relations throughout one's life, influenced by larger cultural dynamics. Harmful patterns of social interaction, when chronic, establish relatively isolated neural networks characterized by negative emotions and chaotic or rigid states of mind that are likely to reactivate in future interactions that resemble the earlier ones (Siegel, 2012). The diathesis-stress theory hypothesizes that ongoing negative social interactions cause cumulative stress (or suffering), which can trigger gene activity in those genetically vulnerable to develop certain disorders, causing changes in neural organization and function that may be sufficient to lead to the emergence of a biopsychosocial disorder (Ingram & Price, 2001).

In addition to these influences, Christians (and humanists) recognize personal/ethical causation that results from personal choices and actions that can also increase suffering and shape neural organization and function. Christians also believe that supernatural agents such as the devil can negatively affect biopsychosocial function (see 1 Sam 16:23).

Levels of Biopsychosocial Damage

Damage can occur to material-biological dynamic structures such as neurons and neural networks, as well as immaterial-psychological dynamic structures such as perception and reasoning, evidenced in mental impairment and incoherent narratives (see Johnson, 2007, chap. 10, for an explanation of immaterial structures). However, we are still far from understanding how problems in the material sphere of the body can cause problems in the immaterial sphere of the soul, and vice versa.

Microlevels of damage. As just mentioned, catastrophic or chronic suffering can lead to alterations in genetic and neural activity and structure that can lead to psychological disorders. These changes include disruption in neurotransmitter production (too much or too little) and reduction in neurotransmitter receptor sites, synapses, and dendritic branching that can be caused by severe stress. Intense suffering in childhood is stored in numerous episodic memories saturated with negative affect and the establishment of increasingly elaborated neural networks that are disposed to activate negative emotion schemes characterized by sadness, shame, anxiety, or anger, and negative beliefs and attitudes about oneself, others, and the future.

Intermediate levels of damage. Years of ongoing psychosocial adversity can lead to the formation of neural networks and their intercommunication that ground maladaptive psychological patterns such as negative moods or states of mind (Cozolino, 2010; Siegel, 2012); a settled negative self-representation;

feelings of depletion, emptiness, or abandonment; perfectionism; a lack of trust in others; discomfort in intimate relations and difficulties empathizing; neediness; affect that seems inappropriate in the setting; defensiveness; restlessness in sleep; limited ability to differentiate self and others or reflect on one's inner life; harsh self-talk; a distorted sense of self and identity; dissociated states of consciousness; and perceptions that God is uninterested in oneself or even hostile (PDM Task Force, 2006; Moriarity & Hoffman, 2007). Adults from such backgrounds may be unmotivated, dispositionally resistant to healing and recovery, internally restless or fragmented, or may perceive a hostile "inner critic" or "saboteur" or identify with and repeat a narrative of failure, rejection, and hopelessness. When poor psychological functioning becomes sufficiently pervasive, an identifiable syndrome may develop.

Syndrome level of damage. In the *Diagnostic and Statistics Manual* (fifth edition; DSM-V)[1] of the American Psychiatric Association, a mental disorder is defined as "a syndrome characterized by clinically significant disturbance in an individual's cognition, emotion regulation, or behavior that reflects a dysfunction in the psychological, biological, or developmental processes underlying mental functioning." In addition, "Mental disorders are usually associated with significant distress or disability in social, occupational, or other important activities" (American Psychiatric Association, 2013, p. 20), including ethical and spiritual activities (though these are largely disregarded in the DSM-V). Only a representative list of the syndromes it identifies will be mentioned to illustrate the wide variety of biopsychosocial damage covered: schizophrenia, bipolar I, major depression, posttraumatic stress, dissociative identity, anorexia nervosa, insomnia, addictions, Alzheimer's, narcissistic personality disorder, and paraphilia.[2] In addition, most Christians committed to classical orthodoxy would continue to recognize same-sex attraction and gender dysphoria as syndromes in spite of their being removed from the DSM and enormous cultural pressure today to normalize them. Their assessment as disorders should have nothing to do with sinful stigmatization, but is simply a function of biblical revelation, natural law, and genetic and developmental norms (to say nothing of evolutionary assumptions).

Degree of damage. People vary considerably in terms of their degree of damage. One way this has been measured clinically is by the assignment of a Global Assessment of Functioning (GAF) score, utilized in the DSM-IV. However, this was dropped in DSM-V. The psychoanalytic community

(PDM Task Force, 2006) has developed a useful continuum regarding the relative damage of personality structure (the P Axis) that corresponds broadly to what we are calling biopsychosocial damage. It begins with a comparative absence of damage constituting a base level of psychological well-being to mild damage (a neurotic level of dysfunction, e.g., having a strong tendency to count steps compulsively that does not interfere with one's life) to moderate (a borderline level of dysfunction, e.g., alcohol addiction) to severe (a psychotic level of dysfunction, e.g., schizophrenia). From a Christian standpoint, human flourishing also includes communion with God and a life and relationships that are genuinely fulfilling. Accordingly, all humans are most profoundly damaged by sin.

Summary. We saw in chapter two that human flourishing, patterned after the triune God, is characterized by vigorous agency and vigorous communion. Any material or immaterial dynamic structure that departs from God's design plan for a flourishing human being constitutes biopsychosocial damage, and there are countless complex ways that human agency and communion can be compromised. In what follows, we will explore the implications of biblical teaching on weakness in order to develop a Christian framework for better understanding biopsychosocial damage.

CHRISTIAN TEACHING REGARDING BIOPSYCHOSOCIAL DAMAGE

There are very few direct references to what we would call biopsychosocial deficits in the Bible (Wilkinson, 1998). "Madness" and "bewilderment of heart" were threatened as punishment for disobedience (Deut 28:28). Saul had repeated bouts with paranoia (1 Sam 18:12; 24:9) and homicidal intentions (1 Sam 18:10-11) due to his disobedience and an evil spirit (1 Sam 16:14-16), which were treated with music (1 Sam 16:16, 23). David, we are told, once feigned madness (1 Sam 21:10-15); and Nebuchadnezzar lost his reason as judgment for his arrogance (Dan 4:29-37). In most of these instances, the cause of the psychological abnormality was designated as personal sin. This inspired perspective is in keeping with the emphasis of biblical revelation, especially in the Old Testament, on the revelation of sin and its destructive consequences, which God gave to form a strong ethical awareness in his people, ultimately to lead them to Christ (Gal 3:24). As a result, we ought not to conclude that these few references provide an exhaustive model of psychopathology according to God. On the contrary, we would not expect to find a comprehensive scientific analysis of biopsychosocial damage in the Bible any more than the periodic table of the elements. The development of science is humanity's God-given calling, part of the creation mandate, and God did not choose to reveal all his knowledge about humanity in the Bible. Rather, through Scripture God gives us a way of seeing the world (Powlison, 2003), including biopsychosocial damage, that accords with his omniscient understanding and that guides us toward his complete understanding and evaluation. We turn next to examine the biblical materials relevant to biopsychosocial damage.

God's View of the "Disadvantaged"

The laws of the Torah taught the Israelites that God was especially concerned with the special challenges facing people with relative disadvantages and disabilities and that he wanted his people to look out for them and their needs. "When you reap your harvest in your field and have forgotten a sheaf in the field . . . it shall be for the alien, for the orphan, and for the widow" (Deut 24:19). "You shall not curse a deaf man, nor place a stumbling block before the blind, but you shall revere your God; I am the LORD" (Lev 19:14). "Vindicate the weak and fatherless; do justice to the afflicted and destitute. Rescue the weak and needy; deliver them out of the hand of the wicked" (Ps 82:3-4). The Israelites were constantly warned not to "oppress the poor" and "crush" or "trample the needy" (Amos 4:1; 8:4; see also Job 24:14; Ps 37:14; Prov 30:14; Jer 7:6; Zech 7:10; Mal 3:5; Ps 10:2; 37:14).

Jesus Christ was well schooled in these teachings (Work, 2002). According to Luke, he officially began his ministry with a visit to a synagogue, where he read aloud, "The Spirit of the Lord is upon Me, because He anointed Me to preach the gospel to the poor. He has sent Me to proclaim release to the captives, and recovery of sight to the blind, to set free those who are oppressed, to proclaim the favorable year of the Lord" (Lk 4:18-19). And when he had finished, he said, "Today this Scripture has been fulfilled in your hearing" (Lk 4:21). His ministry to those with various physical maladies (leprosy, blindness, chronic menstrual bleeding, fevers, numerous kinds of crippling conditions, demon possession) was the fulfillment of Old Testament teaching, so those who saw Jesus' healings "glorified the God of Israel" (Mt 15:31). His associations with the outcasts of his culture showed that he rejected its social stigmas and the social comparisons on which they were based. Christ's life and teachings manifested God's appraisal of human reality, in effect upending and overturning created attitudes about wholeness corrupted by sin. "Blessed are the poor in spirit," he said, "for theirs is the kingdom of heaven" (Mt 5:3). The Israelites, the appointed representatives of humanity, were unable to accomplish God's redemptive agenda, so the Son came to bring in God's reign, where the disadvantaged and disabled would really be helped.

The Biblical Concept of Weakness

The New Testament word *astheneia* (also found in the Septuagint) has generally been translated "weakness," "incapacity," or "infirmity."[3] It is the most common term in the New Testament for physical illness,[4] and occasionally poverty (Acts 20:35), but it can be used to refer to all kinds of limitations: physical, psychological, moral, and spiritual. Jesus, for example, told his sleepy disciples in the Garden of Gethsemane that the spirit is willing, but the flesh is *weak* (Mt 26:41). Paul stated that our natural bodies are sown in dishonor and *weakness* (1 Cor 15:43). He told Roman Christians that when we were *weak*—that is, powerless to save ourselves—Christ died for the ungodly (Rom 5:6; see Rom 8:3). Later in the epistle he wrote that because of our *weakness*, we do not know how to pray as we ought (Rom 8:26). On a couple of occasions, Paul taught churches how to treat *weak* believers, whose consciences were unduly sensitive (Rom 14:1–15:1; 1 Cor 8:1-13). But the relevance of *astheneia* for our purposes is especially brought out in the Corinthian correspondence. In 1 Corinthians, Paul argued that God has chosen the *weak* things of this world, and he admitted to some of his own weaknesses, including feelings of fear and human inadequacy and an absence of rhetorical and intellectual prowess (see 1 Cor 1:17–2:16, esp. 1 Cor 2:3). Then we learn in 2 Corinthians that he was apparently being criticized for his weakness by certain teachers in Corinth, and he conceded to having weaknesses with regard to an unimpressive personal presence (2 Cor 10:10) and a lack of skill in speech (2 Cor 11:6, 21). (More on this below.)

To gain further understanding, let us contrast *weakness* with two of its antonyms in the Bible. In John 5, people were waiting to be healed who were "sick, blind, lame, and withered" (Jn 5:3), and one had a sickness (*astheneia,* Jn 5:5) whom Jesus made "well" (*hygiēs,* Jn 5:9). Here *astheneia* is the opposite of health, soundness, and wholeness (Arndt & Gingrich, 1957), thereby signifying "less than whole" and implying a state that falls short of some standard of well-being. By contrast, Paul a few times compared *astheneia* with *dynatos* (1 Cor 1:26; 2 Cor 12:10; 13:4), which refers to traits such as mighty, powerful, or able (Arndt & Gingrich, 1957). Here, weak denotes a lack of power or ability.

Taken together, the above passages suggest that *weakness* was a rather comprehensive term in the Bible used to denote a variety of physical and psychological conditions that were less than whole or that involved the lack of some competence or ability to accomplish something that most other humans are able to do. So weakness in the Bible refers to *the state of being "less than" in some respect, either less than some ideal—less than complete and whole—or less than what is typical for human beings, and so deficient in some respect to most other people, or both.*

Personal sin and weakness contrasted. It will be instructive to compare the biblical concept of weakness with what we saw in chapter eight regarding personal sin. The most obvious difference is that sin is repugnant to God and entails causal responsibility and personal culpability. Personal sin is an active falling short of God's ethicospiritual standards for humanity (Rom 3:23), a disobedience or lawlessness (1 Jn 3:3) for which humans are held responsible. Weakness, on the other hand, would seem to be a *passive* defect of one's creaturehood, where one finds oneself impaired or disabled in some respect, in comparison with others, a condition resulting from impersonal causes, for which one is therefore not held responsible. Personal sin is an action, whereas weakness is a condition, a limitation in human life. To lack athletic ability or to have Down syndrome is a biopsychosocial problem, not a moral or spiritual one. Weakness is bad in a qualitatively different sense from personal sin and is therefore vastly less problematic on an ultimate scale of significance.

The difference between personal sin and weakness is also revealed in God's respective attitudes toward them. God is opposed to personal sin and punishes it (Ezek 18:4; Rom 2:12). "For You are not a God who takes pleasure in wickedness; no evil dwells with You. The boastful shall not stand before Your eyes; You hate all who do iniquity" (Ps 5:4-5). Then, recall the same God's compassion toward the disadvantaged. He is concerned about their needs and advocates for their rights. So far from rejecting them for their disability, he forbade anyone to curse them. Rather, when on earth in the person of Christ, he associated with the destitute, disabled, and deformed. Indeed, Paul told us that "God has chosen the foolish things [*ta asthenē*] of the world to shame the things which are strong, and the base things of the world and the despised God has chosen, the things that are not, so that He might nullify the things that are, so that no man might boast before" (1 Cor 1:27-29).

Christ's work also distinguishes personal sin and weakness. Matthew outlined a twofold redemptive design that occurred in Christ, writing that he came to "save His people from their sins" (Mt 1:21), and after an evening of healing "he took our illnesses [*astheneias*] and bore our diseases [*nosous*]" (Mt 8:17, quoting Is 53:4 from the Septuagint; ESV). Christians are familiar with the gospel teaching that Christ "was delivered over because of our transgressions" (Rom 4:25), yet his crucifixion also displayed "the weakness of God" (1 Cor 1:25). Being made like humans in every way (Heb 2:17), he can "sympathize with our weaknesses (*astheneias*), since he was tempted in all things as we are, yet without sin" (Heb 4:15). But his identification with weakness culminated in his death, when he was "crucified because of weakness" (*estaurōthē ex astheneias*; 2 Cor 13:4). The Holy and Almighty Son of God became sin and weakness with us and for us, so that we might become righteous and whole and strong in him and with him.

In accordance with God and Christ's differential approach to sin and weakness, Christians likewise are to interpret their personal sins and weaknesses differently.[5] They are to resist their indwelling sinfulness (Rom 6:1-11; Gal 5:17-20), put to death evil desires and deeds (Rom 8:12-13; Col 3:5), confess their sins (1 Jn 1:9)—that is, take responsibility for them—and repent or turn away from them (Mt 4:17). As we have already noted, Paul's approach in 2 Corinthians to his own weaknesses was quite different, for he used them to defend his apostolic calling. Apparently he had been accused of being a weak and therefore unauthoritative apostle. He was not a skilled speaker (2 Cor 11:6); he did not seek financial support when living with them, as a "great" apostle supposedly commanded (2 Cor 11:7-9); and he had been accused of being timid and unimpressive in person but bold and forceful when writing to them (2 Cor 10:1, 9).

Rather than list his apostolic accomplishments to counter these accusations (as he suggests he could, 2 Cor 10:1-6), he turns the criticisms on their head and lists his many difficulties instead (2 Cor 11:23-33). "If I have to boast, I will boast of what pertains to my weakness [*astheneia*]. The God and Father of the Lord Jesus, He who is blessed forever, knows that I am not lying. In Damascus the ethnarch under Aretas the king was guarding the city of the Damascenes in order to seize me, and I was let down in a basket through a window in the wall, and so escaped his hands" (2 Cor 11:30-33) So weak was the apostle Paul that he escaped from his enemies in a basket like a little baby.

Later, to keep him from boasting in his accomplishments, God sent him a "thorn in the flesh." In spite of Paul's pleas for its removal, God famously told him, "My grace is sufficient for you, for power is perfected [or made complete or whole, *teleitai*] in weakness" (2 Cor 12:9). As a result, Paul said,

"I will boast all the more gladly of my weaknesses, so that the power of Christ may rest upon me. For the sake of Christ, then, I am content with weaknesses, insults, hardships, persecutions, and calamaties. For when I am weak [*asthenō*], then I am strong" (2 Cor 12:9-10 ESV; see also 2 Cor 2:5).

The Greek term for "boast," *kauchaomai*, is in the middle voice, and it means to glory or pride oneself in something that pertains to oneself (Arndt & Gingrich, 1957). Paraphrasing Paul, it means to embrace something about oneself and even celebrate it. Rather than weaknesses (such as chronic sufferings, speaking problems, and personality inadequacies) being shameful stigmas and evidence of his lack of calling and suitability for ministry, Paul taught that, at least in his case, they actually demonstrate his calling, for they prove that the tremendous good that he accomplished had to be from God, in light of his considerable limitations.

Recall what he said earlier in the epistle about the gospel:

> We have this treasure in earthen vessels, so that the surpassing greatness of the power will be of God and not from ourselves; we are afflicted in every way, but not crushed; perplexed, but not despairing; persecuted, but not forsaken; struck down, but not destroyed; always carrying about in the body the dying of Jesus, so that the life of Jesus also may be manifested in our body. For we who live are constantly being delivered over to death for Jesus' sake, so that the life of Jesus also may be manifested in our mortal flesh. So death works in us, but life in you. (2 Cor 4:7-12)

Here we see most clearly how personal sin and weakness differ, and in a very striking way. Whereas sins are intrinsically opposed to the glory of God and would seem necessarily to compromise it, and therefore are truly shameful, weaknesses are actually a means of God's glory; in fact, they can uniquely express it, so the shame one feels regarding one's weaknesses is, from a divine perspective, false. Understood aright, the weaknesses of believers are the basis of their unique sharing and participation in the self-glorification of God in Christ, especially his crucifixion. We should infer that every believer has a special calling to glorify God according to his or her own specific weaknesses. As a result, one's path of soul healing involves embracing and even celebrating ("boasting in") one's weaknesses, knowing they are one's own peculiar means of glorifying God. Though both are deficits, sin and weakness could not be more different from each other.

Weakness and psychopathology. So how might we extend the biblical notion of weakness to psychopathology? If weakness is a nonculpable condition or trait that renders one less than whole or deficient in some respect compared to others, then it would seem an appropriate descriptor of various kinds of biopsychosocial damage: genetic abnormalities and dispositions; brain damage and the corresponding mental impairment (as in Down syndrome, Alzheimer's, and schizophrenia); learning disabilities; sleep disorders; all the conditions along the autism spectrum; the tendency toward mood swings that characterizes bipolar disorder; the memory and sleep problems and flashbacks that can occur after severe trauma; and hallucinations and delusions, such as paranoid ideation. And consider the neurological/psychological effects of chronic childhood abuse or neglect, which continue into adulthood, for example the development of an insecure attachment style, a shame-prone personality, a pervasive sense of loneliness, or difficulty regulating one's emotions, all of which are related to genetic vulnerability triggered and constituted by poor childhood socialization (Ingram & Price, 2001). Such damage results in pervasive internal conflict that compromises one's personal agency and capacity for communion.

Whatever the precise causes, we will define psychological weakness as dynamic structures of the soul that are less than complete or whole or that are deficient when compared with typical humans—including cognitive (e.g., memory and reasoning), affective, volitional, and relational capacities. Because such problems are usually grounded on damaged or malformed biological structures (genetic, neurological, and hormonal), psychological weakness is almost always related to some kind of biological weakness (even when the latter was primarily the result of socialization; this phenomenon is the study of social neuroscience). Given the profound interaction between biological, social, and psychological causal influences in human development, we will consider psychological weaknesses to be a function of "biopsychosocial damage."

Some will be concerned that such a broad and inclusive categorization of psychological problems risks being deterministic and minimizes human responsibility and sin in psychopathology, and this is a worthy concern that will be addressed below. However, Christians have historically believed that humans are embodied creatures who develop in a fallen world. If we do not take into sufficient account the creaturely influences of nature and nurture, we run into the opposite intellectual dangers of a radical libertarianism and moralism and treating humans as disembodied spirits who are absolutely free and unconditioned. Both extremes must be avoided if we are to do justice to the complexity of the development of fallen humans into responsible images of God, each of whom has an utterly unique story of influences that constitutes their particular "conditions of glory" (Johnson, 2007, chap. 17).

Fault. Fallen humans are of such complexity that simply distinguishing sin and weakness in psychopathology is not sufficient. We must add a mixed category of psychopathology that includes features of both sin and weakness. We refer here to weaknesses where sin is variously involved. I will refer to this class of phenomena as fault.

The term is borrowed from Ricoeur (1965, p. xvi; 1967), though he used it to label what Christians since Augustine have called original sin.[6] Fault, however, would also seem fitting for the compound of sin and weakness. In both French (*faille*) and English the terms used for this concept have a twofold provenance of meanings. *Fault* in a geological sense denotes a break, a breach in the earth, a line of "brokenness" in the ground. For example, we might say "the light switch is faulty," meaning it is damaged and not working right, and this use is akin to weakness. By contrast, fault in an ethical sense commonly suggests personal culpability and responsibility—"The car accident was my fault." It can also indicate a character defect—"He has his faults"—and these uses point in the direction of sin.

Is there any evidence in the Bible of a third category of psychopathology that is a combination of sin and weakness, a kind of weakness with ethical and spiritual implications?

Poverty, a mixed condition. The book of Proverbs provides a rich, dialectical perspective on the poor. On the one hand, they are viewed with compassion and concern: "Do not rob the poor because he is poor, or crush the afflicted at the gate" (Prov 22:22). "The righteous is concerned for the rights of the poor, the wicked does not understand such concern" (Prov 29:7). In addition, they have a relation with God in common with the rich—"the LORD is the maker of them all" (Prov 22:2)—and with their oppressor: "the LORD gives light to the eyes of both" (Prov 29:13).

Yet Proverbs also teaches that, at least in some cases, poverty is a result of laziness, hedonism, and drunkenness. "He who loves pleasure will become a poor man; he who loves wine and oil will not become rich" (Prov 21:17), and "Poor is he who works with a negligent hand, but the hand of the diligent makes rich" (Prov 10:4, see also Prov 6:11; 13:18; 14:23; 20:13; 23:21; 24:30-34; 28:19). So poverty may be a consequence of personal sin. Perhaps then, at least in some cases, adult poverty may be a kind of fault, a result of social (and perhaps some biological) factors that have disposed people toward it, as well as poor personal choices. A clue that poverty may be a fault could be the absence of any resolution in Scripture to these seemingly contrary approaches to the poor and no set of rules for distinguishing the "worthy poor" from the "unworthy." God is simply concerned about the disadvantaged, even when their poverty may be related to irresponsible living. "He who oppresses the poor taunts his Maker, But he who is gracious to the needy honors Him" (Prov 14:31).

Jesus and sinners. We have already considered Jesus' ministry to the weak. But the Gospels also portray the holy Jesus as a friend to sinners (Lk 7:34). What should Christians make of the difference between his dealings with prostitutes, tax gatherers, and drunkards, and his sharp denunciations of the hyperrighteous Pharisees? The Gospels appear to teach that there are two classes of sinners in the world, those who know they are and those who do not, and Christ's actions would seem to indicate that the self-deception of religious sinners is more reprehensible than the more obvious kind of sin.

Of all the Gospels, Luke included the most accounts of Jesus' dealing with sinners. All three, however, recite the following episode:

> Levi gave a big reception for Him in his house; and there was a great crowd of tax collectors and other people who were reclining at the table with them. The Pharisees and their scribes began grumbling at His disciples, saying, "Why do you eat and drink with the tax collectors and sinners?" And Jesus answered and said to them, "It is not those who are well who need a physician, but those who are sick. I have not come to call the righteous but sinners to repentance." (Lk 5:29-32)

Luke also wrote of a woman who anointed Jesus with perfume. The other Gospels include a similar story, but only Luke's account raises the issue of the woman's moral character:

> And there was a woman in the city who was a sinner; and when she learned that He was reclining at the table in the Pharisee's house, she brought an alabaster vial of perfume, and standing behind Him at His feet, weeping, she began to wet His feet with her tears, and kept wiping them with the hair of her head, and kissing His feet and anointing them with the perfume. Now when the Pharisee who had invited Him saw this, he said to himself, "If this man were a prophet He would know who and what sort of person this woman is who is touching Him, that she is a sinner." (Lk 7:37-39)

Jesus used the Pharisee's reaction as an opportunity to teach about the nature of God's kingdom agenda and his heart toward such people: "For this reason I say to you, her sins, which are many, have been forgiven, for she loved much; but he who is forgiven little, loves little" (Lk 7:47). Referring to this event, Stump (2010) notes that the "sinner has been shown to be someone worthy of more regard than the dinner's host," so that "the pejorative designation 'Sinner' in the end assumes a different connotation" (p. 362).

Luke was also the only author to recount the parable of the prodigal son (Lk 15:3-32). Readers know its gist. A son has squandered his inheritance and returns penniless and ashamed of his folly and profligacy—in light of the book of Proverbs, he was the epitome of the sinful poor—and yet his father (who represents God) does not punish him or even say anything critical but simply rejoices at his return. In the context of the Old Testament law, this parable had to have shocked its first audience. Christ came to fulfill the law, not abolish it (Mt 5:17; an emphasis of Matthew's), but one way he fulfilled it was to tie together the diverse Old Testament strands and reveal a new framework for interpreting sinners and their sin, which Paul, the former Pharisee, built on in his development of the doctrine of what Augustine termed "original sin" (see Rom 1–3; 7; Eph 2:1-3; 1 Tim 1:12-16; Titus 3:3; see also chap. 8 in this volume).

Original sin as *weakness.* This note is picked up in the book of Hebrews:

> For every high priest taken from among men is appointed on behalf of men in things pertaining to God, in order to offer both gifts and sacrifices for sins; he can deal gently with the ignorant and misguided, since he himself also is beset with weakness [*astheneian*]; and because of it he is obligated to offer sacrifices for sins, as for the people, so also for himself. (Heb 5:1-3)

Here *astheneia* refers to *moral* weakness (see also Heb 7:28), suggesting that the tendency to commit personal sins itself constitutes a condition of disability. But in contrast to biopsychosocial weakness, humans are held responsible for this condition, for which they need the propitiatory sacrifice of Christ if they are to avoid God's eventual just punishment for sin (Heb 9:11–10:31).[7]

Conclusion. The Bible, therefore, teaches both that sinful actions are ethicospiritually offensive to God, for which humans are responsible and will be judged (the major theme), and that original sin is an ethicospiritual weakness, with which all humans are born (a minor theme). God's holy wrath is justly directed against sin, because humans repress the truth about God that is being revealed to them, so they are without excuse (Rom 1:18-20). At the same time, God offers salvation to the ethicospiritually weak (unlike the demons), in part because of their disability—"Father, forgive them; for they do not know what they are doing" (Lk 23:34). The weakness of sin, moreover, is expressed through the medium of human weaknesses. Yet God has chosen the weak of this world to express his glory uniquely through their weakness. So, while sin is glory's antithesis, God's glory is manifested to the uttermost in Christ's death for the weak and ungodly (Rom 5:6) and the gradual transfiguration of their sinful and weak selves into his image as they become more holy and more whole.[8]

We are especially interested, however, in fault with respect to psychopathology. In light of the above considerations, perhaps we can hazard a definition. *Psychological fault refers to a biopsychosocial* and *ethicospiritual disorder involving both weakness and sin—a deficient condition influenced by biological and social factors and woven into one's created nature, but having ethical and spiritual significance.* A composite of sin and weakness, faults arise from original sin; physiological, relational, and psychological influences; and possibly personal causation, shaping one's dynamic form and disposing one to certain patterns of thinking, feeling, desiring, willing, and relating to others, and affecting one's personal agency, including efforts to overcome one's sins and weaknesses, as well as one's capacity for communion.

Imagine a Venn diagram of human psychopathology with two circles labeled "weakness" and "sin," and "fault" labeling a large intersection, except that the interrelation between sin and weakness is far more complicated than such a diagram indicates because of the very different ways sin and weakness can co-occur and because there is often (but not always) an inverse relation between them. To begin with, let us eliminate those conditions that can hardly be regarded as sin but do involve some degree of personal agency and responsibility and have mild ethicospiritual implications. Consider, for example, Paul's subtle encouragement to Timothy that "God has not given us a spirit of timidity, but of power and love and discipline" (2 Tim 1:7), or his teaching to the strong regarding the weak, who were technically in doctrinal error, but whom he did not challenge directly (Rom 14; 1 Cor 8). In both cases his comments imply the deficit has ethical and spiritual significance and point to the possibility of improvement through knowledge and agency. However, neither weakness also warrants the label of sin, so they cannot be regarded as a fault. The following cases, however, would seem to qualify.

1. Those conditions that New Testament authors regard as sinful (or what is commonly called a vice), but in light of the knowledge that biopsychosocial damage is involved, we can legitimately infer that they are also

weaknesses. Two prominent examples are homosexuality (Jones & Yarhouse, 2000; Hamer, 2002) and drunkenness (1 Cor 6:9-10).

2. Conditions where sin is involved, but one's culpability is to some extent mitigated by compromised self-awareness or self-deception, such as with false selves or the defenses. Paul implied such a condition: "Even though I was formerly a blasphemer and a persecutor and a violent aggressor . . . I was shown mercy, because I acted ignorantly in unbelief" (1 Tim 1:13).

3. Patterns of living originally initiated by one's own sinful choices but that resulted in a substantial loss of personal agency, making it much more difficult to change the course of action, as occurs in physiological addiction (and really any vice).

4. The problem philosophers have called "weakness of will," when humans know what they should do but do not do it because their personal agency is divided, so that their intention is ultimately thwarted (Charlton, 1988).

5. Deeply entrenched patterns of living and relating to others grounded in biopsychosocial damage that can rightly be characterized as sinful—they hurt others and they are selfish, as is seen in personality disorders.

The marked variety of these subtypes suggests that fault is a fuzzy concept covering many different kinds of challenges. Nevertheless, some term is needed to group together the variety of psychopathology characterized by a conjunction of biopsychosocial damage and negative ethicospiritual significance. When one recognizes one has a psychological fault, the ideal self-understanding would seem to have to reflect both the sense of it being a weakness and the sense of the particular degree of sinfulness involved. Consequently, depending on the fault, it would involve, paradoxically, acceptance (of the weakness) as well as confession and repentance (of the sin), both of which are made possible by redemption in Christ.

The Remediation of Damaged Personal Agency and Communion Capacities

So far we have concentrated on causative factors (including personal causation with fault) that have contributed to biopsychosocial damage (including damaged agentic and communal capacities), but in a book on counseling, consideration must also be given to the present state of one's capacities (including agentic and communal), in order to determine as best as possible the extent to which one can participate in the remediation of one's psychological disorders with others[9]—which by Christians is also done in active receptivity with the triune God (Phil 2:12-13; chaps. 2-4). Damage more or less thwarts one's agency and communion with others. The personhood of some Christians is so severely damaged that they lack the ability to participate with others in their recovery—think of those with the most severe forms of the neurodevelopmental disorders (e.g., autism spectrum disorder and intellectual disability), long-term schizophrenia or bipolar I, or the neurocognitive disorders (e.g., late-stage Alzheimer's). The personal agency and communion capacities of such individuals are so severely damaged that, barring a divine miracle, there can be no hope of recovery, even though as image bearers they continue to warrant our care. By contrast, the agency and communion capacities of most people are much less compromised—how much differs for each individual depending on the extent of biopsychosocial damage (in some cases minimal), their original ethicospiritual resistance (common to all), as well as their current personal agency and communion resources, particularly their effort (Baumeister & Tierney, 2011). Though Christian psychotherapy and counseling relies ultimately on the triune God's creation grace and redemptive grace in Christ, the personal agency and communion capacities of counselees—dependent, as they are, on God and his grace—are usually also necessary and have to be enlisted in order to make progress in overcoming their own ethicospiritual resistance to flourishing more in God and promoting whatever remediation of their biopsychosocial damage is possible. Hence, the mysterious nature of the soul healing journey, which entails riding the bike while we are building it!

SOME THERAPEUTIC IMPLICATIONS

The challenge facing the church today regarding the care of those with biopsychosocial damage is to develop Christian forms of practice within a theocentric edification framework, utilizing relevant biblical teaching and the best scientific literature available, translated accordingly. Let us consider a few directions we might take.

Labels in the Christian Community

Words matter, and the language we use shapes how we understand reality. If we were only to use sin language to describe human psychopathology, we would be unable to grasp the diversity of things that can go wrong with the human soul; we would sound judgmental and moralistic; and we would harm those who are primarily dealing with biopsychosocial damage. As a result, for such problems, in addition to damage, it is important for Christians to use words such as *disorder, brokenness, wounds, internal division,* and for the most severe, *illness.*

Over the past twenty years seminal work has been done by Christians on disability.[10] Though its definition is highly contested (Reinders, 2008), the term conveys to most people the notion of a somewhat intractable deficit or impairment in some human ability. Disabilities are commonly divided into physical and psychological, and the psychological into intellectual and learning (American Psychiatric Association, 2013). But there are also emotional, volitional, and relational kinds of psychological problems that seem more like disabilities than illnesses. While some may be put off by the label in this context (because of the stigma?), when interpreted in light of biblical teaching on weakness, one wonders whether, in the long run, it might help those with and without such damage accept more readily the kinds of semi-intractable limitations in thinking, emotional processing, personal agency, and relationality of those with it. Then, just as those with physical and intellectual disabilities have inspired others with their accomplishments, it might be easier to appreciate the internal barriers those with biopsychosocial damage have overcome in their efforts in Christ to enhance their mental, emotional, volitional, and relational abilities, in spite of their limitations.

Biopsychosocial Damage Hinders and Advances the Glory of God
God is concerned about the disadvantaged. In the kingdom of God, the poor in spirit will be blessed, and those who mourn will be comforted (Mt 5:3-4), and the first shall be last, and the last shall be first (Mt 19:30). So his redemptive and doxological agenda encompasses the biopsychosocially disabled. "Let every valley be lifted up, and every mountain and hill be made low; and let the rough ground become a plain, and the rugged terrain a broad valley; then the glory of the LORD will be revealed" (Is 40:4-5).

Well-adjusted or well-formed people—those without much biopsychosocial damage—have the formal capacity to glorify God well; this is especially true of believers because of the stronger correspondence of the *imago Dei* in them, in terms of its relative unity, strength, and integrity, to the form of God. By contrast, the capacity to glorify God of those who are biopsychosocially damaged is correspondingly compromised, insofar as the relevant structures of their soul that constitute part of the *imago Dei*—their thinking, feeling, willing, and relating—are impaired. All human beings glorify God in some degree, but a fully functioning human can manifest more glory than one whose capacities to resemble God are comparably limited.

At the same time, the "jars of clay principle" (Johnson, 2007, p. 553) suggests that people with various kinds of weakness can glorify God in their own ways, and their wounds have a special value to God, since they show "that the surpassing greatness of the power will be of God and not from ourselves" (2 Cor 4:7; Yong, 2007). Specific biopsychosocial damage provides unique "conditions of glory" that not only render the weak full participants in the manifestation of God's glory through and among his people but also bestow a special role to play. This is particularly the case in terms of the splendor or depth of that glory, since they can especially portray the humble humanity of the Son of God, who came and died in weakness. "The Lord accomplishes witness to the world through our weakness" (Dawn, 2001, p. 47). Well-formed and ill-formed believers together can display more of the immense diversity of God's infinite plenitude and resplendence at work in the world (Hart, 2003; Yong, 2007). Part of the healing of the weak entails their reception and ownership of this unique role, something tragically overlooked in perfectionistic churches, which can only see God's beauty in good form.

Taking Biopsychosocial Damage into Account in Therapy

Since such weakness can be a significant aspect of psychopathology, good Christian psychotherapy and counseling involves identifying its presence in counselees' aptitudes, skills that are enhanced by training and experience. There are a number of benefits to counselees that follow from identifying this kind of damage: (1) It helps them become more accurate in their self-representation and self-evaluation before God as they take responsibility for what they should and learn not to take responsibility for what they should not. (2) It directs the attention of counselees (and interested others, such as spouses) to factors that affect psychological and relational problems other than one's will, providing a more accurate and comprehensive picture of the dynamics involved than moralism can. (3) These factors justly mitigate responsibility and reduce guilt—and since God is just and holds people accountable according to their true desert (Prov 16:11), identifying damage can alleviate false shame and guilt feelings, which can further compromise one's functioning. (4) It helps people understand why progress can be so slow, even when motivation to change is high. (5) Since handling biopsychosocial damage ought to be very different from how one handles sin, it aids the counselor in pinpointing the kinds of interventions that should be used and the degree of challenge that is fitting. And (6) It may help justify the wise use of medication for moderate to severe levels of damage.

Lamenting over One's Weaknesses Before One Boasts

We have seen Paul's encouragement to boast in one's weakness and, in the previous chapter, to rejoice in one's suffering. Both need to be seen as new-covenant goals. However, a canonical orientation requires the integration of all the texts of the canon into one's counseling model. So we should factor the Old Testament teaching on lament into our treatment of psychological weakness, just as we did suffering.

There is a deep pattern at work here. Night comes before the dawn, weeping before rejoicing (Ps 30:5), sickness before healing, and death before resurrection. Similarly, mourning and lament will generally precede boasting. This also makes good psychological sense. If we encourage people to boast in their weaknesses too quickly, we may unwittingly drive them into denial about the harsh realities of their lives, foster more internal dissociation, and strengthen their false selves. Lament is of particular value for those who grew up in dysfunctional families and whose childhood was characterized by chronic negative emotions such as anger, anxiety, disappointment, or contempt. Such early experiences usually lead to some damage in thought processes, emotional experience, relational skills, and self-structure, long before children have the capacity to process such emotions in healthy ways. As a result, when working with those from such backgrounds, counseling in the early phases will concentrate on training in lament and helping counselees to "come to terms" with their weaknesses as well as their suffering before encouraging them to work on the far more challenging goal of boasting in God and their weaknesses honestly.

The Slow Healing of Biopsychosocial Damage in Christ

When we think of personal sin, we often assume that people can just stop it with a single act of repentance. This can happen (though not always), but for many reasons the healing of biopsychosocial damage usually takes much longer. For one thing, some of our deepest patterns of self-understanding and relating to others were established during a "critical period" when our brains were especially susceptible to formative influence, similar to when we learned our native language. And just as learning a second language in adulthood takes much longer than it took to learn the first, and our pronunciation and practice of the second language will always reflect our native language, so learning new-creation patterns of self-understanding and relating to others, including God, are usually very slow, and the old patterns will continue to show up. After all, the old patterns have been practiced for decades, so they don't typically just disappear.

As counselees start to realize this, they can become discouraged. So it may be helpful simply to remind them that changing biopsychosocial damage is slow and, depending on what they are working on and what they are un-learning, may take months or years. Receiving more deeply our union with Christ, our present perfection in him, and our eternal perfection to come, can help us accept the gradual nature of the journey.

"Coming to Terms" with One's Damage

Those with physical disabilities sometimes have a hard time accepting their condition, and this can apply as well to those with emotional, relational, and volitional damage. In some ways, it may be harder with the latter kinds of limitations, because we like to think that God will heal everything in our souls, even if we know he doesn't always heal our bodies. As a result, "coming to terms" with one's biopsychosocial damage is an important part of the process of healing, just as it is with suffering. This doesn't mean resigning oneself to staying the same for the rest of one's life. As long as we are alive, our brains are characterized by some degree of plasticity, meaning they can still be changed. On the contrary, change is strangely facilitated when a person gives up the perfectionistic pressure of being "fixed" now.

Medication and Weakness

Emotional disabilities are a kind of weakness, and drug therapy may be a necessary component in their treatment. However, in a holistic, multiorder framework for understanding humans, even biological deficits should not be separated from the personal agents who possess them. For example, severe depression or anxiety usually requires medication, but most of the time, medication should be used to bring depressed or anxious persons to the point where they can begin to take a more active role in therapy and begin making the kinds of dipolar self-regulatory changes in Christ that will lead to more permanent changes in their brain/soul state than medication alone can provide. Without drug therapy, talk therapy may be useless and even cruel, but carefully managed, it can promote personal activity and responsibility for one's recovery while the person is learning psychospiritual techniques that can supplement and eventually supplant the benefits of the medication. Most folks will eventually be able to be weaned off their medication, while others, particularly those suffering from more serious mental illnesses (e.g., schizophrenia or bipolar disorder), may need to remain on medication their entire lives. Seeing counselees as compromised personal agents can help counselors balance patience and compassion with a fitting degree of strategic challenge to counselees to utilize their personal energy in Christ.

Addressing Fault in Psychotherapy and Counseling

Most recognizable disorders probably involve some biopsychosocial damage. Determining whether a condition is simply a weakness or possibly a fault will depend on all the available information, including relevant biblical teaching, empirical research, and philosophical reflection, as well as individual assessment, which may include tests, observations, and interview data. To demonstrate this kind of analysis, we will take a brief look at four kinds of faults that vary considerably regarding the degree to which fault may or may not be indicated.

Insomnia. Sleep disorders are certainly related to the malfunctioning of sleep mechanisms in the brain and possibly the stresses and strains of the body and the soul. Consequently, insomnia can be like the proverbial canary in the mine, a symptom of a cyst, of suffering past or present, or of sin. A thorough, multilevel evaluation is usually in order, which considers biological, psychosocial, ethical, and spiritual factors, including stress level, lifestyle habits, bedtime routine, and strategies such as relaxation, meditative prayer, exercise, and a healthy diet, as well as the careful use of medication, including a few questions about ethical or spiritual problems that could be affecting the brain.

Same-sex attraction. Western views of same-sex attraction (SSA) and gender dysphoria have changed remarkably over the past fifty years, so that their variations and combinations are now publicly celebrated, much like personality differences.[11] At the same time, contemporary academic discussions assume implicitly that they are disorders needing to be explained, particularly in light of evolutionary assumptions (see, e.g., LeVay & Baldwin, 2011). All this makes SSA a good test case for the notion of fault, so we will examine this problem in a little more depth.

We begin by noting the New Testament teaching that homosexuality, broadly understood, is considered sinful (Rom 1:24-32; 1 Cor 6:9; 1 Tim 1:10; see Gagnon, 2002)[12] (liberal objections to the contrary notwithstanding, e.g., Rogers, 2009), indicating that this form of sexuality is contrary to God's will and his design plan for human flourishing. However, significant evidence of genetic, hormonal, and neurological factors variously involved in SSA has also been discovered in recent decades (Jones & Lopez, 2006; LeVay & Baldwin, 2011), as well as some support for social influence (Jones & Yarhouse, 2000; Hamer, 2002), calling for careful reflection in order to develop a comprehensive Christian understanding that takes into account all the facets of homosexuality and avoids biological reductionism as well as moralism.[13]

A common Christian solution has been the recognition that same-sex-attracted people have an internal disposition, also called a homosexual *orientation* (both terms borrowed from the contemporary science of sexuality), which is contrasted with homosexual *activity*, understood to be personal sin for which the personal agents who engage in it are responsible, whether it involves mental imagery, pornography, or interpersonal behavior—just as with heterosexual sin.

The concept of sexual orientation was a helpful scientific advance from a Christian standpoint, because it provides a label for two phenomena: first, the biopsychosocial predisposition most people have toward opposite-sex sexual expression—largely taken for granted prior to the nineteenth century—and second, the disordered predisposition toward same-sex sexual expression, previously attributed to personal agency. To elaborate, those with SSA have a sexual-desire mechanism that is malfunctioning, since upon its emergence in adolescence, it is directed automatically at the wrong object, one prohibited by Scripture and natural law (as well as evolutionary norms). Natural law is experienced in a sense of sexual normativity based in God's design plan that is conveyed through genetics, bodily form, social development, and the normal means of reproduction (without technological assistance), leading to the emergence of a mature conscience, also in adolescence, that indicates shame about one's SSA and expresses some level of inner conflict in response to one's same-sex desires and activity. However, fallen human development within fallen cultures can obviously overwhelm and suppress this creational awareness, though it can be brought back to life by the Holy Spirit.

The notion of sexual orientation also helps Christians appreciate how the experience of SSA is a kind of temptation. "Each one is tempted when he is carried away and enticed by his own lust. Then when lust has conceived, it gives birth to sin, and when sin is accomplished, it brings forth death" (Jas 1:14-15). James seems to have been describing a temporal process and making a distinction between simply having a desire that could lead to personal sin and the sin itself (Blomberg & Kamell, 2008), indicating they are not identical. What turns one's lust into a personal sin is the addition of consent, that is, the intention to fulfill the desire in some way. *That* is an action. As Augustine is reputed to have written: one cannot prevent a bird from passing over one's head, but one can prevent it from roosting in one's hair. Guilt is not imputed to those who have a sinful desire simply pass through their consciousness, so long as they do not intentionally pursue the desire; so it should be viewed as an internal temptation.[14] But to succumb to such a temptation with action is personal sin, and it can eventually become a vice through repetition.

All of that to say, having SSA by itself fits the category of weakness, whereas consenting to and pursuing one's SSA would constitute personal sin, together warranting the designation of fault. The special tragedy for Christians with SSA is that desire for same-sex partnerships cannot be physically consummated without personal sin, requiring careful differentiation of good created desires for friendship from sexual desires contrary to God's will and design. The problem is compounded by many churches' ambivalence toward those with SSA and lack of efforts to help address their relational needs in accordance with God's design plan. From the human perspective, such loss and such self-denial are no small matters, and it is a form of heterosexism not to appreciate the hardship. But like all forms of significant suffering it also creates a personal Gethsemane—in this case, ongoing—and therefore an opportunity, particularly challenging in the present day, to display the supremacy of the glory of God over all other values. Consequently, Christians who pursue God's will and reject the satisfaction of their SSA sexual desires are virtue exemplars, honoring God (and biblical revelation) over those desires, by putting them to death in various ways (see Col 3:5), in some cases, by concluding that celibacy is part of their divine calling (Hill, 2015).[15]

Major depressive disorder. As is well known, MDD is one of the most common disorders, afflicting nearly 20% of the population at some point in their lives. There is evidence of multiple kinds of influence, including genetics (heritability of 33-45%); hormones; brain function; environment, such as abuse or neglect in childhood; stressful life events (e.g., death of a loved one); parental depression; and culture (Fava & Kendler, 2000; Pennington, 2002), suggesting that MDD should be understood predominantly as a result of biopsychosocial damage. At the same time, after the emergence of personal agency in adulthood, there are any number of personal factors that can compound a disposition to MDD, including bad decisions, difficult relationships, and poor coping skills, as well as personal sins (for example, stealing from one's employer or cheating on one's spouse), which can contribute to anxiety or guilt and shame feelings (whether true or false), triggering an episode of depression. Consequently, there are many aspects to consider in depression and in some cases a diagnosis of fault is warranted, which may help the depressed person take the appropriate kind of action for the condition and its remediation.

Antisocial personality disorder. One of the most difficult examples of fault may be antisocial personality disorder (APD), which is characterized by impulsivity, lack of empathy, hostility, and a capability to commit serious crimes/sins without remorse. Yet there is strong evidence of a genetic component, with a heritability estimate around 50%, which along with poor socialization likely helps to explain the corollary disregard for aversive outcomes, limited attention, and a proneness to violence (First & Tasman, 2004; Vitale & Newman, 2013; Mason & Frick, 1994). Persons who grow up in homes with chronically aggressive parents with moderate or borderline levels of damage themselves (PDM Task Force, 2006) are exposed to repeated emotionally and relationally unpredictable experiences with little empathy, which, it is hypothesized, also contributes to the socioneurological sculpting of brains/souls that appear to have virtually lost the capacity to empathize and feel guilt. As a result, such persons will likely be more neurologically predisposed to verbal or physical aggression than had they grown up in a mostly kind and supportive family climate. The prognosis for those with APD is not good. Nevertheless, such people are made in the image of God just as surely as those with Down syndrome, so Christians ought not despise them. At the same time, adults with APD are much more likely to have desires and cognitions that violate God's ethical norms than those with Down syndrome. Moreover, intellectually normal adults with APD know the violation, even if they do not feel it. As a result, regardless of the biopsychosocial influences, cultures have to hold individuals with APD responsible for their wrongdoing. Yet Christians ought also to have compassion for them, particularly knowing that much weakness is involved, trusting that the good, omniscient God will evaluate them justly and knowing that some have been redeemed.

Differential Treatment for Sin, Weakness, and Fault

We saw above that Christians are to confess their sins and boast in their weaknesses. So what are we to do with the paradoxical condition of faults? It ultimately depends on the particular fault, but generally speaking, boasting in a fault is inappropriate because of the sin involved. Nevertheless, the weakness ought not to be ignored. Instead, one must learn to differentiate one's sin and weakness from each other, so that different strategies can be applied appropriate to their respective targets.

The difficulty on this score, however, is no different for original sin, which, as we have also seen, is a kind of fault. Shame is a fitting emotion when one has an ethicospiritual disorder warranting guilt, confession, and repentance of its consequent sins. And yet, at the same time, mindful of the weakness involved, in Christ Christians can take a resurrection stance toward their weaknesses that turns them upside down for the glory of God and bring that stance courageously into one's confession and repentance, knowing our Savior is on our side and that nothing in all creation "will be able to separate us from the love of God, which is in Christ Jesus our Lord" (Rom 8:39). The characterological outcome of such differentiation will be a noble "resurrection humility" or "resurrection contrition," undaunted by one's faults, being in Christ.

Toward a More Comprehensive Psychopathology, Part Two

Readers may recall from chapter three the assertion that a holistic Christian model of therapy will promote both ethicospiritual holiness and biopsychosocial wholeness. Here we consider the opposite ends of both continua, ethicospiritual disorder (sin) and biopsychosocial damage (weakness), as seen in figure 10.1. Together, sin, fault, and weakness provide Christians with a more comprehensive model of psychopathology than those that focus on only one dimension. Christian psychotherapy and counseling have the resources to address the full spectrum of psychopathology, helping people toward the psychospiritual maturity of quadrant D (more wholeness and holiness) out of quadrant A (both weakness and sin), B (more sin than weakness), and C (more weakness than sin).

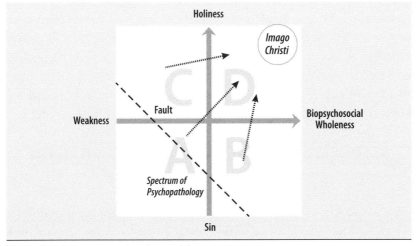

Figure 10.1. A more comprehensive model

Perhaps someday the Christian community will develop its own DSM (like the secular psychodynamic community has done; see PDM Task Force, 2006). Such a work would be the most comprehensive system of psychopathology ever, including biopsychosocial and ethicospiritual disorders within a single diagnostic framework. But much theory building and research has to be done before that can be attempted.

Those Most Vulnerable to Psychopathology

God weaves us in our mother's womb and ordains our days (Ps 139:13, 16), indeed, whatsoever comes to pass (Eph 1:11). And some people are born with genetic predispositions toward psychopathology into dysfunctional families, and they are more likely to develop biopsychosocial damage than others, the effects of which will be with them more or less their whole lives. Some of the most troubled of these people attract plenty of negative attention in the media— for example, the violent mentally ill and, in the church, those whose sin is more manifest as it spills out into their daily lives, families, and other relationships. However, as a class, the biopsychosocially weak are not necessarily the worst kind of people; they have just been exposed to factors that made them more vulnerable to biopsychosocial damage, including more suffering than most children endure. Rather than looking down on the biopsychosocially impoverished (and taunting their Maker; Prov 14:31; 17:5), the biopsychosocially "rich" (those who have benefited from healthier families and more creation grace) might cultivate more of Christ's compassion for such people (including those in mental hospitals and prisons and on the streets), recognizing they could have ended up there had they had the same genetic vulnerability and family life, and honor them as images of God from whom they can gain wisdom by listening to and understanding their stories, and perhaps loving them enough to make a difference in their lives. Conversely, the weak need to strive to see themselves with the just vision of the omniscient God who knows the precise advantages and disadvantages each human has been given and who is mindful that we are but dust. Thankfully, Christ came to seek and to save all the lost (Lk 19:10).

RESOURCES FOR COUNSELORS AND COUNSELEES

Classical

Bridge, W. (2001). *A lifting up for the downcast*. Edinburgh: Banner of Truth Trust.
Sibbes, R. (1998). *The bruised reed*. Edinburgh: Banner of Trust. (Original work published 1630)

Contemporary

American Psychiatric Association. (2013). *Diagnostic & statistics manual: Fifth ed.* Arlington, VA: Author. ‡

Black, D. A. (2012). *Paul: Apostle of weakness* (rev. ed.). Eugene, OR: Pickwick.

Comiskey, A. (2003). *Strength through weakness: Overcoming sexual and relational brokenness.* Downers Grove, IL: InterVarsity Press.

Dawn, M. J. (2001). *Powers, weakness, and the tabernacling of God.* Grand Rapids, MI: Eerdmans. ‡

Manning, B. (2005). *The ragamuffin gospel.* Eugene, OR: Multnomah.

Nouwen, H. (1979). *The wounded healer.* New York: Image.

Packer, J. I. (2013). *Weakness is the way: Life with Christ our strength.* Wheaton, IL: Crossway.

PDM Task Force. (2006). *Psychodynamic diagnostic manual.* Silver Springs, MD: Alliance of Psychoanalytic Organizations. ‡

Stanford, M. (2010). *The biology of sin: Grace, hope, and healing for those who feel trapped.* Colorado Springs: Biblica.

Wardle, T. (2005). *Wounded: How to find wholeness and inner healing in Christ.* Abilene, TX: Leafwood.

Welch, E. (1998). *Blame it on the brain.* Phillipsburg, NJ: P&R.

Yarhouse, M. A., Butman, R. E., & McRay, B. W. (2005). *Modern psychopathologies: A comprehensive Christian appraisal.* Downers Grove, IL: InterVarsity Press. ‡

‡ Recommended more for counselors

—11—

The Breadth of
Psychopathology

Principle 3: Psychopathology is most comprehensively understood from three perspectives:
sin, suffering, and biopsychosocial damage.

*In the day that you eat from it
you will surely die.*

GENESIS 2:17

*They heard the sound of the LORD God walking
in the garden in the cool of the day, and the man
and his wife hid themselves from the presence of
the LORD God among the trees of the garden.*

GENESIS 3:8

*Blessed are the poor in the spirit,
for theirs is the kingdom of heaven.
Blessed are those who mourn,
for they shall be comforted.*

MATTHEW 5:3-4

OVER THE PREVIOUS THREE CHAPTERS, we have seen that, according to Christianity, humans are simultaneously good creatures and fallen, and human fallenness includes the universal condition of original sin and enormous individual differences in personal sins, physical and psychological suffering, and biological and psychosocial damage. While human fallenness includes more than psychopathology (e.g., illness, poverty), disorders of the soul compose the bulk of what Christians think of as the fallen human condition.

TOWARD A MORE COMPREHENSIVE
PSYCHOPATHOLOGY, PART THREE

For theists, human psychopathology can be understood as any deviation from God's design plan for the human body/soul in relationship with others. Sin is an ethicospiritual deviation, whereas created damage is a biopsychosocial deviation. Suffering is a deviation from God's design plan in the sense that, though divinely permitted, he created humans with a motive to avoid it, so that suffering creates tension across all four orders of discourse (biological, psychosocial, ethical, and spiritual; see Johnson, 2007).

Secular psychiatrists and psychologists have made great progress in understanding biopsychosocial damage and the impact of trauma and stress but have largely ignored ethicospiritual disorder. Theologians have concentrated their attention on the disorder of sin and have rarely examined other kinds of psychopathology (McFadyen, 2000, provides a notable exception). The Christian community needs a comprehensive, unified model of psychopathology that addresses all three perspectives by synthesizing the conceptual apparatuses, vocabularies, and wisdom of these two communities' perspectives on the disorders of the soul according to its own worldview assumptions, resulting eventually in a Christian DSM.[1] We finish our reflections on a Christian psychopathology with a consideration of the interrelation of all three perspectives.[2]

To help us understand how each perspective informs a Christian psychopathology, we will consider a brief case study of four persons, each of whom represents a relatively pure type of psychopathology corresponding to each perspective.

Tony is forty-three years old, married with two teenagers, and a vice president of a Fortune 500 company. About six months ago, he went to China, along with two other vice presidents, to find trade partners with some

Chinese businesses. However, on that trip he started an affair with one of the other vice presidents. They have managed to keep their relationship a secret so far. Tony seems happy about the relationship and wants to continue the affair indefinitely, so he is not suffering. In addition, he grew up in a relatively healthy family and has no significant biopsychosocial damage. This is a relatively pure token of ongoing personal sin.

Mary lost her husband of fifty-one years three weeks ago to cancer that was causing him a great deal of pain. She got through the funeral, but though a part of her is thankful that his suffering is over, she cries off and on throughout the day and can hardly stop thinking about him. Within three months she will return to most of her previous activities with friends and at church, so there is no long-term damage. She misses her husband terribly but looks forward to seeing him in heaven. This is a relatively pure token of suffering.

Benjamin is twenty-three years old, has Down Syndrome, lives with his family, and works twenty hours a week in a sheltered workshop. He loves spending time with his family, has a sweet and joyful spirit, and enjoys walking the family dog. He is rarely sad or frustrated, and his parents have few difficulties with his behavior. This is a relatively pure token of bio-psychosocial damage.

Most of the time psychopathology involves more than one perspective. Jenny grew up in a family with an alcoholic father and a mother who worked hard to make sure her husband had no reason to get upset. As a result, Jenny learned very early that her fear and sadness were not important. Once in a while, Jenny would witness her drunk father hit her mother, and this would terrify her. Jenny became a Christian in her twenties and takes her faith very seriously. She got married and has three children. However, when family life does not go as she wishes or has planned, she sometimes "loses it" and runs to her room crying and for a time is inconsolable. Her children know that she loves them, but when they don't do well in school or in sports, she can be severely critical. She especially has conflict with her husband, who has his own struggles with mild depression and lack of self-confidence. When they get in a fight, he tends to withdraw. A couple of years ago, she began to feel a growing sense of anxiety about life, especially her children's physical well-being, and she usually feels distant from God. Jenny has suffered throughout her life, and as a result, she has some biopsychosocial damage that has been woven together with original sin, leading to some patterns of personal sin, called vices, for which she bears some responsibility. Comprehensive Christian treatment would address all three dimensions.

Sin (and sins), suffering (past and present), and biopsychosocial damage constitute three distinct human forms of psychopathology. Table 11.1 summarizes some of the particular features of each, especially with reference to God and redemption.

Table 11.1.

	SIN	SUFFERING	BIOPSYCHO-SOCIAL DAMAGE
The problem with respect to God	God is absolutely free of sin (1 Jn 1:5).	God has eternal characteristics that get expressed in a fallen creation that are analogous to human suffering. A perfect God endures sin and is pained by it; the majestic King suffers empathically, knowing the suffering of humans.	God is absolutely free of defect.
God's attitude to the problem in humans	God is wrathful toward human sin and will one way or another judge all sin.	God is empathic and compassionate toward those who suffer.	God has a special regard for those with disabilities and is their advocate.
The problem with respect to Christ while on earth	Christ never sinned himself but bore the penalty for human sin on the cross (2 Cor 5:21).	Christ suffered during his human life and especially during the last eighteen hours.	Christ had no disabilities, but he identified himself with and was crucified in "weakness" (2 Cor 13:4).
How should Christians approach this problem with respect to themselves?	Confession and repentance	Seek to reduce one's suffering if possible. If not, lament, co-identify with Christ, and reframe.	Seek remediation of one's disability if possible. If not, seek to accept it and boast in it.
What does God do about this problem in the lives of believers now?	God takes away objective guilt and shame from believers, weakens sin, and promotes fewer personal sins through faith and repentance in Christ.	God allows suffering to be unevenly distributed among believers, but comforts them through faith in Christ and seeks to bring good out of it.	There is considerable variation. In some cases the disabilities are allowed to be permanent (mental impairment); in some cases God gradually heals them to some degree; in some cases he takes them away.
What will God do about this problem in the lives of believers in eternity?	God will remove all sin from believers in heaven forever.	God will remove all suffering from those in heaven forever.	We cannot be sure. He may remove all disability from those in heaven, or it may mark our everlasting life (like Christ's wounds), but there will be no shame.

Each perspective has its own unique frame of reference, quality, impact, and resolution, shaped by the triune God's reaction and response to each one. An important goal of this model of therapy is the differentiation of these three kinds of psychospiritual disorders, since each requires its own kind of treatment unified around Christ. Original sin involves the cultivation of fundamental humility, whereas personal sin involves confession, repentance, and mortification. The treatment of suffering entails being authentic in one's response through sharing it with God and trustworthy others so we can learn how to endure it as our calling, to love and forgive those who cause it, and eventually to rejoice in it, in spite of our created resistance to it. And the treatment of damage involves a variety of strategies, depending on the damage, and to the extent that it appears irresolvable, we are to come to terms with it, reframing it as a special site of glory, and gradually learn how to boast in it from the heart.

CHRISTIAN TEACHING REGARDING THE BREADTH OF PSYCHOPATHOLOGY

Building on what we have seen regarding sin, suffering, and damage, we will consider how they are interrelated in psychopathology and their pervasive impact on human beings.

Individual Dramas and a Comprehensive Developmental Psychopathology

Modern developmental psychopathology has tended to study humans as mere organisms, rather than as ethical and spiritual beings, and has limited its considerations to biopsychosocial factors (though see Flanagan & Hall, 2014, for a Christian alternative). As a result, it has not paid enough attention to how the ethicospiritual nature of humans can develop optimally or poorly. A Christian psychology entails a more holistic and comprehensive approach, beginning with a consideration of God's involvement.

Because of his sovereign majesty, God is a perfect personal agent who has absolute or infinite freedom, according to his virtuous nature. Human personal agents, by contrast, possess finite, conditioned freedom—limited by one's location in history, geography, gender, *this* body, and so on—and humans have their agency further limited by original sin and the fallen biopsychosocial conditions within which their capacities developed. We have noted in earlier chapters (and in *Foundations*) that the ethicospiritual orders develop out of the biopsychosocial orders, which temporally precede the former, so that the biopsychosocial orders ground the ethicospiritual. Without a relatively healthy brain, no ethicospiritual orders will develop.

As we have repeatedly observed, though God established this creation as a theater for his glory, he has allowed the display and return of that glory to be extremely difficult, in order to manifest more of his glory than would otherwise have occurred. To create these *advanced* conditions of glory, God set up an "opposition of freedoms"—his sovereign freedom (or personal agency) and the conditioned freedom (or personal agency) of his image bearers (Balthasar, 1988–1998, Vol. 2). The dramatic tension of the theodrama and its ongoing dialogue between God and his images (Vanhoozer, 2005; 2010; 2014) is immeasurably heightened beyond that of a perfect creation by the severe limits of humanity's finite, conditioned agency—its bondage to sin and the particular sins it commits, its sufferings, and its disabilities. How can humans participate in God's glory when their innermost being is antagonistic to it and their actions regularly violate his commandments, when they have a created motive to resist suffering, and when their agentic and communal capacities are compromised in a multitude of ways and degrees? The internal and social conflicts produced by these psychopathological factors frankly give the story of redemptive history a good deal of its dramatic intensity. The particular limits that individual humans become aware of in early adulthood can be termed their "conditions of glory" (Johnson, 2007, chap. 17), but they also afford dramatic opportunities for the role they play in the theodrama.[3]

The goal of the following brief overview of a Christian developmental psychopathology is the tracing of how its main perspectives are complexly interwoven in human development. We shall begin with a restatement (from chap. 8) of its starting point: original sin, which is *a universal, continual, mostly unconscious disposition that pervasively inclines humans to mistrust God and resist his glory, supremacy, and love, and be at enmity with him, others, and themselves, contrary to their own fundamental well-being and that of others, subverting and damaging their created goodness, and leading to idolatries of many kinds.* According to Christianity, the development of all human psychopathology originates from this fundamental disorder.

Original sin tends toward chaos. At the start of the creation, God spoke into chaos and brought order into being (Gen 1:2). The Hebrew term for "chaos" (*tōhû*) denotes that which lies beyond the formative word of God and threatens it from the periphery of the creation (Barth, 1960b; Brueggemann, 2002). One of original sin's effects is the undoing of God's ordering word, bringing chaos in its wake, evident within both body and soul and between self and other. In God's curse on humanity for its sin, he used synecdoche to summarize sin's disordering effects—pain in childbirth, gender warfare, and difficulty in work (Gen 3:16-19). It is now also obvious that some people experience more chaos than others.

Without God's presence to help, one's lower (but good) created psychological powers (biopsychosocial perception/cognition/desires) are stronger
than one's higher psychological powers (moral and spiritual perception/
cognition/desires). As a result, otherwise legitimate created desires become
excessive ("inordinate" in medieval parlance), overriding one's conscience
and awareness of God and his glory in the creation. "Sheol and Abaddon are
never satisfied; nor are the eyes of man ever satisfied" (Prov 27:20). This
disordering turns lower created desires into *lusts*. Without God at the center
of our being, the dominion of original or implicit sin over human persons is
exercised through autonomous creational dynamics and a preference for the
creature over the Creator (Edwards, 1758/1970; Rom 1:25; 5:17-21; 6:6, 12-23).

Original sin and nature: Biological chaos and childhood weakness. We have
already noted that sin's effects extend to our God-created bodies, evident in
the disorder of genetic predispositions to addictions, aggressive behavior,
same-sex attraction, gender confusion, schizophrenia, bipolar depression,
eating disorders, and somatic disorders (Stanford, 2010).[4] These psychopathological tendencies are distributed unevenly among individuals.

In addition, God's perceived absence in human life affects later biological development. Without God as one's ultimate frame of reference,
the natural cognitive limitations of preschool children (e.g., "egocentrism";
Piaget, 1977b) develop into self-absorption in adulthood inappropriate for
an image of God; without the experience of God's love, preschool children's natural desires for love, security, and affirmation become implicit
narcissism in adulthood. Original sin subverts our natural limitations and
yearnings, so that adults live unconsciously alternating between the poles
of seeking to fill an insatiable emptiness and loneliness with other creatures
and despairing in some degree of such fulfillment (Kierkegaard, 1849/1980).
These psychopathological tendencies are common to all humanity.

Original sin and nurture: Psychosocial chaos and early suffering. Original
sin tendencies, genetic deficiencies, and children's natural limitations are
usually combined with disordering socialization to produce abnormal phenotypic outcomes. In a fallen world, the young child's needs for affirming,
responsive, intersubjective union with others (labeled also as attachment,
mirroring, and empathic attunement), as well as for feeding, protection,
training, and norms, are not always adequately met, leading to the possible
emergence of specific kinds of psychopathology.

Arguably the greatest suffering in the world is caused by the physical,
emotional, and spiritual abuse and neglect of children, because of how it

shapes their development. Such treatment conveys meaning that activates emotions, communicating to children they lack created goodness, and to some extent overruling the generally positive orientation of created human life. In addition, repeated negative social experiences and their meaning are likely to get internalized, sculpting the developing brain/soul of the child and possibly leaving behind such long-term biopsychosocial deficits as painful memories, negative-biased thinking and beliefs, intense maladaptive emotion schemes, a lack of appropriate emotion, an inner critic or "saboteur," and other dissociated parts of one's self- and other-representations, defensive interpretations, attachment disabilities, and poor social skills. Nonetheless, their "good-creation orientation" (chap. 7) motivates them toward a positive focus, contributing to the dissociation, defenses, and denial. "The more unhappy childhood was, the more, in self-defense, it is excluded from consciousness and kept from interfering with the life of the present, so far as that is possible. The unconscious . . . is largely built up and structured by the process of burying and forgetting precisely all that was most difficult and disturbing in early life" (Guntrip, 1957, p. 190).

One of the more clinically significant outcomes of negative social experiences is the development of disordered "states of mind" (Siegel, 2012)—also called "self-states" (Wachtel, 2008) or "parts" (Schwartz, 1995). According to Siegel, a state of mind is "the total pattern of activations in the brain at a particular moment in time" (p. 186) that results from repeated, similar experiences. When chronically traumatized children regularly alternate between overwhelming negative emotion states—like anxiety or sadness or shame—and positive emotion states with others, these markedly different "states of mind" form "neuroanatomically distinct sites" (Siegel, 2012, p. 188) that get "clustered into specialized selves" (p. 211) and become more or less dissociated from each other in one's experience—also called "splitting" (Hamilton, 1988). These states of minds are likely to be activated in adult relationships that resemble the earlier dynamics to some extent, providing strong interpretive frameworks of present experiences and relationships, sometimes leading to the arousal of negative feelings that are just as vivid as when those same neural networks were being formed and elaborated in childhood—even when the current triggering events are not nearly so traumatic. States of minds also contribute to the experience of "false selves" that feel inauthentic, when we become aware of them.

Knowing something of these developmental dynamics helps to explain the phenomenon Freud (1920/1959) termed the "repetition compulsion," the tendency for those from troubled backgrounds to seemingly work at re-creating their past in the present by seeking out similarly troubled spouses and friends and acting in self-defeating ways that generate the same kinds of abusive or rejecting responses that hurt them much earlier. Fairbairn (1952) suggested that these repetitions are in part motivated by an unrelenting hope that "the other" will finally change and satisfy the desire for the long-lost connection (or communion), another good created longing.

McFadyen (2000) offers profound Christian explanation of how pathological effects of sexual abuse insinuate themselves into the wills of victims, which can be readily applied to many kinds of mistreatment of children. The personal-agency capacities of children are not yet fully formed, and they lack power, status, and knowledge. As a result, they cannot really resist their mistreatment. However, the power dynamics intrinsic to their relationships with their caregivers create conditions that co-opt what limited agency they possess. Caregivers model certain patterns of action and relational style, providing implicit guides for the actions of children. Since children generally have only one interpretive context within which they come to understand themselves and their capacities, they have no way to form comparative judgments that might qualify and objectify their situation. In addition, the language, emotions, and actions of relatively poor caregivers, often directly associated with the children's deficiencies and misbehavior, correspondingly shape their developing identity and agentic and relational capacities. In some cases, for example with sexual abuse, the children develop an "illusion of consent," since they more or less cooperate with the more powerful abuser, desiring the "good" relationship promised implicitly or explicitly. This results tragically in a false but deep sense of collusion in the evil, distorting the identity and emotions of the abused and subverting their inner resources into patterns of action and relationship that tend toward the self-destructive, get stored in the brain, and will shape their future story mostly unconsciously.

The socialization of children is supposed to prepare them for mature agency, first by training them to act according to the scaffolding of parental guidance and second by gradually relinquishing the close supervision necessary in childhood and providing increased opportunity for older children and adolescents to take responsibility for their choices and actions. Yet, poor parental modeling, abuse, and neglect, particularly given how children are often blamed for their mistreatment in such contexts, shape the pre-agentic volitional capacities of children in ways that incline them toward patterns of personal sin and vice years before they will make adult decisions for which they will be held responsible as mature personal agents. McFadyen (2000) argues that such fallen social influences show how original sin operates, malforming the wills of human beings "by incorporation into concrete, social and material processes of action and by the trajectory of past action. Willing is not merely a personal dynamic; we find it arising out of and being incorporated into pathological dynamics that are inter-, trans-, and supra-personal" (p. 127). What makes one's actions wrong is not whether one absolutely freely choses to do them (contrary to libertarian notions of freedom) but whether one is an adult personal agent willingly doing what God has forbidden.

> [Influences] that . . . originated outside of the will may enter it, altering the structure of intentionality, one's perception of the good and consequently one's internally directed life-orientation. The field of force constituted by the distorted dynamics of sin which surround one and in which one cannot avoid participating disrupts and distorts the internal energies by which one orients and directs one's life from within. (p. 188)

Hence, according to McFadyen, the Christian doctrine of original sin provides a suprapersonal framework within which to understand how individual human agency can be subverted to sinful purposes that transcend individual wills, while maintaining that individual humans are still responsible for their own sinful deeds, though they were shaped more or less by the sinful wills of others. This is a significant part of the tragedy of the fallen human condition.

We might say the sins and unbelief of others that one encounters in childhood resonate and cohere with one's indwelling sin, which can foster greater unconscious collaboration with others in willed loneliness from God, and stronger, usually unconscious, internal opposition to God, inhibiting future faith and the love of God beyond the universal, stultifying influence of original sin. This is, in part, because the sinfulness of those images of God to whom one is exposed and with whom one interacts closely will lead to later distortions in one's God-image (see chap. 6) (as well as one's relational capacities with other humans and one's self-representation).[5] Growing up with religious parents who do not resemble God very well is particularly harmful, because of the inevitable confusion of one's distorted God-image with one's understanding of God (God-concept), *usually obtained from the same persons.*

By contrast, the more creational good to which one is exposed in childhood, the more creation grace (including the repeated experience of positive emotions and the neural networks they establish) will constitute the developing person, leading to the gradual emergence of a more accurate form of creational likeness to God, including one's agentic and relational capacities. However, such is the effect of original sin that the "remaining goodness" of the *imago Dei* is insufficient to enable individuals, even those in skilled counseling relationships, to repair themselves and experience *comprehensive* wholeness apart from Christ—though non-Christians can obviously experience a version of wholeness. Nevertheless, these merely human efforts of soul healing, though beneficial biopsychosocially, are ethically and spiritually inadequate from a Christian standpoint, because human resources alone are not enough to overturn human alienation from the true God due to original sin and its consequent shame and inevitable guilt.

Summary. Sin, suffering in childhood, and damage together contribute to a massive compromise of created human functioning that affects all human relationships—radically and universally with God in the case of original sin, but differentially and with enormous variety, depending on one's degree of early suffering and damage. The threefold relational falsehood of idolatry, the misinterpretation and misuse of others, and self-deception originate in original sin but are exacerbated by suffering and damage, leading all humans to fall short of the form and splendor of God, more or less.

Some Psychological Outcomes of Fallenness

Human agents develop within a fallen social world, in close relationships with humans who are more or less sinful, suffering, and damaged, and this has profoundly affected the nature of their agency and relationships. We noted in chapter seven there is a basic distinction between cognitive and carditive processes (the latter involving emotions, desires, and volition) in created human nature that is directly related to human participation in divine glory, both of which have been profoundly influenced by fallenness.

Cognitive processes in a fallen world. Cognition includes conscious awareness, attention, memory, beliefs, reasoning, and imagination. All are compromised, to one degree or another, especially with reference to one's understanding of oneself, others, and God. Original sin makes it impossible to know God well and correspondingly distorts our knowledge of ourselves and others. It biases our cognitive faculties in autocentric and self-serving ways, particularly in relation to God, exacerbated by personal sins and their effects. In addition, one's cognitive faculties can also be damaged as a result of genetic and other biological influences such as early nutritional deprivation as well as chronic childhood suffering. And pronounced suffering can lead to distortions in one's thinking, recollection, and interpretation of God and others.

Carditive processes in a fallen world. Cardition is the depth dimension of the human soul and includes motives, desires, emotions, core beliefs, the unconscious, intentions, and actions, the phenomena responsible for the direction of one's life. Sin has a greater impact on carditive processes than cognitive, leading humans away from God, confounding human relationships, and inappropriately exaggerating self-love. However, suffering and damage also cause significant distortion in these areas. We will examine two important aspects of the psychospiritual heart: desires and especially the emotions.

Human beings are creatures with desires, and our desires are supposed to resemble God's desires, in certain core respects, and to correspond to his comprehensive design plan for humanity (Lombardo, 2011; Pruss, 2013). That means that, as we have seen, human well-being is tied to a theocentric orientation in which one desires God supremely, and one's other desires (regarding oneself, others, and the rest of creation) are properly ordered in relation to him, the norms of human life, and one's own particular callings and obligations. Human psychopathology, therefore, can be understood fundamentally as consisting of disordered desires (according to God and his design plan). The three kinds of psychopathology we have considered reflect the disordering of human desiring differently. Having original sin means humans desire created things in the heart more than God, leading to inevitable inner conflict regarding competing objects of desire—some good and some evil—whereas personal sins signify and manifest one's disordered heart. Suffering, especially in its chronic forms, can exacerbate this inner conflict, since in sinners who are suffering, unfulfilled secondary desires, based in created needs, can become intensified, leaving persons with conscious and unconscious motives to fulfill those desires. In addition, in those who suffer, the created desire to avoid suffering, combined with the cognitive and carditive effects of sin, can warp one's perceptions of God, self, and others. Biopsychosocial damage can cause further distortions in one's perceptions and desires, resulting in a desire template that deviates more or less from God's design plan, with individual desires falling along a continuum from relative malleability to relative fixedness, so long as we are in this body.

Emotions are signs of evaluative meaning, grounded in distinct neurophysiological states. (A discussion of the semiolinguistic nature of emotions can be found in Johnson, 2007, chap. 9. Also see Roberts [2003] for an excellent analysis of emotion informed by Christian sensibilities.) Greenberg suggests that "emotion identifies what is significant for well-being and prepares people to take adaptive action" (Greenberg, 2011, p. 62). Given their worldview, Christians believe these functions of the human emotion-system were designed by God according to his *complex theocentric* value system: since God and his glory are central, human well-being is found ultimately in him and secondarily in the created order enjoyed accordingly.

In addition, emotions are dichotomous, either positive or negative. Therefore, positive emotions were intended by God to reflect and dispose humans toward that which would promote their genuine well-being, preeminently God and secondarily all else that would contribute to their flourishing, according to his design plan. Negative emotions, by contrast, were intended to reflect and dispose humans away from that which would be harmful to their genuine well-being, preeminently sin and secondarily all else that would compromise their flourishing.

The meaning of negative emotions in a fallen world. Christians might wonder why God would create humans with negative emotions that would have been unfitting in a perfect creation. We might suppose that their presence indicates that he knew that humans would live in an imperfect creation. So God created humans with a few distinct, categorical negative emotions (more distinguished from one another than are the positive emotions) that would be extremely useful in a fallen world. Negative emotions are in fact important signs that human life is "not the way it's supposed to be" (Plantinga, 1995).

In both cases, positive and negative emotions are intended by God to be truth bearing. Just like a belief can be true if it corresponds to reality, so "an emotion is good just in case it 'fits' its . . . object" (Zagzebski, 2004, p. 76). Consequently, an important maturity goal is to cultivate an emotion system with dispositions fitting for the circumstances, corresponding to one's current life space as well as one's life and story, as stored in one's memory.[6] God's evaluation of reality is the only absolutely true, perfectly objective evaluation. But humans are finite, conditioned, and fallen creatures, so their goal should be to approximate God's evaluative response *in light of their own story.* Consequently, five mature Christians might respond to an event mostly similarly and somewhat uniquely, and both the unanimity and the diversity are fitting.

There appear to be at least six universal negative emotions that are part of God's good creation that enable us to live meaningfully in a fallen world—

sadness, anxiety/fear, anger, shame, guilt, and emotional pain—in addition to many cultural variations. We will examine them to determine what they signify.

Sadness. In a fallen world there are no guarantees that one's created needs will be met or one's desires satisfied. Sadness generally indicates the perception of loss, especially a loss of human relationship, but it can also be due to the loss of an accomplishment or a goal or even a material possession. In addition, the perceived loss may be counterfactual, that is, loss of what one *should have had*, for example, as a result of chronic neglect in childhood. When one experiences significant loss, it is God's design that one feel sad and be able to express it productively and appropriately. In a fallen world like ours, great loss can occur, resulting in great sadness.

Fear/anxiety. Various kinds of threats lurk in the future of a fallen world. Fear and anxiety indicate perceptions of the possibility of physical or emotional harm to oneself or someone one cares about. Fear is typically focused on a specific object of potential threat (especially bodily harm), whereas anxiety is a more diffuse state of unease in the face of a more vague menace (Lazarus, 1999). Perceived threats can also pertain entirely to oneself, for example, the potential of a failure of one's personal agency (say, an inability to achieve some goal). In the face of many kinds of danger on earth, periodic anxiety is normal, but those who experience chronic anxiety in childhood may develop trait anxiety later.

Anger. People in a fallen world will also sometimes be treated unfairly by others, and they will at times be prevented from attaining their goals by circumstances or others. People tend to become frustrated or angry on such occasions, especially when both occur, that is, they are unable to attain a goal because of unjust treatment. However, whereas sadness and fear/anxiety (and shame and guilt; see below) tend to lead to inhibition of activity, anger tends to move people to take some action (unless turned in on oneself). In a fallen world like ours, some anger is normal, but chronic mistreatment makes anger more easily triggered.

Shame and guilt. We will consider two kinds of self-conscious or moral emotions.[7] Shame is a feeling of personal deficiency that results from a global negative self-evaluation, whereas guilt is the feeling that one has violated an internal standard (Tangney & Dearing, 2002). Shame is focused on one's *being*, based on beliefs that one has a flawed nature and is defective, and it leads to hiding, whereas guilt is focused on one's *doing* and is a consequence of an action one deems immoral (Harter, 2012; Morrison, 2011; Tangney & Dearing, 2002).

We will examine the moral emotions a little more than the others, because they can signify what we have determined is the worst form of psychopathology—our sin. Shame and guilt, therefore, can be signs with respective transcendent implications, since, according to Christianity, original sin is the greatest universal human deficiency, and personal sins are violations of God's standards for human action. Shame and guilt were the first negative emotions alluded to in the Bible, experienced immediately after Adam and Eve sinned—when they hid—made especially salient by their symbolic embodiment in humanity's sexual and reproductive nature (Gen 2:25; 3:7-8). So while shame and guilt are subjective emotions, they are supposed to correspond to objective valid states as determined by God, and in the eyes of God, humans are truly deficient ethicospiritually and condemned for their sinful actions.[8]

Guilt has received the bulk of attention in the West, which is understandable given the focus of biblical law on personal sins and vices and the greater salience of transgressions than their underlying conditions. However, shame actually signifies a worse feature of the human predicament and is the more destructive emotion. Shame is the opposite of glory, so shame feelings, paradoxically, are a sign both of our created dignity before God and its having been besmirched by original sin. According to Bakhtin, shame reflects *the lie of autonomous being* (Coates, 1998, p. 45). We humans are (mostly unconscious) pretenders to the throne of our souls—where God is supposed to reign—who attempt to cover up the invalidity of our claim (signified by our primordial shame) with an ever-changing set of "fig leaves" (aspects of God's creation behind which we hide). "Shame is man's ineffaceable recollection of his estrangement from the origin; it is grief for this estrangement, and the powerless longing to return to unity with the origin" (Bonhoeffer, 1955, p. 20).

Shame and guilt are good in that they signify our "internal psychic division" (Stump, 2012, p. 142), but they can also motivate us to resist conscious awareness of our deficits and transgressions, contributing universally to self-justification, self-serving bias, and the defenses, and in those with more obvious psychopathology, severe dissociation and delusion. They also compromise our ability to love and receive love, since they lead us to hide and deceive ourselves (Morrison, 2011; Stump, 2012) and fuel the maintenance of our false selves. Tragically, people can also experience *false* shame and guilt, that is, shame and guilt that are excessive, overwhelming, and debilitating (Harter, 2012), according to God's objective knowledge.

Shame feelings are generally more painful than guilt feelings (Tangney & Dearing, 2002), more damaging to the self (Harter, 2012; Tangney & Dearing, 2002), and promote more self-conscious concerns and less empathy (Tangney & Dearing, 2002). While guilt is often associated with depression and anxiety, shame is more strongly associated with psychopathology across the board: in addition to depression and anxiety, bipolar, somatization, obsessive-compulsive behavior, psychoticism, eating disorders, paranoid ideation, hostility-anger, interpersonal sensitivity, and phobic anxiety (Pallanti & Quercioli, 2000; Pineles, Street, & Koenen, 2006; Tangney & Dearing, 2002), drug use (Dearing, Stuewig, & Tangney, 2005), and borderline personality disorder (Rüsch et al., 2007).[9] Therefore, guilt and especially shame's remediation would seem to be of profound importance for human well-being![10] Both shame and guilt—in both their true and false forms—have been removed in Christ: "You will not be put to shame or humiliated to all eternity" (Is 45:17); "Therefore there is now no condemnation to those who are in Christ Jesus" (Rom 8:1). Christian resources for addressing and resolving objective and subjective shame and guilt through Christ are enormous, and simply far richer than anything secular models can offer (see Dearing & Tangney [2011] to consider the comparably limited resources of the best secular models).

Emotional pain. Humans are also vulnerable to pain in a fallen world, including emotional pain, which seems to be a distinct affective experience (Greenberg & Paivio, 1997), irreducible to the other, more traditional categorical emotions, though common in fallen human interactions. Pain, however, is not a sign of anything other than itself—it is simply a form of suffering. In a fallen world everyone knows some emotional pain, and some people live with it chronically, though it may become more or less repressed.

The intensive distortion of negative emotions. Humans now experience negative emotions that seem unwarranted by current conditions and are therefore maladaptive in their lives. When pronounced, this is usually a sign of chronic exposure earlier in life to negative conditions that resulted in the frequent storage of negative emotion schemes. This can manifest itself in adulthood in a proneness to states of mind characterized by strong anger, anxiety, sadness, shame, or guilt, easily triggered but overcome with difficulty. Teaching people how to process these emotions productively is a major focus of contemporary psychotherapy and counseling.

Summary. Emotions are meaningful and evaluative. Though not always totally accurate, they signify a human's relation to and experience of well-being, and negative emotions are especially fitting for life in a fallen world. God designed human beings so that when suffering loss, they should feel sad; when exposed to threat, they should feel afraid or anxious; when treated unjustly or facing an obstacle, they should get angry; when deficient, they should feel shame; when having violated a norm, they should feel guilt; and when hurt emotionally, they should feel it. Negative emotions, then, are created signs of our fallen existence and spiritual death, and the relative absence in our experience of divine and human love, ultimately pointing to and drawing us toward union with the Man of Sorrows and his crucifixion.

Furthermore, since emotions can be stored in memory, we find that those who are currently overwhelmed by chronic negative emotions usually have good reason. Such intense negative emotions generally indicate chronic exposure earlier in life to negative conditions to which their emotions fittingly correspond. Christian psychotherapy and counseling, consequently, involve seeking to understand people, in part by listening empathically to their hearts to discern the meaningfulness in the utterly unique drama of a fallen *imago Dei*, who has lived in a fallen world. A stoic or merely legal approach to one's negative emotions will simply force them into hiding. *Substantial Christian healing of one's brain/soul in adulthood, then, entails becoming aware of one's negative emotions and emotional dispositions; learning how to experience and express them appropriately; understanding to some extent why they are there, in light of one's story; and cultivating compassion toward oneself in Christ.*

Sinful emotions/emotional vices. In addition to good negative emotions, a number of emotions are intrinsically sinful. Examples include envy, jealousy, cruelty, malice, lust, bitterness, hostility, and hatred. Such emotions signify a heart significantly alienated from its Creator and, when consented to and practiced, constitute personal sins and vices. At the same time, because sin is always a parasite on the good creation, counselors must remember that even sinful emotions contain a (corrupted) core of creation goodness (e.g., envy may have its roots in unfair treatment in childhood; lust is a distortion of sexual love; and so on) that does not excuse the sin or vice but must usually be acknowledged and addressed for deeper healing to occur.

The meaning of positive emotions in a fallen world. Since humans were created for positive emotions, they cannot experience negative emotions continually and function well. As a result, humans in a fallen world still tend universally toward the positive emotions (Diener, Lucas, & Oishi, 2002), which dispose them to engage constructively with that world (Fredrickson, 2002). As we have noted, positive emotions were designed by God to signify human well-being and incline humans toward it, ultimately communion with the triune God and secondarily becoming an image of him in community. Having fallen away from our true well-being in God, we find created goods are unable to satisfy our created desires and arouse and maintain sufficient positive emotion to keep ourselves happy. As a result, cognitive distortions arise—defenses, positive illusions (Taylor, 1989), self-serving bias (Aronson, 1988), and the like—as well as a significant expenditure of psychological energy to hold it all together.

By contrast, to become whole persons Christians need to value the relative happiness afforded by created goods, but will be aware of their intrinsic limitations, made manifest within an infinitely larger values framework, with God as the *summum bonum* (greatest good). Christian therapy, then, will promote the cultivation of positive emotions by counselees, guiding them in the enjoyment of created goods with gratitude (1 Tim 4:3-5) while focusing their attention even more on their unlimited redemptive goods in Christ (Eph 1:3-5; Col 3:1-4), in both ways seeking to establish larger and larger "regions" of positive emotional experience from which their counselees can draw when experiencing overwhelming negative emotions and into which the latter can be integrated. More on this in chapters eighteen and nineteen.

Developing into Personal Agents in Communion Having Different Kinds of Psychopathology

God designed humans so that they would become increasingly agentic during childhood into adolescence, as a result of the development of their brain and various relational and cognitive competencies.[11] Scripture informs us that children "have no knowledge of good or evil" (Deut 1:39), using a phrase similar to what was first applied to the tree that Adam and Eve were forbidden to eat (Gen 2:17). However, unless their mental capacities are significantly compromised by brain damage, humans typically cross a threshold in late adolescence or early adulthood at which mature personal agency emerges, and they become ethically and spiritually competent and responsible enough to be held accountable before God and their peers for their actions, in spite of whatever relative biological or social damage they have experienced. One's conscience, our legal systems, and the Bible all hold adults who are not severely mentally impaired accountable for the use of their personal agency. Indeed, the fostering of personal agency is an underlying agenda of God and his word, promoted, in part, through its many divine commands, its implicit assumption that readers are responsible to obey them, and its teachings that objective guilt follows from disobedience.

So, though humans are born with original sin, the commission of personal sins is an emergent capacity, shaped by biological and social influences throughout life, in relation with others and contingent on knowledge and increasing agentic capacity. By holding non–mentally impaired adults accountable for their personal sins, we treat them as personal agents, and in the process actually help them to realize their personal agency. (We noted this very positive, rarely appreciated byproduct of the Christian doctrine of sin in chapter eight.)

Mysterious differences in culpability and the strange effects of personal sins. At the same time, we should also note that personal sins in number and degree are often closely related to the amount of biopsychosocial damage one has experienced. Though all are equally compromised by original sin, there are great differences in the personal sins each individual commits. It is a tragic truism of fallen human development that those who are sinned against are predisposed to sin in similar ways as they develop because of modeling and the internalization of distorted cognition and cardition. Conversely, the more creation grace one experienced in childhood through the love and virtue of parents, the less personal sin people tend to practice later in life. Such a recognition does not lessen the responsibility of mature but damaged personal agents for their personal sins; rather, it intensifies the responsibility of those to whom much has been given.

Complicating matters further, personal sins provide undeniable evidence of one's original sinfulness, and this can lead paradoxically to greater self-awareness and love and gratitude to God (Lk 7:36-50; Berkouwer, 1971). By contrast, those who had greater creation grace early in their development and who therefore do not commit many obvious personal sins, in the absence of much evidence of original sinfulness, may come to conclude, whether consciously or unconsciously, that they are intrinsically better than those who are more obvious sinners, regardless of their explicit theology. Original-sin dynamics like this likely contributed to the self-righteousness of the Pharisees and help explain how "the righteous" killed Jesus rather than "sinners" (Lk 5:27-32). A complex theocentric orientation, consequently, casts an ironic light on sin that cannot be recognized by mere moralism. The bottom line is that only an omniscient God can know the true culpability in a given sinful act. This is why humans generally ought not to judge one another (Mt 7:1), unless there are legitimate social, legal, or ecclesial reasons to do so.

Glory and Human Well-Being Through Psychopathology

God would seem to love a challenge. Sin, suffering, and biopsychosocial damage are each in their own ways hindrances to his glory and human well-being. Yet, they would not have been allowed if he were not going to bring about some greater goods, in spite of them. This all makes for an epic drama!

We have seen that each form of psychopathology leads differentially to the manifestation of divine attributes that would not have been so expressed in a universe absent these evils and dramatic obstacles. Likewise, we have given some attention to the kinds of Christian virtues that can differentially develop from them. Before moving to the therapeutic implications of their interaction in human life, let us tie these threads together and consider how God is able to wrest from them both glory and human well-being.[12]

God's glory is especially manifested in his trinitarian response to the three forms of our psychopathology respectively. In light of revelation history, we might say he responds to sin first with righteousness but also, surprisingly at the time and preeminently we might add, with love: the Son of God humbly assuming our humanity, taking on himself the judgment of our sin, and raising up believers to newness of life by sending the Holy Spirit to dwell in sinners, adopting them and enabling them to live increasingly in accordance with their union with Christ. God responds to human suffering and biopsychosocial damage primarily with love; the Son of God humbly assumed our humanity but also experienced suffering and weakness, along with the rest of humanity; and the Holy Spirit dwells in believing, damaged sufferers, comforting them and enabling them to live better with their suffering and damage. By responding in these ways, God has manifested special features of the beauty of his trinitarian nature and character.

A unique kind of human flourishing originates in Christ's response to our psychopathology that enables our response, in Christ's name. Already holy because of their union with Christ, believers have also been given the Spirit, so that—in spite of original sin, personal sins, and vices—they can learn how to repent increasingly deeply and undermine sin's power in their life and others, through divine forgiveness, so that together they become more Christlike: humble, forgiving, and compassionate toward sinners as well as contrite— virtues, in their case, actually shaped by their sin. Already whole and complete because of their union with Christ, believers have also been given the Spirit, so that, in spite of their created and social motives against suffering and damage, they can learn how to both accept and grow from their suffering and damage, through divine consolation, healing, and power, so that together they become more Christlike: humble, accepting and compassionate toward the suffering and the weak, virtues shaped by their own suffering and weakness. Consequently, the manifestation of God's glory and our flourishing are increased jointly in response to human psychopathology in Christ.

SOME THERAPEUTIC IMPLICATIONS

A psychotherapy model is no better than its model of psychopathology, for without a proper diagnosis of the problem, we cannot reliably apply the appropriate treatment. Therefore, the time we have taken to develop a Christian understanding of psychopathology will hopefully lead us toward the most comprehensive set of remedies possible for the disorders of our souls.

Where Do We Begin?

Though sin is the worst kind of psychopathology within a theocentric framework, that does not mean it should be our sole or even initial focus. Sin's inherent deceptiveness makes addressing it well far more complex than many realize. There are times, of course, when life-destroying personal sin has to be tackled immediately—as in severe addiction, adultery, or ongoing sexual abuse. However, the key to the Christian life and Christian healing is union with Christ, so, generally speaking, when addressing sin, the greatest question facing Christian therapists is how to promote healing *mediated by Christ*, rather than concentrate exclusively on sin and foster moralism (that is ironically human-centered). Because of original sin's pervasiveness (total depravity) and intrinsic deceptiveness (exacerbated by shame), one cannot undermine it directly, for it adheres to every thought and action—*even reflexive action to fight it*—and hides from conscious awareness, necessitating that, most of the time, counselors approach it *indirectly* (Kierkegaard, 1962a), in Christ and with relational wisdom. A more legal orientation may force sin into hiding (from self and others), without actually addressing it at the root. Working with the heart generally requires that sin be addressed only *after* sufficient trust has been formed. Consequently, the counselor's first goal is the development of a therapeutic alliance with the counselee.

At the same time, because sin is absolutely opposite to God's goodness and well-being, it should always be the foremost concern of the Christian therapist, whether or not it is addressed explicitly in a given session. As we noted in chapter eight, successfully addressing it therapeutically through Christ promotes the internal integration of counselees; reduces their guilt and shame, both true and false; and brings associated suffering and damage to the cross and to God. We don't need to be afraid of the doctrine of sin so long as we have Christ.

Fostering Conditions That Facilitate an Open Heart

Working on sin, suffering, and damage is often painful. That is a big reason why so many avoid psychotherapy and counseling. Wise Christian counseling, therefore, aims to keep the inevitable pain of sessions within generally tolerable limits. They do this in part by representing concretely God's general love of broken sinners and his specific love of his children, because of the gospel of Christ. Think of the father's attitude toward his prodigal son upon his return (Lk 15:20-32). This kind of openness toward counselees communicates intersubjectively an accepting personal presence that reduces shame, lowers anxiety, and makes talking about one's psychopathology more bearable, in spite of the pain. In addition, when counselees experience shame in session, which they commonly do, counselors can reduce it tangibly by not panicking themselves and instead maintaining an incarnational presence of love and compassion (Wilson, 2002).

Reference can also be made periodically to the divine ground for such openness described in the gospel and made possible through union with Christ. When doing this, however, counselors must beware of "pulling counselees into their heads," since an intellectual approach to truth can be a defense, and some Christians assume that simply knowing the truth should just take away one's negative emotions rather than facilitate their resolution. Counselors can always get better at speaking truth in love (Eph 4:15; Powlison, 2005).

Accepting One's Psychopathology

We have repeatedly seen that an important part of the healing journey for believers entails coming to terms with all that one is in Christ. According to Kierkegaard (1849/1980), Christian faith is "that the self in being itself and in willing to be itself rests transparently in God" (p. 82). This is made most possible in Christ, and therefore the degree to which one can accept the truth of one's "actual self" is directly correlated to the degree to which one is consenting to God's love and who one is in Christ. The more believers accept God's love and their eschatological perfection in Christ, the more deeply they can recognize, own, and accept their sins, negative emotions, and limitations, and work through them as much as possible, because their ultimate identity is grounded in that of their older brother.

Over time, this can help believers practice distress tolerance (Zvolensky, Bernstein, & Vujonavic, 2011)—which the virtue tradition calls fortitude or endurance—an important part of which is learning to listen to, interpret, and process the meaningfulness of one's negative emotions, which to some extent are a record of one's suffering and story. But distress tolerance is an acquired trait, entailing intentional pursuit, because of humanity's innate, created motive to avoid suffering, including the shameful realization of one's ethicospiritual imperfection (sin) and biopsychosocial imperfection (weakness). As a result, counselees will need a fair amount of encouragement, training, and practice in tolerating distress. This can be facilitated by the counselee's gradual appropriation of her already established union with Christ, through guided imagery with Christ in session and homework assignments such as memorizing Scripture about union with Christ, meditating on one's union with Christ, and spending time in communion with him.

Counselors especially facilitate distress tolerance by role-modeling it concretely in session when the counselee gets distressed. As the counselor dwells with counselees while maintaining a calm presence and an engaged, empathic responsiveness with them without being overwhelmed by their anxiety or sorrow, counselees can experience a supportive intersubjective other—no longer feeling alone, perhaps for the first time—which can be deeply comforting and can provide socioemotional scaffolding that can eventually enable counselees to tolerate and manage their distress and practice emotion regulation on their own (Johnson, 2007, chap. 16). Either way, the key is to work through the distress while experiencing it *with another*, whether with Christ, mindful of one's union with Christ, or with the counselor, Christ's concrete sign or representative.

Differential Treatment of the Three Perspectives of Psychopathology

Given their profound differences, counseling sin, suffering, and damage is very different. At the same time, they are often confounded in human life. As suggested above, unless there are urgent reasons to focus on explicit sin, or therapeutic wisdom dictates otherwise, Christian counselors should trust their counselees to lead them in determining the general course of therapy and the focus of individual sessions. Usually this will eventually draw the conversation toward the counselee's suffering, and this is usually a good thing. The counselor's primary task here is the practice of empathy, by which the counselor accompanies counselees in their pain and helps them explore the significance of their negative emotions. This companionship helps to create what for most counselees is a new kind of emotion experience, where the other does not reprove or run away but dwells with, accepts, and explores, modeling a new way of approaching one's negative emotions. As the counselee grows in reciprocal trust and slowly gains the ability to tolerate distress, the counselor will be able to help the counselee integrate other, more positive considerations and emotions into the negative. The ultimate resolution of the Christian's suffering occurs through its repeated affective identification with Christ's suffering on the cross and his resurrection.

When encountering biopsychosocial damage, psychosocial techniques that gently probe the counselee's story, family-of-origin dynamics, thoughts and beliefs, emotions and relational style are usually called for, in addition to empathic exploration and transformation. Damage that results from childhood maltreatment and trauma (such as poor attachment style or emotion coaching) can be gradually remedied (though not necessarily cured) through the neural reorganization that occurs in psychotherapy and counseling and other positive relationships (Cozolino, 2010). In addition, because of "downward causation" or top-down effects, ethicospiritual activity such as the worship and love of God, identity in Christ, and repentance of personal sin can also contribute to the healing of biopsychosocial damage (Johnson, 2007, chaps. 9, 16). Medical interventions are warranted by severely compromised human functioning or when higher-order strategies are ineffective, ideally to enable counselees to engage in more productive psychosocial and ethicospiritual activity that can restructure their brains, which medications alone cannot do. However, the more intractable the damage (e.g., loss of gray matter in the brain), the less higher-order interventions are called for, in which case, the caregiver's task becomes largely supportive. Christian therapists can also help by reframing damage within the purposes of a loving God and the believer's union with Christ, who was crucified in weakness and makes it a vehicle for his glory.

The foregoing work will also help Christians grow in grace and a deepening repentance and faith in Christ, realized in part through the ongoing discovery of more subtle sin patterns throughout their lives. Christians are to aim at the utter destruction of original sin, while knowing full well that it cannot be destroyed in this life (Owen, 1965, Vol. 6). As Christians increase in their knowledge and experience of God's love and holiness in Christ, accompanied by patient, loving spiritual friends who are concrete signs of God, their defenses can be softened and their shame increasingly resolved, enabling them to identify, grieve over, and mortify personal sins perhaps during their "soul-work" time or when they become aware of them throughout the day, which in turn helps to undermine and weaken the power of original sin. Counselors facilitate this orientation by taking sin seriously, but only within the larger context of the triune God's redemptive agenda, manifested in their kindness, gentleness, and empathic communion that is also taking seriously the counselee's suffering and damage, resembling the twofold ministry of Jesus on earth when he dealt with the sick of both body and soul. We recall from chapter eight that the only way counselees can truly undermine sin and sins—and not just force them into hiding—is with Christ, being mindful of the cross and their forgiveness in him.

Regardless of their precise mixture in individual cases, the resolution of all three kinds of psychopathology is intrinsically both relational and doctrinal, processed in relation to Christ—entailing some knowledge of his person and work—as well as in communion with the triune God, the counselor, and other appropriate persons in the counselee's life.

Repetition/Reenactment or Redemption/New Creation

Psychological research has well established that our experiences with others during the earlier years of our lives contribute profoundly to our adult patterns of feeling, expecting, acting, thinking about ourselves and others, and relating to them. We also have noted that if these experiences were chronically negative, people (unwittingly) tend to act in ways that reproduce the past in their present relationships, for example, pressuring others too much to come closer and thereby provoking them to pull away. In a broader sense, all humans are likely to repeat the pathology they grew up with and more likely to commit sins they have previously committed. This pattern of negative repetition or the reenactment of past trauma is one of the great tragedies of human life.

Part of the therapeutic promise of Christianity is found in the establishment in the soul of the new creation in Christ (2 Cor 5:17), entailing the transformation of one's psychological dynamic structures and story through the gradual building of a new imaginative capacity derived from God's provision of rich, interconnected networks of meaning regarding a new relationship with God and others; new values, desires, and emotions; a different definition of well-being and individual significance; and new options and opportunities in one's personal drama. These can be appropriated and internalized through spiritual reading, prayer, meditation, worship, dialogue with others, imaginative rehearsal, and improvisational practice. Eventually, more positive psychological networks of meaning and then new neural networks on which they are grounded can become more powerful and influential, until they become more compelling than the old pathological networks of negative meaning, and their corresponding neural networks, that were introduced earlier in life.

The Maturation of Personal Agency in Communion in a Fallen World

We have seen that humans are responsible for their personal sins, but not for their original sin (at least not personally), and not for most of their suffering and damage (unless they were caused by their personal sin), particularly that which they grew up with. In addition, humans possess an underlying sense of shame regarding their sin and weakness that makes it difficult to be honest about such matters with themselves, God, and others. Nevertheless, part of the calling of being made in God's image—at least those who are not substantially neurocognitively impaired—entails the emergence of a responsibility for oneself and one's future, at least by early adulthood. As a result, the maturation of Christians in adulthood includes a growing recognition of the current state of one's soul (including one's sinfulness and damage, such as they are) and realization of one's responsibility, from now on, to take care of oneself and take action on one's behalf to obtain whatever possible remediation might be available in this life for one's psychospiritual liabilities, such that the improvement of the soul becomes one of their highest priorities, as important as family and vocation. A corollary responsibility is to grow in caring for others in such a way as to promote a similar recognition and assumption of responsibility in them. And finally, to whom much is given, much is also required (Lk 12:48), so those who have been given significant biopsychosocial and ethicospiritual advantages have a responsibility to mature in a recognition of their giftedness and that which distinguishes them from others (1 Cor 4:7), entailing a greater degree of culpability than those less advantaged and an invitation to serve them like Christ, rather than judge them.

Everyone Is Broken and Wounded

Why did Christ so fiercely confront the Pharisees? Perhaps it was due to his desire to expose their tragic self-deception about their own sinfulness and their pitiless judgmentalism toward those who were more obviously sinful. As we have already noted, one of Christianity's greatest contributions to the self-understanding of humanity is the revelation that everyone is a sinner. So everybody is broken and wounded in the worst way possible, and is therefore fundamentally equal in the worst form of psychopathology.

According to the biological and psychosocial orders alone, this seems obviously false, since there are profound differences between people in terms of their damage. Consider the magnitude of impairment evident in schizophrenia or a personality disorder. And according to the ethical order, this also seems contrary to fact, because the lives of some people are so obviously more morally compromised than others—some people steal habitually, have killed in cold blood, or committed sexual abuse many times without remorse. More to the point, there is a pretty strong correlation between having a troubled family background (and biopsychosocial damage) and greater sinfulness in adulthood. From the standpoint of the spiritual order, however, where all humans are recognized to be autocentric sinners at their core, we can see that the greater damage of some simply allows the pervasive depravity common to all to break out of the normativity that healthier, more virtuous people enjoy, because of God's creation grace (Acts 14:17; 1 Cor 4:7; Jas 1:17), so that the original sin that all share becomes more manifest. How tragic, then, that even we Christians can sometimes be so critical of and care so little for the poor in spirit (Mt 5:4), for sinners such as prostitutes and alcoholics (Lk 7:34), and for the least of these—prisoners, the homeless, the mentally ill, and so on (Mt 25:31-46). I know this to be a deep disposition in my own heart.[13]

Such a diagnosis disturbingly resonates with the analyses of Foucault (1965; 1977) and Girard (1996) that the identification of some members of society as abnormal provides a self-protective function for the society by normalizing everyone else, distracting them from their own abnormalities and frustrations, and reinforcing current power relations. "Normal" people gain psychologically, therefore, by projecting their unconscious shame and sense of inadequacy onto those with schizophrenia or those who have committed crimes, who are identified as having the *real* problems and become a culture's scapegoats. Christians might add that knowing that others are worse than we are—crazy or moral monsters—helps the rest of us pursue more subtly the unconscious, delusional agenda that we (and God) are *together* the good at the center of the universe. For many reasons, we ought to recognize that some people have greater manifest psychopathology than others. Some people need to be hospitalized; others need to be jailed. But a direct implication of the Gospel narratives would seem to be that Pharisaism is worse than schizophrenia and even obvious personal sins, because the former uses the holiest of things—God, righteousness, the Bible—to maintain unconsciously one's remaining autocentrism. So a sight of the plight of others less advantaged than us should make us all put away our stones and weep.

Consequently, God's redemptive agenda includes forming churches that are signposts of the Trinity and beachheads of the new creation, by coming to terms with the remarkable differences there are among all its members and learning to practice soul-healing hospitality together. Those who have been given much are called to genuinely love and help those who have been given little, while realizing that to become wiser, more godly, and more whole themselves, they need to learn from and live with the poor in spirit, sinners, and the least of these, because God's infinite understanding encompasses and transcends all of our finite, fallen perspectives. So help is given mutually, and the goal of every member ministering to every other is closer to becoming a reality. Moreover, Christ's call to *all* those who are weary and heavy-laden to come and find rest in him will grow in concrete credibility to a very skeptical, post-Christian world.

Companionship with All Kinds of Psychopathology

Finally, whether they know it or not, people with psychopathology need friends who will accompany them on their journey of healing. Of special importance are skilled friends, such as psychotherapists, counselors, ministers, and spiritual directors, who have learned how to accept people as they are without abandoning God's design plan. Such companionship requires risk taking and the ability to hold together sometimes enormous sin and negativity along with a fundamentally hopeful and hope-giving stance, derived from Christ's resurrection. Such paradoxical living is not everyone's calling. But it is both a gift of the Holy Spirit and a skill that can be increased.

RESOURCES FOR COUNSELORS AND COUNSELEES

Classic

Bennett, A. (1975). *The valley of vision: A collection of Puritan prayers and devotions*. Edinburgh: Banner of Truth Trust.

Kierkegaard, S. (1980). *The sickness unto death*. (H. V. Hong & E. H. Hong, Trans.). Princeton, NJ: Princeton University Press. ‡

Contemporary

Beck, R. (2011). *Unclean: Meditations on purity, hospitality, and mortality*. Eugene, OR: Wipf & Scott.

Coe, J. H. (2010). A transformational approach to psychopathology, sin and the demonic. In J. H. Coe & T. W. Hall (Eds.), *Psychology in the Spirit: Contours of a transformational psychology* (chap. 14). Downers Grove, IL: InterVarsity Press. ‡

Flanagan, K. S., & Hall, S. E. (Eds.). (2014). *Christianity and developmental psychopathology: Foundations and approaches.* Downers Grove, IL: InterVarsity Press. ‡ A sophisticated but accessible discussion of the issues from a Christian persepctive.

McFadyen, A. (2000). *Bound to sin: Abuse, holocaust and the Christian doctrine of sin.* Cambridge: Cambridge University Press. A profound contemporary treatment of human fallenness.

Roberts, R. C. (2003). *Emotions: An essay in aid of moral psychology.* New York: Cambridge University Press.

Siegel, D. J. (2013). *The developing mind* (2nd ed.). New York: Guilford. ‡

Stump, E. (2010). *Wandering in darkness: Narrative and the problem of suffering.* New York: Oxford University Press. ‡ A brief, challenging but excellent Christian discussion of shame and guilt, and their relation to love, in chap. 7.

Tangney, J. P., & Dearing, R. L. (2002). *Shame and guilt.* New York: Guilford. ‡ The best secular, empirical investigation of these topics there is.

Thompson, C. (2015). *The soul of shame.* Downers Grove, IL: InterVarsity Press.

Welch, E. (2012). *Shame interrupted.* Greensboro, NC: New Growth Press.

Wilson, S. D. (2002). *Released from shame: Moving beyond the pain of the past* (rev. ed.). Downers Grove, IL: InterVarsity Press.

‡ Recommended more for pastors and counselors than counselees

PART IV

The Divine
Intervention

Jesus Christ stands at the center of the Trinity's doxological/
therapeutic agenda, and Christianity makes an extraordinary series of claims
about him. He is an eternal person within the Trinity—the Son of God—who
became a human being and entered human history, while remaining God.
And he lived among us, was murdered by us, condemned for us, suffered with
us, brought back to life so we might live, and is now in heaven with the Father,
bringing in the new creation on earth by the Spirit. His story is the climax of
human history and should be foundational for all psychology and psychotherapy and counseling, because through his story the triune God manifested
his glory in the most remarkable manner of all time; in it Christ is revealed
to be the *true* and *real* human; and by it he has obtained the greatest kinds of
therapeutic blessings for humanity available (Eph 1:3-23; 2:4-10; 4:8-16). Consequently, the life, death, resurrection, and exaltation of Jesus Christ constitute God's primary intervention for the healing of human psychopathology.
The healing benefits of that story get mediated to individual human beings
by means of union with Christ, a work involving the entire Trinity, established by the Father's Word of the Son, and communicated to believers by the
bond of the Spirit (Calvin, 1559/1960, p. 538). Based on the Son's assumption
of human nature, it is a "differentiated union" (Billings, 2011, p. 64) that does
not dissolve the absolute and eternal difference between the divine Son of
God and believers, who are only creatures; it nonetheless joins their interests
together forever (Edwards, 1765/1989, p. 535), a process that believers participate in and further realize by means of the Holy Spirit and faith.

Union with Christ has many glorious aspects, involving (1) a union of
representation, in which Jesus Christ has been appointed by the Father to
act in love and righteousness in heaven on behalf of believers on earth

(Rom 8:34; Eph 2:6; Heb 7:25; 9:24); (2) a union of shared meaning, in which the believer has been identified with Jesus Christ by the Father through the Spirit, in some important respects, by their sharing some of Christ's traits, for example, his perfect righteousness, sanctification, and sonship (Rom 5:21; 1 Cor 1:30; Rom 8:17), indeed, every spiritual blessing (Eph 1:3); (3) a union of mutual indwelling, in which believers and the Trinity share the same intersubjective, embodied space by means of the indwelling Holy Spirit and faith, and act, in some degree, in concert (Jn 17:21-23; 1 Cor 6:19; Eph 3:16; Col 1:27; Gal 5:22-23); (4) a union of *koinōnia*, in which believers are being drawn into and participate in the triune communion (Jn 17:21-23; Eph 1:3-14; 1 Jn 1:3); (5) a dramatic union, in which the believer's story merges with and is transformed by Christ's story (Rom 6:3-8; Eph 2:5-6; Col 3:3, 9-10); and (6) a union of incorporation, in which believers share a unique relationship with one another, as the body of Christ, unified by their common relationship with their head (1 Cor 12:12-27; Eph 4:15-16) (Billings, 2011; Campbell, 2012; Horton, 2011; Purves & Achtemeier, 1999; Ridderbos, 1975; Vanhoozer, 2005).

Such a union, so pervasive in scope and having ultimate significance, changes everything about the believer. The apostle Paul's insights on this score explain his repeated use of phrases such as "in Christ," "with Christ," and "through Christ" with reference to every aspect of the Christian's life (Campbell, 2012), usage that almost makes Christ sound like the believer's continuous "location":

> Christ is the redeemed man's new environment. He has been lifted out of the cramping restrictions of his earthly lot into a totally different sphere, the sphere of Christ. He has been transplanted into a new soil and a new climate, and both soil and climate are Christ. (Stewart, 1975, p. 157)

For Paul, union with Christ was "an abiding reality determinative for the whole of the Christian life, to which appeal can be made at all times, in all sorts of connections, and with respect to the whole church without distinction" (Ridderbos, 1975, p. 59). As a result, that union now defines believers "in their core identity . . . not just in a psychological sense, by which we understand ourselves as Christians, but even more deeply in the sense that our fundamental constitution as persons is framed by our union with Christ" (Purves & Achtemeier, 1999, pp. 9-10).

Over the next four chapters, we will be concentrating on how our union with Christ relates to his story. We noted in chapter five how important narrative is in Scripture, human development, and Christian psychotherapy and counseling. In what follows, we will consider how our union with Christ renders the main episodes and events of Christ's story profoundly relevant to the healing of our souls. Our starting point is found in Romans 6:3-5:

> Do you not know that all of us who have been baptized into Christ Jesus have been baptized into His death? Therefore we have been buried with Him through baptism into death, so that as Christ was raised from the dead through the glory of the Father, so we too might walk in newness of life. For if we have become united with Him in the likeness of His death, certainly we shall be also in the likeness of His resurrection.

Initiated before the creation (Eph 1:4), upon faith in Christ, the Father and Author of history joins believers to Christ's death and resurrection, opening up a new chapter in their lives, a plot twist that entails their own drawn-out death and resurrection (Gal 2:20; Col 3:3), as the meaningfulness of Christ's story comes to infiltrate and permeate their stories (past, present, and future) by their daily participation in his story by the Holy Spirit and on-going faith (Tannehill, 1967/2006, p. 1). This paradoxical joining of eternity, history, and the present is possible because, on the one hand, the triune God is eternally present to the whole of time, two thousand years ago as well as with the believer today, and, on the other hand, according to Kierkegaard (1844/1985), believers are contemporaneous with Christ through faith (pp. 55-71).[1]

The believer's appropriation of Christ's story (its internalization, co-participation, and reflection/manifestation) occurs by means of Christ's living presence (mediated by the indwelling Spirit) as believers come to live and understand themselves, others, God, and the world according to Christ's life, death, resurrection, and exaltation. Christ's story, then, is supposed to become the basis for a significant reorganization and integration of the believer's thoughts, emotions, desires, memories, imaginings, needs, motives, loves and hates, goals and agendas, choices, actions, and relational structures, leading to new ways of living that better foster their well-being and fulfillment. This, in turn, leads to an increasing correspondence of their minds, hearts, and lives to Christ's, who himself perfectly corresponds to the agency in communion of the triune God (Jn 17:21, 23), as we together come to share God's "interests" (Edwards, 1765/1989). The psychological challenge for believers (and their caregivers) is the acceptance of their union with Christ and its significance—deeply, from the heart, throughout their internal world, in spite of the obstacles they encounter there (to say nothing of the obstacles in the world).

According to Calvin, our "mystical union" with Christ is of "the highest degree of importance," since "Christ, having been made ours, makes us sharers with him in the gifts with which he has been endowed" (Calvin, 1559/1960, p. 737). Its relevance and value for Christian psychotherapy and counseling, therefore, can scarcely be overstated. After a long hiatus, the past decade has seen a significant outpouring of interest in the doctrine of union with Christ (see below[2]). Perhaps in no other way is Christian psychotherapy and counseling more distinguished from secular versions of the same than by the prominent role that union with Christ and his story is to play in the soul-healing process of Christians.

RESOURCES FOR COUNSELORS AND COUNSELEES

Contemporary

Billings, J. T. (2011). *Union with Christ: Reframing theology and ministry for the church.* Grand Rapids, MI: Baker.

Campbell, C. R. (2012). *Paul and union with Christ: An exegetical and theological study.* Grand Rapids, MI: Zondervan. ‡ Scholarly, yet devotional!

Fitzpatrick, E. (2013). *Found in him: The joy of the incarnation and our union with Christ.* Wheaton, IL: Crossway.

Hickman, D. (2016). *Closer than close: Awakening to the freedom of your union with Christ.* Colorado Springs: NavPress.

Letham, R. (2011). *Union with Christ in Scripture, history, and theology.* Phillipsburg, NJ: P&R. ‡

Peterson, R. A. (2014). *Salvation applied by the Spirit: Union with Christ.* Wheaton, IL: Crossway. ‡

Purves, A., & Achtemeier, M. (1999). *Union in Christ: A declaration for the church.* Louisville, KY: Witherspoon Press.

Smith, J. B. (2013). *Hidden in Christ: Living as God's beloved.* Downers Grove, IL: InterVarsity Press.

Wilbourne, R. (2016). *Union with Christ: The way to know and enjoy God.* Colorado Springs: David C. Cook. Perhaps the book to start with.

‡ Recommended more for counselors and pastors than counselees

———*12*———

The Life of Christ and
the Perfection of Humanity

Principle 4: The Son of God became a human being and provided the concrete ideal of human life by fulfilling his Father's will, a perfection that is credited to believers through union with Christ and that they also realistically pursue by the Holy Spirit and faith.

*[He] emptied Himself, taking the form of a bond-servant,
and being made in the likeness of men.*

PHILIPPIANS 2:7

IN THE PREVIOUS FOUR CHAPTERS, we have reflected on psychopathology in light of the canonical resources of the Christian faith. We come now to what is at the heart of this book and the heart of the Christian faith: the triune God's most significant, personal intervention to address our psychopathology. As we recall, God is now manifesting his glory by seeking to heal all human beings from their fallen predicament through the Son by the Spirit. For the next four chapters, we will be looking unto Jesus (Heb 12:2) in order to understand better what God has accomplished through him to heal our souls.

To state the obvious: such a focus is unique to Christian psychotherapy and counseling. Whereas all competent, contemporary models will focus attention on the counselee's story and experience, by means of the skills of the counselor, only Christian models will seek to ground this enterprise in the story of another human being, and one who lived on earth two thousand years ago. Such an orientation might be considered bizarre outside the

Christian community, yet hopefully, before we are done, we will see that the person and work of Christ—summarized in his life, death, resurrection, and exaltation—provide therapeutic resources of the greatest value for humanity.

As we noted in chapter five, these four episodes of Christ's story correspond loosely to the main acts of the cosmic theodrama of human history: the creation, fall, redemption, and consummation. The Word of God first identified himself with us in our creatureliness, and then our fallenness (2 Cor 5:21), after which he became the new creation of our humanity through his resurrection and exaltation. Consequently, to know Christ personally is to know him as our incarnate, crucified, risen Lord, and friend in heaven, and we will try to understand how these episodes of Christ's story address our psychopathology. Referring to the first three, Bonhoeffer (1955) wrote, "There could be no greater error than to tear these three elements apart; for each of them comprises the whole. It is quite wrong to establish a separate theology of the incarnation, and theology of the cross, and theology of the resurrection, each in opposition to the others, by a misconceived absolutization of one of these parts" (p. 131). Since then, theologians have also begun to recognize the corollary importance of Christ's exaltation (e.g., Dunn, 1998; Schreiner, 2001; Torrance, 2009). As a result, over the next four chapters we will explore the soul-care implications of these four episodes of the first coming to earth of the Son of God. Figure 12.1 illustrates the agenda.

Respecting Bonhoeffer's wishes, we will strive to avoid separating these four periods and emphasizing one over the other, for they imply one another and together form a whole, indivisible, soul-healing narrative. Focusing too

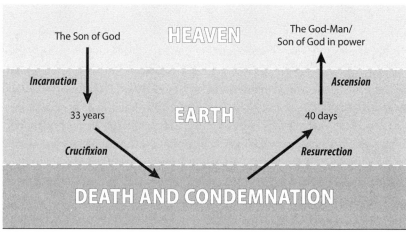

Figure 12.1. Key events in Christ's story

much on Christ's incarnation (as may have happened in the early church, to counter Gnosticism) can lead to a superficial optimism, an implicit minimization of human sin and suffering, and an undermining of the eschatological focus of Christianity on our future life with God in eternity. Too much focus on his crucifixion (as occurred in the Middle Ages) can lead to a stern, morose, and punitive Christianity. Christ's life and work is a unit consisting of four episodes, each with therapeutic significance. Our well-being, therefore, corresponds to getting the right balance regarding their unity and interrelation. The only qualification to make is that the first three are past events, whereas the period of Christ's exaltation is still going on. As a result, this final event ought to have a preeminence corresponding to its contemporaneity. We begin, as one would expect, with a consideration of the therapeutic relevance of Christ's life on earth.

CHRISTIAN TEACHING REGARDING THE SON'S INCARNATION AND HUMAN LIFE

Christ's life is an utterly amazing story of a human being. To begin with, his life had been foretold since human beings became sinners.

God's Messiah Is Coming

The Son of God did not become a human suddenly, without warning. When cursed in the Garden of Eden, the serpent was told that his head would be crushed by the "seed" of the woman, whose heel would be bruised in the process (Gen 3:15). When God initiated a covenant with Abraham, he told the patriarch he would have innumerable descendants and, "In you all the families of the earth will be blessed" (Gen 12:3). God revealed to the Israelites that he would raise up a prophet among them like Moses (Deut 18:18), who would know God intimately (Num 12:8). A few centuries later God promised David that his kingdom would be established forever through his descendants (2 Sam 7:12-16). This king would also be a greater priest than Aaron (Ps 110:1-7). God said he would deliver Israelites from their troubles and disabilities through a righteous Branch (Jer 33:15), a faithful servant anointed with the Spirit, who would bear their sins as a sacrificial offering (Is 52–53; 61:1-2). Consequently, God would establish a new covenant with his people, who would know God personally and would be forgiven and indwelt by the Spirit (Jer 31:31-34; Ezek 36:22-36), a redemption having implications for all of humankind (Is 66:12; Jer 33:9; Mic 4). The New Testament authors recognize that all these disparate prophecies were fulfilled in Jesus Christ (Mt 1:21; 21:9-11; Lk 4:16-21; Jn 1:29; 19:14; Rom 16:20; Heb 3; 7–8; 10). They also realized after his death that his earthly story had its origins in eternity.

The Union of the Divine and Human Natures in the Person of Christ

As the apostles reflected on the relevant Old Testament Scriptures and what Christ claimed and what he had accomplished when he was on earth, they began to ascribe to him a preeminence that far surpassed that of any mere mortal. He was understood to have existed previously in the form of God, but emptied himself to become a human being (Phil 2:6-11); they referred to him as the Lord (*kyrios*) Jesus Christ, a title with divine connotations (Dunn, 1998), and as the Word of God, who was God and was with God in the beginning (Jn 1:1).

Then, as the early church in turn wrestled with the apostolic testimony about Christ in the New Testament, they concluded that the one God of Israel actually consisted of three eternal persons, and that the triune God's messianic rescue centered on one of those divine persons becoming a human being. One of the most important and contested doctrines forged in those earliest centuries of the church was that the person of Jesus Christ involved the union of two natures—one divine and eternal and the other human, the latter of which he had assumed when conceived by the Holy Spirit in a virgin's womb. This "hypostatic union" of two natures in one person (*hypostasis* was the word used by the Greek fathers for what is distinguished in the triune God; the Latin fathers used *persona*) has been termed a mystery throughout Christian history, in part because it is so hard to conceive how the infinite, eternal Son of God could remain what he was while also becoming a human creature in space and time.

Nevertheless, the Son of God indeed became the "divine and perfected creation" (Coakley, 2013, p. 114). Being divine and human, God's doxological and therapeutic purposes were also united in one person. By becoming human Christ made it possible for humanity and deity to commune together (Bavinck, 2006, pp. 304-5). "Ungrudgingly he took our nature upon himself to impart to us what was his, and to become both Son of God and Son of Man in common with us" (Calvin, 1559/1960, p. 465). "In Christ two natures met to be thy cure" (Herbert, 1995, p. 143). He had to become human to rescue and heal humanity; and the human plight was so desperate that only a divine rescuer and healer would suffice. So Jesus Christ is the only therapeutic intervention that is simultaneously human and divine. Consequently, he alone can address our greatest psychological need: the reconciliation of God and humanity. "In Christ, God's nature becomes lovely to us, and ours to God" (Sibbes, 1635/1973, p. 204).

The Story of Jesus Christ as the Fullest Revelation of God

Being eternally begotten by the Father (Jn 1:1, 14), the Son is "the radiance of [God's] glory and the exact representation of His nature" (Heb 1:3), forever a "perfect transcript of the divine perfections" (Edwards, 1994, p. 259). So (as noted in chap. 3), when he became a human being he was *the* image of the invisible God (Col 1:15). "In [Christ] the Father has perfectly expressed Himself: His wisdom, His will, His excellences, His whole being" (Bavinck, 1956, p. 317). Based on Christ's life being a window into the Trinity, Balthasar suggested that "God's 'nature' is something like (that is, analogous to) thanksgiving, something like generosity, something like obedience, something like sacrifice, something like never-ending surprised receipt of self from others, but only as exceeding all that we know as creaturely thanksgiving, generosity, obedience, sacrifice, and surprise" (paraphrased by Quash, 2004, p. 151).

The union of God with human nature in Christ makes him the ideal communication of God to humans. He became the human-shaped Word of God to humanity, and through his story—his actions, relations, teachings, and even his human development—he communicated something of the mission, character, and relations of the triune God. Therefore, the four Gospels constitute the core revelation of God in the Christian canon (Pennington, 2012). What does his life teach us about God that is most relevant to the care of souls?

The humble sovereign of the universe. Perhaps the most amazing message of the incarnation is what it conveys of the humility of the infinite God. "He was Messiah in the form of a servant, in a form and shape which concealed His dignity as Son of God from the eyes of men" (Bavinck, 1956, p. 312). In light of the majesty, greatness, and wrath of God revealed in the Old Testament, *how* the Son came to earth is utterly astounding—not as an adult (like angels appear), but first being conceived as a microscopic zygote, growing for nine months in the "room" of Mary's womb, and finally being born in a barn. He could have been born at least a child of wealth and royalty, a station far more in keeping with his origins, but he entered into the working class. We learn in Christ, better than anywhere in the Hebrew canon, that God is he "whose omnipotence is so great that He can be weak and indeed impotent, as a man is weak and impotent" (Barth, 1956b, p. 129). This act did not contradict his majesty but exemplified it. "Descent to man's lowly position is a supreme example of power—of a power which is not bounded by circumstances contrary to its nature" (Tanner, 2000, quoting Gregory of Nyssa, p. 11).

The foundational text on this theme is in Philippians. After encouraging his readers to be unified in mind and spirit, Paul wrote,

> Do nothing from selfishness or empty conceit, but with humility of mind regard one another as more important than yourselves; do not merely look out for your own personal interests, but also for the interests of others. Have this attitude in yourselves which was also in Christ Jesus, who, although He existed in the form of God, did not regard equality with God a thing to be grasped, but emptied [*ekenōsen*] Himself, taking the form of a bond-servant, and being made in the likeness of men. Being found in appearance as a man, He humbled [*etapeinōsen*] Himself by becoming obedient to the point of death, even death on a cross. (Phil 2:3-8)

The key terms are *ekenōsen* (to empty) and *etapeinōsen* (to humble).[1] The apostle pointed out that the Son of God surrendered his rightful, divinely glorious "form" (*morphē*) and took on additionally an earthly, inglorious "form," to encourage the Philippians to lay aside their individual interests, including presumably their legitimate desires, rights, and privileges, in order to benefit one another (Torrance, 2008). The English theological term *kenosis* is derived from this passage (*ekenōsen*) and refers to emptying oneself, that is, activity that involves turning away from one's own immediate satisfaction, rights, benefits, or goods while procuring the good of another.[2]

God's self-giving love is the eternal source of the Trinity and the basis of all their works, including creation and redemption, and Christ most fully exemplified God's love in human form. In his willingness to lay aside his divine glory on earth, in obedience to the Father and on our behalf, he was manifesting the inexhaustible bounty of the trinitarian community. "What was accomplished in his obedience and death was the outworking of the very character of God, the revelation of divine love" (Wright, 1992, p. 86).[3] In this movement of descent, Christ gave us a remarkable picture of the triune God's virtue of self-denial that is self-donation (Gal 1:4; 2:20). He came to save us but also to share himself with us, to commune with us, and to abide in us.

Because of how this teaching has sometimes been distorted in the Christian tradition, it is necessary to underscore that Christ's kenosis flowed from his vigorous agency in communion: "I lay down My life so that I may take it again. No one has taken it away from Me, but I lay it down on My own initiative. I have authority to lay it down, and I have authority to take it up again" (Jn 10:17-18). Christ "emptied himself" with an earnest determination to express the love of the Trinity to his image-bearers.

Christ's descent into the creation, into weakness, into suffering, and into sin therefore uniquely displayed God's infinite splendor and revealed to what lengths he was willing to go to rescue us. "His whole life, particularly after his baptism among sinners, was a life of intervention in our conflict with God, in which he penetrated into the depths of our personal existence and human society in sin, taking the conflict into his own innermost being, and suffering it in his heart, from the wilderness of temptation right through to the garden of Gethsemane" (Torrance, 2008, p. 112).

The revelation of the heart of God. The incarnation showed that God and humans share many psychological characteristics: reason, speech, emotions, and personal agency. Emotions are especially important in life and in soul care because they indicate one's deepest values and concerns (Johnson, 2007, pp. 300-303; Roberts, 2003; 2007). Christ took to himself "a true and full human nature, one with our own. In this humanity of ours and His, God the Son runs the entire gamut of human experience and human emotions in a true human body with a fully human psychology. In and through that nature He was able to see things as we see them, feel things as we feel them, and experience things as we experience them" (Lewis, 2001, p. 143). Consider the range of emotions he displayed in the Gospels: sorrow (Mk 14:33; Jn 11:35; indeed Isaiah called him a "man of sorrows," Is 53:3), love for individual humans (Jn 11:5), joy (Lk 4:21; Jn 5:11), anger (Mk 3:5; of particular note is his anger with those who were subverting his Father's worship, Jn 2:13-22), irritation or annoyance (Mt 20:24), compassion (Mk 1:41), and wonder (Mt 8:10) (Erickson, 1983–1985, p. 708; Warfield, 1970). Christ was no stoic but instead a person of deep, rich, emotional experience and expression.

Because emotions reflect one's deepest concerns, their relative presence and absence are important ethicospiritual barometers. Notably, Christ is never said to have felt fear, and even rebuked his disciples for their fearfulness in a storm because it revealed their "little faith" (Mt 8.26). Christ's faith, by contrast, was unshakable—he trusted his Father even unto death (Lk 23:46)— yet that faith is compatible with the most extreme anxiety he experienced in the Garden of Gethsemane as he contemplated the impending propitiatory sacrifice involved in his death (Mt 27:46; Rom 3:25; 1 Jn 2:2).[4] Vicious emotions, on the other hand, such as envy, sexual lust, arrogance, ingratitude, greed, or insolence, were never attributed to him. Christ's heart was calibrated by true virtue (Edwards, 1746/1959; 1989), giving us a remarkable narrative portrait of the heart of God.

Jesus also demonstrated a fierce regard for God's holiness and honor. He was devoted to doing his Father's will unto death; he never sinned (Jn 8:47) and encouraged others not to sin; his life was intensely focused on upholding God's purity and fostering it in his life. For example, he fearlessly attacked those who most dishonored God with their hypocrisy and greed through their oppression and mistreatment of others.

His behavior on many occasions also underscored God's intense compassion for the weak (children, the poor, the sick, the demon possessed, the grieving) and the sinful (thieves, prostitutes, and drunkards). Consider how Christ's denunciations of those who put stumbling blocks in front of children (Mt 18:6) complement, fulfill, and transcend Old Testament teachings that encourage children to honor and obey their parents (Ex 20:12; Prov 6:20; 13:24; 19:18; 23:13).

The Son of God's willingness to die on behalf of sinners (Mt 1:21; 26:28) also revealed that God seeks the well-being of those to whom he is simultaneously opposed on ethical grounds. Christ's life led to the ancient Christian truism worth repeating: God hates sin but loves the sinner (Augustine, 1958, p. 304) and demonstrated concretely that God's love and grace can exceed and incorporate his righteous condemnation of sin, and its shame and guilt. This is good news to all human beings.

The Archetypal Human

Besides providing the best picture of God in the universe, Jesus Christ was (and is) the epitome of a human being. In the incarnation, "God becomes man, real man" (Bonhoeffer, 1955, p. 71; see also Barth, 1960a, pp. 132-202). As *the* image of God, Christ is the prototype, ideal, fulfillment, and telos of human nature. In Christ, "we see man as he was made to be" (O'Donovan, 1986, p. 54): the "concrete universal" of human nature (p. 150), the only embodied actualization of God's design plan for humanity the world has ever seen. "It is Jesus' own life that irradiates the authentic features of humanity's own form of being" (McIntosh, 2004, p. 34). Let us consider some of the implications of Christ as the archetype of humanity.

Adam—Israel—Christ. All humans prior to Christ failed in their calling to obey God and fulfill his design for their existence. Adam and Eve sinned, and their children were like their parents. "Every intent of the thoughts of his heart was only evil continually" (Gen 6:5). So God chose one group of human beings—the Israelites—on whom to concentrate his energies, revealing himself, giving his law, and lavishing them with his love (Ezek 16:1). But the best of them sinned—Abraham, Moses, David—and as a group, they failed this project utterly and so were sent into captivity. In the fullness of time, a seed of Eve and of Sarah came on the scene who, because he was a human united to the divine, could fulfill the failed callings of those who came before and after. He entered no Garden of Eden, just Gethsemane, and before that a wilderness, where he endured much more severe temptation than Adam and Eve or the people of Israel, and he obeyed his Father and God, the first human to do so: "I glorified You on the earth, having accomplished the work which You have given Me to do" (Jn 17:4). The Father finally has a faithful human image on earth: the second Adam, the true Israel, and so the Son of Man.

The goodness of humanity. We have already considered that human nature was created good, but the fact that the holy Son of God could assume it especially underscores this point. His becoming human validates the created goodness and capacities of human beings. The incarnation proves that there remains a primordial goodness in human nature, in spite of human fallenness, that serves as the basis of human life and shows that all human faculties are capable of being sanctified by the Holy Spirit (Lk 1:35).

The significance of Christ's development. We are also told in Luke that as a child Christ "continued to grow and become strong, increasing in wisdom; and the grace of God was upon Him" (Lk 2:40), so he seems to have developed normally in childhood, increasing naturally in complexity physiologically, mentally, emotionally, and as a personal agent. After his twelfth birthday, he demonstrated a precocity and wisdom beyond his years in his dialogue with some of the religious teachers of that day. Afterward we are told "He continued in subjection" to his earthly parents (Lk 2:51), and the brief narrative of his pre-adult years concludes with, "Jesus kept increasing in wisdom and stature, and in favor with God and men" (Lk 2:52). Irenaeus inferred from these limited observations that

> he passed through every stage of life: he was made an infant for infants, sanctifying infancy; a child among children, sanctifying those of this age, an example also to them of filial affection, righteousness and obedience; a young man among young men, an example to them, and sanctifying them to the Lord. So also among the older men; that he might be a perfect master for all, not solely in regard to the revelation of the truth, but also in respect of each stage of life. (Bettenson, 1963, p. 30)

Though Christ did not grow old, he attained full physical and neurological maturity, so his maturation validated, in principle, all aspects and stages of human development and underscored their role in the realization of God's design plan and doxological purposes. In addition, following Irenaeus, he purified each stage of human life as he developed, blazing a path of maturing holiness and inviting us to follow him.

In the likeness of sinful flesh yet without sin. One of the great puzzles of the faith concerns how a perfectly holy being like the Son of God could assume human nature when that nature is corrupted by sin. The New Testament reveals that the Son of God assumed a human body (see Lk 1; Jn 1:14; Rom 1:3; Gal 4:4; 1 Jn 4:2). We are told in Hebrews that "since the children share in flesh and blood, [Christ] Himself likewise also partook of the same" (Heb 2:14), and he "had to be made like His brethren in all things" (Heb 2:17). Paul directly highlighted the problem when he wrote that God sent "His own Son in the likeness of sinful flesh and as an offering for sin, He condemned sin in the flesh" (Rom 8:3). The fallen body is, of course, the source of many temptations (Jas 1:14; 2 Pet 2:18) and the medium of much sinful human activity (Rom 6:19), so Paul could say a few verses later that the mind set on the flesh is death and hostile to God (Rom 8:6-7). By using the phrase "likeness of sinful flesh," Paul was able to claim that Christ "participated fully in sinful flesh" (Schreiner, 1998, p. 403) but without denying his perfect holiness. He had a truly human body and lived in the "old age" of human fallenness, so he was subject to death and to fleshly temptations of all kinds. With a human body Christ could experience physical pain, biological needs, natural desires for pleasure (presumably including sex), and physical and verbal mistreatment by others. Indeed, all three of the devil's overt temptations were related in some way to his embodiment (felt severe hunger, challenged to throw himself off the temple roof, and offered worldly power, Mt 4:2-9).

Paul's use of this phrase, however, underscored Christ's solidarity with sinners, a fact communicated repeatedly in the Bible. Christ submitted himself to the baptism of John, unnecessary for a sinless human being but significant as a public testimony of his intimate association with sinful humanity (though John too was puzzled by it, Mt 3:14). Shortly before he died, Christ said, "For I tell you that this which is written must be fulfilled in Me, 'And He was numbered with transgressors'" (Lk 22:37, quoting Is 53:12), and then he was crucified alongside two thieves. Perhaps the strongest statement on this score is found in 2 Corinthians: God "made Him who knew no sin to be sin on our behalf" (2 Cor 5:21), conveying the closest possible identi-fication of the Son of God with sinfulness, while maintaining his lack of personal acquaintance with sin.

What is at stake here? As the early church fathers grasped, "that which He has not assumed He has not healed; but that which is united to His Godhead is also saved" (Oden, 1989, quoting Gregory Nazianzus, p. 128). The rescue of humanity from its sinful predicament could only be accomplished within our actual human condition. His incarnation, then, was Christ's first act of redemption, the beginning of the saving of his people from their sins (Mt 1:21). "His was not the human nature of Adam before the fall; rather God sent his Son in the likeness of sinful flesh, that is, in flesh that was the same in form and appearance as sinful flesh" (Bavinck, 2006, p. 310).[5] The only human nature he could assume was what he received from Mary, with the Holy Spirit cleansing it as Christ entered it, raising it out of its corruption, and restoring it to its divinely intended purity. He now enters analogously into our sinful flesh through his Spirit to cleanse us from our remaining sinfulness, though much more gradually, to bring us into a better state of communion with God than that which sinless Adam and Eve enjoyed.

Christ did this well. He "recapitulated in himself the ancient formation of man, that he might kill sin, deprive death of its power and vivify man" (Oden, 1989, quoting Irenaeus, p. 128). In contrast to Adam and Eve and Israel in the wilderness, the second Adam and the true Israel endured temptation and overcame it without sinning. As a result, Satan had "nothing in [Him]" (Jn 14:30).

Christ proved that antagonism or indifference toward God is not nec-essary to human nature as such. "Christ recapitulates humanity's struggle against evil, and in so doing achieves the victory that humanity could not" (Hart, 2003, p. 326). Having assumed and purified human nature, he de-veloped and lived in holiness, and now he enables his people to follow him by his indwelling Spirit, who works out in us what was accomplished for us by Christ in his humanity.

He showed us how to be human. We saw in chapter three that as the *imago Dei*, Christ is the fundamental pattern of human life. We briefly noted that Jesus did "nothing *of Himself*" (*aph heautou*, Jn 5:19) or "*on My own initiative*" (Jn 5:30; see Jn 8:28; 14:10; 12:49). These phrases convey Christ's human self-understanding. He did not live as an independent or auton-omous being—even *he* was not a "self-actualizer." Rather, God was the source of all he was and did, so the actualization of his human personhood in relationship to God and others occurred through active receptivity.

This theme of Christ's life calls into question the universality of secular theories of motivation, attribution, and personal agency, which assume that the goal of human maturity is fundamentally either self-determining (e.g., Bandura, 1986; DeCharms, 1968; Ryan & Deci, 2000) or socially determined (Gergen, 1992). While helpful in their descriptions of many aspects of created human agency, they also reflect a nontheistic worldview. "He who speaks *from himself* [*aph heautou*] seeks his own glory," but Christ sought "the glory of the One who sent Him" (Jn 7:18) and lived in transparent dependency on God: "He who practices the truth comes to the Light, so that his deeds may be manifested as having been wrought in God" (Jn 3:21). In all of this, the Son of Man, the *imago Dei* exemplar, demonstrated the ideal explanatory style for humanity (Buchanan & Seligman, 1995) according to God's design plan. Christ showed us the end for which God made humanity (Edwards, 1765/1998, pp. 201-2). By the Spirit, we too can abide in him (Jn 15:1-7), so that his explanatory style more and more becomes ours.

Because of Christ's role as the archetypal human, in a multitude of ways, believers discover their humanity and their individual calling by learning from him (Mt 11:29). His story is the story of humanity living in perfect, face-to-face communion with God; so his story is the revelation of *our* story, both as the gift of perfection that God gives believers in Christ and as the goal of our lives. Indeed, because of their union with Christ, believers now find their "fulfillment through participation in the Word's own calling or mission given him by the Father" (McIntosh, 2004, p. 26). So, the unique life of each believer is to be an analogue and extension of the mission of Christ, which altogether constitute a dazzling array of glorious callings, so that we "may grow into full personhood precisely by following Christ into relationship with the Father" (McIntosh, 2004, p. 35). We can do this because by the Spirit Christ is being formed in us (Gal 4:19).

The maturation of perfection. The Scriptures teach (Mal 3:6) and the classical Christian tradition has assumed that the divine nature is incapable of development because he exists already in a state of absolute perfection. However, God became a human creature who could and did develop. As a result, the life of Jesus Christ presents the wonderful paradox of the "perfecting" of a morally perfect person. We read of this in Hebrews: "It was fitting for [God], . . . in bringing many sons to glory, *to perfect* [*teleiōsai*] the author of their salvation through sufferings" (Heb 2:10), and "In the days of His flesh, He offered up both prayers and supplications with loud crying and tears to the One able to save Him from death, and He was heard because of His piety. Although He was a Son, He learned obedience from the things which He suffered. And *having been made perfect [teleiōtheis]*, He became to all those who obey Him the source of eternal salvation" (Heb 5:7-9). The root word *teleioō* in these passages means "to bring to its goal, or to accomplishment" (Arndt & Gingrich, 1957, p. 817) and indicates in these passages that the sinless Christ became a *better* human being—in a developmental sense—through obediently submitting to his Father's will and undergoing suffering and temptation (Heb 4:15). Christ's character was tested and improved through the testing, much like the blade of a sword is strengthened by placing it in a fire. In response to his physical, relational, emotional, and spiritual suffering, the human Christ could have rejected his Father's calling. By persevering self-consciously in loving fidelity to his Father in the power of the Spirit, he continually had to deny his natural human desires to avoid pain and seek relief, and in the process he realized a more virtuous character, presumably a process that could have continued. Finally, this thread of biblical teaching also tells us that human suffering has been part of God's design plan from the beginning, an important part of the realization of the human *telos*.

Christ and psychopathology. So, what is the relation of this perfect human archetype to the likes of us, marred as we all are with some degree of psychopathology? First, while Christ had no sin—he was not drawn away from God by original sin, he did not commit a single transgression, and he never developed any vices—yet he was tempted in every dimension of human life, and he was made to be sin on our behalf (2 Cor 5:21). Second, though he was infinitely rich in heaven and free of all biopsychosocial damage on earth, he became poor (by contrast) for our sakes (2 Cor 8:9), climaxing his life on earth by being crucified in weakness (2 Cor 13:4). However, he experienced enormous suffering, immeasurably and most intensely during the last twenty-four hours of his life. As a result, while the epitome of psychological well-being and the model of mental health, the Son of God came to know personally our psychopathological condition and emerged from it a therapist of incomparable capacities and resources for all three kinds of psychopathology.

Christ, the healer of bodies and souls. One of the most remarkable features of Jesus' ministry about which all Jesus scholars agree—liberal to conservative—is that Jesus was considered to be a healer of sickness.

Matthew reports that early on, Jesus was "proclaiming the gospel of the kingdom, and healing every kind of disease and every kind of sickness among the people" (Mt 4:23). Half of the first five chapters of Mark deal with healings of sicknesses and demonic possession. This activity was foundational to his ministry on earth. Beyond showing us a concern for our health and his ability to cure such ills, why was this activity such a prominent feature of his earthly ministry?

The Gospel authors interpret Christ's physical healings as metaphors of spiritual healing (see Jn 9; Mk 2:1-12). Christ was a physician for broken sinners (Lk 5:31; 8:43). Consider the story of the healing of the paralytic, who was lowered into a home in Capernaum where Jesus stayed for a few days (Mk 2:1-12). Readers will recall that before healing him, Jesus told him his sins were forgiven (a fascinating response to the assertive faith of his four friends, Mk 2:5). Some of those present were appalled at Christ's absolution, so he asked them which was easier to do: forgive sins or heal the man's paralysis? Then Jesus said, "So that you may know that the Son of Man has authority on earth to forgive sins," and turning to the paralytic he said, "Get up, pick up your pallet and go home." And the man became also physically healed.

In John 9 we read of Jesus healing a man of blindness on the sabbath. However, John crafts the story to show that more importantly Jesus heals those who are spiritually blind. Hearing of the miracle and objecting to such "work" being performed on the sabbath, the Pharisees interviewed the man newly healed, and he confounded and irritated them with his ironic response. Jesus later found the man and said to him, "For judgment I came into this world, so that those who do not see may see, and that those who see may become blind" (Jn 9:39).

These miracle accounts show the close connection in Jesus' (and the Gospel authors') mind between physical and spiritual healing. His physical healings were a sign (Jn 4:54) that he could restore wounded and broken sinners to wholeness and holiness. By taking away objective shame and guilt, Christ made possible the most thorough removal of their subjective shame and guilt. This link between Jesus' physical and spiritual healing has been the focus of untold therapeutic sermons over the centuries and serves as the ground of Christian psychotherapy and counseling. And as the poor in spirit come to the true physician of souls and believe on him and abide in him more and more, they too will hear Jesus say, "your faith has made you well" (Mt 9:22, 29; 15:28; Lk 7:50; 17:19).

SOME THERAPEUTIC IMPLICATIONS

We saw early in the book that the Son of God is the medium through which the Father created humanity, the word of God about God and humanity, the form and ideal of humanity, and the saving and healing mediator between God and humanity. Consequently, down through the centuries the church's thinkers and caregivers have recognized that the story of Christ's life on earth is fundamental to the Christian life and maturation, and therefore to Christian soul care. "Our salvation is 'from outside ourselves' [*extra nos*]. I find salvation, not in my life story, but only in the story of Jesus Christ" (Bonhoeffer, 1996, p. 62). Christian psychotherapy and counseling is most sharply distinguished from secular therapy by the fact that it brings the life of Another directly into its therapeutic considerations. In her classic book on Christian therapy, Probst (1988), for example, hopes that "the reader will be able to discern a central role for the figure of Christ. Indeed, it is my intention that Jesus the Christ represent the backbone of the counseling relationship. This centrality of Jesus Christ reflects my assumptions [*sic*] that it is ultimately to Jesus Christ that we turn for healing" (p. 14). Let us explore some ways in which this orientation can be realized.

God Desires Our Well-Being

The willingness of God to so identify himself and enter into solidarity with our fallen humanity through Christ's incarnation is an encouragement to all humans regarding God's sincere and wholehearted commitment to foster their ultimate well-being in Christ (Jn 3:16). Whatever one's story, personality, disability, or sin, Christ the great Physician came to draw all people to himself (Jn 12:32) in order to heal them and enable them to find the fulfillment for which they were created. We might say that the overture of grace manifested in the incarnation was God's clearest goodwill gesture, intended to communicate to broken sinners his good intentions toward them in Christ and to give them the hope that, no matter the evidence of their past or of their opposition to him, he genuinely desires that they truly flourish.

Christ, My Representative and Life

The imitation of Christ has often been considered to be the primary focus of the Christian life. However, this orientation by itself can easily become moralistic or depressing, depending on the evidence of one's psychospiritual maturity.[6] Underlying the believer's imitation of the life of Christ in the Christian scheme of salvation is the believer's union with the life of Christ

348 Part IV—The Divine Intervention

by the bond of the Spirit (Horton, 2007, p. 183; Heb 2:14-18; 4:14–5:10). *Christ's* life of faith is to be understood, first and foremost, as the basis and substance of the believer's life of faith, rather than as an exalted model that we are to emulate by our own power.

As broken sinners such as Bonhoeffer (1966) have recognized, "Jesus' work leads to despair in myself, because I cannot imitate his pattern" (p. 39). This insight was one of the most important outcomes of Martin Luther's earnest dedication as a monk to be like Christ, which led eventually to the Reformation. He came to realize that "the main point and the foundation of the gospel is that you first encounter and recognize Christ as a gift and present, which is given you by God and is now your own possession, long before you can think of him as an example" (quoted by Bayer, 2008, p. 64); so that "mine are Christ's living, doing, and speaking, his suffering and dying, mine as much as if I had lived, done, spoken, suffered, and died as he did" (Luther, 2005, p. 135). Rather than being primarily our goal, Christ's life is to be viewed and appropriated vicariously *as our own*. Christ is "the LORD our righteousness" (Jer 23:6; 33:16). The healing Word spoken by God that now describes those who are in Christ Jesus is our "wisdom from God, and righteousness and sanctification, and redemption" (1 Cor 1:30).

Christ on earth was the perfect image, son, human, and servant/king. By faith, his ethicospiritual perfection and beauty are received by his siblings. "Now believers are so closely united to Christ that they are the same in the Father's account; and therefore what Christ has done in obedience is the believer's, because he is the same. So that the believer is made happy, because it was so well and worthily done by his Head and Husband. This is a great doctrine of Christianity" (Edwards, 1994, p. 174).[7] And it is also a great doctrine of Christian soul care, since it means all true guilt and shame, and therefore the grounds of much of our anxiety and sadness, have been taken away and replaced with Christ's perfect love and obedience. As a result, we need no longer hide from God, ourselves, or others.

The Gospels, therefore, give Christians a portrait of the perfection that God has *already* given to them (declaratively) in Christ, received in toto prior to any activity of their own. The believer now on earth is considered by God to be already as good as Christ was on earth. Consequently, one way to read the Gospels is to interpret each of Christ's deeds as if it were one's own, on account of their having been transferred to one's own "account." The psychological benefit for this divine gift is enormous, as it gives all believers the right to release to God their psychological shame and guilt, and to undermine their false self, since their ontological basis has been *wholly* subverted by Christ *already*—though this takes time to realize experientially.

Experiencing the Christ of the Gospels

Christian counselors can also help counselees consider the implications of Christ's life for their personal relationship with him. Edwards wrote that Christ became incarnate so that our love of God may be not only the "adoration of a glorious being" but "friendship" with a "companion" (quoted in Jenson, 1988, p. 118). Jesus laid down his life for his friends and not for mere servants (Jn 15:15). He is believers' "older brother" (see Rom 8:17), who is now always with them in this life (Mt 28:20), their hero with whom they can joyfully identify. Though, depending on past relationships or present difficulties, they may be unable to experience it at present, followers of Christ have been placed in a profound and meaningful relationship of infinite love and holy acceptance, which is theirs in principle at all times. "The figure of Christ works [in therapy] in a multitude of ways. The presence of Christ can bring needed clarity into the darkness of emotional pain. The figure of Christ can also be the model of appropriate behavior in a confusing environment. Finally, the presence of Christ can be an assurance of acceptance in the midst of both our own and others' condemning voices" (Probst, 1988, p. 14).

As a result, Christian psychotherapy and counseling is more than a model of good therapeutic practice or skillful relating—though it is hopefully both those things. The primary relational agenda of Christian therapy is to help others develop a close relationship with the best counselor/friend imaginable—the remarkable protagonist we read of in the Gospels. Counselors promote this end best, of course, by loving their counselees as Christ has loved them (Jn 13:35)—entailing their own experience of Christ's friendship!—as well as training in the appropriate spiritual disciplines. They might also foster this agenda by encouraging counselees to read the Gospels imagining themselves as witnesses and even participants in the stories, for example, being (spiritually) healed or invited to walk on water or allowed to wash Christ's feet with their tears (Benner, 2004).

Participating with the Christ of the Gospels

Having noted that Christ's perfect life has become the ultimate word of God about the believer, we turn to consider how it is also, secondarily, a description of the *telos* or goal of the believer's life. The dialogue that God has initiated with the world called the Christian faith entails a response, and our

gradual conformity to the image of Christ is an important part of that response, made possible by the life of his Spirit. "Christ . . . is a persuasion, a
form, . . . a real and appealing form of being, a way of dwelling among others,
a kind of practice" (Hart, 2003, p. 147); indeed, *he is to be formed in us* (Gal
4:19). So we are taught repeatedly in the Bible to imitate Christ (Mt 10:38; Jn
8:12; 13:14-15, 34; Eph 5:2; Phil 2:5-8; 1 Pet 2:18-25). The True Human is the
"concrete universal" pattern of the ethicospiritual life of believers, so Christians are to strive to be "like Jesus" in their behavior, thoughts, desires, emotions, choices, loves, and character.[8] "To be conformed with the Incarnate—
that is to be a real [hu]man" (Bonhoeffer, 1955, p. 81). But how does this work
with someone who lived on earth two thousand years ago and is therefore
someone we have to read and hear about and whose presence we can only
experience psychospiritually rather than physically? As developed in Johnson
(2007), God intends for us to internalize the form of God spoken first in
Christ, then recorded in the stories of his life in the Bible, and alluded to
throughout the canon, and imputed to the believer. Its internalization *begins*
with understanding this word and seeking to "keep" it (Jn 15:10), by modeling
one's actions after Christ's (while resting in the gift of his perfection). However,
its inward deepening is fostered by more affective and relational processes,
such as admiration, attachment, introjection, and identification (see Johnson,
2007, chap. 16), grounded in our union with Christ, which is sealed by the
Spirit, enabling us to participate with him in that deepening.[9]

According to social, cognitive, and relational developmental research and
theory, the above processes shape the formation of the self and one's relational
capacities, beginning in early childhood. Admiration is the process of es-
teeming or respecting someone; attachment is the affective bond we form with
someone who is close to us; introjection involves internalizing one's experience
of that person; and identification consists of taking in the characteristics of him
or her. How might such processes contribute to one's conformity to Christ?

The Gospels are written in the genre of narrative rather than scientific
discourse. The noted psychiatrist and narrative researcher Robert Coles
(1989) was fascinated with the formative value of story. He believed that the
ideals, values, and moral sensitivities of a story's characters can become
those of its readers, shaping and ennobling their own character as the characters in the story become "imbedded in their mental life" (p. 138), sometimes having an influence for years to come. As an example, Coles wrote of
a student of his who turned the characters of a novel he was reading into his
"buddies" or "soulmates." During the period he was reading the book, the

student found he could almost hear one of the admirable characters speaking to him as he weighed morally significant choices. (This "voice" is similar to an "introject" by object relations theorists; Hamilton, 1988; St. Clair, 2000.)

The Gospels of the life of Christ were written with just such a formative agenda (Mt 10:38; Jn 8:12; 13:14-15, 34; Pennington, 2017). It was God's authorial intention to mold believers by Christ's character as they read and meditate on the stories of his life. Followers of Christ naturally admire him and presumably regularly esteem him in public and private worship. Asymmetrical experiences of God are likely intrinsic to the formation of an attachment relationship with him (Granqvist & Kirkpatrick, 2008). However, in order to be healed (promoting earned secure attachment; Hesse, 2008), experiences of him also likely entail a sense of proximity, safety, and security (Granqvist & Kirkpatrick, 2008), made possible by love, that is, the mutual sharing of attention, personal presence, and thoughts, feelings, and desires with God (Stump, 2010), which are facilitated by *lectio divina*; intimate, meditative prayer; and imaginative elaboration (Boa, 2001)—though of course such experiences are always interpreted, usually unconsciously, in light of one's prior attachment history (Granqvist & Kirkpatrick, 2008).

The more one experiences the Christ of Scripture in active receptivity, the more he becomes an "introject," that is, a *psychologically real* person—rather than just a historical figure—whose presence, along with his beliefs, values, attitudes, and actions as found in the Gospels, carries significant emotional weight within the believer. Finally, believers come to identify with Christ as his beliefs, values, attitudes, and action dispositions become more and more their own, and their actions and practices come to reflect this internal reorganization (in conscious dependence on him: dipolar identification).[10]

Perhaps the greatest danger here remains the deadly combination of our inborn created desire for perfection with the deceitfulness of original sin that perpetually inclines all humans, including Christians, toward the usually unconscious delusion that they are good independently of God, leading people to imitate the life of Christ, mostly unconsciously, "out of" *themselves*, in some cases while relying consciously on God, grace, and the gospel. Though we cannot escape from this self-deceptive dynamic completely on earth, we can increasingly recognize its influence and remind ourselves of the true state of affairs and talk about it with others.

Abiding in the story and life of Christ. Altogether these obstacles render the exemplary life of Christ an insurmountable peak, far higher than the comparatively meager laws given on Mount Sinai (which Paul said kill us, Rom 7:5, 11; 2 Cor 3:6-7). As a result, the imitation of Christ, understood as the *unmediated* reproduction of his character in ours, is absolutely beyond our capabilities. We cannot climb this mountain.

But Christ's story is intended by God to *encourage* believers, not discourage them. So, to belabor the point, there must another way: the mountain must come to us (originating in the word of Christ's perfect life of filial love and obedience) and also enter into us (as the gift of the life of the Spirit). As Danielou (1969) suggestively wrote, "The Father begets the Son eternally. And since He begets us too, through our participation in the life of His Son, He allows us to partake mysteriously of this eternal process of generation. Thus, our life is essentially participation in the life of His Son." It is as if "the mystery of the nativity has perpetuated itself in the recesses of the soul" (p. 57).

Based on the believer's union with Christ, our participation in the life of Christ consists, from our perspective, in the reciprocal abiding of Christ in the believer and the believer in Christ (Jn 14:20; 15:1-7; 17:21, 23; 1 Jn 3:24; 4:12-13), which is analogous to the process in the Trinity, noted in chapter two, that the ancient church called *perichoresis*. But what shall we call the mutual indwelling of the triune God and the believer? While *perichoresis* may be too lofty, the terms that refer to analogous human processes— *intersubjectivity* and now *introjection*—are too paltry to do justice to the unique ontological dynamics being referred to here. It is less a taking something in from the outside (like introjection) or sharing simultaneously the same experience (as in intersubjectivity) than a realizing that the Christ we are reading about is already truly present within us by the Spirit. This abiding, in the corpus of the apostle John, includes being saturated in the word of God and Christ (Jn 15:7; 1 Jn 2:14, 24), feeding on his death and all that it accomplished (Jn 6:54), and actively receiving him (Jn 14:20; 15:7) and the gift of the Spirit he obtained for us (Jn 14:17; 1 Jn 2:27).

Conformity to Christ, according to Bonhoeffer (1955), "is achieved only when the form of Jesus Christ itself works upon us in such a manner that it molds our form in its own likeness" (p. 80). However, while Bonhoeffer rightly underscored its fundamental basis on the work of God outside us and within us, it remains our responsibility to realize it by "abiding in Christ."[11] So, to summarize this section, abiding in the story and life of Christ involves (1) becoming familiar with the stories of his life; (2) worshiping him and growing in our attachment to him through love, that is, by mutual sharing of attentional focus, personal presence, and thoughts, feelings, and desires; (3) consciously welcoming the (already present in the Spirit) Christ of the Gospels into our souls; (4) listening to his input (like introjection); and (5) consciously identifying ourselves (in dipolar fashion) with him and his mission, beliefs, values, attitudes, and actions, and practicing his way of life in our daily life, so they more and more become ours.[12]

Abiding in Christ imaginatively. Finally, we should underscore that this participatory imitation of Christ's life involves the believer's imagination. Christians will never face the identical situations of Christ, so imitation also involves wisdom or discernment (*phronēsis*) to envision how to live out one's own life as an analogy to the life of Christ, given one's current life context, so that there is a "fitting" correspondence to the life of Christ. In some sense, this is the thrust of the whole New Testament (e.g., Eph 5:23-33; 1 Pet 2:21-23; see Vanhoozer, 2005; 2014). An important task of the counselor is to help counselees imagine new courses of thought and action that flow from and resemble the overall death-resurrection pattern of Christ's life (Vanhoozer, 2010), sometimes using mental imagery, planning, and rehearsing future courses of action.

Christ's *Kenosis* and Ours

"To be more human in the way Jesus calls us to be human is to be willing to live with a holy indifference toward our own plans as we give up our agenda, to join the dreams of others" (Allender, 1999, p. 197). The descending form of Christ's incarnation and life is a revelation of the paradox that the greatest, most intense form of being is the all-powerful mutual loving and glorifying of the triune life, which is manifested supremely in Christ when he divests himself of his rights for the other, first and foremost his Father, and secondarily us. Rather than being destructive of the self-regard built into human beings, *kenosis* realizes the highest form of self-regard (LaPorte, 1997). In Christ's self-giving, we can discern the infinite strength and self-subsistence of the Son, as well as the infinite solidarity, interdependence, and mutual regard of the triune communion. "Sending Christ to us is the most potent cure for pride. Christ teaches the eternal truth that humility is superior to pride when, by divesting himself of power and taking on weakness, he gains our allegiance and persuades us to do likewise" (Charry, 1997, p. 139). *Kenosis*, then, is arguably the most significant way that believers can imitate Christ (LaPorte, 1997). "If anyone wishes to come after Me, he must deny himself, and take up his cross and follow Me" (Mk 8:34).

***Pseudo*-kenosis.** The virtue of self-denial, however, comes across as nearly incomprehensible to a culture that has long promoted self-fulfillment as among its highest values (Yankelovich, 1981). The cultural and therapeutic ethic that has evolved over the last fifty years generally encourages people today to be true to themselves above all else and to stand up for themselves and their rights, rather than to sacrifice themselves in significant ways for others. Self-love—a good, created motive—has become absolutized, isolated from its proper ethicospiritual context of the love of God and neighbor within which it thrives, evidenced in, among other things the long-standing relatively high divorce rate of the West.

At the same time, the criticisms of secular therapists and feminists sharing this orientation have helped Christians to recognize that some examples of self-denial are unhealthy and in some cases abominable. Consider, for example, people who lack a strong sense of their identity and have difficulty expressing their preferences or opinions; or spouses who remain in physically or sexually abusive relationships, popularly described as "codependent." Persistent tendencies toward self-destructive behavior seemingly for the sake of others have been called "masochistic personality disorder" (PDM Task Force, 2006). Christians can be thankful for such insights into the opposite extreme, all too common in the Christian community.

Self-sacrifice, of course, is hard for everyone. It seems to go contrary to the good created motivation to advance one's own interests, which became magnified to narcissistic levels by original sin, leading to an underlying motive to advance one's interests at all costs, including the well-being of others, though often masked by social norms and kept in check by creation grace. However, the Christian virtue of self-sacrifice is especially confusing for counselees whose selves never properly developed and were severely damaged because of growing up with parents who chronically exploited them for the parent's self-serving (rather than self-giving) purposes, and who consequently did not develop a healthy sense of self-other boundaries that are a prerequisite for healthy self-giving. Such tendencies are compounded by continuing to live in relationships with difficult and demanding spouses, relatives, coworkers, supervisors, or neighbors who try to manipulate them for their own purposes. How should one respond, for example, to an insensitive spouse who insists on having sex late at night with his wife, in spite of her obvious exhaustion and mild protest to the contrary. A misunderstanding of the *kenosis* principle might lead a codependent Christian to give in to the pressure, whereas the most loving and godly thing to do may be to stand up for oneself and say, "Sorry, but I can't tonight." To consider a biblical example, when the apostle Paul was arrested on unjust charges for disturbing the peace, he was not passive but advocated for his rights and appealed to Caesar for justice (Acts 25:11).

Unfortunately, many in the church over the centuries have had difficulty properly understanding and applying Christian teaching on this score, and in the process promoted neurosis more than *kenosis*, tragically justifying and perhaps promoting future abuse in the name of Christ. Some Christians, as a result of this distorted understanding, could be said to suffer from a "*kenosis* complex," serving others out of an unhealthy and ungodly servility, seeming to live in penance, and punishing themselves out of shame and guilt while believing they are being "like Christ." Such a stance can be the fruit of growing up in legalistic Christian homes that mandated self-denial before the child's self had fully developed, and often without providing the Trinity-like love and affirmation that are the developmental prerequisites for healthy self-denial. Having grown up in such conditions, people are prone to divest themselves of their rights in destructive ways, not virtuously but out of fear or an intense desire to be loved, and they may allow themselves to be mistreated, without a proper regard for their own well-being. They are not givimg themselves *freely*, so this can only be termed "pseudo-*kenosis*," and it has to be distinguished from the genuine self-giving for which we were designed.

Such individuals are led by relational compulsions that demonstrate a lack of mature personhood and the presence of deterministic residue that hinders the free love of the other, and therefore they manifest less glory than they might think. Immature individuals who have not developed the structures of full personhood are incapable of laying down their lives for others *well*. As some Christian counselor has quipped, someone who lays down his or her self for another must first have a self to lay down.

A better, stronger kenosis. Perhaps the caution we are raising here can be made most clear by drawing out some of the developmental/maturational lessons regarding human *kenosis* of Christ's life. First, Christ's *kenosis* began in heaven when, as a perfect divine being, the Son of God laid aside his divine privileges. Second, the kenotic agenda of his human life encompassed the entire span of his life on earth, issuing in a self-giving climax on the cross. He did not enter into public service until around the age of thirty, and it seems appropriate to consider him *at that time* the fullest picture of human well-being. Yet his years of preparation were not wasted. They resulted in a well-developed and mature human self that was able to assume God's call to *kenosis at that age* with the greatest deliberation and commitment. Consequently, he gave himself to the world as only a mature, strong self is able to. Christ's life manifested not codependent ambivalence but the unsurpassable power of perfect self-giving. As a result, though *sent* by the Father to die, Christ wholeheartedly, actively accepted his mission, so he *laid down* his life *of his own accord* and *by his own authority* (Jn 10:18). We conclude then that the fullest *kenosis* entails a vigorous sense of one's competence, significance, and purpose in God.

Rather than naively reinforcing their pathology by challenging them to sacrifice themselves for others, counselees with underdeveloped selves need the kenotic love and support of God and others to help them build more whole selves and identify and surrender to God the masochistic motivation that has driven them in the past, as steps toward healthier self-denying activity in the future. In the long run, such individuals will contribute more to God's glory for they are becoming *genuinely* more other-oriented and God-centered than if they were neurotically attempting "great things for God" with an extremely damaged and self-deceived soul. How are Christian counselors to guide their counselees toward Christian notions of well-being?

Mindful of the above qualifications, Christ-centered therapists will nevertheless maintain that *kenosis* is an important part of the therapeutic *telos* toward which they seek to guide their counselees. God's nature is self-giving, and Christ came to display the kenotic splendor of the Godhead. So humans made in God's image and being conformed to Christ's image are created to find their greatest fulfillment in self-giving too. Children need parents who give of themselves in healthy ways. Marriages can improve when at least one spouse learns how to live more truly kenotically. So Christian soul caregivers will practice *kenosis* and seek to draw those with whom they work into an increasingly kenotic orientation.

Fortunately, Christians have resources that make healthy self-giving possible (beginning with the indwelling Spirit of Christ). One strategy entails "reframing" one's situation and actions by recognizing the potential there to glorify God precisely by resembling Christ's story (Vanhoozer, 2005). This metaphoric reinterpretation can give additional motivation that enables one to give of oneself in strength, rather than falsely, and to bear with self-denial and even suffering by sensing its transcendent value. In addition, though there are no guarantees here, over time this agapic initiative may have the benefit of softening the heart of the resistant or unloving other.

Secondary Incarnations

We are warranted in seeing those who counsel in Jesus' name as his redemptive representatives, as contemporary incarnations of Jesus Christ, as the only Jesus some people will ever see. The term *incarnation* simply means "in-fleshed," and all humans are that. When we use the term in the present context, we are obviously making an allusion to Christ's sui generis incarnation. Some would argue that we should, therefore, avoid applying such a term to ourselves because it risks obscuring the absolute difference between the Son of God and his people. However, rejecting such usage obscures the equally profound truths of Christ's joining himself to our humanity and his remarkable willingness to have us represent him. So long as we are clear about the first truth, we should allow the other two truths to humble and amaze us.

RESOURCES FOR COUNSELORS AND COUNSELEES

Classic

Irenaeus. (1990). *The scandal of the incarnation: Irenaeus against the Heresies* (H. Urs von Balthasar, Ed.; J. Saward, Trans.). San Francisco: Ignatius. ‡

Contemporary

Blomberg, C. L. (2005). *Contagious holiness: Jesus' meals with sinners*. Downers Grove, IL: InterVarsity Press. ‡

Fitzpatrick, E. (2013). *Found in him: The joy of the incarnation and union with Christ*. Wheaton, IL: Crossway.

Issler, K. (2013). *Living into the life of Jesus: The formation of Christian character*. Downers Grove, IL: InterVarsity Press.

Johnson, M. P. (2013). *One with Christ: An evangelical theology of salvation*. Wheaton, IL: Crossway. ‡

Miller, P. E. *Love walked among us: Learning to love like Jesus*. Colorado Springs: NavPress.

Tanner, K. (2000). *Jesus, humanity and the Trinity: A brief systematic theology*. Minneapolis: Fortress. ‡ Weak on the atonement, but strong on the incarnation and its implications for human beings.

Torrance, T. F. (2008). *Incarnation: The person and life of Christ* (R. T. Walker, Ed.). Downers Grove, IL: InterVarsity Press. ‡

Wellum, S. (2017). *God the Son incarnate: The doctrine of Christ*. Wheaton, IL: Crossway. ‡

‡ Recommended more for counselors and pastors than for counselees

—*13*—

The Death of Christ and the End of Psychopathology

Principle 5: Christ's atoning death overcame sin and its penalty, and, to some extent in this age, many of its soul-disordering consequences, through union with Christ by the Holy Spirit and faith.

In this is love, not that we loved God, but that
He loved us and sent His Son to be the propitiation for our sins. . . .
There is no fear in love; but perfect love casts out fear,
because fear involves punishment, and the one
who fears is not perfected in love.

1 John 4:10, 18

By His wounds you were healed.

1 Peter 2:24

Most murderers have a recognizable rationale, at least partially explained by understanding the motive, whether money or hate or ideology. Far more disturbing are those murders that are seemingly gratuitous, where no motive is apparent. But perhaps most perplexing are those times when someone is murdered for his or her *virtue*. Such killings happen periodically in every culture, and there is no shortage of them in the West: Socrates, Thomas Becket, Abraham Lincoln, Martin Luther King Jr. Just such a murder, of course, was the founding event of the Christian religion, and over the centuries its significance has been variously interpreted, resulting in different models of the atonement, the relative merit of which has been a subject for debate. Our interest in these perspectives on the atonement is due to their respective soul-care value. The great irony of Christianity's founding is that the early Christians understood the murder of this universally regarded virtuous person to have been the most salutary event in human history.

CHRISTIAN TEACHING REGARDING CHRIST'S DEATH

Indeed we see throughout the earliest writings of the Christian church what might seem from the outside as a sustained obsession with Christ's death. Four canonical biographies were written of him, and somewhere between 25 and 50% of their content is focused on his death and the events leading up to it. This same interest is sustained throughout the New Testament. The apostle Paul, for example, wrote to the Corinthians, "I determined to know nothing among you except Jesus Christ, and Him crucified" (1 Cor 2:2). All the apostles were agreed that Christ's death was the fulfillment of the sacrificial system established by God in the Pentateuch. Peter told his readers they were redeemed "with precious blood, as of a lamb unblemished and spotless" (1 Pet 1:19), and John wrote that "the blood of Jesus . . . cleanses us from all sin" (1 Jn 1:7). The book of Hebrews is pervaded with the redemptive-historical significance of Christ's death. And an early vision in the book of Revelation is centered on "a Lamb standing, as if slain" (Rev 5:6).

Consider further Christianity's religious rites. Compared to most religions, it has very few—by most Protestant reckonings, only two, and both are focused on Christ's death. Baptism symbolizes the believer's original identification with Christ in his death, burial, and resurrection, and the Lord's Supper is a remembrance specifically of his death. Significantly, this is the rite that is practiced regularly throughout a Christian's life. Like a seed found in the core of an apple, the main theme of the earliest Christianity would seem to be the death of Christ. In light of this emphasis, Brunner (1934) suggested that the test of a theology's being Christian is whether the cross was central to its formulation (p. 437). Perhaps the same test could apply to models of Christian psychotherapy and counseling.

English-speaking theologians have used the Anglo-Saxon term *atonement* to refer to the salvific significance of Christ's death with respect to God and humanity, and the Bible contains many metaphors and networks of meaning that illuminate different aspects of the atonement. As a result, over the centuries, a number of "models" of the atonement have developed, most of which are complementary (Marshall, 2008) and have relevance for Christian healing of the soul. In what follows, we shall order the most relevant models conceptually, from simpler to more complex, and developmentally, from more foundational to more personal. Let us consider how the cross figures in the Christian care of souls.

Christ's Death as an Act of War and Prisoner Rescue

The simplest model of the atonement, and the first to be developed in the early church, begins with the recognition that humanity is in the midst of a cosmic spiritual conflict. As we saw in chapter eight, the biblical authors believed that there is a world system opposed to God, operating across all cultures (Gal 1:4; 1 Jn 2:15-17; 5:19), ruled by Satan (Jn 12:31; 2 Cor 4:4), and managed by evil spiritual forces, including demons, powers, and principalities (Eph 6:12). They have enslaved humans and blinded their eyes to their rebellious agenda (2 Cor 4:4), influencing them through sin and the flesh (Rom 6:16-17; Gal 5:17-19) and negative emotions such as fear (Rom 8:15; Heb 2:15), and using them to fight against God and undermine his influence on the earth (Eph 2:1-3). The creation, however, belongs ultimately to God, and he has been engaged in a long-term war with Satan and the evil forces under his control, over which God will eventually completely triumph (Boyd, 1997).

The *Christus victor* atonement model—significantly revived within the last one hundred years and also termed the classical or dramatic model (Aulen, 1931)—focuses on the role that Christ's death plays in this cosmic battle by setting humans free from their ethical and spiritual captivity through faith in Christ (Lk 4:18; Eph 4:8). In this perspective, the death of Christ is interpreted as the climax of a divine drama of deliverance, which harks back to the typological deliverance of the Israelites from Egyptian bondage. We recall that just before their exodus, God "passed over" the homes of Israelites who had wiped the blood of a lamb over the door, protecting them from the judgment he brought on the Egyptians. Christ's death (as we just noted, often represented by his blood) provided a ransom or payment[1] that somehow procured[2] the ethicospiritual freedom of believers (Murray, 1988; Vos, 1980). In the New Testament Christ is understood to be the Passover lamb (1 Cor 5:7). This redemption has cosmic implications as well, for through his death Christ rendered "powerless him who had the power of death, that is, the devil" (Heb 2:14) and "disarmed the rulers and authorities, . . . [God] having triumphed over them through Him" (Col 2:15).

Within this dualistic universe, believers have been set free from their imprisonment, have changed their allegiance, and are now fighting on God's side against his enemies. Through the cross the "world" has been crucified to them and they to the world (Gal 6:14) so that, in principle, its values and motives no longer have the absolute power in their lives they once did, because of the fundamental paradigm shift that occurred in their being. Through faith Christians advance the realization of this supernatural transfer from the dominion of darkness into the kingdom of God's beloved Son (Col 1:13).

Bondage to sin is manifested every time humans are unable to do what they want to, or when they do what they don't want to, and Christ alone can set them free from their wretched powerlessness (Rom 6:6–7:25). Addiction provides a telling example (and metaphor) of this aspect of sin (Plantinga, 1995, chap. 8; Welch, 2001). People are also in bondage to fear: the fear of death (Heb 2:15), of condemnation (Rom 8:1, 15), and of punishment (1 Jn 4:18), from which the work of Christ also sets people free. And the liberating dynamic of Christ's death can aid in the resolution of all negative emotions that enslave, including anger, despair, shame, and guilt.

Christ's Death as Punishment on Behalf of Others

Within the context of the cosmic war outlined above, the death of Christ is also interpreted in the New Testament as a sacrifice that pays the ultimate penalty for human sin. In the Garden of Eden humanity first learned that the wages of sin are death (Gen 2:17; Rom 6:23)—spiritual death immediately and physical death eventually. To teach the Israelites the terrible seriousness of sin, to promote personal agency and responsibility, and to point ahead to Christ's redemption, God revealed himself as someone who gets angry with sin—signifying his fundamental opposition to it—and he also gave them the law, including hundreds of commandments, and punishments or substitutionary ceremonies for when they violated it (depending on the commandment). Pervading the covenant made with Moses and the people of Israel was a system of retributive justice intended to promote an ethic of reciprocal exchange, both epitomized in the expression "eye for eye, tooth for tooth" (Ex 21:24). Within the Mosaic covenant, God's people were schooled in basic moral understanding: their sin required some form of recompense. For example, Israelites who committed an unintentional sin were to bring an unblemished animal to the priest "for his sin which he has committed" (Lev 4:28), which would then be killed, and "the priest shall make atonement for him, and he will be forgiven" (Lev 4:31). The death of the animal substituted for the punishment of the sinner.

Centuries later, when John the Baptist first met Jesus Christ, he called him "the Lamb of God who takes away the sin of the world" (Jn 1:29), an unblemished lamb, since he never sinned (2 Cor 5:21; 1 Pet 2:21-25). Later the apostles wrote that Christ "bore our sins in His body on the cross" (1 Pet 2:24), and he "died for the ungodly" (Rom 5:6), having "become a curse for us" (Gal 3:13). In this substitutionary role, Jesus was "pierced through for our transgressions" and "crushed for our iniquities" (Is 53:5; cited by Peter in 1 Pet 2:24), rendering himself as a "guilt offering" for our sins (Is 53:10). The Father, we are told, sent the Son "as an offering for sin" and then "condemned sin in [his] flesh" (Rom 8:3). It was the Father, therefore—and not Satan—who rendered a verdict of guilty on the innocent Christ when he was on the cross, and his temporary abandonment by the Father and ultimately his death were the consequences of that verdict. The New Testament authors, therefore, interpreted Christ's death as a substitution for the punishment of sinners, analogous to a sacrificial animal in the Torah, except that in the case of Christ, *we* did not bring the substitute but the triune God offered himself up as the substitutionary sacrifice in the person of the Son!

As a result, God's wrath against sin has been resolved. The resolution is indicated by the Greek word *hilastērion*, used four times in the New Testament to refer to a shift in God's attitude toward the sinner from wrath to acceptance: God "displayed [Christ] publicly as a *propitiation* in His blood" (Rom 3:25; see also Heb 2:17; 1 Jn 2:2; 4:10). "To propitiate means both to cover and to conciliate" (McDonald, 1985, p. 78), so (in contrast to expiation) it has the connotation of removing God's just displeasure toward sinful human beings (Gaffin, 2004; Kistemaker, 2004).

On the basis of Christ's death, the apostles concluded that God the Father can justly release believers from their sin (Rev 1:5), having forgiven "all our transgressions, having canceled out the certificate of debt consisting of decrees against us, which was hostile to us; and He has taken it out of the way, having nailed it to the cross" (Col 2:13-14). As a result, God's perfect justice has been satisfied, and all the ethicospiritual impunity of all who believe—their true shame and guilt—is removed, they are spared from his wrath and condemnation (Jn 3:16-36; Rom 8:1), and they now have peace with him (Rom 5:1).

This model of the atonement has been labeled *penal substitution*, since it asserts that sin and its corresponding shame, guilt, and deserved punishment[3] were transferred to Christ, and he suffered, therefore, in their place (Denney, 1911; Letham, 1993; Schultz, 2014; Tidball, 2001).[4] Packer (1974) nicely summarized the perspective: "Jesus Christ our Lord, moved by a love that was determined to do everything necessary to save us, endured and exhausted the destructive divine judgement for which we were otherwise inescapably destined, and so won us forgiveness, adoption and glory" (p. 35).

In spite of the strong biblical evidence for this perspective (Jeffrey, Ovey, & Sach, 2007), many thoughtful Christians today are critical of it (e.g., Girard, 1996; Milbank, 2003) and liberal Christianity has uniformly rejected it. Its critics believe its basis in retributive justice and reciprocal morality is deeply problematic. Such a religious framework to them seems to entail an angry and vindictive (male) deity, who exemplifies relatively primitive motives, such as vengeance, in the punishment of sin, even if in a substitute, rather than taking the more virtuous path of forgiveness (Johnson, 1993; Lotufo, 2012). Some have also suggested this model implies a division in the Trinity between a wrathful Father who unfairly punishes his self-sacrificing Son (e.g., Brown [1992] called it "divine child abuse"). Such a god looks downright dysfunctional compared to twenty-first-century parents who can regulate their children's behavior without resorting to punishment. Even worse, such a model, they allege, ultimately sacralizes violence against others (Girard, 1996; Weaver, 2001).

The issues surrounding the interpretation of this model are far too complex to address adequately here.[5] However, given the criticism it has attracted in recent decades, a few remarks are in order. First, the principles of retributive justice and reciprocal exchange might be easier to appreciate if one recognizes their universality and developmental significance. They did not originate in the Mosaic covenant but are found across cultures and across time (Otterbein, 1986; O'Donovan, 2005; Myers, 2012; Roth, 2015)—*basically, wherever wrongdoing is punished*—because they are likely embedded in the human genome, contributing to what some have termed natural law (Rom 2:12-13; Levering, 2008). Moreover, children's understanding of agent causation and responsibility that lead to the development of personal agency entails a world where good actions have positive consequences and evil actions negative (what Coe & Hall [2010] called the sow-reap principle, which pervades much of the Old Testament, for example, the book of Proverbs). So, the fact that Christ's death is interpreted in the New Testament as a resolution of retributive justice for the sinner shows that it addresses a deep logic at the core of human nature.[6] Outside the secularized West, few reject the notions of retributive justice and reciprocal exchange. As a result, Christian opposition to this model would seem to be more a reflection of modern tastes than of either empirical evidence or scriptural revelation.

Ultimately, a theocentric framework may be required to grasp the validity of the penal substitution model, one that assumes God's utter transcendence and uniqueness; his infinite dignity and worth; and his sovereign majesty, righteousness, and rightful authority over human creatures. The awfulness of sin would seem directly related to God's transcendent greatness. From that vantage point, total opposition to sin manifested in a cosmic system of retributive justice would seem to be a necessary response of the righteous Creator of humanity, given sin's antagonism to his glory and its destructiveness to our well-being. While there is more to the atonement than the penal substitution model can explain, there cannot be less.

Nevertheless, as Packer reminded us, righteousness is not God's only attribute, so the model of penal substitution must not be isolated from the other models of the atonement, or we will end up with a distorted theology. "The cross is a window opened into the very heart of God" (Torrance, 1992, p. 112), precisely because it demonstrates the unity of God's righteousness and his love. The cross resolved God's righteous indignation against sin *by means of his self-giving love*. The cross demonstrates God's love (Rom 5:8) because he "covers up" or "takes away" our sin and its ethical meaning before God *himself* in the joint operations of the missions of the Trinity, so that we do not have to suffer them fully ourselves. So the triune God is able to forgive our sins out of his love without undermining the deep, equally primordial logic of his righteousness (Rom 3:26). What a beautiful, paradoxical accomplishment![7] As Denney (1902/1951) understood, there can be no gospel "unless the integrity of God's character be maintained" (p. 98).

The Relational Significance of Christ's Death

The foregoing leads us to the most important outcome of substitutionary atonement from our standpoint: it removed the transcendent obstacle to our having a personal relationship with the triune God—his offended righteousness. Sin necessarily separated humans and the righteous God (Is 59:2), so that we were by nature "children of wrath" (Eph 2:3), storing up wrath for ourselves through our disobedience (Rom 2:5). Nevertheless, because of his great love for us (Rom 5:8; Eph 2:4), God removed the ultimate cause of the enmity between himself and sinners, so that he could now invite all humans to return to him through faith in Christ, without violating his righteous nature (Jn 3:16, 36; 2 Cor 5:18; Eph 2:15; Vos, 1980). "While we were enemies we were reconciled to God through the death of His Son" (Rom 5:10), having been saved from his wrath (Rom 5:9).

At the same time, our alienation from God has a corollary, subjective side. Humans are now "alienated and hostile in mind" (Col 1:21), "enemies of the cross of Christ" (Phil 3:18), and unable to subject themselves to his law (Rom 8:7). Consequently, reconciliation with God also entails the therapeutic reversal of our internal opposition to him—initially in some form of conscious conversion, and then gradually, more and more deeply, by practicing faith in him (Eph 2:8), the love of God being poured out within our hearts through the Holy Spirit (Rom 5:5; see 2 Thess 3:5) as we learn how to abide in Christ as he abides in us (Jn 15:1-7). So, because of the cross, God is fully reconciled to believers, while they are becoming reconciled to him.

Perhaps one more relational observation is in order. Because the penal substitution model assumes that divine wrath is ultimately something positive, Christians who were exposed to excessive parental anger in childhood, which got internalized and is still fundamentally unresolved, may experience a strong affective repulsion *or* attraction to it. Those who have consciously disidentified with the anger of their family of origin may be strongly disposed to reject or reinterpret this model, regardless of the biblical evidence. It *can't* be valid because it feels like it confirms the abusive anger one experienced earlier in life (at an unconscious level). Such a reaction is understandable if not the healthiest response. Eventually, through greater healing, the ability to accept more of biblical revelation may emerge. In the meantime, such persons need our compassion and patience. On the other hand, those with uncontested, unresolved anger, of which they may not be very aware, may be more attracted to this model because it permits an unconscious identification of their pathological anger with God's righteous anger, legitimizing it. Such a stance makes it easy to be critical of others, including other Christians, so long as it is for a "good" cause. But they too can find greater healing and learn how to question and better understand the roots of their critical disposition. These persons also warrant our compassion and patience. I should add that I know the latter phenomenon very well, having been emerging from it throughout my adult life, I am persuaded, by means of the healing found in the atonement and its increasing resolution of my guilt and shame in Christ.

Christ's Death as a Therapeutic Intervention

Another model of the atonement especially relevant to the care of souls has been termed the "healing view" (Reichenbach, 2006). The origins of this model can be traced to the Hebrew Testament, where God promised the Israelites, "Behold, I will bring . . . health and healing, and I will heal them. . . . I will cleanse them from all their iniquity by which they have sinned against Me, and I will pardon all their iniquities by which they have sinned against Me and by which they have transgressed against Me" (Jer 33:6, 8; cf. Is 57:18-19; Jer 30:17; Hos 14:4). They were also told that the Messiah would be involved in this restoration: "the chastening for our well-being fell upon him, and by his scourging we are healed" (Is 53:5, which Peter related to Christ's atonement, 1 Pet 2:24), and then "the sun of righteousness will rise with healing in its wings" (Mal 4:2).

Such teachings provide the backdrop for interpreting Christ's healing ministry, touched on in the previous chapter. His healing of the body was symbolic of his healing of the soul—the primary reason he came—a healing grounded in forgiveness (Mk 2) and faith in Christ (Jn 9:38). This model of the atonement highlights the consequences for believers of their appropriation of the forgiveness obtained by Christ on the cross through faith in him. So this would seem to be a transitional model that relates the more objective models of the atonement to the more subjective. The cross has delivered believers from the domain of darkness (Col 1:13) and divine judgment and alienation from God, making possible the freedom to return to God, overcome sin, and resolve the feelings of true shame and guilt that sin caused. As we saw in chapter eleven, such feelings, especially shame, are significantly correlated with various forms of psychopathology (Tangney & Dearing, 2002). Christianity uniquely provides an objective *ground* for the resolution of subjective shame and guilt, one that is *outside the self* and located in the transcendent, saving work of God, the only one ultimately with the authority to pronounce the total forgiveness of his sinful creatures (Ps 51:4; Mk 2:7).[8] Christ's healing, on this account, occurs as the *objective* transfer of sin (that is, its true shame and guilt) to Christ by the Father is actively received and appropriated by believers, so that it is *subjectively* transferred from one's self to Christ, mentally and affectively, as the shame and guilt feelings of believers are experientially taken to the cross and released there. The gospel itself, therefore, provides believers with *theological* scaffolding that helps them to objectify, mentalize, and disidentify with their shame and guilt and surrender them to God, knowing their activity is grounded in what *God* has already accomplished. But it is the responsibility of believers to promote their own internal resolution of their remaining shame and guilt.[9] "Daughter, take courage; your faith has made you well" (Mt 9:22).

What can secular psychotherapy and counseling offer counselees who struggle with shame and guilt feelings, such as those found in depression (Tangney & Dearing, 2002)? In *Cognitive Therapy for Depression*, Beck, Rush, Shaw, and Emery (1979; pp. 177-79, 187-88) argued that "the sense of 'wrong-doing' is based on highly idiosyncratic and arbitrary standards" (p. 177) that are often unrealistic, and "shame, in a sense, is self-created" (p. 178). Both are deemed to be irrational, and neither is given any credence. The goals of therapy, therefore, are to challenge the belief or reasoning that underlies the feelings of guilt and shame and to "normalize" the thoughts or behaviors that are the source of the feelings.[10]

Depressed people do typically deal with false shame and guilt. However, they also know—often better than their happier neighbors (and therapists!) —that they really do have some deficiencies and that they really have done some wrong deeds, for their sadness is also due in part to a sense of the objective reality of their true shame and guilt, their hopelessness compounded by the recognition that they feel incapable of removing them. *But this is true from a Christian standpoint!* One cannot overcome one's ethicospiritual uncleanness simply by being convinced that to do so is "adaptive," or by self-referential affection and absolution: love yourself and forgive yourself; for at some level a depressed person thinks, *What does it matter if I love or forgive myself, since I really am bad?* While secular therapy can lead to improved functioning, its underlying worldview simply does not provide the resources to address adequately the sense humans have of their genuine ethicospiritual deficits. Only the healing found in the atonement can address the sense of personal continuity humans have with their past sins, while simultaneously communicating that every ground for self-loathing—true and false—has been removed by a transcendent God in Christ (Reno, 2002).

The healing of Christ's atonement is clearly concentrated on sin, the worst form of psychopathology, and so is primarily concerned with people's *ethicospiritual deficits*—one's relation to God, the ultimate direction of one's life, sins and vices, and true shame and guilt. However, its scope is greater still. Having been reconciled to God, much that pertains to other forms of psychopathology has been addressed and recontextualized in Christ. His death means believers are no longer fundamentally alone. Their lives, suffering, and damage are no longer ultimately meaningless (as naturalism entails). The negative trajectory of their stories has been authoritatively reversed. Their relationship with God can address attachment problems and other relational disabilities. Negative emotions—all signs of living and developing in a fallen world—can also be taken to the cross experientially, creating a novel pathway for their modification and transformation. *All* that is negative in one's soul, life, and relationality has been *in principle* overcome by God in Christ and therefore can be experientially modified and transformed. Such healing exemplifies top-down change processes that can affect one's thoughts, emotion schemes, memories, self-understanding, action dispositions, values, relational patterns, and story—as well as one's underlying neural architecture (Johnson, 2007, chaps. 8-9). The cross, therefore, also leads to some measure of healing one's *biopsychosocial damage* and ability to cope with suffering. How much is hard to say, and it depends on a host of factors, as we noted in chapter eleven, including the degree of suffering and the precise kind of damage under consideration. Nevertheless, all this suggests that the experiential appropriation of Christ's death could have a significant impact on the Christian soul and warrants considerable research.

Union with Christ's Death and the Death of the Autonomous Self

We move on to an even more subjective perspective on the atonement, though one that is still grounded in the objective work of Christ, which pertains to the death of the believer's "old self" (*palaios anthrōpos*, Rom 6:6; Hoekema, 1975; Chamblin, 1993a). Paul argued that because believers were united to Christ's death (Rom 6:5), they also had "died" in a spiritual sense (Col 2:20; 3:3). Their "old self was crucified" (Rom 6:6); they had been crucified to the world and the world to them (Rom 6:14); they have put off the old self with its practices (Col 3:9); and therefore they have died to sin (Rom 6:2, 10) and to the law (Rom 6:14; 7:4, 6). As a result, believers are no longer "still in [their] sins" (1 Cor 15:17). Put most paradoxically, Paul said, "I have been crucified with Christ; and it is no longer I who live, but Christ lives in me" (Gal 2:20). This model concerns the believer's self-representation, so we will call it the *psychological* view of the atonement.

Because the implications of this model will be explored in more detail in chapters seventeen to nineteen, I will only make a few brief observations here. What *is* the old self? We might define it as the false, autonomous self-understanding, identity, and way of life and relating to others that originated in the fall and that was condemned and overruled in Christ's death by the Father. On the cross, "the old man, the old mode of existence of sin, was then judged and cursed" (Ridderbos, 1975, p. 63). As soon as humans believe in Jesus Christ, they are mystically joined to Christ's death two thousand years ago and given a transcendent, spiritual basis for a fundamental reorganization of their self-understanding, identity, and way of life and relating to others. At that moment, their autonomous way of life becomes fatally compromised, making possible a new direction of life and the gradual construction of a new self. We might say that the believer's old self was given a "death blow" at conversion.[11]

The death of each believer's old self, however, is not just a once-for-all event, like Christ's death. It is also a process, begun definitively at conversion but continuing throughout one's life on earth and contingent on one's faith/ activity. "Consider yourselves to be dead to sin, but alive to God in Christ Jesus. Therefore do not let sin reign in your mortal body so that you obey its lusts" (Rom 6:11-12). It is a semiodiscursive and eschatological death—the sentence of execution pronounced by the Father with respect to his Son on the cross, and a judgment announced in the gospel but then received and internalized by faith ("consider yourselves"), fulfilled only in eternity. In the meantime, the death of the old self is gradually realized through what Catholics have called "purgation" (Groeschel, 1993) and the Puritans called "mortification" (Owen, Vol. 6, 1965). This involves self-examination; the identification of sinful and dysfunctional thoughts, desires, emotions, actions, and relational patterns; and their being "put to death" (Col 3:5 ESV) or "put off" (Eph 4:22 ESV), cognitively (or decisionally) and affectively, by means of deepening confession and repentance. More will be said about these therapeutic processes in later chapters.

Christ's Death as the Form of New Life

We have already considered the suffering of Christ on the cross in chapter nine in order to understand God's purposes in suffering. Here we will focus on how Christ's suffering constitutes an aspect of the atonement. What was God saying to us through Christ's actions from the time he was in Gethsemane until he yielded up his spirit to the Father that makes us one (at-one-ment) *experientially*?

In some respects Christ's actions were the final realization of his *kenosis.* "[Christ] humbled Himself by becoming obedient to the point of death, even death on a cross" (Phil 2:8). In spite of his natural, profound antipathy to the infinite suffering he would endure, he surrendered to the Father's will to save his people from their sins and, in so doing, also surrendered himself to the wills of those who wished to kill him. Though Christ had done nothing worse than challenge the faulty religious traditions and assumptions of the representative leaders of his people, he was condemned to an excruciating death, whipped and beaten and humiliated and mocked, with diabolical irony— "Hail, King of the Jews!" (Mt 27:29)—and most of his closest followers betrayed or abandoned him. Given the extraordinary honor of this divine-human dignitary, this event was easily the greatest calumny ever to occur on the planet. Nevertheless, throughout the violent persecution and abuse, he endured, mostly silently, taking the blows and insults without responding reciprocally. Instead he focused on others: caring for his mother's well-being after his death (Jn 19:26-27), reaching out to a criminal with whom he was crucified (Lk 23:43), and asking his heavenly Father to forgive his persecutors (Lk 23:34).

The atonement model that has focused on Christ's character manifested during this episode and its implications for our life and relationships has been called the moral exemplar or moral influence perspective. However, these rather vague labels might convey the impression that the goal is merely our moral emulation. Perhaps a better label for this model would be *cruciform love* (Gorman, 2001), which directs our attention more clearly to the supreme ethicospiritual *telos* of the atonement: the laying down of one's life for the sake of others in conformity to the crucified Christ by the power of the Spirit.

Measured by doxological criteria, this atonement model highlights what is the pinnacle of Christ's glory manifestation. His excellence was arguably more concentrated here than anywhere else in his life. That the infinite sovereign of the universe would be willing to subject himself to such violence and abasement for the ultimate well-being of his subjects is the greatest sign of virtue imaginable. Here he demonstrated the infinite excess of his love for his infinitesimal, image-bearing creatures (Jn 3:16), especially for his followers: "Greater love has no one than this, that one lay down his life for his friends" (Jn 15:13).

In the end, how did Christ finally defeat Satan and his forces, resolve sin and its desert, heal psychopathology, and kill the old self, that is, how did he finally overcome the violence and evils of this world and their opposition to him? *Not* by crushing his enemies in a concrete show of his inestimably greater power, and *not* by responding *to them* reciprocally and retributively.

Rather, manifesting his matchless humility, mercy, and compassion, he made himself vulnerable to them, submitting to their abuse; absorbing sin, suffering, and human weakness into his infinite being; and *in himself* destroying their power. His final act of *kenosis* demonstrated the immeasurable superiority of his sovereign majesty and power far more thoroughly (and ironically) than a military or judicial show of force could have. He will come again "in glory" to judge humankind (Mt 25:31-46), but until then, this display of omnipotent vulnerability serves as a call to all his human subjects to surrender to this beautiful King and find their eternal well-being in him.

The suggestion was made that retributive justice is foundational to human life and development, written into the fabric of the moral universe. However, we must recognize its misuse by us sinners who are inclined to view ourselves through the lens of self-serving bias as righteous and justified and to view others as the ones acting out of selfish and evil motives (Baumeister, 1997). Consider the contemporary conflict between Jews and Muslims in Israel/Palestine—they are locked together in a seemingly endless cycle of retributive justice. The only way to transcend this system of negative reciprocal exchange is for one party to act out of an ethicospiritually higher framework and sacrifice one's rights for the other. The problem is that one party has to develop a sufficient capacity of virtue to perceive and receive the sacrificial and virtuous act of the other for reconciliation to occur; otherwise the sacrificial act will be misinterpreted and taken advantage of. Nevertheless, the sovereign of the universe did exactly that for us, in spite of humanity's immediate inability to benefit from it rightly, because his self-donation is precisely that which would enable us to transcend the ethic of reciprocal exchange and live according to that *highest* ethic, *while confirming the validity of the lower ethic.*[12] So Christ maximally exemplified his admonition to love our enemies (Mt 5:44), and he did so in part to melt and remold our self-justifying hearts and our opposition to him and toward others, more and more, throughout our lives, as we receive the "word of the cross." In this most benevolent act of all time, his all-powerful, overcoming, and ultimately victorious act of weakness was the decisive "undoing of the cycle of violence" in human history (Horton, 2005, p. 195; 2 Cor 13:4).[13]

At the same time, Christ demonstrated a profound solidarity with sufferers, the weak, and the mistreated. His quotation of Psalm 22:1, "My God, my God, why have You forsaken Me?" tips us off to interpret the cross as the fulfillment of the entire lament tradition. In the crucifixion anguish of the God-man we discover the perfection and fulfillment of humanity's perennial lament to God, evident in Job's despair and the representative cries of the Jews—in their groans in Egypt and sinful complaints in the wilderness, to the perplexities and confessions of the psalmists, the lamentations of the prophets, and up to the horror of the Holocaust. Christ also became the *ultimate* (willing) *victim* of sin and its *conqueror*, simultaneously identifying with the abused and victimized and bearing away the sin of the world. In that event all violence and oppression and abuse throughout history became a metaphor of the cross, and their meaning was in principle transformed. Christ "bore unspeakable distress, sorrow, horror, and hellish torment on the cross in order that he might redeem us from them" (Bavinck, 2006, p. 416).

And he was exemplary even in his suffering. He experienced with perfect integrity intense negative emotions in Gethsemane, so extreme they produced bizarre physical symptoms, while surrendering his struggling human will to his Father. Then, throughout the mistreatment and torture of the next day, he showed just as extreme a capacity for self-control and fortitude, indicating the most remarkable ability to regulate his human emotions *fittingly*, that is, with regard to his own needs (in the garden) and the virtuous exigencies of the public situation (throughout Friday). Sufferers can hide themselves in this Rock of authentic emotion experience, expression, and regulation, knowing by faith they are united to his perfection and can learn from him how to rest (Mt 11:28-30) and where to cast their anxiety (1 Pet 5:7). Reflecting a cruciform model of the atonement, the author of Hebrews challenged his readers to look to "Jesus, the founder and perfecter of our faith, who for the joy that was set before him endured the cross, despising the shame. . . . Consider him who endured from sinners such hostility against himself, so that you may not grow weary or fainthearted" (Heb 12:2-3 ESV; see 1 Pet 2:21-25).

The underlying unity of all these models of the atonement is demonstrated in an important aspect of its *telos*: the formation of local communities— called churches—characterized by love, peace, and unity, and modeled on the life (and death) of their servant-Lord (Jn 13:13-15, 34-35). People formerly guilty, ashamed, and alienated are being made one—"now in Christ Jesus you who were formerly far off have been brought near by the blood of Christ" (Eph 2:13)—to resemble the Trinity (Jn 17:21-23). Committing oneself to this community entails the subordination of all other earthly relationships to one's membership in the family of God, even one's biological family (Mt 10:34-39; Mk 3:31-35; Rom 8:16-17; Eph 3:15). "He who does not take his cross and follow after Me is not worthy of Me" (Mt 10:38). These bodies of believers are to grow up into Christ, the head (Eph 4:11-16), learning how to regard one another as more important than themselves (Phil 2:4-5), being "kind to one another, tender-hearted, forgiving each other, just as God in Christ also has forgiven you" (Eph 4:32), and sharing the word of reconciliation with their neighbors (2 Cor 5:18-20). Boersma (2004) calls this living out of the cross *hospitality*.

A final word of caution, however, might be in order here regarding the needs of certain counselees (already discussed in the previous chapter). While conformity to Christ's cruciform pattern of life is a universal goal of the Christian life and the church, persons who suffered and were damaged before they became personal agents will likely need *first* to develop a stronger sense of self, greater differentiation of self and others, and better self-understanding, before being encouraged too much to live self-sacrificially for others, so that they don't do so mostly out of their own woundedness and pathology. Feminists have helped the church to recognize there is a kind of self-sacrifice that is very unhealthy.[14] Let it be said again and again: people need to develop a self in order to sacrifice it. There is a dialectic here, to be sure, but rightly emulating Christ's cruciform love entails the ingression of at least some of his vigorous agency by the healing of the Spirit, and naturally strong Christians are often unaware of how interdependent redemptive dynamics are with creational. Christ surely would not want his cross used to break bruised reeds (Mt 12:20).

SOME THERAPEUTIC IMPLICATIONS

The renowned nineteenth-century Baptist preacher Charles Spurgeon (1971) recognized that "the precious blood of Christ is useful to God's people in a thousand ways" (p. 34). Let us consider a few.

Dying to Get to the Tree of Life

One of George Herbert's most striking poems is called "The Sacrifice," where he imagines Christ taking the reader through the events of the last day of his life on earth. He ends each short stanza with "Was ever grief like mine?" At one point, Christ says,

O all ye who pass by, behold and see;
Man stole the fruit, but I must climb the tree;
The tree of life to all, but only me;
Was ever grief like mine?

At the heart of the Christian faith is a paradox that is deeply counterintuitive both to our nature as fallen beings created good and to secular models of psychotherapy and counseling: we have to die in order to obtain spiritual life. As Herbert recognized, this pattern is grounded in Christ's death and resurrection on our behalf.

The Christian life is radically discontinuous, *continuously* (Harrisville, 2006). This means that Christian healing of the soul does not consist merely in a gradual improvement of natural abilities, simply adding more information or more skills. It is not first about *finding* ourselves but about *losing* ourselves in order to find ourselves (Mt 10:39; 16:25; Mk 8:35; Lk 9:24; 14:26; 17:33). "Truly, truly, I say to you, unless a grain of wheat falls into the earth and dies, it remains alone; but if it dies, it bears much fruit. He who loves his life loses it, and he who hates his life in this world will keep it to life eternal. If anyone serves Me, he must follow Me; and where I am, there My servant will be also; if anyone serves Me, the Father will honor him" (Jn 12:24-26).

Christian psychotherapy and counseling, at the core, therefore, are cruciform, involving a radical, conscious, and ongoing identification with Christ on the cross. "To be formed in the likeness of the Crucified—this means being a man sentenced by God" (Bonhoeffer, 1955, p. 81). This is how Christ's disciples follow him. Everything in life has to be reorganized and approached from a nonnatural perspective. Most paradoxically, this death is not once and for all (e.g., only occurring at the beginning of the Christian life); it is daily (Lk 9:23) and continual. It is a learning to live by dying to the old self and its way of life.

How does this happen? In a thousand ways. For example, while doing "soul work" in meditative prayer, we can consciously surrender our lives, our relationships, our emotions, our bodies, and so on, to God in Christ, afresh, every day, little by little, experiencing a shift in our consciousness from the old to the new. Gradually, this virtuous practice of cruciformity trains us how to live more transparently before God and others, and enables us to better confess our sins, take appropriate responsibility, acknowledge our weaknesses, and become more self-aware, vulnerable, and authentic through disidentifying with old beliefs, emotions, and relational patterns. This is the death of the old self that makes way for the new. "It is only as one who is sentenced by God that man can live before God. Only the crucified man is at peace with God. It is in the figure of the Crucified that man recognizes and discovers himself. To be taken up by God, to be executed on the cross and reconciled, that is the reality of [being human]" (Bonhoeffer, 1955, p. 75).

In our union with Christ's death we discover that our entire life before God—our sin, suffering, and damage, as well as our good gifts and graces—has been crucified and is being transformed accordingly through faith in what he has done for us and is doing in us by the Spirit.

Overcoming shame and guilt through peace with God. As we saw above, Christ's death on the cross has objectively removed from believers their shame and guilt before God by means of the penal substitution of Christ. God "made peace" with sinners through Christ (Col 1:20), who "Himself is our peace" (Eph 2:14), so that now "having been justified by faith, we have peace with God through our Lord Jesus Christ" (Rom 5:1). Because of the cross, now God "tenderly excuses us, and he always shields us from blame in his eyes" (Julian of Norwich, 1998, p. 173).

However, the objective declaration of peace and divine forgiveness does not necessarily lead to experiential appropriation. The fact is many Christians continue to feel overwhelmed and beaten down with an awareness of their shame and guilt, sometimes leading to clinical syndromes such as depression and anxiety. Consequently, Christian psychotherapy and counseling is concerned with helping counselees learn how to receive divine peace and forgiveness.

Internalizing peace with God in one's conscience. We noted in chapter eleven that feelings of shame and guilt are a product of the psychological module called the conscience (*syneidēsis*; Rom 2:15). Contrasting Christ's death with the Old Testament sacrificial system, the author of Hebrews wrote, "If the blood of goats and bulls and the ashes of a heifer sprinkling those who have been defiled sanctify for the cleansing of the flesh, how much more will the blood of Christ . . . cleanse your conscience from dead works to serve the living God?" (Heb 9:13-14). And a little later: "Therefore, brethren, since we have confidence to enter the holy place by the blood of Jesus, by a new and living way which He inaugurated for us through the veil, that is, His flesh, . . . let us draw near with a sincere heart in full assurance of faith, having our hearts sprinkled clean from an evil [*ponēros*, which the NIV translates as "guilty"] conscience and our bodies washed with pure water" (Heb 10:19-20, 22).

These passages suggest that the changes effected by the cross were not only objective (resulting in a forgiven status before God) but also subjective, reaching into the heart and purifying the conscience from the felt contamination of sin. "The New Testament sacrifice has an inward efficacy" (Denney, 1902/1951, p. 128). The gospel of the cross is intended by God to be a conscience scrubber and wash away one's experiential shame and guilt, so that the believer's conscience becomes "clear" (2 Tim 1:3; Heb 9:9) or "good" (1 Tim 1:5, 19), that is, free of shame and guilt, so that one has confidence before God (Heb 10:19-22; 1 Jn 3:21). Paul analogously prayed that "the Lord of peace Himself continually grant you peace in every circumstance" (2 Thess 3:16). The experience of peace is a fruit of the Holy Spirit's work within the believer (Gal 5:22). "The kingdom of God is not eating and drinking, but righteousness and peace and joy in the Holy Spirit" (Rom 14:17). Consequently, believers are encouraged to appropriate this peace: "Let the peace of Christ rule in your hearts" (Col 3:15). The perennial challenge of Christian soul care, then, is how to help people appropriate such peace so that they experience it *in their heart*.

For believers, the death of Christ becomes an objective site where they can leave behind their guilt and shame by releasing these negative affects "into" the cross and allowing themselves to be "cleansed" by Christ's blood. Such conscious activities enable believers to distance themselves—that is, their new selves—from their felt guilt and shame, with God's authoritative approval and without denial. This objectification of guilt and shame is essential to their losing their power over the believer. What the Bible calls faith (and what Edwards called consent) is the means by which the objective realities of peace with God and forgiveness become subjective and realized within.

Yet this gospel subjectivization is generally very gradual. An absence of shame and guilt may be due to any number of factors (including dissociation and sociopathy!), but the deep resolution of the believer's experiential shame and guilt is not automatic, particularly for those who have shame-prone personalities. For neurological and psychological reasons, the process takes time and intentional effort in self-examination and meditative prayer with reference to God and the cross, bolstered by the acceptance of other humans, especially other believers (Rom 15:7), and cases of severe abuse may take years for noticeable healing to occur because of the overwhelming exacerbation of *false* shame and guilt in one's family of origin. Moreover, because Christians are still "in the flesh," peace may be hard to come by in one's daily experience, for some more than others. One's biology, early experiences, cognitive and emotional habits, and choices continue to shape one's experiences of shame and guilt throughout life, as well as one's ability to receive the peace already available in Christ. Central to a Christian therapeutic approach to the resolution of such problems, then, is the realization that the peace already exists objectively, outside one's experience of it, on account of Christ's death two thousand years ago. If the infinitely great Creator of the universe declares that all believers are forgiven in Christ, then believers have God's permission to "turn to" their consciences, so to speak, and take the time it takes to apply the blood of Christ to their underlying, inarticulate feelings of shame and memories of guiltiness. The distinction between objective and subjective peace is therapeutically valuable. It gives biblical and Christian counseling a strategic advantage over secular models of therapy, which do not have the transcendent ground to make the distinction.

The Resolution of Loneliness and Alienation in the Cross

Based on the "great exchange" between Christ and the believer, the cross has also removed the enmity that exists between believers and God and between believers themselves. However, once again, we note that this objective accomplishment has to be appropriated and internalized and uniquely contextualized within each believer's story. We observed in chapter eight the relational fallout from human sinfulness. The cosmic loneliness and shame due to original sin; the normal frustrations, anxieties, and sad experiences of the earliest years; the great variation people experience in attachment and child rearing; and personal guilt together result in remarkable differences in adult relational capacities, sense of loneliness, detachment, and isolation from God and others, and conversely, tendencies toward co-dependence and enmeshment. Unhealthy earlier patterns are then reenacted in marriage and with one's own children, friends, coworkers, and therapists, until they get resolved.

By bringing about reconciliation between believers and the archetypal and perfect Father, the cross provides a comprehensive, spiritual basis for the resolution of some fundamental aspects of one's relational difficulties through the knowledge and experience of absolute forgiveness and the transcendent abolition of one's existential alienation, suffering, and rejection, vertically and horizontally.

Because of the cross, believers have an objective basis to work through their sense of God's distance and neglect, as well as whatever negative emotions toward God they may experience. All believers, it appears, experience periodically some degree of alienation from God, so long as they are in the flesh. In addition, because of difficult attachment and relational histories, some believers have especially chronic and pervasive problems experiencing the favor and love of God (Moriarity & Hoffman, 2007). Such sufferers might find some consolation in the fact that perceived alienation from God

PART IV—The Divine Intervention

is quite common in the Bible and in church history. The Psalms abound with such spiritual experience (e.g., Ps 13; 22; 77; 88), and then there is Job: "O that I knew where I might find Him, that I might come to His seat! . . . Behold, I go forward but He is not there, and backward, but I cannot perceive Him; when He acts on the left, I cannot behold Him; He turns on the right, I cannot see Him" (Job 23:3, 8-9). Such periods of alienation have been called "spiritual desertions" by Protestants (Voetius & Hoornbeeck, 2003) and "dark nights of the soul" by Catholics (St. John of the Cross, 1959). Personal sins can also lead to a renewal of felt alienation, since they grieve the indwelling Holy Spirit (Eph 4:30; see also Deut 32:20; Ps 51:9-11), requiring confession, repentance, and forgiveness (1 Jn 1:9). When the alienation believers feel seems to them to raise questions about their standing with God, it has been historically termed a "problem with assurance," at least by Protestants (Demarest, 1997). Whatever the cause, believers can be encouraged to take to the cross their sense of loneliness and alienation from God, their sin as well as their negative emotions, and identify with Christ in his Godforsakenness, knowing that in Christ nothing can separate them from the love of God.

The body of Christ that is being crucified. The cross also undermines alienation among and between humans. Perhaps we could call this the intersubjective aspect of the atonement. This began in the reconciliation of Jew and Gentile. Writing to some Gentiles, the apostle Paul wrote,

> But now in Christ Jesus you who formerly were far off have been brought near by the blood of Christ. For He Himself is our peace, who made both groups into one and broke down the barrier of the dividing wall, by abolishing in His flesh the enmity, which is the Law of commandments contained in ordinances, so that in Himself He might make the two into one new man, thus establishing peace, and might reconcile them both in one body to God through the cross, by it having put to death the enmity. (Eph 2:13-16)

As we have seen, a critical part of the mission of God is the perennial formation of local assemblies (and relations among all Christians in the universal church) that increasingly resemble the unity of the Trinity (Jn 17:21). How does this happen? It requires cultivating a unique approach to one's relationships that flows from our crucifixion to our autonomous self and the world (Gal 2:20; 6:14): "Do nothing from selfishness or empty conceit, but with humility of mind regard one another as more important than yourselves" (Phil 2:3); "forgiving each other, just as God in Christ also has forgiven you" (Eph 4:32); "love covers a multitude of sins" (1 Pet 4:8). Such behavior requires Christians to die to their own needs, desires, and rights. This lofty ethicospiritual ideal cannot be fulfilled by immature and broken Christians until they personally experience some substantial healing through Christ or in relations with some of his people (e.g., a therapist).

As they listen to their hearts, many believers become aware of negative emotions they have toward others: anxiety, anger, and sadness, as well as some that are sinful—envy, bitterness, rage. All of these can be taken to the cross through meditative prayer, since Christ bore them there. One can also use the cross preventatively. Before entering into an intimidating situation, a counselee can be encouraged to surrender to the cross the sense of anticipatory anxiety she is feeling. With a brief imagery exercise, she can lower her arousal level and be better prepared for entering into the fearful situation, a routine that, with practice, can become internalized and automatized.

Of special importance is forgiveness. The Psalms teach Christians that the first stage of processing injustice is taking one's sadness, fear, and anger to the cross as one comes to terms with what has happened and surrendering the individual (and psychological object) to God. However, Christ's words on the cross—"Father, forgive them; for they do not know what they are doing" (Lk 23:34)—teach that the *telos* of such experiences is the eventual forgiveness of the offender. The benefits of such forgiveness have been well documented (Worthington, 2009). But for the Christian, human forgiveness is grounded in and facilitated by one's own forgiveness by the Father (Eph 4:32).

The counselor's role in the communication of divine reconciliation. Christians share in Christ's ministry of reconciliation by sharing "the word of reconciliation": "Therefore, we are ambassadors for Christ, as though God were making an appeal through us; we beg you on behalf of Christ, be reconciled to God" (2 Cor 5:19-20). We might also say this is a special calling of Christian psychotherapy and counseling.

Recalling the relational triangle (God, self, others), counselors can play a pivotal role in the communication of God's love and favor toward the counselee obtained in the cross by embodying and signifying it through the nature of their dialogue and interactions with their counselees. Counselors are to be a welcoming presence—"welcome one another as Christ has welcomed you, for the glory of God" (Rom 15:7 ESV)—curious and interested, committed to others' fundamental well-being, accepting of all that they bring into the counseling room without undermining God's standards for human conduct. Christian counselors represent a loving, reconciled, holy God. This can make an especially powerful impact when counselees share

unpleasant and shameful memories, activating the related negative emotions and their corollary neural regions, while their counselor models empathy, love, and acceptance. Such counselor behavior can modify the associated biopsychosocial dynamic structures with a new experience of social
support in the midst of distress, perhaps periodically making explicit that
the counselor is a sign of God's love of the counselee.

The Internalization of Redemption

We noted earlier that Christ conquered his spiritual enemies on the cross
and, as a result, redeemed or freed believers from bondage of various kinds.
How does that redemption become subjectively realized? The first thing to
note is that Christ's redemption was purchased for us and is a gift, so it is not
ultimately *our* task. Recognizing that the origin of one's freedom is "from
above" can reduce anxiety and grant some peace, simply because of the relief
that comes from knowing the solution is not up to us. As believers learn how
to appropriate and properly focus their attention on this dipolar dependence,
the resultant peace itself can promote some freedom.

Second, as believers come to accept and receive Christ's victory on *their*
behalf, more and more deeply, the capacity to undermine the believability of
the lies they grew up with—and still believe—likewise grows. Particularly
worthy of undermining are the false selves people maintain unconsciously to
hide the subjective shame and guilt that haunt their souls and continuously
seep quietly debilitating messages: *Bad. Invalid. I don't belong. Unlovable.*
Christ the Truth died for us, bearing and removing all our true, objective
shame and guilt on the cross, and the omniscient Truth also knows the unresolved subjective shame and guilt we continue to carry—both true and false.
In a sense, because of the cross, *it is all false now*, and our victorious Prince
seeks to communicate new messages into our hearts by faith, to gradually set
us free from our remaining subjective shame and guilt, and from our corresponding false selves, so that they become experientially unnecessary. In this
process, Christ's acceptance and belovedness by the Father is becoming ours.

The redemption of the cross also offers a useful narrative therapy strategy:
the believer has entered into Christ's story of deliverance. As Moses led the
people of Israel out of slavery into the Promised Land, so Christ is leading
believers out of their various kinds of bondage into the freedom of the glory
of the children of God (Rom 8:21). As Christians believingly enter into this
story, their identity, values, and relationships are becoming discretely transformed; meaning is gradually being made of their past, and hope for the

future slowly emerges. "I was once a slave, powerless and helpless; no wonder I did not make any progress. But I'm now on a journey of growth in Christ. Because of the cross, I'm not just 'turning over a new leaf.' A transcendent break has been made between me and my past, and I am learning I don't have to repeat it, because Christ has given me new possibilities." The formation of this "redemptive self"[15] may be particularly helpful for those who have lived chronically defeated lives due to highly debilitated personal agency, as seen in long-term addiction. Such repeated failures of agency can lead to deterministic and fatalist self-attributions. For such individuals, the narrative power of theodramatic redemption may enable them to reframe their life and provide a way out of their self-defeating belief/habit loop, giving them new action-potential in Christ.

Killing the Old, False Self

As we saw above, union with Christ's death warrants believers to consider themselves to be "dead to sin" (Rom 6:11). They are not to lie to one another, "since you laid aside the old self with its evil practices" (Col 3:9); so now, "lay aside the old self" (Eph 4:22), and "put to death therefore what is earthly in you: sexual immorality, impurity, passion, evil desire, and covetousness, which is idolatry. . . . But now you must put them all away: anger, wrath, malice, slander, and obscene talk from your mouth" (Col 3:5, 8 ESV). Such teachings suggest that believers need to reorganize their self-representation according to Christ's death as part of separating themselves from their vices.

Reflecting this therapeutic agenda, Luther (1535/1963) wrote, "Let us learn, therefore, in every temptation to transfer sin, death, the curse, and all the evils that oppress us from ourselves to Christ, and, on the other hand, to transfer righteousness, life, and blessing from Him to us" (p. 292). Though forgiven, believers still have what we might call "old-self-representations," which were forged in childhood and are reinforced in everyday life as broken, sinful adults, whenever they think, feel, and practice sinful patterns. As a result, believers are to *own* the death of their old self and old identity and *disown* specific old beliefs, surrender old emotions, and weaken false selves they have trusted. This requires identifying and focusing one's attention on elements of one's old self, ideally whenever it is activated, and undermining them in consciousness by connecting them affectively with Christ on the cross and distancing oneself psychologically from them. This process involves "disidentifying" with what belongs to their former way of life. The apostle Paul directed this disidentification process toward sin (Rom 6:2, 10; Col 3:4-9) and the law (Rom 6:14; 7:4, 6), which gives sin its power (Rom 7:5, 9, 11, 13), but this process can also focus on desires, beliefs, memories, and actions, and their associated emotions. Such a framework allows believers to accept their fallenness and distance themselves from it at the same time by acknowledging it but then approaching it as if it were that of *another person* and that person has died, so the believer is ultimately *no longer that person*. More will be said about processes such as disidentification in chapters seventeen to nineteen.

Entering into Christ's Lament

We have already considered much about the suffering of believers in chapter nine, and we need not repeat that material here. However, we cannot remind ourselves too often that our suffering—past, present, and future—is divinely joined indissolubly to Christ's on the cross (Rom 8:17; 2 Cor 1:5; Phil 1:29; 1 Pet 2:21; 4:12-19).

Lament in the new covenant, therefore, involves the conscious joining of our sorrows to Christ's on the cross and the growing realization that it is not only taken seriously (as the psalmist believed), but that God took them on himself and absorbed and resolved them in his power and love. This conscious identification with the cross, in turn, makes it possible for our laments to be transformed through the therapeutic practices of faith, consent, and surrender.

Perhaps the most profound lesson suffering believers can take away from the cross is the thought that if God did not spare his own Son from suffering, we will likely experience it as well. Indeed, as Paul realized, "For your sake we are being put to death all day long; we were considered as sheep to be slaughtered" (Rom 8:36)! Rather than viewing suffering as an anomaly, truth be told, it is one of the believer's callings—in Christ we are being experientially joined to the heart and doxological agenda of God to bring us from death to resurrection. This message is too complex and profound to be used with believers who are in the earliest stages of their recovery, particularly from early childhood abuse. But eventually, as their new selves become stronger and they enter more and more into their cruciform identity, their sufferings can become transfigured.

The End of Psychopathology

Christ's death signifies the end of the believer's psychopathology in a few ways. Since it has all been joined mystically to Christ's death—sin, suffering, and biopsychosocial damage—it finds there either its *telos* and meaning-fulness (suffering and damage) or its final judgment (sin). The cross is also a divine promise that all three kinds of psychopathology will be resolved someday. At the same time, Christ's death reminds us that the resolution will not happen completely in this life, but only in the life to come—it is escha-tological. It will be banished from the new creation, and that end has begun through faith in Christ. Believers therefore are now to reinterpret their psy-chopathology accordingly, realizing that the old is passing away and losing its power (2 Cor 5:17; 1 Jn 2:17).

RESOURCES FOR COUNSELORS AND COUNSELEES

Classic
Anselm of Canterbury. (n.d.). *Why God became man*. Albany, NY: Magi Books. ‡
Aulen, G. (1961). *Christus victor*. New York: Macmillan. ‡
Julian of Norwich. (1998). *Revelations of divine love*. New York: Penguin.
Murray, J. (1955). *Redemption accomplished and applied*. Grand Rapids, MI: Eerdmans. ‡
Schilder, K. (1945). *The Lenten trilogy (Christ in his sufferings; Christ on trial; Christ crucified)*. Grand Rapids, MI: Eerdmans. ‡

Contemporary
Boersma, H. (2004). *Violence, hospitality, and the cross*. Grand Rapids, MI: Baker. ‡
Crabb, L. (2009). *66 love letters*. Nashville, TN: Thomas Nelson.
Driscoll, M., & Breshears, G. (2008). *Death by love: Letters from the cross*. Wheaton, IL: Crossway.
Fitzpatrick, E. M., & Johnson, D. E. (2009). *Counsel from the cross*. Wheaton, IL: Crossway.
Gathercole, S. (2015). *Defending substitution: An essay on atonement in Paul*. Grand Rapids, MI: Baker. ‡
Gorman, M. J. (2001). *Cruciformity: Paul's narrative spirituality of the cross*. Grand Rapids, MI: Eerdmans. ‡
Hill, C. E., & James, F. A., III. (Eds.). (2004). *The glory of the atonement: Biblical, theological and practical perspectives*. Downers Grove, IL: InterVarsity Press. ‡
Leithart, P. J. (2016). *Delivered from the elements of the world: Atonement, justi-fication, mission*. Downers Grove, IL: InterVarsity Press. ‡
Lewis, A. E. (2002). *Between cross and resurrection: A theology of Holy Saturday*. Grand Rapids, MI: Eerdmans. ‡

Longman, T., III, & Reid, D. (1995). *God is a warrior.* Downers Grove, IL: Inter-Varsity Press.

Mahaney, C. J. *The cross-centered life.* Wheaton, IL: Crossway. A very short book, useful as a homework assignment for shame-prone counselees to help them understand how the penal substitution model resolves guilt and shame.

Reno, R. R. (2002). *Redemptive change: Atonement and the Christian cure of the soul.* Harrisburg, PA: Trinity Press International. ‡ A philosophically informed treatment of why the atonement matters for the healing of the soul. Should be widely read by Christian counselors up for the challenge.

Stott, J. (2006). *The cross of Christ.* Downers Grove, IL: InterVarsity Press.

‡ Recommended more for counselors and pastors than counselees

—*14*—

The Resurrection of Christ and the Beginning of the New Creation

Principle 6: The new creation began in Christ's resurrection and through union with him is being realized in and among believers by the Holy Spirit and faith.

He is the beginning, the firstborn from the dead, so that He Himself will come to have first place in everything.

COLOSSIANS 1:18

God . . . made us alive together with Christ (by grace you have been saved), and raised us up with Him.

EPHESIANS 2:4-6

ACCORDING TO EDWARDS (1993), the created order is filled with "signs" or "images" of spiritual reality, many of which are revealed in the Bible (e.g., marriage signifies the relation of Christ and the church, water symbolizes cleansing). Reading "the book of nature" like this shows it to be filled with spiritual metaphors. As we learn how to read when spending time outdoors and seeing with the eyes of faith, such metaphors can feed and heal our soul.

Reading in this way, Teresa of Àvila (1577/1961) pointed to the spiritual truth found in the life of a butterfly (pp. 104-8). She saw in an ugly caterpillar's wrapping itself up in a cocoon, never to be seen again, a symbol of the believer dying and being hidden in Christ, and she drew an analogy between the beautiful butterfly breaking out of the cocoon and the believer being transformed into a new person through union with Christ. There would appear to be many created metaphors of spiritual resurrection: awakening after a night of sleep, the stunning growth of plant and animal life in springtime, and the profusion of flowers that rise up in the desert after a rain, to name a few. We cannot be certain about such suppositions without an authoritative interpretive guide, and Scripture does not give us an exhaustive list of divinely inspired metaphors. Nevertheless, how wonderful that the Father has filled his creation with remarkable symbols of the resurrection of his Son and its impact on the human creation. In what follows we will explore some of the psychospiritual implications of what the Son accomplished at this point in his story.

CHRISTIAN TEACHING REGARDING CHRIST'S RESURRECTION

Within the Roman Empire crucifixions were a relatively common occurrence. Accounts of resurrections, however, are very rare. The very novelty of Christ's resurrection makes it a sign of his divine vindication (1 Cor 15:14-17; 1 Tim 3:16) and proves that he was the long-promised Messiah who would bring in a new era of God's reign and eventually a new creation (Is 40–66; Jer 31; Ezek 34–47). So all four Gospels report that Christ was raised from the dead and met with his disciples a number of times afterward and continued to teach them over a period of forty days (Acts 2:3).

The evangelical and soul-care significance of the death of Christ is widely appreciated in the church. But the gospel is also about Christ's resurrection (1 Cor 15:3-4), and the two events are indissolubly connected (Gaffin, 1978). The Christian initiatory rite of baptism brings them together, underscoring their dual importance to the Christian life. Moreover, in a significant sense the resurrection is the Christian's starting point for doing soul care, because it begins the repair of God's corrupted and damaged creation. In Christ's resurrection, rebellious, suffering, and broken humanity was repaired, healed, and brought back into communion with the triune God, thus bringing human nature to its greatest fulfillment and restoring it to its divinely intended end.

The resurrection altered the status before the Father of the human Jesus Christ. He was "declared [*horisthentos*; appointed, established] the Son of God with power by the resurrection from the dead, according to the Spirit of holiness" (Rom 1:4). The sonship of the God-man Jesus Christ was expanded in the resurrection, through which he was invested with greater power and authority than he had in his precrucifixion, incarnate life (Mt 28:18; Gaffin, 1978; Murray, 1959), having overcome the law's deadly condemnation of fallen humanity (Torrance, 2009, pp. 109-14) and confirming that he was the Davidic warrior-king prophesied in the Old Testament (Schreiner, 1998, p. 165). Through the resurrection, he became a "life-giving spirit" (1 Cor 15:45) who can now himself give new life to others (Jn 5:21-29) through the gift of his life-giving Spirit (Jn 7:37; 16:7), with whom he has become especially identified (2 Cor 3:18; Dunn, 1998, p. 262). All that he had accomplished through his resurrection from the dead entailed this new authoritative designation.

So radical was the resurrection in the apostle Paul's mind that he repeatedly contrasted the resurrected Christ with Adam (Rom 5:12-21; 1 Cor 15:12-28, 35-57)—"For as in Adam all die, so also in Christ all will be made alive" (1 Cor 15:22)—since Christ fulfilled God's intentions for Adam, the first son of God (Lk 3:38)—intentions that the rest of humanity, helpless and sinful, did not and could not fulfill (Rom 5:6, 8). So he called Christ the "last Adam" (1 Cor 15:45) and the "second man" (1 Cor 15:47), implying that the resurrected Christ is the archetype of a new race of humanity: "the beginning, the firstborn from the dead" (Col 1:18), the "first fruits" of the coming harvest (1 Cor 15:20), having gone before his followers and opened up a "new and living way" of life for them (Heb 10:20), forever joining their future to his own. In the resurrection Christ became the pioneer and inaugurator (Ridderbos, 1975, p. 56), the "progenitor of a new kind of humanity—resurrected humanity" (Dunn, 1998, p. 261).

A New World Order

The resurrection of Christ "is characteristic of the beginning of a new order of things" (Vos, 1980, p. 105). It altered time and space and opened up a new era or age—the last days have begun (Acts 2:15-17; 2 Tim 3:1-9; Jas 5:1-9); "the ends of the ages have come" (1 Cor 10:11)—and it initiated a radical breakthrough into this fallen creation in which a "new creation" has dawned "in an overwhelming manner, as a decisive transition from the old to the new world" (Ridderbos, 1975, p. 55).[1] As a result, believers in Christ are brought into the new creation now through union with him. "If anyone is in Christ, he is a new creation. The old has passed away; behold, the new has come" (2 Cor 5:17 ESV). "God has willed that the restored creation should take form in, and in relation to, one man. He exists not merely as an example of it, not even as a prototype of it, but as the one in whom it is summed up. To participate in the new creation, not provisionally only but forever, is to participate in Christ" (O'Donovan, 1986, p. 150). For Paul, "a new creation is everything" (Gal 6:15 NRSV). So perhaps the Christian era—*Anno Domini*—should have begun with the year of our Lord's resurrection rather than his incarnation!

What is the new creation? The beginning of a new order of human life, finally functioning according to God's design plan by the drawing of humans into the holiness, love, and communion of the triune God by the Holy Spirit through faith. Believers are God's "workmanship, created in Christ Jesus for good works" (Eph 2:10); they are *already* new selves "being renewed to a true knowledge according to the image of the One who created him" (Col 3:10); and their new selfhood is in the process of *becoming*, having been "created in righteousness and holiness of the truth" (Eph 4:24). Consequently, the long-ago prophesied apocalyptic establishment of the new heavens and new earth (Is 65:17; 66:22) has started in Christ—and in the minds, hearts, lives, and relationships of those who are in Christ, long before its total realization occurs (Rev 21:1).

Vos (1952) suggested that the apostle Paul's teachings about the new creation were so far-reaching that it implied that "not merely individual subjective conditions have been changed. . . . There has been created a totally new environment, or, more accurately speaking, a totally new world, in which the person spoken of is an inhabitant and participator. It is not in the first place the interiority of the subject that has undergone the change, although that, of course, is not to be excluded" (pp. 46-47). It involves "an incorporation into a new system of reality" (p. 47). However, this reality is *semiodiscursive* (Johnson, 2007), that is, like the first creation, it too is the realization of God's Word/words.

The Spiritual Order of Discourse

The apostle John was the canonical author clearest about the discursive nature of the new creation. He drew a direct parallel between the first creation in Genesis and a new creation established by Christ (Köstenberger, 2009): "In the beginning was the Word, and the Word was with God, and the Word was God. . . . All things came into being through Him, and apart from Him nothing came into being that has come into being" (Jn 1:1, 3; see Jn 1:14). In Genesis we read that God created light and life by means of his word, and in John's Gospel we read that "in [the Word] was life; and the Life was the light of men" (Jn 1:4). But the Word is now bringing in a new form of human life: *eternal* life (Jn 3:36; 10:28). Christ taught that people needed to be born a second time, spiritually (Jn 3:3-6), which is a kind of resurrection. Christ's miracles were signs of his glory (Jn 2:11) and soul-healing power (Jn 9:38-39), culminating with the resurrection of Lazarus (Köstenberger, 2009, p. 334). Before raising him, Christ announced that he was "the resurrection and the life" (Jn 11:25), and then "he cried out with a loud voice, 'Lazarus, come forth'" (Jn 11:43), bringing him to life with words. But the climax of John's narrative, of course, is the resurrection of Christ himself (Jn 20). John understood that the resurrection of Jesus Christ, the Word of God, *was* the word that brought in the new creation. Christ's resurrection, then, was a divine speech-act that announced the arrival of the long-promised new creation (Is 65:17-25) that includes all who believe in him (Rom 10:9).

So the new creation is a spiritual order of discourse (Johnson, 2007, chaps. 8-9). Just as the Spirit was present at the first creation (Gen 1:2), bringing into being the words of the Father, so the Spirit brings about the new creation. As he raised Christ from the dead (Rom 1:4), he is now the power raising believers from the deadness of their fallenness (transforming their sin, suffering, and damage). "If the Spirit of Him who raised Jesus from the dead dwells in you, He who raised Christ Jesus from the dead will also give life to your mortal bodies through His Spirit who indwells you" (Rom 8:11). To be "in Christ" is to be also "in the Spirit" (Rom 8:9), and the Spirit is the link between Christ and the spiritual blessings that believers enjoy because of their union with him (Rom 8:4-7, 15; 1 Cor 6:11; Gal 3:5; Eph 1:3; Tit 3:5-6).

The relation between the first and second creations is of great importance to the care of souls. As we have seen, the first creation has been corrupted and damaged and is characterized by suffering. One can imagine a new creation that is radically unrelated to the old. However, redemption seems intended by God to overrule and remediate the effects of the fall, so that *this* creation is being transfigured and enabled to realize more of its original God-intended potential. "The eschatological transformation of the world [in Christ] is neither the mere repetition of the created world nor its negation. It is its fulfillment, its *telos* or end. It is the historical *telos* of the origin, that which creation is intended for, and that which it points and strives toward"

(O'Donovan, 1986, p. 55). At the same time, the effects of redemption necessarily transcend the scope of the original creation, for example, the believer's
union with Christ. "The transformation [due to redemption] is in keeping
with the creation, but in no way dictated by it" (O'Donovan, 1986, p. 64).
Indeed, because of the Son of God's personal participation in redemption,
the glory of the new creation immeasurably exceeds the glory of the original
creation (as great as that is!).

The completion of the new creation nonetheless awaits the consummation, the beginning of which is signaled by the second coming of
Christ. As a result, the resurrection and consequent new life of the believer are intrinsically eschatological, pointing ahead to their fulfillment
in a bodily resurrection and everlasting life with the triune God in the
new heavens and new earth (Jn 5:21; Rev 21:1), themes to be discussed in
this book's final chapter.

The Believer's Union with Christ Resurrected

The resurrection of Christ contributes to the psychospiritual well-being of
Christians because of their union with Christ. "All of us who have been
baptized into Christ Jesus have been baptized into His death. Therefore we
have been buried with Him through baptism into death, so that as Christ
was raised from the dead through the glory of the Father, so we too might
walk in newness of life" (Rom 6:3-4). "Having been buried with Him in
baptism, in which you were also raised up with Him through faith in the
working of God, who raised Him from the dead. When you were dead in
your transgressions . . . He made you alive together with Him" (Col 2:12-13).
"Even when we were dead in our transgressions, [God] made us alive together
with Christ . . . and raised us up with Him . . . in Christ Jesus" (Eph 2:5-6).

These passages refer to a mystical joining together of Christ and believers
by means of his resurrection. Christ's role is obviously primary and constitutive (Gaffin, 1978, p. 57), but in the purposes (and speech-acts) of God in
Christ, believers have themselves been raised from spiritual death and
alienation from their Maker into a living relationship with him. This coresurrection is foundational to Paul's understanding of the Christian life and
soul care (Maddox, 1994). However, the resurrection of believers has two
installments (Gaffin, 1978). One is ethicospiritual: the renewal of their inner
life (2 Cor 4:16; Rom 7:22; Eph 3:16), manifested in virtuous action in relationships (Eph 4:25–5:2; Col 3:12–4:6). But it is only partial, since believers
continue to struggle against the internal and external powers of the flesh

(Rom 8:5-8; Gal 5:19-21) in this present evil age (Gal 1:4). The other is material: the renewal of their bodies (Rom 8:23; 1 Cor 15:35-44; 2 Cor 5:1; Phil 3:21)—indeed a renewal of the entire cosmos (Rom 8:21)—which will occur in the age to come (1 Cor 15:23), bringing about complete physical and spiritual perfection (1 Jn 3:2). "Behold, I am making all things new" (Rev 21:5).

Reconciliation Through Resurrection

In the previous chapter, we considered reconciliation with God with reference to Christ's death, to which it is indissolubly linked because its prerequisite is the resolution of human sin. However, reconciliation is also tied to Christ's resurrection and the new creation (2 Cor 5:15-21). The Greek root word for reconciliation, *katallassō*, and its cognates refer primarily to the peace and renewal of fellowship between believers and God, instigated by "the Father's good pleasure . . . through [Christ] to reconcile all things to Himself, having made peace" (Col 1:19-20). The peace was obtained "through the blood of His cross" (Col 1:20), true, but the peace itself is the substance of the resurrection. God's goal has always been relational. We "exult in God through our Lord Jesus Christ, through whom we have now received the reconciliation" (Rom 5:11). Ultimately, resurrection life involves participation in trinitarian *koinōnia* (1 Jn 1:3; communion, fellowship). The love of the Father for the Son is now in believers, for Christ himself is now in them (Jn 17:26), and they are in the Father and in the Son (Jn 17:21) by the indwelling Spirit (1 Cor 6:19; 2 Cor 13:14; Phil 2:1).

From God's standpoint, reconciliation has been accomplished: God has already "reconciled us to Himself through Christ" (2 Cor 5:18). Yet from our standpoint, subjectively, it is a process, so Paul said to *believers*, "we beg you on behalf of Christ, be reconciled to God" (2 Cor 5:20). Reconciliation, therefore, has profound psychological implications, since a restored relationship with God is the most significant social relationship one has, providing a kind of friendship and kinship that in principle transcends all other relationships in value and potential impact. Yet because of their remaining sin (that is, their usually unconscious, unresolved antagonism toward God), believers have to work out their salvation (Phil 2:12), in part by undermining and overturning their resistance, which has been made possible now in Christ.

In the restoration of that ultimate, preeminent relationship, believers can experience relational healing of an utterly unique kind. The Bible announces that believers are reconciled to God in Christ, but gradually, through communion with him, believers discover *experientially* what that means. "We have come to know and have believed the love which God has for us. God is love, and the one who abides in love abides in God, and God abides in him" (1 Jn 4:16). As a result, believers now have access to an intersubjective relationship with the God who loves them, through the indwelling Holy Spirit, an interpenetration (Witherington, 1994, p. 277) that we have seen is analogous to the trinity's *perichoresis*, intentionally designed to fulfill and transcend infinitely the psychological symbiosis infants had with their mother in the first year of life (see Mahler, 1968[2]).

Believers now are being raised from the dead as they grow in knowledge and experience of the invisible God as their loving Father and Brother through worship, *lectio divina*, and meditative prayer, accepted by divine members of their new family who are perfectly righteous, loving, and sovereign. Admittedly, the relationship is not with a physically tangible person, and this conditions the psychological impact it has in this life. Over the long term, however, it is God's intention that his relationship with his children becomes the most influential, since only in him can they receive an inexhaustible, increasingly intimate, perfectly virtuous love, particularly as it is mediated and confirmed through loving relationships with tangible brothers and sisters. "Not only does [Christ] cleave to us by an indivisible bond of fellowship, but with a wonderful communion, day by day, he grows more and more into one body with us, until he becomes completely one with us" (Calvin, 1559/1960, p. 570).

The Resurrected Self

Just as the believer's union with Christ led to the death of his or her old self through cocrucifixion with Christ, union with Christ has led to the creation of the believer's *new self* (*kainon anthrōpon*; lit. "new man")—"which in the likeness of God has been created in righteousness and holiness of the truth" (Eph 4:24[3]), through its coresurrection with Christ (see Rom 6:1-11; Col 2:12; 3:1; Eph 2:6). The apostle Paul referred to this event repeatedly: "If any man be in Christ, there is a new creation! Old things have passed away. Behold, new things have come" (2 Cor 5:17; translation from Vos, 1952); "for we are His workmanship, created in Christ Jesus for good works" (Eph 2:10). In response to Jewish Christian leaders teaching that Gentile Christians had to be circumcised, Paul wrote that whether or not one gets circumcised is irrelevant; the only thing that matters is "a new creation" (Gal 6:15). Having been identified in the mind and heart of the Father with the resurrected Son of God, the believer's self has been in some analogous fashion transformed by the resurrection and made part of the new creation.

At the same time, we read in Colossians 3:10, which parallels Ephesians 4:24, that the new self (*neon anthrōpon*) "is being renewed [*anakainoumenon*] to a true knowledge according to the image of One who created him" (Col 3:10). Here the context and the verb form (present passive participle) suggest that the believer's new self is now "not in its final state: it is in a state of 'becoming'" (Moo, 2008, p. 269). It therefore has to be realized throughout this life. More on that below and in chapter seventeen.

Paul's labeling of the Christian's self as "new" had no parallel in the non-Christian religions of that day (O'Brien, 1982), nor in the self-theory of modern psychology (see Baumeister, 1999; Harter, 2012). At the same time, Paul's comments on this score are relatively cryptic and are far from a comprehensive, scientific description of the new self. That remains a post-canonical task to be worked out by the church, based on scriptural revelation and relevant scientific knowledge. Nevertheless, believers have been given sufficient information, with the power of the Spirit, to begin the process of realizing the new self in their lives.

The Already/Not-Yet Dynamic of the Christian Life

So believers now are living in the new creation; however, in this age it is only partially realized. Theologians have labeled this salvation paradox the "already/not-yet" dialectic or dynamic (Horton, 2002; Ladd, 1974; Schreiner, 2001). The word of the new creation has been uttered by God in Christ and has taken root in believers, whose spiritual maturation is tethered to the depth of their reception of that word. Unlike the establishment and mainte-nance of the original creation, where God's word has an immediate effect, the *new* creation occurs in believers in three "stages": (1) the initial regeneration, (2) the ongoing process of Christiformity, and (3) its perfection in eternity. Christians now live "between the times" (Dunn, 1998, p. 461), in which the new creation—though entirely dependent on the Holy Spirit—is generally a gradual development, conditioned by temporality, embodiment, indwelling sin, biopsychosocial damage, personal faith, and social influences. As a result, the process of transformation is usually slow, uneven, and ultimately imper-fectable in this life. So, while believers are *already* experiencing some degree of new-creation renewal, it is *not yet* the perfection that all humans desire.

One of the primary reasons for the already/not-yet tension is that the physical body of Christians is not yet redeemed (Rom 8:23), which will occur only at the end of this age (1 Cor 15:42-44). Consequently, many bodily desires incline the believer away from God and toward sin and lesser goods (Rom 6:12-22; 7:5; Col 2:11; 3:5). So the resurrection life of believers pertains in this age fundamentally to the ethicospiritual orders. Yet through consent to the resurrection word of God more and more deeply, its power spreads top down, gradually transforming psychosocial dynamic structures (thinking, feeling, relating, and so on) and brains, potentially permanently, as the changes get stored in one's neural architecture. As a result, believers live in a unique conjunction of temporal frameworks, "the time of this passing world and the time of the new creation" (Torrance, 2009, p. 256), out of which some eschatological change can always emerge. Living in the "between times" can transform created time itself, through visions and contemplation, in which we are "lost" in communion with God and experience a foretaste of eternity.

The Validity and Renewal of the Original Creation
Christ's resurrection brought together creation and redemption. For one thing, it "tells us of God's vindication of his creation, and so of our created life" (O'Donovan, 1986, p. 13). The resurrection is a reaffirmation of God's good will toward the human creation, in spite of its sin. It demonstrates that neither sin, death, nor damage, nor Satan's power over human nature, are necessary to human life, and their chaos, meaninglessness, evil, and pain, and the tragedy of fallenness can (and will) be overcome. The resurrection transposes human nature out of the ethical judgment it deserves into the spiritual order of redemptive grace, where created human beings can find their highest fulfillment in union with Christ and communion with God and one another.

The new creation now is the old creation renewed. The created human psychological systems that are now corrupted and often damaged by sin—memory, emotion, cognition, volition, and relationship—have been given a new legitimation in Christ's resurrection. Though they are still fallen, Christians are entitled to the hope of partial restoration in this age and complete restoration in the age to come. Moreover, God's delight in creation, underscored in the resurrection, can keep believers from a naturalistic fatalism held captive by a belief in the supposed determinism of genetics or socialization, as well as the legalist's obsession with personal sin (whether one's own or the sin of others), by fostering a realistic, resurrection optimism that is simply more confident in the possibility of the recovery and flourishing of humanity in God's new creation than in humanity's constraints due to the evil, suffering, and damage of the present age, as significant as they are. He is risen! And therefore we believe that we can also be raised from the dead.

SOME THERAPEUTIC IMPLICATIONS

The importance of Christ's resurrection for Christian psychotherapy and counseling can scarcely be overstated. In addition to validating the created dynamic structures that constitute human life and demonstrating that God's doxological-therapeutic agenda involves their fulfillment and realization through divine renovation, the resurrection of Christ initiated a *new* creation— a new kind of created being—wounded by the fall but healed in Christ, who overcame human sin, suffering, and weakness by the Spirit, legitimizing hope for therapeutic change in this age while also pointing to a perfected life in the age to come. Christ's resurrection, therefore, signifies a way of therapy that transforms human nature "from above."

"Believer, Come Forth!"

The resurrection of the Word of God is still being realized. God the Father has uttered a cosmic revolution in his Son. This time he said, "Light shall shine out of [human] darkness," and the light was "the knowledge of the glory of God in the face of Christ" (2 Cor 4:6). When God's glory passed before Moses on Mount Sinai, God proclaimed his character (Ex 34:6-7). Out of Christ's tomb flowed another manifestation of divine discourse, this time the beauty of the triune God designating and establishing the beauty of all who are united with the resurrected Christ. The new creation is a world of meaningfulness, the outshining of the light of Christ's glory on human life, transforming it through "face time" with him (2 Cor 3:18; Ford, 1999). As believers receive the gospel and commune together with the resurrected Christ, they become new creatures (2 Cor 5:17) and enter into a new "sphere" of meaning, the spiritual order of discourse (Johnson, 2007, chaps. 8-9). As a result, believers no longer know people "according to the flesh" (2 Cor 5:16). Everything about them is different now because of their union with Christ's resurrection, making it possible for believers to transpose themselves by the Spirit from the old creation into the new (Johnson, 2007, pp. 366-69), understanding God, themselves, their relationships, and their entire body and soul in the light of Christ. God in Christ has provided remarkable therapeutic resources for Christians to experience their "old, unsettled conflict, but with a new ending" (Alexander & French, 1946, p. 338): an ongoing resurrection to new life.

Sons and Daughters of God

Reconciliation with the triune God is further ennobled through adoption into God's family. Christ was designated the "Son of God with power" by the resurrection from the dead (Rom 1:4), which uniquely confirmed his eternal sonship through its being joined to a resurrected human nature. Union with Christ in his resurrection therefore includes being brought into the divine family of Father and Son, by means of the Holy Spirit. "You have received a spirit of adoption as sons by which we cry out, 'Abba! Father!' The Spirit Himself testifies with our spirit that we are children of God, and if children, heirs also, heirs of God and fellow heirs with Christ" (Rom 8:15-17; see Gal 4:6) The Holy Spirit makes experientially real believers' objective status that they are in fact children of God.[4]

We recall that Christ is the "firstborn from the dead" (Col 1:18). "Firstborn" here implies both preeminence and the existence of siblings. In his resurrection, Christ became the firstborn child in God's soon-to-be greatly expanded adoptive family. In the human sphere, when a child is adopted into a family, the adopted child has the same rights and privileges that a biological child has. Likewise, in the family of God, adopted children who were formerly alienated and ultimately alone are now given the same rights and privileges as Jesus, the only-begotten human son of the Father (Jn 1:14; Moore, 2009)! God has adopted believers to be "His heirs, to see and share the glory into which His only-begotten Son has already come" (Packer, 1973, p. 182).[5]

Experiencing God's presence is so important for the healing of our souls, because deep relational experiences are necessary to repair dysfunctional relational patterns and self-understanding derived from poor past experiences of oneself in relation to others. Regular communion with a perfectly loving, righteous, and sovereign Father can uniquely compensate for harmful experiences with poor parents, while providing transcendent fulfillment of one's lifelong positive relational experiences, analogous to our early psychological merging and identifying with our parents.

A merely intellectual apprehension that one is adopted by God simply cannot change one's attachment style, and while communion with other, healthier humans (such as counselors) can be extremely impactful over time, every human relationship has significant limits (e.g., contact only one hour a week), whereas God is the true fulfillment of an ideal father (the significance of which Freud tragically misinterpreted; Vitz, 1988). Ongoing meaningful contact with him—the more emotional the better—can slowly contribute uniquely to the rewiring of one's attachment system, creating new neural networks and pathways that, over time, can become influential in one's everyday self-understanding and human relationships, eventually overriding those laid down earlier in life. Constructive experiences in adulthood with God the Father, such as symbiosis, attachment, intersubjectivity, empathy, and dipolar identification, grounded in the God/*imago Dei* relation, can be profoundly corrective, providing a "transmuting internalization" of the transference relationship (Kohut, 1971), analogous to a human clinical relationship, that can uniquely help promote recovery from the relational deficits derived from earlier in one's life, given God's perfections and our union with Christ.

At the same time, as we have already noted (e.g., in chap. 6), poor earlier relationships with parents may create a catch-22 for humans—especially if they were religious—by compromising their "God image,"[6] making it difficult to relate to God constructively without first getting healing (see Moriarity & Hoffman, 2007). In such cases, loving relationships with other humans (for example, a trained therapist or possibly a mentor or small group) may be extremely helpful (not surprising given Gen 2:18), affording another God-ordained pathway into the healing of a person's self-in-relationship matrix. Ideally, one's participation in the new creation is facilitated by the formation of healthy relationships with God and our fellow heirs, which reciprocally enable us to love them back (Eph 4:15-16).

The Spread of the Resurrection

We turn next to consider the unfolding impact of Christ's resurrection on the healing and flourishing of his followers.

The new birth. Believers have been made spiritually alive by God in Christ (Eph 2:6), raised in their soul from the spiritual deadness of their earlier life, evidenced in unbelief, disobedience, and unconscious autonomy, into an awareness and experience of the true God, including loving dependence on him and healthy submission to him as Lord. The new birth (1 Pet 1:3) is the beginning of a consciousness that has been awakened to the reality and claims of God through Christ.

The most well-known metaphor of the new life is being "born again" (Jn 3:3, 7; 1 Pet 1:3, 23). However, the biblical meaning of that phrase has become obscured. Within evangelicalism it has come to mean a one-time supernatural event in which the believer turns to God from a life of sin and is saved. This use aptly brings out the divine and mystical origin of the Christian life, in contrast to a merely socialized version. Unfortunately, in some quarters, this has led to the false impression that a Christian must know the exact day and time when one was, in fact, born again. Yet, as Hoekema (1994) has pointed out, since the new birth is "a change in the subconscious roots of our being" (p. 104), one may not actually know when it occurred.

Nevertheless, the metaphor suggests that becoming a Christian is as profound and radical as the birth of a child, introducing a new mode of existence into a person's life, the veritable beginning of a new human being. Theologians have termed this revolutionary transition that began in Christ's resurrection "regeneration," based on the Greek word *palingenesia* (Titus 3:5), which means literally "a birth again." Jesus taught that this birth is "from above" (Jn 3:3), that is, it is not a merely natural process (see also Jn 1:12-13) but is caused by the mysterious power of the Holy Spirit (Jn 3:8, though this does not rule out the influence of any number of biological and psychosocial factors; see Hood, Hill, & Spilka, 2009).

In spite of its mysterious nature, few aspects of assessment in Christian psychotherapy and counseling are more important than discerning whether a counselee is actually regenerated. Of course, sometimes it is impossible to know for sure, but counselees cannot avail themselves of gospel resources unless they are actually, subjectively alive in Christ. If it is clear that they are not, Christian counselors will have to rely on merely creational therapeutic processes, as Christian parents do in child rearing before their children become Christian, and look for opportunities to point them to a new life in Christ. Powerful secular influences in graduate school and public mental health have convinced some Christians that they cannot advocate the Christian faith in therapy. But secular therapists share implicitly their naturalistic/humanistic worldview in every session, but because the discourse lacks reference to supernatural entities and processes, it is commonly supposed they are being religiously neutral. However, metaphysical claims are necessarily being made covertly, whether one is aware of it or not, for they are unavoidable in the promotion of psychological change. Consequently, Christian counselors should also be free to share their faith with their counselees, with the hope of introducing them to the power of divine regeneration, while always respecting their needs and desires. Someday, hopefully, the current rules of secular therapy will be changed to allow for greater worldview diversity.[7]

The nature of resurrection life now. C. S. Lewis (1952) characterized true Christianity as "Zoe," from the Greek word for life, found in the New Testament (Jn 14:6). The new life in Christ is a human kind of life, but a kind qualitatively different from the life humans can experience on their own apart from Christ.

We saw above that the resurrection made possible a new relationship with God, and this new relationship constitutes the substance of the new life. Christ claimed to be "the bread of life" (Jn 6:35), "the resurrection and the life" (Jn 11:25), "the way, and the truth, and the life" (Jn 14:6); he said repeatedly that he came to give people eternal life (Jn 3:16; 5:24, 40; 6:27; and so on); and in his high priestly prayer, he defined eternal life as to "know You, the only true God, and Jesus Christ whom You have sent" (Jn 17:3). The apostle Paul later referred to Christ as "your life" (Col 3:3). So the new life is obviously centered on Christ and might be said to consist of the realization of the believer's union and communion with him. We experience the resurrection life, then, by living our daily life mindfully and emotionally in the presence of the Lord, in such a way that *his everywhere saving presence permeates our souls*—our thoughts, affections, memories, imagination, relational capacities, actions, story, and self-understanding—our entire way of life. This is what it means to abide in Christ (Jn 15:1-7).

Like everything in the Christian life, this occurs by the Word of God. Believers were "born again not of seed which is perishable but imperishable, that is, through the living and enduring word of God" (1 Pet 1:23), and they are to continue to "receive the word implanted, which is able to save your souls" (Jas 1:21). "Let that abide in you which you heard from the beginning. If what you heard from the beginning abides in you, you also will abide in the Son and in the Father" (1 Jn 2:24). So the new life consists of the enjoyment of communion with the triune God and the blessings that Christ obtained for us, and it advances in our souls the more thoroughly and deeply *his saving word also permeates our souls*. The new life is both relational and semiodiscursive.

Another way to think about the resurrection life relates to the receiving of and living according to the ethical and spiritual orders (see Johnson, 2007, chaps. 8-9). Both are being appropriated and internalized in the new life. The focus of the ethical order is obedience to God's law—something humans can attempt on their own—whereas the spiritual order is especially concerned with redemptive grace and communion with God. However, these two orders are hierarchically related, with the spiritual order being ultimate ("where sin increased, grace abounded all the more," Rom 5:20), so that the *new* life involves the transposition of the ethical order into the spiritual order. The result could be called the "gospelization of the law." This means that the obedience of the new life is increasingly characterized by a radical, supernatural sense of God's grace, favor, and love, in which one's sense of deficit, unworthiness, guilt, and shame is being swallowed up in union with Christ. The new life, therefore—and therapy working with the new life—is like a gradual, ongoing conversion to God (Snell & Cone, 2013, pp. 124-27, following Lonergan).

Finally, the new life is characterized by glory. As Christ was "raised from the dead through the glory of the Father" (Rom 6:4), an event that singularly manifested that glory, so the believer's new life consists of participation in God's glory. God has shined into believers' hearts "the Light of the knowledge of the glory of God in the face of Christ" (2 Cor 4:6; see also Eph 3:16; 1 Thess 2:12; 1 Pet 1:8). The new life is thoroughly doxological.

As Edwards (1746/1959) pointed out, the resurrection life does not involve the creation of a new spiritual faculty or module. Rather, it consists of the regenerating or enlivening or transposition of one's original, created faculties, the most important of which is the module for perceiving God, what Calvin called the *sensus divinitatis*, which was damaged and benighted by original sin. God implants "a new foundation" (Edwards, 1746/1959, p. 206), a theocentric motive that has been lacking since the fall, which enables us to use our created capacities for their originally designed purposes, God's glory and our true well-being. So the new life is characterized by a new conscious direction toward God—antithetical to the way of the flesh (Rom 8:5-9; Toon, 1987)—a grace-based way of life that can transform everything and involves drawing steadily nearer to God with more and more of our created being in love, worship, obedience, and fellowship out of God's own life.

The new life is complicated, of course, by the fact that resurrected believers still live in the flesh and so are still sinners living in the "in-between times"— the already/not-yet—in unredeemed bodies, with one foot in the new creation and the other in this present evil age. Consequently, though grace is ultimate, the new life on earth involves a law-grace dialectic (Bonhoeffer, 1985): alternatively (periodically?) focusing on conviction of sin and perfection in Christ, repentance and faith, mortification and vivification, dying to the old life of narcissism and autonomy and living to God in grateful dependence—though grace is always the last word for believers (Rom 5:15-21). Chapters seventeen to nineteen explore some of the clinical implications of this dialectic.

The "seed" of resurrection life. Another metaphor applied to regeneration is that of a seed: "No one who is born of God practices sin, because

His seed [*sperma*] abides in him" (1 Jn 3:9; see also 1 Pet 1:23). This suggests that God has implanted something within believers that constitutes the beginning of their new life in God. It could refer to the indwelling Holy Spirit or the Word of God (Edwards, 1959, p. 201; Marshall, 1978) or perhaps the love of God in the heart (Rom 5:5), leading to a fundamental change in the ultimate direction of the soul.

The seed metaphor might also imply that regeneration begins as a very small (but radical) internal change—small perhaps in comparison to the rest of the soul, which is still "of the flesh" (to use Paul's terminology). Psycho-spiritual maturity increases, then, as the life of this seed grows, spreading slowly throughout the soul, so that more and more of one's thoughts, feelings, desires, and motives become similarly transformed. This also leads to an analogous, isomorphic "spreading" that occurs to neural tissue as memories, thoughts, and emotions are recontextualized within Christ, forming new neural networks created by the gospel of Christ, linked by new neural pathways to previously formed but now modified neural networks. To extend the metaphor we might consider the goal of Christian soul care to be the fostering of the growth of that seed into a sprout, a sapling, and gradually a tree, throughout the process increasing the percentage of the brain/soul that is brought under the sway of the new life, knowing that complete enlivening—often called glorification—awaits us in heaven (1 Jn 3:2).

No matter how small the new life, it is sustained by an omnipotent God. The Puritan pastor Richard Sibbes (1630/1998) encouraged weak saints: know "that a spark from heaven, though kindled under greenwood that sobs and smokes, yet it will consume all at last. Love once kindled is strong as death. . . . That little that is in us is fed with an everlasting stream" (p. 97).

Faith, the human medium of resurrection life. While the new creation is instituted by God's Word/words and made possible by the Spirit, the receptive activity of believers plays an essential role in its realization. Sometimes after healing people Jesus would say, "Your faith has made you well" (Mk 5:34; Lk 17:19). Though God has the power to heal unilaterally, he desires our participation through our faith/consent/active receptivity, since his doxological/therapeutic agenda is furthered through our active conformity to Christ. According to Ridderbos (1975), faith is "the mode of existence of the new life" (p. 231); it is "the way in which . . . the new creation is being realized" (p. 233). At the same time, the faith of believers is simultaneously the faith of Christ (Purves, 2004). Rightly understood, all Christians should be advocates of physical healing, but the only kind that God *guarantees* down here is the healing of our neural networks through their reorganization by faith in the gospel of Christ.

At the same time, doubt remains a "normal" condition for believers in this age (Mk 9:24). Sin, finitude, and growing up with poor images of God can all play a role in this inclination. Christ is our goal, and even he agonized in prayer with his Father, asking him anguished questions (Mt 26:38-39; 27:46). But nowhere is he described as doubting. So doubt ought not to be lauded as a virtue in the new creation. Yet doubt is often a stepping stone, mixed with faith, and asking questions is good. All that to say, counselors need great discernment, patience, and compassion when helping believers with their doubts and struggles.

The gradual diffusion of resurrection life. The new life is expandable, and it expands by the internalization of the word of God by the Spirit through faith. As the word of Christ is heard, read, received, believed, consented to, meditated on, kept, obeyed, and shared with others in love, the new creation spreads. So, wherever the word of God is taking root in the dynamic structures of the brain/souls of the first creation, we find evidence of the expansion of the second creation.[8] The Reformation tradition has termed the growth of the new life *vivification* (Calvin, 1559/1960, p. 595; Goodwin, 1861–1866/1996), in contrast to mortification, the corollary process that corresponds to the crucifixion. In the following section we will trace some of the psychological aspects of vivification.

New beliefs, values, and behaviors. The first (and easiest) changes to occur after becoming a Christian are cognitive. As new believers hear preaching, read their Bibles, sing hymns and spiritual songs, memorize Scripture, dialogue with other believers, and read other Christian literature, they learn to think differently about God, themselves, the way they live their lives, and the rest of the world.

In addition, depending on age and family life, vivification also generally leads to changes in one's behavior, including public and private liturgical practices such as attending church, taking the Lord's Supper, sharing one's faith, and practicing the spiritual disciplines. (In addition, there is usually a corollary decrease and eventual elimination of significant immoral behaviors such as premarital sex, but this process is called mortification and was discussed in the previous chapter.) Many believers make little additional progress in vivification beyond thinking and behaving in these basic Christian ways.

New emotions and desires. Through new experiences of God, themselves, and others, emotions and desires will be inevitably awakened and stirred, some of them relatively novel and hopefully increasingly fitting, according to Christian values: guilt, contrition, gratitude, love of God and his beauty, and so on. Edwards (1959) argued that such emotional experiences indicate a spiritual understanding and provide evidence of the new life *in the heart*. Gradually, there will also likely be changes in feelings about other people, oneself, and one's activities (e.g., work and recreation).

However, emotions can be episodic and will not persist unless they are cultivated into emotion dispositions, and this requires some intentionality. Moreover, they cannot be pursued too directly or for their own sake, or they will disappear. Emotions can only really be pursued indirectly or mediately, as byproducts of what one is doing, for example, in worship or reflecting on a close relationship. In addition, those who have a damaged emotion system as a result of maltreatment in childhood will generally need to pursue more substantial healing and restoration of their emotions, and this usually takes additional time and therapy.

New imaginings. New thinking, behavior, feelings, and desires can lead to the development of new plans and goals, and the envisioning of a new way of being in the world. Actual changes in one's life are, of course, much slower, but they begin in one's imagination, where one considers new possibilities and projects oneself into the future, using mental images and mental rehearsal (Vanhoozer, 2005). A realist Christian imagination takes seriously the tension of the already/not-yet and pictures new actions and relational patterns before they occur.

New action and relational patterns. The new creation continues to expand through new actions and ways of relating to others, through experiencing the love of healthier persons, practicing ahead of time, and taking risks and trying out novel courses of action. Gradually, as believers grow in self-awareness in Christ and learn how to dismantle their defenses (part of mortification), deeper healing can occur in their self-understanding and deep perceptions of others, and they can begin to care more genuinely for themselves and others with decreasing narcissism and defensiveness, gradually acting more and more for the true benefit of God, self, and others.

A new story. Usually the most profound narrative change of the new life that occurs is one's initial conversion, particularly if one was not raised in a "good-enough" Christian family.[9] One's conversion is a story of resurrection, and it naturally leads to the construction of a "testimony," the retelling of one's story in light of the new life: "I once was lost, but now I'm found, was blind, but now I see!" The psychological power of such a narrative is obvious.

For one thing, it offers a fresh, novel sense of meaningfulness to the individual. As Baumeister (1991) noted, "Adding new meaning to one's life typically brings a period of great happiness, euphoria, exhilaration, and even bliss" (p. 297). Admittedly, the more dramatic the conversion, the more narrative value it will likely have, since the change itself will be more notable and so redefining. A radical shift in the plot of one's story can be especially helpful for people whose earlier life was particularly compromised by devastating sin or whose addictions had dominated their activities, relationships, and identity. A conversion narrative can also help to undermine the unresolved guilt and shame associated with one's pre-Christian past by objectifying and distancing oneself from one's previous sinful deeds, sealed with fresh consent to one's forgiveness in Christ with regard to those pre-resurrection actions. Conversion makes it possible to say, "That was who I was *then*, but I'm heading in a new direction now." So one's conversion can contribute to a valid, contemporary sense of self-affirmation—originating in God's word in Christ—that can be very helpful in the reconstruction of a new story, given our created need to feel in harmony with God's perfections.

The narrative implications of the resurrection continue throughout one's life. Eventually, as believers more and more come to think, feel, desire, remember, and act according to their resurrection life in Christ, their story likewise begins to take on a new form that differs increasingly from their old story (depending on how contrary to the Christian faith it was) and "the world."

As we noted in chapter five, the Christian's story is being transformed by its incorporation into the grand story of God's plan of redemption for humanity, and like Augustine in his *Confessions*, Christians can capitalize on the therapeutic benefits of that incorporation by interpreting their story in light of their resurrection with Christ. Their following of Christ should be seen as an ongoing resurrection, a "walking in newness of life" (Rom 6:4). One's resurrection with Christ ennoblizes, dignifies, and heightens the significance of the events and actions of one's life, since it brought one's story into a far more momentous context than that of one's autonomous life (O'Donovan, 1986, p. 257; Balthasar, 1988–1998), and this metanarrative significance applies to all Christians, regardless of the dramatic details of their own story.

A new self. As we noted above, the resurrection of Christ has already had an enormous impact on the believer's self—there is a new creation (2 Cor 5:17; Col 3:10; Eph 4:24)!—and the new self is also in the process of becoming. The apostle Paul called this entire process "putting on" the new self (Eph 4:24).[10] How do believers do that? As new beliefs, behaviors, emotions, imaginings, actions, and relational patterns flowing from Christ's resurrection get stored in one's memory system, forming new, corresponding episodes of one's story, new dynamic structures are laid down in the brain/ soul that come to constitute the new self—neural network by neural network. But participation requires the believer's intentional, dependent activity.

What precisely is the new self? According to Paul, it is the believer viewed ethicospiritually in Christ, consisting of "true righteousness and holiness" (Eph 4:24 ESV), mediated by "true knowledge" (Col 3:10) and calibrated to the image of Christ. Indeed, Christ *is* the new self in its perfection! Experientially, having been captured by the divine love, the believer's new self is the aspect of the self that is centered on God in worship, love, active receptivity, and virtuous resemblance. In addition, being holy and righteous, the new self is in principle without sin, shame, and guilt. It is not naked (Gen 3:7) like Christ was on the cross but is "clothed . . . with Christ" (Gal 3:27) and his righteousness (1 Cor 1:31) (Philip Jamieson, personal conversation, January 20, 2011). The new self is one of the first fruits of glorification, an eschatological anticipation of the perfection that will be the believer's in the age to come.

The new self, therefore, is fundamentally relational,[11] made according to the image and likeness of God (Eph 4:24; Col 3:10) and "created in Christ Jesus" (Eph 2:10). Analogous to Christ's dipolar relation with his Father as a human and the believer's dipolar dependence on God the Holy Spirit, we might say the believer's *new self* has two poles: Christ, the ultimate and defining pole, and the irreducible personhood of the believer, which lives and grows by looking to its divine "doppelgänger." Union with Christ is like a mirror that is improving the image it reflects. Christians see new aspects of *themselves* as they look on *Christ*: they are righteous, holy, wise, and loved by the Father, just like Christ. Union with Christ provides the real basis for Kierkegaard's (1849/1980) declaration, "The greater the conception of Christ, the more self" (p. 114). Christians become more truly themselves—more truly a new self—as they participate in and appropriate their union with Christ.

New selves in community. The above diffusion is actually also a social process. In his death and resurrection, Christ abolished the "law covenant" with Israel and brought Jews and Gentiles together into a united body "that he might create in himself one new humanity" (*kainon anthrōpov*, Eph 2:15 NRSV; the same phrase used in Eph 4:24). As a result, the new selves of believers also have a corporate dimension, for they are to grow "into a holy temple in the Lord, in whom you also are being built together into a dwelling of God in the Spirit" (Eph 2:21-22), "to maturity, to the measure of the full stature of Christ" (Eph 4:13 NRSV). This is made possible through "the proper working of each individual part [by which Christ] causes the growth of the body for the building up of itself in love" (Eph 4:16).

There is, therefore, in fact a trinitarian-like "one-many" dialectic intrinsic to the new self, by which the new creation is realized in community as believers learn how to view, address, and act toward one another according to the resurrection, rather than in terms of individual, gender, racial, or cultural differences or out of envy, domination, or slothful passivity.

Fostering an Atmosphere of Resurrection in Session

The foregoing also reminds us of the role that the counselor plays in facilitating resurrection life through kind, patient dialogue and persevering love. Christ overcame the condemnation of the law in his resurrection (Torrance, 2009), so new-creation discourse is characterized by grace (corresponding to the spiritual order) more than law (corresponding to the ethical order, unresolved by redemption). Counselors of the resurrection are learning how to put their questions, probings, and challenges in increasingly kind and gentle ways to avoid triggering a defensive reaction. (Wachtel, 2011, shows how secular therapists grow in this way, and Christians will benefit from his creation-grace wisdom, combining it with divine redemption as its basis when working with believers.) Christ's resurrection triumph over sin, suffering, and weakness, and the counselor's personal experiences of its power justify a measured degree of excitement, an eye for God's glory and the counselee's good, resilience in the face of setbacks or resistance, and the assumption of long-term progress, even in the face of short-term stagnation. However, Christian therapists also must tether their resurrection optimism to the counselee's present experience, or their enthusiasm will be experienced as unreal or threatening. The cross and the resurrection are dialectically related, so they should not be too far separated in our experience.

Christ Our Mediator Within the Old Creation

The believer's union with Christ's resurrection helps us to make sense of Bonhoeffer's (1963) point that Christ is the mediator not only between God and believers but between believers and the rest of reality, including other people. "Since [Christ's] coming man has no immediate relationship of his own any more to anything, neither to God nor to the world" (p. 107). The cruel words or thoughtlessness of those we care about typically automatically activate feelings of pain, shame, or hurt. However, living in Christ believers are, in principle, spiritually detached and insulated from what others say or do to them. In the new creation, Christ is their psychological "boundary." When criticized, for example, believers can remind themselves (usually after the activation of an automatic negative response) that that criticism is no longer valid. Even if empirically accurate, the criticism is not the ultimate truth, for ultimately they are now new persons in Christ, regardless of their performance, their participation in Christ, or the evaluations of others. By faith, criticized Christians can envision Christ as their protective shield (Ps 18:2), since union with him relativizes any criticisms and prevents them from truly defining them. Instead, they can imagine such criticisms hitting Christ and stopping. This offers a transcendent therapeutic strategy, enabling believers to objectify and disidentify with criticisms and undermine their tendency to be overwhelmed emotionally by them. Eventually, this strategy can enable believers to hear whatever partial truth is being communicated in otherwise hurtful remarks.

How Much Resurrection Change Should Believers Reasonably Expect?

The already/not-yet dialectic encourages believers to rest in what they currently possess in Christ, to seek greater experience and growth, and at the same time, to be realistic about their remaining limitations. Grasping this dialectic with both genuine hope and a spirit of trusting resignation is an important part of healing and maturation. To summarize the process: the therapy journey is generally slow, involving the development of new neural networks through the internalization of new thoughts, beliefs, imagery, memories, affections, motives, desires, self-regulating abilities, goals, strategies, and actions—a new self and new patterns of relating to others—all of which shapes a new story. Together with others, this can lead to a communal way of life where we increasingly reciprocally and collaboratively help each other along the way into a growing God-centeredness, practicing the Christian virtues, living in transparency, improvising shaped by the gospel, and gracious and courageous dialogue with others. But genuine change happens very gradually for embodied, finite, sinful creatures with a prior history written on our brains.

Only the "inner person" of believers enjoys resurrection renewal in the present age (2 Cor 4:16); for now their bodies are "decaying" (2 Cor 4:16) and will continue to do so until *their* resurrection renewal at the end of the age (1 Cor 15:42) (except for the corollary change in neural structures that can happen now alluded to above). Consequently, part of our maturation hinges on coming to terms with the relative lack of change that may happen over the rest of one's life, especially when dealing with severe damage to one's self and relational capacities. Our experience now, after all, is said to be only the "first fruits" of the new creation (Rom 8:23), and that—along with the testimonies of godly believers over the centuries—should temper the expectations of how much deep transformation believers can expect in this age. Unrealistic optimism can actually be a kind of defense mechanism, so sharing this reality with counselees takes tact and good timing, but in the long run it is extremely valuable to know that significant change takes time and that sometimes we will go for long periods without any appreciable change. Such information is especially helpful for perfectionists or those who have been exposed to some form of perfectionism (whether explicit or not), for they may struggle with an unconscious sense that there is something particularly deficient with them or that God is not interested in helping them, adding to the negative affect they may already be dealing with and compromising their ability to believe that they really are new selves-in-process. Such self-acceptance and realism is made possible by our current perfection in Christ and our actual perfection in the age to come.

RESOURCES FOR COUNSELORS AND COUNSELEES

Classic

Augustine. (2009). *Confessions* (Henry Chadwick, Trans.). New York: Oxford University Press.

Owen, J. (1965). The grace and duty of being spiritually-minded. In *The Works of John Owen* (Vol. 7). Edinburgh: Banner of Truth Trust. (Original work first published 1850–1853)

Contemporary

Anderson, N. (2000). *Victory over the darkness*. Ventura, CA: Regal.

Breaux, M. (2007). *Identity theft: Reclaiming who God created you to be*. Grand Rapids, MI: Zondervan.

Ferguson, S. (1982). *The Christian life*. Edinburgh: Banner of Truth Trust.

Forde, G. O. (1988). The Lutheran view. In D. Alexander (Ed.), *Christian spirituality: Five views of sanctification*. Downers Grove, IL: InterVarsity Press.

Gaffin, R. B., Jr. (1987). *Resurrection and redemption: A study in Paul's soteriology* (2nd ed.). Phillipsburg, NJ: P&R. ‡

Leiter, C. (2009). *Justification and regeneration* (2nd ed.). Hannibal, MO: Granted Ministries Press.

Manning, B. (1991). *Abba's child.* Colorado Springs, CO: NavPress.

Payne, L. (1995). *The healing presence: Curing the soul through union with Christ.* Grand Rapids, MI: Baker.

Peterson, E. (2010). *Practicing resurrection: A conversation on growing up in Christ.* Grand Rapids, MI: Eerdmans.

Piper, J. (2009). *Finally alive.* Minneapolis: Desiring God Foundation.

O'Donovan, O. (1986). *Resurrection and moral order.* Grand Rapids, MI: Eerdmans. ‡

Smith, J. K. A. (2013). *Imagining the kingdom.* Grand Rapids, MI: Baker. ‡

Torrance, T. F. (2009). *Atonement: The person and work of Christ.* Downers Grove, IL: InterVarsity Press. Contains an excellent theological discussion of the resurrection and its implications. ‡

Wachtel, P. L. (2011). *Therapeutic communication: Knowing what to say when.* New York: Guilford. A remarkably insightful secular book filled with creation-grace wisdom in how to improve one's therapeutic speech.[1] ‡

Warnock, A. (2010). *Raised with Christ: How the resurrection changes everything.* Wheaton, IL: Crossway.

‡ Recommended more for counselors and pastors than counselees

—*15*—

The Exaltation of Christ and the Spread of the New Creation

Principle 7: The spread of the new creation is being guided by the exalted Christ in and among those who are united to him by the Holy Spirit and faith.

Fixing our eyes on Jesus, the author and perfecter of faith,
who for the joy set before Him endured the cross,
despising the shame, and has sat down at
the right hand of the throne of God.

Hebrews 12:2

[God] raised us up with Him, and seated us
with Him in the heavenly places in Christ Jesus.

Ephesians 2:6

From [Christ's ascension]
our faith receives many benefits.

John Calvin,
Institutes of the Christian Religion

LIFE IN CONTEMPORARY CULTURE is characterized by many paradoxes. For example, on the one hand, humans in technologically advanced cultures today are influenced by more and more people outside their immediate social world, and on the other hand, they have more personal options to explore and freely pursue than ever before. In stark contrast to previous centuries, the lives of people today are profoundly shaped by the decisions, actions, values, and dialogues of people they will never meet: politicians, business leaders, writers, scientists, and entertainers are constantly acting and interacting and changing the lives of others. Yet, at the same time, people are faced with an increasingly complex array of choices regarding the vocations they can pursue, the places they can live, the kinds of people they can associate with, as well as the foods they can eat, the music they can listen to, the kinds of video they can watch, and the ways they can spend their free time. It seems as if cultural influence, individual freedom, and technology mutually enhance each other, affecting people separated by great distances.

This dynamic is a little analogous to a major feature of the Christian life. Much of the most important and influential activity, decisions, values, and dialogues pertaining to an individual Christian's life currently occur far outside his or her immediate presence and social circle—in the realm of heaven, with the Father and the Son—and yet their activities are affecting believers' lives slowly but dramatically and intended to lead to their increasing freedom to realize their true selves in Christ, which in turn fulfills the Trinity's doxological-therapeutic agenda.

CHRISTIAN TEACHING REGARDING CHRIST'S EXALTATION

In this chapter we will focus on the period of Christ's existence that began forty days after he was raised from the dead, when he ascended into heaven (Acts 1:3). That episode, uniquely, has become an era, continuing now for twenty centuries, and enduring until Christ returns to earth to wrap up human history as we know it. The teaching concerning this aspect of Christ's redemptive work reminds us that "the heavens" are an important part of the creation (Gen 1:1), from which the Son of God came and to which he returned—now as a human. As a result, the eyes of Christ's followers here are drawn increasingly toward the heavens.

The Ascent and Reign of the Resurrected Christ

Over the nearly six weeks following his resurrection, Christ repeatedly visited his disciples to teach and edify them. However, on the fortieth day after, something just about as astounding as the resurrection happened: after sharing a few more thoughts with them, "He was lifted up while they were looking on, and a cloud received Him out of their sight" (Acts 1:9). Christ left this world in dramatic fashion, back to heaven to rejoin his Father, from whose immediate presence, from an earthly vantage point, he had been absent for around thirty-three years.[1]

The Bible tells us that at this point in human history, the Son of God re-entered the heavenly realm or temple (Heb 8:2), returning now as a divine-human being, and he sat down at the right hand of the Father (Mk 16:19; Heb 8:1; 10:12; 12:2; 1 Pet 3:22) "to appear in the presence of God for us" (Heb 9:24), to pray on our behalf (Heb 7:25), and to be our advocate with the Father (1 Jn 2:1). Though omnipresent in his divine nature, the embodied Christ is representing, ruling, and blessing his people from a distance. He is their forerunner (Heb 6:20), guiding them to the heavenly realm as well, which he has prepared for them (Jn 14:2). He is able to do this because of the work he has already accomplished through his once-and-for-all sacrifice (Heb 1:3).

Christ's sitting down at God's right hand (commonly called his *session*) was the final act of his ascension and together with his resurrection is called Christ's *exaltation* (Bavinck, 2006; Braaten, 1984), for after his death, "God highly exalted Him, and bestowed on Him the name which is above every name, so that at the name of Jesus every knee will bow, of those who are in heaven and on earth and under the earth, and that every tongue will confess that Jesus Christ is Lord, to the glory of God the Father" (Phil 2:9-11). All authority has been given to him in heaven and on earth (Mt 28:18); he is now the Lord of lords and the King of kings (1 Tim 6:15; Rev 17:14).[2]

In Psalm 110 the Israelites were told of their future Messiah, a fearsome king whom God would bless with victory over his enemies and who would some day sit at the right hand of Yahweh (Ps 110:1). Christ applied this passage to himself (Mt 22:44; Mk 12:36; Lk 20:42), and the early church reflected a lot on its implications (Acts 2:34; Heb 5:6; 7:7; 8:1). Yahweh told the Messiah, "Rule in the midst of Your enemies" (Ps 110:2), and prophesied that he would "shatter kings" and "judge . . . the nations," filling them "with corpses" (Ps 110:5-6). We now understand that these enigmatic sayings refer to a holy war waged against Satan and the world—not flesh and blood (Eph 6:12)—that was ironically advanced by his death and, after his resurrection, by leaving the battlefield to conduct the military campaign *through us* from his headquarters in heaven; and the war will not be over until he comes again to judge the entire human race. His sitting at God's right hand indicates a position of royal honor and power—he is a prince (Acts 5:31)—and that his reign has been securely established. So his eventual victory over his spiritual enemies was begun in his life (Mt 12) and furthered in his death, resurrection, and ascension: these events were the beginnings of their end.

Yahweh also purposed that the messianic king would be "a priest forever, according to the order of Melchizedek" (Ps 110:4³). Much of the book of Hebrews is a sermonic exposition of this psalm, particularly focusing on Christ as the high priest of the new covenant (Heb 5:1-10; 6:13-20; 7:1–10:18). There were, in effect, two phases of his priestly activity. The first occurred when he offered himself up once and for all (Heb 7:26), laying down his life on the cross and allowing his blood to be shed, and the second began when he entered the heavens as the eternal high priest, continuing throughout this age to go before the Father on behalf of his people, applying by the Spirit the effects of his self-offering to their ongoing needs. "When He had made purification of sins" (Heb 1:3), "through His own blood, He entered the holy place once for all, having obtained eternal redemption" (Heb 9:12), and "He sat down at the right hand of the Majesty on high" (Heb 1:3). As a result, "Humanity is elevated to that which it has never enjoyed before, the seat at God's right hand which belongs to his Son" (O'Donovan, 1986, p. 57). Both priest and sacrifice, Christ continues to minister in the heavenly temple (Heb 8:2) as a mediator between God and his people by offering up himself and so making eternal propitiation and intercession for the sins of the people (Heb 2:17). So Christ's once-and-for-all offering is "taken up eternally into the life of God, and remain[s] prevalent, efficacious, valid or abidingly real" (Torrance, 1976, p. 115).

The significance of Christ's exaltation for humanity. The Son of God left heaven a divine being and returned a human being too, bringing human nature with him into the eternal communion of the Trinity. Now in heaven, "the humanity of Adam is carried forward to its 'supernatural' destiny precisely as it is rescued from its 'sub-natural' condition of enslavement to sin and death" (O'Donovan, 1986, p. 57). In Christ, "humanity is elevated to that which it has never enjoyed before, the seat at God's right hand which belongs to his Son" (O'Donovan, 1986, p. 57). In Christ "man himself is exalted, not as God or like God, but to God, being placed at His side, not in identity, but in true fellowship with Him" (Barth, 1958, p. 6).

PART IV—The Divine Intervention

On account of his life, death, and resurrection Christ was "made perfect forever" (Heb 7:28), and then "became to all those who obey Him the source of eternal salvation" (Heb 5:9). As the fulfillment and pinnacle of created humanity brought back to fellowship with God, but now in the fellowship *of* God, Jesus Christ is the vicarious basis, substance, and goal of the believer's well-being, offered to all and consummated in eternity.

Christ's exaltation also further established the eschatological overthrow of Satan's rule, the return to subjection of the powers and principalities, and the liberation of humans from the dominion of sin. Christ's sitting down signifies the beginning of his reign as the earth's rightful Prince and Savior (Acts 3:15; 5:31), a coming kingdom being realized through the love, obedience, and healing of his subjects by the Spirit,

> which [the Father] brought about in Christ, when He raised Him from the dead and seated Him at His right hand in the heavenly places, far above all rule and authority and power and dominion, and every name that is named, not only in this age but also in the one to come. And He put all things in subjection under His feet, and gave Him as head over all things to the church, which is His body, the fullness of Him who fills all in all. (Eph 1:20-23)

There remains much about the rest of humanity that is incongruent with the Christ's virtuous humanity. Justice does not yet roll down like waters (Amos 5:24): tyrants still oppress their people; children are still being abused. Those outside the faith still need Christ; sinful and broken Christians still need divine therapy. There is an enormous gap between the perfected humanity found in heaven and the very imperfect humanity that lives on earth. During this age Christ's seemingly distant activities in heaven are nonetheless focused on the ongoing application of his perfection to what remains unredeemed among believers and within the world, through conversion and his mediatorial kingship, all for the realization of God's doxological purposes for creation that will be finally accomplished only in the consummation.

This prolonged, proleptic phase of Christ's reign before the end signifies that the *telos* of human life is not to be found on earth in this age but lies above and will be attained only in the age to come. The focus of the monastic tradition on heaven was half-right. Where it went wrong was its failure to grasp the eschatological orientation of *this* life and the potential fullness (*plērōma*) of splendor available to begin bringing in the new creation down here into this world, precisely by directing humanity's thoughts and affections to the things above (Col 3:1-4; Vanhoozer, 2010, p. 243).

Christ's intercession for us. One of Christ's pivotal activities in heaven is his perpetual praying to the Father on behalf of his people: "he [now] always lives to make intercession for them" (Heb 7:25). The Son of God is always active on our behalf, dialoguing with the Father about us, asking him to help us, and continuously forgiving and cleansing us of our remaining sin (1 Jn 1:9–2:1). He intercedes for us (Rom 8:34) to bring about our greater good. "Every need of the believer and every grace requisite to consummate his redemption are brought within the scope of Christ's intercession"; his "intercession must have regard to the distinctive situation of each individual" (Murray, 1959, pp. 329-30). His ministry of prayer continues the intercession he began on earth, in John 17, where we read a foreshadowing of his heavenly prayers in his requests to his Father to protect and preserve his people in faith, sanctify them, and foster their unity and communion with the Trinity and one another (Elwell & Comfort, 2001).

At the beginning of his heavenly intercession, Christ asked the Father to send the Holy Spirit to his disciples (Jn 14:16), and presumably the fruit and the gifts of the Spirit (Gal 5:22-23; Rom 12:6; 1 Cor 12:1-31; 14:1-12; Eph 4:8-16) are throughout this age dependent on Christ's ongoing prayer on their behalf. Part of the authority in heaven and on earth he was given by the Father (Mt 28:20) entails his freedom to bestow on his people the first fruits of the glory he has obtained for them (Jn 17:22), the fullness of which they will inherit at the consummation.

The author of Hebrews suggests that Christ's intercession is shaped by his prior experiences down here: "For we do not have a high priest who cannot sympathize with our weaknesses, but One who has been tempted in all things as we are, yet without sin" (Heb 4:15; see also Heb 2:18). His human suffering affected him by increasing his personal, experiential understanding of the challenges we face in our journey to glory and conditioning his motivation to plead for us personally aware of what we need. In addition, his omniscience guarantees that no one knows better what we are going through, our problems cannot overwhelm him, and he is irrevocably on our side. He is, therefore, the best person imaginable to pray on our behalf.

Christ's vicarious humanity. So believers have a "friend in high places" who speaks for them to advance their ultimate interests. "If anyone sins, we have an Advocate [*paraklēton*] with the Father" (1 Jn 2:1), who is "the atoning sacrifice [*hilasmos*] for our sins" (1 Jn 2:2 NRSV). His heavenly activity during this age, therefore, resembles that of both a "counsel for the defense" (Marshall, 1978, p. 116) and a priest, uniquely obtaining ongoing clemency through his own blood (1 Jn 1:7) and the sacrifice of himself for those who continue to commit sins (1 Jn 1:10), still being sinners (1 Jn 1:8), while the general trajectory of their lives is characterized by "[walking] in the light" (1 Jn 1:7) and confession (1 Jn 1:9). Consequently, their good standing with God cannot be jeopardized, so long as they never finally turn away from Christ (Heb 6:6-9; 10:26-39), which the elect will never do (Eph 1:4-5; Phil 1:6; Col 3:12).

In addition to the negative aspect of his intercession—the continuous removal of sin, guilt, and shame—there is the positive aspect: as the exalted Son of Man, he represents believers before the Father in all his goodness. On our behalf Christ offers to the Father his beautiful, self-giving, and redeeming life. In him, their imperfect prayers, worship, love, righteousness, and holiness are

> laid hold of, sanctified, and informed by his vicarious life of obedience and response to the Father. They are in fact so indissolubly united to the life of Jesus Christ which he lived out among us and which he has offered to the Father, as arising out of our human being and nature, that they are *our responses* toward the love of the Father poured out upon us through the mediation of the Son and in the unity of his Holy Spirit. (Torrance, 1983, p. 108; see also Purves, 2004; Torrance, 2009)

As a result, the superabounding goodness of Christ's humanity infinitely more than compensates for the limitations of believers' own faith, love, and good works, filling in their deficits to overflowing. Given their union with him in heaven, the triune Jesus can say to imperfect believers with no need for qualification, "Come to me, and all that you bring with you is welcome! I have taken care of everything and will show you what that means for you."[4]

With Christ in heaven. Because of their union with Christ, believers are also said to be "seated . . . with [Christ] in the heavenly places in Christ Jesus" (Eph 2:6). By the Father's unifying fiat, believers on earth physically and consciously are present in heaven in the mind and heart and life of God— and since the sovereign Creator is able to call reality into being, God has spoken in Christ, and they are there! On the basis of their presence in Christ in heaven, the Father now considers them to be saints, justified, and children of God, possessing all the rights of their co-heir and brother Jesus Christ (Rom 8:17). Consequently, believers are to "keep seeking the things above, where Christ is, seated at the right hand of God. Set your mind on the things above, not on the things that are on earth. For you have died and your life is hidden with Christ in God" (Col 3:1-3).

Phrases such as "the things above" and "the heavenly places," according to Lincoln (1981), refer to "a transcendent dimension with its own reality" (p. 124), encompassing the eternal salvation that Christ obtained through all he has accomplished. While the New Testament reveals many specific benefits believers possess in Christ, there is no reason to conclude the list is complete—the primary theme is that believers have already obtained their superlative good; it is just reserved in heaven (1 Pet 1:4-7). "Blessed be the God and Father of our Lord Jesus Christ, who has blessed us with every spiritual blessing in the heavenly places in Christ" (Eph 1:3). Paul's "eulogy" states that believers already possess in Christ everything spiritually beneficial, inclusive of all the redemptive and therapeutic goodness that can be appropriated now, as well as the total inheritance package, which they will not obtain in toto until the end of the age, that is, the final, comprehensive salvation of their souls (1 Pet 1:9).[5] Consequently, the above/heavenly things would include the triune God's favor and communion with him, union with Christ, the indwelling Holy Spirit, and all his fruit, including forgiveness, repentance (Acts 5:31), faith, righteousness, and love of others, realized through transparency, freedom, healthy boundaries with others, and the development of new desires and emotions. The above/heavenly things, then, also provide the resources of the new self (Lincoln, 1981, p. 126). In a word, these blessings constitute *salvation*, "the sum-total of the benefits bestowed on believers by God" (Marshall, 1988, p. 610), already obtained by Christ and now residing in heaven, to be entirely manifested only in the coming age of perfection-fulfillment, in the completed new creation. The Christian life, then, is one of ascent (Canlis, 2010), following Christ up to heaven, living out one's heavenly union with him on earth by faith (as much as possible), and utilizing the resources there to heal, grow, and flourish here.

The Gift of the Holy Spirit in History

In chapter four we looked at the therapeutic significance of the gift of the Holy Spirit and his indwelling activity within believers. Here, we consider the significance of the timing of his being given to humans at Pentecost.

Before his death, Jesus told his disciples of the coming of a third divine person. He had to go back to heaven, he said, where he would ask the Father to "give you another Helper" (*allon paraklēton*). *Allon* means another of the same kind, and *paraklēton* is the same word we noted above that was used elsewhere of Christ. This divine person will be with you and in you forever (Jn 14:16-17). This would not happen, however, unless the incarnate Son went back to heaven (Jn 16:7).

So, forty earth days after his arrival up there, a new era of the Holy Spirit's public manifestation was initiated. Up until Jesus' time, the Spirit was "not yet given, because Jesus was not yet glorified" (Jn 7:39). The Spirit, of course, had been active since the creation (Gen 1:2) and came upon individuals and spoke through prophets throughout the Old Testament period of redemptive history. However, in the age of the Spirit, believers would *receive* the Spirit *within* (Jn 7:39), and as a result, "from [their] innermost being will flow rivers of living water" (Jn 7:38).

We call the day on which the Spirit was sent to the church *Pentecost* because of the day of the Hebrew calendar on which the Spirit was poured out; and the significance of the Spirit's coming was underscored by the manifestation of extraordinary signs (Acts 2). The disciples were "filled with the Holy Spirit" (Acts 2:4), and Peter explained that Christ, "having been exalted to the right hand of God, and having received from the Father the promise of the Holy Spirit, He has poured forth this which you both see and hear" (Acts 2:33). "Christ's ultimate mission . . . was to draw the Spirit into man and man into the Spirit, that man might truly become a living being" (Farrow, 1999, p. 60).

As a result, the new covenant blessings that Christ had obtained for believers could now be released: "When He ascended on high . . . He gave gifts to men" (Eph 4:8), and these gifts were mediated by the Gift of gifts, the Holy Spirit. They include "spiritual gifts"—meaning sometimes extraordinary practical capacities of leadership (Eph 2:11), miracles, healing, prophecy, and tongues (1 Cor 12:8-10, 28)—as well as the more exalted ethicospiritual gifts, the fruit (or virtues) of the Spirit (Gal 5:22-23) and, we might add, any healing of biopsychosocial damage of believers in Jesus' name.

Through his life and death the Son of God made possible the indwelling of the Holy Spirit in fallen human temples by cleansing them of their sin and guilt and shame. Then the Father sent the Spirit so the Spirit could give them Jesus—"It is no longer I who live, but Christ lives in me" (Gal 2:20); "Christ in you, the hope of glory" (Col 1:27)—and access to many of the spiritual blessings that they possess in Christ in heaven. However, the apostle Paul called them the "first fruits" (Rom 8:23) and "down payment" (2 Cor 1:22), suggesting that enjoying them in their fullness will come later. Perhaps they could also be called the disbursements in this age of the trust fund of our coming inheritance—our experiential perfection and glorification in eternity.

The Spirit's advocacy for us. Before considering in more detail some of the spiritual blessings believers have now, we should note another way the Spirit's work is similar to that of Christ. "The Spirit also helps our weakness,"

Paul wrote in Romans, "for we do not know how to pray as we should, but the Spirit Himself intercedes for us with groanings too deep for words; and He who searches the hearts knows what the mind of the Spirit is, because He intercedes for the saints according to the will of God" (Rom 8:26-27). The Holy Spirit is praying for believers from within their innermost being (Jn 7:38; Rom 8:9-11, 16, 27; 1 Cor 3:16; 6:19).

Paul indicated that the weakness (*astheneia*) of believers limits their ability to pray knowledgeably and wisely. The Spirit, however, is not so limited, so he is able help believers by praying for them from the depths of their being, in the midst of the internal obstacles (sin, suffering, and emotional and relational damage) they carry around within them. Jesus Christ is the believer's Advocate (*paraklētos*) in heaven, and the Holy Spirit is the believer's Advocate on earth. God the Son and God the Holy Spirit, then, are both speaking up as one on behalf of believers to the Father from their respective "vantage points" on earth, thinking and "speech-acting" about their well-being in order to bring them good. What would explain this degree of divine interest and investment? What else but God's intensely personal love?

We have noted that the metaphor of speech is central to the revelation of God's triune activity: the Father speaks, the Son and all he has done is the content of that speech, and the Spirit carries out the word (God's breath). In the intercession of the Son and the Spirit on behalf of every believer, we discover just how particular and personal the divine dialogue is, for the Christian life is situated in the midst of trinitarian conversation. "Union with Christ is dialogical" (Vanhoozer, 2010, p. 291). One of the challenges facing believers is to learn how to participate in this intratrinitarian dialogue and to gradually learn the language and practice of how to pray to the Father along with the Spirit and the Son for our well-being, the well-being of our brothers and sisters, and the well-being of everyone in the world (particularly their salvation)—according to the will of God (Rom 8:27), that is, according to the praise of his glory (Eph 1:5-14). So our flourishing entails our entering into and participating in the conversation of the triune God, who speak and act together, transcendently and intersubjectively, advocating for us and helping us to address well the challenges and problems of our lives.

Union with the Exalted Christ and the New Creation

In the previous chapter we saw the close linkage between Christ's resurrection and the new creation, and the Spirit's role in both. We noted above that soon after his resurrection, Christ ascended to heaven and then asked the Father to send the Holy Spirit to his followers, and this, in turn, began the next step in the new creation. At Pentecost the new creation of humanity that began in the resurrection of Christ was extended to other humans, starting with the "reception of the word" that Peter preached (see Acts 2:41), encouraging repentance and baptism in Christ's name, followed by the gift of the Spirit (Acts 2:38-41). Through faith in Christ humans are united to him and all he did, by the Father, symbolized by baptism, and the Spirit who raised Jesus raises them from the dead of their sin (Rom 8:11; Eph 2:1), enabling them to live the new life (Rom 6:4; 2 Cor 5:17). For Paul union with Christ is synonymous with the gift of the Spirit (Vos, 1980). So we might say that the Spirit brings Christ in heaven down to earth and the future age into the present, by bringing believers into heaven and the future now.[6] The result of this process is the gradual conformity of believers into the image of their heavenly archetype, initiating in this age what they will become in fullness in the next. "To be 'in Christ' is to be the vanguard of a new creation animated by the Holy Spirit for the purpose of realizing—communicating—the image of God in and to the world" (Vanhoozer, 2010, p. 57). We will consider salvation under four headings to understand better how the gradual realization of the new creation of believers occurs since the Father spoke in Christ and they sent the Spirit to earth.[7]

The new-creation word: declarative salvation. "God's working is God's wording" (Horton, 2007, p. 231). Christ's death and resurrection was God's word that began the destruction of the old world of sin, the curse of the law, Satan's dominion, and the flesh, and uttered in a new world order. Analogous to the original creation, God brings about the new creation also "by his Word and Spirit" (Bavinck, 2008, p. 33). "It is not a different Word that renews and glorifies, but the same Word in its different operations and effects" (Horton, 2007, p. 279). This word was first spoken in God's promises uttered to Adam and Eve, Abraham, Moses, and David (among others), and those promises are now being fulfilled in God's declarations in Christ. Declarations are speech-acts that accomplish what they say upon their being uttered, such as "I now pronounce you husband and wife" (Searle, 1969; Horton, 2007; Johnson, 2007, pp. 289-91; 2011; Vanhoozer, 2002). God's creating and providential speech consists of declaratives: "Let there be light!" and there was light! So it is with God's salvific/new-creation speech. Paul recognized the connection between the first and second creations: "God who said, 'Light shall shine out of darkness,' is the One who has shone in our hearts to give the Light of the knowledge of the glory of God in the face of Christ" (2 Cor 4:6). One of the main differences between the two creations is that God's declarations in the second are all interpersonal and have to be actively received by faith in order for them to be realized on earth. In the first creation God declaratively spoke everything into being, and humans were simply told to implement his creation-mandate imperatives; but when the Son of God assumed human nature, a new era of human life began, so that human beings in union with him—personal-agents-in-community—are now enabled by the Spirit to participate with God in the constitution of the new creation.

Declarative salvation, then, refers to the Father's redefinition and reappraisal of individual believers on the basis of Christ's life, death, resurrection, and exaltation upon receiving (hearing and understanding, Mt 13:23) the word of the gospel, the word of the cross (1 Cor 1:18), the message that Christ came into the world to save sinners (1 Tim 1:15).

When sinners believe, what does the Father declare? The summary utterance is that the believer is united to Christ (Eph 1:3; Murray, 1955). Many metaphors are used to picture this union: marriage (Eph 5:32), a father and firstborn son (Rom 8:16-17), a branch that gets its life from the vine (Jn 15:4-5), and a living body and its head (Eph 4:15-16) (Campbell, 2012).[8]

Upon faith in Christ, a host of ethicospiritual benefits are immediately bestowed on believers: reconciliation with God (Col 1:22), acceptance by God (Rom 14:3; 15:7) and communion with the Father and Son (1 Jn 1:3); forgiveness of their sins (Eph 4:32); the righteousness of Christ (Rom 1:17; 5:1-2; Titus 3:7); adoption by God (Eph 1:5; Rom 8:16-17); sanctification (1 Cor 6:11); chosenness[9] (Eph 1:4; Col 3:12); being seated with him in the heavenly court (Eph 2:6); being led in God's triumph (2 Cor 2:14); membership in Christ's body (Rom 12:4-5); citizenship of a heavenly city (Eph 2:19; Heb 12:22); they are heirs of an eternal or heavenly inheritance (Gal 3:26; Eph 1:11, 18; 1 Pet 1:4; Heb 9:15); co-heirs (and siblings) with the Son of God (Rom 8:17); saints (1 Cor 1:2; Eph 1:1); and more. God declares a dazzling array of blessings to be true of believers in Christ. Indeed, they have been given *every* spiritual blessing there is (Eph 1:3); all the promises of God in Christ are yes for them (2 Cor 1:20), so that they are complete (*peplērōmenoi*, Col 2:10) and perfect (*teteleiōken*, Heb 10:14). All this is a description of the believer's *real* self, the new self eschatologically complete and perfect in Christ, which will be discussed in more detail below.

Thus, declarative salvation is the Father's affirmation of the believer in Christ that creates what it says. It is, of course, not a description of how good believers *already actually are*, but rather an utterance that *establishes* and *bestows* on them Christ's goodness and beauty by *fiat*. As a result, all believers are equally considered by God to be as loving, patient, kind, humble, good, and gentle as Jesus Christ is. "We possess in Christ all that pertains to the perfection of heavenly life," Calvin (1559/1960) wrote, "and yet faith is the vision of good things not seen" (p. 426), for faith is the dialogical response by which humans appropriate the gift of salvation offered them in Christ.

The perlocutionary effects of God's new-creation word. Human speech-acts often have consequences; divine speech-acts *always* do, except to the extent that sinful humanity (including believers) resists God's word and pursues lives of autocentric independence (though even then God mysteriously constrains what is possible; Prov 16). By the Spirit, however, believers are enabled to resist their own resistance and receive, experience, and fulfill the word of God, so that it accomplishes God's intentions after all. Faith is simply our Spirit-enabled reception.[10]

Readers of *Foundations* (Johnson, 2007, pp. 289-91) may recall that declarative speech-acts are a kind of *illocution* (in terms of their intended meaning) and a *perlocution* (in terms of their actual effects on their hearers/readers),[11] so the consequences of speech-acts have been called their "perlocutionary effects" (Searle, 1979). In the following subsections, we will be considering the progressive perlocutionary effects of the Father's declarations regarding those who are in Christ, realized by the Holy Spirit (Horton, 2007; Vanhoozer, 2005). God works in believers in two ways: "within, through his Spirit; without, through his Word" (Calvin, 1559/1960, p. 322). The Bible is an inerrant record of God's declarations. His word therefore is the sword of the life-giving Spirit (Eph 6:12; Jn 7:38), who makes the declarative words of God alive with meaning, so that their divinely intended perlocutionary effects can be realized through the believer's faith. Salvation, then, entails the perlocutionary effects of the Spirit, and there are at least four phases that, for therapeutic reasons, ought to be distinguished.

Harré, Clarke, and De Carlo (1985) describe the process of psychological symbiosis, in which mothers interact with their infant not as it actually is but "rather with a being of her own invention to whom she has ascribed quite sophisticated thoughts and feelings" (p. 75), treating it as more mature than it actually is. Over time, the infant comes to assume the characteristics that were earlier ascribed to it. It would appear that God does something analogous with his children with declarative salvation and his Spirit.

The new-creation word and catechesis. The first phase in the realization of the new creation begun in declarative salvation in Christ is simply understanding God's word in Christ.[12] *It is to know with the knowledge of Christ.* While also a work of the Spirit,[13] Christians have to spend time hearing, reading, and meditating on scriptural texts, grasping their meaning, and then storing in long-term memory the biblical teaching relevant to Christian maturation. For example, the fact that Christians are righteous and loved by God in Christ provides divinely revealed information for their new-self self-understanding (Anderson, Zuelke, & Zuelke, 2000; McGee, 1990). Part of this educational process also involves learning and adhering to biblical ethical norms. In the early church this educational process was called catechesis; evangelicals today call it discipleship; paedo-baptist Christian traditions have called it confirmation and aimed it at young teens. Edwards (1959) called this kind of cognitive or intellectual knowledge of the faith "notional understanding," and he did not believe it was sufficient for genuine Christianity, but it was necessary and "of infinite importance, in this respect, that without it we can have no spiritual or practical knowledge" (1974, Vol. 2, p. 158).[14] Catechesis is the cognitive appropriation of God's word (Johnson, 2007, pp. 499-502).

The new-creation word and experiential salvation. The next phase consists of the *affective* appropriation of declarative salvation. Experiential salvation refers to the conscious, emotional processing of the cognitively grasped word of God through faith by the Spirit. *It is to appraise and feel with the appraisal and emotions of Christ.* This phase of salvation is realized when one's consciousness is meaningfully engaged with the triune God and his salvation, such that God's glory shines into one's brain/soul, moving one emotionally by what one knows about God and one's salvation. Like catechesis, experiential salvation occurs in consciousness, but the affections are involved, so this phase is the beginning of *carditive* internalization (Johnson, 2007, pp. 502-7).

Though often neglected in modern discussions of salvation, this aspect was celebrated in earlier times (see Sibbes, 1635/1973; Edwards, 1959). Its old-covenant expression is found in the Psalms, where all kinds of experiences in the midst of life—joyful, thankful, anxious, and sad—are expressed verbally to God, processing them, in some degree, in relation to him. However, in contrast to declarative salvation, which is eternally established in Christ in heaven and described in the Bible, experiential salvation is temporal, embodied, and sporadic. "The calling to image or reflect the divine life is only momentarily present, in each instant that the self is in motion towards God"

(McIntosh, 2008, p. 158). It usually only happens as the result of intentional pursuit, perhaps occurring in public worship or private devotions, singing or listening to Christian music, in loving relations with other Christians, walks in nature, or when practicing the presence of God in everyday life. Experiential salvation is distinguished from catechesis neurologically by the former's engagement of those regions of the brain where emotion is processed, in the limbic system and the cingulate and frontal cortices (Siegel, 2012). Edwards (1959) called such experiences "spiritual understanding."

In what does experiential salvation consist? On the positive side of the emotion spectrum, it includes the heartfelt perception of the beauty of the triune God (Edwards, 1959, 1765/1960); the worship and love of God and communion with him; a sense of one's adoptive relationship (Rom 8:15: "Abba! Father!"); the encouragement of one's own declarative salvation; the experience of freedom, joy, peace, being loved by God, and a clean conscience (Heb 9:14; 10:22); seeing life afresh in its relation to God; and the love of others. Such happenings are an experiential sharing in Christ's resurrection (Phil 3:10).

On the negative emotion side, experiential salvation includes the fear of God, conviction of sin, and contrition. In light of the Psalms, Job, Ecclesiastes, and Lamentations, it also includes the awareness of one's spiritual malaise and distress due to felt distance from God, and the bringing of negative emotions (sadness, anxiety, shame and guilt, disgust, and anger; chap. 11) transparently into God's presence. "Pour out your heart like water before the presence of the Lord" (Lam 2:19). We shall see that such processing of one's negative emotions with God by the Spirit is one way Christians participate therapeutically in the sufferings of Christ (2 Cor 4:10-11; Phil 3:10), and also forms an important part of Christian therapy.

Emotions are signs of *depth* processing and therefore indicate that the more determinative aspects of one's soul—the heart—are being renewed by the Spirit (Edwards, 1959; Johnson, 2007, chap. 9). Experiential salvation, therefore, would seem to be a necessary bridge to the long-term change that is God's desire and design. As Thomas á Kempis (c. 1480/1864) prayed, "I cheerfully receive [your words] from your mouth, that they may be more deeply implanted in my heart" (p. 270).

The new-creation word and Christiformative salvation. Understanding and experiencing God and his salvation can be temporary events and are not ends in themselves. God's primary perlocutionary intent is that they lead to lasting change in his children's neural architecture and the form of their souls (i.e., their long-term memory, thinking, emotions and desires, and patterns of living and relating to others). This aspect of salvation is being called Christiformative,[15] since its goal is conformity to Christ. As believers participate in Christ's life, death, resurrection, and exaltation consciously, and enter into the trinitarian communion—individually and communally— the more deeply and the more permanently "Christ is formed in [them]" (Gal 4:19), and they grow into Christ's likeness. This transformation is the temporal realization of the new creation in the believer's heart, life, and re- lationships, which Kierkegaard called "inward deepening," and it cannot occur apart from the Holy Spirit, as well as the believer's faith (unless God miraculously bypasses the believer's agency). *It is the impress left on the brain/soul by participating over time in Christ's life.*

Catechesis, experiential salvation, and Christiformative salvation typi- cally involve conscious processing. However, each temporal step accesses deeper neurological and psychological dynamic structures than the pre- vious one, with the later phases activating core beliefs, scripts, emotion schemes, dispositions, defenses, and relational patterns and promoting di- polar self-regulation abilities (Johnson, 2007). Consequently, the last phase of Christiformative change is much slower than mere education and more enduring than ephemeral emotional experiences, since it involves the gradual alteration of brain/soul structure manifested in greater Christ- likeness in one's living and loving.

"The beginning of every good is from the second creation, which we attain in Christ" (Calvin, 1559/1960, p. 298). Over time (months, years, and decades) and through repeated experiences of the second creation (communion with God and others and experiences of God's truth that gradually transform one's understanding of God, self, and others in the context of meaningful life events), subsequent Christiformative change will be evident in a stronger kind of faith that can accept greater mystery and ambiguity and contributes to a decreasing need for personal control; a more thorough and genuine repen- tance that makes it easier to apologize with less defensiveness and to forgive others more readily; greater trust in God's goodness and sense of existential security, allowing for more distress tolerance and willingness to expose oneself to negative emotions, painful memories, and the suffering of others; increased ability to regulate one's negative emotions without being overwhelmed or shutting down and dissociating; greater range of emotion, and emotions that are increasingly fitting in various kinds of settings; greater resolution of one's negative emotion schemes, leading to less shame-proneness and irritability, and fewer periods of overwhelming sadness or anxiety; greater self-awareness and transparency with others; greater tolerance of others' imperfections and selfishness; greater empathy, a more sensitive dialogical style, and a greater willingness to help others without personal gain; greater wisdom and sense of irony, and the ability to see more clearly God's doxological/therapeutic agenda in life events; and increasingly consistent virtuous and loving deeds. All of the foregoing contributes to an ethicospiritual character that is simply more beautiful than the person exhibited earlier in life. Nevertheless, one's maturational possibilities on earth are constrained by one's remaining sin and biopsychosocial damage, so that perfection will always elude us down here. The "final" phase of salvation on earth—ecclesial—will be discussed in the next chapter. See table 15.1 for an outline of how these four aspects of salvation are related.

SOME THERAPEUTIC IMPLICATIONS

Promoting Upward Mobility in Christ

In *Metaphors We Live By* Lakoff and Johnson (1980) demonstrate that human thought and life is grounded in embodied, spatial metaphors that orient us largely unconsciously. *Up* and *high* are among the most basic, conveying notions such as greater ("That's a high number"), good ("We have hit our peak"), improvement ("His vital signs are up"), virtue ("She has high standards"), and happiness ("I'm feeling up"), likely based on our earliest physical and social experience. From a Christian standpoint, this fundamental metaphoric orientation is part of God's design, and it helps explain why humans pray to God "up in heaven" and similarly assume this orientation regardless of their location on earth.

How intriguing, then, that Christ literally ascended from the Palestinian region of the earth into the sky and that, according to the biblical authors, he is now seated "up in heaven." The Creator of human development is utilizing this primordial metaphor to communicate to believers something deep and basic, which seeps "into their bones" accordingly, by means of this aspect of Christ's exaltation. As we have seen, the attention of Christians is especially directed to the "above things" (Col 3:1-4): their calling is from above (Phil 3:14); every spiritual blessing, including their citizenship and inheritance, is in heaven (Phil 3:20; 1 Pet 1:4; Eph 1:3; Gal 4:26); and they are mysteriously seated up there with Christ (Eph 2:6). As a result, beyond the natural tendency of all theism to look upward to God, the Christian's life is now uniquely

Divine Declarations In Christ ——————→ *The Realization of the Father's Perlocutionary Intentions Toward Us in Christ*

The Father's Word → *Faith by the Spirit* → *Substantial Change by the Spirit* → *Communal Realization of the Word*

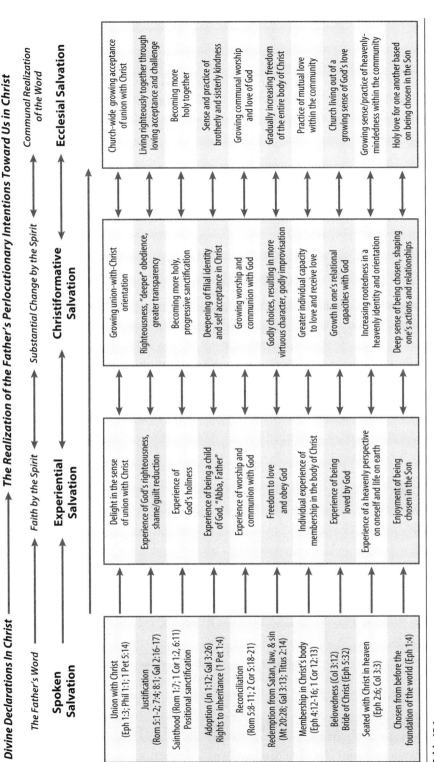

Spoken Salvation	Experiential Salvation	Christiformative Salvation	Ecclesial Salvation
Union with Christ (Eph 1:3; Phil 1:1; 1 Pet 5:14)	Delight in the sense of union with Christ	Growing union-with-Christ orientation	Church-wide growing acceptance of union with Christ
Justification (Rom 5:1-2; 7:4; 8:1; Gal 2:16-17)	Experience of God's righteousness, shame/guilt reduction	Righteousness, "deeper" obedience, greater transparency	Living righteously together through loving acceptance and challenge
Sainthood (Rom 1:7; 1 Cor 1:2, 6:11) Positional sanctification	Experience of God's holiness	Becoming more holy, progressive sanctification	Becoming more holy together
Adoption (Jn 1:12; Gal 3:26) Rights to inheritance (1 Pet 1:4)	Experience of being a child of God, "Abba, Father"	Deepening of filial identity and self acceptance in Christ	Sense and practice of brotherly and sisterly kindness
Reconciliation (Rom 5:8-11; 2 Cor 5:18-21)	Experience of worship and communion with God	Growing worship and communion with God	Growing communal worship and love of God
Redemption from Satan, law, & sin (Mt 20:28; Gal 3:13; Titus 2:14)	Freedom to love and obey God	Godly choices, resulting in more virtuous character, godly improvisation	Gradually increasing freedom of the entire body of Christ
Membership in Christ's body (Eph 4:12-16; 1 Cor 12:13)	Individual experience of membership in the body of Christ	Greater individual capacity to love and receive love	Practice of mutual love within the community
Belovedness (Col 3:12) Bride of Christ (Eph 5:32)	Experience of being loved by God	Growth in one's relational capacities with God	Church living out of a growing sense of God's love
Seated with Christ in heaven (Eph 2:6; Col 3:3)	Experience of a heavenly perspective on oneself and life on earth	Increasing rootedness in a heavenly identity and orientation	Growing sense/practice of heavenly-mindedness within the community
Chosen from before the foundation of the world (Eph 1:4)	Enjoyment of being chosen in the Son	Deep sense of being chosen, shaping one's actions and relationships	Holy love for one another based on being chosen in the Son

Table 15.1.

oriented upward, heavenward, and away from this world of sin, sorrows, and difficulties, operating unconsciously and subtly seasoning Christian discourse and thought with an optimistic flavor and a sense of improvement.

Following Christ, the Christian life is an ascent to the "above things" and "the heavenly things," where the life of Christians is "hidden with Christ in God" (Col 3:3; Canlis, 2010). "Our redemption would be imperfect if he did not lead us onward to the final goal of salvation" (Calvin, 1559/1960, p. 503). This orientation is part of our embodied human nature that we assume in our quest to become heavenly minded in the right way, living as strangers and exiles in this world (Heb 11:13; 1 Pet 1:1), since we have an eternal home up there. In addition to the positive connotations of this upward orientation, it provides a cognitive strategy to detach ourselves from immediate access to the "worry of the world" (Mt 13:22) and develop a more objective perspective on inferior and sinful pleasures, as well as our own desires.

Therapists and counselors can make use of these assets by tying this biblical language and spatial orientation naturally into conversations about the therapeutic journey with their counselees: "Your progress is part of Christ's drawing you into his communion up there in heaven with his Father." In addition, counselees can be invited to view themselves from their heavenly vantage point, seated with Christ and as they are viewed by him: "Imagine yourself in heaven with Christ looking down at you on earth the next time you feel rejected by your spouse. How might you and Christ encourage yourself?" This imaginative vista is one way to "set one's mind" (*phroneō*) on the above things (Col 3:2),[16] a cognitive activity that has "connotations of sober consideration and firm purpose" (Lincoln, 1981, p. 125). A therapeutic agenda creates opportunities for Christians to inquire into all the ways in which healing in Christ's name might occur through deliberate cognitive activity by taking the "above things" by faith into new regions of the brain/soul, where Christ's redemptive accomplishments may not yet have reached, at least experientially, thus furthering the kind of Christiformative changes that Paul advocated later in the passage (Col 3:5-17).

Meditating on one's present eschatological position up in heaven in Christ provides Christian counselees with another perspective on the discouragement they feel because of their sins and problems down here, none of which present barriers to God and his desire to bring about their psychospiritual healing and well-being. Knowing that Christ the beloved is their advocate in the heavenly places provides believers with a new-covenant strategy to detach from and disidentify with their sin, suffering, and damage in this earthly sphere of existence—without dissociation—and ground their life orientation in a divinely established, transcendent order, which provides a new-creation basis for hope and optimism.

Perfection in Christ Can Undermine Perfectionism

As we have repeatedly seen, most humans have a yearning for wholeness, completeness, and perfection, yet because humans are fallen, that yearning is unsatisfied, and often mollified by various degrees of distraction and dissociation. In addition, many persons (including many Christians), struggle with maladaptive perfectionism (Winter, 2005), a tendency to have unrealistic and inflexible standards for oneself, self-esteem dependent on performance, fear of failure, and severe self-criticism when one's standards are not met (Flett & Hewitt, 2002). God's declarative word about their completeness and perfection in Christ corresponds to and in principle satisfies these human yearnings, *but in another* with whom the believer is joined by the Spirit. This orientation provides transcendent resources to undermine maladaptive perfectionism and modify one's negative self-appraisals. The new self of Christians (we have noted) is dipolar in nature, in which their self-representation has a transcendent, relational pole or ground outside the self, in Christ, sanctioned by our Creator-Redeemer, a "rock" (Ps 18:2) of ethico-spiritual perfection, which both meets our creational-"legal" need for integrity and reduces the fallen desire to cover up one's imperfect state and pretend one is complete in oneself. Communion with God and meditation on declarative salvation—ideally along with corresponding, emotionally significant experiences of complete acceptance by important others, such as a good therapist and understanding friends—can therefore gradually reshape one's self-representation and help to resolve long-standing, harmful negative emotion schemes such as shame-proneness and perfectionism.

The Coming of the Holy Spirit in Christ

We have already examined some of the therapeutic implications of the indwelling Holy Spirit in chapter four. We revisit the topic to explore how its relation to union with Christ multiplies its benefits. As Calvin (1559/1960) noted: "As long as Christ remains outside of us, and we are separated from him, all that he has suffered and done for the human race remains useless and of no value for us. . . . Therefore, to share with us what he has received from the Father, he had to become ours, and to dwell within us" (p. 537). If the Spirit alone dwelt in us, we might be inclined to perceive the indwelling God impersonally, as merely God's "power" within us. However, this is the Spirit of Christ, and having read about Jesus in the Gospels, we know him as a person, and this helps us to correctly interpret his activity within us as a person. Because of the *perichoresis* of the Trinity, Christ is a friend (Jn 15:12) who really *is* closer than a brother (Prov 18:24). So we can know Christ via the Spirit as a companion within, who knows our joys and sorrows intimately and with whom it is only natural that we consciously share everything.

In light of our previous discussion on sin, we might also note that the Holy Spirit's indwelling fills in the existential hole created by original sin that lies at the core of every human being. The vacancy left by the alienation of human beings from their Creator led to a profound sense of shame that haunts all humans and that unconsciously motivates people to try to fill it with created things turned idols. Only an infinite God can fill that void, so the Holy Spirit is alone capable of adequately addressing that universal ethicospiritual need. As a result, Christians no longer *have* to feel that primordial shame, so when they do, they can reflect meditatively on how the Spirit dwells in them far deeper than that sense of shame and prayerfully imagine him resolving and undermining it from within. The same Word of God who sanctified them—declaratively—has also sent the *Holy* Spirit into their hearts to sanctify them experientially, over time, through his immediate presence within. From both vantage points, they are rendered holy, so their objective shame has been removed—they are whole and complete, also because they are indwelt by their God.

There are also extraordinary gifts that the Holy Spirit may bestow on Christian counselors, for example, exhortation, encouragement, healing, wisdom, knowledge, discerning of spirits, and mercy (Payne, 1995; Tan, 1999). Many Christian counselors report "inner promptings" of the Holy Spirit that help guide the counseling process and can direct the counselor in what to pursue that might best promote psychospiritual healing. The Holy Spirit may also be poured out on counselees in session, leading to an immediate experience of peace, insight, or the forgiveness of someone who troubled them. Such experiences sadly will fade, so the experience itself is not the goal, but it may be interpreted as an encouragement to seek deeper, longer-lasting "structural" change through the ongoing, "ordinary," deepening work of Christiformic salvation. In light of the biblical record of physical healing, and sporadic but well-documented accounts of such healing throughout church history, Christians should pray for extraordinary, miraculous psychological healing by the Holy Spirit, nevertheless mindful that God generally seems to prefer to use ordinary, creational means to heal the embodied souls of his children.

Tan and Ortberg (1995), Payne (1995), and Smith (2002) also advocate explicit reliance on the Holy Spirit during counseling sessions to guide the use of mental imagery regarding Christ and the healing of the soul. Scripture provides a wealth of relevant metaphors and images that can also be suggested by counselors who rely on the Spirit less directly (see Beck, 2011; Ryken, Wilhoit, & Longman, 1998). Either way, the Spirit can make the truth of the gospel more emotionally and relationally meaningful, in part because of the utilization of other emotion regions of the brain, in concert with the discursive regions, that can lead to therapeutic breakthroughs as well as more gradual transformation in counselee perceptions, values, feelings, and loves.

The Complexity of the Christian Self-Representation

To summarize some key themes of the chapter: union with Christ and all its spiritual blessings are given to all believers equally and immediately upon faith in him, providing essential resources for the building of their new self. The Lord Almighty says who they are now, so they now have the transcendent right—established outside themselves and their limitations—to appropriate their divine calling, including participation in the trinitarian communion and the construction of a new-self self-understanding, and make it the basis of their well-being and healing. Such appropriation is not easy because of sin, and particularly if there are substantial biopsychosocial obstacles in the way, but God has established transcendent conditions that entitle them to do so, even though they may still feel inadequate.

The self is the sum total of all the self-representations or self-schemata that a person possesses (Harter, 2012; Markus, 1977). The challenge facing believers is the reorganization of their self-representations according to who the Father says they are in Christ. *That* is who they are most truly. We might call this subset of self-representations the believer's "real self."[17] Consider Mary, a Christian, a grandmother, a diabetic, a tennis player, a director of human relations, conscientious and agreeable, a member of a local orthodox church, and a sinner. But who Mary *really* is, who she is most truly, is *Mary-in-Christ*: child of God, holy and beloved, seated with Christ in heaven and so already ethically and spiritually perfect and complete. The most influential components of the self-understanding and self-evaluation of believers are to be derived *from above*, and not from anything on earth, so not from their own unique attainments (which are gifts of God anyway, 1 Cor 4:7) or from their sinfulness, which has been resolved in Christ. "Belonging to Christ renders negligible every other source of security—wealth, education, noble birth, or political or ecclesiastical power. One stands tall in the world because one is God's own" (Charry, 1997, p. 42).

This suggests that one's *real* self, seated with Christ in the heavens, should be kept consciously differentiated from one's actual, empirical self (James, 1890). The *actual* self is a composite of all that one actually is, here on earth. For Christians this includes the good created infrastructure of oneself that gives them unique personal identity (their strengths, personality, body, good motives, ideals, and desires, and so on, what we might call one's created self), all about them that is fallen (what Paul calls the "old self" that is still being corrupted, Eph 4:22), and all about them that pertains to the new creation, realized up to this point (what Paul calls the "new self" that is still being re-newed, Col 3:10). As a result, one's actual (earthly, empirical) self is much "messier" than one's real (heavenly, above) self. One's actual self is not yet empirically, existentially righteous and holy (though it *is* in Christ). While the actual self of Christians possesses creational and redemptive good and is able to perform some good (acceptable to God), and it generally images God better than before conversion (on account of some measure of conformity to Christ), it is still capable of significant selfishness, and it sins because of re-maining sin. Consequently, a *primary* focus on one's actual self for one's sense of self and identity will be discouraging for some and encouraging for others, but either way it hinders becoming a new self in Christ. Nevertheless, it is probably the case that most Christians most of the time base their self-understanding and -evaluation on what and how their actual self is doing. After all, the actual self is close at hand and what the Christian is continuously perceiving and getting feedback about (Bem, 1972).

Christians, however, as we noted above, are to set their minds on the above things, and this includes their self-understanding and -evaluation.[18] Consequently, Christian therapists will want to focus the attention of their counselees periodically on their real self and emphasize its supreme impor-tance within the Christian self-system. The first step is to understand this cognitively. However, eventually believers will need deeper appropriation of their real self than the merely cognitive. The most shame-prone in particular will have to overcome strong, unconscious resistance to this agenda because of as-yet-unresolved guilt, shame, and felt unworthiness that can make identity-in-Christ teaching feel inappropriate, if not cruel. Healing prayer or Christian emotion-focused therapy (e.g., Kim & Johnson, 2013) may be useful in undermining the deep obstacles to real-self internalization that counselees experience, as well as the loving acceptance of the therapist, which is a concrete sign of the Father's acceptance.

At the same time, believers ought not to focus exclusively on their real self and ignore their actual self. Ongoing self-perceptions (Bem, 1972) of one's actual self are automatic and invaluable—at least to the degree they are accurate—for they tether one's self-awareness to how one is actually living and relating to others. One's actual self is also one's *true* self, that is, who one is existentially, honestly and authentically without the hiding and pretense so common among humans, what is sometimes called one's "false self."[19] Indeed, grounding one's self-understanding primarily in one's real self best enables one to come to terms with and accept one's actual self, since in Christ one's actual self is declared to be perfect and complete, and therefore one does not need to *pretend* that one is. The key to developing a mature Christian self would seem to be finding the right balance in the experience of one's real self and one's actual self, so that the former has greater "weight" within one's overall self-representation, while becoming increasingly open to who one actually is. To facilitate the proper ratio, time and effort have to be devoted to incorporating emotionally loaded *real-self* self-representations into one's self-schemata, through communion with God, Scripture reading, meditation, journaling, guided imagery,[20] and the empathic acceptance of the therapist.

Comparison with secular self-theory. The terms "actual self" and especially "real self" have also been used by secular psychologists (e.g., Harter, 2012; Horney, 1950; Masterson, 1988; Rogers, 1961), and a comparison between the secular models and the above Christian formulation may prove instructive. Though there is some variance in terminology, the secular models all posit something analogous to the "actual self." Horney (1950), for example, defined the actual (or empirical) self as "everything that a person is at a given time: body and soul, healthy and neurotic" (p. 158).[21] However, their notion of the real self (or whatever is analogous in the respective system, with the exception of Harter, who has no comparable component) is unsurprisingly markedly different from the Christian real self outline above. Horney, for example, defined the real self as "that most alive center of ourselves" (p. 157), "the 'original' force toward individual growth and fulfillment" (p. 158), and "the spring of emotional forces, of constructive energies" (p. 173).[22]

These secular models of the self (Harter excepted) posit a dynamic set of positive motives and desires at their core that are basic to humanity and that were unfortunately overlaid with defenses and inhibitions due to early pathological social experiences and unhealthy ethical constraints (the "fall" according to secularism). Trusting in this core, whatever it is called, is an analog to faith in their secular therapeutic system (see Horney, 1950, pp. 157-58; Masterson, 1988, pp. 38-50; Rogers, 1961, pp. 118-19, 175).

Interpreted Christianly, secular psychologists have highlighted valuable aspects of creation grace—the progressive goodness of the created self—which we discussed in chapter seven (e.g., self-regard, a positive orientation, and intuitive wisdom, all of which are part of the law of God within). However, as we have repeatedly noted, sin has warped these good created, maturational dynamics, so that they are bent toward religious autonomy and self-sufficiency, and secular psychology has developed models of the self that reflect and support that agenda. With the self at the center of human life, some of them elevate our created goodness to a quasi-mystical, "redemptive" life force, which can be trusted to guide one to well-being. But from a theocentric Christian standpoint, at their best, these models are promoting a more subtle, enlightened, and socially adaptive form of narcissism. By contrast, Christian models of the self are fundamentally relational and exocentric. The healthiest self, according to Christianity, is learning how to ground its search for its well-being and identity ultimately in real relationship, outside itself: in the triune God and one's relation with him, in one's real self in Christ in heaven, and in its relations with others, with whom it is learning reciprocally how to love them as it loves itself. The created self, with all its gifts and powers, is best able to become itself and find its greatest fulfillment and happiness, given by grace, within this relational matrix because that is its design plan.

Fasting for Psychospiritual Growth

During the time Jesus was ministering on earth, people raised questions about the fact that his disciples did not fast even though the most devoted to God of that time commonly fasted. Jesus heard about these questions and responded by saying that while he was with them, it was not the time to fast. "But the days will come when the bridegroom is taken away from them, and then they will fast in that day" (Mk 2:20), and that time is now.

Consequently, fasting has been used for centuries by Christians to promote spiritual formation by focusing on the bread of heaven rather than the bread of earth. Christian counselors might consider recommending it as a therapeutic intervention for those who would be open to it.

"Jesus Christ and the Holy Spirit Are Praying for Me"

As we have seen, the ascension initiated a unique era of human history, one in which both the Son of God and the Holy Spirit are praying to the Father on behalf of their children. This astounding fact has relevance for therapy. Many therapants feel lonely, unlovable, and unnoticed by God and others. Simply being informed of the interest of two members of the Trinity in their lives will not necessarily change the sense of abandonment from which they suffer. However, they can be encouraged to "keep" this truth by meditating on it periodically. Reflecting deeply and opening up one's soul to the "possibility" that the Son in heaven and the Spirit in our hearts are personally interested in our concerns, our needs, and our failings, and advocating on our behalf before the Father, provides one more strategy to help facilitate the deep, psychosociospiritual paradigm shift that is one of the aims of Christian therapy. *I am not alone. I am cared for by God. I matter to him.* Counselees might use their imagination to picture Jesus above and sense the Holy Spirit within praying for them with deep desires for their good, *for them* with greater intensity and deliberation than anywhere else in the universe, letting this realization seep into the loneliest and most remote parts of their soul.

RESOURCES FOR COUNSELORS AND COUNSELEES

Classic
Owen, J. (1965). The grace and duty of being spiritually minded. *The works of John Owen* (Vol. 7). Edinburgh: The Banner of Truth Trust.

Contemporary
Anderson, N. (2000). *Victory over the darkness.* Ventura, CA: Regal.

Appleby, D., & Ohlschlager, G. (2013). *Transformative encounters: The intervention of God in Christian counseling and pastoral care.* Downers Grove, IL: InterVarsity Press.

Campbell, C. R. (2012). *Paul and union with Christ: An exegetical and theological study.* Grand Rapids, MI: Zondervan. ‡

Canlis, J. (2010). *Calvin's ladder: A spiritual theology of ascent and ascension.* Grand Rapids, MI: Eerdmans. ‡ A thorough treatment of Calvin's understanding of relational participation in God's communion through our union with Christ's ascension.

Chester, T., & Woodrow, J. (2013). *The ascension: Humanity in the presence of God.* Ross-shire, UK: Christian Focus.

Farrow, D. (1999). *Ascension and ecclesia*. Grand Rapids, MI: Eerdmans. ‡

Kapic, K. M. (2010). *God so loved, he gave*. Grand Rapids, MI: Zondervan.

O'Donovan, O. (1986). *Resurrection and moral order*. Grand Rapids, MI: Eerdmans. ‡

Prime, D. (1999). *The ascension: The shout of a King*. Surrey, UK: Day One.

Purves, A. (2004). *Reconstructing pastoral theology: A christological foundation*. Louisville, KY: Westminster John Knox. ‡ Though Purves misses the point of penal substitution, this otherwise remarkable book makes union with Christ and his ongoing representative intercession for his people basic to our Christian life.

Torrance, T. F. (2011). *Atonement: The person and work of Christ*. Downers Grove, IL: InterVarsity Press. ‡

‡ Recommended more for counselors and pastors

PART V

The Divine Therapy

BASED ON THEIR UNION WITH THE LIFE, DEATH, resurrection, and exaltation of Christ, by the Father's declaration and the Spirit's indwelling, believers have been brought into the communion of the triune God and the new-creation community and tradition called the church, and are now being formed into the image of Christ primarily in the context of these two primary relationships. As a result, their lives are now marked, all the way down, by a fundamental redemptive-historical conflict between their old way of living in the world—their psychopathology—and their new way of life, into which they have been incorporated and in which they are learning to participate by the Holy Spirit and faith. Christian psychotherapy and counseling facilitates the ongoing resolution of the conflict and the transformation from old to new by *redemptive differentiation*, which involves deeply distinguishing the new—personally owning one's individual created goodness and all the blessings of one's union with Christ—from the old—putting one's sin to death and redeeming one's damaged created goodness and promoting its healing, where possible; and *redemptive integration*, which involves the increasing purification and unification of one's body/soul by means of communion with the triune God, bidirectional love with other believers (as well as others made in God's image), and a new self-understanding, through coming to terms with and owning all that they are now by the Spirit and faith.

—16—

The Holy Embrace
of the Body of Christ

Principle 8: The church is the body of Christ—
the new creation becoming visible—its members
being conformed to Christ individually and to the
Trinity communally by the Holy Spirit and faith.

The whole body, being fitted and held together
by what every joint supplies, according to the proper
working of each individual part, causes the growth
of the body for the building up of itself in love.

Ephesians 4:16

Social life in a fallen world is fraught with such promise and
peril. Humans cannot develop without the help of others, yet others are
often the cause of their most painful suffering. As Augustine (1958) put it,
"There is nothing so social by nature, so anti-social by sin, as man" (p. 268),
and both these realizations are repeated throughout the Christian tradition. Extolling solitude in the late Middle Ages, Thomas á Kempis
(2003) quoted Seneca, "As often as I have been among men, I have returned less a man" (p. 17). By contrast, the Puritan pastor Richard Sibbes
(1635/1973) asked, "If God in the state of innocency thought it fit man
should have a helper, if God thought it fit to send an angel to comfort
Christ in his agonies, shall any man think the comfort of another more
than [he] needs?" (p. 195).

Given Christ's redemption, one might hope that *Christian* social life would be a substantial improvement over its unredeemed forms, and it can be (e.g., "individuals regularly involved with a congregation have larger social networks, interact with network members more frequently, receive more diverse types of support, and find their support networks more satisfying and more reliable that those who do not attend services regularly"; Park & Slattery, 2013, p. 548). Yet, perhaps because of heightened expectations, the conflicts and scandals that occur periodically in the church have led to a heightened sense of disappointment. Many in the West are disillusioned with the institutional church, and even many Christians do not consider their churches to be places of psychological healing and flourishing. It is no small irony that God has appointed the church to be the best proof of his existence on earth and made it the site of the community of embodied signs of the coming new creation, the primary manifestation of his glory, and his soul-care clinic for humanity! What was he thinking? Let us probe into this mystery.

SOUL-CARE TEACHING REGARDING THE CHURCH

A Definition
There are many different Christian understandings of the church (Dulles, 1991; Volf, 1998). Following Allison (2012), the church in this book is defined as "the people of God who have been saved through repentance and faith in Jesus Christ and have been incorporated into his body through baptism with the Holy Spirit" (p. 29).

The Trinity as the Archetype of the Church
In chapter two the Trinity was described as one God who is a communion of persons, and it was suggested human beings were created to be an image of this God as they become individuals in communion. The church is specially designated to be the site of this actualization. We recall that one of Edwards's rational arguments for the Trinity was based on beauty or excellence: "One alone cannot be excellent," he wrote (1994, p. 284), and minds in community are "the only proper . . . beings" (1758/1970, p. 206), because "the highest excellency . . . must be the consent of spirits one to another" (1758/1970, p. 337). This beauty is found superlatively in the Father and Son, who share an eternal delight in and consent to each other, a love that, according to Edwards (and Augustine and Aquinas before him), is the Spirit

(1758/1970, p. 364).[1] Edwards also argued that a perfectly good being would have "an inclination to communicate all his happiness" (1994, p. 263), which could not be perfectly realized except in another equal to himself, and this we only find in the Trinity (McClymond & McDermott, 2012). As a result, together the three form an "infinitely sweet and glorious society" (Edwards, 2006, p. 153) or "family" (Edwards, 2000, p. 367).

Such a happy being, Edwards (2000) reasoned, would also be pleased to manifest his beauty by bringing into existence a created image of their mutual personal consent and happiness, and "it seems to be God's design to admit the church into the divine family as his Son's wife" (p. 367). Terribly complicating the family drama, of course, is the fact that the wife has a notorious background (highlighted in Ezek 16 and Hosea). The drama's action is then immeasurably heightened in the fullness of time (Gal 4:4) by the bridegroom's sacrificial rescue and purification of his bride (Eph 5:25-26). Through his death and resurrection, those who participate by faith with the Trinity's consent are brought into that conjugal union with Christ and, in turn, are "admitted into that glorious society" of the Trinity (Edwards, 2006, p. 153)! "As You, Father, are in Me and I in You," Jesus prayed, "that they also may be in Us, . . . that they may be one, just as We are one; I in them and You in Me, that they may be perfected in unity, so that the world may know that You sent Me, and loved them, even as You have loved Me" (Jn 17:21-23). So, the church's own communion/fellowship/*koinōnia* is a reflection of and participation in the communion/fellowship/*koinōnia* of the Trinity (1 Jn 1:3) (Danaher, 2004; McClymond & McDermott, 2012).

Our union with Christ, however, "is not something that happens only to isolated individuals but to a company of people that together form the 'body' of Christ: the church. Union with Christ implies union with others" (Vanhoozer, 2010, p. 292). The new creation is a "new humanity" (Eph 2:15) that has a necessarily corporate dimension (Lincoln, 1990, p. 287; see also Ridderbos, 1975)—only *together* are they the "church of the firstborn" (Heb 12:23).

The "body" is one of Paul's key metaphors used to communicate the corporate dimension of union with Christ. Believers "are one body in Christ" (Rom 12:5), "Christ's body, and individually members of it" (1 Cor 12:27). The analogy carries rich associations that underscore the church's diversity-in-unity; communion, harmony, and cooperation; mutual service to one another; and submission to its head—all of which also express the mutual consent and corporate likeness of the members-in-community in the Trinity. Paul also suggestively linked this body metaphor to another: the bread of the Lord's Supper that symbolizes Christ's death (1 Cor 10:16-17; 11:24-29; and Mt 26:26). This linkage of metaphors accentuates the church's redemptive origin[2] and unity (1 Cor 10:17), and perhaps also its calling to suffer with Christ (Phil 3:10).

Paul likewise taught that believers are baptized into the body of Christ "by one Spirit" (1 Cor 12:13). The church therefore is not merely a voluntary human association—like the Lion's Club—but is brought about ultimately by the Spirit, in order to be "built together into a dwelling of God" (Eph 2:22).[3] The Spirit extends the boundaries of the Trinity's communion by mediating grace through local communities of indwelt believers who are ideally growing together to become more vigorous personal agents in vigorous communion (Jn 17:21-26; 1 Jn 1:3). In church services where God is present among his people, more than anywhere else on earth, his glory (his meaning-fullness) is being consciously appropriated, enjoyed, and shared.

The Church as the Ektype of the Trinity

Edwards observed that "no reasonable creature can be happy, we find, without society and communion," and "the happiness of society consists in this, in the mutual communications of each other's happiness" (1994, p. 264). With Christ in heaven, the church is now the preeminent site within the creation appointed by the triune God to display his communal happiness. Admonitions to be "of the same mind," maintain "the same love, united in spirit, intent on one purpose" (Phil 2:2), promote "the unity of the Spirit in the bond of peace" (Eph 4:3), and love one another (Jn 13:34-35) are expressions of God's doxological agenda to reproduce analogues of the Trinity in this age throughout this world.[4]

In chapter two we noted that the Trinity is the archetype for humanity, providing a distinctly Christian maturity model for human life that promotes a beautiful harmony and balance between the dialectical/reciprocal ideals of vigorous personal agency within vigorous communion, in dependence on the triune God. The church was created anew to become the primary *ektype* of the triune God's personal-communal form on earth.

Because of creation grace, however, good models of personal and communal agency can be found outside the church. A major feature of the church is its receptive reflection of God's ethicospiritual character, that is, his holiness (or, we could say, his splendor or his supreme devotion to himself as Trinity), found preeminently in Jesus Christ. The *quality* of Christian maturation is different from secular maturity. "'Formation' . . .

means in the first place Jesus' taking form in His church" (Bonhoeffer, 1955, p. 83) by his character being manifested "within the patterns of the community's life together" (McIntosh, 2008, p. 10). Precisely through the course of their interactions with one another, the members of Christ's body are now the primary *visible* protagonists in the divine drama of the manifestation of the form and splendor of the Trinity.

Called into Being by the Word of God and Empowered by the Spirit

As the first creation was brought about by the Word of God, so the second creation, the church, and that in three ways. First, the church is constituted by Jesus Christ, the Word of God, in whose life, death, resurrection, and exaltation it exists. Put another way, it is established by the Word of the Father, whose declaration of salvation in Christ is uttered over all who believe and (we add here) who gather together in Christ's name (Mt 18:20). Second, the church is being transformed into the image of the one it loves, through union and communion with Christ. And third, it is becoming reconstituted by its deepening appropriation of Scripture. In its various genres and two Testaments, Scripture articulates the form of the church—its membership criteria (repentance and faith in Christ); its rites of initiation (baptism) and commemoration (the Lord's Supper); the general structure of its main gatherings (its liturgy, including preaching and teaching, worship, singing, prayer, confession, the ordinances, and conversation together); its center (God) and the basis of its life (union with Christ); its form of life (Scripture's description of its virtues and maturity ideal, ethics, boundaries, violations, and rules for excommunication); and the general pattern of its soul healing.

However, by itself the letter kills; only the Holy Spirit makes it come alive (2 Cor 3:3-18, esp. 2 Cor 3:6). The church is also *pneumadynamic* (Allison, 2012, borrowing from Coe, 2000)—empowered by the Spirit to bear fruit for God (Jn 15:5; Gal 5:22-23). As Christ was raised from the dead according to the Spirit (Rom 1:4), so the Spirit now is raising from the dead "the body of Christ," the church, by anointing its worship, teaching, liturgy, and relationships with the first fruits of the new creation, through the Spirit's gifts and the healing of its members, so they reflect more and more of Christ's glory.

Ecclesial Salvation

Humans are equally personal beings and social beings, so salvation is both personal and social.[5] In the previous chapter we focused primarily on the personal side of salvation. Here we consider its social corollary. With rare exceptions, declarative, experiential, and Christiformative salvation happen to persons in significant relationship with other Christians. The personal appropriation and internalization of union with Christ is generally correlated with its social appropriation and internalization. *Ecclesial salvation, then, is the formation of communities of friends, united to Christ, bound together to God by the new covenant, and is supposed to be characterized by a gradually increasing theocentrism, unity, holy love, and transparency by the Holy Spirit through faith.* From the beginning, the triune God's design has been to raise up out of a sinful, suffering, and broken humanity a new-creation community, by means of Christ's life, death, resurrection, and exaltation, that would increasingly resemble the triune communion.

Personal and social salvation are promoted by the receptive practice of God's holy love in Christ *together* within the body of Christ. The apostle Paul wrote that God has appointed the church's leaders

> for the equipping of the saints for the work of service, to the building up of the body of Christ; until we all attain to the unity of the faith, and of the knowledge of the Son of God, to a mature man, to the measure of the stature which belongs to the fullness of Christ. As a result, we are no longer to be children, tossed here and there by waves and carried about by every wind of doctrine, by the trickery of men, by craftiness in deceitful scheming; but speaking the truth in love, we are to grow up in all aspects into Him who is the head, even Christ, from whom the whole body, being fitted and held together by what every joint supplies, according to the proper working of each individual part, causes the growth of the body for the building up of itself in love. (Eph 4:12-16)

Here Paul put forward a beautiful ideal of a continually growing community of holy love, experiencing reciprocal, interactive, spiral growth, in which the individual members of the church *together* learn how to practice Christiformity, "speaking the truth in love"—a pregnant phrase, if there ever was one—with members doing the best they can to build one another up in holy love.[6] There is no better description in the Bible of the therapeutic/reciprocal development of Christ's community of broken sinner-saints into his image and into a society of friends like him (Jn 15:15).

The communal appropriation of Christ's salvation occurs formally, in the liturgy of the public assembly of local churches, through preaching, teaching, singing, reading Scripture, reciting, sharing, baptizing, confessing, and taking the Lord's Supper. However, it also occurs informally in everyday life, as evidenced by the many "one another" commands of the New Testament: love (1 Thess 3:12; 1 Pet 1:22), submit to (Eph 5:21), teach and admonish (Col 3:16); exhort (Heb 3:13), comfort and agree with (1 Cor 13:11), show hospitality to (1 Pet 4:9), encourage and build up (1 Thess 5:11), be kind and forgive (Eph 4:32), serve (Gal 5:13; 1 Pet 4:10), bear with (Col 3:13), do good to (1 Thess 5:12), confess one's sins to (Jas 5:16), bear the burdens of (Gal 6:2), and stir up to love and good deeds (Heb 10:24).[7] These are examples of practices for becoming more like Christ (more whole and more holy) that can only be performed *together*. Ecclesial salvation turns Christians into *ecclesial selves* (Grenz, 2001) whose identity is grounded in the love of God and the life of their church.

A Community of Paradox and Irony

At least, that is God's design. But we all know the present reality falls far short of God's glory. Paradox and irony pervade the church (Allison, 2012), much of it due to the already/not-yet tension that also characterizes the church in this age, as well as the finite and temporal nature of social life, both of which require a developmental model of church life—rather than a perfectionist one. "And *we all*, with unveiled face, beholding the glory of the Lord, are being transformed into the same [personal-communal] image from one degree of glory to another" (2 Cor 3:18 ESV).

A conflicted community becoming centered on God. The church is the social institution that, more than any other, has as its main agenda the worship of God. As this orientation characterizes its teaching and liturgy and permeates its life, a church's members are drawn more and more into that orbit. And as they grow closer to him, they grow closer to each other. God is their unity.

The remaining sin of its members, however, serves as a constant centrifugal force, drawing them to competing idols, agendas, and preferences. Even an emphasis on God-centeredness can become an unconscious basis for unresolved narcissism. So local churches have to pursue their theocentric agenda self-critically, mindful that their knowledge and love of God is mysteriously but directly correlated with their self- and other-knowledge and love in Christ. Indeed, we could conceive of the ideal church as the social/dialogical space within which the relations between the knowledge and love of God, self, and others are most deliberately being reciprocally cultivated in Christ.

Local sites of the universal church. A local church is a group of believers who physically gather together regularly in a specific location to worship, hear the Word, and celebrate the Lord's Supper and baptism, having covenanted together with God to love and serve him and one another.[8] Most attention is usually directed to the gatherings for worship (Sunday for most churches, Saturday for Adventists). But thriving communities have members who find other reasons for getting together during the week.

Local assemblies, however, are microcosms of the universal church, composed of all believers living on earth at any point in time, encompassing and transcending all local churches and denominations.[9] Both poles of this dialectic are important. Nevertheless, the local church needs to have functional priority in our values, since it is the only place where the church *does* what it has been "called out" to *do*.[10] With respect to a therapeutic agenda, Christians need social/dialogical places where they can worship God with others and experience face-to-face communion with one another over a sufficient period of time to influence their brain/souls with new-creation discourse and love, and the local church is the place where God especially intends for that to happen—in the name of Christ.

A community of unity in diversity. "The Holy Spirit unites us in Christ even as the Holy Spirit encourages the uniqueness of our persons by a diversity of gifts of the Spirit" (Tanner, 2001, p. 83). God created humans with remarkable diversity to be naturally attracted to similarity. Consequently, humans tend to form homogenous groups that differ from each other, a created inclination the fall turned into a vice. Forging supernatural unity out of this fallen diversity is part of the doxological agenda of the Trinity. Jesus prayed that his followers would be "one; even as You, Father, are in Me and I in You, that they also may be in Us" (Jn 17:21). So the unity of the church was emphasized a lot in the New Testament (e.g., Eph 2:13-16; 4:3-6, 13-16; Phil 2:1-5; Col 3:14), and disunity (division, strife, and enmity) is severely criticized (e.g., 1 Corinthians; Gal 5:19-21; 1 Tim 6:3-5; 2 Tim 2:23-24). Likening church members to different body parts that need each other to flourish was, therefore, a strategic metaphor, turning individual differences that can alienate people into goods that can bring them together (see, e.g., 1 Cor 12:12-31).

Appreciation of diversity has become commonplace in our day (and we might note that Christian assumptions helped to shape that agenda, though the story is a complex one). But even here God focuses our attention: "Is not this the fast which I choose, to loosen the bonds of wickedness, to undo the bands of the yoke, and to let the oppressed go free, and break every yoke? Is it not to divide your bread with the hungry, and bring the homeless poor into the house; when you see the naked, to cover him; and not to hide yourself from your own flesh?" (Is 58:6-7). Old Testament teachings such as this were foundational to the Messiah's message and ministry (Mt 25:31-46; Lk 4:18). "Blessed are the poor in spirit, for theirs is the kingdom of heaven" (Mt 5:3). The apostle Paul exulted in God's preference for the foolish of the world, the weak, the base, and the despised (1 Cor 1:26-29). We might, therefore, expect churches today to be characterized by significant bio-psychosocial and ethicospiritual diversity, with members falling all along a psychospiritual maturity continuum, resembling the normal curve. The variety of biologically and relationally shaped persons brought together in a local church will typically cause many problems—and also create a prism through which the infinite glory of God can shine in seemingly endless combinations (Hart, 2003).[11] To its creational diversity the Spirit adds redemptive diversity through gifts he distributes "as He wills" (1 Cor 12:11), given "for the common good" (1 Cor 12:7; see Rom 12:3-8; 1 Cor 12:4-11; Eph 4:11-16).

A community of fallen friends. True friendship consists of reciprocal love. Therefore, the Trinity's love for one another serves as the eternal standard for true friendship as well as the life of the local church. Yet, unlike the Trinity, the members of a local church are fallen. This makes psychospiritual church growth extremely challenging! In chapter two we learned some things about love that can be practiced in the church. First, benevolent love desires the well-being of the beloved and rests in that well-being and in its love being fully reciprocated (Aquinas, 1945, Vol. 1, p. 217; Edwards, 1765/1960). Therefore, to the degree the beloved is not flourishing or reciprocating that love, the desire of benevolent love is unfulfilled. Love at its best—the love of the Trinity—is fulfilled and completely reciprocal. By contrast, the love among fallen humans cannot be fully reciprocated and therefore cannot be fulfilled. Consequently, the benevolent love of God toward humans seeks to promote their well-being and their reciprocal love, and love among true friends does likewise.[12] Such friendship, therefore, has to be more than unconditional positive regard.

We also learned that love desires a differentiated union with the other (Aquinas, 1945, Vol. 1, p. 217; Edwards, 1765/1965). Stump (2010) suggests that such union involves being mutually present, entailing an I-Thou relation and shared attention, and mutual closeness, that is, the desire to be with one another, the sharing of thoughts and feelings, and the internal integration of both persons around the good. Internal integration, we recall, includes substantial self-awareness (a prerequisite for sharing thoughts and feelings) and the proper ordering of one's desires around the good. Sharing thoughts and feelings is intrinsic to love because the lover must know the beloved as he or she actually is if the lover is to love *the beloved*. Otherwise, one is loving an illusion, a mutually constructed projection, a false self.

Sharing one's mind and heart is facilitated by the gospel of grace and mutual humility and empathy. Referring to what we now call empathy, Sibbes (1635/1973) wrote that it "has a strange force, as we see in the strings of an instrument, which being played upon, as they say, the strings of another instrument are also moved with it" (p. 193). Empathic listening affirms the created goodness of the other by taking his or her emotions seriously and communicates that those emotions are meaningful—they signify values—even when they misrepresent *current* reality to some extent, because present emotional meaning often re-presents experiences from one's story (Johnson, 2007, chap. 9). Becoming a better friend, therefore, also involves face-to-face dialogue: taking turns mutually sharing one's mind, heart, and story, and empathic listening.

Finally, we noted in chapter two that complacent love entails delight (Edwards, 1765/1960; Pruss, 2013). Delight is "value-responsive" (von Hildebrand, 2009), corresponding to the beauty of its object, and since God is infinitely the greatest beauty, delight in him is in principle unbounded. The fitting love of all other persons being in God's image, created beauty is proportional to that person's being in God's image, created beauty, love of God, and resemblance to him. So the holy love of friends necessarily includes appreciation and affirmation of the other.

Christian love is regulated by the highest ethicospiritual standards—it is "the fulfillment of the Law" (Mt 5; Rom 8:4; Gal 5:14). Yet, that fulfillment (or obedience) flows from its completion and perfection in Christ, in which there is simultaneously "no condemnation" (Rom 8:1). Therefore, because saints are still sinners (Emlet, 2009), the holy love of friends entails forbearance and forgiveness. "Love covers a multitude of sins" (1 Pet 4:8). "The very life and soul of friendship stands in freedom, tempered with wisdom and faithfulness. Love with compassion and patience to bear all, and hope all, and not to be easily provoked by the waywardness of him we deal with" (Sibbes, 1635/1973, p. 193).

In the extreme case of grave, ongoing, unrepentant sin, holy love may lead, reluctantly, to church discipline (1 Cor 5; Leeman, 2010).[13] Love cares too much to sit back and watch a friend reject his or her own well-being and destroy him- or herself; compassion, pity, and action are called for. When the church is forced to respond to a grievously wayward member, the communication of its love must be paramount, with tears and pleading. A merely judicial handling of a member's falling away comes across as condescending and ultimately antagonistic; a grace-saturated approach, by contrast, conveys humility and a genuine desire for the person's good. And whenever church discipline becomes necessary, the church must ask itself how it failed this member. Like divorce, it is not God's ideal, but sometimes it is necessary.

From a Christian standpoint, the love of God, neighbor, and self are reciprocally interrelated, for desiring the good of God, the other, and oneself aims at the wholehearted differentiated union or consent of all three. All love in the creation, in whatever degree, consciously or unconsciously, originates in and resembles God's love for himself in his threefold personal nature, and God intends that the members of his churches participate increasingly consciously in his love and together increasingly consent to becoming better friends and "dear to [one] another" (Edwards, 1989, p. 129).

A community of the broken and beloved.[14] "The church of Christ is a common hospital, wherein all are in some measure sick of some spiritual disease or other" (Sibbes, 1635/1973, p. 34): perfect in Christ, called to holy love yet characterized by remaining sin and degrees of suffering and biopsychosocial damage. What kind of atmosphere in local churches would best promote the development of such complex self-understanding? In theory, we might suppose that knowing the free love of God in the gospel would automatically facilitate the emergence of communities of honesty and transparency, which are continuously accepting, forbearing, and forgiving one another, in the context of their union with Christ and pursuit of Christlikeness. Yet Christians who know the gospel well intellectually can still resist transparency, because of high levels of unresolved, unconscious[15] shame and guilt, evident in defensiveness, judgmentalism, passive-aggressive behavior with others, and harshness and arrogance with one's family members.[16] How does that happen?

We have seen that shame especially causes humans to want to hide (Gen 3:8). But how does one know one is deficient? Paradoxically, the good law of God, when combined with sin, can actually intensify shame and guilt by exposing one's sinfulness (Rom 7:7-24), and that in turn can easily activate shame about one's biopsychosocial damage, particularly with shame-prone personalities. As a result, members of churches with the highest ethical standards often have the greatest difficulty opening up with one another about their imperfections.

Yet the solution here is not lower standards. Churches that *only* emphasize acceptance and grace, without ever challenging their members, tend to create communities of unconscious hopelessness and despair, which show little evidence of resurrection over time. Finding the balance here requires supernatural discernment, and we should add that it is likely part of God's design that different churches meet different kinds of needs for believers at different stages of their Christian life.

Nevertheless, biblical narratives and the epistles make abundantly clear that believers on earth are characterized by imperfection. "Therefore we must expect an imperfect church" (Kuyper, 1948, p. 54). Coming to terms with and accepting the weaknesses of one's church and giving up the search for a perfect one are important markers of Christian maturation. "Only that fellowship which faces such disillusionment, with all its unhappy and ugly aspects, begins to be what it should be in God's sight, begins to grasp in faith the promise that is given to it. . . . A community which cannot bear and cannot survive such a crisis, which insists upon keeping its illusion when it should be shattered, permanently loses in that moment the promise of Christian community" (Bonhoeffer, 1954, p. 27). That is because God's holy love can be received only to the degree of one's honesty and transparency about oneself (and one's church).

Funded by the knowledge of the gospel, deepening experiences of union and communion with Christ by the church's leaders and a critical mass of its members gradually enable a community to practice acceptance, forbearance, confession,[17] and forgiveness of one another, knowing believers are already perfect in Christ and will be perfected in heaven, while striving to enter the "rest" of Christlikeness (Mt 11:28; Heb 4:11). The cross and the resurrection have created a new social/dialogical space, where the law's "hostility" of condemnation, guilt, and shame has been divinely removed (Col 2:10-23),[18] opening up new possibilities for genuinely free speech (Jn 8:36) that fosters relational healing and psychospiritual progress. In that space lies the possibility of differentiated union with other humans, involving mutual closeness (empathy, sharing of thoughts and feelings), gracious dialogue that undermines internal conflict and promotes internal integration, delight in another, ideally no matter how broken, and increasingly successful pursuit of one another's good. Out of our experiences with the crucified and resurrected Christ of Scripture and our reciprocal experiences of the holy love of one another, we just might gradually "grow up . . . into Him who is the head, even Christ" (Eph 4:15).

Even so, we must confess that the reality of our churches differs consid-erably from the goals of Scripture. Taking a cue from Kierkegaard (Evans, 2009, pp. 39-40), we might view our churches (and ourselves) ironically. What absurdity and presumption for such imperfect communities as ours to claim to represent the perfect God in this world! And yet this too is part of God's glory, and accepting the paradox and the irony helps us along the way.

The Church to Come

The church is also an eschatological community (*eschatos*: "last," referring to the "last things")—a sign pointing ahead to the perfect city of God in the age to come. The bride of Christ—the church universal—will become ac-tually whole and holy at the time of her marriage to the Lamb (Eph 5:26; Rev 19:7-8), a community of supreme beauty (Rev 21:9-21), "having the glory of God" (Rev 21:11). Then there will be no more hindrances to receiving, par-ticipating in, and giving back God's holy love and sharing it with one another. There will be perfect internal integration and complete transparency—we will know fully as we have been fully known (1 Cor 13:12), and we will have the rest of eternity to grow in holy love with God and one another.

As a result, local churches now, at their best, are anticipations of that eternal community; at their worst, they make us long for it. In the meantime, they are missional, cities set on a hill (Mt 5:14), whose members penetrate and participate in all legitimate aspects of their cultures, loving their neighbors and inviting them to Christ so they too would become members of his body before the end.

SOME THERAPEUTIC IMPLICATIONS

Assembling Together Is Good for the Soul

"Magnify the LORD with me, and let us exalt His name together" (Ps 34:3). Therapy can happen in public worship settings in many ways unlike anywhere else. To begin with, being guided in worship by a church's liturgy and skilled ministers can draw one out of the narrow confines of one's private subjectivity to consider soul-healing realities that one needs but would not have occurred to oneself given the present state of one's soul. Public gatherings of the church create opportunities for a fresh perspective on God and experiences of him to break into our habits of thought and routines: an encouraging sight of God's beauty, gratitude for Christ, conviction for sin, the awareness of one's distance from God, the recognition of unresolved anxiety or bitterness, leading to a new awakening and resolve. Good preaching instructs about God, humans, and salvation; provides ethical and relational guidance; gives detailed applications of the gospel to everyday life and soul problems, and trains how to read the Bible for soul healing. Fundamentally, it is a public proclamation of the law and gospel of Christ that aids in self-examination and invites hearers to accept afresh that they are right with God in Christ, simply through believing God's promise (Paulson, 2011). Hymns and songs can cheer one's heart, move it to tears, and help people surrender their burdens.[19] The Lord's Supper is designed to remind us of our fallenness, Christ's love, and the gift of our union with him. Through the course of a well-designed service (and church calendar), members will have opportunity for praise, thanksgiving, lament, confession, forgiveness, encouragement, and celebration, providing weekly preventative therapy and implicitly training the saints how to practice their own Christian soul care.

Becoming a Better Community of Friends

Given that the members of every local church are still fallen, how can they grow more into a society of friends? To begin with, God's ongoing delight in those members in Christ (Zeph 3:17; Eph 1:7) provides the ground for the church's communal love, which is nothing other than a participation in and representation of his delight. But that representation is also a key part of God's doxological agenda for their healing. As church members celebrate God's goodness in one another and on behalf of Christ, by practicing mutual respect and affirmation, recognizing and practicing their gifts, challenging each other, yet overlooking and enduring each other's sins, weaknesses, and mistakes, they give each other new kinds of social experiences—which are also concrete experiences of the Spirit of Christ in one another. These experiences may help to resolve one's pathological relational patterns and negative emotion schemes more powerfully than worship and meditation alone, because of the greater neurological impact of interaction with embodied beings than an immaterial one, even God—who designed human life in this way! "Though sometimes the Spirit of God immediately comforts the soul, which is the sweetest, yet for the most part the 'Sun of righteousness that hath healing in his wings' (Mal 4:2) conveys the beams of his comfort by the help of others, in whom he will have much of our comfort to lie hid; . . . God often suspends comfort to us to drive us to make use of our Christian friends, by whom he purposes to do us good" (Sibbes, 1635/1973, p. 195).

Well-functioning churches offer a range of "social support," defined as "emotional, informational, and instrumental assistance" that we receive from others (Dunkel-Schetter & Bennett, 1990). Instrumental help refers to tangible support (e.g., money, physical assistance), informational help is knowledgeable advice, and emotional help consists of expressions of care and concern. Of special value, according to Sarason, Pierce, and Sarason (1990), is the communication of a sense of acceptance. Empirical evidence abounds showing that social support is related to positive physical and mental health outcomes (Leach, 2015; Uchino, 2004), and local churches are ideal "mediating institutions" for its provision (Berger & Neuhaus, 1976).[20] What distinguishes churches from other supportive cultural institutions is their basis in the gospel of Christ, which gives believers transcendent grounds for the acceptance of one another.

The therapeutic value of belonging to a community that seeks to cultivate genuine friendship is manifold. Such support can help to undermine a legalistic/perfectionist orientation that afflicts many Christians, especially in early adulthood. It can also help to resolve shame by means of face-to-face acceptance of one another (Rom 15:7). Research on "earned secure attachment" (Hesse, 2008) suggests that significant, long-term friendships in local churches might help repair deficits due to earlier unhealthy relationships. "There is a sweet sight of God in the face of a friend" (Sibbes, 1635/1973, p. 192). Believers are, ideally, "transitional objects" for one another with respect to God. "A ministry of healing which understands itself as the cure of souls in [a] christological sense is nothing less than the continuing of Christ's own ministry through our lives as the Spirit of Christ lives and works in us" (Anderson, 1982, p. 201).

Because of their finitude, weakness, and remaining sin, believers also need dialogue with others that involves mutual accountability and challenge. Therefore, churches that promote friendship might want to provide training in how to graciously challenge one another to be honest with their experiences, fight against immoral desires, lament and persevere in suffering, practice psychospiritual disciplines, forgive each other when called for, and so on. Gracious challenging is an art and takes practice and requires feedback (again, see Wachtel, 2011, for some remarkable creation-grace wisdom on this art).

How do churches become better communities of friends? In addition to drawing their members to their greatest communal good—the holy, loving God—Stump's (2012) model of love would suggest they need to encourage members to have regular "face time" together, where they practice being intentionally present with and attending to one another and sharing their thoughts, feelings, concerns, and stories with mutual acceptance and compassion (e.g., in small groups [requiring good leader training] and weekend seminars). Finally, church staffing and programming reflect and communicate a church's priorities. Churches serious about cultivating genuine friendships will structure opportunities for them to develop naturally and hire someone to oversee their soul care and spiritual formation ministries if they can afford it.

A Continuum of Care Within the Local Christian Community

While local churches have a special role to play in the soul healing of God's people, few churches can do everything. Next we will consider the range of soul-care services that a decent-sized and equipped Christian community of churches can provide in a local region.

Pastoral leadership. God established the office of pastor (Eph 4:11; also called overseer [Acts 20:28; 1 Tim 3:1-7] and elder [1 Tim 5:17]) to guide local congregations into increasing conformity to Christ and soul healing in his name. Of course, denominations disagree about such matters. This description represents a "congregational" understanding. From the church's beginning this office was associated with being a "shepherd of souls" (Acts 20:28; Heb 13:17; the Greek word for "pastor"—*poimēn*—means "shepherd"), and later a "physician of souls" (Gregory of Nazianzus, 1996). Much of pastoral work is concerned with promoting the psychospiritual well-being of God's people, whether preaching, visiting, administering the ordinances, or conducting weddings or funerals, in addition to the most obvious soul-care task of counseling. Even in contemporary Western culture, where the mental health field has become radically secularized, pastors are still often the first one called when someone has a mental health crisis (Stanford & Philpott, 2011). The most valuable pastors conduct all their ministerial duties mindful of their therapeutic significance. Some pastors nowadays sadly see their role as more of a teacher, motivational speaker, or CEO than a shepherd of souls.

Nevertheless, pastors are charged with leading and guiding God's people into psychospiritual maturation in Christ (Eph 4:11-16). As a result, their responsibilities include reflecting on the soul-care significance of all they do and making a soul-care agenda a high priority in the life of their church. This can be communicated in many ways, such as praying publicly (sensitively) regarding general mental health issues; having a "Mental Health Sunday"; bringing in speakers and holding seminars on common soul-care topics such as depression, anxiety, and addiction; and organizing the church so as to facilitate as much soul care *in house* as possible (e.g., in small groups). In addition, most ministers should probably do some one-on-one counseling every week. If they do, they will generally practice what today is called "biblical counseling"—soul care that works primarily with biblical teachings—since they are trained in the Bible, God's soul-care guidebook, containing the "first principles" of Christian soul care (2 Tim 3:15-17). Ideally, pastors will embrace a progressive form of biblical counseling that is critical of secularism but open to valid empirical research, interpreted Christianly (see materials by the faculty of the Christian Counseling and Educational Foundation; MacDonald, Kellemen, & Viars, 2013; Kellemen, 2014). Even so, this will usually mean that most pastors will need more counseling training than they get in a typical seminary program. Some of the most gifted should consider spending extra time developing their counseling skills and perhaps becoming more broadly educated in soul-care matters, following the example of Richard Baxter (1981; 1990).

Complicating their work immeasurably, pastors (and their families) are often put on pedestals and expected to be idealized representations of the members of their congregation—and so without flaws. This can create strong psychosocial pressures, strengthening previously learned defenses, which can make it difficult for them to be honest with themselves and with the church about their remaining sin, and even their suffering and biopsychosocial damage. This undoubtedly contributes to much pastoral frustration and burnout.

Such perfectionistic dynamics actually inhibit the self-awareness necessary for genuine Christian maturation, setting up in many churches a tragic, reciprocal pattern in which self-ignorance ends up being implicitly reinforced, inauthenticity becomes normative, and mere outward performance the goal. Because leaders cannot take others further than they have gone, such churches will tend to plateau psychospiritually, and otherwise good substitutes for genuine maturity will take precedence (e.g., Bible knowledge, good works, tongues). Consequently, pastors will need encouragement from their peers, and ideally from the church's lay leadership, to maintain an openness to fresh experiences of Christ and wise self-disclosure and transparency.

Additional soul-care staff. Larger churches are also able to hire additional skilled personnel whose main responsibility is counseling or spiritual direction,[21] and who may also be the primary overseer of other kinds of soul-care activity at the church (such as small group leader training, lay counseling, or marriage mentoring). There are healthy differences of opinion in the field regarding the relationship between church-based and professional counseling; for example, some caution churches not to hire licensed counselors to avoid the perceived liability associated with licensure, and instead to simply refer out to Christian mental health professionals (MHPs such as counselors, psychotherpists, physicians, and psychiatrists) (Hannaford, 2009). On the other hand, some churches employ MHPs to offer a level of therapeutic expertise to Christians beyond that of the typical pastoral staff member, to provide the greatest range of Christ-centered soul-care services within the oversight of the pastoral leadership. Whichever path a church takes, the key is finding God-centered licensed counselors who are as well informed about the therapeutic resources of the Christian faith as they are about the contemporary science of human beings and able to interpret the latter according to the former.

Every-member ministry. In addition, New Testament teaching (and the book of Proverbs) suggests that Christian maturation in the church involves every member becoming better equipped to be a spiritual friend to one another (Eph 4:12-16; Kellemen, 2016). Though not everyone in a church is gifted for counseling, small groups of various kinds provide regular opportunities for members to practice love and basic counseling skills, and engage in "troubles talk," that is, "conversations in which individuals talk about problems, from the hassles of daily life to the major life events that pose stressful challenges, threats, or losses" (Goldsmith, 2004, p. 4). Different philosophies of ministry dictate the kinds of small groups churches develop, from teaching to evangelism to social support, but the healthiest churches strive to find a balance between inreach and outreach, knowing that ministry outward is best fueled by the mutual love of its brothers and sisters.

Churches with the appropriate resources may also elect to train lay counselors to help people with relatively basic psychospiritual problems through biblical counseling and social support, as well as to provide such help for any who would benefit (Kellemen, 2012; Tan & Scalise, 2016). Mentoring programs provide similar structure to enable wiser, experienced laypersons to help those earlier on the journey.

Local-church soul care for the local region. Many megachurches offer the widest range of psychological services available at one site within a region, from one-to-one counseling to gender-based and age-graded ministries to small groups that address all kinds of problems. Such churches provide their communities with a remarkable array of explicit soul-care resources, mostly for free, that sadly are going largely unrecognized within the field of community mental health.[22] But even medium-sized churches can make their counseling resources available to the surrounding community, as well as offering special seminars periodically on topics such as marriage, child rearing, and various mental health topics. Churches are also ideal places to help educate and provide guidelines for the Christian community (and others) regarding the wise use of psychotropic medication and when to refer to a professional counselor or physician.

Referral outside the local church. Well-trained ministers are usually the best qualified to deal with most ethical and spiritual problems, such as significant moral failures, spiritual struggles, and assurance, as well as many, if not most, psychospiritual problems, such as shame and guilt; grief; mild depression, anxiety, and addiction; stress; and marriage, family, and relational difficulties until they prove to be more severe than originally thought. However, most ministers do not have the time to address such problems long term, to say nothing of more complex kinds of psychopathology, which are often rooted in biological and developmental issues—such as schizophrenia, bipolar disorder, personality disorders, eating disorders, severe trauma, moderate to severe depression and anxiety, dissociative disorders, and severe addictions—since the complexity of their treatment needs often transcends the knowledge and counseling expertise of those trained primarily in biblical exposition and preaching. As a result, the best care for such conditions usually requires the help of others with more advanced training in counseling or medicine.

Nevertheless, because of their unique location on the front lines of the mental health field (Stanford & Philpott, 2011), ministers have opportunities regularly to perform three critical, soul-care tasks: (1) evaluation, requiring a basic understanding of the various kinds of psychopathology; (2) triage, determining the severity of the problem; and (3) referral, making a recommendation regarding who to see for this problem, if its treatment requires competencies beyond those of the minister (McMinn, Vogel, & Heyne, 2010). Some training in these tasks, therefore, is highly desirable.

Some Christians believe that such referral amounts to an abdication of ministerial responsibility or of the sufficiency of Christ or Scripture or the local church for soul healing. However, recognizing the limits of one's knowledge, training, and skill and the gifts of others in the body of Christ may be a mark of humility and wisdom, and pastors over the centuries have often happily collaborated with those with relevant expertise beyond their own.[23]

In a perfect world, ministers would be able to refer counselees with problems beyond their soul-care expertise to those whose counsel would be just as Christ-centered as theirs but who also have advanced training in neuroscience, human development and family systems, psychopathology diagnosis, and clinical techniques. Unfortunately, such professionals are currently rarer than we might wish. As a result, ministers might consider interviewing prospective referrals in their regions about how Christ fits into their therapy, as well as prayer, Scripture, and meditation; their favorite counseling authors; their training in psychology and theology; and their counseling specializations (e.g., eating disorders, trauma, personality disorders, children, and so on). Ministers could then develop a referral list that takes into account the Christ-centeredness and biblical understanding of the counselors in their area, along with their psychological sophistication and specializations, humbly acknowledging the challenges of being skilled in two disciplines (theology/spirituality and psychology/counseling) and being willing to work with those who are the best qualified to address specific problems. Moreover, ministers can continue to provide spiritual guidance to those they have to refer elsewhere for specialized care. Conversely, Christian MHPs ought to cultivate relationships with ministers in their area in order to build their practice and inform them about their expertise (McMinn & Dominguez, 2005). The need for greater collaboration within the body of Christ as well as for more dual-qualified counselors (both theologically and psychologically skilled) cannot be overstated!

Called to truth and holiness and love. In chapter three it was suggested that Christlikeness proceeds along three dimensions: holiness, love (agency in communion), and active receptivity. Because of their vocation (and probably their giftedness), pastors and theologians are those in the Christian community most likely to be the standard bearers for truth and holiness, encouraging a radical commitment to God and the gospel, distinctive service to God, and fidelity to orthodox teachings and ethical norms and practices that are particularly defining of Christianity. The Christian community needs such prophetic leaders who are well trained in the Bible and theology and who call us back, again and again, to God's grace and to purity of heart in Christ by the Spirit. Because of their vocation (and probably their giftedness), MHPs are those in the Christian community most likely to have the greatest understanding and expertise for working with the dynamics of the human soul and loving others in ways that promote their trust, self-exploration, and resolution of inner conflicts. The Christian community needs such compassionate leaders who have great capacity to accept others as they are, in spite of their brokenness and sin, who can recognize defensive activity, tolerate strong emotion (or no emotion) in others, interpret the nuances of emotion expression and the presence of unconscious dynamics due to early trauma, skills that can develop only after years of training, experience working with others, and, usually, self-understanding.

Sometimes these two groups of leaders are frustrated with and mistrustful of each other. However, their respective callings and expertise provide another example of how different members of Christ's body need each other and have gifts to be shared through mutual respect and dialogue. Yet to benefit from each other, members of each group have to recognize the giftedness of those in the other group. Let us pray that the Holy Spirit will bring many leaders in these groups together and unify their agendas in the twenty-first-century church. A noble outcome could be the formation of local and regional soul-care networks in which ministers and their churches, MHPs, and parachurch organizations (rescue missions, counseling and training centers, and residential programs) collaborate to offer a broad continuum of Christ-centered and Bible-based, psychologically sophisticated and compassionately guided soul-care services, addressing the widest range of psychospiritual problems possible.

Psychospiritual Variation Within Local Churches

If the measure of a culture is its care of its poor, the measure of a church is its care of its poor in spirit. We have seen that most churches are composed of believers who differ widely in their psychospiritual maturity. How this variability is dealt with illustrates a church's understanding of the Christian faith. The psychospiritual variation of the church is addressed frequently in the New Testament (e.g., Rom 14; 1 Cor 3:1-4; 8; Phil 3:15; 1 Thess 5:14; Heb 5:12-14). What if it is part of God's design to bring *these* different kinds of Christians together in the body, so that they might benefit one another? "The eye cannot say to the hand, 'I have no need of you.' . . . On the contrary, . . . the members of the body which seem to be weaker are necessary. . . . God has so composed the body . . . that there may be no division in the body, but that the members may have the same care for one another" (1 Cor 12:21-22, 24-25).

Yet one finds a sort of psychospiritual "caste system" in many churches, where the more "honorable" members (1 Cor 12:23) look down on the "weaker members" (with more visible psychosocial and ethicospiritual problems) who hide in shame (and struggle with envy). A little investigation, however, usually reveals that the weaker have often had fewer advantages in life, perhaps having been exposed to more childhood abuse or neglect than the more honorable. Conversely, the more honorable have tended to grow up in healthier families than the weaker, and suffered less in childhood, so that the success of their lives has more to do with God's grace than they are able to fully appreciate (at least in this life). Consequently, their advice to the weak, while technically true, can sometimes come across as superficial and shaming, possibly doing more harm than good.

In a gospel-saturated atmosphere where every believer is equal before God in Christ and has something to contribute to the life of the body, one wonders whether these two groups could also learn to value and benefit from the other. The weaker members could exemplify (and teach) transparency and vulnerability, taking risks to share their stories and struggles, while the more honorable could learn from their suffering and the evil of this world, from which they were comparatively spared, adding more wisdom and compassion to their goodness. Perhaps the more honorable could spend significant time with the weaker, bringing them into their lives, where possible, in substantial ways, loving and accepting them but also gently and compassionately mentoring them in self-reflection, emotion regulation, and social skills, without judgmentalism and with a care and patience that the weak have rarely experienced. This kind of reciprocal relating would enhance the Christiformitive salvation of both groups.

This will most likely occur in churches where growing psychospiritually is a highly valued good, wise authenticity and transparency are modeled and overtly encouraged, the stigmas associated with having psychospiritual problems and seeing a counselor are publicly challenged, and counseling is regularly advocated as a periodic "social spiritual discipline." More formally, regular liturgical confession communicates the truth that believers are still broken sinners, and periodic reference to various soul-care struggles in public prayer or sermons helps to normalize them. A good sign that such an atmosphere is being cultivated is that the weaker folks feel welcome.[24]

Viewing One's Church as a Mirror into One's Soul

Local church involvement also benefits believers by creating opportunities to gain insight into their psychological, relational, and spiritual dynamics. The church is a kind of social laboratory where we can learn about our strengths and weaknesses and practice and refine our gifts and skills, ideally within an environment of "no condemnation . . . in Christ" (Rom 8:1). For instance, how do I feel in relation to the rest of the church: Like I belong or like I am unwanted? And where is that coming from—the church or me (or both)? Do I engage with God in the worship service, or am I distracted and thinking about everything else under the sun? Does praising God make me feel joy or condemnation? Am I open to God speaking to me through the sermon or when fellow small group members share, or do I tend to be critical? Do I perceive other church members as forgiven saints, indwelt by the Holy Spirit, or as potential sinners, liable to mess up? At the end of a service, do I seek to meet new people, or do I leave quickly? What emotions do I feel as I am arriving or leaving the assembly, and why? Am I trying too hard to keep myself busy at church to avoid being with God or going deeper with others? Then, how hard am I on myself, when I realize I have such struggles? At the end of a service, do I look for others to connect with me, or do I reach out to connect with them, and either way, why? Am I able to apply the gospel to myself?

All of this has therapeutic potential, and our experiences at church can bring to light unresolved issues from our past, core beliefs about ourselves and others, or perhaps a gap between our God-concept and our actual God-image. Our local church, then, can create opportunities to process such dynamics redemptively and also help us understand and accept the other saints at church who struggle with some of the same things we do.

At the same time, how one feels at church usually has some basis in external reality too, and as already noted, human fallenness and brokenness of all kinds show up there. So believers ought not to assume that their negative experiences at a church originate entirely from themselves. The New Testament itself teaches us that churches can have significant psychosocial problems (e.g., the existence of cliques; 1 Cor 3:3-4), as well as spiritual. Churches can unwittingly convey an atmosphere of arrogance, xenophobia, perfectionism, or intellectualism. Pastoral leadership can be severely compromised by narcissism, defensiveness, passivity, or the domination of members (sometimes called "spiritual abuse"; Johnson & Van Vonderen, 2005), oblivious to how church problems may reflect the psychological deficits of the ministers. As a result, sometimes members may reluctantly determine that they can no longer remain at a church and serve well. Ideally, leaders and members would be characterized by an openness to feedback, from whatever source, so they might grow in self-understanding, humility, and wisdom and abuse become less likely.

The Role of the Church and Its Members in the Mental Health Field
The local church is in a very strategic location in the mental health field (Weaver, 1995). Consider the incalculable societal and mental health benefits—both preventative and supportive—provided by an average local church to its members: the pastor as an on-call, "first responder" crisis resource; free

counseling; a social support network; well-defined guidelines for living that prioritize love; material aid; and weekly meetings of celebration that focus people's attention on a good, loving, powerful God (Park & Slattery, 2013). There is currently no comparable organization or institution in most communities that addresses such a range of mental health needs (Franklin & Fong, 2011).

In addition, some churches are very intentional and deliberate about playing a more direct role as a mental-health "mediating institution" in their communities through the services they offer to the broader community. Such care might begin with an initial psychospiritual screening and triage[25] for those who come to the church seeking help, leading to a discussion of the best referral options available within the church and the community, ending with a more or less informed decision by the person seeking help (Runnels & Stauber, 2011). Such a process is obviously enhanced by the knowledge of local resources of the persons doing the screening (usually a minister) and their relationships with local MHPs. In addition, larger churches can offer to the public either free or fee-based Christ-centered counseling; seminars or special groups on disorders such as depression, schizophrenia, or sexual addiction; classes on practical topics such as parenting skills, budgeting, and marriage building, utilizing their own or local Christian MHPs; and sports activities and material help such as financial assistance, crisis housing, a food bank, a clothing closet, literacy classes, and basic car-maintenance services (sometimes called "mercy ministries," Keller, 1997).

Churches with the most expansive vision can set up, or at least participate in and contribute to, Christian rescue missions, women's shelters, pro-life clinics, or sheltered workshops and halfway houses for prisoners or those with mental illness. Networks of churches, of course, can also be formed to pool resources to meet regional needs. I am aware of one church that built a community center for their town, instead of a new sanctuary, with an indoor walking track, pool, disc-golf course, fitness center, meeting rooms for festive occasions, and a coffee shop, in addition to free biblical counseling services, classes of various kinds, sports leagues, and a residential treatment program for teenage and young adult women in a variety of situations. Local judges have been known to make this last program a voluntary option to those who are in trouble with the law and they think might benefit from this kind of support.[26]

Most local churches cannot build a community center, but churches and individual members can elect to work with many underserved and neglected populations in their region in Jesus' name—for example, the poor (in the inner city and rural areas), the homeless, the mentally or physically ill, prisoners, victims of sex trafficking, the elderly, or those with chemical dependency, either directly or through collaboration with and support of local parachurch organizations. In addition, many Christian therapists feel called to work within the public mental health system in a wide variety of ways, seeking to help people as Christians, most probably implicitly and some more explicitly, depending on their calling and the openness to Christianity at their place of employment.

God Loves the World Outside the Church

The life of Christ, the Word of God, is God's message to the world, that he loves the world and desires to forgive and heal all those who are alienated from him (Jn 3:16; 1 Tim 2:4; 4:10; 2 Pet 3:9). Christians believe that message is at the core of the most helpful therapeutic agenda on the planet. Whether working in the church or in public mental health, Christian therapists should have the right to share that message in session, because clients have the right to consider the psychospiritual benefits of the therapist's worldview as a part of their therapy, even if that worldview differs from some version of naturalism, so long as the client's therapy preferences are always respected. This pursuit of the counselee's ultimate therapeutic good is based, ultimately, on the relationship all counselees have to their Creator God and his desire to heal them from their sins and their damage and give them rest (Mt 11:28). At the same time, counselors working in public mental health facilities must be mindful of the current ethics standards in their field that continue to prohibit therapist initiation of such exploration, as well as the particular standards at one's workplace, and take into account the risks involved in sharing God's therapeutic program in such contexts. Eventually, it is hoped that there will be an increasing openness to worldview-based therapy in public mental health that will replace the current mandate of "worldview-neutral" therapy (which actually promotes secularism), so that Christian therapists (among others) are free to counsel according to all of their therapeutic values, wisely and considerately, just as good secular therapists are currently able to do.

RESOURCES FOR COUNSELORS AND COUNSELEES

Classic

Bonhoeffer, D. (1996). *Life together*. Minneapolis: Fortress.
Edwards, J. (1978). *Charity and its fruits*. Edinburgh: Banner of Truth Trust. (Original work published 1852)

Contemporary

Allison, G. R. (2012). *Sojourners and strangers: The doctrine of the church.* Wheaton, IL: Crossway. ‡

Baker, J. (2005). *Celebrate recovery: Leader's guide.* Grand Rapids, MI: Zondervan.

Burke, J. (2007). *No perfect people allowed: Creating a come-as-you-are culture in the church.* Grand Rapids, MI: Zondervan.

Crabb, L. (1997). *Connecting.* Waco, TX: Word.

——— (1999). *The safest place on earth.* Nashville, TN: Thomas Nelson.

Dever, M. E. (2005). *Nine marks of a healthy church.* Washington, DC: IX Marks. Strong emphasis on the theological and ethical dimensions of church life.

Franklin, C., & Fong, R. (Eds.). (2011). *The church leader's counseling resource book: A guide to mental health and social problems.* New York: Oxford University Press. ‡ An uneven but helpful initial resource for those interested in enhancing church involvement in mental health services.

Journal of Biblical Counseling. The premier resource for God-centered, local-church soul care. www.ccef.org.

Kellemen, R. W. (2011). *Equipping counselors for your church.* Phillipsburg, NJ: P&R.

Lane, T., & Tripp, P. (2012). *Relationships: A mess worth making.* Greensboro, NC: New Growth Press.

McMinn, M. R., & Dominquez, A. W. (Eds.). (2005). *Psychology and the church.* New York: Nova Science Publishers. ‡

Purves, A. (2004). *Reconstructing pastoral theology: A christological foundation.* Louisville, KY: Westminster John Knox. ‡

Scazzero, P. (2003). *The emotionally healthy church.* Grand Rapids, MI: Zondervan.

Thrall, B., McNicol, B., & Lynch, J. (2004). *True-faced: Trust God and others with who you really are.* Colorado Springs: NavPress.

Volf, M. (1998). *After our likeness: The church as the image of the Trinity.* Grand Rapids, MI: Eerdmans. ‡

Wachtel, P. L. (2011). *Therapeutic communication: Knowing what to say when* (2nd ed.). New York: Guilford. ‡ A secular book that communicates creation grace in a way that can teach believers how to communicate redemptive grace better.

Wilkerson, M. (2011). *Redemption.* Wheaton, IL: Crossway.

‡ Recommended more for counselors and pastors than for counselees

—17—

The Old-New Division
of the Christian

Principle 9: Conformity to Christ is the personal realization of the new creation through redemptive differentiation and integration in Christ by the Holy Spirit and faith.

For the flesh sets its desire against the Spirit,
and the Spirit against the flesh; for these are
in opposition to one another, so that you
may not do the things that you please.

GALATIANS 5:17

JOHN BUNYAN IS BEST KNOWN for writing *Pilgrim's Progress*, an allegory of a Christian's journey from conviction of sin to becoming a Christian, through various dangers and blessings, until he arrives at his final destination in heaven. But Bunyan later wrote another allegory—little read today—of the inner side of the pilgrim's progress, called *The Holy War*. Both books recognize that the road to the celestial city is not an easy one, even with the grace of God. *The Holy War* tells the story of the town of Mansoul, which falls under the control of the enemies of the king of the realm, headed up by Diabolos. The king's son, Emmanuel, lays siege to the town, eventually setting it free. A good third of the book focuses on overcoming the remaining resistance in the town to the king and the gradual transformation of the conscience, thinking, and feeling of the town.

Bunyan understood that every believer was in the midst of such a holy war, and Christian soul care is especially involved in this battle.

THE CAUSE OF THE CONFLICT IS CHRIST

What started this war? The answer to that question is explored in the four chapters that constitute the thematic center of this book. Christ in his life, death, resurrection, and exaltation initiated the new creation in the midst of a fallen old creation alienated from its Creator. Because of believers' mystical union with Christ, their stories—inwardly and relationally—are becoming analogies to Christ's story of conquest and victory.

We have seen that God is at war against all that is against him—any other stance would compromise his sovereign majesty and righteousness. However, God devised a plan that would best manifest his glory-love: the Father's sending of his Son to be condemned in human flesh (Rom 8:3) to put an end to human rebellion and turn the hearts of his image bearers back to him by uniting them to his Son through faith. By that means God destroyed the power of sin and overturned the rule of Satan (Col 2:15), and in his resurrection Christ began a new form of humanity (Rom 1:4). Now, by the gift of the Holy Spirit through faith, believers are enabled to follow Christ into the new creation, but because they are still "fleshly," that journey is hampered by many obstacles—biological, psychosocial, ethical, and spiritual (Johnson, 2007, chap. 16). Consequently, believers now experience a profound internal conflict, indicating that the new creation has begun in their hearts and that they are on the way of healing. "He Himself bore our sins in His body on the cross, so that we might die to sin and live to righteousness; for by His wounds you were healed" (1 Pet 2:24). Christ bore all of sin's shame and guilt in his flesh *for the purpose that* (*hina*) we would participate in and advance his continuing work of overcoming human sin and brokenness and bringing in the new creation—by his Spirit in union with him—*within our minds and hearts and lives and relationships.*

Christ the Word speaks judgment that exposes our sin and death and speaks resurrection by reinterpreting our created goodness, suffering, and weakness and creating new motives, thoughts, emotions, desires, identities, and stories. A two-edged sword comes out of Christ's mouth (Rev 1:16), a word of law and grace that is to go deep into our hearts, piercing "as far as the division of soul and spirit, of both joints and marrow, and able to judge the thoughts and intentions of the heart. And there is no creature hidden from His sight, but all things are open and laid bare to the eyes of Him with whom we have to do" (Heb 4:12-13). This leads to an internal division: "I am separated from the 'I' that I should be by a boundary which I am unable to cross. This boundary lies between me and myself, between the old 'I' and the new 'I.' . . . At this place I cannot stand alone. Here Christ stands, in the centre, between me and myself, between the old existence and the new" (Bonhoeffer, 1966, p. 61).

So, "all believers have, as it were, a double form—that of sin and that of grace" (Ames, 1629/1997, p. 170). Christ's work of redemption has created a division in the believer's heart and life, establishing a new reality within where God is supreme and is seen as supremely lovely, enabling believers to wage war on the desires of the flesh and to bring healing into their souls so that they can become more whole in Christ. "The new creation into which believers have been inserted, far from the end of strife, is the beginning of inner conflict, since the will that was once bound to sin and death is now liberated to pursue righteousness yet not free from the presence of sin" (Horton, 2007, p. 250). Our next task is to study the "great division" of the believer's soul, because a proper understanding of it is critical to making progress in Christian psychotherapy and counseling.

BIBLICAL TEACHING REGARDING THE DIVISION

"We have in us our risen Lord Jesus; we have in us the misery of the harm of Adam's falling and dying" (Julian of Norwich, 1998, p. 125). Over the centuries, few Christians have doubted the existence of a marked internal division within the Christian. However, for various reasons, this dominant position in the Christian tradition has received some criticism, particularly in the twentieth century. Consequently, in this chapter we will examine the biblical evidence very carefully before considering its therapeutic application in the two chapters to follow.

We could examine the narrative evidence in the Bible of an inner conflict in believers prior to Christ's resurrection. Just think of Abraham, Moses, Samson, David, and Peter. However, the Christian's internal dynamics could only be described after Pentecost, since that is when the indwelling Holy Spirit was given to all believers (Jn 7:37; Acts 2). The apostle Paul, as usual, was the most thorough biblical psychologist of this internal conflict, so we will concentrate on some key passages in his writings.[1]

The Flesh and the Spirit

We begin by examining Paul's contrast between the flesh and the Spirit. In the three passages where he deals with this contrast, we find significant differences in emphasis.

The flesh and Spirit fighting: Galatians 5. One of Paul's clearest passages regarding the ongoing internal conflict of the Christian is found in Galatians:

> Walk by the Spirit, and you will not carry out the desire of the flesh. For the flesh sets its desire against the Spirit, and the Spirit against the flesh; for these are in opposition to one another, so that you may not do the things that you please. . . . Now the deeds of the flesh are evident, which are: immorality, impurity, sensuality, idolatry, sorcery, enmities, strife, jealousy, outbursts of anger, disputes, dissensions, factions, envying, drunkenness, carousing, and things like these, of which I forewarn you, just as I have forewarned you, that those who practice such things will not inherit the kingdom of God. But the fruit of the Spirit is love, joy, peace, patience, kindness, goodness, faithfulness, gentleness, self-control. (Gal 5:16-17, 19-23)

Here Paul highlights the role of the Holy Spirit in this internal warfare. Without the Spirit, people are only "flesh." Paul taught that before becoming believers, we "lived in the lusts of our flesh, indulging the desires of the flesh and of the mind" (Eph 2:3; see Col 2:13). But now the Holy Spirit, who resides in the believer's body (1 Cor 6:9), has brought in an alternative motivational orientation, guiding the believer toward God, consisting of theocentric desires, emotions, thoughts, and action-dispositions. We ought to note that Paul does *not* point to the "goodness within" (as a secular humanist might) or even to the new self. His choice of terms emphasizes that God, and not the believer, is the ultimate source of Christian virtue and the resistance against the flesh. Believers have a role to play (after all, Paul just exhorted the Galatian Christians to walk by the Spirit and not the flesh, Gal 5:17), but it is fundamentally secondary, and grasping the hierarchical relationship between divine and human causation is paramount to Christian maturation (as we saw in chap. 4). As dependent co-agents with the Holy Spirit, believers become increasingly free by directing their energies to the sphere of the Spirit rather than the flesh, a process itself the work of the Spirit. But this passage suggests that believers are truly caught in the middle, as it were, being pushed and pulled by two opposing systems of desire.

That which opposes the Spirit is the flesh (*sarx*). Paul used that term here in a rather novel way (Dunn, 1998). Reminiscent of Plato's very dim view of the material world, in which the body is understood to be the prison of the soul, Paul selected the term *flesh*, rather than *sin* (for example), to describe that within that resists the Spirit. The choice indicates his recognition that the body does play a role in this spiritual conflict. Without God at the center of human life, natural, biological (and socially conditioned) motives become dominant, since there is nothing more influential in the system than prudent self-interest and perhaps some ethical considerations to restrain them. Without the Spirit's power, created human life is by nature thoroughly corrupt, so that even bodily desires now can become ultimate and lead us astray (O'Donovan, 1986). However, in the Spirit, believers have a measure of freedom they did not have before to subdue the natural desires of their bodies and subordinate them to God's desires. So, in contrast to Plato, the body can be redeemed (see Rom 6:19; 8:23; 1 Cor 6:9-11).

Significantly, Paul personifies the flesh. One can easily understand that the Spirit fights against the flesh, since the Spirit is a person. However, Paul here juxtaposes their activities, suggesting that from Paul's perspective the flesh in believers has some felt measure of autonomy, with its own intentions that are antagonistic to God's design. Such an analogy cannot be pressed too far. Paul is not suggesting the flesh is a distinct person like the Spirit, but his phenomenological description highlights the felt power of an indwelling, quasi-independent nexus of an antiglory/antiflourishing dynamic that behaves like a destructive parasite, pushing believers away from God and resisting his purposes, aptly describing fallen human nature.

Paul was also teaching us here that the Spirit and the flesh are in ongoing conflict in this age. "A great battle wages in the hearts of believers" (Schreiner, 2010, p. 343). The flesh "sets its desire against" (*epithymei kata*) or, more literally, "desires against" the Spirit, and the Spirit desires against the flesh. These two desire systems are "opposed to [*antikeitai*: withstand; lie opposite to] one another" (*allelois*). The "passions" or "desires" of the flesh (Gal 5:17, 24) are fundamentally contrary to those of the Spirit, having different motives and goals, "so that" (*hina*) believers do not always do what they consciously want to (Gal 5:17). It appears, then, that the desires of neither the flesh nor the Spirit will be fully realized during this "present evil age" (Gal 1:4; Schreiner, 2010, p. 344), teaching us that this conflict is "irreconcilable" (Ridderbos, 1956, p. 204) and will continue throughout the earthly lives of believers.

At the same time, God is right there in the middle of this conflict. The Holy Spirit is the member of the Trinity charged with being the divine warrior *within* the believer, fighting against the flesh with the word, the sword of the Spirit (Eph 6:17), and producing its own virtuous "fruit" (Gal 5:22-23). For believers there is a "necessity of having something in the soul above itself" (Sibbes, 1635/1973, p. 160). Personal faith that depends on the Holy Spirit's energy brings in the new creation. The Spirit therefore is especially implicated in the internalization and realization of Christ's death and resurrection and the growing of Christ's virtuous character. "Here Paul indicates in fairly stark terms that flesh and Spirit constitute two dimensions of the believer's present existence that is in the process of salvation" (Dunn, 1998, p. 481).[2]

"You are not in the flesh, but in the Spirit": Romans 8. Paul shed further light on the contrast between the flesh and the Spirit in Romans 8:4-13:

> [We] do not walk according to the flesh but according to the Spirit. For those who are according to the flesh set their minds on the things of the flesh, but those who are according to the Spirit, the things of the Spirit. For the mind set on the flesh is death, but the mind set on the Spirit is life and peace, because the mind set on the flesh is hostile toward God; for it does not subject itself to the law of God, for it is not even able to do so, and those who are in the flesh cannot please God.
>
> However, you are not in the flesh but in the Spirit, if indeed the Spirit of God dwells in you. But if anyone does not have the Spirit of Christ, he does not belong to Him. If Christ is in you, though the body is dead because of sin, yet the spirit is alive because of righteousness. But if the Spirit of Him who raised Jesus from the dead dwells in you, He who raised Christ Jesus from the dead will also give life to your mortal bodies through His Spirit who dwells in you.
>
> So then, brethren, we are under obligation, not to the flesh, to live according to the flesh—for if you are living according to the flesh, you must die; but if by the Spirit you are putting to death the deeds of the body, you will live.

Paul's contrast here between the flesh and the Spirit emphasizes the redemptive-historical transition that has occurred to all those in Christ because of all that God accomplished in him. As a result, believers are to regard themselves *fundamentally* as those who are "in the Spirit" and not "in the flesh."[3] Because of their union with Christ, believers have entered a radically new state of being, characterized by the Spirit's influence. The apostles varied in their denomination of this state: a new creation (2 Cor 5:17), a future era or eon, which has already begun (Heb 6:5), in which the true light is shining (1 Jn 2:8), a new realm or kingdom (Col 1:13), or a new community (Eph 1:23; 3:6; 5:30). But the most important feature of this state is the indwelling presence of God in the person of the Holy Spirit, given exclusively to believers (Dunn, 1998;

Vos, 1980). One at a time, through faith in Christ, the Holy Spirit frees people from a way of life dominated by sin and their autocentric desires (characterized as "hostility toward God," Jas 4:4) and delivers them into a whole new way of life, where God is being restored to a place of absolute preeminence. As a result, the new life in Christ has a redemptive-historical/cosmic/eschatological dimension that Paul called being "in the Spirit." "The *pneuma-sarx* antithesis, then, while it has important anthropological implications, is fundamentally a historical contrast" (Gaffin, 1978, p. 109).

However, Paul does not draw a sharp distinction between the redemptive-historical/cosmic and the anthropological/psychological. Rather, the former transition provides the basis of the psychological conflict going on in believers' souls. So, for example, in the context of the present passage, Paul reminded his readers that since the Spirit now indwells them (Rom 8:9), they must not live according to the flesh but by the Spirit must put to death "the deeds of the body" (Rom 8:13). So even in this passage, the holy war is clearly not over. There remains both an indicative/historical and an imperative/personal dimension to this ongoing transition, and the indicative/historical is the source, basis, and cause of the imperative/personal so that these two dimensions are actually inseparable (Dunn, 1998; Schreiner, 2001).

In fact, with Christ in heaven, the redemptive-historical/cosmic now generally advances *by means of* the anthropological/personal, that is, through the Spirit-empowered communal agency of believers. The Spirit's transforming work typically begins cognitively and consciously, then carditively, in the heart (that is, into the emotions and desires and inner recesses of the unconscious, a process that is incomplete as long as we are "in the body"), and outward into improving interpersonal and sociocultural relationships.

The practical import of Romans 8 is the news that the flesh and the Spirit are not equal forces in the Christian life. Now that believers are indwelt by the Spirit, the deepest and truest part of themselves is their new spiritual state of being in union with Christ. Believers therefore are able to define themselves fundamentally as members of the new creation, those who have entered into the realm of the Spirit, in spite of the evidence of remaining fleshliness. They have entered a new stage of their story and have been given a new identity. Indeed, their inner conflict proves they are now "in the Spirit."

"You are still fleshly": 1 Corinthians 3. Finally, the apostle Paul used similar language in 1 Corinthians 3:1-4 to describe what may be a developmental course in the Christian life:

And I, brethren, could not speak to you as to spiritual men, but as to men of flesh, as to infants in Christ. I gave you milk to drink, not solid food; for you were not yet able to receive it. Indeed, even now you are not yet able, for you are still fleshly. For since there is jealousy and strife among you, are you not fleshly, and are you not walking like mere men? For when one says, "I am of Paul," and another, "I am of Apollos," are you not mere men?

After discussing the wisdom that believers possess by the Spirit (1 Cor 2), the apostle turned to admonish the Corinthians for their divisiveness. Though they were spiritual brothers (1 Cor 3:1), their lives were still so char-acterized by the "deeds of the flesh" (Gal 5:19) that they could be charac-terized as "fleshly" persons (*sarkikoi*) whose divisiveness was so marked they were behaving as those who had no Spirit at all—as mere men. His remarks convey a developmental understanding of their problems: their "fleshliness" was due to their immaturity—they were still infants who needed milk; they had not matured to the point that their lives could be characterized as more thoroughly "spiritual." Even so, the admonition was based on the assumption that they were indwelt by the Holy Spirit (1 Cor 3:16), and since God is the source of all growth (1 Cor 3:6-9), they have the capacity to overcome this division within the church.

This passage suggests that Christians can be dominated by old patterns of living. At the same time, Paul later makes clear that Christians generally will not live in explicitly sinful patterns of life (such as adultery, homosexu-ality, drunkenness, and so on; 1 Cor 6:9-10), so there are limits to the "flesh-liness" that can characterize believers (indeed, in cases of unrepentance, they may even warrant church discipline for the purpose of restoration; 1 Cor 5). However, Paul's teaching here seems to suggest that Christians can get stuck in this "stage" throughout their life, a state signified by a divisive spirit. Apparently ignorance of one's redemptive-historical, internal division can lead to social division by its projection outward onto others.[4]

The "I" and the Law of Inner Sin in Romans 7

We turn next to discuss one of the most debated passages in the New Tes-tament. The exegetical problems are indeed complex (Moo, 1996; Schreiner, 1998), but the passage cannot be avoided, because its content bears directly on our considerations. Because of its length, the passage will not be written out here, so readers are asked to read Romans 7:1–8:2 before proceeding.

The context of this passage is crucial for determining its relevance for our purposes. In Romans 4 to Romans 6, Paul described many key features of the salvation obtained for believers by Christ. After discussing the Old Testament basis for justification by faith (Rom 4), Christ's role as the head of a new race of redeemed humanity (Rom 5), and the believer's union with Christ's death, burial, and resurrection (Rom 6:1-10), Paul begins to reflect on the inevitable impact of these realities on how believers live. Before going very far, he considers the role of God's law in the Christian life. While vigorously affirming its goodness (Rom 7:12), Paul points out that, apart from the Spirit, human nature was completely stymied by the law, because of how indwelling sin reacts to it.

"While we were in the flesh," Paul writes, "the sinful passions [*ta pathēmata tōn hamartiōn*] . . . were aroused by the Law" and were bearing fruit for death (Rom 7:5). Then, for the rest of the passage, in an unusual rhetorical move, Paul speaks autobiographically, saying that sin took "opportunity through the commandment," producing sin "in me" (Rom 7:8). I was once alive, he said; however, sin "killed me" through the law (Rom 7:11). In response to God's commandments, Paul found himself doing what he knew he shouldn't and not doing what he knew he should. He agreed with the law consciously—with his mind (Rom 7:23), "confessing that [it] is good" (Rom 7:16). But because he still did things with which he consciously did not agree, he argued that "no longer am I the one doing it, but sin which dwells in me" (Rom 7:17; see also Rom 7:20). Indeed, "nothing good dwells in me, that is, in my flesh" (Rom 7:18), Paul writes, recognizing that he was powerless to fulfill the law in himself, for "I cannot do what I want" (language very similar to Gal 5:17).

Paul concluded from this experiential evidence:

> I find then the principle [law: *nomon*] that evil is present in me, the one who wants to do good. For I joyfully concur with the law [*nomō*] of God in the inner man, but I see a different law [*heteron nomon*] in the members of my body, waging war against the law of my mind [*tō nomō tou noos*] and making me a prisoner of the law of sin [*tō nomō tēs hamartias*] which is in my members. Wretched man that I am! Who will set me free from the body of this death? Thanks be to God through Jesus Christ our Lord! (Rom 7:21-25)[5]

Many have wondered whether Paul was referring to fallen humanity in general or to his own personal experience, and if to the latter, before or after he became a Christian. But those questions miss the main point of the passage (Moo, 1996). The overall context indicates that Paul's theme was the "fleshliness" and powerlessness of *all* humanity, including Christians, before

God's law.[6] Apart from Christ, humanity is doomed, since the law at best only incites disobedience in us sinners rather than leading to conformity (if we could really see what was going on in our hearts, contrary to our conscious self-assessment). Paul was using his own experience to teach that all human beings—on their own, independent of Christ's redemption—are unable to obey God's law (Schreiner, 1998).[7]

Paul reports here of a marked distinction between two aspects of himself that he still experienced: the good within (e.g., the law of one's mind, Rom 7:23) and the sin within (the evil present in me, Rom 7:21; the law of sin, Rom 7:23, 25), a duality that applies to non-Christians as well as Christians. For non-Christians, the good within is the created law of God written on everyone's heart (Rom 2:12-13); for Christians, in addition to the created law, the good within includes the virtue of the Spirit (see Jn 16:8; Gal 5:22-23; Eph 4:30). So this passage teaches that humans cannot rescue themselves—"Who will set me free from the body of this death?" (Rom 7:24)—because we all have a principle of sin or evil within us that seeks to kill us, which we are powerless to resist in ourselves, though it can be overcome through Christ (Rom 7:25). Following Paul, believers will continue to recognize their native fleshiness and cry out for deliverance and in thanksgiving throughout their lives.

In addition, Paul made some significant observations in this passage regarding the evil aspect of human beings, which he termed here "sin": (1) it indwells humans and so differs from a sin *deed*; (2) sin works in "the flesh" (Rom 7:18) or "the members of my body" (Rom 7:23); (3) it is personified—referred to as a power that operates independently of Paul's self (Rom 7:17, 22); it fights against his better inclinations and is antagonistic to his well-being; (4) sin's power enslaves him to its agenda; (5) sin is a "law" (*nomos*), a principle, authority, or orientation, analogous in some way to the law of God that Paul served consciously (Rom 7:25); (6) yet that law surprisingly utilizes *God's* law to oppress and destroy (Rom 7:5, 8-13); (7) sin can be differentiated from the created and redeemed "I" (Rom 7:17-18, 20); and (8) it is only overcome through the salvation found in Jesus Christ (Rom 7:24-25), in whom there is no condemnation (Rom 8:1).

While Paul makes clear before and after this passage that believers have resources in Christ to resist sin that are unavailable outside Christ, they are still susceptible to the destructive law of sin common to humanity. Cranfield (1985) observes:

When Christians fail to take account of the fact that they (and all their fellow-Christians also) are still slaves under sin's power they are especially dangerous both to others and to themselves, because they are self-deceived. . . . [Their] very best acts and activities are disfigured by the egotism which is still powerful within [them]—and no less evil because it is often more subtly disguised than formerly. (p. 165)

This, the holy war of the Christian, according to Romans 7. We next consider the division from the standpoint of the self, hinted at by Paul in just a few brief but related passages.

The Old Self and New Self

In chapters thirteen and fourteen, we discussed the death of the old self and the creation of the new self in relation to Christ's crucifixion and resurrection, respectively. We saw that the old self is the believer *considered as a sinner*—an autocentric person who lives psychologically independent from God[8] (whether consciously or unconsciously), who was crucified with Christ, whereas the new self is the believer *considered as a saint*—a theocentric person made alive in Christ and living in dependent communion with God. We also saw that the new self can be considered the image of Christ into which the Christian is being formed inwardly and outwardly. In what follows, we will take a close look at the sharp contrast the apostle Paul drew, for the sake of Christian practice, between these two fundamental aspects of the Christian self in a couple of parallel passages.

Colossians 3:9-10. In the first half of Colossians Paul presents some foundational truths about Christ and salvation, whereas in the last half, he challenges the Colossians to live out their implications. After encouraging the Colossians to set their minds on Christ in heaven, where their life is hidden (Col 3:5), he exhorted them to put to death vices incompatible with their eternal life. "Do not lie to one another," he wrote in Colossians 3, "since you laid aside [*apekdysamenoi*; aorist middle participle] the old self [*ton palaion anthrōpon*; lit. "old man"] with its evil practices, and have put on [*endysamenoi*; aorist middle participle] the new self [*neon (anthrōpon* implied); lit. "new man"[9]] who is being renewed [*anakainoumenon*; present passive participle] to a true knowledge [*epignōsin*] according to the image of the One who created [*ktisantos*; an aorist active participle] him" (Col 3:9-10).

Ephesians 4:20, 22-24. The letter to the Ephesians has a similar structure to Colossians as well as a number of analogous passages, such as the ones we are considering. After a remarkable discussion on the Christian way of life in the church, leading to reciprocal love in Christ (Eph 4:1-16, discussed in the previous chapter), Paul contrasts that with the Gentile way of life in the world, characterized by darkened understanding, sensuality, and greed. "But you did not learn Christ in this way, . . . that, in reference to your former manner of life, you lay aside [*apothesthai*; aorist middle infinitive] the old self, which is being corrupted [*phtheiromenon*, present passive participle] in accordance with the lusts of deceit [*apatēs*], and that you be renewed [*ananeousthai*; present passive infinitive], in the spirit [*tō pneumati*] of your mind [*noos*], and put on [*endysasthai*; aorist middle infinitive] the new self, which in the likeness of God has been created [*ktisthenta*; aorist passive participle] in righteousness and holiness of the truth [*alētheias*]" (Eph 4:20, 22-24).

Paul's language here implies the existence of two "individuals . . . identified either with the old or with the new order of existence," and that *at the same time* believers are fundamentally "new people who must become in practice what God has already made them" (O'Brien, 1999, p. 285). We learn further that both God and believers are concurrently involved in the fundamental transformation of believers from an old way of being to a new way of being.[10] The change originates in God's act of (new) creation (Col 3:10; Eph 4:24), sustained in an ongoing process of divinely caused renewing,[11] rooting all the desirable human activities ultimately in God's activity. However, the present verb form for the renewing underscores that it is a gradual and ongoing process (Best, 1998; O'Brien, 1999); though divinely caused, the renewal is temporal because of its correlation to human activity, which is affected by sin, suffering, and damage. The temporal point of reference for the two different verb forms for putting off the old self and putting on the new self (aorist participles in Colossians, infinitives in Ephesians) has to be determined by the context (Campbell, 2015).[12]

Both of these passages are based on the assumptions that the believer's internal division is based on Christ's life, death, resurrection, and exaltation, and that therefore the activity Paul is calling for involves our participation in the story of Christ, who has already died and been raised and is now acting on our behalf in his glorified humanity in heaven. Given that context, we should note the contrast between the two passages: Colossians teaches us that believers have already been brought into the realm of the new creation— they have put off the old and put on the new (Bruce, 1984; Moo, 2008; O'Brien, 2000). Ephesians instead emphasizes the need for believers to participate in that redemptive-historical transition in an ongoing way: continue to put off the old and put on the new (Arnold, 2010; Bruce, 1984; Lincoln,

1990; Thielman, 2010). This difference forms a redemptive-historical, asymmetrical dialectic that is basic to the Christian life and that makes the ongoing human activity dependent both on the prior divine accomplishment in Christ and in the believer and on the Spirit's ongoing enablement.

We also learn of the twofold nature of the renewal activity: negative (putting off) and positive (putting on). Its object is also twofold: an old self and a new self—as well as their corresponding set of action patterns—vices and virtues (which assumes their respective thinking, desiring, feeling, intending, acting, and relating to others) that were Paul's primary focus in the context of the passages we are examining; and back of it all, implicitly, "an old and a new order of existence" (O'Brien, 2000, p. 189), the fallen creation and the new creation.

Third, both passages strongly suggest that the ongoing renewal activities require much human effort—albeit only made possible by the Spirit—to resist one's predispositions, rooted as they are in one's fallen history.[13] There is a constructive irony, for example, in the extended series of imperatives in these sections to stop practicing patterns of living that were "old," "former," "in which you once walked," for if they were just "former," why the imperatives? Paul was addressing the perennial problem of all counseling: significant change takes time and effort to replace the old patterns of life stored in one's brain/soul with new patterns. So Paul's point was that "this renewal is a continuing process" (Ridderbos, 1975, p. 64).

Fourth, Paul's pedagogical priority here, as elsewhere (2 Cor 5:17; Gal 6:15), is to persuade believers that they are fundamentally identified with the new creation rather than the old because they are now in Christ. In light of that union, "believers can be exhorted to put off the old self that they no longer are and to put on the new self that they already are" (Lincoln, 1990, p. 291).

Also of note is Paul's focus of intervention on a renewal of "knowledge" (Col 3:10), "in the spirit of your mind" (Eph 4:23), "in . . . truth" (Eph 4:24). But we must be careful not to import modern intellectualism into the passages. His holistic Hebraic anthropology meant the renewal involves "a person's innermost being" (Lincoln, 1990, p. 287) and, I would add, *through one's consciousness*. The pattern for the renewal is the entire image of God in Christ—indeed, the form of Christ himself (2 Cor 3:18; Gal 4:19)—and believers participate in that renewal through a conscious, *experiential* knowledge and understanding of God in Christ, their salvation, others, and themselves given by the Spirit.

Paul, the apostolic psychologist par excellence, taught that, since the old self was crucified (Rom 6:6) and the new self has already been created in Christ (Eph 2:10), believers have been given the task to "actualize" this "redemptive-historical transition, effected in Christ's death and resurrection, that is working itself out in this process" (Ridderbos, 1975, p. 64). As a result, the new self "is not in its final state: it is in a state of becoming" (Moo, 2008, p. 269). The terms "old self" and "new self" pertain primarily to redemptive-historical/cosmic ages or orders of religious being, akin to "flesh" and "Spirit." But they also appear to refer to psychological dynamic structures that co-exist within the experience of believers, each implicitly with its own corresponding memories, thoughts, feelings, desires, and patterns of thinking, feeling, acting, and relating to others—and underlying neural architecture.

A surprising number of commentators and theologians argue against the notion that the old self and new self are psychological "parts," preferring to interpret them solely as redemptive-historical/cosmic categories.[14] But why limit their scope in that way? Could not a cosmic redemption include personal psychological transformation? Moreover, is that not precisely what Paul is suggesting in these passages by encouraging that believers put off and put on the respective old-self and new-self patterns of vice and virtue? The renewal process initiated by Christ's resurrection and carried out now by the indwelling Spirit involves an exchange of kingdoms/worlds/ages that believers are to receptively actualize, at least in part, by their internalization, appropriation, and participation in what Christ has done.

Contemporary self-theorists are in broad agreement that the normal adult self is actually multiple, consisting of a set of relatively distinct "sub-selves" that develop based on different experiences, contexts, and activity domains, unified by a single consciousness, and that this healthy multiplicity tends to increase throughout life (Harter, 2012; Robins, Tracy, & Trzes-niewski, 2008; Showers & Zeigler-Hill, 2003).[15] In these two passages, the apostle Paul has given us the seeds for a distinctly Christian theory of multiple selves and a twofold identity, grounded in redemptive history and union with Christ's death and resurrection/exaltation.

Love and Fear/Shame

We finish this section with two short passages written by different apostles on closely related topics. "For you have not received a spirit of slavery leading to fear again, but you have received a spirit of adoption as sons by which we cry out, 'Abba! Father!'" (Rom 8:15); and "There is no fear in love;

but perfect love casts out fear, because fear involves punishment, and the one who fears is not perfected in love" (1 Jn 4:18).

Both passages refer to fear, most likely before God, and though only John mentions judgment, that is probably implicit in both. We might suppose that behind this New Testament gospel realization is the awareness of the law's condemnation that has been removed by Christ, and back of everything is humankind's original fear, when Adam and Eve were ashamed and hid in the garden from God. So one may legitimately interpret the source of this fear to be humanity's primal and universal shame before God. Both apostles are alluding to a psychological/emotional orientation that can haunt the consciousness of believers, and both point to an alternative orientation that is curative.

The redemptive alternative that Paul highlights is relational and trinitarian, and it pertains to the believer's adoption into the family of God, in which the indwelling Spirit enables the believer to look and pray to the Father as a joint heir with the Son (Rom 8:17). John's relational emphasis is remarkably similar conceptually, yet lexically dissimilar, for he states that the triune God is love (1 Jn 4:8), and the Father who loved us sent the Son, who procured our needed propitiation (1 Jn 4:10) and gave us his Spirit (1 Jn 4:13). The perfect love of the triune God abiding in us enables us to cast fear out, so that wherever fear remains, John sensitively and therapeutically suggests, love has not yet attained its *telos*. Believers have access to two very different emotion orientations: one characterized by the autonomous affect of fear and bondage related to shame, and the other characterized by the relational affect of love and adoptive freedom, pervaded by communion with the triune God through the humanity of the Son.

Summary

The passages we examined above reveal that a radical rupture has occurred in human history and in the lives of believers in Christ. As we have seen, this far-reaching event can be approached in a few different ways. First is the *redemptive-historical/cosmic* perspective, according to which "the flesh" (Rom 8:5-9), "the world" (Jn 17:14, 16), and "domain of darkness" (Col 1:13) label the sphere of human (and satanic) alienation from God into which all humans are born (Eph 2:1-3; 1 Jn 5:19), along with the newer sphere of Christian existence, established by Christ, entered by faith, and designated by the phrases "in Christ," "in the Spirit," and "new creation" (2 Cor 5:17), as well as "the kingdom" (of God, Mt 12:28; of heaven, Mt 23:13; and of God's beloved Son, Col 1:13). Believers, consequently, exist in both spheres, though *ultimately* only in the second (Rom 8:9). As a result, their personal story is now also marked by this fundamental transition.[16]

In addition, the redemptive-historical/cosmic perspective leads also to a *social* perspective on the great division (Rom 8:5-16; Eph 2:2; Jn 17:14; Col 3:1-17). Because of faith in Christ, humanity is now composed of two fundamentally different people groups: those who are "of the world" and living "in the flesh," and those who are "in Christ" and living "in the Spirit," the latter having been altered forever by Christ's life, death, resurrection, and exaltation. This distinction formed the basis for Augustine's (1958) notion of the two cities. Everyone is born in the city of humanity, and God desires and made possible the migration of everyone still living there to the city of God (Ezek 18:23, 32; 33:11; 1 Tim 2:4; 2 Pet 3:9).

However, we might consider the *psychosocial* division that characterizes believers to be the most important perspective for directly therapeutic purposes, since it pertains to their understanding and experience of themselves and others, based on and derived from the redemptive-historical division created by Christ and fostered and supported by the social division. Most of the passages discussed above reflect primarily the psychosocial perspective (including Gal 5:16-24; 1 Cor 3:1-4; Rom 7; Col 3:1-11; and Eph 4:22-24). Though there are many valid ways to characterize a Christian personality theory, it is certainly a conflict model (Maddi, 1996). For the rest of this chapter and the next two, we will explore the implications of the psychological perspective on the division for Christian psychotherapy and counseling. Table 17.1 displays the major redemptive-historical categories.

Table 17.1.

THE OLD	THE NEW
Sin that indwells me (Rom 7:20, 21, 23)	Law of the mind (Rom 7:23, 25; creation)
Law of sin (Rom 7:23, 25)	Law of the Spirit of life (Rom 8:2, redemption)
Flesh (Gal 5:16-21; Rom 7:18, 25)	Indwelling Spirit (Gal 5:16-17, 22-23; Rom 8:11)
Old self (Rom 6:6; Col 3:9; Eph 4:22)	New self (Col 3:10; Eph 4:23-24)
The world (Jn 17:14)	In Christ, in the Spirit
Fear/shame, bondage, punishment	Love, the freedom of God's child, abiding in the communion of the triune God

SOME THERAPEUTIC IMPLICATIONS

One of the great challenges facing a Christian psychology is the elucidation of scientifically complex models of human experience and activity that are legitimate extensions of and elaborations on the seminal teachings of the Bible, on which they are based, since the authors of the Bible wrote in everyday discourse rather than scientific. Such a project is fraught with danger and difficulty. Yet Christian theology and much Christian philosophy are based on just this kind of work. If the Bible was inspired especially to aid Christians in their psychospiritual maturity (2 Tim 3:15-17), then few topics are more worthy of such development than the believer's internal conflict, particularly for the sake of Christian psychotherapy and counseling.

Distinguishing the Old-New Division

I will suggest in this chapter, and the following two, that a primary task of Christian psychotherapy and counseling is to help Christians recognize, foster, and come to terms with the redemptive-historical division within which they live and that they find within themselves.

The old-self system. Let us review and insert what we have seen regarding just the negative aspect of the division. In Romans 7 sin is described as a tyrannical, self-destructive principle, authority, or orientation—a *nomos* antagonistic to, yet activated by, the *nomos* of God—distinct from one's sense of self that nonetheless works within, preventing people from living according to their best intentions. The term *flesh* in Galatians 5 (along with "body of sin" [Rom 6:6] and "body of this death" [Rom 7:24], mentioned in Rom 8) underscores the embodied (and implicitly physiological) side of this inner orientation that resists the Spirit. Evidence of the believer's fallenness also shows up in a sense of bondage, fear, punishment, and shame. The most comprehensive term would seem to be the "old self." The apostle Paul taught that the old self was crucified (Rom 6:6) and on another occasion that he himself was crucified (Gal 2:20), suggesting that the old self involves the whole person. According to Dunn (1996), the term denotes "what belonged to life prior to faith in Christ" (p. 220); to O'Brien (1999) it means the "whole personality of a person when he is ruled by sin," the person's "whole way of life" (p. 328); and to Lincoln (1990), the person "under the dominion of this present age" (p. 287). Perhaps we could say that the old self refers to the whole person of believers viewed from the standpoint of their remaining fallenness, all that has not yet been integrated and resolved into one's union with Christ, including their bodies, minds, hearts, and social interactions, insofar as they are still living autonomously from God (whether consciously or unconsciously).

Altogether the above terms of fallenness offer a number of distinct perspectives on the "old" way of being in the world, an orientation that characterizes all believers in spite of their redemption. It refers to their remaining sinfulness and biopsychosocial damage, their current life and experience still "under the Law" (Gal 4:5) and not yet healed in Christ. This old-self system[17] begins with the pervasive, mostly unconscious, contamination of original sin, possibly shaped by early maltreatment, and pertains to all that has been stored in one's memory and grounded in corresponding neural architecture, according to the old orientation: episodes of one's life, one's thoughts, emotions, desires, attitudes, and sinful actions experienced before one knew Christ (or before one could process one's experiences *in Christ*), as well as the ongoing experience and practices of one's fallenness throughout one's life as a Christian.

We have seen that fallen action dispositions called vices are identified in Scripture with the flesh or old self. In addition, as discussed in chapter eleven, these vices are often woven together with damaged neurological and psychological dynamic structures. The old-self system therefore includes all the remaining sinfulness and disordered embodied, physiological, and psychosocial functioning of believers, for example, poor neurotransmitter processing and malformed neural networks experienced as overwhelming emotion schemes; extreme moodiness; severe self-criticism; dissociation; addictive patterns of acting and relating; affect phobia; false core beliefs; inner wounds; intergenerational patterns of sinful acting and relating; distorted self-representations, other-representations, and God representations; insecure attachment patterns, and so on, prior to their resolution in Christ. Finally, it includes all their goodness not yet surrendered consciously to Christ. ("Beware of the leaven of the Pharisees and Sadducees" [Mt 16:6]!)

In addition, the old-self system reflects, participates in, and contributes to the "old-world system," which transcends individual experience, permeating social relations and cultures, connected ultimately to the cosmic battle God is waging "against the rulers, against the powers, against the world forces of this darkness, against the spiritual forces of wickedness in the heavenly places" (Eph 6:12). Interpersonally, our old-self system engages with the fallenness of others, activating and being activated by their sin and brokenness. Growing up in the old-world system means we suffer and may develop biopsychosocial damage. This psychosocial, ethicospiritual complexity justifies the tendency for Christian psychotherapy and counseling to work generally with the whole person and address the counselee's entire way of being and relating, rather than approaching people mechanistically and atomistically by treating their problems solely as medical or just the result of faulty beliefs or behavior. While it is true that the old orientation is undermined therapeutically one belief (or affect or memory or action) at a time, believers are personal agents composed of a fundamentally interconnected system of beliefs, emotions, memories, actions, in relation with others, all of whom live in a fallen "order of existence" (Ridderbos, 1975, p. 66), so they need to be treated as whole persons and enlisted in the therapeutic process to whatever degree possible.

The new-self system. We next consider the nature of the new creation aspect of the great division. First, earlier in this chapter (and chap. 4) we learned that the indwelling Spirit has the preeminent role to play in the establishment of this new orientation: fighting against the flesh and undermining its resistance, and producing the virtuous fruit of the new life, including the spirit of adoption (Gal 5:17-23; Rom 8:15). Though absolutely distinct from the believer's new self, the Holy Spirit is ultimately the one who enables it to be actualized.

What is the new self? According to Lincoln (1990), it is "the person under the dominion of the new creation and its life" (p. 287). Based on our previous considerations, the new self refers to the whole person of believers viewed from the standpoint of their life in Christ under the Spirit's sway, including their bodies, minds, hearts, and social interactions, insofar as they are living in a dependent, loving relationship with the triune God, free from felt condemnation under the law.[18]

The new-self system, therefore, encompasses all the biopsychosocial dynamic structures of embodied believers—their old memories, beliefs, emotions, desires, action tendencies, relational style, and narrative—from well formed to damaged, that are being redeemed and transformed with respect to Christ (to the degree possible), as well as the new memories, beliefs, emotions, and action tendencies that are developed consciously in Christ by faith, all of it grounded on corresponding neural architecture. *Redemption brings the remaining good, created dynamic structures of believers to their proper fulfillment in Christ.* So the believer's new-self system is the interrelated, developing union of the first creation with the new creation. As a result, an important part of the personal task of redemptive renewal is seeing oneself as the good created/redeemed/*being*-redeemed person that one is, through union with Christ by the Spirit.

The term *new* ties the renewal project of the Christian self to the new creation (Meyer, 2009), underscoring that the believer's individual subjectivity is situated within divided interpersonal, cultural, and cosmic contexts and that their redemptive-historical transitions were established in eternity (2 Tim 1:9), prophesied for centuries, begun in human history in the accomplishments of the life, death, resurrection, and exaltation of Christ, and are being brought to ongoing fruition by the Spirit.

Living in Division

The divided quality of the redemptive-historical experience of believers runs through their entire lives: they live in two worlds and have two worlds within. However, more psychologically minded believers have tended to be especially aware of the internal. For example, "This twofold nature of man is so evident that some have thought that we had two souls" (Pascal, 1941, p. 132); and "We must conceive in a godly man, a double self, one which must be denied, the other which must deny; one that breeds all the disquiet, and another that stills what the other has raised" (Sibbes, 1635/1973, p. 103).[19] A growing awareness of this division within the person/self would seem to be necessary for Christian maturation.

To make sense of the division, however, believers are faced with a unique whole-part paradox. Are the two aspects of their soul two parts of one person or two wholes experienced sequentially? On the one hand, experienced believers have distinct memories, beliefs, desires, and emotions that reflect each orientation, grounded in corresponding neural networks. This reality can give one the sense of two different parts of oneself, with one's conscious mind (one's ego) mediating between them, seemingly free to choose which network of associations to activate at any given time. Yet the way consciousness works, these aspects are experienced as wholes, and biblical language often reflects that wholeness: "Let us . . . walk by the Spirit" (Gal 5:25); "I have been crucified . . . and it is no longer I who live" (Gal 2:20). From the latter vantage point, the two orientations are experienced as gestalts, alternately and discontinuously, as mutually exclusive wholes, either of which is fully "online" in the believer's consciousness for a certain period of time. Both of these perspectives would seem to capture something valid about the Christian's experience of the division.

The goal for the Christian, as we know, is to "walk in the Spirit," which entails focusing one's consciousness on God and "the things above," as much as possible, and living out of that awareness. Unfortunately, it is difficult to sustain such intentionality, since "our former connection [with the old man] brings us in frequent contact with him" (Kuyper, 1900, p. 483).[20] The old-self system seems to remain the default orientation. A wife, for example, may strongly desire to respond lovingly to a husband's habitual harshness only to react aggressively again at the next provocation, particularly when tired or stressed. A good way to approach this problem is to redefine the goal as a gradual transfer of consent from the old orientation to the new, based on one's perfection in Christ rather than the immediate attainment of a perfect state of Christ-centered consciousness (corresponding to God's law). Put another way, the goal should be a gradual, but realistically uneven, increase in the proportion of one's total psychospiritual resources influenced by the Spirit, over the course of one's life, so that more and more of the believer's memories, thinking, emotions, relationality, and narrative are becoming oriented to the new-creation life, resulting in corresponding changes in one's neural architecture and activity.

Creation structures developed under the old way of life will continue to serve the flesh until and to the degree they are self-consciously brought under the lordship of Christ and surrendered to him, and even then, it is a matter of degree, and there is often stagnation and regression. The new self is not pristine—just as Christ's resurrection body bore the marks of his crucifixion—since it includes biopsychosocial dynamic structures that were previously warped by fallenness but are now being brought into the believer's union with Christ experientially/neurologically.

At the same time, the division can be too much emphasized (though some will think it too late for this qualification!). Humans normally have a single consciousness, a relatively unified sense of self and identity, and substantial coherence and continuity in their narrative, and increasing integration is a goal of Christian maturity and so of Christian psychotherapy and counseling (as we will consider in chap. 19).

Moreover, believers need reminding that regardless of current experience, the old-self and new-self systems are not equally *valid*. The old system has been crucified, and the believer's life is now hid with Christ in God (Col 3:1-4). According to God's declarative word, believers are ultimately united to Christ. Their remaining fallenness is a penultimate reality, fundamentally subordinate to their relationship with the triune God (Bonhoeffer, 1955). Therefore, believers are not *ultimately* a divided self, but unified new creations, seated with Christ in heaven (in their *real self*), whose redemptive activity helps to bring about greater unity of purpose and purity of heart. Which aspect should be the focus of the attention of counselees at a given point in time will vary, depending on their most pressing needs. Those overwhelmed with their fallenness will need to focus far more on their perfection in Christ and the new self, whereas those in greater denial about their remaining fallenness may need help to attend more to identifying and owning their old self.

Might we liken the believer's situation to that of a dog owner? Mary has a dog named Bruno, but she has no confusion about who she is and who Bruno is, and is properly differentiated from her dog. However, she is responsible for all that she does and *also* for all that Bruno does. If Bruno escapes from her backyard and is found digging a big hole in the neighbor's yard, Mary will owe the neighbor an apology and may need to help repair the damage. Perhaps this bears an analogy to the believer, who is primarily a new self in Christ yet is still responsible for her old self (that dog!).

Splitting and the redemptive-historical division. Secular object-relations theorists have discovered a maladaptive kind of psychological division that is a result of exclusively created and fallen processes, including poor socialization, called *splitting* (Hamilton, 1988; St. Clair, 2000), and Christians need to distinguish that disunion from the redemptive-historical division outlined in the New Testament.

Fonagy, Gergely, Jurist, and Target (2002) define splitting as "the partial representation of the other (or the self)" (p. 364). It occurs for two created reasons: positive and negative affect are processed early on in distinct neural systems, and infants can only experience one affect—for example, pleasure or frustration—at a time because of their limited psychological capacities. Consequently, early mental representations of self and others come to be formed and elaborated, characterized by sharply distinct emotion schemes, either positive or negative, and their corresponding neural regions. The problem is these dichotomous socioemotional representations are oversimplified and polarized. As children grow, they naturally develop greater capacity to integrate more complex socioemotional representations and experiences. Parents assist this by mirroring and labeling their children's emotions as they interact, and soothing them when they are distressed. Such responses facilitate their children's understanding and acceptance of their polarized states of mind, which makes it easier for them later to be integrated.

Poorly skilled and self-absorbed parents, by contrast, are less likely to mirror and label their children's emotions, especially when the child is distressed, because their own negative-emotion states of mind tend to get activated, so they respond by either aggravating their children's negative emotion, causing a different one (as when a parent gets angry and the child becomes fearful), or discounting the emotion ("Stop crying. It's not that bad."). As a result, their children's negative socioemotional schemes will be strengthened by similar negative experiences, as well as sharply separated from positive schemes, so that the latter are not contaminated. Eventually, such children develop increasingly dissociated and polarized socioemotional states of mind. Chronic experiences of these kinds generally result in the development of the defense of splitting, in which one's experience of self and other are inflexibly split into different kinds of all-good or all-bad selves and others, paired in some form, resulting in adulthood in relatively rigid ways of feeling in relationship with others. Depending on the quality of one's typical interactions with one's early caregivers, splitting can occur in a variety of permutations, falling into basically four categories: self/good and other/good (everything is okay), self/bad and other/bad (everything is hopeless), self/good (judge or comforter) and other/bad (rejected or needy), or self/bad (rejected) and other/good (idealized judge/persecutor). "The great price to be paid for this defensive construction of social experience is, of course, the ensuing distortion of reality [in adulthood] and the generation of mistaken and maladaptive responses when actions are anticipated incorrectly based on the split representations of the [self and the] other's mind" (Fonagy, Gergely, Jurist, & Target, 2002, p. 365).

Christian splitting. The complexity of splitting is even greater within Christian models than those that arise from secular/naturalistic systems of interpretation, since the above dynamics are interpreted as creational damage related to humanity's alienation from God and one's fallenness. As a result, splitting in adult Christians lies within the sphere of the old self. While biblical authors did not describe these complex internal dynamics, they are known by an omniscient God, and implicit evidence of splitting is found throughout the Bible. The Pharisees provide perhaps the most glaring example, since they viewed themselves as all good and more obvious sinners as all bad. And the apostle Paul linked such dynamics to the flesh, teaching that its "works" consist of "enmities, strife, . . . disputes, dissensions, and factions" (Gal 5:20), implying that Christians still have a proneness to split the world into "us" versus "them," leading even to fights in the church over matters of faith (see 1 Cor 3)![21]

One of the greatest challenges Christians face is learning to recognize the "stolen" good that the old self uses to maintain itself. We have seen that the combination of primordial created goodness and sin inclines fallen humans to maintain an image of themselves as all good, though as sinners, this no longer holds. As a result, their created goodness now gets subverted by a fallen agenda, even corrupting the good things of Christianity. When created dispositions to avoid pain and maintain a strong all-good self-understanding are combined with the extraordinarily positive riches of salvation in Christ, human fallenness is given incomparable resources to disguise its agenda, making it extremely difficult for Christians to come to terms with their remaining fallenness and extremely likely that the more subtle forms of fallenness will be repressed, like self-righteousness.

These universal tendencies are only exacerbated by early relationships with caregivers who frequently shifted in their attitudes toward their children, one moment displaying hostility, the next care and concern, leading to dissociation that is strongly motivated to maintain itself, made even easier, paradoxically, by the antithesis between Christianity and "the world." Consequently, Christians who had parents characterized by inconsistent emotion regulation may find they have a strong tendency to view themselves or others unconsciously as all good or all bad, regardless of their explicit theology or self-awareness. One way this can manifest is in a conscious focusing of one's self-understanding only on one's union with Christ, while subtly ignoring and minimizing evidence of one's remaining sin and damage, and maintaining a subliminal awareness of one's badness but unconsciously projecting it onto others (family members, those outside the faith), leaving one with consciously good feelings about oneself. (For the record, over the course of my adulthood I have come to realize the pervasive presence of this dynamic in my life.) On the other hand, other believers who come from such families, particularly if the abuse was severe, may come to reject their created and redeemed goodness and maintain an all-bad view of themselves (and certain others), whether consciously or unconsciously, also regardless of their explicit theology.[22] Though seemingly opposite in symptoms, both extremes can perpetuate unconsciously a simplistic sense of oneself and the divine other, in the first case "God and I are both absolutely good," and in the second, "I'm absolutely bad, but at least God is absolutely good." They also both illustrate the differential complexity of the old self of believers operating quite unconsciously.

The Christian's true self and false self. One way to address the divided complexity of Christians is with the corollary concepts of the true self and the false self. Thomas Merton (1961a; 1961b), a gifted Cistercian monk, may have been the first to write about the Christian's true self and false self from the standpoint of union with Christ. Remarkably, roughly around the same time, Winnicott (1965), an important secular object-relations theorist, independently came up with a naturalistic model of the true self and false self concentrating on the early childhood dynamics that lead humans to lose touch with themselves and their actual experience.[23]

Winnicott recognized that parents who are relatively insensitive to their young children's needs and limited capacities can pressure them in various ways into conforming their behavior prematurely to their parent's expectations, causing their children to focus their young attention on the parent's emotions more than their own. This parenting strategy, while effective in the short term, promotes self-deception and a lack of emotion awareness in the long term and gives birth to the false self—a way of living that is more outer-directed and performance oriented than integral and authentic, squelching childhood spontaneity and initiative and leading eventually to adult relational patterns that feel vaguely deceptive to others and leave the individuals themselves feeling empty and disconnected.

Merton, by contrast, linked the false self ultimately to human alienation from God: "To say I was born in sin is to say I came into the world with a false self. I was born in a mask" (1961b, p. 33). The false self is the rejection of who God has called me to be, in his love and grace; it is an illusion used to conceal my nakedness and emptiness (p. 35; Vaden, 2015). Consequently, the false self is also part of the "old order of existence." As the child grows older, the shame and anxiety of God-alienation due to sin, combined with the despair caused by the perfect law of God written on the heart, intensify the fallen developmental dynamics, which Winnicott described, that become more elaborate and refined through our socialization.

The true self, Merton believed, is the person God knows and loves, including the person that God is calling into being—in relation to Christ—in light of his or her particularity. "The secret of my identity is hidden in the love and mercy of God" (Merton, 1961b, p. 35). One's true self, therefore, has not yet been fully realized.

The most comprehensive Christian model of the true self and false self will include developmental and theological aspects. The false self is a function both of sin and distorting developmental pressures. The true self known by God emerges on earth from the increasing fusion of *all* that one *actually* is (one's *actual* self in chap. 15)—a composite of one's old self (and its false selves) and new self (including one's to-be-realized created potential and creativity)—along with who one *really* is in Christ (one's *real* self): beloved by God, perfect and complete. Ideally, all these dynamics reciprocally lead to ever greater transparency, courage, and resolve to actualize the unique, created person one is in union with Christ's glorified humanity within the community of the church.

Only by tracing such complexity can adequate accounts be given of the conflicted nature of the church and its members on earth and of a realistic pathway for healing and maturation for which they may reasonably hope. Based on such a psychology, a Christian psychotherapy and counseling will seek to promote the redemptive differentiation of the fallen aspects of the soul from the genuinely good (both created and redemptive), and the proper integration of it all, in union with Christ (the summaries of which, it just so happens, we will be considering for the next two chapters).

RESOURCES FOR COUNSELORS AND COUNSELEES

Classic

Bunyan, J. *The holy war.* (Any edition)

———. *The pilgrim's progress.* (Any edition)

Calvin, J. (1960). *The institutes of the Christian religion.* Philadelphia: Westminster Press. See pp. 602-7, 688-89, 776-77, 805 for helpful, honest discussions of the problem of remaining sin in believers.

Merton, T. (1961). *The new man.* New York: Farrar, Straus, & Giroux.

Newton, J. (1960). *Letters of John Newton.* Edinburgh: Banner of Truth Trust. Newton was remarkably transparent regarding his inner life, especially in letters 22-25.

Owen, J. (1965). On the mortification of sin in believers; Remainders of indwelling sin in believers. In *The Works of John Owen* (Vol. 6, pp. 5-86; 152-322). Edinburgh: Banner of Truth Trust.

Sibbes, R. (1973). The soul's conflict with itself. In *Works of Richard Sibbes* (Vol. 1, pp. 119-294). Edinburgh: Banner of Truth.

Winnicott, D. W. (1965). Ego distortion in terms of true and false self. In *The maturational process and the facilitating environment* (pp. 146-52). New York: International Universities Press. ‡

Contemporary

Bland, E. (2009). The divided self: Courage and grace as agents of change. *Journal of Psychology and Christianity, 28*(4), 326-37.

Campbell, C. R. (2012). *Paul and union with Christ: An exegetical and theological study*. Grand Rapids, MI: Zondervan. ‡

DeGroat, C. (2016). *Wholeheartedness: Busyness, exhaustion, and healing the divided self*. Grand Rapids, MI: Eerdmans.

Ferguson, S. (1987). *John Owen on the Christian life*. Edinburgh: Banner of Truth Trust. ‡

Lloyd-Jones, D. M. (1973). *Romans—an exposition of chapter 6: The new man*. Grand Rapids, MI: Zondervan.

Lundgaard, K. (1998). *The enemy within: Straight talk about the power and defeat of sin*. Phillipsburg, NJ: P&R.

Plass, R., & Cofield, J. (2014). *The relational soul: Moving from false self to deep connection*. Downers Grove, IL: InterVarsity Press.

Seifrid, M. A. (2011). Romans 7: The voice of the law, the cry of lament, and the shout of thanksgiving. In T. L. Wilder (Ed.), *Perspectives on our struggle with sin: 3 views of Romans 7*. Nashville, TN: B & H.

Stump, E. (2010). *Wandering in darkness: Narrative and the problem of suffering*. New York: Oxford University Press. ‡ An overall excellent Christian philosophical discussion of the psychic division, particularly in chapter seven on "willed loneliness."

‡ Recommended more for counselors and pastors than for counselees

—18—

Redemptive Differentiation

Principle 9: Conformity to Christ is the personal realization of the new creation through redemptive differentiation and integration in Christ by the Holy Spirit and faith.

Consider yourselves to be dead to sin,
but alive to God in Christ Jesus.

ROMANS 6:11

In much wisdom there is much grief,
and increasing knowledge results in increasing pain.

ECCLESIASTES 1:18

The old man perishes day by day,
but in Christ the new man is renewed day by day.

T. F. TORRANCE, *ATONEMENT*

IN 1886 THE SCOTSMAN ROBERT LOUIS STEVENSON published a now-famous horror story about a relatively good man and scientist named Dr. Henry Jekyll who took an elixir that brought out an evil side of his person, which emerged fully formed as the violent, malevolent Mr. Edward Hyde.

Toward the end of the story, after discovering that Mr. Hyde has committed another murder, Dr. Jekyll comes to the conclusion that he is unable to control this evil personality he carries within him and that Mr. Hyde will eventually take over permanently, so he kills himself. Though Stevenson had long abandoned the Presbyterian faith of his youth, this novella, extremely popular in its day, reflected something of the ethically divided view of human beings with which he grew up, but without God and the Christian hope of redemption, so it ends tragically.

But the story is not far off the mark as an allegory of a biblical psychology of unredeemed humanity. Christians, as we saw in the previous chapter, have a similar inner conflict. The apostle James challenged his Christian readers: "Purify your hearts [*hagnisate kardias*], you double-minded [*dipsychoi*; lit. "two-souled"]" (Jas 4:8). Because of their union with Christ and the indwelling Holy Spirit, however, Christians have resources to do something about the division within their hearts. We consider next the process of "heart purification" believers can use to undermine the division. The first part of this therapeutic agenda (practiced throughout life) involves the *promotion* of the division, so that its features are better recognized, making it easier to address. We will call this *redemptive differentiation*.

DIFFERENTIATION DEFINED

The term *differentiation* is borrowed from developmental theory, usually paired with integration (see Hamilton, 1988; Harter, 2012; Kegan, 1982; Siegel, 2012; Werner, 1957). Differentiation is the individuation of related entities, whereas integration is their later, increasing interrelationship in a system. As a baby develops in utero, for example, its earliest form is a ball of undifferentiated cells (called a zygote). Genes in the cells begin to trigger protein production that causes the cells to become differentiated, some turning into bone cells, others into neurons, still others into muscle cells, and so on. As this process continues, the various types of cells become integrated with one another, working together within organs and within major body subsystems (skeletal, nervous, muscular, and so on), eventually working with one another within a coordinated system, resulting in a mature, well-integrated body. Similar stages occur in a child's psychological development, with the infant's soul largely undifferentiated, but developing gradually into a set of distinct systems: cognitive (evolving further into perceptual modalities, memory, reasoning, and so on), emotion (four basic emotions that increase to as many as twenty), action (and countless action tendencies), and many others, all of which become increasingly integrated, gradually forming a relatively unified person.

As social beings, humans also naturally differentiate themselves from other humans. Object relations theory suggests that within the first few months of infancy, children experience an undifferentiated social world in which they are one with their primary caregivers. Over the next three years or so, children typically form a relatively stable sense of self and other that are substantially differentiated, shaped by one's early relationships (Hamilton, 1988). Social differentiation and integration gradually increase reciprocally throughout childhood, until a spike in differentiation occurs in adolescence, when teens begin the process of leaving the nest by seeking greater psychosocial independence from their families. Later, again based on one's relational history, adults settle into a relatively stable configuration of self-other perception and relational style, exemplified especially in one's most important relationships (Titelman, 2015; Tyson & Tyson, 1990) (though adults vary considerably in the quality of that configuration).[1] A mark of mature personal agency is the capacity to pursue greater social differentiation and integration throughout life, which can be facilitated through therapy.

No human ever becomes completely differentiated and integrated psychologically or socially (at least in this life), because of finitude and sin. Perhaps only the uncreated, holy, and simple triune God can be fully differentiated and integrated, existing in three persons who know and love themselves and each other as one, absolutely, exhaustively, and eternally.

REDEMPTIVE DIFFERENTIATION EXPLAINED

Christians engage in another kind of differentiation, distinguished by its dependence on God's redemption in Christ and flowing from their union with him. But similar to psychological and social differentiation, it is realized through human activity. Christ himself taught, "He who loves his life [*psychē*] loses it, and he who hates his life in this world will keep it to life eternal" (Jn 12:25; cf. Lk 14:26-27). This drastic language points to a radical, gestalt-like reorientation in which believers "hate" their (old) life of autonomy from God and obtain a new life of communion with God.

The apostle Paul incorporated this teaching of Christ's into his own, tying it to his union with Christ's crucifixion, so that while he no longer lives, yet "the life which I now live in the flesh I live by faith in the Son of God" (Gal 2:20). Later in the same epistle he wrote that he was also crucified with Christ to the entire world, and the world to him (Gal 6:14), showing that this transition transcends individual subjectivity.

In Romans 6 Paul went into more detail about this ongoing death and life of faith. Because of their union with Christ's death and resurrection (Rom 6:4-10), he challenged the believers in Rome to

> consider [*logizesthe*] yourselves to be dead to sin, but alive to God in Christ Jesus. Therefore . . . present [*parastēsate*] yourselves to God as those alive from the dead, and your members as instruments of righteousness to God. For . . . you are . . . under grace. . . . Present your members as slaves to righteousness, resulting in sanctification. (Rom 6:11-14, 19)

Paul encouraged believers to further participate in their spiritual death and resurrection with Christ in two ways, first by "reckoning themselves" to be dead to sin and alive to God. Believers are to focus their cognitive and carditive resources consciously and continually on who they are in light of Christ's work, in order to promote its actualization in their lives. They are to think and feel about themselves in ways that actualize the old self's crucifixion and the new self's resurrection.

Second, believers are to "present [themselves] to God as those alive from the dead" (Rom 6:13) and the "members [of their body] as slaves to righteousness" (Rom 6:19). Roberts (2001) points out that the root word *paristēmi* meant "to present, yield, let rule, or let dwell" (which also resembles "surrender"), and he suggests it conveys a kind of "active passivity," that "believers should let themselves be carried in a certain direction rather than, or at least as much as, they should do anything positive" (p. 140). Moreover, "considering" participates psychologically in the eschatological transfer from old creation to new, while "presenting" enlists the body's participation through actions visible to others.

Paul advocated similar strategies in Colossians 3:1-3: "Therefore if you have been raised up with Christ, keep seeking the things above, where Christ is, seated at the right hand of God. Set your mind on the things above, not on the things that are on earth. For you have died and your life is hidden with Christ in God." Being united to Christ's death and resurrection, believers are now to set their minds (*phroneite*) on the "things above." Paul also directs believers to "put to death" (*nekrōsate*) the members of their bodies to sin (Col 3:5) and "lay aside" (*apothesthe*) sins (Col 3:8), since they have put off their old selves and put on their new selves (Col 3:9-10). To participate in Christ's resurrection now, they are told to "let the peace of Christ rule in your hearts" (Col 3:15) and "let the word of Christ richly dwell within you" (Col 3:16). Here, as in Romans, we learn that believers are to actualize an inner resurrection of their minds and hearts and an outer resurrection of their bodies—their tongues, faces, arms, and legs—so that external actions manifest internal renewal.

This sounds familiar. In the previous chapter, we examined the believer's responsibility to "put off the old self" and "put on the new self" (Eph 4:22-24), because they already have (Col 3:9-10). Many verbs were used by biblical authors to label aspects of redemptive differentiation (RD): *dying, hating, believing, considering, yielding, presenting, seeking, setting one's mind, laying aside, putting to death, putting off,* and *putting on.* All these actions, one way or another, foster Christian inwardness and outwardness (Johnson, 2007) that "recapitulate" Christ's death and resurrection internally, behaviorally, and relationally and are the means by which believers actualize Christ's healing of their souls.

SOME ADDITIONAL DISTINCTIVES OF REDEMPTIVE DIFFERENTIATION

Merton (1961a) remarked that the spiritual journey involves the development of one's "interior vision" (p. 18), and this surely applies to the therapeutic journey as well. To see well within, however, Christians need light: the light of the glory of God in the face of Jesus Christ (2 Cor 4:6). As believers open up their hearts by faith to Christ, the enlightening Word (Jn 1:9), the indwelling Spirit's outshining (*doxa*) of Christ's glory (Jn 16:14) casts an interior radiance that enables them to see, highlighting the glory already there, revealing hindrances to glory that need to be removed or repaired, and conveying new glory. God's glory gives an inward *clarity* necessary for Christian therapy (the Greek word *doxa* was sometimes translated *claritas* in medieval Latin; Scholl, 2009).

Interior vision also entails what Kierkegaard called "double reflection" or "second reflection" (1846/1992, p. 73; Evans, 2009).[2] Part of Christian maturity, according to Kierkegaard, involves the development of "the right emotions, the right kind of 'subjectivity'" (Evans, 2009, p. 163), including a right understanding of how one's "objective knowledge" pertains to oneself.[3] This is crucial regarding the knowledge of one's union with Christ.

We should also note the dialogical dimension of these activities. The Father began the differentiating conversation by speaking union with Christ to believers by the Holy Spirit. The indwelling Spirit then seeks to deepen the divide (Gal 5:17) by drawing believers into the trinitarian dialogue, teaching them how to listen to God using the law and gospel in Scripture to open their soul up to God's presence (Heb 4:12-13), and how to speak with God (see the Psalms and the prayers of Jesus), themselves (modeled in Ps 42; 103), and one another (Eph 4:11-16).

At this point, we might also remind ourselves of the distinction made in chapter seven between conscious/intentional/cognitive processing (head-level/explicit/intellectual knowledge—what I am aware I believe about God, self, others, and reality) and unconscious/automatic/carditive processing (heart- or gut-level/implicit/experiential knowledge and love—what I really, most deeply believe and feel about God, self, others, and reality). Early in the Christian life, redemptive differentiation (RD) tends to focus on the more easily identified aspects of human life, distinguishing, for example, between godly and sinful beliefs, attitudes, and conduct. However, the trajectory of the Bible (and so of Christian therapy) is heading toward the heart. As a result, RD eventually focuses more on the unconscious/carditive/characterological realm, addressing desires, emotions, the defenses, and self and relational dynamic structures.

Redemptive Differentiation and the Recapitulation of Christ's Story

As we have repeatedly noted, God has established a new creation "characterized by the steady reclaiming of individuals for an ever closer conformity to the risen Christ. In some sense the event of Christ's passion and resurrection has to be reenacted in believers until the renewal of the new age is complete" (Dunn, 1998, pp. 403-4).[4] We might say that the Christian life is a continuous eschatological conversion from the old creation that is passing away to the new creation to come, realized through two parallel activities of believers. Historically these processes have been called vivification and mortification. Vivification, according to Calvin (1559/1960), "comes to pass when the Spirit of God so imbues our souls, steeped in his holiness, with both new thoughts and feelings, that they can be rightly considered new" (p. 600). Mortification involves our being "violently slain by the sword of the Spirit and brought to nought," (p. 600) and includes a hatred of sin and "continual repentance" (pp. 614-15). "Both things happen to us by participation in Christ" (p. 600). However, as we have seen, the identification of believers with Christ's crucifixion pertains to their suffering and their weakness, as well as their sin. As a result, we will need a model of healing and recovery that incorporates suffering and weakness more explicitly into its agenda. So, alongside the mortification of sin, we will add the process of "surrender" to our understanding of the negative aspect of RD, that is, the surrender of one's suffering and biopsychosocial damage to the crucified Christ. Together, mortification and surrender will refer to the believer's cocrucifixion with Christ.

Christian psychotherapy and counseling, then, seeks to promote the recapitulation and suffusion of Christ's story throughout the believer's body and soul and every relationship. This happens by deeply consenting to what Christ has done with respect to me and all that I am, involving my behaviors, memories, core beliefs, emotions, attitudes, complex psychological dynamic structures (such as the inner critic, dissociated parts of one's personality), relational dynamic structures (attachment and self/object patterns), family relationships, work activities, and story, up to and including my religion and view of God (including God-concept and God-image).

Such conscious work on one's heart is necessarily a slow process, unfinalizable in this life. Discriminations have to be made between what is good and comes from God and what is a result of fallenness. With regard to the good, Christians need to discriminate between creational and redemptive goodness, and with regard to fallenness, among sin, suffering, and biopsychosocial damage.

In *Foundations*, chapter fourteen, these activities were categorized as aspects of self-examination. The relevant categories, slightly modified, are represented in figure 18.1.

The psychological phenomena of each of these quadrants require a different sort of faith response, depending on whether they originate from God's goodness, either creational

	UNITED TO CHRIST	PSYCHOPATHOLOGY
STRUCTURAL FEATURES	Creational Goodness	Suffering and damage
DIRECTIONAL DYNAMICS	Redemptive Goodness	Sinfulness

Figure 18.1. Internal dynamic structures

or redemptive, or are aspects of human psychopathology, either sin or suffering and damage. Faith re-visions everything according to union with Christ, so it seeks to put sin to death (mortification) and actively receive God's goodness (vivification). Of greatest complexity is the upper right quadrant, since both suffering and weakness are undesirable, but faith recognizes their relation to God's good creation and their redemptive potential. Consequently, part of the challenge of the Christian therapy process is changing our interpretation of them through surrender, so that they are "resurrected" and "transferred" from the right column to the left. Without engaging in some such process of redemptive differentiation and making these kinds of inner (and outer) discriminations, believers will live in some level of unresolved inner conflict and chaos and their old/false selves will likely exert more influence than they will be aware of, perhaps operating on the basis of defenses such as denial, rationalization, and overidentification with God and his perfection.

PROMOTING REDEMPTIVE DIFFERENTIATION

So, in keeping with the old-new division of believers resulting from their union especially with Christ's death and resurrection, redemptive differentiation (RD) proceeds in two directions: the believer's participation in Christ's resurrection, consisting of the development of the new self (vivification), and the believer's participation in Christ's crucifixion, consisting of the death of the old self (mortification) and the transformation of one's suffering and damage in Christ (through surrender).

Promoting Therapeutic Participation
in Christ's Resurrection

We have already considered the nature of the believer's new self in chapters fourteen and seventeen. Redemptive differentiation begins with God's word about the believer in Christ, its ultimate source, which initiates the bringing into being of the believer's new self by the Spirit and faith, a process termed "vivification." The new self is not an eternal ideal, existing only in heaven, but includes the created goodness and biopsychosocial damage of believers, insofar as they have been incorporated consciously into their union with Christ by faith. The resurrection of the new self of believers, therefore, is dependent on the reception of God's word about who one is in Christ (Johnson, 2007, chap. 16).

We saw in chapter fourteen that the new self has a dipolar nature. Because of union with Christ, believers (viewed in themselves) are no longer alive, but Christ lives in them (Gal 2:20). With the apostle Paul, they have experienced a radical "change of subject" (Ridderbos, 1975, p. 232). Paul obviously still had a self after his conversion that had temporal continuity with his preconversion self (1 Tim 1:13). However, it experienced a fundamental re-organization with respect to Christ, signified by a change of name—from Saul to Paul. He no longer had "confidence" in his religious accomplishments (Phil 3:4-7; in contrast to the Pharisee in Lk 18:11-12). He became a new person, with a self-understanding now so saturated with Christ that on occasion he spoke *only* of Christ with reference to himself.

And he is an apostolic role model (1 Cor 11:1). With Paul believers are invited to reconceive of themselves in Christ, using gifts/materials outside the boundaries of their own empirical self and its story and incorporating the holy and beloved characteristics of Christ and his story. Christ is now "the believer's confidence, goodness, righteousness, strength, love, and worth" (Johnson, 2000, p. 16). However, these features cannot benefit believers psychologically apart from their personal appropriation. As believers actively receive the Word, their new selves gradually get constructed and take shape: this process proceeds as believers consent to, participate in, and practice who God says they already are in Christ, the beloved of the Father.

This also means the new self has been brought forever into the trinitarian communion, whether or not the believer is consciously aware of it (chaps. 1–4). Nevertheless, the new self only grows by conscious reliance on and relationship with the triune God, enabled by the Spirit to hear and receive the constructive and affirming voices of the Trinity and others and distinguish them from the destructive voices of Satan, the world, previous abusers, and the old self. The new self of believers is given life through their knowing and experiencing the delight of the triune God, as they are in themselves, in spite of their sins and limitations; his desire for their well-being; his pursuit of reciprocal intimacy with them through mutual sharing of thoughts, emotions, desires, and stories; and his promotion of their internal integration, all of which also draws them further into the trinitarian communion.

The new self is the transformation of one's created self. Yet, in contrast to the original creation that was formed "out of nothing," the new self is grounded on and builds on (supervenes on) the now redeemed "created self" (the good, created dynamic structures of one's body/soul) that, though corrupted by original sin, has been developing throughout life, providing one's unique sense of who one is (including a sense of identity, continuity, narrative, and personal agency) (Johnson, 2007, chaps. 8–9). As we saw in chapter seven, the created self is that which most basically distinguishes an individual from all other persons and includes one's created strengths, weaknesses, and personality. It is the *who* that has a name and that God loves and seeks to redeem. One's new self is built upon and realized through the created infrastructure and narrative that gives it its particular form. Redemption based on union with Christ's death and resurrection, we might say, is the gradual raising by the Spirit of the created self from the deadness of its fallen existence and transforming it into a new self in Christ. Consequently, the building of the new self includes the grateful reception of all of one's created goodness from God, the reclaiming of one's story and bio-psychosocial damage, and the conscious incorporation of it all into one's new-self identity and way of life.

As discussed in chapter fourteen, new-self development entails faith, which with respect to that development includes active receptivity, acceptance, and ownership of one's created goodness (one's unique created being) and one's redemptive goodness (which all believers share in Christ), as well as the product of the dipolar collaboration of the created-redeemed self and the Holy Spirit, including the formation of new beliefs, episodic memories, desires, emotions schemes, imaginings, dispositions, and actions, leading to a new story—to the degree such material gets stored in one's memory and fixed in corresponding neural structures. Just like anything worthwhile, this therapeutic development process takes time and intentional activity, in this case, worship, prayer, Bible reading and meditation; contemplation; alone and with others; through relevant dialogue with other believers (including therapists) and involvement in local church services and ministry; at work and at leisure. By these means they form new, healthier psychological structures—analogous to those derived from relatively healthy parent relationships earlier in life—the process in adulthood is just much slower, in part because a self is already present and because the brain is less plastic than it was in childhood, much like second-language acquisition is slower. And this development, of course, is far from smooth and steady; everyone experiences periods of stagnation and regression, and some make more progress than others

The new self's dipolar relationship with God, in particular, is difficult to grasp and experience, especially for those with a poor relational history and borderline levels of self/other disorganization (PDM Task Force, 2006). On the other hand, such individuals have the most to gain from such a relationship, analogous to the healing possible in healthy human-human psychotherapy. Furthermore, as suggested in chapter six, it seems likely that skilled human relational therapy (i.e., with relatively accurate imaging of God) would interact positively with communion with the triune God, so that both horizontal and vertical relationships together would be most likely to facilitate earned security attachment status (Hesse, 2008; Granqvist & Kirkpatrick, 2008; though research is needed to document this interaction). The point here is that the new self is the locus of this tripolar, relational active receptivity.

Secular therapy has recently highlighted the role that acceptance of self and reality play in the healing process (Hayes, Strosahl, & Wilson, 2012; Linehan, 1993). Christianity just has its own version of acceptance, which Edwards called *consent*, based fundamentally on divine providence, Christ's redemption, and one's unique gifts and calling in Christ.

New-creation work: Strategic participation in Christ's resurrection. The following exercise provides an example of how counselees might be guided in homework during the week by their focusing on some aspect of who they are in Christ, to facilitate their participation in Christ's resurrection.

Step 1: Identifying God's goodness toward oneself. As part of their daily "soul-work" time, Christians can be "glory hunters," looking for evidence of their Father's love through the gifts, strengths, and blessings they have received from him (Voskamp, 2011), whether through creation or redemption. Perhaps depending on what is going on in one's life space or what one reads in one's devotions, one can take time each day to identify one created strength or one redemptive blessing in Christ.

Step 2: Reception of God's goodness in Christ. After believers have selected a creation strength or redemptive blessing to focus on, they can spend some time owning and identifying with that strength and meditatively incorporating it more deeply into their self-structure. However, as we have seen, such identification for Christians is dipolar, since all their strengths and blessings are derived ultimately from the Son of God, with whom they have been identified by God through union with him. Consequently, Christian ownership of a strength or blessing entails taking the time to trace it back to its source in him and building the sense of its dipolar connectedness through active receptivity.

Step 3: Thanksgiving. The verbal recognition of God's goodness in one's life is a common occurrence in the Psalms, and this points new-covenant believers to also take time to put into words their gratitude for the created goodness or redemptive blessing they are focusing on in their soul work for a given day. This can be done verbally or in writing, perhaps in a gratitude journal (Emmons, 2007). Such articulation can weave together verbalized understandings and positive emotional experiences of God's goodness into the new self, laying down increasingly elaborate "islands" of psychological structure on which the new self gets built and which can be integrated with the infrastructure of the created-redeemed self already realized.

Step 4: Celebration with Christ. To complete the foregoing exercise, one can imagine Christ's delighting over the particular created strength or redemptive blessing of focus. "He will rejoice over you with gladness, he will renew you in his love; he will exult over you with loud singing as on a day of festival" (Zeph 3:17-18 NRSV). More than human parents who delight in the traits and accomplishments of their children, God relishes the outshining of his glory being returned to him in love by his children. This is the end for which they were created and the end for which the Son of God came to save them. Believers consolidate the development of their new self as they take time to recognize and receive their God's enjoyment of them.

There are countless other strategic exercises by which believers can participate in Christ's resurrection and experientially differentiate their new self from their old, and it is part of the church's glory to use those that are available and to develop new ones.

Figure 18.2 presents a flow chart of therapeutic participation in the resurrection.

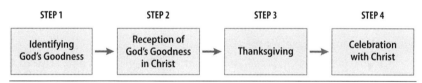

Figure 18.2. New-creation work

Promoting Therapeutic Participation in the Cross

We begin this next section by noting that the resurrection process of vivification is the basis for the crucifixion processes discussed below. In contrast to their temporal order in the life of Christ, there is an efficient priority of resurrection over crucifixion in that the participation of believers in Christ's crucifixion flows from the newness of life they have been given in Christ.

We recall from the previous chapter that the old self is the believer considered as a sinner, insofar as he or she lives autocentrically, psychologically independent from God (whether consciously or unconsciously), encompassing the believer's remaining sin. Just as one must clear away and pull out unwanted vegetation in order to cultivate a garden, the Christian must "put away" or "put to death" the old self in order to grow a new one. Suffering and biopsychosocial damage, by contrast, are forms of psychopathology that are the effects of fallenness on good, created dynamic structures. So, for example, the negative emotions associated with one's suffering and biopsychosocial damage are often valid and meaningful signs of life in a fallen world, and so are not intrinsically sinful and part of the old self. Therefore, they are not to be put to death; to do so would amount to a slash-and-burn approach to the Christian life that can do more harm to our created nature than good. Rather, they are to be redeemed. Nevertheless, negative emotions associated with suffering and weakness *are negative* and require some kind of process that "puts away" their negative effects. Let us consider, then, how believers' union with Christ's death can be used to "put away" or "distance" ourselves from all three kinds of psychopathology.

A number of terms, phrases, and concepts in the Bible label aspects of psychological distanciation: *confession* (Ps 32:5; 38:18; Jas 5:16; 1 Jn 1:9), *repentance* (Job 42:6; Ps 7:12; Mt 3:2; Acts 2:38; Rom 2:4; Rev 2:5; see also Calvin, 1559/1960; Colquhoun, 1826/1965), *denying one's self* (Mt 16:24; Lk 14:23; Calvin, 1559/1960), *carrying one's cross* (Mt 10:38; Lk 14:23), *losing one's life for Christ's sake* (Mt 10:39; Lk 14:24), *hating oneself*[5] (Jn 12:24-25), *mortification* (Rom 8:13; Col 3:5; see also John of the Cross, 1935; Calvin, 1559/1960; Owen, 1965, Vol. 6); *lament* (see Job; Ps 13; 22; 88; Lam); *yielding* (Rom 6:13); *cocrucifixion with Christ* (Rom 6:1-6; Gal 2:20; 6:14), and *laying aside the old self* (Eph 4:22). Paul also seemed to reflect a distanciation agenda when he referred to "the flesh" (rather than himself) that fights against the Spirit (Gal 5:17), and perhaps most strikingly, in Romans 7, where he stated that *he* no longer did the evil he did, but "sin which dwells in me" (Rom 7:17, 20).[6]

In addition, a family of related postbiblical terms emerged in the Christian tradition, for example, *detachment* (Thomas à Kempis, 2003; Tanquerey, 1930; John of the Cross, 1935; Merton, 1961b), *discrimination* and *dispassion* (Evagrios, 1979a), *purgation* (John of the Cross, 1935; Francis de Sales, 1619/1955), *renunciation* (Cassian, 1985; Merton, 1961b), *resignation* (Thomas à Kempis, 2003; John of the Cross, 1935), *surrender* (Caussade, 1861/1986; Smith, 1870/1952), *transparency* (Kierkegaard, 1849/1980), and *watchfulness* (Evagrios, 1979b).[7] Sometimes these terms were unfortunately used to help Christians distance themselves from legitimate created desires, such as marriage, for example, in the monastic traditions. However, they are quite apt for addressing suffering and biopsychosocial damage, fallen effects on the good human creation, as well as for sin.

Any precise ordering of these two families of overlapping terms/concepts is problematic, but to address all three aspects of psychopathology through the cross will require more than one category of treatment. Consequently, mortification and surrender will be used to distinguish two different kinds of distanciation, depending on the object, whether sin or suffering and damage.

Every complex soul-healing system has discovered strategies that are analogous, in some respects, to the Christian processes of mortification and surrender (e.g., see Hinduism, Buddhism, Stoicism). Over the past century, secular psychotherapy has developed some of its own. Psychoanalysis was originally thought to benefit people by bringing into conscious awareness the underlying, unconscious motives or reasons for one's thoughts and behavior, the simple understanding of which was thought to free one from the control of one's defenses and resolve one's inner, archaic conflicts. More recently, psychodynamic therapists have recognized that Freud's emphasis on rational understanding may have actually obscured the true value of his model (Wachtel, 2008). Today a variety of labels are used by secular therapists of different orientations for this distanciation process, including *exposure* (Wright, Basco, & Thase, 2006), *mentalization* (Fonagy, Gergely, Jurist, & Target, 2002), *mentalized affectivity* (Fonagy, 2006), *defusion* (Hayes, Strosahl, & Wilson, 2012), *mindfulness* (Linehan, 1993), *deactivation* (Young, Klosko, & Weishaar, 2003); *desensitization* and *expression* (McCullough et al., 2003), *symbolization* and *articulation* (Greenberg & Paivio, 1997), *"finding the right distance"* (Leijssen, 1998), and *disidentification* (Assagioli, 1965; Walsh & Shapiro, 2006). Christians of course are free to use these terms too, but they have to interpret them *Christianly* rather than *secularly*. However, most of the corresponding Christian terms and phrases are generally more reflective of the believer's union with Christ and his story.

What the classic Christian terms and their analogues in secular therapy share in common is their discovery of a therapeutic procedure that entails the conscious objectification of harmful and unwanted elements of one's inner life (e.g., thoughts, attitudes toward self and others, feelings, behaviors) in such a way that they lose their hold on oneself. The therapeutic goal of this reorientation is the conscious, internal distancing of oneself from one's harmful inner dynamics, without denial or dissociation. It entails recognizing that one's harmful inner dynamics are part of oneself but not absolutely, identifying them, and then personally disidentifying with them, so that one is no longer embedded in them psychologically and influenced by them unconsciously, freeing one from the sense that one's distorted perceptions of oneself and external reality are true.

As the Christian terms above indicate, however, the therapeutic shift in viewpoint toward one's psychopathology is understood quite differently from within a Christian worldview, particularly with respect to sin. Samuel Rutherford (1664/1984) illustrates the Christian stance: "I see there is a necessity that we protest against the doings of the Old Man, and raise up a party against our worst half, to accuse, condemn, sentence, and with sorrow bemoan, the dominion of sin's kingdom; and withal make law, in the New Covenant, against our guiltiness. For Christ once condemned sin in the flesh, and we are to condemn it over again" (p. 465). This denunciation of the old self reflects ethical and spiritual considerations—including an antagonistic evaluation—that are absent in the secular versions of distancing activity. Indeed, most naturalist and humanist therapists would probably be concerned that the strong evaluative tone of the Christian approach, reflected in Rutherford's quotation, would compromise the therapy process by activating shame and defenses and so hinder self-awareness. But this issue gets at the heart of the worldview differences between Christian and secular therapy. All experienced therapists are aware of the inhibiting role that shame plays in therapy. The question is, how is it best addressed for the long-term healing of counselees? Naturalism and humanism tend to treat ethical and spiritual deficits as simply the result of biology or poor socialization, so therapy resolution typically involves training counselees to distance themselves by developing a nonjudgmental stance toward them. Yet what if one feels guilt, for example, over sexually abusing a child? Such a stance, at its core, would seem to be, at least implicitly, at odds with contemporary ethics codes in the field, as well as the implications of secular psychological research on the phenomenon of evil (Baumeister, 1997; Miller, 2005).

By contrast, Christianity generally takes ethical and spiritual deficits more seriously, because they reflect a falling short of norms given by our Creator. In addition—and here is where Christian psychotherapy and counseling are most distinctive—Christianity teaches that their transcendent resolution has been provided by God in Christ. Consequently, for believers, Christian therapy is practiced within the dialectical paradox of "judgment resolved," attaining the same therapeutic end of "the resolution of shame and guilt" (Rom 8:1), but without minimizing or justifying our ethical and spiritual failings. At the same time, a sharp distinction is made in this book between sin and weakness/suffering. As we saw earlier, though all three fall short of God's design plan for human well-being, the later two aspects of psychopathology are to be understood as good-creation realities affected by the fall, and so fundamentally different from sin. Therefore, regarding the treatment of suffering and biopsychosocial damage, Christian and secular psychology have more in common than in the treatment of sin, though Christians assume a theistic universe with all three. Nonetheless, it is noteworthy that both the Christian and the secular psychology traditions have developed their own respective terms/concepts to help persons distance themselves from their psychopathology.

Cross work: Strategic participation in Christ's crucifixion. What follows is the other half of redemptive differentiation, a model to guide counselees through the personal appropriation of Christ's work on the cross, depending on the kind of psychopathological issue they are working on, using the process of surrender to address their suffering and damage and mortification to address their sin. There are a hundreds of ways to participate in the cross by faith. In this model the attention of believers is focused on their negative emotions as meaningful signs of fallenness that can be identified with Christ's work, because of their union with Christ. The following steps encourage persons to bring their negative emotions into their consciousness and working memory, where their emotional experience (desires and emotions) and related thoughts and attitudes can be processed, interpreted, disidentified with, and worked through redemptively, with Christ and in light of his story. Depending on the issue, the entire sequence could take as long as twenty to thirty minutes.

Step 1: Negative emotion awareness. As we saw in chapter eleven, emotions[8] are signs of evaluative meaning or significance (also Johnson, 2007, chap. 9); negative emotions are especially associated with our fallen condition—that which in one way or another is contrary to God's glory and our well-being. Because they can be stored in memory, they also serve as a record of our exposure to and experience of fallenness, and those emotion schemes can only be modified when they are being currently experienced. As a result, negative emotions drive believers to the healing of the cross, where Christ suffered and was crucified in weakness and for our sin.

Yet some negative emotions (guilt, anxiety, and especially shame) incline humans to hide, especially when they are intensified by poor socialization. As a result, fallen humans come to deny aspects of themselves, including their negative emotions. This can result in a "restricting, foreshortening, and fragmenting (that is, dissociating) of experience," so that, "certain things we 'know' do not really influence very much what we do or what we tell" (Wachtel, 2008, p. 143). Research has confirmed that "opening up" to one's emotions improves one's well-being (Niederhoffer & Pennebaker, 2002). This includes becoming aware of one's emotions, taking responsibility for them, and experiencing them in productive ways. This confirms the evidence found within the canon, where remarkable transparency with God regarding one's negative emotions is demonstrated in the Psalms, Job, and the Prophets. The modeling of such honesty in Scripture invites Christians to open up their hearts to God, themselves, and trustworthy friends, regardless of what comes up, and suggests that such transparent faith is integral to their salvation. Knowing they are loved by God and their deficits are resolved in Christ, believers have transcendent grounds to take such risks. As Kierkegaard (1849/1980) keenly grasped, "Faith is: that the self in being itself and in willing to be itself rests transparently in God" (p. 82). Such faith—and love—help resolve our shame and fear (1 Jn 4:18), enabling us to listen to the signs of our heart in order to uncover what may be hidden. As a result, the first step in strategic participation in the cross is simply to become aware of one's negative emotions and understand their meaning.

We saw that suffering causes negative emotions, which can be stored in memory, so the chronic presence of such emotions in adulthood is meaningful and valuable, invariably signifying suffering and possible biopsychosocial damage that occurred earlier in one's story. Their adult emergence is a function of a deep, created wisdom/law that brings them into consciousness, so that they can be addressed and purged. Therapists honor their counselees, their stories, and the created goodness at the core of their emotions by listening and helping them accurately interpret the meaning they convey. Good questions can help counselees identify emotions embedded in their experience that they were previously not aware of. Once the emotion is identified, skilled therapy seeks to evoke and accentuate emotional arousal to promote the fullest understanding possible (Greenberg & Paivio, 1997).

In addition, negative emotions may also reveal the old self, since much of its psychopathological structure developed in association with them. Shame and guilt, in particular, are of special semiotic value here, since if true from a divine perspective, they are signs of sin, and if false, at least of a *perceived* lack of wholeness (shame) or ethical violation (guilt). In addition, some negative emotional experience is sinful, for example, envy and bitterness. On the other hand, sometimes the problem is a lack of negative emotion where it should be present, for example, the absence of guilt after harshly criticizing someone.

Step 2: Negative emotion evaluation. As counselees become aware of their emotion, the next step is to determine whether the emotion itself is sinful or legitimate (and a function of suffering and damage). Secular therapy typically takes a different route at this point, for example, with mindfulness. However, Christian emotion evaluation is conducted *in Christ*, so in principle whatever one finds has already been resolved in him, thus there is no

ultimate reason to be afraid or ashamed (though, of course, being able to
accept this is part of the Christian therapy journey).

We have noted each negative emotion conveys a different kind of meaning.
Therefore, an emotion has to be explored to determine, as best as possible,
whether it is a function of sin or our created nature. Cultivating such discernment takes time and practice and benefits from grace and good questions, and can be helped by journaling.

We have seen that suffering and weakness are nonsinful deficits based in
creation that may lead to a number of negative emotions that are legitimate
responses to fallen experience and a result of growing up in a fallen world,
recorded in one's brain/soul. During this step counselees are encouraged to
accept the validity of those negative emotions in light of the cross. Often
counselees will need help allowing themselves to reexperience these emotions with God, because they are unpleasant, and they have usually been
avoided automatically, perhaps for decades.

Identifying sin can be extremely challenging, because it tends to hide
(chap. 8). Even sinful behaviors and thoughts can be difficult to recognize
because of our tendency to interpret them from a self-serving standpoint.
But the problem is even greater with more subtle old-self dynamics such as
sinful emotions and attitudes; lusts, vices, and idols; and unconscious identification with God's perfection. Shame and guilt are important signs here,
if present. But false shame and guilt are usually signs of suffering, rather than
original or personal sin. So, even shame and guilt must be evaluated to determine, as best as possible, whether they are valid or a distortion and instead a function of one's suffering and damage, or both.

When true shame and guilt are identified, contrition is warranted, if not
already present. This is what the Puritans called "loading the conscience"
(e.g., Owen, 1965, Vol. 6, pp. 56-59). Allowing one's wrongdoing to weigh on
one's soul is unpleasant, but it can promote a healthy sense of one's sinfulness
that can lead to behavior and character change and reconciliation, so long as
Jesus is kept in the center of such a process (something not all Puritans understood!). But counselors have to guard against the activation of excessive
and unproductive guilt and shame (Tangney & Dearing, 2002; what Paul
called "worldly grief" that "produces death," 2 Cor 7:10 ESB; see Narramore,
1984, for a Christian analysis), especially for those with shame-prone personalities, usually developed in abusive families. Consequently, when necessary,
such counselees may initially have to practice this step mentally, suppressing
the negative emotions until their new self is strong enough to tolerate and

engage them productively in working memory, without getting overwhelmed. A kind, empathic therapist is especially helpful here, providing emotional scaffolding, "containing" the negative emotion, modeling how to think and feel about it and to regulate it, and pulling back when the counselee's emotion system gets flooded. While our guilt and shame may be extreme from God's standpoint, our finite capacities cannot handle such realizations, and God's goal in such awareness is not to overwhelm us (Mt 12:20).

Faults, we recall, are characterized by both sinfulness and weakness. Because believers have fallen bodies and grow up in a fallen world, much of their old-self system probably consists of fault. One of the great tragedies of human life is that the more sin humans are exposed to when young, the more their adult brain/souls will be correspondingly disordered. In adulthood, for example, a man may become aware of "the destructive power of undermining past experiences perpetuated in his mental make-up in the form of . . . the destructive emotions and impulses they arouse in him, and the often equally self-destructive defenses he is obliged to build up within himself" (Guntrip, 1957, p. 185). Though not necessarily responsible for causing such fallen damage, as a personal agent in adulthood, one can learn how to grieve one's wounds and the suffering of one's story and also take responsibility for perpetuating one's fallen damage and seek healing and resolution, as well as forgiveness if needed. Faults, therefore, are especially complex to work through, because they are simultaneously something for which one bears responsibility, but not entirely. At the same time, the weakness of faults indicates they are also potential sites for God's glory.

Step 3: Verbal expression from the heart. After discerning the ethicospiritual quality of one's current emotion state, the next step is to make explicit in words what has been implicit, and this usually includes a declaration of ownership, though one's sin is processed markedly differently from one's suffering and weakness.[9] Secular research has documented the therapeutic value of expressing our thoughts, emotions, and memories (Fonagy et al., 2002; Neiderhoffer & Pennebaker, 2002; Prochaska & Norcross, 1994). But given the importance of words and discourse in the Christian scheme of things, the verbal articulation of one's emotional experience makes even more sense in a Christian therapy framework.

Lament of suffering and biopsychosocial damage: As we saw in chapter nine (and in Job, the Psalms, and the Prophets), lament puts into words one's negative emotions—signs that one lives in a fallen world—and shares one's burdens with God (and trustworthy others), perhaps describing the circumstances (a trial of some kind, a recognition of one's brokenness), and usually requesting his aid and relief, *while feeling the feelings.*

Lament can be spoken or written down in journaling. Some Christian therapists recommend counselees write out their own psalm of lament focused on a part of their story or a dilemma they are going through, but the key is to lament *with feeling.* Part of the therapeutic value of lament is that it integrates different parts of one's brain/soul by connecting emotion, linguistic/conceptual, and relational regions, which may be dissociated (Siegel, 2012). Lament allows us to more deeply "own our affects" (Fonagy et al., 2002, p. 440), by facing them and vulnerably bringing them into the presence of God (and others), so it undermines hiding, defensiveness, and dissociation.

Confession of sin: This is the first official step in the process of mortification, the putting to death of one's sin (Owen, 1965, Vol. 6). Confession is the verbal acknowledgment to God and oneself (and possibly others) of one's personal sins and sinfulness, analogous to lament. Confession occurs in many forms in Scripture: "I have sinned against the Lord" (2 Sam 12:13); "I despise myself and repent in dust and ashes" (Job 42:6 NRSV); "I am a sinful man" (Lk 5:8); "Father, I have sinned against heaven and in your sight; I am no longer worthy to be called your son" (Lk 15:21); "God, be merciful to me, the sinner!" (Lk 18:13); "Wretched man that I am!" (Rom 7:24). Christian confession is "a free, soul-opening acknowledgment" of one's sin in the light of the gospel of Christ (Owen, p. 372) and typically includes taking responsibility for one's sinful action or character, without qualification or excuse, so that the "heart is made free" (Owen, p. 374).[10]

Confession also undermines hiding, defensiveness, and dissociation, and someday research on the confession of sin will document its therapeutic benefits (see Watson, Morris, Loy, & Hamrick, 2007, for a study on the positive effects of sin awareness), since it also promotes the mentalization of particularly deleterious aspects of the soul (e.g., shame and guilt), which are better ameliorated when put into words. However, confession does more, first by addressing as-yet unresolved shame and guilt by bringing one's sinfulness out of hiding into one's relational space with God, and second by contributing to one's personal agency and communion, because the self "stands up" before God and says, *I have done it!* Confession, therefore, is generally good for the soul. It is "grace, not law. It is not a work we do in order to become perfect Christians; it is a grace which leads to certitude, conversion, fellowship, and joy. Confession is divine sadness which leads to divine joy" (Bonhoeffer, 1985, p. 64).

Christianity also commends interpersonal confession. "Confess your sins to one another, and pray for one another so that you may be healed" (Jas 5:16). Transparency before trustworthy others can promote humility, deepen our mortification, and encourage others to open up as well.[11]

We might wonder who does the confessing, the old self or the new? Perhaps both, since confession would seem to be intrinsically a transitional event, signifying in one's consciousness both death and resurrection. The old self is responsible, after all, for our sinfulness, but it cannot confess, for it lives in shame and denial. Only the new self, confident in God's forgiveness, can take responsibility for the whole self before God. Consequently, though a part of mortification, confession also signifies the new life of vivification.

Finally, our negative emotions can also be a mixture of sin and woundedness, or fault, a condition suggested in the cry, "I believe; help my unbelief!" In such cases, lament *and* confession are both called for, where we talk with God (and others) about what is distressing, alternatively lamenting and confessing, depending on the immediate focus, for example, grief and bitterness; a sense of betrayal and hatred; feelings of injustice and a desire for revenge.

Step 4: Repositioning oneself with respect to the old and the new. To further the inward deepening of one's participation in the cross, another action is needed regarding one's negative emotional experience that establishes one's transition from death to life.

Surrender of suffering and biopsychosocial damage: In light of Christ's teaching about the poor in spirit, his example, and his own suffering, after believers lament sufficiently, they can take their negative emotion schemes associated with their suffering or brokenness and release them to Christ (Ps 55:22; 1 Pet 5:7). During the previous steps, they may also discover false shame and guilt that they have borne regarding their suffering and weaknesses, which can also be taken to the cross. Because our story, damage, and suffering are not intrinsically sinful, they are to be incorporated into the new self, rather than rejected and put to death, in contrast to sin—we recall that Christ's wounds from his crucifixion are permanent marks on his resurrection body—so one's suffering and psychospiritual wounds have to be mentalized differently from sin. In meditative prayer, surrender repositions oneself with respect to one's freshly owned and articulated suffering and biopsychosocial damage and wounds, uniquely distancing oneself from them by releasing them into God's hands in Christ (Caussade, 1861/1986; Cole & Pargament, 1999). Something like this step has become universally recognized as therapeutically beneficial. The action can be facilitated by a variety of means, including dialogue, psychodrama, art therapy, guided imagery, chair work, journaling, and meditative prayer. As an example, at the right time in the therapy journey, it may be helpful to guide a counselee to surrender memories of events of which the counselee remains ashamed, including sins that were committed against him or her in childhood. Counselees can use their imagination to recall such an event to activate its associated shame or guilt, objectify it and its negative affect, and yield it to Christ, allowing him to detoxify and transform the memory—though care must be taken not to retraumatize the person (see Gingrich, 2013).

Repentance of sin: The New Testament word for repentance is *metanoia*, and its root meaning is literally a "change of mind" (*meta* = change, *nous* = mind) (Arndt & Gingrich, 1957). In the New Testament it refers to a conversion of mind, heart, and life—a turning away from sin, idols, and the old way of life (Acts 8:22; 2 Cor 12:21; Rev 2:21), and a turning to God (Acts 3:19). Repentance, therefore, constitutes a fresh alteration of one's consciousness, in which, after owning one's sin (or old self or flesh) in confession, one personally disavows one's recent sin or sinfulness and repositions oneself by "turning away" from it, indicating, in effect, *That is no longer me! With Christ I repudiate what I once was.* In repentance one disidentifies with the old-self system and takes the position of one's new self again. It is a radical, internal reversal,[12] a decentering of the self that recenters on God by the Holy Spirit who "brings the cross of Christ into the heart of a sinner by faith, and gives us communion with Christ in his death" (Owen, 1965, Vol. 6, p. 19).

Repentance should be viewed as a depth variable, since one can repent with different levels of intensity and integrity, and one can grow in earnestness by which the power of sin is weakened. *Primary or direct repentance* is the most basic kind and involves "an active, aggressive disavowal of all of one's contaminated life" (Johnson, 2007, p. 485). It is a direct attack on sin by refraining from it. "Beloved, I urge you . . . to abstain from fleshly lusts which wage war against the soul" (1 Pet 2:11). Primary repentance involves making a cognitive-decisional break with sin, akin to what addicts must do at some point to give up their addiction.

However, primary repentance is essentially behavioral and legal; it is like an amputation and works through avoidance but does not necessarily change much in the heart. For that one needs a greater internalization of God's mercy and love. *Secondary or indirect repentance* flows more from grace than law and is birthed out of a deeper appropriation of God's love in

Christ (Colquhoun, 1826/1965).[13] If primary repentance is fleeing from the dragon, secondary repentance is more like entering the dragon's lair with Christ in order to slay it. However, in contrast to the "just say no" approach of primary repentance, secondary repentance utilizes a more subtle and indirect class of repentance activities—active receptivity, detachment, relinquishment, resignation, surrender, yielding—entailing more advanced inwardness skills, usually learned in meditative prayer, and in the experiential knowledge that God in Christ is for me, no matter what (Rom 8:31). But in order to actually kill the dragon one has to get very close to it! So secondary repentance does not just cut off or repress the sinful emotion or desire but goes after it and aims to do it harm, using Scripture meditation, guided imagery (e.g., to actually nail it experientially to the cross), or contemplation on God's love or the harm it has caused. The key to secondary repentance is that one can feel the death of the sin by the change in one's emotion state.

Unfortunately, repentance is not a one-time event. There will be inevitable setbacks in the Christian life, along with seasons of recovery. Calvin wrote that Christians are on a "race of repentance, which they are to run throughout their lives" (Calvin, 1559/1960, p. 602), indicating it is to be an ongoing practice. "To be formed in the likeness of the Crucified—this means being a man sentenced by God. In his daily existence man carries with him God's sentence of death, the necessity of dying before God for the sake of sin. . . . Every day man dies the death of a sinner" (Bonhoeffer, 1955, p. 81). All this also suggests that repentance can increase in quality over the course of one's life.

Repentance and surrender of fault: Humans usually develop specific defenses in childhood, based on difficult family experiences—when they are weaknesses—but most adults are more or less responsible for their maintenance, as well as for seeking help to overcome them (Johnson & Burroughs, 2000). So the defenses of most adults should be considered faults. Helping others relinquish their defenses is one of the great challenges of psychotherapy (Vaillant, 1997; McCullough et al., 2003). God's love and union with Christ's perfection provide transcendent support to undermine shame and anxiety about one's general badness. In addition, therapists can help counselees explore the costs versus benefits and secondary gains of defenses, take responsibility for maintenance, and grieve the losses due to defenses, while taking it all to the cross more deeply, to promote a deepening, ongoing oscillation between repentance and surrender of one's defenses (and other kinds of faults).

Step 5: A transformational emotion shift. Cross work is ideally not finished until the counselee attains a positive emotion state congruent with Christ's resurrection, such as a felt sense of reconciliation with God, comfort, contentment, or hope, thereby recapitulating in a small way Christ's story in the believer's life. This is what therapy theorists call a "corrective emotional experience" (Alexander & French, 1946).

Receiving comfort from Christ in relation to one's suffering or damage: Cross work with one's past or present suffering or biopsychosocial damage concludes with some kind of emotion resolution made possible by the appropriation of some Christian consideration, for example, a fresh sense of God's compassion toward oneself in this state, the felt realization that God is using it for good, the recognition that God will compensate one superabundantly in heaven (2 Cor 4:17), or an interpersonal experience of Christ's blessing. Two features distinguish this resolution from defensive activity or dissociation that simply turns off and represses the unresolved negative emotion: first, the preceding conscious processing of the negative emotion that accepted and owned the emotion; and second, the transition to a modified, more positive emotion state. The goal is a transformed emotion scheme in which the negative emotion that one was working on is mixed together with a positive emotion based on God's love or peace, or Christ's work, enabling the believer to "come to terms with" and accept the suffering or damage with Christ, as best as possible. We see here again that Christian therapy can attain the same outcome, formally, as certain kinds of secular therapy (acceptance: Hayes, Strosahl, & Wilson, 2012; Linehan, 1993) but gets there through an altogether different route.

The counselor has a responsibility to discern the counselee's readiness for cross work. For many reasons, people are at different places in coming to terms with their suffering and damage, so the goal of resolution must not be pressed too quickly on struggling saints or we risk promoting harm or inauthenticity, not accepting them just as they are, and indirectly shaming them for not being further along on the journey. At the other end of the spectrum are those mature individuals who will be able to join the apostle Paul in the shift he experienced regarding his own weaknesses (2 Cor 12:8-10) when he moved from praying for their removal to boasting in them, knowing they were sites of divine glory and strength. But those with the greatest weaknesses know what a lofty goal that is and how easy it is to fake it. Authenticity is key.

Receiving forgiveness for one's sin: Decades ago now, the noted behaviorist O. H. Mowrer (1961) discovered that confession and repentance helped him recover from depression, and he began recommending them as secular techniques to promote psychological healing. Christian confession and repentance are distinguished from his secular insight by their relational quality and their transcendent basis and result: the gift of forgiveness by God through Jesus Christ. "If we confess our sins, [God] is faithful and righteous to forgive us our sins and to cleanse us from all unrighteousness" (1 Jn 1:9; see 1 Jn 2:2). As a final step in cross work with regard to sin, believers are to personally appropriate their forgiveness by God, so that they realize experientially their "new" standing before God as a "former sinner" and now righteous and loved in Christ. In contrast to a merely intellectual understanding of one's forgiveness, its carditive reception results in some degree of affective resolution—a felt sense of relief, gratitude, joy, signifying that the conscious appropriation has reached the neural basis of one's emotion system. Christian therapy aims at facilitating this internalization, using a variety of techniques, including meditative prayer, *lectio divina*, imagination, even Christian music. Regardless, the endpoint of such cross work regarding one's sin is an emotion shift, from shame and guilt to restored communion with God. Since the old self has already been put to death in step four, this step is actually a return to vivification.[14] "If Christ is the Lamb of God Who takes away the sins of the world, then surely He sends His Spirit to deliver our souls from obsession with our feelings of guilt" (Merton, 1961a, p. 43). This model is a guide to help believers participate in that deliverance.

Some Christians, as we know, are so burdened by self-hatred and chronic shame that they seem unable to feel forgiven by God, though they believe the gospel mentally (Payne, 1995). Such incapacity is usually explained, at least in part, by childhood mistreatment, while their personal agency was developing, thus compromising the form of their agency-in-communion in adulthood, making it difficult to benefit psychologically from the gospel. Such bruised reeds (Mt 12:20) need the most skilled Christian counselors to help them through their internal obstacles. Simply pressuring them with more gospel truth will only make matters worse, even though the gospel is exactly what they need! Fortunately, our forgiveness is not based on our faith or our ability to receive forgiveness but on Christ's intercession on our behalf. "If God is for us, who is against us?" (Rom 8:31), and that includes ourselves! Their counselors will simply have to try out a number of different therapeutic interventions, maybe for a long time, including the witness of their patient compassion. Already believing intellectually the truth of the gospel, such counselees may find their reception of Christ's forgiveness deepened by agentically "facing themselves" and forgiving themselves in the name of Christ, perhaps while looking at themselves in a mirror, and disavowing their sense of unforgivableness. Or while their shame is engaged, reading one of the relevant Gospel accounts and imagining they are the one hearing Christ say to them, "Your sins are forgiven" (e.g., Lk 5:20; 7:48). But there are a thousand other strategies that can be employed to promote such an emotion shift.

Receiving forgiveness and consolation for faults. When both sin and damage are present, the final stage is doubly positive: letting in Christ's word of forgiveness and empathy to modify and transform the fault and its associated negative emotions, so that the person experiences a fresh resurrection. Figure 18.3 presents a flow chart of therapeutic participation in the cross.

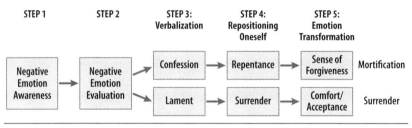

Figure 18.3. Cross work

THE PRACTICE OF REDEMPTIVE DIFFERENTIATION

The overall goal of RD is a more complex and comprehensive self-understanding and self-practice from the standpoint of Christ's redemption. This means reinterpreting and reorganizing one's internal world, as well as relations with others, according to Christ's death and resurrection. This should lead to the development of an increasingly influential and elaborate new self, grounded on one's creation goodness in Christ and the weakening of one's old self by the transfer of one's suffering and biopsychosocial damage into the new self, and their corresponding transformation, and the killing of one's sinfulness. Christians have practiced aspects of RD for centuries, often calling it purgation or sanctification. The purpose of this chapter has been to elaborate and extend historic Christian thought and practice by showing how they might contribute to a Christian model of psychotherapy and counseling. Perhaps we could sum up RD by rewording a psychodynamic motto: "Where the old self was, there the new self shall be."

The RD goal in session is to create enough psychological distance between their new self and old self to permit counselees to see themselves in a new way and to practice corresponding new actions. Too much distance and the dialogue will be abstract and intellectualized, collaborating with the tendencies of both participants to dissimulate; too little distance risks over-whelming counselees with shame and guilt, and other negative emotions, which can short-circuit or even shut down the therapy process.

Christian therapists are trail guides and companions on the soul-care journey who walk with their Christian counselees into the valley of the shadow of their old self's death, which entails, in part, the differentiation of their new selves from their old. Christian counselors are embodied represen-tatives of Christ whose encouragement, comfort, and challenge, along with their expertise, help counselees to make the requisite kinds of internal and external discriminations. In the context of a strong therapeutic alliance, skilled therapists can look for and comment on the good created abilities and strengths of their counselees and regularly direct their counselee's attention to their union with Christ in session and through homework. They can also provide scaffolding by guiding them through feeling, acknowledging, verbal-izing, positioning themselves with respect to, and shifting in their emotions regarding their new selves and their old selves, and helping them to distin-guish their sins, suffering, and biopsychosocial damage, through patient, transparent, and compassionate dialogue. So, the counselor's role in helping counselees to die and to live in Christ is of inestimable importance.

RESOURCES FOR COUNSELORS AND COUNSELEES

Classic

Bennett, A. (1975). *The valley of vision: A collection of Puritan prayers & devo-tions*. Edinburgh: Banner of Truth. Remarkable transparency before God, though it leans to the dark side. A collection is needed that focuses more on the resurrection.

Calvin, J. (1960). *The institutes of the Christian religion* (F. L. Battles, Trans.). Phila-delphia: Westminster Press. Pp. 595-602. Classic discussion of vivification and mortification and the need for ongoing repentance throughout the Christian life.

Colquhoun, J. (1965). *Repentance*. Edinburgh: Banner of Truth Trust. (Original work published 1826)

Newton, J. (1960). *Letters of John Newton*. Edinburgh: Banner of Truth Trust. Transparency is needed for differentiation, and the author of "Amazing Grace" had it! See especially letters 22-25.

Owen, J. (1967). On the mortification of sin in believers. In *The Works of John Owen* (Vol. 6, pp. 5-86). Carlyle, PA: Banner of Truth.

Sibbes, R. (1973). The soul's conflict with itself. In *Works of Richard Sibbes* (Vol. 1, pp. 119-294). Carlyle, PA: Banner of Truth.

Contemporary

Allen, J. G., Fonagy, P., & Bateman, A. (2008). *Mentalizing in clinical practice.* New York: American Psychiatric Association. ‡

Allender, D., & Longman, T., III (1998). *The cry of the soul.* Colorado Springs: NavPress.

Groeschel, B. (1993). *Spiritual passages: The psychology of spiritual development.* New York: Crossroad.

Lundgaard, K. (1998). *The enemy within: Straight talk about the power and defeat of sin.* Phillipsburg, NJ: P&R.

Paulson, S. D. (2011). *Lutheran theology.* New York: T&T Clark. With *simul peccator et justus*, Luther was an important proponent of redemptive differentiation. ‡

Payne, L. (1995). *The healing presence: Curing the soul through union with Christ.* Grand Rapids, MI: Baker.

Plass, R., & Cofield, J. (2014). *The relational soul.* Downers Grove, IL: InterVarsity Press.

Roberts, R. C. (2001). Outline of Pauline psychotherapy. In M. R. McMinn & T. R. Phillips (Eds.), *Care for the soul* (pp. 134-63). Downers Grove, IL: InterVarsity Press.

Stump, E. (2010). *Wandering in darkness: Narrative and the problem of suffering.* New York: Oxford University Press. ‡ Excellent description of psychic division.

Webster, J. (2016). Mortification and vivification. In *God without measure: Working papers in Christian theology*, Vol. 2, *Virtue and intellect* (pp. 103-22). London: Bloomsbury T&T Clark. ‡

‡ Recommended more for counselors and pastors than for counselees

—19—

Redemptive Integration

Principle 9: Conformity to Christ is the personal realization of the new creation through redemptive differentiation and integration in Christ by the Holy Spirit and faith.

Our inner self is being renewed day by day.

2 Corinthians 4:16 nrsv

Therefore from now on we recognize no one according to the flesh;
even though we have known Christ according to the flesh, yet now we
know Him in this way no longer. Therefore if anyone is in Christ,
he is a new creature; the old things passed away;
behold, new things have come.

2 Corinthians 5:16-17

Germany today is very different than it was in the aftermath of World War II. Devastated by a crazed tyrant hell-bent on destroying the Jewish people and subjugating the rest of world to his narcissistic designs, Adolf Hitler brought judgment on his head and all the German people. When the country finally surrendered and the fighting was halted, it was clear that the back was broken of one of the greatest cultures ever to exist. Germany had lost nearly 10% of their population; their economy was in ruins; many of their artistic and architectural treasures were lost under piles of rubble; and the German people themselves awoke to the realization that they had been duped by a demonically inspired orator. It would have been easy to collapse in self-condemnation and despair.

But with the help of their former enemies, the surviving German people began the grueling process of reclaiming their country and rebuilding their culture by reunifying it under a new government. Cities that once held Nazi parades and were flattened by bombs were reconstructed, and the country that was once morally and materially bankrupt has become now one of the world's great economies and a state loath to act aggressively in world affairs.

We have been considering the ethicospiritual division that exists in the Christian heart and the therapy work needed there, an important aspect of which consists of recognizing and promoting that division through faith, a process that has been called redemptive differentiation (RD). As discussed in chapter eighteen, RD is a therapeutic elaboration of three practices of the Christian tradition. We saw there that Christians are being healed by differentiating their new self from their old self and disidentifying with the latter through mortification or surrender (or both) and co-constructing (with God and others) the new self based on their union with Christ and by the Spirit, a process called vivification. In this chapter, we extend further the practice of vivification, which transcends mortification in the Christian life much as Christ's resurrection transcended his death, referring to this extension as redemptive integration (RI).

Calvin (1559/1960) defined vivification as "the desire to live in a holy and devoted manner, a desire arising from rebirth, as if it were said that man dies to himself that he may begin to live to God" (p. 595). The concept is based on apostolic teaching about the new life in Christ and the new creation. Believers have been joined to Christ so that they might "walk in newness of life" (Rom 6:4). They have been brought into the new creation. "The old things passed away; behold, new things have come" (2 Cor 5:17; see 1 Jn 2:8, 17). Though believers still have to deal with their old self, its authority over the believer was dissolved by divine fiat, and it is passing away through faith, so we are not equally old and new. From the eschatological standpoint of Christ in heaven and union with him, the old has become ultimately false, and only the new is true about believers.

As a result, the emphasis of Christian therapy should be on the reception and construction of a resurrection/ascension way of life based on God's love toward them in Christ, though this entails coming to terms with one's (as yet) unresolved sin, suffering, and damage, accordingly. This orientation contrasts with a more negative orientation, common throughout the Christian tradition, which is fixated on our sin or the evils of this age. But we are following here the emphasis of the apostle Paul, who, though he knew the destructive and deceptive power of the old way of life well (1 Tim 1:12-15) and could describe his own internal conflicts with great transparency (Rom 7:7-25), encouraged believers to focus their attention on "whatever is true, whatever is honorable, whatever is right, whatever is pure, whatever is lovely, whatever is of good repute, if there is any excellence and if anything worthy of praise, dwell on these things" (Phil 4:8).

INTEGRATION DEFINED

In the last chapter we noted that integration is a developmental outcome that follows differentiation (see Hamilton, 1988; Harter, 2012; Kegan, 1982; Siegel, 2012; Werner, 1957), a necessary consequence of being finite creatures who grow in complexity biologically and psychologically. Integration is "linking differentiated parts into a functional whole" (Siegel, 2012, p. 9), and such linking occurs in psychological functioning throughout life. According to Siegel, it happens normally in a host of domains, including within one's consciousness and the integration of body and brain: left and right brain hemispheres, limbic system and cerebral cortex, one's memory systems, episodes of one's life, forming a coherent narrative, along with experiences of others, one's sense of temporal continuity (past, present, and future), and the "transpirational" integration of all these forms of what Christians might call creational integration. Skilled parenting promotes such integration in childhood (termed "assimilation" by Van der Hart, Nijenhuis, & Steele, 2006).

However, as we have seen, fallen persons are also born with a fundamental kind of spiritual dissociation, due to original sin, that obscures aspects of one's relationship to God and one's true motives with respect to him. Stump (2010) adds that the willed loneliness of fallen human beings leads to a divided heart, mind, and will, fragmented by conflicting desires for the plethora of creational blessings available, and this internal fragmentation compromises our ability to love God, others, and ourselves well.

Compounding this ultimate problem, fallen persons growing up in a fallen world differentially develop neural networks that resist integration due to early suffering (or trauma) organized according to the relational style of their early caregivers and the associated emotions and beliefs that form, resulting in relatively dissociated subsystems and states of mind (evidenced in defenses and false selves, and in the extreme, dissociative disorders) (Siegel, 2012; van der Hart, Nijenhuis, & Steele, 2006). The presence of chronic internal chaos or rigidity in adult functioning that is developmentally immature signifies a special need for the integration that can come through therapy (PDM Task Force, 2006; Siegel, 2012).

How does therapeutic integration occur? Siegel (2010) contends that humans change their brains by means of what they consciously focus their attention on. By bringing into consciousness two or more psychological aspects of oneself that were previously unassociated (e.g., beliefs, images, affects, actions, memories), a more complex psychological structure can be formed. Van der Hart, Nijenhuis, and Steele (2006) call this mental action "binding." They divide binding into "personalization" (owning one's experience) and "presentification" (being consciously present in the moment).[1] An example of therapeutic integration would be the recollection of a memory of childhood sexual abuse with the feeling of its associated shame and the addition, for the first time, of the realization that "it was not my fault," while owning the entire experience in the present—"that really happened to me" and "I'm different now." Like many developmental processes, the more integrated or whole one is, the better one can integrate one's experiences, and vice versa, so that the process of integration is very much like trying to ride one's bicycle while still building it.

Many words have been used for psychological integration or its aspects, including *linkage, joining, coherence, cohesion*, and *resonance* (Siegel, 2010); *exposure* and *modification* (Barlow et al., 2011); *therapeutic alliance, empathy, metabolization*, and *mentalization* (Fonagy, Gergely, Jurist, & Target, 2002); *mindfulness* (Linehan, 1993); *desensitization* and *expression* (McCullough et al., 2003); *synthesis* and *realization* (van der Hart, Nijenhuis, & Steele, 2006); and *transformation* (Greenberg, 2011); as well as the verbs *fold* (Stump, 2010) and *bind* (van der Hart, Nijenhuis, & Steele, 2006).[2]

REDEMPTIVE INTEGRATION EXPLAINED

In addition to the above kinds of creational integration that as gifts of God's creation grace are natural to human beings, humans have a need for another kind of integration, instigated through Christ's redemption—necessary because humans are also fundamentally ethicospiritually divided—and that also provides the ultimate spiritual context for the creational integration of Christians.[3] Let us consider the many ways Christianity promotes the creational and redemptive integration of believers in Christ.

To begin with, the entire enterprise of redemptive integration (RI) originates in God's simplicity, beauty, and love (Jn 3:16; 17:1-26; 1 Jn 4:10). God is supremely attractive and draws beings like us to himself (in spite of sin), being a transcendent center of gravity that unifies our desires, emotions, beliefs, actions, and relationships. Furthermore, our created nature is made to glorify God through drawing closer to him in worship and love. According to Stump (2010), such love entails intimacy. For us finite, fallen personal agents, this involves the conscious opening up of ourselves to God. This takes time and involves the reorganization of our individual lives— including all that lies within our brains/souls—into an increasingly theocentric configuration through union with Christ and communion with God. Our love of him is his love of us in Christ received and returned (Lopez, 2014). However, because Christians are still fallen beings living in a fallen world, this wholehearted surrender now includes all of our bad as well as our good. Only God's perfect love can overcome the fear and shame that would keep broken sinners away (1 Jn 4:18). The loving surrender of every aspect of ourselves to God in Christ is the core of RI.

God-centeredness brings an additional therapeutic benefit. God provides a transcendent nexus to which everything in our lives is related and to whom we owe everything: "Whether, then, you eat or drink or whatever you do, do all to the glory of God" (1 Cor 10:31). As he is worshiped and loved mindfully, through the course of our lives, his glory links together our daily experiences, thoughts, feelings, relationships—indeed, our whole lives—and so helps to unify our souls in the midst of internal conflicts, diverse activities, and fragmented lives and relationships. In addition, the Christian virtues of "purity of heart" (Ps 24:4; Mt 5:7; 2 Tim 2:22; 1 Pet 1:22) and single-mindedness (Mt 6; the opposite of double-mindedness, Jas 1:8) are synonyms of integration, flowing from God being the center of the universe and corresponding analogously to his simplicity.[4]

Second, the Scriptures also contain many commands that encourage RI indirectly, for example, "seek first the kingdom of God and his righteousness" (Mt 6:33 ESV); "set your mind on the things above" (Col 3:2); and take "every thought captive to the obedience of Christ" (2 Cor 10:5). Third, the redemptive truths of Scripture that shape our understanding and love of the triune God, others, and ourselves provide a divinely authorized system of therapeutic discourse within which one can situate dissociated memories, emotions schemes, reasoning, imagination, relational patterns, and action dispositions, and the neural regions on which they supervene, and forge

linkages. Fourth, the theodrama of God's redemption in Christ offers a metanarrative context within which the individual's story is being incorporated.
Fifth, interpreting one's life and its activities, relationships, and obligations as
God's calling binds them together and bestows transcendent meaning across
the particulars of one's life. Sixth, as human fallenness—signified by shame
and guilt—is resolved through redemption, the law of God written on the
heart is being gradually interpenetrated with God's grace.[5] Seventh, love is
the supreme Christian virtue, and loving others and receiving their love integrates minds and facilitates seeing others and oneself as whole persons,
composites of created goodness, fallenness, and redeemed goodness in Christ
(the latter if they are Christians). The Christian counselor plays an important
part in this process by loving counselees well, if not perfectly, and forming a
friendship and working alliance, cocreating a trusting, empathic relationship
that enables counselees to explore themselves and their relational style safely.
Finally, one's union with Christ in his life, death, resurrection, and exaltation
provides an all-encompassing, soul-healing medium intended by God to be
consciously suffused throughout one's brain/soul by faith and love to connect
everything in one's life to Christ, bringing it all into his loving presence.
Christianity essentially provides an integrative framework that promotes
natural/creational forms of integration through redemptive integration.

Many terms have been used within the Christian tradition for redemptive
integration and its aspects (and a few we must coin), including the knowledge
and love of God; union with Christ and communion with God and their
suffusion and saturation throughout one's being; providence and concur-
rence; recollection and consolidation; surrender, faith, and consent; and the
folding of one's desires into God's will (Stump, 2010), along with the goal of
purity or singleness of heart, single-mindedness, and the unification of one's
will with God's will.

THE PROCESS OF REDEMPTIVE INTEGRATION

One reason why Christian transformation is so slow is that both RD and
RI entail that believers consciously open up more "places" within their
brain/soul to Christ: thoughts, memories, motives, and relational structures, some of which have been cordoned off for years and so hidden from
themselves. The slow suffusion of Christ's healing throughout one's brain/
soul occurs one memory, emotion scheme, or belief (and corresponding
neural network) at a time. We might say that RI is the deepening

appropriation and synthesis of Christ's resurrection within the believer's self-understanding and self-evaluation.

The goal of RI (unfinalizable in this life) is for believers to know and evaluate themselves comprehensively and at the same time as created thoroughly good; crucified thoroughly in their sin, shame, and guilt; and thoroughly resurrected and seated in Christ. Only the omniscient God is able to know and evaluate Christians in Christ in this way simultaneously; as finite, temporal beings, we must begin the slow process of integration by knowing and evaluating ourselves one perspective at a time. Over time though, through practice, we can learn to know ourselves dialectically, that is, in an alternating fashion, in which each perspective is grasped in relation to the others. Eventually, as we repeatedly alternate these gestalt-like self-perspectives sequentially, they become more and more joined together and blended in our self-understanding and self-evaluation (Fauconnier & Turner, 2002), facilitating the overcoming and resolving, in some degree, of our remaining internal division and dissociation due to sin, suffering, and damage. As a result, believers are enabled by the Spirit to unify the disconnected and disassociated parts of their *actual self*—all that the believer still is in this world (both old and new)—in relation to Christ, so that more and more of the current state of their brain/soul is brought under the reign and into the presence of Christ, becoming more and more part of the new creation and freeing up the combined creational and redemptive resources available for greater healing and conformity to Christ (and their *real self* in heaven).

I noted above that integration involves one's attention. Christian therapy is distinguished by that to which Christians direct their attention. "Our whole life of faith is a life of attentiveness, of 'listening' in order to receive the word of God into our hearts" (Merton, 1961a, p. 123). The Christian's new self is realized by a Christ-saturated consciousness, that is, by knowing and evaluating more of oneself, one's activities, and one's relationships in relation to one's union with Christ, so that they become "Christologized," united experientially to the resurrected Lord of the new creation by faith— including what remains of the old self after surrender and mortification. RI is basically the ongoing realization of one's union with Christ by the growing consolidation of all that pertains to oneself *in Christ*. This involves redeeming the created goodness of the believer, including that which underlies the old self, and "bringing it over" into the new self, and uniting that with all that the believer has been given in creation and in Christ.

How does this happen? Like RD, RI occurs within one's consciousness or working memory, where one focuses on present experience or material from one's long-term memory system and processes (or reprocesses) it consciously by faith in (relation to) Christ, at a sufficient depth of processing that the present experience or previously stored dynamic structures come to be stored in long-term memory (and the brain) in some degree according to the new creation. This processing enables one to come to terms with and accept oneself more and more the way that God does in Christ.

This does not mean that RI is the only way believers change therapeutically. On the contrary, humans are being influenced unconsciously and automatically all the time (Bargh & Chartrand, 1999), and powerful factors in therapy like the therapeutic alliance occur largely outside of awareness. Nevertheless, conscious, intentional change is one of the best predictors of change, and most forms of therapy utilize it.

It should be obvious that RI involves more than the addition of pieces of knowledge about oneself, whether subjective or theological. RI promotes relational knowledge and evaluation, and includes one's "location" in the new creation vis-à-vis Christ and therefore one's body, callings, roles, obligations, and so on, in the midst of the thoroughly interpersonal universe within which one lives (with God and others, including one's family, friends, and neighbors as well as oneself).

It is predicted that, when RI is pursued with some diligence during early and middle adulthood, a deepening paradigm shift will occur over the course of one's life—a transposition centering on the spiritual order—enabling one to think, feel, act, and relate increasingly out of one's new self and less out of one's old self, contributing to greater personal and narrative coherence, more access to and acceptance of one's own body and soul, a truer trust in God and a more realistic trust in self and others, and a greater capacity to receive the love of God, others, and oneself and practice the love of God, others, and oneself in Christ. However, this transformation results from the gradual accumulation of thousands of stepwise carditive identifications with Christ, and the details of this process will, of course, differ for everyone.

THE REDEMPTIVE INTEGRATION OF
THE CHRISTIAN'S ACTUAL SELF

RI, then, is the linking together of the diverse elements of all that the Christian actually is in the present in the believer's consciousness. In what follows much of RI is organized according to the Christian metanarrative.

Its Origin Is Outside Us

Given that RD and RI are reflexive human activities, it bears repeating that the driving force in RI is the holy love of God, both objectively and subjectively. Out of his own eternal unity and harmony, the triune God seeks to share himself with those made in his image but who are characterized by internal and interpersonal conflict. "Love, therefore, is the name for what God does to man in overcoming the disunion in which man lives" (Bonhoeffer, 1955, p. 52). So, God's love of himself incorporates believers into itself in Christ (1 Jn 4:10) and then realizes its *telos* as they learn how to receive it and return it to him and share it with others (1 Jn 4:12). "The life of love to God and neighbor is a true participation in the restored order of creation, a responsive love to the divine love in which the divine mode of life becomes our own" (O'Donovan, 1986, pp. 248-49).

Recollection with the triune God. The carditive experience of dialogical communion with God—when we can get it—opens us up to God and welcomes him in. Through such interaction, believers are redefined in his holy love of us and our responsive love of him, guided by the discourse of Scripture. But our participation is based on Christ's mediatory presence in heaven before the Father. Our hearing him, therefore, from heaven and from the cross speaks to us forgiveness, affirmation, validation, and encouragement; and because of our union with him, enables us—from a transcendent vantage point—to gradually break down our resistance to God and others and undermine our self-destructive attitudes and defenses, all of which brings increasing unity and harmony within.

Recollection, a Catholic spiritual formation practice, has been called "integration in depth" (von Hildebrand, 1948/2001, p. 137), for it involves pulling away from the secondary "distractions" of life and "gathering together the fragments of one's soul" in order to direct one's attention exclusively on God. This concentration of one's attention promotes subjective peace and enables believers to see reality more accurately, including what occurs within, by subordinating all of our other activities to this supreme aim, making it easier to distinguish the superficial from the real and the false from the true, and fostering surrender and release of all the particulars of one's life into God's hands. Recollection is a theocentric therapeutic alternative to Buddhist mindfulness, which results in an analogous clarity but is devoid of God and a personal relationship with God.

Surrendering One's Entire Actual Self in Christ to God

We have already noted that Christ still bore evidence of the wounds of his previous suffering after his resurrection (Jn 20:20, 27), and so do we. Our union with Christ does not take away our scars but transposes them into the spiritual order—*and makes them a part of the new creation.* Everything that believers are, their actual self—their created good, created damage, fallen dispositions—all that one is in Christ and all the fruits of redemption that one enjoys now have been taken up by God into Christ. As we consent to his prior divine activity with regard to us in Christ—in our creation, in judgment on our sin, in his suffering with us, and in the renewal of our resurrection and ascension—we are given divine warrant to accept all that we actually are here on earth, including our old self and our remaining sinful dispositions and weaknesses, as well as our new self, the gift of his perfect salvation along with our personal gifts from him (our strengths and virtues) and redemptive development, and so we become more consolidated and increasingly organized according to the meaningfulness and fulfillment of the will and word of God.

A large part of RI, therefore, involves the acceptance of one's actual self; using Bonhoeffer's (1955) language, we might say one's "penultimate self" (one's self before the eschaton). The great challenge now for many Christians, of course, is to believe that they are beloved by God in Christ and ultimately who God says they are in Christ, our incarnate High Priest, in spite of what remains of their old self—in spite of their previous histories and the fallen self-knowledge stored in their memories, previously defining episodic memories, emotion schemes, core beliefs, and unconscious attitudes, and even in spite of their current compromised thoughts, feelings, and actions. Immeasurably complicating the transposition of oneself from old to new is the fact that this process moves from cognitive levels into carditive levels of one's deepest self-other relational structures, often in dialogue with God and others. By such means the old can be owned but not cherished; recognized but not viewed as "who I *really* am"; acknowledged to be a part of one's actual self but only as peripheral, rather than central to one's identity.

Integrating one's created self into one's new self. In the previous chapter, we noted that aspects of the created self need to be identified and separated out from one's old self. Here we reflect on how these created aspects get reintegrated into the new self. One's created self—all that one is as a creature and image of God—provides the *personal* basis and infrastructure of one's new self. The new self would be nothing but an abstraction apart from an individual with a name, a unique body, specific strengths and weaknesses, and a particular story. Believers are creatures who belong to God twice over, having been created by him and then purchased by God in Christ's death

(1 Cor 6:20). RI therefore involves conscious reflection on and validation of one's created strengths and weaknesses, body and story, in light of Christ's death and resurrection. This goes beyond mere gratitude, since RI entails bringing specific aspects of our created natures into relation with Christ, flowing to us from our gracious Creator and Savior.

Most believers have experienced a virtually continual outpouring of creation-grace blessings throughout their lives, new every morning (Lam 3:23). Consequently, opportunities to consolidate them redemptively are occurring all the time. The challenge is to practice attending to these blessings *in Christ*. The fact that many of them are constitutional and relatively permanent features of the individual's life does not reduce their integrative value for therapy, since the old self has enjoyed these blessings autonomously, without a true regard for their origination in God (Lopez, 2014). As a result, fresh experiences of God's creation mercies provide occasions to walk into the new creation that one is becoming in Christ (2 Cor 5:17). But to be effective, it has to be personal and affective, and not merely intellectual. New-creation stewardship recognizes that this creation grace is not "over there," but right here, given to me and placed by God in my name. The fact that these gifts are mine is intended by God to release me to a grateful celebration of my created being, without the halting and qualification that often characterizes the fallen imitation of humility. In Christ one can relish all that one is, because one's intelligence, athletic ability, friendliness, or good looks have been united to Christ and are suffused with the Spirit's sanctifying presence in our bodies.

The created self-love of those who have been redeemed seeks God as its predestined fulfillment, and the celebration of ourselves in the context of theocentric gratitude and praise is the proper response to the word of the Son and the gift of the Spirit. Self-love, mediated by Christ, is both a necessary motive for Christian soul healing and one of its goals, for it ensures the unifying engagement of the believer's created capacities and personal agency. Moreover, whatever a person's good created desires, they can be "reshaped by being woven into the deepest desire of that person's heart," which is communion with God (Stump, 2010, p. 443).

Integrating one's redemptive gifts into one's created self. A more unified self is also promoted by receiving the gifts of one's union with Christ and weaving them more thoroughly into one's created being. First, we are brought into a new relationship with the triune God. He loves me—Eric Johnson; I am in you and you are in me—my body, my face, my personality, my story, my limitations and created strengths. Second, declarative truths about me in

Christ are also intended by God to be integrated into my created identity. I am perfect in Christ! I am as loveable as Christ!—with my body, face, story, limitations, and created strengths. The point here is to avoid mere abstract theological generalizations and to take the general truths regarding all believers in Christ and personalize them by binding them to and blending them with one's own created and historical particularity, as thoroughly and deeply as possible. Similarly, the unique fruit of the Spirit that is expressed in our lives and unique personalities is to be affirmed in Christ. Whatever love, joy, kindness, and patience we manifest are integratively celebrated with gratitude to God and relished as his working in us. "For we are His workmanship, created in Christ Jesus for good works, which God prepared beforehand, that we would walk in them" (Eph 2:10). How remarkable that God allows me to collaborate with him in the fostering of his new creation. This applies to whatever good we do, in spite of how it may at first feel to us and regardless of whether others, even non-Christians, do the same things better than we do. Part of our healing involves accepting *our* virtue, though given by God, in spite of sometimes strong internal pressure to criticize it. The fact is, it is new!—simply because it now comes from Christ and so participates in him and his perfect future for us. Feeding one's mother-in-law with dementia for the five hundredth time can still be new eschatologically.

Why do believers not experience more actual change in their internal and relational worlds? First, Christians typically do not know who they are in Christ well enough to see themselves in these strikingly different ways. Second, the knowledge that we do have is often relatively isolated and cordoned off from the rest of our brains/souls. As a result, our heavenly inheritance (Eph 1:3) has relatively little impact on our actual lives and experience. Consequently, Christian therapy includes encouraging counselees to spend time focused on improving their well-being in Christ, given their life space and other responsibilities. Without such intentional soul work, relatively little change will occur.

Integrating one's sinfulness and sins into one's new self. In the previous chapter, we saw that RD included the mortification, or putting to death, of sin. So, sin is not incorporated directly into the new self. Most Christians realize that so long as we are in fallen bodies, we will have original sin and commit sins. Yet, combined with the law of God on our hearts and our shame, sin inclines most humans—including Christians—to hide their sinfulness from themselves and others and to work hard at appearing modestly virtuous. The best remedy for this tendency is actually to bring the knowledge of one's remaining sin into the light of Christ and fold it into his love. Rather than promoting hopelessness or complacency, such self-awareness unites with gratitude and glory in the desire to participate in what Christ has done on our behalf, returning love for love. One's union with Christ, in addition, makes it possible to reinterpret one's old self as a disidentified part of oneself—acknowledged to be relevant to one's actual self but no longer pertaining to oneself ultimately. The old self of believers is like electronic equipment that has been sold to a new owner but is still being stored in one's garage. My old self is still part of me—part of my continuing story and part of all that I currently, actually am—but it has been recontextualized and redefined by Christ by being joined to his per-fected humanity, so that it is foreign to me now, and I am not related to it in the immediate way I once was.

We saw that confession and repentance of sin is one path of RD. However, these actions can also promote the integration of the knowledge of one's fallenness into the new self. As we noted, when believers confess, they are saying: *I am the one who sinned!* And when they repent, they are saying, *I disavow my sin. That is me no more!* RD is a psychological action of discontinuity in one's story, mediated by union with Christ. With RI, we consider the same actions in terms of the continuity of the one acting: the created-redeemed self with a particular name. Though paradoxical, the new self of believers is consolidated and strengthened as they take responsibility for themselves and their sin and, through confession and repentance, break from it—as only new selves can do—because of their union with Christ. The continuity and discontinuity of the Christian self is illustrated in the apostle Paul's classic statement "I have been crucified with Christ," yet "the life which I now live . . . I live by faith in the Son of God" (Gal 2:20).

As a result, as believers mature in Christ, they become better able to take ownership for their sin and at the same time become more deeply freed of its guilt, shame, and power. Our union with Christ can also prevent repeated sins from becoming either a cause for carelessness or a source of unresolved shame and despair. Instead, by driving us back to our holy friend and Savior, working through our sinfulness in Christ cleanses our conscience of guilt and shame and humbles us over time, making us more honest and realistic about ourselves, and yet less desirous of sinning in the future. As a result, Christian maturity is itself paradoxical: while one's remaining sinfulness (one's old self) gradually becomes less frequently manifest in discrete actions, the automatic response of hiding (due to our old-self defenses) is also being undermined, so that our new selves are also characterized by greater transparency regarding our remaining struggles with sin.[6]

In the old self, the moral law is either experienced as an introject (as an "inner critic" that chronically condemns oneself and fosters self-punishment) or is overidentified with, so that one feels perfect like God (unconsciously), even if one believes otherwise consciously. As the law of the ethical order is more and more transposed in Christ by grace into the spiritual order, sin's distortion and misuse of the law (Rom 7) get undermined. This allows the law itself to be increasingly integrated with grace in the heart, so that it becomes the law-in-Christ and a source of genuine, heartfelt joy, in spite of a simultaneous awareness of one's remaining sin and brokenness, producing a beautiful combination of contrition, humility, gratitude, and self-affirmation in Christ.

All this is based on the biblical teaching that the old self is *old*. "The darkness is passing away and the true Light is already shining" (1 Jn 2:8). When Christians sin, we confess (as we have seen in the previous chapter), but our confession turns the sin into something old, former, passing away—not our true self, who we are forever in Christ. This complex self-understanding allows Christians to maintain (imperfectly) a clean conscience alongside an awareness of their sinfulness and an openness to self-examination. The Christian's old self is of vastly secondary importance compared to their new self. This is no different from what relatively healthy persons do with any other "lesser" aspects of their self-representation. Those who are not very good at something, say basketball, relegate their "basketball self" to the periphery of their identity, whereas something they are good at, say piano playing, they tend to bring into the center (Harter, 2012).

Integrating one's suffering into one's new self. We have seen that suffering is of great significance in the kingdom of God (Mt 5:3-4, 10-12), because it is a sharing in Christ's sufferings, so it also needs to be incorporated into one's new self. The apostle Paul understood that suffering was part of his calling, and he strategically made reference to it in his epistles (2 Cor 1:5-11; 4:11-15; 11:23–12:10; Phil 1:12-14). When believers have suffered in the past or as they suffer in the present, they are to consider themselves as cosufferers with Christ (Rom 8:17), and over time this should impact their new identity—the greater the suffering, the greater the impact—contributing uniquely to the kind of new person they are becoming, increasing their capacities to suffer well and to refold their desires into the love of God (Stump, 2010), which in turn fosters consolation and can even modify the pain of suffering to some extent (Coakley, 2005).

Integrating one's biopsychosocial damage into one's new self. True and sound wisdom includes, at least in part, a recognition of one's limitations, as well as one's strengths and sins, so the development of the new self also includes coming to terms with one's biopsychosocial damage. A more realistic hope is forged in such realizations. Neural plasticity guarantees some potential for change in most biopsychosocial disorders, though it varies according to many factors, including the disorder's deterministic resistance to change or, put conversely, its susceptibility to influence by agency and interventions as well as available treatments. Humans live within an unpredictable dialectic of determinism and determination. Kierkegaard (1849/1980) believed that the form of the self was shaped by how this dialectic is negotiated. We might just add that the form of the new self is that negotiation in Christ.

In addition, life in Christ provides a transcendent context for the reinterpretation of our disabilities. As we become aware of them, they too can be integrated or refolded into our new self and on into the love of God. The weaknesses of believers are analogous to the wounds or scars on Christ's crucified body—indeed, they are the wounds of his other body, the church. Consequently, counselees can appraise them, as much as possible, as Christ does. For example, a believer who stutters might be burdened with shame about the problem. Whenever activated, the shame could be folded into a positive emotion scheme tied to Christ, for example, by reflecting on his compassionate treatment of the weak in the Gospels, resulting in the formation of a complex emotion scheme that over time can come to dominate his appraisal of the weakness (which in turn may positively affect the stuttering).

More mature believers may even be able to modify their appraisals of their weaknesses to the point that they can "boast" with Paul in them, that is, recognize and consent to their positive value in Christ to God. Christians can make mistakes and do not have to be as good as someone else, because their weaknesses are bestowed with divine glory. By refolding them into our perfection in Christ and his love, we can undermine the false shame that we may be more aware of. However, whatever shame one feels is a sign of something unresolved in Christ. So if the created damage is really to become honestly valued, that shame has to be intentionally modified experientially— the only alternative is to force ourselves into some degree of unconscious denial. Moreover, people often cannot legitimately consent to a weakness until they have grieved over it and perhaps the losses that it may have caused them. As we have already noted, boasting is a lofty, virtuous goal, and the counselor needs to gauge counselee readiness to move from grief, for example, to acceptance, before boasting can even be considered.

Integrating one's faults into one's new self. Because faults are both sin and damage, their incorporation into one's new self is complex and paradoxical. Consider a disposition to lose one's temper (rather than a specific unwarranted angry outburst, which is usually considered a sin). A tendency to harm others in that way is grounds for true shame, while its dispositional nature is cause for interpreting it as a site for Christ's glory—as paradoxical as that is. So, while reflecting on the periodic manifestation of this tendency over many years (perhaps spurred by a spouse's offhanded complaint) and feeling some legitimate shame about it, a believer could allow the reflection and shame to lead first to a deeper realization of how this tendency characterizes his actual self and has marred his life and relationships—in spite of his love relationship with Christ—and then on to confession of it to Christ and requests for forgiveness and the eventual ability to overcome it, finishing up, perhaps, with the sense that Christ wants to help him become more aware of this tendency and reduce the frequency of its expression, and transform the trait into discernment.

As believers acknowledge their faults and bring them to Christ, such knowledge can be "metabolized" and incorporated consciously into their new-self structure. This makes one's fault more salient and weakens it by undermining the associated shame and fear and enabling believers to talk more freely about it with others, while increasing their appropriation of God's love and their hope that God will overcome the fault, while patiently bearing with it and learning to live in that paradox.

Integrating one's story into Christ's story. Research has documented the importance of one's narrative to one's identity and relational style and the role that narrative plays in personal integration (see Cozolino, 2010; Siegel, 2012; van der Hart, Nijenhuis, & Steele, 2006). Narrative processing requires sufficient cognitive and linguistic ability, the temporal sequencing of events, narrative logic, imagery, agency, and interpersonal relations, which together integrates many different regions of the brain. Just talking through (or journaling) one's story promotes brain integration, because narrative processing occurs more in the right hemisphere and language in the left. There is also strong evidence that attachment experiences in particular exert a profound effect on one's ability to develop a coherent personal narrative, and some evidence that psychotherapy can be reparative and foster more coherent narratives (Hesse, 2008)—and a likelihood that one's relationship with God can do likewise (Granqvist & Kirkpatrick, 2008).

We noted in chapter five that the union of believers with Christ is a critical pillar in the triune God's theodramatic, doxological agenda, in part through the weaving together of each believer's life story with the life story of Christ's life, death, resurrection, and exaltation—in their place and on their behalf as their great High Priest, who became like them in every respect except sin. Some of this narrative retelling (which Ricoeur [1984] called *emplotment*) involves the present, and some involves the past. Regarding the present, Christians give their story new-creation unity as they interpret everything that happens—their actions, relationships, and events they experience, including their current suffering—as participation in God's theodrama. This redemptive narrative framework bestows a grand sense of purpose to one's life and actions and grants curative meaning to one's suffering, damage, and even one's sins. Moreover, believers are coauthors of their own story. Through the dramatic improvisation possible with freedom in Christ, conditioned as it is by biological and social influences, they are continuously writing much of the plot line of their story, as well as contributing to their own character formation by loving others and working on and accepting their psychopathology. Every good deed is a manifestation of one's created, redeemed self. "Whatever you do in word or deed, do all in the name of the Lord Jesus, giving thanks through Him to God the Father" (Col 3:17). Such a frame provides a Christ-centered narrative coherence for one's story.

Another narrative type of RI is the reinterpretation of the past events and actions of one's story in light of one's union with Christ. Paul did this. "I am the least of the apostles, and not fit to be called an apostle, because I persecuted the church of God. But by the grace of God I am what I am, and His grace toward me did not prove vain; but I labored even more than all of them, yet not I, but the grace of God with me" (1 Cor 15:9-10). God's grace turned his story in a direction no one could have predicted and empowered him to act very differently than he had.[7] In his *Confessions*, Augustine engaged in a more thorough Christian emplotment, where he reinterpreted the details of his pre-Christian and Christian life according to a biblically based understanding of God and his purposes.

Such emplotment is basic to Christian narrative therapy. Memories from childhood abuse or of one's own sinful actions earlier in life are usually laden with negative emotions such as shame, guilt, sadness, anxiety, and anger, which can reactivate and reinforce toxic messages stored in one's brain/soul until they are resolved: "You're to blame!" "You can't do anything right!" "You're unlovable!" Just knowing intellectually that Christ has redeemed believers from their past will not go very far in resolving the deep emotion schemes associated with specific events in one's past and modify the negative emotions associated with them. Yet one's union with Christ bears on all that one currently is, including all of one's emotion memories, and applying the work of Christ to them extends its reach further and deeper. Integration with one's narrative can be done by letting some Christian truth modify the emotions associated with a particular episodic memory, for example, by applying the atonement to a memory of a terrible sin one committed long ago but cannot forget, leading to forgiveness; or inviting Christ into a memory of abuse and bringing in justice, redemption, or love (see Tan & Ortberg, 1995, for a model that invites Jesus into the memory); or allowing some aspect of the meaningfulness of Christ's story (e.g., his unjust mistreatment) to give new meaning to one's own story ("My unjust mistreatment is analogous to Christ's"). Regardless of how it is done, we might call the healing of memories an example of *retroactive redemptive integration*.[8]

Conclusion

The overall developmental goal of images of God is to know and love God, friends and neighbors, ourselves, and his creation as much like God as possible, for the sake of his glory (ultimately) and our personal and communal flourishing. As finite and fallen beings, however, our capacities are severely limited, particularly when compared with God's omniscience and perfect appraisal. The best we can do is to know and love as much as possible what and how God knows and loves; for us that means that our knowledge and love are as thoroughly interrelated as possible, corresponding in a finite degree to God's simple, unified knowledge and love. When we consider our self-understanding and self-appraisal, this entails knowing and valuing ourselves as created good; as sinful, suffering, and damaged; as redeemed in Christ; and as perfected in heaven—in relation to each simultaneously. Though it is impossible to realize this *telos* fully, to whatever degree it is possible, it will entail some form of redemptive differentiation and integration.

INTEGRATION THROUGH HUMAN RELATIONSHIPS

Because of the profound interconnection between divine-human relations and human-human relations, and between creation and redemption, RI is also promoted by human relationships and dialogue. This is because dialogue with relatively healthy others tends to activate the interpersonal regions of one's brain, connecting with one's subjectivity (Siegel, 2012) and providing an *inter*subjective experience with a stabilizing external but personal reference point that can facilitate one's exploration of one's emotions, the practice of emotional regulation, and the conscious integration of the experience with one's union with Christ.

Christian therapists have a special role to play in this process. To begin with, they promote integration by accepting their counselees (as Christ has accepted them), acknowledging and affirming their created gifts, offering therapeutic insight and progress, assigning homework, promotiong in-session accomplishments, and regularly reminding them of God's love for them and—if they are Christians—of their forgiveness and justification in Christ. Furthermore, by means of therapist love, empathy, and responsiveness, the therapist and counselee can negotiate and create a safe intersubjective space in which deep connection occurs while the counselee divulges matters of which they are ashamed. Christian therapists seek to create a theocentric holding environment in which their holy love—in the context of Christian discourse—represents for their counselees their holy, loving Father, allowing them to experience themselves as the whole persons they are perceived to be by him in their union with the Son's humanity. Further integration can occur as they talk together about themselves and their stories in light of their union with Christ and the therapeutic implications of Christian truth, while simultaneously experiencing loving "resonance" together in their states of mind (and brains) (Lewis, Amini, & Lannon, 2000; Siegel, 2012). Without any human relational support or scaffolding, theological truth talk will most likely remain merely cognitive and not forge new connections with emotional, self, and relational regions of the brain/soul.

The relational modality can also be utilized to help counselees learn how to experience others as whole persons too. As we noted in chapter seventeen, many who come for counseling tend to engage in "splitting" and experience people alternatively as all good and all bad, which in turn affects which parts of themselves get activated and how they relate to others. Such self-other dynamics can only be worked on during their activation, and it can be helpful if they are activated with someone who is relatively healthier and can guide them through to some resolution, such as a therapist. As counselees talk about what they are experiencing, the therapist can respond with understanding and kindness and so help counselees learn how to manage and eventually bring about healing in their internal-relational conflict. With training and practice, spouses and very close friends may also successfully facilitate such intersubjective integrative activities together. And the more integrated we are, the better we can help promote the integration of others.

AN ILLUSTRATION OF REDEMPTIVE DIFFERENTIATION AND INTEGRATION

Let us consider Todd, a thirty-six-year-old married counselee, who with his wife has two young boys. He came to counseling complaining of overwhelming sadness and exhaustion. He also had difficulty sleeping and was taking medication for an ulcer. He said he often felt like a failure and was ashamed that he had made so little of himself. He also reported carrying on a nearly continual argument within himself of self-criticism and half-hearted rebuttal. Most of his life he had been scarcely aware of this internal conflict, but in recent years it had been growing stronger, and he said that lately he couldn't "get a handle on it" and was desperate to get it to stop.

Todd worked fifty to sixty hours a week as a quality-control engineer at an industrial chemical company, but he was haunted by the belief that he did not work hard enough, and he was convinced that if he let up on his efforts, a catastrophe would ensue, ruining his career, which though very unlikely was possible. Todd described his wife as "cold and distant," but he did not want a divorce. Communication was tense at home, so he mostly "stayed out of everyone's way." He admitted to deep regret for his lack of involvement with his family, but he felt he would just do more harm than good. However, he insisted that the family attend church every week and a small group on Thursdays, though it felt to him like God "never showed up." With regard to his family of origin, Todd's stay-at-home mother took care of him as a child, but she "never had a nice thing to say," and he grew up feeling incapable of satisfying her demands. His father traveled a lot for his job, and Todd remembers him mostly watching TV when he was home. Todd also shared that he was converted to Christ when he was nineteen, but after the first few years, which were a high point in his life, a dark cloud descended on him that he has never been able to shake. Though he said he knew better, he confided to feeling like there wasn't much point to having personal devotions, for he perceived God to be pretty frustrated with him. Nevertheless, he was convinced from his first years as a Christian that God could make a difference in one's life. Todd continued in therapy for a few years, and the following summary is intended to illustrate how redemptive differentiation and integration was promoted.[9]

Sensing Todd's significant feelings of alienation and anxiety, the counselor believed her primary task for the first few months was to represent the compassionate, relational side of Christ when they were together, as someone who was deeply interested in him, so she spent a lot of time asking Todd questions about his background, his relationship with his parents past and present, and the tension that existed in his current family, and listening intently to what he had to say.

Over the following months, the counselor probed gently into Todd's thoughts and feelings and got to know pretty well his inner world, his beliefs about himself, and his experience of others. The counselor was keen to commend Todd whenever he had an insight or shared something positive that he had accomplished. Some time was spent in most sessions talking about an aspect of the gospel: union with Christ, the significance for Todd of what Christ had done on the cross and in the resurrection, or something about the Christian's old and new selves, sometimes pulling out the Bible to illustrate a theme from that session, and usually concluding with prayer. During those early months Todd was also taught how to meditate and encouraged to get into a daily routine of some Bible reading, prayer, and meditation. This took months to become a consistent part of his life.

At the end of a particularly difficult session filled with self-criticism, in which it became obvious that Todd could not think positively about himself, the counselor gave him a homework assignment to write out two lists, one of his created gifts and strengths and the other of important salvation blessings that he had received from God the day he became a Christian (he was also given a handout with many of those blessings on it), and for homework he was to spend time in his daily devotions reflecting and journaling about both lists, with the goal of more deeply appreciating and owning these aspects of himself. On another occasion Todd was asked to maintain a readiness throughout the coming week to actively receive compliments from others and to identify and appreciate his own accomplishments. Whenever he was complimented or accomplished something, he was first to listen to his automatic negative internal response and, if he had the time, to label it as his old self, surrender it to Christ on the cross, and then reflect again on the strength that had been manifested and thank God for it. Later that day, he was to take ten to fifteen minutes and journal about his positive features that had been identified during the day and whether they were a result of creation, redemption, or both.

One week Todd came in filled with shame and guilt over how he had hurt his son with some sharp criticism that brought him to tears. After talking through the event, the counselor encouraged Todd to take some time right then to confess his sin to God and then receive forgiveness from him. Before they finished, the counselor asked him to read through a devotional book in the coming week that explained how the cross resolved our sin and was involved in our forgiveness and justification in Christ. During another session, the counselor and Todd read together 2 Corinthians 12, about Paul's thorn in the flesh, and Todd was asked to come up with list of some of his own weaknesses and reflect and journal about God's attitude toward him because of them, which they talked about in the next session.

After they had developed a strong therapeutic bond, and as opportunity arose, they would also periodically discuss Todd's tendency to criticize himself and others, identifying this pattern as a reflection of Todd's story as well as his old self. He developed a disposition to attend to the impact of his words on others and apologize to them if he had hurt them, and then seek forgiveness and reconciliation with God. Eventually, he grew to recognize and own when he got into a critical mood and would then disidentify with it, labeling the emotion structure as a part of his old self, and seek to replace it with a more benevolent state of mind based on God's love of him in Christ.

Throughout the first year of therapy Todd thought his relationship with his parents was great. However, whenever he talked about either of them, his tone and facial expressions suggested all was not well. As they explored this incongruity together, Todd became aware of significant, unresolved anger toward them. Pointing to the Old Testament model of the Psalms, the counselor guided Todd through a phase, lasting a few months, where he was encouraged to experience and own his anger toward his parents activated in response to specific mistreatment by them—whether recent or recalled from the past—and express it to God with emotion, and then surrender the entire episode into his hands. Over time he began to sense that God was validating his sense of injustice but also that God didn't want him to stay there. Eventually, Todd was invited to consider again the virtue of forgiveness as advocated in the New Testament (which he had embraced as a young Christian), this time using Worthington's (2009) REACH model, augmented by reflection and journaling about Christ on the cross, his union with him, the death-resurrection narrative pattern, and how the transformation he was undergoing was contributing to the strength of his new self.

In a number of sessions Todd was asked to think of an emotionally painful episode from his life and bring it into his working memory while activating the associated mental images and feelings, and then was invited to introduce some aspect of the Christian faith into that emotion scheme, so that he might experience a resolution signified by a positive emotion shift, transforming the original negative emotions (associated with the cross) into a sense of God's peace, consolation, or compassion (associated with Christ's resurrection). Periodically, the counselor would also have Todd engage in conversations between his old self and his new self, both in session (using the two-chair technique) and at home (looking in the mirror), helping him to better distinguish them. After a couple years of therapy, Todd would be invited to share a recent event in his life where he felt he had failed, and the counselor would ask him to close his eyes and imagine, first, what Jesus might say to him about it, and second, what his new self might do in a similar situation in the future.

Throughout the time they met together, the counselor sought to cultivate a relationship where Todd felt accepted and safe, reflected in periodic sharing of her own struggles and liabilities as well as her personal appreciation for the grace of God in her own life. On the few occasions that Todd criticized her, the counselor did her best to model an openness to such feedback, recognizing the validity in Todd's comments and owning and apologizing where she could, but reminded herself that she was holy and beloved in Christ and that Todd was somewhat distorted in his views of others.

By the time Todd decided to wrap up the therapy, he had become much more aware of his complexity—his created strengths, his sinfulness and sins, his relative biopsychosocial damage, the suffering and blessings of his story, the immense benefits he had as a saint and a child of God, and the progress he had made. In addition, most days he was experiencing less internal conflict than when he had begun, was less anxious, angry, and critical (validated by feedback from his wife), had greater access to his story and his defenses and a growing sense that he and his future were going to be okay, and he felt closer to God and others than he had for a long time. With Christ, and the counselor's help, he was becoming more of a whole person—a personal agent in communion—what Christians call living out of his new self.[10]

RESOURCES FOR COUNSELORS AND COUNSELEES

Classic

Kierkegaard, S. (1938). *Purity of heart is to will one thing.* New York: Harper & Row. ‡

Owen, J. (2007). *Communion with the triune God.* Wheaton, IL: Crossway. ‡

Thomas à Kempis. *The imitation of Christ.* (Any version)

von Hildebrand, D. (2001). *Transformation in Christ: On the Christian attitude.* San Francisco: Ignatius. ‡

Contemporary

Allen, J. G., Fonagy, P., & Bateman, A. (2008). *Mentalizing in clinical practice.* New York: American Psychiatric Association. ‡

Appleby, D. W., & Ohlschlager, G. (Eds.). (2013). *Transformative encounters: The intervention of God in Christian counseling and pastoral care.* Downers Grove, IL: InterVarsity Press. ‡ The best survey of distinctly Christian therapy models available in one location.

Billings, J. T. (2007). *Calvin, participation, and the gift: The activity of believers in union with Christ.* New York: Oxford University Press. ‡

Coe, J. H., & Hall, T. W. (2010). *Psychology in the Spirit: Contours of a transformational psychology.* Downers Grove, IL: InterVarsity Press. ‡ Discusses many themes that promote internal integration by the Spirit.

DeGroat, C. (2016). *Wholeheartedness: Busyness, exhaustion, and healing the divided self.* Grand Rapids, MI: Eerdmans. A contemporary Christian classic on integration.

Siegel, D. J. (2012). *The developing mind* (2nd ed.). ‡ New York: Guilford. ‡ Chapter twelve discusses the nature of neurological and psychological integration, though based on the worldview of naturalism.

Stump, E. (2010). *Wandering in darkness: Narrative and the problem of suffering.* New York: Oxford University Press. ‡ A marvelous Christian discussion of internal integration.

Thrall, B., McNicol, B., & Lynch, J. (2004). *TrueFaced: Trust God and others with who you really are.* Colorado Springs: NavPress.

Zeiders, C. L. (2004). *The clinical Christ.* Birdsboro, PA: Julian's House.

‡ Recommended more for counselors and pastors than for counselees

PART VI

The Divine Cure

Integral to the infrastructure of a Christian approach to well-being and healing is the assumption that believers are heading toward a stage of life that will be immeasurably better than life on earth: where all the evil and sorrow of this world will have been removed, including all their own sin, suffering, and shame, and where they will enjoy the greatest happiness imaginable in completely satisfying communion with the triune God and one another, to which all the goodness enjoyed in this age weakly points. Believing by the Spirit that this stage is coming is intended by God to transfigure how those in Christ interpret everything in this life, to help them cope with their earthly limitations, struggles, and obstacles, and to promote the coming of Christ's kingdom through their lives, their relationships, and their culture, including inviting others to join them on this journey.

—20—

Living in the Future

Principle 10: Already being a part of the new creation orients believers to an eternal future with God and radically reframes their lives on earth.

"Behold, the tabernacle of God is among men, and He will dwell among them, and they shall be His people, and God Himself will be among them, and He will wipe away every tear from their eyes; and there will no longer be any death; there will no longer be any mourning, or crying, or pain; the first things have passed away." And he who sits on the throne said, "Behold, I am making all things new."

Revelation 21:3-5

In spite of all our feelings, weal and woe, God wants us to understand and believe that we are more truly in heaven than on earth.

Julian of Norwich (1998)

One of the earlier hits of the rock group U2 puzzled some of their Christian fans with lines like the following:

> You loosed the chains
> Carried the cross of my shame . . .
> But I still haven't found
> What I'm looking for.

Complicated, to be sure, but this seems a pretty apt description of the restless longing in this life of the Christian heart. With all the spiritual riches and therapeutic resources available to the Christian we have surveyed in this book, at best Christians still experience now only a shadow of what they will. All that we can obtain through the Holy Spirit—our only access to those riches and resources in this age—is likened by the apostle Paul to a down payment or first installment (*arrabōn*; 2 Cor 1:22; 5:5; Eph 1:14) and the first fruits (Rom 8:23, *aparchēn*) of the coming harvest. Here we sin, knowingly and unknowingly; disabilities are thrust upon us; we have unsatisfied desires and unrealized goals; we suffer a variety of miseries; we are victims of various evils; we are divided, conflicted beings; and we lack consistent intimacy with God and others. As a result, "we . . . groan within ourselves, waiting eagerly for our adoption as sons, the redemption of our body" (Rom 8:23), "longing to be clothed with our dwelling from heaven" (2 Cor 5:2)—even the Spirit now groans within us (Rom 8:26)! Bono was right. We still haven't found what we're looking for.

As a result, some dissatisfaction is normal down here. We were made for holiness and wholeness, and for relational fulfillment with a big-hearted God and good friends, but because of human sin, things are now set up in such a way that we are simply unable to find in this life all the good for which we were made. Instead, we must look forward to a future state of blessedness, flowing from mutual closeness with the Father, Son, and Holy Spirit—then we shall know fully just as we also have been fully known (1 Cor 13:12). That future state will be experienced as praise, joy, delight, and gratitude scarcely comparable to anything we have tasted down here. At best, our foretastes are inconsistent and rarely intense, and they are unpredictably mixed together with the sorrow and frustration and anxiety and pain—our own and others'—that characterizes so much of this present evil age.

The biblical authors, therefore, often encouraged their readers to look ahead, toward their eternal future, and console themselves by taking to heart their divinely promised, everlasting flourishing, teaching us that this kind of hopefulness is fundamental to the Christian life in this world. While there is much to celebrate in creation and redemption, there is also great value in concentrating our attention on the consummation as we travel through this dry and weary land, especially since in Christ we are already living "ahead of time," in the new creation.

Theologians call this concentration on the future "eschatological," derived from *eschatos*, the Greek word for "last" or "final." Many Christians of the last century have understood eschatology to be the divining of the historical events that portend and accompany the second coming of Christ and the ending of this age (as in the Left Behind book series). But that kind of speculative inquiry seems far removed from the actual eschatological agenda of Scripture and has little value for the healing of the soul.[1] At the very least, such a focus seems a distraction from both the realities of the present life—good and bad—as well as those of the future that have been more clearly revealed to us. But before considering the latter, we will take a look at the secular psychological alternative to see what we can learn and as a standard of comparison.

IMMANENT HOPES

It is commonly recognized that humans are future-oriented beings (Haith, Benson, Roberts, & Pennington, 1995; Heidegger, 1962; Markus & Nurius, 1986). However, that orientation is inevitably shaped by worldview assumptions. According to the Catholic philosopher Charles Taylor (2007), Western culture is currently in the grip of an "immanent frame," within which people can only conceive of human life and well-being according to the ontological and temporal limits of the natural world. Within such a frame, human happiness can only be found in this life, creating an unconscious desperation to "get your best life now."[2] Most commonly, this means people realize themselves solely by working more or less diligently toward having a successful family and career and obtaining significant material prosperity, aided by enjoyment of the comforts of Western life: good food and entertainment, and a nice house and car. For many this is the extent of the meaningful universe. Some of the less fortunate may cope by losing themselves in what Kierkegaard called "immediacy": living for the weekend, trying to win the lottery, looking forward to a buzz or the next orgasm (and this near-future orientation seems to be growing in influence in the West). The immanent frame also creates a crisis of care for those who are chronically sick or in pain or severely depressed, so that it becomes easier to imagine they might simply be better off dead. At a more abstract level, Western culture gives hope with the promise of continual human and cultural improvement through education, science, and the latest versions of technology. Yet in the immanent frame people can only share in such hopes as long as they live, and after that, there is no personal existence, the terrifying implications of which are mostly consciously avoided, according to terror management theory (Greenberg, Koole, & Pyszczynski, 2004).[3]

Nevertheless, a number of secular models of hope and optimism have arisen, in part to improve people's quality of life under these circumstances (e.g., Carver & Scheier, 2002; Seligman, 1991). Snyder (1994, 2000) developed a cognitive model of hope, defining it as "a positive motivational state that is based on an interactively derived sense of successful (a) agency (goal-directed energy) and (b) pathways (planning to meet goals)" (Snyder, Irving, & Anderson, 1991, p. 287). Subsequent research (Snyder, 2000) demonstrated that people with these two features of hope are better able to succeed in a variety of human endeavors, including therapy, school-based achievement, and athletic performance, and in spite of illness, disability, trauma, and maladaptive development. Such findings confirm that humans were created for hope and optimism. However, according to a biblical frame, without God humans lack *true* hope (Eph 2:12). In comparison with a Christian model, the secular hope models lack content, sounding vague and empty, as if the goal were just to be "hopeful." In light of terror-management theory, such models could be interpreted as contributing to the denial of death (Becker, 1973). Moreover, as legitimate as many "immanent hopes" are, they are distorted if they are based solely on one's own, autonomous resources. In addition, they are inadequate to fulfill human life as it was designed if their scope does not extend beyond this age, especially for those who are severely damaged or who have sinned or suffered greatly, as well as for those who are the most self-aware. Within this life, we just can't find what we're looking for.

CHRISTIAN TEACHING REGARDING THE FUTURE

While love is supreme, the apostle Paul (1 Cor 13:13) famously included hope and faith in his short list of the primary Christian virtues. He even said that Christians are saved in hope (Rom 8:24). In contrast to the exclusively immanent hope described by a secular psychology, we will examine some of the distinctive features of biblical hope.

Christian Hope and Death

The first "last thing" to consider is the last event of our earthly life. Though people are dying around us every day, it is eerily easy to forget about our own inevitable demise and to give it little serious reflection. We are indebted to existentialist psychologists who have studied this stunning, pervasive defense (Greenberg, Koole, & Pyszczynski, 2004). Yet, to be fair, it may be impossible for humans to conceive of their own nonexistence (Jenson, 2003), suggesting there has to be more for each of us.

When Christians think of the inescapable end of their life, they are also always to think of their forerunner, Jesus (Col 1:18), who walked into death before them and emerged from it a new man. And since his resurrection is ours (Rom 6:4), as well as his death, thoughts about our own physical death should be integrated and transposed into thoughts about our own resurrection (Jenson, 2003).

The Preeminent Focus of Christian Hope

Christian hope begins with trust in the triune God (1 Tim 4:10; 5:5; 6:17). It is (unsurprisingly) theocentric, exulting "in hope of the glory of God," mediated by Christ and what he has accomplished (Rom 5:2). The final age of human history is still to come—what we called in chapter five the consummation and is sometimes labeled the eschaton (Schwarz, 2000)—beginning after the Son of God returns to earth. Then there will be a public manifestation of God's glory unlike anything in this age, where his sovereign majesty, righteousness, and love will be displayed for all to see, and universal worship will result: "every created thing which is in heaven and on the earth and under the earth and on the sea, and all things in them, I heard saying, 'To Him who sits on the throne, and to the Lamb, be blessing and honor and glory and dominion forever and ever'" (Rev 5:13).

Because of the believer's union with Christ's death and resurrection, and what they portend, Christian hope is especially focused on the Lamb who was slain and raised (Rev 5:6; see 1 Jn 3:3; Eph 1:12). "What has happened to Jesus is what will happen to the whole creation" (Bauckham, 2009, p. 309). So Christ is the "first fruits" of the final resurrection of believers (1 Cor 15:20-23). His resurrection was "the sign that God has stood by his created order [and] implies that this order, with mankind in its proper place within it, is to be totally restored at the last" (O'Donovan, 1986, p. 15). So Christ himself is the believer's hope (1 Tim 1:1), and his indwelling now through the Holy Spirit is called "the hope of glory" (Col 1:27). König (1989) concludes that "the *eschatos* is a person, not just a set of forthcoming *things*" (p. 39). So, Christian hope is optimistic about oneself and one's future, but in relation to Christ; we might therefore also call it a dipolar hope. Of special importance is the preeminent role Christ plays in bringing in the age to come. "Jesus himself has a future with the world that is both his own future and the future of the world. He himself as the coming savior and judge of all determines the final future of all things" (Bauckhum, 2009, p. 318). Like everything else having to do with believers' lives, the future is first and foremost about the God with whom they are reconciled and then secondarily about themselves and their relationship with him.

Christian Hope Looks Forward to the After-Age

Hope in the New Testament is especially oriented toward what will happen to believers after this age, a state termed "eternal life" (Titus 3:7) and "salvation" (1 Thess 5:8; see Rom 8:24), brought about by the triune God after Christ comes back again (Rev 21–22).[4] Positively, eternal life will consist of a happiness or blessedness with God and other believers that will last forever and immeasurably transcends happiness in this age; negatively it includes deliverance from the major problems of this age—sin and suffering—and from a just condemnation due to sin. Believers are therefore now encouraged to "fix your hope completely on the grace to be brought to you at the revelation of Jesus Christ" (1 Pet 1:13). At the same time, Christian hope does not reject life in this age—current blessings, for example, are to be enjoyed as foretastes of eternal blessings—but it also looks beyond them, to their fulfillment promised but currently unattainable in their fullness:

> For I consider that the sufferings of this present time are not worthy to be compared with the glory that is to be revealed to us. For the anxious longing of the creation waits eagerly for the revealing of the sons of God. For the creation was subjected to futility, not willingly, but because of Him who subjected it, in hope that the creation itself also will be set free from its slavery to corruption into the freedom of the glory of the children of God. For we know that the whole creation groans and suffers the pains of childbirth together until now. And not only this, but also we ourselves, having the first fruits of the Spirit, even we ourselves groan within ourselves, waiting eagerly for our adoption as sons, the redemption of our body. For in hope we have been saved, but hope that is seen is not hope; for who hopes for what he already sees? But if we hope for what we do not see, with perseverance we wait eagerly for it. (Rom 8:18-25)

God's glory will be finally manifested to believers when their secret of being the children of God is fully disclosed. They will experience a complete eschatological healing and will finally attain the freedom to love God well, which they have long sought. Christian hope, therefore, focuses on what is hidden now—it cannot be seen—but what God promises is coming. In addition, the natural order would seem to participate in it. Using "poetic language" (Cranfield, 1985), the apostle personified the entire creation

(Schreiner, 1998) to underscore that it also has been affected by human fall-enness and therefore also has much at stake in the coming redemption, teaching us that Christian hope is about more than just one's own future happiness. Cosmic in scope and in continuity with life in this age, Christian hope is intended to influence our lives now.

The Redemption of the Body
In the above passage in Romans the apostle Paul also linked together the redemption of the bodies of believers with their becoming a fully realized child of God. Though formally already adopted by God, there is a fuller sense of sonship that awaits them, tied mysteriously to their obtaining a new body.

The future redemption of our bodies underscores their primordial goodness and suggests a new kind of embodiment. They will no longer be "fleshly," no more tainted by sin and its effects, and so freed from God's pri-mordial curse (Gen 3:16-19); they will be "immortal, incorruptible, spiritu-alized, and glorified" (Bavinck, 1956, p. 563; 1 Cor 15:42-44). As a result, there would seem to be no more bodily damage that compromises human func-tioning, so no new genetic abnormalities to trigger, no neurotransmitter deficits or maladaptive neural networks. This means no more somatic dis-orders, eating disorders, gender dysphoria, or same-sex attraction.[5] Part of our final redemption, then, includes our biological and embodied well-being.

No More Suffering or Additional Damage
One of the best changes brought in by the coming of eschaton is the removal of all the evil of the present evil age. "There will no longer be any death; there will no longer be any mourning, or crying, or pain; the first things have passed away" (Rev 21:4). God will destroy death (Is 25:8). "Shall I ransom them from the power of Sheol? Shall I redeem them from death? O death, are your thorns? O Sheol, where is your sting?" (Hos 13:14, cited in 1 Cor 15:55). These promises, of course, hark back to the curse pronounced on humanity in Genesis 3. A day is coming when death will be taken away, and "there will no longer be any curse," and "there will no longer be any night" (Rev 22:3, 5).

Part of that final redemption includes the release of God's children from whatever evil remains of their psychopathology, including all their sin and suffering. We are not, however, told that God will remove all the effects of their damage—perhaps because they are not intrinsically evil. We recall that Christ still had the wounds from his crucifixion on his resurrection body. Some Christians with mentally impaired loved ones have suggested that there must be some continuity between their form on earth and their form in heaven; otherwise they will not be recognizable (Yong, 2008; Young, 1990). Until then, we cannot know for sure, but we do know that God will "wipe away every tear" from his people's eyes (Rev 21:4), poignantly signifying that he will personally comfort us and be intimately involved in our final healing, tenderly resolving the negative emotions that affected us in this life. Sadness and pain are specifically mentioned, but also anxiety (there will be nothing there to fear), anger (no more injustice), disgust (everything there will be beautiful), and shame and guilt (we will be free of sin and perfectly beloved).

Completeness and Flourishing with God

So, in the coming age all that is truly bad in the lives of believers will be gone. However, in that day, they will also be given unfathomable good, the greatest of which is the immediate presence of the triune God.

Eschatological discourse necessarily "deals in the symbolic and the imaginative" (Bauckham, 2009, p. 316), since it refers to realities that vastly transcend current human life. Metaphorical language, for example, runs riot in the book of Revelation. The age to come is likened at one point to a marriage ceremony, when the people of God will be "made ready as a bride adorned for her husband" (Rev 21:2), and she will be adorned with God's greatness and beauty. The apostle Paul also used this trope, teaching that Christ died for the church "that He might sanctify her, having cleansed her by the washing of water with the word, that He might present to Himself the church in all her glory, having no spot or wrinkle or any such thing; but that she would be holy and blameless" (Eph 5:26-27). Such passages imply that the future age will be an incredible celebration, where the cleansing, enlivening grace believers have only begun to enjoy will be realized fully in the perfection of the bride's beautiful character manifested on that day. Also implied is the consummation of the bride's everlasting union with her husband, Jesus Christ, suggesting that that age will be characterized by a climactic joy far transcending the greatest physical pleasure of this age. At their best, even the joys of this earth are no more than metaphors pointing faintly toward that blessed age of complete fulfillment.

The bride of Christ is also likened to the holy city—a new Jerusalem (Rev 21:2, 10-27)—a vast, grand metropolis made of gold, clear as glass; bedecked with jewels and precious stones; fifteen hundred miles high, wide, and long (Rev 21:16), "having the glory of God" (Rev 21:11). And there, "God Himself will be among them" (Rev 21:3). God Almighty and the Lamb shall be their temple (Rev 21:22); their servants "will see His face" (Rev 22:4), and all shall be illuminated by God and the Lamb and their glory (Rev 21:23; 22:5).

At that time, all of God's doxological therapeutic purposes will finally be accomplished. God's many promises of future reconciliation and restoration—spoken in the covenants and the Old Testament, in redemptive history to Israel, and in Christ's life, death, resurrection, and exaltation—will be fulfilled. How? "They shall be His people, and God Himself will be among them" (Rev 21:3). God's original design for Adam and Eve to be children who resemble him will also be finally realized and fully experienced: "I will be his God and he will be My son" (Rev 21:7)—all because of the Son—and as God's royal sons and daughters, believers "will reign forever and ever" with the triune God (Rev 22:5; see 2 Tim 2:12). He will be our sovereign friend, whose never-ending, face-to-face presence will continually fill us to overflowing with joy unspeakable, full of glory (Col 3:12; 1 Jn 3:2; Rev 21:3; 22:4).

The Coming Inheritance

Another metaphor used to picture life in the coming age completes the declarative process of our adoption by God (Rom 8:23): the obtaining of our inheritance. Paul prayed that the Ephesians would know "what is the hope of His calling, what are the riches of the glory of His inheritance in the saints" (Eph 1:18). The children of God are "heirs according to the hope of eternal life" (Titus 3:7), "heirs of God and [incomprehensibly] fellow heirs with Christ" (Rom 8:17), which means that like Christ we are *royal* heirs.

So what does this royal inheritance consist of? The specifics are obscure; in fact, we are told it is unfathomable: "Things which eye has not seen and ear has not heard, and which have not entered the heart of man, all that God has prepared for those who love Him" (1 Cor 2:9). But we know that it is glorious—we will receive an "eternal weight of glory" (2 Cor 4:17)—a sharing in the glory of Christ (Rom 8:17), which is the glory of the children of God (Rom 8:21). So it has to do with meaningfulness and love. We will obtain the greatest sense of significance and the greatest mutual closeness with God possible for a creature, elevated into the immediate communion of the Trinity. With Christ, we will hear the Father say, "You are my beloved child, with whom I am well-pleased" (Mt 17:5), "in whom My soul delights" (Is 42:1). Moreover, we will be perfectly conformed to the image of Christ (Rom 8:29), making it possible for us to participate in God's glory and reflect it fully, according to our finite, respective capacities. But whatever those are, all believers will experience a fullness of joy, such that all their earthly joys and pains will be perceived as utterly insignificant in comparison.

Contemporary positive psychologists have developed measures of subjective well-being or happiness, on a scale from strongly negative affect to strongly positive. In this age the majority of people are a little above neutral on average, euphoria or ecstasy are quite rare, and "happy people report mild-to-moderate pleasant emotions most of the time" (Deiner, 2000, p. 36). Scripture suggests that the subjective state of believers in the age to come will be undiminishable bliss. Over the centuries of Christian reflection, this eschatological fulfillment came to be known as the *beatific vision,* a transcendently satisfying happiness derived from the unmitigated sight of God's splendor (Ex 34:20-23; 1 Jn 3:2). However, why limit the state to one sensory modality? Perhaps a better term would be "beatific consciousness," since, whatever we are doing, our attention will be joined forever to God's,[6] so that we will always be aware of his being as infinite, interpersonal Goodness, Beauty, and Truth. We will dwell in continual communion with him and enjoy perfect, actively receptive felicity through the constant infusion of his goodness toward us in Christ, so that, lacking nothing, "nothing can remain to be desired" (Aquinas, 1947, p. 112). The stupendous changes that believers will enjoy in eternity have been called *glorification* by theologians, and for good reason, since they involve a participation in God's glory so radical as to render them glorified (Rom 8:17, 30), like Jesus now in heaven (Jn 7:39).

Consequently, believers now are to be "looking for the blessed hope and the appearing of the glory of our great God and Savior, Christ Jesus" (Titus 2:13) and its incomparable bestowal of grace (1 Pet 1:13) and never-ending life, light, and love (Rev 21–22). At that time they will finally flourish according to God's design plan: holy and whole partakers in the divine nature (2 Pet 1:4), filled with all the fullness of God (Eph 3:19). The positive psychology of that era will vastly transcend the positive psychology of this one, though of course not for all.

Christian Hope Is Optimistic in the Face of the Final Judgment

We also learn in the Bible that the coming age begins with divine judgment, in which all the personal agents God brought into being and sustained throughout their lives are held accountable for their "deeds in the body" (2 Cor 5:10), an appraisal of the good and bad of their lives that takes into account the degree of their knowledge and privilege. One's works (Mt 25:35-46), words (Mt 12:36), and thoughts (Rom 2:16; 1 Cor 4:5) will be assessed, and given the misuse of our being and gifts, no personal agents will escape condemnation, unless they have submitted to God's judgment in Christ and allowed him to take their place. So those who united themselves to Christ and his atonement by faith can eagerly wait "for the hope of righteousness" (Gal 5:5), and though blameworthy in themselves, clothed in Christ's righteousness they will be "blameless in the day of our Lord Jesus Christ" (1 Cor 1:8), rendered "beautiful and lovely" (Edwards, 1974, p. 888). As a result, they can contemplate that day with confidence that it will go well with their souls.

Even more astounding, believers will be given rewards corresponding to the quality of their lives on earth. We noted in chapter nine that God mysteriously compensates suffering in this life with incomparable blessings in the age to come (2 Cor 4:18). However, though interpretations vary, it looks as though believers will also be evaluated according to another reward system that corresponds to the ethicospiritual quality of their actions.

> Now if any man builds on the foundation with gold, silver, precious stones, wood, hay, straw, each man's work will become evident; for the day will show it because it is to be revealed with fire, and the fire itself will test the quality of each man's work. If any man's work which he has built on it remains, he will receive a reward. If any man's work is burned up, he will suffer loss; but he himself will be saved, yet so as through fire. (1 Cor 3:12-15)

Though in the context Paul was referring to the work of ministers, it has historically been applied to the lives of all believers. Having been saved from the wrath to come (Rom 5:9), believers were "created in Christ Jesus for good works" (Eph 2:10); their personal agency set free in Christ, they can now learn how to pursue virtue in active receptivity—a slow, uniquely Christian process of virtue formation—though in an absolute sense, in themselves, they will continue to fall short of God's glory and need Christ's cleansing throughout their lives (1 Jn 1:6-10).[7] As a result, God renders their postconversion agency significant by "rewarding" believers in heaven for the good they have received from God on earth. Hence, "He who sows sparingly will also reap sparingly; and he who sows bountifully will also reap bountifully" (2 Cor 9:6); "Let us not lose heart in doing good, for in due time we will reap if we do not grow weary" (Gal 6:9; see also Lk 19:17; 1 Cor 3:10-15; 2 Cor 5:10).

In what will that reward consist? "We shall have him [God] for our reward" (Julian of Norwich, 1998, p. 174), and that is surely enough! However, that applies to everyone there. Edwards (1852/1969; 1974) thought that the heavenly rewards to be distributed referred to the relative capacity of one's character in heaven to love and enjoy God in true happiness, which would correspond precisely to one's grace-based ethical and spiritual attainments in this life. At first glance, this might seem to perpetuate in heaven the inequality and unfairness of life in this age, but "shall not the Judge of all the earth deal justly?" (Gen 18:25). Indeed, finally there will be perfect justice, since he who knows the respective advantages and disadvantages given to each believer, as well as their secret thoughts and deeds, will perfectly compensate them all, including the poor in spirit—for theirs is the kingdom of heaven—rendering satisfyingly meaningful everyone's postconversion agency.

Edwards reflected on heaven frequently, and he understood there will be no pride or envy there. Totally sanctified, everyone there will be filled with happiness, according to their respective capacities. As a result, everyone will be completely satisfied. The most blessed will have the greatest happiness, along with the greatest humility, while the least blessed will rejoice forever, and seeing the perfect justice in the greater blessedness of others, they will be genuinely happy for them without reserve. True delight in the greater well-being of others guarantees that heaven will be a happy place for everyone. The love of one's neighbor as one's self will finally be fully realized.

One more point. We recall from chapter five that, according to Bakhtin, characters in a story could not know the significance of their lives from within their own horizon. Only from the standpoint of the author, who exists outside each character's story, knowing it in its entirety, can its "consummated" meaning be grasped. Vanhoozer (2010) applies this framework to the relation between God, the author of history, and humans, the other characters in his story. We note here that the unique meaningfulness of our lives—its glory—cannot be fully known by anyone but God, and it cannot be known adequately by us until we are also outside human history, in the eschaton. Only then will the full significance of our lives be grasped, and that too will be a part of our reward. Until then, we must generally judge ourselves and others with great charity, since we simply do not know the whole story.

Judgment Against Perpetrators

God's sovereignty over all that happens in the world can be confusing for those who have been grievously wronged by others, because they wonder why God allowed it to happen. With such cases, it may be helpful to bring up the coming judgment in session, for they need to know that God is fundamentally opposed to the sins that were done against them and they can pray to him for justice, just like the Christian martyrs pray for judgment on those who murdered them (Rev 6:10). Justice is an eternal concern, and a Christianity that rejects the revelation of God's judgment in biblical history and at the end will be patently inadequate to address the real evils of this world and the suffering of its victims. Only a high view of humanity holds personal agents responsible for their wrongdoing, and arguing that all wrongdoing is a function of biopsychosocial damage, as is surprisingly common in our day, adds layers of injustice to the world that functionally minimize the wrong done. When God's glory passed before Moses, God declared that he "will by no means leave the guilty unpunished" (Ex 34:7). Those who were abused in childhood often have little other recourse than to take their abuse and emotional pain to God. The trajectory of God's healing will lead eventually to the forgiveness of one's abusers (Mt 6:14-15; Lk 23:34), but genuine Christian forgiveness never minimizes the mistreatment (Worthington, 2009). Christ reserved his fiercest condemnation for those who have harmed children, and this includes child abusers: "whoever causes one of these little ones who believe in Me to stumble, it would be better for him to have a heavy millstone hung around his neck, and to be drowned in the depth of the sea" (Mt 18:6)! Abuse survivors are better enabled to work through their fear and anger if they know that God hated the abuse and will punish it in the end—though in some cases by having taken its penalty on himself.

The Future of Those Who Rejected the Messiah

Secular terror-management theory limits its focus to the influence of death-related anxiety on human behavior (Greenberg, Koole, & Pyszczynski, 2004). Christian terror-management theory goes further to argue that our anxiety about the future includes the denial of a future judgment for our sins and the terror of final separation from God and his goodness. Physical death, as bad as it is, signifies a far worse demise called the "second death" (Rev 20:6, 14-15; 21:6). Jesus himself repeatedly warned his hearers about this outcome, using metaphors from this life to express something of its anguish: "outer darkness" (Mt 22:13), "eternal fire" (Mt 25:41), "where [the] worm does not die" (Mk 9:48) and there is "weeping and gnashing of teeth" (Mt 22:13).

Without this teaching, there is no ultimate justice in the universe, and it really doesn't matter whether we have lived like Hitler or Mother Teresa (Kreeft & Tacelli, 1994, chap. 12). At the same time, the Bible says we have all fallen short of God's holy standards and so deserve eternal separation from him (Rom 3:23). God's solution was to resolve that alienation himself in Christ, while at the same time respecting and promoting our personal agency, and therefore requiring that we surrender our lives to him and consent to his way of reconciliation and healing. As a result, the only ones who will end up condemned are those who persist in their autonomy and reject him and his judgments and his remedy for reconciliation (Heb 9:27).

Why even mention this subject in a therapy book? Because Christian counseling seeks to promote the well-being of all its counselees, and there is no soul-care agenda more important than one's eternal destiny. As a result, wherever employed—whether in public mental health or a local church—we need to wisely love others the best we can, giving counsel that is always implicitly Christian and, whenever possible, explicitly (Tan, 1996), being mindful of both our institutional obligations and everyone's future destiny.

God desires to redeem everyone in Christ from this judgment (2 Pet 3:9), so we should earnestly regularly pray for the conversion of counselees who are not Christians and ask him to pour out his Spirit in a massive way in our culture to fulfill his promise that "the earth will be filled with the knowledge of the glory of the LORD, as the waters cover the sea" (Hab 2:14).

Christian Hope Rests in a Future That Has Already Begun

While the primary eschatological focus of the canon is the age to come, there is another perspective of biblical eschatology that is simultaneously concerned with this age. Like many other Christian teachings, this bifocal orientation is a result of the person and work of Jesus Christ. We learn in the New Testament that the coming of the Messiah prophesied in the Old Testament actually occurs in two phases, and the first has already happened. As a result, the end of the ages actually began in Christ's life, healing, and preaching (Jn 3:19; 9:39; 12:48) and especially in his death (Gal 3:13; Col 2:14), and as we have seen, the new creation began with his resurrection and exaltation (2 Cor 5:17) and advanced with the gift of the Holy Spirit (Vos, 1952).

So Christ's first coming was interpreted as a partial fulfillment of the Old Testament prophecies about the age to come (regarding the Messiah, Mt 1:20-23; the Davidic kingdom, Mt 12:28; Acts 15:16-18; and the Holy Spirit, Acts 2:47). The New Testament authors concluded that the "last days" had already begun, in a significant sense (Acts 2:47; Heb 1:2), since the Messiah (Son of Man, Servant of the Lord), whom the prophets foretold would usher in the final age, had just come and gone.[8] The apostles therefore understood that the establishment of God's eternal reign on earth, previously prophesied, had arrived *spiritually* (Col 1:13)—that is, *through the Spirit*—and Christ was now actively extending that reign one person at a time (Rev 1:6, 9; 5:10). This means that new-covenant believers now live in two, overlapping eras (Gaffin, 1978), the continuation of the "present evil age" (Gal 1:4)—along with all other humans and that will end when Christ comes a second time—and the eschatological age of the new creation, into which one is "born again" through faith and that will continue forever.

Cullman (1964) famously compared Christ's first coming and his second with D-Day and V-Day in World War II. The combined event of Christ's life, death, and resurrection, he suggested, was the decisive battle (like D-Day) that began the eventual total overthrow of Satan's reign over humanity and the destruction of sin and its effects that will be finally realized at the end of this age (like V-Day).

Living between these "days" creates the already/not-yet tension of the Christian life that we have repeatedly noted. On the one hand, believers have already won the war (Rom 8:37; 2 Cor 2:14). They have eternal life (1 Jn 5:13), "every spiritual blessing" (Eph 1:3), a heavenly inheritance and citizenship (1 Pet 1:4; Phil 3:20), and their real self seated with Christ in heaven.[9] On the other hand, the war is not yet over, and a great deal of fighting remains to be done in order to finish up what Christ started two thousand years ago. Believers are still suffering sinners, more or less damaged, and sometimes persecuted by others more or less alienated from God and hostile to him.[10] As we would expect, this is a war of words. "The eschatological dialogue that accompanies the interjection of God's word into human history generates the distinct temporality of the 'already/not yet'" (Vanhoozer, 2010, p. 328). God is speaking the future into existence now, first by inviting alienated and sinful images of God to Christ; second by declaring believers to be new creations—holy, righteous, complete, and beloved children in Christ; and third by making its actualization depend on the Spirit and their faith in that word, in spite of their remaining psychopathology and the challenges of living in a still-fallen culture. "New covenant time" is a way of living temporally in which the already/not-yet dynamic of redemption is becoming deeply integrated.

A smooth blending of present and future eschatology is found in 1 Peter:

> Blessed be the God and Father of our Lord Jesus Christ, who according to His great mercy has caused us to be born again to a living hope through the

resurrection of Jesus Christ from the dead, to obtain an inheritance which is imperishable and undefiled and will not fade away, reserved in heaven for you, who are protected by the power of God through faith for a salvation ready to be revealed in the last time. In this you greatly rejoice, even though now for a little while, if necessary, you have been distressed by various trials, so that the proof of your faith, being more precious than gold which is perishable, even though tested by fire, may be found to result in praise and glory and honor at the revelation of Jesus Christ; and though you have not seen Him, you love Him, and though you do not see Him now, but believe in Him, you greatly rejoice with joy inexpressible and full of glory, obtaining as the outcome of your faith the salvation of your souls. (1 Pet 1:3-9)

Believers, then, are called to live consciously in the tension between these two eschatological realities—the future that has already come and the future that lies at the end of this age (Schwarz, 2000), banking on a perfected and consummated life in eternity while living out of their present perfection in Christ and sporadic communion with God in an unredeemed body and world.

Eschatological Development

Developmental psychologists have identified stages that distinguish qualitative psychological progress in a number of areas of human functioning, including neurological, cognitive, sexual and psychosexual, social and psychosocial, and in one's self-representation, moral reasoning and agency, and spirituality. However, from a Christian standpoint, all this creational development has to be subsumed under the first stage of a more radical two-stage human developmental framework—human life in this age and in the one to come. Christianity posits a radical rupture in the believer's life and story that separates a relatively brief period of life on earth and an infinitely longer stage, about which we know comparatively little.

"I shall be one day better than before" (Herbert, 1995, p. 165). Though the first creation was good, the new creation will be far better. We groan down here in this body, the apostle Paul wrote, being "naked," "burdened," and "absent from the Lord." Since the current stage of human development is characterized by shame, suffering, and distance from God, we should long, therefore, for the heavenly stage of existence that awaits us. By contrast, in the next stage, we will be "at home with the Lord" (what a phrase!) and have a wondrous, heavenly body that will apparently feel better—unburdened, "clothed," free of pain, and more fully alive (1 Cor 15:40-54; 2 Cor 5:1-9).

In addition, current human development on earth is transfigured by focusing on its next stage. Believers are becoming on earth, to some degree, who they already really are in Christ—seated with him in heaven—and who they actually will be when dwelling with him in the age to come. "We will be like Him, because we will see Him just as He is. And everyone who has this hope fixed on Him purifies himself, just as He is pure" (1 Jn 3:2-3). Knowing we will be fully conformed to Christ in eternity guides our current, gradual conformity to him. Consequently, "what is most true about human nature is not its primordial past but its eschatological future, an arriving determination that addresses us and calls us to spiritual union with God in Christ" (Shults, 2003, p. 242). We change our brains/souls by attending to things above and things to come.

Will there be any development within the second stage of human life in eternity? The Scriptures do not say. However, the Eastern Orthodox tradition and Jonathan Edwards (1852/1969) have reasoned that once all our sin has been removed, conformity to Christ will continue forever, simply because finitude can always be drawn into greater approximation with infinite perfection (without obscuring the Creator-creature distinction). Though we cannot be sure about this, it would make heaven that much better and contradicts neither Scripture nor reason.

SOME THERAPEUTIC IMPLICATIONS

To summarize: Christianity is a future-oriented way of life in which present and future perspectives are united. That is the case because Christian "doctrines are intellectual habits that draw upon the synthetic power of the imagination to enable us to see this world in otherworldly—which is to say, eschatological—terms" (Vanhoozer, 2005, p. 377). From the Christian point of view, everything in this world—perhaps obviously redemptive good, but even creational good and, most surprisingly, sin, suffering, and damage—can all be interpreted as signs of the age to come, guiding us toward that city whose builder and maker is God (Heb 11:10). How does this future orientation affect Christian psychotherapy and counseling?

The Triune God Will Finally Be Everything to Us

At their conversion, Christians left the city of self-determination and have been traveling ever since to the city of God, where he is the true center of life. "The throne of God and of the Lamb will be in [the city], and His bondservants will serve Him" (Rev 22:3). God's glory, honor, and beauty will be immediately palpable, and believers will happily worship the triune God there forever (Rev 4:6-9; 5:8-10, 14; 7:11-12) without any psychopathology getting in the way. In that day, God will be seen as the sovereignly majestic, righteous, and loving being that he is, and believers will finally fully and self-consciously praise him with gratitude proportional to their unhindered capacity, itself a gift that they have received from him. The triune theodrama will be over; he will have overcome all evil and suffering on the earth. Jesus Christ will be seen as the hero of heroes, God's beauty will be clearly manifested to his human creatures, and his followers will celebrate his love forever. The end for which God created the world will finally have been attained.

Best of all, we will have consistent experiential communion with the triune God in Christ, in contrast to the rather ephemeral experiences with God most of us have now. No more willed loneliness, we will be fully internally integrated, able to know and love God as we have been known and loved by him: we will have beatific awareness all the time, our attention continuously joined to his, and we will experience full mutual closeness with him, sharing thoughts and feelings with full transparency, wholly delighting in and consenting to one another, limited only by our finite capacities (Stump, 2012). Our attachment needs will be met, our debts erased, our shame taken away, no more sin or old self in the way, our suffering (with Christ) will finally make sense, consummated in a way that can only happen after it is all over. We will joyously boast in our previous weaknesses (and maybe those we still have), finally understanding to some degree how God's glory was being manifested through them, and we will love our neighbors as we love ourselves. Our participation in God's glory, love, and joy will reach total saturation. We will finally have found what we were looking for.

In the meantime, everything in this life is a relatively brief preparation for eternity (2 Cor 4:17). As a result, Christian psychotherapy and counseling helps guide believers in recalibrating their lives according to that *telos*, training them how to cope with suffering, loss, mistreatment, and pain—past and present—in light of the future, and encouraging meditation on their future estate, journaling about present circumstances while thinking about eternity, and reprioritizing their lifestyle and standard of living according to a "wartime mentality." Though there will be times when counselees will be overwhelmed by their past or present challenges, in principle, nothing is so bad—no disfigurement or disability, long-term rejection by a parent or a spouse or a child, no failure—that it cannot be transfigured by its reinterpretation in light of communion in eternity with the infinite God.

Nonetheless, we cannot reap the psychological benefits of this principle without practicing it in personal "soul-work" time and in public worship.

Every Believer's Story Is a Divine Comedy

Comedies in the West were classically defined by their having a positive ending, so Dante accordingly understood that human history is a divine comedy, since it ends with God's final triumph over all that was wrong in this fallen creation. Yet the stories of some believers have seemed predictably tragic, beginning with insecure attachment, damaged further by years of abuse and neglect, leading to poor impulse control, emotion regulation, and social skills, long before full personal agency developed, just about guaranteeing that difficulties would follow them into marriage and continue to compromise their adult lives. Particularly painful are the lives of those individuals whose adult suffering was severely compounded by their own personal agency—repeated substance abuse, withdrawal from others, aggressive behavior, promiscuity, or adultery.

Yet, no matter how bad, every believer's story has been taken up into the divine comedy, which, even if change is modest in this life, always turns stunningly positive in the final act: their sin gone and suffering over, ethically and spiritually perfect—truly happily ever after! The eschaton provides an invaluable future frame for Christian narrative therapy that is vastly more encouraging than the final act of secular narrative therapy based on a naturalistic/humanistic worldview: nonexistence.

Stories of suffering turned eternally good. In chapter nine we reflected on one of the most astonishing aspects of our incorporation into the theodrama: the revelation that our suffering now "is producing for us an eternal weight of glory far beyond all comparison" (2 Cor 4:17; and Rom 8:18). The acceptance of such a possibility would provide a unique religious coping strategy that can reconfigure present suffering by linking it to transcendent glory. Calvin (1559/1960) suffered many trials and illnesses in his life, and he was helped by such a promise: "In harsh and difficult conditions, regarded as adverse and evil, a great comfort comes to us: we share Christ's sufferings in order that as he passed from a labyrinth of all evils into heavenly glory, we may in like manner be led through various tribulations to the same glory" (vol. I, p. 702).

Unfortunately, those who have suffered the most down here, having been designed for perfection, become to some extent neurologically wired to a more or less compulsive pursuit of immediate well-being, which they cannot see is counterproductive to their immediate, as well as long-term, aims. Life is incredibly hard for those who constantly re-create the chaos with which they grew up. With patience, kindness, and compassion Christian therapists can gently draw such counselees into an increasing eschatological orientation, without minimizing their current suffering. Life down here *is* grossly unfair in terms of its distribution of blessings and sufferings. Christians who have suffered a lot need to know that God will someday more than compensate them for their trials now. According to Stump (2010; and Aquinas), eternal joy with God alone makes the Christian explanation for the problem of suffering work. Counselors have the opportunity to help great sufferers grasp and begin to benefit now from God's eternal investment program.

The eschatological self of believers. Markus and Nurius (1986) pointed out that mature humans form "possible selves," self-knowledge that pertains to who they believe they will become. God has revealed in Scripture enough about their future for Christians to form an eschatological "possible self": in eternity they will be ethically and spiritually perfect (Heb 12:23), freed of sin and suffering, conformed to the image of Christ (Rom 8:29), and members of the royal family who have ascended to the throne.[11]

One's future selves can have a significant impact on one's life in the present, according to Markus and Nurius (1986), by motivating and guiding activities that lead to the realization of those selves. Focusing on one's eschatological self could affect the lives of Christians now in at least a few ways. First, understanding that one will be continually in communion with God forever might make present communion with God more plausible, perhaps helping to justify its pursuit. Second, recognizing that they will be royal children of God and perfectly good, holy, and righteous forever could contribute to a sense of dignity and self-confidence in the present. Believers have inherited the right to carry themselves on earth with a noble, royal bearing in their relations with others. Finally, knowing they will be free of sin and suffering might help Christians now come to terms with and consent to their present degree of fallenness, even while inclining them to work toward alleviating suffering and overcoming sin that will be banished in the future. Christians may be enabled to strive now for greater healing and virtue, by resting in their present and future perfection in Christ and thus undermining the anxious, legalistic pressure that drives so much Christian activity.

Eternal happiness. The believer's story concludes with a never-ending chapter of joyful participation in the fullness of God's glory and love, experiencing an ectypal share in the triune communion with one's divine

Father, lover and husband, comforter and advocate, along with all other believers. "The tabernacle of God is among men, and He will dwell among them, and they shall be His people, and God Himself will be among them" (Rev 21:3). We will finally be "at home with the Lord" (2 Cor 5:8).

Aquinas (1949, pp. 175-78) wrote that being in the presence of the greatest Good for our souls, and experiencing him directly in that way, will so transform us that we will never want to leave him. His beauty has a delightfully compelling quality to it that will make us so much happier than anything we have ever known. The use of the metaphors of gold and jewels throughout heaven in Revelation are meant to convey that the goodness of the afterlife far exceeds that of our life on earth. We simply lack the categories down here to appreciate adequately how intense will be our happiness there. What can we say? It will be better than pizza, better than first falling in love, better than a hike in the Grand Tetons, better than being voted most popular by thousands, better than cocaine, better than a mutual orgasm with the spouse one has loved for a lifetime. Fully experiencing communion with the most beautiful, virtuous being there is will be a shared ecstasy, without guilt or side effects, a kind of sober co-euphoria that will intensify our perceptions, understanding, and love, rather than distort them.

Put differently, believers will enter into the joy of their Master (Mt 25:23), that is, they will share in a portion of the effulgent, unsurpassable delight that the triune God shares among the three persons of the Godhead to the fullest of their finite capacities. They will experience far more of his infinite form and splendor than it is possible to imagine now. At the same time, believers then will know their own belovedness, seen in God's absolute affirmation and approbation of them, individually, in Christ, symbolized by their each being given a "new name" (Rev 2:17), a "crown of life" (Jas 1:12), and a "crown of glory" (1 Pet 5:4). So Christians can look forward to a future experience of positivity that vastly exceeds anything attainable in this life.

In the meantime, Christians may be able to increase their appreciation for their future by using their imagination now to focus and meditate on their coming eternal happiness. Imagining what our lives in the eschaton will be like—as best we can, given what has been revealed—can foster a sense of peace and contentment and strengthen the new self. In addition, one can highlight, purify, and deepen the joys of created blessings by recognizing they are also intended to point to their greater fulfillment in eternity.

This World Is Not Our Home

In *Pilgrim's Progress*, Bunyan's great allegory of the Christian life, Bunyan gave worldly society the name Vanity Fair. The contemporary world seems to hold out the hope, at least implicitly, of problem-free living and total happiness and success now, by means of money and possessions, power to influence others, health care, sex according to any of one's desires, beauty enhancement, legal and illegal drugs, and unceasing entertainment. Some of these means are created by God; all of them are divinized by sin. But they work as well as they do because they bring some short-term pleasure. Nevertheless, from ancient times, sages have told us such objects and activities cannot satisfy the deepest needs of the human soul, and at least some empirical research has documented that truth (Myers, 2000). Our yearning for the transcendent, established in the human heart (Eccles 3:11), can only be satisfied by an infinite God in eternity; everything else amounts to vanity (Eccles 1:2-10). Christ himself taught us that "the worry of the world and the deceitfulness of wealth" are inimical to the reception of the gospel (Mt 13:22). Even religion is compromised on earth, where our motives can be masked and distorted: "Do not be excessively righteous, and do not be overly wise. Why should you ruin yourself?" (Eccles 7:16). "Beware of the leaven of the Pharisees and Sadducees" (Mt 16:6). At least a portion of the stress, anxiety, and sadness of our counselees is due to their having accepted the lie that complete fulfillment on earth is possible.

There is, therefore, therapeutic good in helping others recognize the vanity of this earthly life and pointing to a future of eternal fulfillment. There is greater mental health in seeing ourselves, in the right way, as "strangers and exiles on the earth" (Heb 11:13), having our ultimate citizenship in heaven (Phil 3:20), so that it contributes to our identity. We are creatures of God's good creation and free to enjoy it, but we live with a tension now, for we are also eschatological creatures, and our best life is found above (Col 3:3), where we really belong, more than we do down here.

Those who were severely mistreated as children sometimes have a hard time recalling what happened to them and being sure about what they do remember, in part because of the distortions of perpetrators and others who were complicit, as well as their own fears and defenses. As a result, they can be haunted by questions and misgivings about their stories: *Did that really happen? Am I the bad one? Maybe I made it up.* However, the omniscient and compassionate God knows everything that happened with perfect accuracy. We can trust that he will deal justly with perpetrators and that the survivors of abuse will finally be exonerated and vindicated. Such outcomes will contribute to the eschatological healing of survivors and give us another reason why God will be wiping tears away. Knowing that now can bring some consolation in an often unjust and unfair world.

The Gifts of Doubled Perfection and "Sufficient Power" in Christ

Being made for perfection, our imperfection can be overwhelming, especially for shame-prone personalities. We have repeatedly observed that believers have been declared to be ethicospiritually perfect in Christ already. In this chapter we have noted that believers will become actually ethicospiritually perfect in Christ in eternity. This gives believers another way to think about themselves and one more reason to accept themselves as they are in this age, in spite of their imperfections. Whether we look above in the present or we look ahead to the future, we can see ourselves as righteous, good, and holy persons in Christ, now because God declares it to be so and then because he will actually make it so. As a result, our created need to be perfect ends up being satisfied in two ways, helping us to come to terms with where we are at currently on our therapeutic and maturational journey, with all our limitations.

With those two transcendent anchors of ethicospiritual perfection providing the doubled "rest" (Mt 11:28) they need, those united to Christ can better rely on "the secret energy of the Spirit" (Calvin, 1559/1960, p. 538) enabling them now to participate in their present and future adoption, righteousness, and communion with God, and practice the ennobling life of a faithful disciple in community. Thought imperfect by absolute standards, this participation and practice can be powerful enough to give hope of increasing Christlikeness, in holiness and wholeness, as long as they live.

Learning to Live in the Future in Head and Heart

A strange irony of the Christian life is that we are to be "grounded in heaven." For the Christian, the universe is upside down. Psychological well-being results from an honesty about ourselves on earth made possible by focusing our attention on Christ in heaven and our real union with him there (Eph 2:6). So, one of Paul's cognitive therapy strategies was to encourage believers to "set their minds on the things above," those realities that are already true of believers in Christ (Col 3:1-4). "He that is much in heaven in his thoughts is free from being tossed with tempests here below" (Sibbes, 1635/1973, p. 164). In worship, meditation, and conversation, believers can fold these eschatological truths into their suffering and negative emotions, creating another way to objectify them, leading hopefully to greater stabilization of one's internal experience.

Developing such an orientation begins with a cognitive reframing of one's life and eventually moves into the much slower process of a carditive modification of one's values, emotions, and desires. Eternity can put things on earth in a different light, relativizing their importance. Mistreatment by others, a sick spouse, limited skills, even one's sinful dispositions can be reinterpreted in light of eternity, not by denying the pain but by transposing it—first in the mind and then in the heart—into a higher, more meaningful order: the spiritual, that is, the eschatological or eternal order, set in place by Jesus Christ, the new Adam.

Christian Soul Care Is Eternally Momentous and Temporally Warranted

The consummation bestows on Christian soul care ultimate significance. All counseling seeks to improve the quality of human life in this age; because of its eschatological orientation, Christian counseling is also concerned with the quality of human life in the age to come. As important as the amelioration of current suffering and psychological and relational problems is, the amelioration of eternal suffering and its attendant psychological and relational problems is immeasurably more important. While counselees obtain some measure of psychological healing in this life, it is intended by God to lead them to a fuller restoration with him in eternity (Acts 14:15-17; Rom 2:4). How tragic, then, if their temporal healing simply leads them to become more autonomous from God.

Consequently, Christian counselors have to be mindful not only of the presenting problems and the underlying dynamics before them but also of their eternal significance and everlasting resolution. To be a Christian counselor means neither conflating nor dissociating temporal and eternal concerns. Both are important, but the latter are of infinite import.

Such a stance is grounded, ultimately, in God's love for the world and his desire that everyone should find him to be their great soul physician. He joined himself eternally to humanity as a sign of that love and desire, died for the sins of all (1 Jn 2:2), and throughout history he continues to seek and to save the lost (Lk 19:10).

Consequently, Christian therapists and counselors are warranted in sharing the gospel at opportune times with their counselees. As suggested before, such a claim seems controversial in our day only because of the current dominance of secularism. *From a Christian perspective, bringing God's love in Christ to others is the most therapeutic thing one can do.* The current prohibition against counselor initiation of religious or worldview conversations is not only unjust; from a Christian standpoint it is antithetical to the client's everlasting well-being, for the Creator God of all humans is seeking the temporal and eternal therapeutic good of all humankind. (Ironically, research shows that religion also has temporal psychological benefits too; Myers, 2000.) Of course Christian therapists will have to be wise and sensitive, both to the rules of the institution within which they work and to the openness of their counselees to explore an alternative worldview. But in our contemporary pluralistic world, public mental health needs to become more truly pluralistic and reject mandated worldview "neutrality," allowing all counselors the freedom to work explicitly according to their prudence, compassion, and worldview assumptions (especially if they have already been shared in their informed consent).[12]

Comprehensive Christian soulcare seeks also to promote the greatest eternal welfare of believers possible, as well as their earthly well-being. This means including ethical (virtue) and spiritual formation as part of therapy and tackling the psychopathology of sin, as well as seeking to alleviate as much counselee suffering and damage as possible. How might such psychotherapy and counseling differ from contemporary mainstream soulcare? Ongoing sinful practices would get addressed along with DSM diagnoses; medication would be used more to augment treatment than as the sole treatment; divorce would more frequently be seen as a last resort, because of greater hope for recovery; and coming to terms with and accepting one's suffering and biopsychosocial damage would be seen more as legitimate therapeutic ends, just to give a few examples. Such therapeutic emphases are more than justified by an incomparable afterlife, and they also reflect God's patience, perseverance, and interest in bringing about good where it seems unlikely. Conducting our counseling as if eternity matters more than life on earth helps everyone involved to lay up for themselves treasures in heaven, like greater flourishing.

Therapists on a Caravan to Eternity

Understood eschatologically, an important divine purpose for human life seems to be the cultivation of endurance through delayed gratification as we prepare for eternity with God. This end cannot be achieved without the help of friends, particularly those skilled in the journey. The church is to be sort of an eschatological caravan, particularly in a culture so strongly fixated on the things of this world, helping its people to hope in a glorious future that vastly transcends the best this world can offer. We finish the chapter and the book by touching on the role counselors, therapists, and ministers play on that journey. Having facilitated the co-construction of a relationship of mutual trust through empathic listening and humble transparency, counselors can convey an eschatological orientation by valuing eternity themselves, vigorously accepting where they and their counselees are on the journey, periodically talking and praying about eternity in session, and assigning reading and meditation on life with God in heaven.

What a privilege to be a friend on this caravan. Christian psychotherapy and counseling gets to participate directly in the triune God's agenda of manifesting his glory. God personally invested himself in the redemption and healing of broken sinners so that they would come to participate and flourish, individually and communally in the trinitarian communion as fully as possible. To counsel another well, therefore, is to be like our God.

Come, Lord Jesus, and by the Spirit grant us more of your holiness and wholeness. And more of your Father's love.

RESOURCES FOR COUNSELORS AND COUNSELEES

Classic

Baxter, R. *The saints' everlasting rest.* (Any version)

Edwards, J. (1969). Heaven is a world of love. The last chapter in *Charity and its fruits.* Edinburgh: Banner of Truth Trust.

Lewis, C. S. *The weight of glory.* (Any edition)

Owen, J. (1965). The grace and duty of being spiritually minded. In *The works of John Owen* (Vol. 7, pp. 261-497). Edinburgh: Banner of Truth Trust. (Original work published 1681)

Thomas à Kempis. *The imitation of Christ.* (Any version)

Contemporary

Alcorn, R. (2004). *Heaven.* Carol Stream, IL: Tyndale House.

Bauckham, R., & Hart, T. (1999). *Hope against hope: Christianity eschatology in contemporary context.* London: Darton, Longman & Todd. ‡

Gaffin, R. B., Jr. (1987). *Resurrection and redemption: A study in Paul's soteriology.* Grand Rapids, MI: Baker. ‡

Kreeft, P. (1989). *Heaven: The heart's deepest longing.* San Francisco: Ignatius.

Lewis, C. S. (2009). *The great divorce.* New York: HarperOne.

Milne, B. (2003). *The message of heaven and hell.* Downers Grove, IL: Inter-Varsity Press. ‡

Moll, R. (2010). *The art of dying: Living fully into the life to come.* Downers Grove, IL: InterVarsity Press.

Nichols, S. J. (2006). *Heaven on earth: Capturing Jonathan Edwards' vision of living in between.* Wheaton, IL: Crossway.

O'Donovan, O. (1986). *Resurrection and moral order.* Grand Rapids, MI: Eerdmans. ‡

Tripp, P. D. (2012). *Forever: Why you can't live without it.* Grand Rapids, MI: Zondervan.

‡ Recommended more for counselors

Notes

PREFACE

[1] The term actually makes more sense in a worldview that still believes humans are embodied souls.

[2] I say Christian *tradition* (singular) because the book was written for all Christian counselors, regardless of their particular Christian tradition. However, each of us will interpret the Christian faith according to our own tradition, and I am no exception, favoring Reformational and Baptist traditions, while maintaining a strong appreciation for all orthodox expressions of Christianity.

[3] Cortez (2016) argues that for an anthropology to be christological, its "beliefs about the human person (anthropology) must be warranted in some way by beliefs about Jesus (christological)" (20). Furthermore, the model should be applied to a broader range of areas than has traditionally been done in theology. The current project meets both criteria. However, according to the customs of my disciplinary training and probably most of my readership, I will use the terms *psychology, psychotherapy*, and *counseling* over *anthropology*.

[4] *Secular* has a number of meanings, and this negative meaning is only one of them. It can also refer to aspects of reality that stand in contrast to those aspects that are explicitly spiritual or religious or sacred. And Taylor (2007) has argued that *secular* in our day means the recognition that there are many fundamental options for understanding the nature of things.

[5] In retrospect, now that this project is drawing to a close, I regret that I did not early on seek out a theologian with whom to collaborate. Over the years of my writing, it became increasingly clear to me that good transdisciplinary Christian scholarship requires multiple authors with complementary expertise to produce disciplinary texts for the Christian community that reflect the formative influence of the Christian metadisciplines, particularly biblical studies, theology, and Christian philosophy. I hope to spend the rest of my career sharing the lessons learned.

CHAPTER 1: THE ORBIT OF THE HUMAN SOUL

[1] In a devotional explanation of God's agenda in the Bible, Larry Crabb (2009) has God making this very point to the reader: "You are more Ptolemaic than Copernican. Claudius Ptolemy, a first-century astronomer, thought the sun revolved around the earth. You naturally assume My agenda revolves around yours. Sixteen centuries later, Nicholas Copernicus realized the earth revolves around the sun. It takes a long time to understand that I am not here for you, but that you are here for me" (p. 38).

[2]Something analogous to this realization, but much more personal, occurs with each human life. Human consciousness emerges in the first years of life from a basic sense of one's physical needs to the gradual recognition that the world is other than oneself, that it is populated by other persons who also have rights and to whom one has obligations, and—depending on one's culture and family—all of it, including oneself, was somehow brought into being.

[3]Many other terms besides *worldview* could be used to designate this psychological structure, including *episteme, language-game, order of love, paradigm, being-in-the-world, social imaginary*, and *life-world*. And there are problems with *worldview*, one of which is its objectivistic, perceptual connotations. Nonetheless, because of its wide use and because of the normative role of beliefs and discourse in human life, I have chosen to use *worldview*.

[4]The phrase "*late* modernism" is used to distinguish it from early modernism, which was more open to the theism from which it arose.

[5]Christianity bears some responsibility for the development of modernism, both good and bad (Milbank & Pickstock, 2001; Stark, 2004; Taylor, 1989).

[6]It is customary to distinguish modern and postmodern forms of discourse and practice, and there are certainly important distinctions between them. But for our purposes here, postmodernism is understood as simply a more pessimistic and relativistic, and more community-sensitive, stream within late modernism, compared with, say, naturalism and humanism, two other streams. Its communal sensitivities dispose postmodernists to respect communal differences a great deal and even to question the existence of a "self" (see Gergen, 1992). However, contemporary secular postmodernism promotes communities because they are contexts that offer the contemporary secular individual the materials by which it can choose to construct itself, arguably an advance in understanding the construction of the individual self (protests to the contrary notwithstanding). But secular postmodernism is no less opposed to communal systems that recognize an absolute religious and ethical state of affairs to which the self is obligated and beholden, such as Orthodox Islam, Judaism, and Christianity, than is humanism or naturalism.

[7]The transition from Christianity to modernism is discussed in more detail in *Foundations for Soul Care* (Johnson, 2007) and the introductory chapter of *Christianity and Psychology: Five Views* (Johnson, 2010).

[8]As mentioned in note 5 in this chapter, one can also argue that Christianity is, ironically, in part responsible for the current state of affairs, by so valuing all human beings (and not just those in power) because all are created in the *imago Dei*. This was fine so long as God was the infinitely glorious center. But when God was relegated to the periphery, the West was left with highly valued human beings and nothing greater in the universe to keep our native narcissism in check.

[9]Though I have been referring to the worldview of *late* modernism, for simplicity's sake, and because the psychology and psychotherapy to which I turn are commonly called simply *modern*, I will generally avoid the appellation "late."

[10]It is instructive to consult some of the founders of late-modern psychotherapy such as Rogers, for they were still living in the midst of the secular revolution (Smith, 2002) and so were more explicit about its religious implications than is common today. Of special interest in this opening chapter on glory is the first chapter of Horney's (1950) magnum opus, *Neurosis and Human Growth*, titled "The Search for Glory."

But while the religious implications of secular psychotherapy are less explicit today, they continue to undergird its activities, as evident in the following quote: "Experiential theory is dialectically constructivist in nature, emphasizing that change is an inherent aspect of all systems, that meaning is created by human activity, is created in dialogue, is constrained by a bodily felt emotional experience, and ultimately is created by synthesis of experience and symbol. Emotional experience thus is seen as both creating and being created by its conscious symbolization and expression. This view thus casts us as creators of the self we find ourselves to be" (Greenberg, Watson, & Lietaer, 1998, p. 453).

[11]This bias is evident in Kohut's (1971; 1977) remarkable term "healthy narcissism," in spite of the fact that Narcissus drowned because of his self-absorption!

[12]There are, of course, voices within contemporary psychology, including object relations theory, family-systems theory, and social constructivism, that advocate for a more socially attuned orientation. But this is still a minority protest.

[13]Theists are, of course, very appreciative of the heightened interest in religion and spirituality in contemporary psychology over the past two decades (e.g., Richards & Bergin, 2000; Shafranske, 1996). Explicitly religious or spiritual counseling and therapy is being promoted by some as a legitimate option for clients who desire it, and here we can see that postmodernism has provided a corrective to the excesses of late modernism, advocating for a more formative role for community in psychology and the need to incorporate the perspectives of minority groups, such as women, racial and ethnic minorities, and gays and lesbians, as well as religious groups, involving a criticism of modernism's goal of universal knowledge (in particular, a universal psychology that applies to all people) (Cushman, 1995; McNamee & Gergen, 1992). APA has even published materials on religious diversity (Richards & Bergin, 2000) and two that are explicitly Christian (McMinn, 2006; Miller & Delaney, 2004)!

Such accommodations are to be welcomed by all people of faith; in fact, one might hope it portends a paradigm shift in the field, where a genuine pluralism might be promoted (see Johnson, 2007, chap. 7). But we must not let our appreciation blur our vision of the present. For those committed to historic Christianity, postmodernism's openness to religion is less helpful than it might first appear, because at the same time, its hard-core proponents typically vehemently reject any specific metanarratives and explicit claims to universal truth, paradoxically making the orientation fundamentally antagonistic to any *particular* religious stance, especially one such as Christianity that assumes it has been entrusted with a mission from the triune God to seek the conversion of the world to Christ. As a result, most of this growing body of psychotherapy literature ends up promoting a generic "spirituality" that shares relatively few distinctives with any *actual* religion (except those liberal versions that have arisen in the modern era that are willing to accept all faiths as valid in principle; see, e.g., Fowler, 1982; Miller, 1999).

[14]This orientation also distinguishes a Christian understanding of created reality from a modern one (Oliver, 2013).

[15]A sign is anything that points or refers to something else. So, smoke is a sign of fire; *barn* is a linguistic sign of a building on a farm used for animals and equipment. Being created in God's image means that humans are the best signs of God in the creation.

[16]*End* (as used in the subheading) was used in Jonathan Edwards's day to mean "goal."

[17]In his magisterial treatment of glory, Hans Urs von Balthasar (1982–1991) made an important distinction, following Aquinas, that glory is manifested according to two dimensions: form and splendor. Form is the pattern or configuration of elements that makes something beautiful, like the complex and novel arrangement of shapes and colors of a great painting, whereas splendor is the "depth dimension" of the form—the inner meaningfulness that is expressed by means of the form—like the subject matter that is movingly portrayed in a great painting. Imagine a human being and an excellent wax figure of that human both having identical physical form, but the actual human has *far* more splendor. "As another illustration, consider two siblings who are taking care of their dying mother, one in order to guarantee a large inheritance and the other out of loving devotion. The actions may have the same form, but their moral splendor is considerably different. Form and splendor are inseparable, since a thing's splendor is dependent on its form" (Johnson, 2007, p. 312). Form, we might say, is the surface beauty and complexity of a thing, whereas splendor is its inner beauty or complexity, the density of the form's significance.

Two centuries earlier, Edwards (1974) defined excellency as an "admirable conjunction of diverse excellences," *so dissimilar* that they "would have seemed to us as utterly incompatible in the same subject," and "impossible to be exercised to the same object" (Vol. 1, p. 680). Excellency sounds like an important aspect of splendor. In a sermon titled "On the Excellency of Christ," Edwards argued that the greatness of Christ's glory is seen in the harmony in him of seemingly opposite characteristics, for example, his "infinite majesty and transcendent meekness" (p. 680) and "infinite worthiness of good and the greatest patience in the suffering of evil" (p. 681). Edwards understood that the greatness of God's glory was disclosed precisely in the complex depth of his character manifested in Jesus Christ. A lesser god would not have become a baby and suffered and died.

To summarize, God's splendor or excellency is the deep union and harmony of the extreme diversity of his characteristics, perhaps especially evident to humans by the presence of real or apparent oppositions or contrasts. Throughout this book, we will try to plumb some of the depths of God's splendor, in order to tap its soul-healing benefits, considering, for example, the Trinity (chap. 2), Christ's incarnation (chaps. 3 and 11), God's perfections (chap. 6), his just and redemptive response to human sin (chaps. 8 and 12-14), his willingness to suffer (chap. 9) and become weak (chap. 10), and perhaps most surprisingly, his communion with and indwelling of sinners (chaps. 4 and 15), as well as the associated paradoxes, ironies, and dramatic reversals that the manifestation of his glory in "this present, evil age" entails.

God has both infinitely beautiful form (given his infinite meaningfulness or signification, his immensity, and the quality of his perfections and virtues) and infinite splendor or depth (that is, infinite significance, personal presence, and earnestness). All creatures share in a little of God's glory, but they necessarily have infinitely less form and splendor than God. Humans, nevertheless, being made in God's image and able to know and freely respond to God in love, have the potential, through that relationship, to develop greater form and splendor. Moreover, their sin, suffering, and weakness provide a rich and complex context for the manifestation of God's form and splendor through his interactions with them and through their own increasing form and splendor as they "work through" their sin, suffering, and weakness—overcoming sin and coming to terms with their suffering and weakness—through faith in Christ. So God has plenty to work with in his doxological (and therapeutic) drama of doctrine (Balthasar, 1988–1998; Vanhoozer, 2005), and psychotherapy and counseling play a special role in this agenda.

[18]The full story, of course, includes the triune relations of the Trinity—a wondrous development in revelation. However, Christianity is a trinitarian *monotheism*, and it is fitting that we acknowledge that God is one God who loves himself supremely. In the next chapter, we will consider the trinitarian implications of God's glory, where we examine in some detail how God's glory is intrinsically relational and that the Father, Son, and Holy Spirit know, love, and value each other absolutely, infinitely beyond anything else, and yet, such is the nature of their glory, they seek to draw others, made in their image, into their fellowship.

[19]"God alone is His own goodness, and He alone is essentially good. All other beings are said to be good according as they participate, to some extent, in Him" (Aquinas, 1947, p. 116).

[20]At the same time, as we shall see in the next chapter, the glory of the persons of the Trinity is shared and social (Jn 17:5).

[21]The opposite problem occurs when we apply concepts to ourselves that can only apply to God. For example, some Christians have suggested that humans are of infinite worth. But necessarily only God can be of *infinite* worth, so this assertion unwittingly implies that human beings have the same worth as God.

[22]The concept of a *fitting* union is based on the Christian assumption that mere humans cannot become one ontologically with God, in contrast to the once-for-all incarnation of the Son of God, in which the divine and human natures were united in the person of the Son by means of his assumption of human nature. Unorthodox understandings of union with God confuse the divine and human natures and are similar to distorted human-human relational experiences, for example, codependent relationships, where there is a lack of proper boundaries between self and other.

[23]God and believers are united through Christ in holiness, righteousness, and love, while remaining absolutely different from each other in essence.

[24]There are, admittedly, different Christian understandings of participation with God. Assuming the absolute Creator-creature distinction, we must be careful to reject any implication of absorption into the divine that one finds in the most extreme forms of Christian mysticism. At the same time, by grounding human activity in absolute dependence on God, it is equally far removed from any notion of a kind of human-divine collaboration, in which humans and God each contribute their respective part.

[25]As a result, the term *participation* is best used only for human activity intentionally dependent on God's goodness. To use it, as is sometimes done, to refer to the automatic dependence of the nonhuman creation on God's goodness is anthropomorphic. One cannot participate in something when one lacks consciousness, and the rest of creation lacks the self-awareness that participation requires. Using *participation* to refer to all of creation minimizes the uniqueness of the image of God and harks back to a pre-Christian view of the world that is enchanted rather than held together by God's word.

[26]In theology, the word *analogy* is used to refer to the relation of humans to God, since humans are creatures who are similar to God in some respects and dissimilar in other respects, though their dissimilarity is infinitely greater than their similarity.

[27]We could call it a theocentric-eudaemonistic therapy paradigm, in which God's glory and the realization of our happiness are interrelated. (*Eudaemonism* is the term for Aristotle's view that human happiness is the chief goal of humanity.) Augustine, Aquinas, Edwards, and others understood that a Christian framework led to a radical reconceptualization of eudaemonism in which God's glory was the final end, but that our happiness was directed related to that glory.

[28]He first made this distinction in 1518 in what has been called the Heidelberg Disputation, an early defense of his Reformational ideas.

[29]Elevation is an emotion triggered by witnessing acts of moral virtue. It involves a warm or glowing feeling in the chest, and it causes people to want to become morally better themselves (Haidt, 2003).

[30]Piaget recognized that proper cognitive development entails the process of "decentration" (Kegan, 1982), in which the child's egocentric mental orientation is gradually overcome and a broader and more objective framework is developed that takes into account the existence and perspectives of others. The egocentric orientation of a preschool child is not sin; it is intrinsic to the limited cognitive capacities of a child. So Piaget is referring to a creational process, not a result of the fall. However, this created egocentrism provides a creational metaphor for the self-centeredness that characterizes fallen adult life, for which we are held responsible before God. Similarly, the cognitive processes of decentration, "the loss of an old center, and what we might call 'recentration,' the recovery of a new center" (Kegan, 1982, p. 31), also have later redemptive analogues in the ethicospiritual orders that are only realized through faith in Christ and, though dependent on those cognitive capacities, transcend them.

[31]A mixed evil is fundamentally evil but includes some good (Chisholm, 1986). The pain of suffering is unpleasant, but good can come from it.

[32]At the same time, God can also be glorified by a divorce, say in response to adultery, since that would picture God's justice. The fact that glory can be manifested in different ways is why those outside the marriage must be cautious in their assessments.

CHAPTER 2: THE GLORIOUS MISSIONS OF THE TRINITY

[1]Readers familiar with *Foundations* will recall that the Trinity was discussed in chapter twelve, but there the focus was on the precise psychological roles of the Trinity in our relationship with them. Our focus in this chapter is the specific glory manifested by the triune God in the healing of the soul.

[2]Horton (2011) summarizes: "biblical revelation identifies each of these persons as a thinking, willing, and active agent" (p. 303). Though paradoxical from our standpoint, we learn from Scripture that the one God is a threefold "I" and two "Thous" with one essence.

[3]Theologians have continually acknowledged that these terms have their limitations as designations for the members of the Trinity. Nevertheless, they seem to present the fewest problems from among the available options (Bavinck, 1956, p. 158; Thompson, 1994; Te Velde, 2011).

[4]The distinction must not be pressed too sharply, since there is only one Trinity.

[5]Meaning "arrangement, order, plan," from the Greek word *oikonomia* (Arndt & Gingrich, 1957).

[6]This point is essential to the Christian religion, for God's eternal relations within the divine life are the basis of his activities with reference to humanity, and not the reverse. Otherwise, God's being would be dependent on his creation.

A major qualification, however, must also be made, for many theologians since Rahner (1970) have tended to equate the economic relations with the immanent, arguing that our understanding of the Trinity must be based on God's revelation to us through his works of creation and redemption, and in Scripture, to guard us from speculating about God's intratrinitarian relations, beyond the few statements about the immanent Trinity found in Scripture. There is wisdom in this caution. At the same time, we ought not ignore the biblical texts that make reference to the eternal relations of the Trinity, and the historic church has rightly recognized the necessary, ontological priority of God's eternal relations within the Godhead over how those relations are expressed to the creation. This provides another safeguard that would keep us from radicalizing "Rahner's Rule" and interpreting God's essential being solely in terms of his missions in history (Vanhoozer, 2010).

[7]The Son of God is called the *Word* of God, existing with God at the beginning (Jn 1:1-14), and the radiance of God's glory (Heb 1:3), suggesting that the Son is the "expression" of or "issues forth" from the Father. Jesus said, "As the Father has life in Himself, even so He gave to the Son also to have life in Himself" (Jn 5:26; see also Jn 1:4), implying that the Son's self-sustaining being is a gift from the Father. Christ is also called "the only begotten God who is in the bosom of the Father" (Jn 1:18; see also Jn 1:14; 3:16, 18; 1 Jn 4:9). Because the Son *is* God (Jn 1:1; Rom 9:5), he cannot have been created but is described as eternally *begotten*, a special term used to differentiate the eternal origin of the God the Son from the bringing forth of creatures in time.

We have much less information about the Spirit's eternal relations with the Father and the Son. The Holy Spirit is described as the breath of the Almighty (Job 33:4). Jesus said that the Holy Spirit will be sent by the Father in the Son's name (Jn 14:26), and "when the Helper comes, whom I will send to you from the Father, that is the Spirit of Truth who proceeds from the Father, He will testify about Me" (Jn 15:26); he is also called the Spirit of Christ (Rom 8:9), suggesting that both Father and Son are involved in the Spirit's eternal existence, but since these references pertain to the Spirit's work in redemption, we must infer what the Spirit's eternal relation is with the others.

[8]The Eastern Church disagrees with this Western understanding, maintaining that the Father alone sends both the Son and the Spirit.

[9]Edwards (1852/1969) argues that the Father's love "flows out, in the first place, necessarily and infinitely, towards his only-begotten Son; being poured forth, without mixture, as to an object that is infinite, and so fully adequate to all the fullness of a love that is infinite. And this infinite love is infinitely exercised toward him. Not only does the fountain send forth streams to this object, but the very fountain itself wholly and altogether goes out toward him. And the Son of God is not the infinite object of love, but he is also an infinite subject of it. He is not only the beloved of the Father, but he infinitely loves him. The infinite essential love of

God, is, as it were, an infinite and eternal, mutual, holy, energy between the Father and the Son: A pure and holy act, whereby the Deity becomes, as it were, one infinite and unchangeable emotion of love proceeding from both the Father and the Son. This divine love has its seat in the Deity, as it is exercised within the Deity, or in God toward himself" (pp. 332-33).

[10]The *perichoresis* of the Trinity helps us understand how Christ could say, "He who has seen Me has seen the Father," for the Father was literally fully present within the Son. This also explains how Christ dwells in believers through the Spirit's indwelling (Col 1:27) and how Jesus can be identified with the Spirit (2 Cor 3:17).

[11]This model fits well into the triad: subject, object, and the relation between subject and object, whether one considers love (Lover-Beloved-Love) or knowledge (e.g., knower-known-knowledge or law). However, at best, this abstraction is a very weak analogy for the Trinity, falling far short of the Trinity's actual nature (Frame, 2002).

Some have objected that this model relegates the Holy Spirit to an impersonal term in the triad and essentially undermines his personhood and deity (see Thompson, 1994). To prevent that, I think, we must diligently remind ourselves of the Spirit's personhood and deity. The Trinity is the most profound mystery there is. All our models are no more than analogies, which correspond in some respect to the triune God but are unable to represent him fully. There is nothing we can think about the Trinity that corresponds perfectly to it (to think otherwise would be to affirm univocal knowledge about God). On the other hand, we must not assume that the Trinity is so beyond our thoughts that our understanding in no way corresponds to his nature (that would be to affirm multivocal knowledge about God). Rather, we must expect that all our models for the Trinity are deficient, without despairing of the analogical knowledge of which we are capable. As the Fourth Lateran Council taught, our analogical knowledge of God (and analogies for God) has far greater dissimilarity to God than similarity. We will have to remind ourselves of this humbling limitation of our knowledge of God throughout this book.

[12]Consider the lonely divine alternatives: the conflict between the gods one finds in the polytheisms, the ultimately impersonal nature of the Brahmin, or the eternal silence of a monotheistic deity before the creation. Rightly understood, the revelation that God is triune informs us that at the basis of the universe is a God of infinite and mutual delight in the other. While beyond our full comprehension, what we *can* grasp points us to the fulfillment and intended destiny of those made in his image.

[13]Particularly regarding salvation, Bavinck distinguished the persons of the Trinity as follows: "The 'good pleasure,' the foreknowledge, the election, the power, the love, and the kingdom all belong to the Father. The mediatorship, the atonement, salvation, grace, wisdom, and righteousness pertain to Son. And regeneration, renewal, sanctification, and communion is from the Spirit" (Bavinck, 2004, p. 270).

[14]Being one God, all three are of one mind and heart, and there is no temporal sequence involved in their cooperation to accomplish their singular agenda.

[15]John records Jesus making reference to the Father sending him *twenty-seven times* (Jn 4:34; 5:24, and so on). In a few of those passages, Jesus referred to the "Father who sent Me" (Jn 5:36-37; 6:39, 44; 7:29; 8:18; 17:3, 8, 18, 21, 23). From such Scripture Reformed theologians determined that the Father and the Son made an agreement in eternity in which the Father sent the Son to earth to do what he wanted done to save human beings, and the Son consented. As an agreement, it bears a similarity to the kinds of covenants that God has enacted with humans in history (see Berkhof, 1939; Horton, 2002; Robertson, 1980), so they termed it the "covenant of redemption" and believed it to be the ultimate trinitarian basis for redemption. This covenant shows how the agency of both was involved in their joint work of redemption and lays a distinctly Reformed foundation for the recognition of the persons of the Trinity as distinguishable agents and, further, for the covenantal nature of human life and redemption.

[16]"Thus the divine original creates for itself a copy in the creaturely world. The Father and the Son are reflected in the man Jesus" (Barth, 1960a, p. 221). Put differently, "'The whole personality of Jesus as expressed in the Gospels is also totally relational, dialogical, *toward the Father*.' There are therefore good Trinitarian grounds for taking 'person' as the key metaphysical principle" (Vanhoozer, 2010, p. 226, quoting Clarke).

[17]"Only in Christ Jesus as our Lord can we know the embrace and bond of this love of God" (Murray, 1959, 1:335).

[18]By archetype, I am following the Protestant scholastics who understood God's knowledge to be the archetype of human knowledge, which they called the ectype (Muller, 2003). I am just extending it to include the divine and human forms. Therefore, I am not here referring to Jung's notion of archetype.

[19]This is because the incarnate Son of God's relationship to the Father is reciprocal (since he is necessarily fully divine) and yet radically asymmetrical (since he is also fully human), so that, during the time of his earthly life, he lived as a servant of God (Phil 2:7). Consequently, the relationship of Jesus to the Father cannot tell us everything about personal relationships that exist at the same ontological level. Here, we must take advantage of the limited biblical revelation given to us regarding the immanent Trinity, since the three persons of the Trinity are absolutely equal, just as all human persons are absolutely equal. At the same time, even here Christ's earthly life gives us information about human-human relationships, because the pattern of service is normative for how we are to treat one another. We must maintain, then, a dialectic between Christ as the archetype for humanity and the Trinity as the archetype for humanity, depending on the precise issue in question.

[20]Because of this evolution, *person* does not mean exactly the same thing it did in the early church, and how Christians interpret and evaluate that evolution varies considerably (see, e.g., Emery, 2011; Gunton, 1998; Holmes, 2012; LaCugna, 1991; Thompson, 1994). Barth (1936) questions even using the word *person* today for the members of the Trinity, believing that the contemporary concept amounts to a distortion of what the creeds actually taught about God. On the other hand, we can acknowledge that some cultural influence on Christian understanding is inevitable and not necessarily deleterious. Just as the early church borrowed the concept of person from its culture, shaping it to meet its needs to capture what the Christian canon revealed about God, the subsequent development of *person* in the West has been further influenced by the Bible and the church's understanding of the Trinity (Grenz, 2001; Heims, 2011; Rolnick, 2007; Taylor, 1989), so contemporary understandings of person may helpfully illuminate contemporary Christian understandings of human beings and even the Trinity to some degree, so long as the church remains under the primary authority of Scripture and the secondary authority of the early creeds, which provide necessary guides to Christian discourse and limit how much variance can be tolerated in any age. For example, such submission currently necessitates interpreting the radical individualism of modernity as heretical.

[21]In the modern era, the terms *person, personal agent, human agent,* and *moral agent* are commonly used interchangeably to refer to a mature human being, in whom human nature has realized a central part of its potential (see, e.g., Braine, 1992; Sprague, 1999; Taylor, 1985a), virtuous in some degree, and in love with God. A more extensive discussion on these matters can be found in Johnson (2007), pp. 341-44, 472-73, 476-77, 543-44.

[22]While Christians must begin with Scripture in terms of its authoritative primacy, Frame (1987) has argued that no one reads Scripture abstracted from the world within which it was written and which we live, but our understanding of God and Scripture are themselves related perspectively to everything else we know. Those who claim to base all their knowledge about God on the Bible, that is, exclusively on knowledge "from above," must be unaware of the necessary role that their extra-biblical knowledge has in informing their understanding of Scripture. We cannot get outside our preunderstanding to get a purely biblical understanding of anything. However, classical Christians can acknowledge such dynamics without embracing antirealism by believing that God has created human knowing in such a way that it corresponds in a limited, analogical way to his own knowing. This position is problematic only to the extent that our (and our culture's) preunderstanding of Scripture is *distorted* by our understanding of the creation. Of course, some distortion is inevitable for finite, sinful creatures. But if we believe that God designed the world to help shape our analogical understanding of him and his ways, that we are made in

his image, and that grace improves our finite, fallen capacities in some degree, then we can accept an analogical model of knowing and be reasonably confident that our knowing yields some measure of knowledge, and can confidently reject equivocal (skeptical) and univocal (positivist-biblicist) models.

[23]What follows will appear to some to reflect a "social trinitarian" perspective, an interpretation of the Trinity that has emerged over the past forty years (Gunton, LaCugna, Moltmann, Volf) that makes a greater distinction among the persons—even referring to them as a community—than has historically been the case in classical theism. So a word of explanation is in order. While committed to the early church's creedal descriptions of the Trinity, there is enough latitude within those careful but simple boundary statements of orthodoxy to allow for a range of understandings of the persons of the Trinity and their relations. On the one hand, for various reasons, the dominant authors on the Trinity in the Western tradition (e.g., Augustine, Aquinas, and Barth) have strongly emphasized the oneness of God (an emphasis that, if taken too far, is called "modalism"). On the other hand, the materials of a more social understanding of the Trinity can also be found in the tradition (e.g., Richard of St. Victor and Jonathan Edwards). Consequently, it would seem that both stances fall within the boundaries of orthodoxy, so that, so long as both the unity and the threeness of the Trinity are equally affirmed, a position should not be considered heterodox. My own approach to the Trinity has been influenced by Van Til, Frame, and McCall, who have seen the Trinity as the transcendent origin and pattern for the unity and diversity of the created order, and I am simply extending such an orientation to the understanding of human individuality and relationality in the fields of psychology and counseling, approached from a distinctly Christian perspective. Consult Van Til (1955), Frame (2002), and McCall (2014) for fuller discussions that have shaped my views.

[24]A number of psychologists from very different standpoints have concluded that there are two fundamental characteristics of human life—agency and communion (Bakan, 1966), power and intimacy (McAdams, 1993), and the interpersonal circumplex model consisting of two continuums: dominance-submissiveness and love-hate (Leary, 1957)—perhaps a confirmation of the psychological validity of the divine-human analogy developed in this chapter.

[25]A priori rejection of such endeavors is often rightly motivated by a concern with univocal understanding—that human characteristics are being simplistically equated with and projected onto God (Te Velde, 2011). But just because the doctrine of the Trinity can be used for bad political purposes (justification of tyranny) or to say opposite things by different authors (equality of humans and hierarchy among humans) (criticized by Tanner, 2010) does not prove there is no basis for using the Trinity as the archetype for our understanding the human ectype in its individuality and relationality.

An analogical approach recognizes that our understandings of God fall far short of God's nature but maintains that there can be some degree of correspondence between human understanding and the nature of God. As always is the case, concerns with univocal understanding have to balanced with concerns about equivocal understanding: that we can understand nothing about the nature of God because human understandings are completely inadequate. Christians have to steer between these two extremes in order to make use of theological revelation in our formulation of ideals for human life, psychology, and psychotherapy and counseling. Taking an analogical stance entails a humble, self-critical confidence in our ability to make measured claims about God and allows us to safeguard the Christian doctrine of God as transcendent while we utilize that doctrine to shape our understanding of human life, for it is in such utilization that we best regulate human life and also participate in God's glory.

[26]Theologians have historically distinguished between two ways of describing God. The "positive way," or *via positiva*, is the assertion of what God *is* (a description of his traits or attributes). The *via negativa* is the assertion of what God *is not*, by reference to how he differs from aspects of the creation.

[27]Even Barth (1969) could say, "Precisely in Himself, from eternity, in His absolute simplicity, God is oriented to the Other, does not will to be without the Other, will have Himself only as He has Himself with the Other and in the Other" (p. 483).

Scripture and the Christian tradition emphasize both the divine unity and relationality of the Trinity. Contemporary work on the Trinity based on scriptural revelation and within the broad parameters established by Scripture and the early creeds should not be rejected as heterodox.

[28]Many theologians are uncomfortable with the use of the term *perichoresis* to refer to human experience. Vanhoozer (2010), quoting Volf (1998), says: "'Another human self cannot be internal to my own self as subject of action. Human persons are always external to one another *as subjects.*' The divine persons indwell human beings in a qualitatively different way than they do one another." Vanhoozer continues, "We are not internal to Christ as acting subjects," since the "relation is non-reciprocal" (p. 153). However, the concept of analogy would seem able to serve the same end here as it does when we use terms such as *person* and *shepherd*. In human participation in the divine communion, humans and God form a profoundly asymmetrical divine-human kind of *perichoresis*, different from that of the Trinity's *perichoresis* but still analogous to it. In fact, the language in John 17 would seem to require such a claim. So long as we make clear its analogical nature, it would seem appropriate and illuminating to refer to human-to-human communion through language and empathy as a finite kind of *perichoresis*.

[29]A much more in-depth discussion of the roles of each member of the Trinity in the psychospiritual healing that derives from Christian salvation can be found in chapter twelve of Johnson (2007).

[30]Research and reflection on children's development suggests that their inter-subjective experiences with their caregivers come to constitute their internal world, affecting their experiences for the rest of their lives. Some have conjectured that in the first year of life, unable to distinguish themselves from others, infants experience their relations with others as a subject-object fusion: "Mother and I are one" (see Guntrip, 1971; Lewis & Brooks-Gunn, 1979; Mahler, Pine, & Bergman, 1975). This original, unified, self-other intersubjective experience is due to the lack of cognitive structures that enable older children to distinguish self from other. Out of this primordial relational union all other relational experiences flow.

Later, through the course of ongoing experiences with their caregivers, infants form an emotional bond with them called an attachment. This bond, which forms around the age of one, is made possible by the infant's increasing memory abilities and constructive interactions with caregivers/image bearers, enabling the infant to recognize whether the attachment figure is present or absent. As a result, when the caregiver leaves, a child with secure attachment cries in distress because it knows the caregiver is leaving, and the child's sense of itself is bound up in the current representation of the caregiver now absent, causing some emotional pain. This is evidence of a kind of cognitive/affective union the child experiences with the other, a degree of psychological identification with the caregiver that Stern (1985, p. 188) calls "being-with." Gradually, the child's self-structures begin to emerge, continuously shaped for good as skilled caregivers gently and sensitively "enter into" the subjectivity of the child, sharing the same thoughts and experiences (Rogoff, 1998; Stern, 1985).

According to Kohut (1971), parents need empathy to promote healthy kinds of intersubjectivity, and in this shared psychological state, some of their most important tasks occur, including mirroring the child's affect back to the child and generally affirming and enjoying the child's actions. The parents' interest in the child and lavishing of joy on it analogically resemble the eternal, mutual joy experienced among the members of the Trinity, except that the child's limited capacities at this age render the relationship profoundly asymmetrical. As a result, these childhood experiences formally resemble more the quasi-*perichoresis* experienced by God and believers.

Vygotsky (1978) and others (e.g., Wertsch, 1998; Rogoff, 1998) have investigated how all higher mental functions are shaped in childhood within the intersubjectivity of close social relationships. Rogoff (1998), for example, has studied "scaffolding," in which a more intellectually competent individual provides guidance, motivation, and strategies (or some other mental structure) for the less competent, enabling the latter to accomplish more than they otherwise could have (within the Zone of Proximal Development) and also training them for future independent performance. Through joint attentional focus, conversation, and a corresponding emotional tone, the older person "enters into" the soul of the younger, supplementing their mental structure with their own. According to this well-documented model, the whole of our early intellectual development (and the corollary shaping of our affective, volitional, and axiological structures) is conditioned and made possible by such "dwelling in" cognitive-affective-relational processes. Another simple kind of human-human quasi-*perichoresis* is labeled "psychological symbiosis" by Shotter and Newson (quoted in Harré, Clarke, & De Carlo, 1985). This refers to the common occurrence when parents talk to infants beyond their competence, acting as if they could understand and, in so doing, drawing the child into the world of more mature human discourse and understanding.

Relational agency begets relational agency. Assuming normal physiological development and "good-enough" social interactions with persons/image bearers, children develop an increasingly complex sense of self (Harré, 1984; Harter, 2012; Stern, 1985), and slowly the capacities of personal agency emerge (a process Vitz [1997] called *personagenesis*). Consequently, children become increasingly distinct individuals, forming their own values and making their own choices (though, significantly, always within the context of others, primarily family and peers). This process of individuation-within-relationship (first within one's family of origin, in interaction with family members, and later with peers and others outside the family) continues through adolescence and into adulthood, expanding into additional relational contexts and reaching full maturation in early to middle adulthood. So in many ways, human beings experience something somewhat analogous to divine perichoresis, and such experiences come to constitute the form of our souls. It is the job of a counselor to try to cultivate such experiences to aid in the healing of the soul in therapy.

[31]"Love both presupposes union and likeness between lover and beloved, and causes deeper union. It causes mutual indwelling between lover and beloved, and even an ecstasy that draws the lover out of himself and toward the beloved" (Sherwin, 2005, p. 80). However, as we have learned from those with various kinds of psychological damage, unhealthy relations are characterized by an inordinate union with the other, such that the proper boundaries of self and other are in some measure lost. Consequently, therapy has as one of its goals the development of proper boundaries.

[32]Even Tanner (2001) acknowledges, "Reflecting in our lives the goodness of God's own triune being, we do so as the free active agents we are. Our agency is part of the gifts God gives in imitation of God's own dynamic life; we reflect, then, the goodness of God in those actions" (p. 70).

CHAPTER 3: THE WORD OF THE SON

[1]Every therapeutic model "holds up a concept of the ideal person and aims therapy toward helping the client to develop in the direction of that ideal" (Charry, 2001, p. 121).

[2]Some Christians have attempted to appropriate the terms *self-realization* or *self-actualization* for Christianity by arguing for their similarity with the Christian term *progressive sanctification*, at least in part to show a genuinely common interest in human maturation. However, the respective processes are hardly identical. The most significant distinction is that the modern versions were understood by their originators to be exclusively activities of the self; that is, the "self" within both terms refers both to the self as *object* (that which is being realized or actualized) and the self as *subject* (the self which realizes or actualizes *itself*). But the latter is contrary to a Christian understanding of maturation, since humans are ultimately dependent on God's grace for all maturational good. Humans, of course, necessarily participate in their maturation. However, naturalistic accounts leave God entirely out of that process. Few terms of modern psychology, therefore, are *more* antithetical to a Christian orientation than *self-realization* and *self-actualization*. (See Johnson, 2007, chap. 7, for a more thorough discussion on this score.)

[3]Unfortunately, it is impossible here to attempt a full evaluation of contemporary PP and contrast it with a *Christian* positive psychology. At a minimum, according to a Christian worldview, all human positivity is ultimately a function of God's grace—either creation grace or redemptive—but it also necessarily falls short of God's design for the highest kind of human flourishing found alone in union and communion with the triune God, because of the fundamental psychospiritual disorder known as sin (see chap. 8). See the special issue of the *Journal of Positive Psychology*, "Toward a Christian Positive Psychology," in volume 12, no. 5.

[4]"This is the *anapsuxis*, the *apokatastasis pantōn*, the revivification, the restitution of all things, Acts 3:19,21; the *anakephalaiōsis*, or the gathering of all things in heaven and earth into a new head in Christ Jesus: Eph 1:10" (Owen, 1965, Vol. 1, pp. 61-62). "Upon the prospect of the ruin of all by sin, God would in and by him—as he was fore-ordained to be incarnate—restore all things. The whole counsel of God unto this end centered in him alone" (p. 62).

[5]Christ provided a stark contrast with the rest of humanity on this score, for he did "not receive glory from men" (Jn 5:41), and he did not seek his own glory (Jn 8:50) or glorify himself (Jn 8:54), but sought "the glory that is from the one and only God" (Jn 5:44).

[6]"The eternal, firstborn Son furnished a pattern for man as a royal glory-image of the Father. It was in his creative action as the Son, present in the glory-Spirit, making man in his own son-image that the Logos revealed himself as the One in whom was the life that is the light of men. Not first as incarnate Word breathing

on men the Spirit and re-creating them in his heavenly image, but at the very beginning he was quickening spirit, creating man after his image and glory" (Kline, 1986, p. 24).

[7]Historically, the *imago Dei* has been treated under the heading of theological anthropology rather than Christology. However, in the twentieth century, beginning with Bonhoeffer and Barth, that categorical determination has been rethought. In a book on Christian psychotherapy and counseling, it seems especially important to show how all lines of thought trace back to Christ, hence the discussion on the *imago Dei* in this chapter rather than in the chapter on creation (chap. 7). There, however, we will consider the developmental nature of the *imago Dei*.

[8]"The likeness of God extends to the whole excellence by which man's nature towers over all the kinds of living creatures." It included "right understanding," "affections kept within the bounds of reason, all his senses tempered in right order, and he truly referred his excellence to exceptional gifts bestowed upon him by his Maker" (Calvin, 1559/1960, p. 188).

[9]The following is a summary of some of this research. To begin with, human reason and memory require brains that have developed normally; perception of the physical and social worlds; attentional focus; encoding, storage, and retrieval of information; the ability to understand distinctions among and relations between things, including conceptual things; language comprehension and production; the use of logic to draw valid conclusions, see patterns and regularities, and solve problems; the ability to manipulate images and other sensory information; creativity; and wisdom (Ashcraft, 1994; Baltes, Gluck, & Kunzmann, 2002; Gazzaniga, 2000; Pinker, 1994; Sternberg, 1998). Intelligence is the comprehensive term used to refer the sum of these mental abilities (more than just human reason), and if the foregoing is true, we would seem warranted in concluding that the more intelligent a person, the more fully is the omniscient and exhaustively rational God imaged by that person (though all humans have image-bearing potential, including severely mentally impaired people, and even the brightest of humans is a weak analogy to God given our relatively minuscule capacity as finite creatures) (though Erickson, 1983–1985, disagrees with the latter point).

The Scripture also represents God as emotional. Given God's perfection, we should understand him to be omnipathic; that is, he possesses an infinite capacity for all possible divine emotions including those that are evoked in response to specific events. Since humans have emotions, mature image bearing includes having a rich and well-developed emotional life, capable of experiencing temporally a range of affective states similar to God's: positive affectivity and optimism, anger, interest, contentment, sadness, awe, and disgust, to name a few, in appropriate ways at appropriate times (e.g., experiencing sadness in the loss of a friend, rather than joy, Vander Goot, 1984).

Dynamic-structural features of the *imago Dei* would also seem to include being moved by certain motives for action, including self-affirmation, a sense of competence and self-efficacy, affiliation, curiosity, and the joy of creating something new (Bandura, 1977; McAdams, 1993; Murray, 1938; Weisberg, 1993; White, 1959). Similarly, this dimension would also entail self- and other-understanding and relationality: a degree of self-awareness, inwardness, and ego-strength; a sense of personal continuity and personal and narrative identity; high social skills; an ability to trust and love others, empathize, form friendships, behave prosocially, and understand the feelings and perspectives of others (Damon, 1988; Maccoby, 1980; Parker, Mitchell, & Boccia, 1994). Image bearing would seem, as well, to involve action structures: the capacities to recognize and commit to certain ends, to establish particular goals, to delay gratification, to initiate actions with a certain vigor, to keep oneself on task, to terminate action when necessary, to change one's mind appropriately, and to work on new projects (Brandtstadter, 1998; Cantor & Banton, 1996; Carver & Scheier, 1981; Heckhausen, 1991; Mischel, 1974). As we saw in the previous chapter, these capacities make it possible for humans together to image a triune God who consists of three absolute persons in absolute communion, who is utterly self-sufficient and yet exists in self-giving love for eternity, and who has exhaustive self- and other-knowledge (is absolute subjectivity), and is maximal purposiveness, indeed, the supreme personal agent and the source of all creativity in the universe.

Lastly, dynamic-structural features of the *imago Dei* are also manifested through just and prudent dealings with others; honesty; empathy; genuineness; advanced moral reasoning; care for the well-being of others; an ability to take appropriate responsibility for oneself and one's actions; an affirmation of social justice; a delight in goodness, truth, and beauty; patience, self-sacrifice, and other virtues (Damon, 1988; Kreeft, 1992; Kruschwitz & Roberts, 1986; Rest, Narvaez, Bebeau, & Thoma, 1999; Turiel, 1998). Such moral capacities and virtues, even in sinful and flawed human beings, signify the God who is their Archetype and origin.

All of the foregoing dynamic structures are combined in the form of a mature human being (Johnson, 2007). The above list is obviously selective, but it consists of characteristics that are necessary for the highest levels of human functioning, and they are also, for the most part, finite signs in humanity of God's superior, transcendent, and triune personhood. In light of the above, it would seem that a fuller understanding of the dynamic-structural aspects of the *imago Dei* is available to us now than was available in previous eras because of the contributions of twentieth-century psychology. At the same time, a few qualifications are in order. Some may have noticed there are a number of features in the list above that are not actually characteristics of God (e.g., a sense of personal continuity, which only a self-conscious, temporal being would have). However, they are included in a discussion of image bearing because such are necessary for temporal, finite human beings who are created to image God. If these are not, strictly speaking, features of the *imago Dei*, perhaps we could call them supplemental components, without which the *imago Dei* could not be properly sustained in creatures over time. (Another supplement would be the body, without which we could not image God in space.) This temporality suggests another aspect of the *imago Dei* that does not apply to God: it is developmental. Finite humans must grow more fully into the *imago Dei* as its dynamic structures emerge and unfold. In addition, there are also emotional and attitudinal states that would seem to be qualities of a healthy human personality but that God could not possess, such as guilt, shame, remorse, and regret, that are the result of wrongdoing or mistakes. Nevertheless, it can be virtuous for sinful humans to feel guilty (when one has done wrong) and shameful (when one is a sinner). Perhaps we can say that there are some ideal human psychological states that a perfect God *would* experience if he *were* capable of the sin or error that lead to them. Given that God is a holy, true, responsible personal agent, guilt feelings *would* be his response to sin were he to commit it. So, humans who legitimately feel guilt after sin are in fact imaging God's holy *disposition*. It would seem, then, that the human conscience is also a part of the image of God. Finally, we must also note that no single finite creature could image the infinite God, as well as a host of such creatures. God can only be imaged by an infinite being; this is why the Son of God is the only one who can be *the imago Dei*.

[10]We might add that relationships can only occur between persons, and without the dynamic structures of the human body/soul, we would have no more capacity to have meaningful relationships with others and with God than a newt. So there is little point in rejecting the structural approach in favor of the relational. A better course of action is to figure out how these different "representations" of God are themselves related to one another and form a unitary whole.

[11]This point was also recognized by Aquinas: "Since the divine goodness could not be adequately represented by one creature alone, on account of the distance that separates each creature from God, it had to be represented by many creatures, so that what is lacking to one might be supplied by another. . . . Of course, not even the entire universe of creatures perfectly represents the divine goodness by setting it forth adequately, but represents it only in the measure of perfection possible to creatures. . . . Therefore multiplicity and distinction occur in things not by chance or fortune but for an end, just as the production of things is not a result of chance or fortune, but is for an end" (Aquinas, 1947, p. 105).

[12]Calvin (1559/1960), for one, rejects the functional as a sufficient explanation of the *imago Dei*: "Nor is there any probability in the opinion of those who locate God's likeness in the dominion given to man, as if in this mark alone he resembled God,

that he was established as heir and possessor of all things; whereas God's image is properly to be sought within him, not outside him, indeed, it is an inner good of the soul" (p. 190).

[13]The term *biopsychosocial* has been used over the past thirty years by modern psychologists to label models of human beings that include the most comprehensive set of psychological phenomena (see, e.g., Block, 1999; Coleman & Miner, 2000; Renfrew, 1996; Sarafino, 1990, among many others). Unfortunately, these models typically do not recognize the unique features of personal agency, the emergence of which enables humans to take responsibility for themselves and act intentionally in light of their own values.

[14]We see here the limitation of the metaphor of a mirror, since a mirror reflects its image passively, whereas the *image Dei* is an *active* reflection; indeed, we are actors whose task in the theodrama is to imitate the general way of life of the main protagonist (Vanhoozer, 2005; Torrell, 2003, p. 89).

[15]Christian therapists and counselors, therefore, cannot be entirey content to work exclusively on the formal aspects of the *imago Dei*.

[16]Particularly emphasized by the Reformational wing of the Christian church.

[17]This obviously needs to be distinguished from legitimate "mercy ministries" (Keller, 2015), which directly assist with biopsychosocial well-being but do so without promoting an alternative religious or secular belief system.

[18]As Balthasar (2004) argued, "There can be no question at all of certain Christians specializing in the transcendent aspect (the so-called 'eschatological' or contemplative aspect) while other Christians specialize in the immanent aspect (as active and 'turned toward the world'). To propose something of this sort would be to tear Christ in two and to render his image unintelligible in both directions. There is only one form of *agape*, which is lived in its wholeness" (p. 136). In an otherwise perceptive book, Dueck and Reimer (2009) make an Anabaptist case for Christian therapists to promote explicitly the religious system of the counselee. On this score, such a "peaceable psychology" has far more in common with contemporary postmodern values than the radical intentions of the original Anabaptists. Genuine dialogue requires more of both counselor and counselee.

[19]Interpersonal knowledge with humans does not change the infinite, triune God any more than creation, the cross, or forgiving us changed God. But God's omniscient knowledge cannot be reduced to the scientific. Knowing a person is different from knowing facts about a person, and God knows all things. See Stump (2010).

CHAPTER 4: THE GIFT OF THE SPIRIT

[1]Most contemporary psychologists would consider this a methodological issue, but from a Christian worldview standpoint, it is better understood as the result of worldview bias. The same kinds of methodological claims prevented modern psychologists from studying the virtues for decades.

²This shows that worldviews affect how one interprets research findings and the nature of well-being. While naturalists have tended to interpret this self-serving bias or "positive" illusion solely in terms of its adaptive value and commend it (see, e.g., Taylor, 1989), the partial self-deception involved in an optimistic explanatory style would seem to be intrinsically *unhealthy* psychologically, according to a Christian interpretation, since accurate perception and integrity is also a feature of a Christian account of human well-being.

³Following Seligman, an explanatory *style* is a personal attributional orientation that may be helpful or hurtful. An explanatory *framework* is derived from one's worldview and therefore reflects the assumptions about human beings shared by the intellectual community with which one identifies. Humans from different worldview communities may share analogous attributional styles (optimistic or pessimistic) while differing in their fundamental framework.

⁴From a Christian standpoint, we might consider the tendency of humans to attribute their good actions to themselves, without regard to God's involvement, to be the *ultimate* fundamental attribution error.

⁵Calvin (1559/1960) followed Augustine closely on these issues: "You act and are acted upon. And if you are acted upon by one who is good, then you act well. The Spirit of God who acts upon you is the helper of those who act. The name 'helper' indicates that you also do something" (p. 334); and again: "To will is of nature, but to will aright is of grace" (p. 335).

⁶This is usually termed the "Creator-creature distinction."

⁷Some think this understanding of the Spirit does better justice to the full personhood of the Holy Spirit than does the traditional Augustinian interpretation of the Holy Spirit as the bond of love between Father and Son, since love is not itself a person. But see chapter two, note eleven.

⁸"It can be said that in the Holy Spirit the intimate life of the Triune God becomes totally gift, an exchange of mutual love between the divine Persons, and that through the Holy Spirit God exists in the mode of gift. It is the Holy Spirit who is the *personal expression* of this self-giving, this being-love. He is the Person-Love, He is the Person-Gift" (Pope John Paul II, cited in Grenz, 2001, p. 328).

⁹Perhaps one reason why he is the only person of the Trinity whose name is consistently given the adjective *holy* is to make clear that the holiness that distinguishes God is in no way compromised by our remaining sinfulness. Another reason may be to remind us that the God who lives in us is holy and is always drawing us into more holiness. We should surmise that the only way he can dwell in us is because we have been definitively sanctified by the work of Christ.

¹⁰Some have suggested that the Holy Spirit's indwelling is a kind of *perichoresis*. Such language will be avoided here since the Spirit's indwelling of the believer is absolutely asymmetrical rather than perfectly reciprocal, but the believer's relationship with the Spirit (and the communion of the Trinity) is certainly *analogous* to their *perichoresis*.

[11]*Pneuma* is the word used for the Spirit in the Greek Old Testament (the Septuagint) and the Greek New Testament.

[12]This is as good a psychological example of natural law as any.

[13]"Faith and Spirit are the two sides of the same coin" (Dunn, 1996, p. 649).

[14]Natural science methods require uniformity and the predictability of the norms of the natural order. Therefore, one cannot expect that they will be the best methods to study the freedom of the Spirit. Human science methods—e.g., phenomenological reports, narratives, participant observation, and discourse analysis—will be more helpful. Natural science methods are, however, quite useful in studying the Spirit's more routine providential work throughout the created order, so that there is an underlying unity and harmony in natural laws and so-called supernatural interventions, since everything that happens within the creation, aside from sin, is the Spirit's work.

[15]Pargament (1997), for example, has found that people can engage in a "transformation of significance," a kind of interpretive control, that reduces the perceived importance of something, making the problem less problematic.

[16]Over the past few decades, Pargament (1997) and his colleagues have put together a significant number of studies closely related to religious attribution but focused more practically on religious problem solving. He distinguishes between *self-directing* (a more individualistic stance, in which the person solves problems independently of God), *deferring* (a more passive stance, in which the person trusts God to solve his or her problems), *collaborative* (a stance of joint problem solving, where God and the person both actively engage), and *spiritual surrender* (in which the person actively gives the problem into God's hands) (Cole & Pargament, 1999). The latter two styles have been associated with positive life adjustment.

Dipolar problem-solving style has many affinities with the more generic collaborative and surrender styles of religious coping. However, dipolar problem solving is distinguished by its trinitarian orientation in which God the Holy Spirit is wholly and ultimately active and the human is wholly but dependently active within the believer's union in Christ. Future research needs to document dipolar attribution.

[17]Pelagianism was the view of human nature and the Christian life taught by a British monk named Pelagius, among others, around AD 400 that denied that human sinfulness was native and universal and asserted that humans were essentially able to improve themselves without the necessity of supernatural help from God.

CHAPTER 5: STORIES OF GLORY

[1]This is not the place to discuss in detail the creation-evolution intellectual conflict, but a few words must be said. The majority of proponents of evolution hold to the philosophy of naturalism, which assumes that "everything that exists is a part of nature and that there is no reality beyond or outside of nature" (Goetz & Taliaferro, 2008, p. 6). Therefore, confessional Christians must reject *naturalistic* ET, which

entails the belief that the earth's biological diversity arose entirely from natural agents and processes, specifically natural selection and random genetic mutation. Good Christians disagree about exactly *how* God was involved in the formation of human life—whether as a six-day Creator, an intelligent Designer, or the One who holds all things together, including evolutionary processes—but they agree that God is absolutely necessary to the formation of the creation. We might add that few Christians reject evolution absolutely because of the evidence that at least some evolution is occurring even now, for example, in the emergence of new strains of bacteria. But aside from creedal adherence, the empirical evidence itself calls into question a purely naturalistic account of such things as the information system known as the genetic code; the irreducible complexity of the cell; the Cambrian explosion; air-breathing lungs; flight in insects, birds, and mammals; four distinct lines of the development of eyesight; the genetics and energy necessary for four stages of insect development; the repeated, robust rehabitation of the earth after global catastrophes as recorded in the fossil record; and the emergence of the massive neocortex of human beings that makes possible capacities to do far more than was necessary for mere survival on the African savannah, including extensive language skills, reading, music, complex mathematics, aesthetics, recognition of a transcendent Good, and religion. Naturalistic evolution is simply incapable of explaining the emergence of these phenomena based solely on its own principles, a conclusion being drawn even by some naturalists (Nagel, 2012). For further Christian discussion, see Cunningham (2010); Dembski (1999); Plantinga (2011); and Fowler & Kuebler (2007).

[2]Dooyeweerd, however, focused primarily on creation, fall, and redemption.
[3]The Christian metanarrative is also called redemptive history and salvation history.
[4]The Greek word for consummation, interestingly, is a cognate of *telos*.
[5]"When he became incarnate and was made man, He recapitulated in Himself the long history of mankind and, in that summing up, procured for us the salvation that we lost in Adam" (Ireneaus, 1990, p. 59).
[6]"We cannot speak of the being of man except from the standpoint of the Christian and in the light of the particular being of man in Jesus Christ" (Barth, 1956b, p. 92). Such quotes could be greatly multiplied.
[7]"Our concern, therefore, is with the real man, sentenced and made new. The real, sentenced and renewed man exists nowhere else save in the form of Jesus Christ and, therefore, in the likeness of this form, in conformation with Him. Only the man who is taken up in Christ is the real man. Only the man who suffers the cross of Christ is the man under sentence. Only the man who shares in the resurrection of Christ is the man who is made new" (Bonhoeffer, 1955, p. 110). Bonhoeffer referred to this archetypal narrative pattern in many ways. The complete form of Christ is "the incarnate, crucified and risen God" (p. 85). "Christ as the centre of

human existence means that he is man's judgment and his justification" (Bonhoeffer, 1966, p. 63). So Christ is "himself the end of the old world and the beginning of the new world of God" (Bonhoeffer, 1966, p. 67). The problem with both Barth and Bonhoeffer is that they spoke of this happening in Christ without making clear its relation to personal faith in him, and so undermined the role of receptive human activity.

[8]There is, of course, an enormous tension bound up in Christ's assuming human nature and dying for sinners that has led Christians to divide regarding whether Christ died for all or died just for the elect. Scripture supports the former position (Ezek 18:23; Jn 3:16; 1 Tim 2:4-6; 4:10) as well as the latter (Jn 3:36; Eph 1:3-11; Col 3:12), teaching us that this matter is a mystery, and our task is to consent to and live according to both truths and leave their reconciliation with God. Such a stance fosters a missionary agenda around the world and encourages Christians to seek the salvation of everyone, knowing that God is calling on all of his image bearers to take responsibility for themselves before God and to repent of their sins and receive the Son, confident that none of God's righteous purposes will be thwarted by sin.

[9]Barth made this theme central to his *Church Dogmatics*. "In [Christ] we encounter the history, the dialogue, in which God and man meet together and are together, the reality of the covenant *mutually* contracted, preserved, and fulfilled by them. Jesus Christ is in His one Person, as true *God,* man's loyal partner, and as true *man, God's.* He is the Lord humbled for communion with man and likewise the Servant exalted to communion with God. He is Word spoken from the loftiest, most luminous transcendence and likewise the Word heard in the deepest, darkest immanence" (Barth, 1960c, pp. 46-47).

[10]Before moving on, we might note the loose analogy there is between the main epochs of the Christian metanarrative and the main episodes of Christ's story on earth. Christ's incarnation was his entrance into the creation; his crucifixion was related to his becoming sin for us (analogous to the fall); his resurrection was the beginning of our redemption; and his exaltation to heaven draws upward the attention of believers to await his return and the ushering in of the consummation.

[11]Calvin (1559/1960) traces many of the practical connections between Christ's life and our new life: "We see that our whole salvation and all its parts are comprehended in Christ (Acts 4:12). We should therefore take care not to derive the least portion of it from anywhere else. If we seek salvation, we are taught by the very name of Jesus that it is 'of him' (1 Cor 1:30). If we seek any other gifts of the Spirit, they will be found in his anointing. If we seek strength, it lies in his dominion; if purity, in his conception; if gentleness, it appears in his birth. For by his birth he was made like us in all respects (Heb 2:17) that he might learn to feel our pain (cf. Heb 5:2). If we seek redemption, it lies in his passion; if acquittal, in his condemnation; if remission of the curse, in his cross (Gal 3:13); if satisfaction, in his

sacrifice; if purification, in his blood; if reconciliation, in his descent into hell; if mortification of the flesh, in his tomb; if newness of life, in his resurrection; if immortality, in the same; in inheritance of the Heavenly Kingdom, in his entrance into heaven; if protection, if security, if abundant supply of all blessings, in his Kingdom; if untroubled expectation of judgment, in the power given to him to judge. In short, since rich store of every kind of good abounds in him, let us drink our fill from this fountain, and from no other" (pp. 527-28).

[12]"The covenant of grace . . . is indeed unilateral" in its basis. "But it is destined to become bilateral, to be consciously and voluntarily accepted and kept by humans in the power of God. This is the will of God, which so clearly and beautifully manifests itself in the covenant in order that the work of grace may be clearly reflected in the human consciousness and arouse the human will to exert itself energetically and forcefully" (Bavinck, 2006, p. 230).

[13]Centuries ago the great Puritan pastor Richard Sibbes (1629/1982) described mature Christian self-awareness in the following way: "In every Christian there are three men. (1.) First, the natural man, the good creature of God, having understanding, will, and affection. (2.) There is nature under the 'spirit of bondage,' which we call 'the old man.' (3.) There is the 'new man,' framed by the 'Spirit of God,' which doth strive against the corruption of his nature" (pp. 55-56).

[14]The church's performance is an ongoing "creative extension of the definitive form of communicative action embodied in the history of Jesus Christ" (Vanhoozer, 2005, p. 261).

[15]"The whole into which all else fits is none other than Jesus Christ, the definitive and comprehensive display of the wisdom of God" (Vanhoozer, 2005, p. 257). The form we seek to fit is "the history of Jesus Christ, a history that represents the whole and complete divine action from creation to consummation: *the Christo-drama*" (p. 257).

CHAPTER 6: THE BEAUTY OF GOD AND HUMAN FLOURISHING

[1]Calvin, of course, was not alone in this insight. Zwingli asserted the very same thing before Calvin, and both were influenced by Augustine, whose writings are suffused with the recognition that the knowledge of self and of God are interrelated. One can discern this theme throughout the Middle Ages, and in the Catholic tradition in Pascal, up to Tanquerey, a twentieth-century Catholic monk (1930, pp. 213-32), who made the same observation as Calvin. Perhaps the most comprehensive Christian psychologist on this score was Søren Kierkegaard (1849/1980), who, in addition to recognizing the mutual relationship between knowledge of God and self-knowledge, understood with greater developmental awareness that genuine selfhood (what is referred to in this book as "personal agency") *grew* only in relation to God (and vice versa). "The greater the conception of God, the more self there is; the more self, the greater the conception of God" (p. 80). Kierkegaard

believed that the more we come to know God, the more aware we are of our du-
plicity and our actual creaturely qualities, and the more our self matures, enabling
us to live more transparently before God and grasp more of him.

[2]Today Christian theologians and psychologists might clarify and advance Calvin's
insight in four ways. First, knowledge of God and self are also interdependent with
the knowledge of others, which, along with the knowledge of self, begins developing
in the first year of life, both together preceding the knowledge of God. Second, the
knowledge and love of God are also interdependent. Calvin's concentration on
knowledge seems, in retrospect, an overemphasis, unreflective of the biblical focus
on the love of God as the chief command. Even the more philosophical Aquinas
made the equilateral relation of love and knowledge clearer. Third, our knowledge
and love of God are preceded logically and temporarily by being known and loved
by God (a truth Calvin affirmed elsewhere in the *Institutes*). Finally, being known
and loved by God and knowing and loving God is mediated through the knowledge
and love of *Christ*, through whom all our true and sound wisdom is made possible
(which Calvin also discussed later in the *Institutes*).

[3]"[God] is beautiful, divinely beautiful, beautiful in His own way, in a way that is
His alone, beautiful as the unattainable primal beauty, yet really beautiful" (Barth,
1957a, p. 650).

[4]For Edwards, *excellency* is a synonym for *beauty* (Daniel, 1994) and denotes
"harmony, symmetry, or proportion" among a set of things (Schafer, 1994, p. 53).

[5]Along with Julian of Norwich (1998): "For of all else, beholding and loving our
Maker makes the soul see itself as most puny, and most fills it with reverent awe
and true meekness, with abundance of love for its fellow Christians" (p. 50).

[6]This assumption has shaped Acceptance and Commitment Therapy in our day.

[7]Those familiar with contemporary evangelical theology will recognize how this
coheres with Frame's perspectivalism (1987) and Poythress's "symphonic" theology (2001).

[8]However, this superior translation was taken from Balthasar (1982–1991, Vol. 2,
p. 136).

[9]I have great sorrow for the hindrances I have caused my own children by my lack
of correspondence to Christ.

[10]There is also some interesting confirmatory empirical evidence in two studies that
found that stronger belief in Satan was related to higher religious well-being and
associated negatively with complaints against God (Beck & Taylor, 2008).

CHAPTER 7: THE WAY IT'S SUPPOSED TO BE

[1]Temporal personal agents require conversations in order to communicate, whereas
the eternal persons that compose the Trinity communicate eternally.

[2]Science involves the elucidation of the divine discourse of the Son of God embedded
in the created order. So, humans encounter a communicating God throughout the

creation (Ps 19:1-2; Rom 1:20), albeit indirectly, and are continuously being invited to live in joyful, creative dependence on him. Their being addressed within a meaningful world suggests that humans are not best understood as "meaning makers" (as secular constructivists like to put it) but as "meaning receivers" or, we might say, "meaning artists," who use the given meaning in creative ways. By contrast, naturalism assumes that existence is ultimately meaningless. This presents a problem for secular therapy, since even many secularists recognize that humans live for meaning (e.g., Baumeister, 1991). Christian assumptions on this score would seem to fit human nature better than naturalistic assumptions.

[3]By natural law I mean all the norms found in the created order, but especially those that pertain to the ethicospiritual orders of human life.

[4]"The formula that describes the state of the self when despair is completely rooted out is this: in relating itself to itself and in willing to be itself, the self rests transparently in the power that established it" (Kierkegaard, 1849/1980, p. 14). See the parallel: "Faith is that the self in being itself and willing to be itself rests transparently in God" (p. 82).

[5]Plantinga (1993) defines the proper function of human faculties in this way: "they are working properly when they are working in the way they were intended to work by the being who designed and created both them and us" (p. 197).

[6]Unity in diversity is nowhere signified more profoundly than in the one-flesh union of husband and wife, the human embodiment of the union of Christ with his bride (Eph 5:22-32). Moreover, these considerations fit well with the functional aspect of the *imago Dei*, which involves "being fruitful and multiplying" (Dempster, 2003, p. 61). If true, it would seem to have profound implications for marriage, sexuality, individuation, gender identity, and sexual orientation, and might put on a stronger footing classical Christian values regarding psychopathology and healing in these areas (Anderson, 1982). However, we must add that singleness is also a Christian sign. Our Savior was single, and singleness points ahead to the eschatological fulfillment of humankind (see O'Donovan, 1986, p. 72).

[7]Kohut (and others in the Freudian tradition) used the term *idealization* rather than *admiration*. However, I think this implies too strong an individualist-constructivist orientation and does not do justice to the strong relational/contextual realities within which humans develop. As Taylor (1989) points out, goods are not experienced as posited (or idealized) by the self but as existing outside the self—that is why theists and other realists refer to them as *goods. Admiration* brings out a little more clearly than *idealization* the fact that children esteem what they perceive to be actually worthy of esteem.

[8]Calvin (1559/1960, p. 188) concedes that "sparks" of the divine image glow in the human body. This is at least in part because the body communicates some of the

glory or meaning of God, for example, behaviorally. Paul made this point indirectly when he told believers to yield the members of their body to God as instruments (means) of righteousness. Through godly actions God's glory is displayed. Second, the body also communicates glory/meaning inwardly. The somatic marker hypothesis (Damasio, 1994) suggests that emotional meaning is conveyed viscerally, by means of the neural system throughout one's torso. As a result, we feel our emotions, such as joy in God and conviction of sin, *in our bodies.*

The Old Testament makes repeated reference to the psychological and ethico-spiritual significance conveyed by one's internal organs (Prov 14:33; Jer 4:14), liver (Lam 2:11), and kidneys (Ps 7:9; 16:7; 73:21; Jer 20:12; see Wolff, 1974). Paul similarly said he longed for the Philippians "with the affection of Christ Jesus" (Phil 1:8; see 2 Cor 6:12). The Greek word here for affection, *splanchnois*, literally means "bowels." Jesus said regarding one who believes in him that "from his innermost being [*koilias*] will flow rivers of living water" (Jn 7:38). *Koilias* means stomach, belly, or "the hidden, innermost recesses of the human body" (Arndt & Gingrich, 1957, p. 438). These are suggestive clues in the lay psychology of the Bible that point to the *bodily* representation and experience of human meaning that was designed to be a vehicle of God's glory. Counseling involves being alert to such messages (e.g., in the counselee's body language and "felt sense") and training counselees how to interpret them accurately.

[9]One problem in listing these processes this way is the false impression it gives they are static structures. Since humans are temporal beings, these psychological processes are *dynamic* structures, necessarily temporal themselves, and many of them have the ongoing potential of being modified.

[10]According to Fredrickson (2002), positive emotions tend to "broaden an individual's thought-action repertoire," leading to interest, exertion toward goals and projects, creativity, and collaboration, which in turn contribute to the building of enduring positive traits, personal resources, and social bonds. Christians would only add the theocentric telic context for which humans were created that provides the ultimate end of one's positive emotions.

[11]Negative emotions were created to signify that which takes one away from God and goodness, which were hardly needed prior to becoming fallen, with the exception of temptation.

[12]As discussed in Johnson (2007, chap. 9), the above elemental and intermediate dynamic structures of the embodied soul can be perceived and conceptually organized from different perspectives, forming distinct psychological wholes or gestalts, which are called *forms*: personality architecture, personality signature, self, personal agent, narrative, and character. The soul as a set of forms is termed a *pluriform* (Johnson, 2013).

[13]Freud labeled consciousness the ego.

[14]Following Edwards (and Augustine; see O'Donovan, 1980), proper human self-love is absolutely asymmetrical to God's self-love given what we have called the archetype-image distinction. It is fitting that God love himself supremely, whereas human self-love is supposed to be subject to and calibrated by the love of God, who alone ought to be loved supremely. So proper human self-love (as it was designed) is theocentric.

[15]"The greatest baseness of man is the pursuit of glory. But it is also the greatest mark of his excellence; for whatever possessions he may have on earth, whatever health and essential comfort, he is not satisfied if he has not the esteem of men. He values human reason so highly that, whatever advantages he may have on earth, he is not content if he is not also ranked highly in the judgment of man. This is the finest position in the world. Nothing can turn him from that desire, which is the most indelible quality of man's heart" (Pascal, 1680/1941, p. 128, no. 404).

[16]No one doubts that a positive orientation is adaptive in many respects. However, adaptiveness is a very plastic measuring stick, so it can be used to justify just about any phenomena. The pure naturalist also has the burden of explaining the pervasiveness of the idealism evident in these findings. Would it not be adaptive to be accepting of reality? Why the tendency to see the world better than it currently is? Christian theism would seem to offer a better account with its assertion of a good human creation now fallen.

[17]While this chapter is concentrated on processes of creation grace, it is also necessary to consider the processes of redemptive grace when considering the development of *imago Dei* capacities now, because redemptive grace undermines sin and the damaging effects of the fall among Christians and so works closely together with creation grace to facilitate *imago Dei* development. This interrelationship will be discussed somewhat below.

[18]Though strictly speaking the narrow aspect of *imago* development now pertains to redemption rather than creation, it presumably would also have developed in human beings as they developed from children into adulthood had humanity never fallen. The love of God, for example, would necessarily develop in unfallen humans as their created capacities for knowing God increased.

Interestingly, the Reformed tradition has long had a developmental model of this aspect of the *imago Dei* called "progressive sanctification" (Hodge, 1874/1993; Murray, 1977). However, this concept tended to be discussed in the soteriology section of a systematic theology rather than where the *imago Dei* was usually discussed, under the heading of biblical anthropology. As a result, the progressive nature of sanctification was rarely linked to the narrow model of the *imago Dei*, so the developmental nature of the latter was left largely unexplored.

[19]"The Child continued to grow and become strong, increasing in wisdom; and the grace of God was upon Him" (Lk 2:40). "And Jesus kept increasing in wisdom and

stature, and in favor with God and men" (Lk 2:52). "It was fitting for [God] . . . to perfect the author of their salvation through sufferings" (Heb 2:10). "Although he was a Son, He learned obedience from the things which He suffered. And having been made perfect . . ." (Heb 5:8-9).

[20]Some have resisted the idea that people can differ in terms of their likeness to God and grow into greater likeness. Erickson (1983–1985), for example, writes, "There is no indication that the image is present in one person to a greater degree than in another. Superior natural endowments, such as high intelligence, are not evidence of the presence or degree of the image" (p. 513). This may be because they think that any acknowledgment of individual differences in imaging could be used to undermine the truth that *all* humans are made in God's image. Recognition of the ontological sacredness of all human life has to be maintained. However, that valid concern ought not contribute to conceptual confusion that evacuates the words *image* and *likeness* of their meaning. The terms are surely intended to denote that humans bear some recognizable, substantive similarity to God. To reduce the *imago Dei* only to some kind of ethereal quality that one is born with, which one then continues to possess throughout life without change, renders the concept virtually meaningless (except that it means "very special!"). On the contrary, one can maintain that God has established a unique relationship with all human beings by designating them all his images (including the unborn and mentally impaired), such that they are all worthy of special protection and regard, and simultaneously affirm that the *imago Dei* in its fullest sense consists of an emergent set of capacities—some creational and some the fruit of redemption—that must develop over time and through faith in order for mature image bearing to be realized. An acorn is of the same species as a mature oak tree, but there are noticeable differences between them.

[21]Bavinck discussed the concept of the *imago Dei* in some detail. He (2004), for example, believed that it could be seen in the use of human faculties—reason, emotions, will, language, attachments, and action (pp. 556-57).

"In all these psychic capacities and activities of human beings we can see features of the image of God as well. The very diversity and abundance of these forces reflect God. . . . Precisely because man is so wonderfully and richly endowed and organized, he can be conformed to and enjoy God in the fullest manner—from all sides, as it were, in all God's virtues and perfections" (p. 557).

"So the whole human being is image and likeness of God, in soul and body, in all human faculties, powers, and gifts. Nothing in humanity is excluded from God's image; it stretches as far as our humanity does and constitutes our humanness" (p. 561).

While he did not discuss the developmental implications of these aspects, they all entail development. However, Bavinck (1956) did recognize that the *imago Dei* required a historical unfolding and social proliferation in order for it to be most fully exemplified (see pp. 215-16; 2004, p. 577).

Pannenberg (1985) discovered in Herder a developmental notion of the *imago Dei*. However, it was not until the late twentieth century that the implications of this approach to the *imago* began to be more thoroughly explored, by theologians as diverse as Pannenberg, Moltmann (1985), Gunton (1998), Grenz (2001), Shults (2003), and Horton (2005). Grenz's work in particular is a remarkable tour de force on the development of the *imago Dei* in the context of the fall and redemption.

[22]"It is not a thing contrary to Christianity that a man should love himself, or, which is the same thing, should love his own happiness. If Christianity did indeed tend to destroy a man's love to himself, and to his own happiness, it would therein tend to destroy the very spirit of humanity; but the very announcement of the gospel, as a system of peace on earth and good-will toward men, shews that it is not only not destructive of humanity, but in the highest degree promotive of its spirit. That a man should love his own happiness is as necessary to his nature as the faculty of the will is; and it is impossible that such a love should be destroyed in any other way than by destroying his being. The saints love their own happiness. Yeah, those that are perfect in happiness, the saints and angels in heaven, love their own happiness; otherwise that happiness which God hath given them would be no happiness to them; for that which any one does not love he cannot enjoy any happiness in" (Edwards, 1969, p. 159). Edwards goes on to point out that the law of God itself uses self-love as the standard by which one evaluates one's neighbor love (Lev 19:18), and since neighbor love is next to the love of God, a proper self-love ought to be very strong, and will be, since it will be subordinate to and dependent on the love of God.

[23]Pascal (1680/1941) thought much about such matters: "When I consider the short duration of my life, swallowed up in the eternity before and after, the little space which I fill, and even can see, engulfed in the infinite immensity of spaces of which I am ignorant, and which know me not, I am frightened, and am astonished at being here rather than there" (p. 74).

[24]"[God] did not leave Himself without witness, in that He did good and gave you rains from heaven and fruitful seasons, satisfying your hearts with food and *gladness*" (Acts 14:17, italics mine).

CHAPTER 8: SIN AND PSYCHOPATHOLOGY

[1]These messages are conveyed throughout our culture in many ways, directly and indirectly. One place to look is children's movies, where our culture's implicitly religious values about humanity's unbounded potential and high self-esteem are repeatedly taught to its youth.

[2]The classic Christian understanding of sin as privation is perplexing but has many benefits. It honors God as impeccably holy who cannot be the cause of sin (1 Jn 1:5; Jas 1:13-14). It also helps us avoid problems that come with thinking of sin as a substance, something ontological, something that one can objectify and identify

over there—distant from *me*—for example, a part of the creation or culture or behaviors that *others* do. Such dualistic/moralistic thinking tragically underestimates the deceptive danger of sin. As a result, Christians at least since Augustine have preferred to understand sin as the absence of human well-being—and that sounds a lot like a psychological problem. The problem with sin as privation is that it cannot explain how sin has such destructive force, so more must be said.

[3]Some Christians sharply distinguish relationship and law (and the forensic qualities of salvation), but this obscures their fundamental unity in a theocentric universe. Disobedience is relational and judicial, since God is our Father and friend, as well as our king and judge. While relationship and law might seem like contrary orientations to us, requiring us to choose one over the other, childlike submission to our loving, righteous God assumes their unity in his mind, heart, and action.

[4]Bonhoeffer (1966) said that there are basically only two possibilities for human life: "either man must die or he kills Jesus" (p. 36).

[5]Some Old Testament scholars have questioned whether the original tempter should be identified with Satan, since the figure in Genesis 3 is just referred to as the serpent. However Jesus considered the serpent to be the devil (Jn 8:44), so we will follow the majority of historic Christian interpreters and regard the original foe of the human race as the Satan of later biblical revelation.

[6]Jesus once said, "You seek to kill Me, because My word has no place in you" (Jn 8:37).

[7]Some non-Christian intellectuals have actually considered the serpent to be a hero in the story, for he was guiding humans to their true enlightenment (Halstead, 1984).

[8]Freud, of course, is commonly credited with discovering the unconscious, but it was already widely recognized by the time he came on the scene (Ellenberger, 1970). The Bible taught about it, without using the term, but usually tied it to sin. "The heart is more deceitful than all else, and is desperately sick; who can understand it?" (Jer 17:9). One subversive agenda of the gospels is the exposure of the corrupt, unconscious motives of human religion (Johnson, 2016). See also Johnson, 2007, chap. 13.

[9]Commentators have speculated whether the favor was due to Abel's bringing animal sacrifices, symbolically indicating he understood the need for blood-sacrifice for his sins—in contrast to Cain's grain sacrifices. However, the text is unclear about the reason for God's favor, and that is just as well, since God's favor cannot always be explained.

[10]As we noted in chapter four, this is the *ultimate* fundamental attribution error.

[11]We cannot go into much detail here, but it should be added that the loss of freedom that sin entails doesn't rob humanity of every kind of freedom, just the freedom to move toward God. A secondary, and less important, freedom is retained: the freedom to make all the other kinds of choices that sinful personal agents can make: what cereal to eat, what job offer to take, what person to pursue for marriage.

However, sin can also compromise and limit this secondary freedom, and extend its bondage (e.g., in addiction). Sin in the Christian perspective "is the attempt to conceive and exercise freedom outside the acknowledgment of [one's] relation (to God). When this happens, finite freedom condemns itself to frustration; it binds itself in an inability to be dependent and to receive, so cuts itself off from its roots" (Williams, 2004, p. 42).

[12]O'Donovan (1986) calls it a "divided consciousness" (pp. 109-12).

[13]The Puritans also called this disposition "indwelling sin" and in Christians "remaining sin" (e.g., Owen, 1965, Vol. 6). The Eastern Orthodox call it "hereditary sin," though today that seems to suggest biological causality, which would be misleading. But even Calvin (1559/1960) used biological metaphors for original sin, considering it an "inherited corruption" (p. 246), an "inborn defect" we bear "from our mother's womb" (p. 247), and a "disease" with which "we are infected" (p. 248). Though he considered original sin to be guilt-worthy, these metaphors indicate the determined nature of our fallen predicament.

[14]A number of theories have been put forward to try to explain this mystery, including biological transmission and federal imputation. Regardless of how original sin is passed on, Christianity teaches that all humans are infected and, once they become personal agents, are participants in it.

[15]In psychiatry "endogenous" refers to a disease or symptom not attributable to any external or environmental factor.

[16]In *The Mortification of Sin*, Owen (1965, Vol. 6) similarly emphasized that the Christian's greatest enemy is indwelling sin. "If we are not always killing sin, it is always killing us" (p. 9). However, Kierkegaard had a better understanding of the unconscious dynamics of sin.

[17]This is why Kierkegaard argued that the opposite of sin is not good works or virtue but faith (p. 82; based on Paul's comment, "whatever is not from faith is sin," Rom 14:23). The book's entire analysis, he said, was guided by faith, defined as "that the self in being itself and willing to be itself rests transparently in God" (p. 82), which alone can undermine "the continuance of sin," but not remove it.

[18]Christians recognize that this teaching is one of the more offensive doctrines to those outside the faith, since it asserts humans are born alienated from God, before they commit personal sins. Pascal (1680/1941) responded to such complaints: "Original sin is foolishness to men, but it is admitted to be such. You must not then reproach me for the want of reason in this doctrine, since I admit it to be without reason. But this foolishness is wiser than all the wisdom of men, *sapientius est hominibus*. For without this, what can we say that man is? His whole state depends on this imperceptible point. And how should it be perceived by his reason, since it is a thing against reason, and since reason, far from finding it out by her own ways, is averse to it when it is presented to her" (p. 147). But Pascal may be conceding too

much, given Chesterton's oft-cited observation that there is more empirical evidence for the Christian doctrine of sin than any other! Though it may seem unfair from our perspective, three points must be kept in mind: (1) Creatures simply have no right before God to complain about the quality of their existence, for existence of any kind is better than none and pure gratuity. (At the same time, we must balance that truth with the awareness that Job and the Psalms in inspired Scripture imply that God invites us to take all of our concerns to him.) (2) If the doctrine is true, our perspective is biased by sin, which raises questions about our ability to perceive the situation aright. And (3) God was himself so moved by our calamity that he devised a rescue plan in which the Father sent the Son to become sin for us so that we might be restored to him and his love.

[19]Paul wrote similarly that "the sinful passions . . . were at work in the members of our body to bear fruit for death" (Rom 7:5), and he encouraged the Galatians to "not carry out the desire of the flesh" (Gal 5:16).

[20]The Hebrew word for sin, *ḥāṭṭāʾ* (e.g., 1 Sam 2:17), and the Greek word, *hamartia* (e.g., Lk 15:18), both bring out the notion of violating a standard. See also 1 Jn 3:4, where John defines sin as "lawlessness."

[21]The apostle James focused on an especially troublesome part of the body: "the tongue is a fire, the very world of iniquity; the tongue is set among our members as that which defiles the entire body, and sets on fire the course of our life, and is set on fire by hell" (Jas 3:6).

[22]Pascal reflected brutally on the paradox of present humanity's goodness and badness: "What a chimera then is man! What a novelty! What a monster, what a chaos, what a contradiction, what a prodigy! Judge of all things, imbecile worm of the earth; depository of truth, a sink of uncertainty and error; the pride and refuse of the universe!" (Pascal, 1680/1941, p. 143).

[23]According to Dunn (1998, p. 111), Paul is the major biblical psychologist of sin.

[24]We need not follow Barth, however, in his rejection of the traditional redemptive-historical approach to sin. Barth fails to recognize the biblical dialectic created by counterposing the redemptive-historical and the christocentric approaches. Both are true, and together we get the most comprehensive understanding of sin. In retrospect, either one by itself would seem to be a distortion.

[25]Some theists believe that God can forgive sin without punishment, just as humans often do in their everyday lives. However, to think so is to fundamentally misunderstand God's utterly unique nature and role. He is the absolute guarantor of justice in the universe. For him to bypass any sin without punishment would be to countenance it. We learn that in part from what happened to Christ.

[26]Calvin (1559/1960) went on to say, "There is no danger of man's depriving himself of too much so long as he learns that in God must be recouped what he himself lacks" (p. 267).

[27]All that secularists can offer is the suggestion that counselees don't need to feel so bad about themselves because there's no *true* shame and guilt. Yet this does not actually respect and address the felt shame and guilt but promotes defense mechanisms instead (minimization and rationalization).

CHAPTER 9: SUFFERING AND PSYCHOPATHOLOGY

[1]In a masterwork on the problem of suffering, Christian philosopher Eleonore Stump (2010) argues that suffering is better understood as that which undermines (or destroys) what the sufferer cares about, either her flourishing or the desires of her heart or both (p. 11). Moreover, she suggests that what someone cares about can be distinguished *objectively* (what is actually the case, say, from God's perspective) and *subjectively* (according to the perspective of the sufferer), because we can be confused about what we actually care about—about what actually contributes to our flourishing or the desires of our hearts—in part because of sin. I prefer this more nuanced definition, and I know of no better treatment of suffering than hers. However, for counseling purposes, I think it is sufficient to work with the looser, more commonly held understanding of suffering, since the majority of the time, objective and subjective accounts of suffering overlap considerably, and more subtle distinctions would be lost on most counselees.

[2]In a remarkable essay, "The Love of God and Affliction," Simone Weil (1951) distinguished suffering from *affliction*, which she defines as "an uprooting of life, a more or less attenuated equivalent of death, made irresistibly present to the soul by the attack or immediate apprehension of physical pain" (p. 118). This sounds like what we now call trauma. A lifelong sufferer of migraines, she may not have known survivors of severe childhood abuse, some of whom might prefer chronic physical pain over the chronic psychological pain they have endured and carry. So, rather than limiting her notion of affliction to physical pain (especially since all psychological pain has a physical-neurological element), it makes good sense to see its distinguishing feature as having in some sense *overwhelmed* the capacities of the sufferer.

[3]*Stress* is the term usually used within modern psychology for the human experience of adversity. However, it was borrowed from the physical world, where it refers to a force that causes an object to change shape (e.g., a "stress fracture"). As a metaphor for human adversity it is fine as far as it goes. But terms like *suffering*, *adversity*, and *trial* convey the unique meaningfulness of human difficulties that are absent in the term *stress*. This is another example of how the naturalistic worldview that undergirds modern psychology has subtly distorted contemporary understandings of human beings, resulting in a human science that is not just less religious but less human.

[4]For a survey of the relevant concerns, see Dodds, 2008; Frame, 2002; Lister, 2013; Weinandy, 2000.

⁵"Christianity is committed, in the first place, to a view of divine providence which expects it to act 'arbitrarily.'" This simply means that "God exercises *arbitrium*, the right of decision in matters where there is no reason for him to do one thing rather than another." Some die and some live, and so on. "It is pointless to say 'It isn't fair'—and that not because God truculently exempts himself from the canons of fair behavior, but because such canons are inappropriate to judge the nature of the events. . . . If God were not free to do this, the differentiation of one individual biography from another would be purely a matter of chance; but the Christian doctrine of vocation teaches us to understand it in terms of particular callings received as individual gifts from God" (O'Donovan, 1986, p. 42). This is very illuminating. However, this would need to be more nuanced when discussed in counseling.

⁶The Hebrew verb here (*wayyinnāḥem*) means "to be sorry," and it is in the *niphal* form, so it probably should be translated as reflexive, that is, he "let himself be sorry" (von Rad, 1972, p. 118).

⁷The phrase here is *wayyit'aṣēb 'el-libô*. The verb, *'ṣb*, is in the *hithpael*, which has both a factitive (causal) and reflexive sense, so it could be translated, "he brought himself pain into his heart" (Peter Gentry, personal communication, January 22, 2013).

⁸We recall from the semiotic orientation of *Foundations* that emotions are signs of significance. God's revealed emotions, therefore, convey important meaning about God and reality.

⁹Theologians who strongly emphasize God's sovereign majesty, such as Calvin (1979, Vol. I), have tended to label such narratives "anthropomorphic" or "anthropopathic," arguing that they do not portray God in his essence, since he has planned and therefore knows all that comes to pass in human history and therefore cannot be disappointed. So when it says that "God was affected with grief," that cannot be strictly true. "Certainly God is not sorrowful or sad; but remains for ever like himself in his celestial and happy repose." This was written instead to show how "great is God's hatred and detestation of sin," so "the Spirit accommodates himself to our capacity" (Calvin, 1979, p. 249). One could argue, however, that this stoic-sounding interpretation of God is driven by an *over*emphasis on God's sovereign majesty—and possibly a discomfort with emotion—and is insufficiently respectful of the biblical text in its approach to the particular paradox involved here. As a result, its reading is foreclosed to the possibility of a more comprehensive, post-formal "resolution" regarding God's nature (Johnson, 2002). Rather than consider this passage anthropopathic, let us suppose that it reveals true aspects of God's nature (certainly his hatred and opposition of sin, but also his sorrow and disappointment at human sinfulness and the pain of his thwarted desires for his glory and the flourishing of those made in his image) that are logically subordinate to other aspects (such as his sovereign majesty and predestination of human history, as well as his eternal blessedness and contentment) but are nonetheless *real*, given

the perfection, infinitude, and omni-competence of God, who therefore possesses all virtuous emotion-states simultaneously. See Carson (1991, pp. 184-88; 2008b, pp. 47-49) for a more detailed critique of the traditional "stoic" view of God. Calvin is generally a reliable interpreter, but here his understanding of God (and Scripture) is being limited, ironically it seems to me, by an anthropocentric interpretive framework that assumes God can have only one emotion-state at a time—like humans—which in God's case is that of contentedness (though one wonders why hatred is compatible with God's "happy repose," but not sorrow!).

[10]We learn from the Old Testament that God experiences something analogous to anger, sorrow, and pain. But nowhere do we read that God experienced anything analogous to fear. That is a negative emotion incompatible with the omnipotent ruler of the universe.

[11]See Van Til (1969). The Chalcedonian creed takes no stance regarding the suffering of Christ. While traditionalists have emphasized the assertion that Christ has two natures "without confusion," one can just as well emphasize that the natures "came together in one person and one hypostasis." The sharp disjunction between Christ's divine and human natures with regard to suffering generally held by the classical tradition was maintained to protect the transcendence of God, believing God cannot be affected by his creation. However, the sharpness of this disjunction made it difficult to understand how the singular person of the Son of God could suffer and to articulate the hypostatic union with regard to his suffering, seeming to posit a questionable ontological division in the person of Christ. However, the greatness of Christ's work results precisely from the union of the divine person and nature of the Son of God with human nature, so that God became fully a human being. As a result, we cannot understand properly what happened on the cross without concluding that in some meaningful sense the Son of God suffered in Jesus Christ. Tanner (2000) would seem to treat this as a matter of linguistic reference: "Since this particular human being and the Word are one, it is certainly also true that the Word does and suffers all that—there would be nothing saving to Jesus' life otherwise—but the Word does not do and suffer them as a [mere] human being would, in a fashion like that of a human being, forming opinions, taking action, moving one's lips to speak, disguising one's omniscience, etc. . . . That the Word is the subject here simply means that what Jesus does is attributed to the Word in the same way the Word's own properly divine predicates are attributed to the Word; the human being Jesus acts but these are God's own works" (Tanner, 2000, p. 26, my bracketed addition). What is said of Christ must refer to the one who is both the Son of God and a human being.

[12]Christ experienced some kind of anxiety in Gethsemane, and here we have to say this was uniquely the perspective solely of his humanity. From the standpoint of the Son of God, he could not dread or fear anything, but while reflecting on his

coming condemnation on our behalf and consequent death, he was perceiving them from the standpoint of his humanity. This view is compatible with the teaching that Christ had two wills, called dyothelitism, which was affirmed in the Third Council of Constantinople, the Sixth Ecumenical Council of the early church (Crisp, 2007). But this insight need not apply to suffering per se, because suffering is compatible with the divine nature; at least, that is what is being alleged here.

[13]The resolution of the Nestorian controversy hammered out in the Constantinopolitan Creed (AD 451) affirmed the differentiated unity of Christ's two natures in his person, but Greek assumptions regarding impassibility prevented the early church from applying that hard-won understanding to the suffering of Christ on the cross *as the Son of God.*

The complete solution on this score is found in the distinction between *enhypostasis* and *anhypostatis*, used to describe the incarnation. *Enhypostasis* refers to the insight that the Son of God is necessarily a divine person with a divine nature. When he became a human being (without ceasing to be a divine being), he assumed a human nature that was *anhypostasis*, without personhood (McCormack, 1998; Torrance, 2008). Such a distinction gives the church the conceptual tools to understand how the divine person of the Son of God could actually experience human life in Jesus Christ, including his suffering. Consequently, even if it were true that the divine nature could not suffer, the suffering of Jesus Christ on earth means that the divine person of the Son of God suffered in his human nature, so that Christians can justly claim that God suffered. Nevertheless, it is hoped that the evidence surveyed in this chapter will justify the stronger claim, based on biblical revelation, that a kind of divine suffering analogous to human suffering is not only ontologically possible for the sovereign God of the Bible but fitting for a God who is perfectly virtuous, and activated upon the occasion of human evil and suffering.

[14]The real problem here is the extent to which the early church was influenced in its thinking on the nature of God by classical pagan concepts and assumptions, some arguing for significant corruption (e.g., Van Til, 1969) and others that Christians transformed and corrected them (e.g., Wilken, 2003). Central to the concerns of the early church was the attribution of change, emotions, and suffering to God. Back then and there, suffering implied weakness and vulnerability and was understood to be incompatible with perfect contentment. In the context of ancient thought and religion, where the mythical gods were often characterized by very human passions, and the classical moral and metaphysical ideal was complete freedom from passion—God as the "unmoved mover"—this is quite understandable. Even more important was the assumption that if God suffered it meant he was influenced by events outside himself, making the Creator subject to his creation, ultimately reversing their absolutely asymmetrical relationship. Rejecting the latter notion is basic to orthodox Christianity.

A closely related corollary claim is the classical linkage between immutability and impassibility: God cannot change, and therefore he cannot have emotions, which are intrinsically labile. Part of the confusion here stems from the difference between ancient and contemporary understandings of emotions. In the ancient world, what we today call an emotion was called a passion, and it entailed the characteristic of being affected by something. Consequently, Christians in the early church could not affirm that God had a passion, since that would mean God is affected by his creation—something outside himself—and therefore is dependent on it in some way. The contemporary notion of emotion, however, does not have that entailment (one can feel emotion about a mental image, e.g.). Moreover, it simply is not necessary to interpret God's emotional response to a temporal event (which is referred to repeatedly in the Bible) as necessarily indicating an ontological change in God or a dependence on his creation. There are ways to make sense of those texts that better respect their revelational content.

This is necessary, for the God of the Bible is often portrayed as a very emotional being. Indeed, the same arguments against God's sorrow over human suffering could be made against the notion of God's wrath, yet few orthodox Christians have rejected belief in God's wrath. Moreover, many otherwise classical, contemporary Christians maintain some kind of belief in God's sovereign majesty and allow that he suffers (see Frame, 2002; Horton, 2005; Plantinga, 1985; Zagzebski, 2004). Horton (2011) asserts that there has been a "stoic thread" of discomfort regarding divine emotion running throughout the Christian tradition (p. 247). So, today, the existence of God's emotions is affirmed by at least some orthodox Christians while they maintain that divine emotions are necessarily only analogous to ours—that is, they are similar in some meaningful respects but not identical, since given the infinite differences in our respective natures, they have to be more different than similar (e.g., our emotions are tied to the activation of bodily states, and God has no body apart from the incarnation). As a result, we cannot claim to know very much about God's emotions, beyond what the Scriptures convey.

Another approach to this subject is to argue that as a perfect being, God is infinite and omni-competent with respect to his emotions. Therefore he experiences all emotions befitting a holy, perfect being *eternally* (Spiegel, 2005). (Some emotions, of course, are unfitting for a perfect spirit, e.g., anxiety, shame, or lust.) However, being simple and eternal, this implies no change in his essence, including his emotions. Therefore, in his sorrow he is simultaneously content and in his contentment is sorrowful, but without a sense of loss. His perfection and omni-competence entail that (1) he eternally feels whatever a perfect being would feel with respect to a temporal event, so that, for example, he eternally would sorrow when faced with human suffering (Plantinga, 1985; Zagzebski, 2004); yet (2) he never experiences anything as a true loss, for he is the sovereign majesty who will bring all things to a victorious and glorious end (Frame, 2002; Horton, 2005). To repeat what was said previously: the Bible has simply recorded some historical occasions of the manifestation of God's eternal nature.

Therefore, we ought not consider the biblical depictions of God's emotions as mere "passionless" anthropomorphic facsimiles of human emotions. On the contrary, "In the light of the doctrine of the imago Dei ̦ then, perhaps the Bible's depiction of divine suffering is less a matter of anthropopathic projection than it is a case of human suffering being theopathic (God-like)" (Vanhoozer, 2010, pp. 77-78). One ought to argue instead that God's emotions constitute the evaluative ground of the universe, since they reflect his perfect values and virtues and convey a meaningful similarity between his values and ours. The difference is that he cannot be overcome or engulfed by his emotions or the suffering of this world. Horton (2005), for example, defines impassibility simply as "the incapacity for being overwhelmed by suffering" (p. 195).

On the other side of the spectrum, we must also avoid post-Hegelian views of God common to many who have also noted Greek influence on early Christian thought but have rejected the classical attributes that I am summarizing with the term "sovereign majesty" (involving his meticulous control over the creation, known as providence), asserting instead that God has novel experiences and emotional reactions, and increases in knowledge, as argued by process and open theism (see Huffman & Johnson, 2002; Vanhoozer, 2010).

[15]We of course should not conclude from the foregoing that suffering is therefore an unmitigated good. God himself intervened in human history precisely to avert our eternal suffering in hell, and we are told he will personally wipe away the tears of his people in heaven (Rev 21:4), so the avoidance and alleviation of suffering are goods to be pursued in imitation of God. Suffering, therefore, should never be sought out (in marked contrast to a pronounced theme in medieval and monastic Christianity). God is pursuing simultaneously countless agendas in this creation. Our challenge as his children is to participate in as much of his complex orientation to suffering as we can.

[16]Spiegel (2005) likens God's experience of human emotions with God's omniscience and calls that "God's omnipathy," and the way he is using this term seems valid. However, he makes some needed clarifications and qualifications, the most relevant of which I summarize and modify for the purposes of this chapter. God's omniscience is widely accepted by orthodox Christians. Yet, when we assert that God knows all human thoughts, we must add that he also knows that he is not their subject and that he does not personally endorse them if they are false or sinful. Can we make similar moves regarding God's omnipathy? God knows and feels (empathizes) all the emotions of his creatures (Spiegel points out there is usually a cognitive component in human emotion, and I would add, that would always be the case with God), but God does so also knowing that he is not the subject of human

emotions and does not endorse them to the extent they are inaccurate or sinful. One of the benefits of divine omnipathy, Spiegel notes, is "the obvious source of psychological comfort for the believer who suffers" (p. 178).

[17]*Empathy* means "the ability to understand and share the feelings of another," whereas *sympathy* means "feelings of pity and sorrow for someone else's misfortune" (*Concise Oxford English Dictionary*, p. 467, under "empathy").

A number of orthodox theologians are critical of the idea that God empathizes with humans in their suffering, in part because it also seems to imply that God has a deficit and changes, and perhaps also because process and open theists have argued the same for their positions and because it is a strong value in a secular therapeutic culture. However, another approach is to understand empathy, within a network of other virtues such as justice and compassion, as a social virtue necessary to a perfect, omniscient, and compassionate God. Virtuous empathy is an important component of good parenting and good therapy. Conversely, the lack of virtuous empathy is a distinguishing mark of certain kinds of psychopathology, e.g., sociopathy. Therefore, it may be compatible with a Christian virtue framework and need not have the stigma it seems to have for many.

[18]Indeed, to the wise, Job's created motive to avoid pain would be ultimately realized in learning to love God more deeply and truly and become more like God.

[19]Modern hermeneutics has unfortunately often encouraged such abstraction by treating Old Testament texts as interpretable solely in terms of the understanding of the original human author, and usually neglecting to consider the understanding of the original divine author, who inspired the entire canon and who was ordering revelation history to issue in the glorification of the Son of God.

[20]Stump (2012) makes an important distinction between being completely unwilling to suffer, that is, unwilling *simpliciter*, and being unwilling to suffer in a certain respect, unwilling *secundum quid*. This latter, more mature unwillingness is paradoxical: it still considers suffering an evil that should be avoided if possible, but it is also characterized by a measured acceptance of suffering "as a means to inner healing and greater closeness with other persons, including God" (p. 383). The first kind of unwillingness is unqualified resistance, and such a stance prevents therapeutic healing.

[21]The accent indicates the different meanings. To per*fect* is simply to improve, whereas to be *per*fect is to be beyond need of improvement. Because of the serious problems of perfectionism in the church and in psychopathology, I generally avoid both words.

[22]Moser (2013) argues that human suffering is intended by God to lead to a similar "Gethsemane union" of the divine and human wills. God desires our righteousness so much that he is willing for us to suffer to bring it about. Given the salutary benefits of suffering for Christ, the archetype for the *imago Dei*, perhaps we should

consider faithful suffering to constitute another dimension of the active receptivity of the *imago Dei* (see chap. 3).

[23]The *teleios* root in the word translated here "perfect" likewise emphasizes the never-ending goal of the Christian life, without implying that we can actually attain perfection here on earth.

[24]Suffering, then, is intended to drive the self beyond its (created) egocentrism and out of its (fallen) self-centrism into an increasing new-self theocentrism.

[25]From "Affliction (II)." *Imprest:* payment in advance.

[26]Brother Lawrence's (1895) passivity toward suffering is typical of this approach. "I do not pray that you may be delivered from your pains, but I pray God earnestly that He would give you strength and patience to bear them as long as He pleases. Comfort yourself with Him who holds you fastened to the cross. He will loose you when He thinks fit. Happy those who suffer with Him. Accustom yourself to suffer in that manner, and seek from Him the strength to endure as much, and as long, as He shall judge to be necessary for you" (p. 39).

[27]"Aesthetic consummation—the process by which authors confer wholeness, and therefore meaning, on the lives of their heroes—is to literature as grace is to theology. . . . Only someone who stands outside a person's finished life can 'consummate' or complete it by construing the whole in a particular way. Authorship consists in just such a bestowal of meaningful form" (Vanhoozer, 2010, p. 326).

[28]"God is now the heavenly father who is *over me* and can be merciful to me and justify me where I, from within myself, cannot be merciful to myself" (Vanhoozer, 2010, p. 326, quoting Bakhtin). Bakhtin believed "outsideness," and not empathy, is the vital condition for an author's having compassion on the suffering of his or her heroes. Empathy only "repeats"; it does not consummate the suffering (Vanhoozer, p. 328). "To relieve suffering, by contrast, requires authorship: a return to one's own position, from which location one can then console, assist, or consummate—perhaps to redeem?—the hero's suffering recasting it in meaningful (i.e., salvific) form. . . . There is nothing meritorious, or redemptive, in experiencing another's suffering. A fusion of horizons would result in 'an infection with another's suffering, and nothing more'" (Vanhoozer, quoting Bakhtin, p. 328).

There is a transcendent insight here in Bakhtin's notion of outsideness with respect to suffering. However, Bakhtin (and Vanhoozer) underestimate the role that divine empathy *does* play in the healing of the human soul by rendering one's suffering bearable as it is shared with God and God enters into it, comforting and consoling by "being with" his child. Communion with God, together with divine consummation, enables believers to "overcome the world" (Jn 16:33).

[29]These are some of Christ's fiercest words, directed at perpetrators of childhood abuse: "Whoever causes one of these little ones who believe in Me to stumble, it

would be better for him to have a heavy millstone hung around his neck, and to be drowned in the depth of the sea."

[30]Frame's (1987) perspectivalism offers a good framework for understanding the healing of the soul in Christian psychotherapy: human healing occurs through the integration of the normative dimension (biblical discourse) with the situational (adversity in one's narrative) and the existential (personal suffering). More on that in note one of chapter eleven.

[31]This is part of what Luther called a theology of glory, in contrast to a theology of the cross (see chap. 1).

[32]Two friends, Kay Warren and Amanda Forrester, have taught my wife and me much on this score.

CHAPTER 10: BIOPSYCHOSOCIAL DAMAGE AND PSYCHOPATHOLOGY

[1]In light of misunderstandings about the DSM, perhaps a few comments are in order. As is well known, American psychiatry has been working for decades on an evolving diagnostic system for what it labels "mental disorders," the most recent of which is the fifth edition. Like each previous edition, the DSM-V has received significant criticism (e.g., its focus on symptoms rather than the whole person, comorbidity, problems with a categorical model, the absence of reference to biological markers; Lilienfeld, Smith, & Watts, 2013; PDM Task Force, 2006); and as already noted in chapter eight, Christians have their own concerns, including the assumptions of naturalism and positivism that have shaped it and the absence of any reference to personal, ethical, and spiritual dynamics. Nevertheless, by any criterion of scientific accomplishment, the latest edition is a work of enormous value and clinical importance. Those Christians who basically reject the DSM seem to be relatively unfamiliar with the challenges of the human sciences and so are skeptical of their deliverances, and their discourse evidences a dualism that so prioritizes the problems of sin that the damage to created human nature that can occur in a fallen world seems negligible by comparison (Johnson, 2007, chap. 3). But as a manual describing the symptoms of biopsychosocial damage it is enormously useful.

[2]As Calvin said of ancient philosophy, we might say of modern psychiatry, "If we regard the Spirit of God as the sole foundation of truth, we shall neither reject the truth itself, nor despise it wherever it shall appear, unless we wish to dishonor the Spirit of God" (p. 273). "Shall we say that the philosophers were blind in their fine observation and artful description of nature? . . . No, we cannot read the writings of the ancients on these subjects without great admiration" (p. 274). The ancient philosophers to whom he referred held many beliefs with which he fundamentally disagreed. Recognizing the truth in non-Christian writings with significant distortions or lacunae from a Christian standpoint is not necessarily compromise.

³The seeds of this section can be found in Johnson, 1987.

⁴Dawn (2001) counts nine times. See for example Mt 10:8; Lk 5:15; Jn 5:7; Jas 5:14.

⁵It is also instructive to consider how Paul taught Christians to treat the unrepentant sins of other believers and their weaknesses. Regarding the Corinthian who committed adultery with his father's wife, Paul told the Corinthians to remove him from their midst until he repents (1 Cor 5; see 2 Cor 2:5-10). And he said to "reject a factious man after a first and second warning" (Titus 3:10).

But regarding the weak, he wrote, "Now accept the one who is weak in faith [*asthenounta tē pistei*], but not for the purpose of passing judgment on his opinions. One person has faith that he may eat all things, but he who is weak [*ho asthenōn*] eats vegetables only. The one who eats is not to regard with contempt the one who does not eat, and the one who does not eat is not to judge the one who eats, for God has accepted him. Who are you to judge the servant of another?" (Rom 14:1-4). He concludes his discussion: "Now we who are strong ought to bear the weaknesses [*asthenēmata*] of those without strength [*adynatōn*] and not just please ourselves" (Rom 15:1). Addressing a different topic on another occasion, Paul stated that "some, being accustomed to the idol until now, eat food as if it were sacrificed to an idol; and their conscience being weak [*asthenēs*] is defiled. But food will not commend us to God; we are neither the worse if we do not eat, nor the better if we do eat. But take care that this liberty of yours does not somehow become a stumbling block to the weak. For if someone sees you, who have knowledge, dining in an idol's temple, will not his conscience, if he is weak, be strengthened to eat things sacrificed to idols? For through your knowledge he who is weak [*asthenōn*] is ruined, the brother for whose sake Christ died. And so, by sinning against the brethren and wounding their conscience when it is weak, you sin against Christ" (1 Cor 8:7-12).

What do we learn from these passages? Paul recognizes that some believers have an overly sensitive conscience, but that weakness is not to be ridiculed, and they are not told to repent of it, even though it is clear that the weak hold sub-Christian beliefs. Instead, he encouraged the strong to care for the weak, going so far as to tell the strong *they* are sinning if they do not show consideration to them in their weakness.

On at least two other occasions, Paul told Christians to "help the weak" (Acts 20:35; 1 Thess 5:14), likely a more generic use of the term. Throughout his epistles Paul applies strong pressure on believers to resist and turn from their sin, but he is understanding and kind to the weak in the church.

⁶This also seems apt, since, contrary to Adam and Eve's primal sin, humans ever since have been born into a fallen condition, to which they necessarily become enslaved—so original sin is a kind of necessity in human experience for which humans are responsible. Consequently, sin itself can legitimately be considered a

kind of ethicospiritual defect or weakness (Blocher, 1997; Shuster, 2004). We will explore this supposition later in the chapter.

[7]Paul made a similar point: "For while we were still weak, at the right time Christ died for the ungodly" (Rom 5:6 ESV), which was underscored in the parallel of Romans 5:8. See also Romans 6:19, where he referred to his readers' "weakness of the flesh" to explain why he was arguing the way he was. As Calvin (1559/1960) acknowledged, Paul "knew that there is always some weakness in believers" (p. 1313).

[8]Calvin (1559/1960) pointed out with concern that Augustine referred to the desire to sin (concupiscence) as only a weakness, and designated sin as that which is enacted or consented to. "We, on the other hand, deem it sin when man is tickled by any desire at all against the law of God. Indeed, we label 'sin' that very depravity which begets in us desires of this sort" (p. 603). In light of the present category of fault, we could say they are both correct. Concupiscence is both sin and weakness.

[9]Distinguishing between causation and participation in remediation was inspired by the distinction made in Brickman, Rabinowitz, Karuza, Coates, Cohn, & Kidder (1982) between attributions of causation and solution.

[10]For example, Reinders (2008), Yong (2008), and Brock and Swinton (2012), though Vanier (1971) and Hauerwas (1986) initiated this focus decades ago.

[11]More space is devoted to this problem because of contemporary controversy about how to interpret its normativity, increasingly even among Christians.

[12]In addition to Gagnon's (2002) systematic overview, standard orthodox commentaries that support these assertions include Cranfield (1985), Kasemann (1980), and Moo (1996) on Romans 1; and Thiselton (2013) and Fee (2014) on 1 Corinthians 6:9; and Quinn & Wacker (2000) and Witherington (2006) on 1 Timothy 1:9.

[13]This disorder is probably best understood as a result of epigenetics (Rice, Friberg, & Gavrilets, 2012), which may include socialization. For example, the fact that concordance for the homosexuality of monozygotic twins is about 50% suggests there are factors in addition to genetics.

[14]Some are critical of the notion of sexual orientation, believing that it reduces a sin problem to a natural condition without ethical implications (Burk & Lambert, 2015; Butterfield, 2015). As a result, they advocate rejecting the term, arguing that biblical teaching leads to the conclusion that homosexuality is sinful in every respect. Their caution is warranted, particularly given the unreliability of secular discourse on sexuality in our day, and they rightly note that a homosexual *desire* is sinful (Gal 5:17-19), not neutral, regardless of the explanation of its origins. In addition, their many expressions of compassion for believers with SSA indicate that their judgment that SSA and homosexuality activity are ethically equal is motivated by genuine concern. But the assumption that SSA is an exclusively ethicospiritual problem would seem to minimize the particularly tragic dimension of having a sinful condition that one has done nothing to create and would therefore

seem to add a layer of false guilt and shame to their already difficult predicament, at least given the distinctions being made in this book between sin, weakness, and fault. Butterfield's personal story and Christian conversion give her a particularly valuable vantage point. However, her reasons for rejecting the term *sexual orientation* sound strangely similar to the kind of antirealist/postmodern arguments that feminists and LGBTQ activists have used against sexual essentialism.

While scientific terms can certainly be used for political purposes antagonistic to the Christian faith, Christians can also reinterpret and use them within a theocentric discursive system. Sexual orientation is a good example of one that should be redeemed to prevent our adding burdens to those already burdened with SSA. The postbiblical development of a more complex understanding of a human condition addressed in the Bible need not be interpreted as necessarily a contradiction of biblical teaching, but could be simply its outworking, just like the orthodox elaboration of biblical teachings on the Trinity that occurred in the history of Christian doctrine. God knows everything, including many things he chose not to reveal in the Bible, for example, the biopsychosocial dimensions of SSA, and he is glorified by our growing conformity to his perfectly comprehensive understanding.
[15]This is not the place to discuss in detail the possibility of sexual orientation change, but some Christians with SSA have reported a lessening over time, and some have gotten married and had a family (e.g., Butterfield, 2012; Comiskey, 1992). Jones & Yarhouse (2007) reported that one-third of a sample of SSA men in weekly Christian support groups experienced movement toward greater heterosexual desire and lesser homosexual desire over a two-year period (that means, of course, that two-thirds of the sample did not change or returned to a gay identity. We should also note, however, that the intervention was only a support group and not an actual therapeutic treatment). Yarhouse & Burkett (2003) have developed a cognitive model of treatment that focuses on change in one's identity, rather than SSA, recommending that Christians base their core identity on their relationship with Christ and interpret SSA as simply one part of their experience. Reparative therapy (RT), by contrast, seeks to promote change in SSA through the therapy relationship, in principle, a legitimate creation-grace/common-factor resource. Unfortunately, the RT approach has not always been conducted by trained mental health professionals and with realistic expectations given the degree of homosexual orientation, and it has been severely criticized in the public square (and by some Christians). However, RT has many supporters and case studies of effectiveness in promoting a stronger heterosexual orientation among some with SSA (Hamilton & Henry, 2009; Nicolosi, 2009). In addition, as just mentioned, others have advocated acceptance of one's SSA without consent and opted for celibacy. Burk and Lambert (2015) and Butterfield (2015) advocate repentance as the best response to the condition of SSA, and this stance toward one's same-sex desires

undoubtedly helps some to resist them. However, repentance would seem to be most fitting for those who have consented to and pursued SSA—where SSA has become homosexual activity, and eventually a vice—since repentance is a kind of counteraction, involving an intentional severance from one's sinful activity. By contrast, the mere experience of SSA without consent would seem more to warrant lament and surrender than repentance. Some, of course, will need to practice all three. Nevertheless, depending on the needs and desires of their SSA counselees, Christian therapists have a variety of options that together utilize creational and redemptive resources, leading hopefully to the best possible outcome in individual cases. Much will depend on the degree of SSA, which differs considerably among individuals. Some kinds of disorder are, tragically, more resistant to change than others, and our grief for those afflicted should correspond to the intractability.

CHAPTER 11: THE BREADTH OF PSYCHOPATHOLOGY

[1]We might note that the theologian John Frame (1987) has developed a tri-perspectival framework for understanding reality—focusing on law (normative), subject (existential), and object (situational)—that corresponds fairly well with the model of psychopathology developed over the past few chapters. With regard to our concerns, the normative perspective (regarding the *norms* of human life) refers to the lawfulness of human life (the most important principles of which are revealed with greatest clarity in the Bible); psychopathology here is concerned with sin and has been the focus of theology. The existential perspective (regarding the *subject* of human knowledge) refers to human experience; psychopathology here concerns suffering, and has been the focus of psychotherapy and counseling, as well as research psychology (as *stress*). The situational perspective (regarding the *object* of human knowledge) relates to the setting (understood most broadly) of human persons; psychopathology here refers to biopsychosocial damage and has been an important focus of psychiatry and research psychology. According to Frame, each perspective is irreducible to the others, and each bears on every aspect of human life. [2]For some additional reflection on this project see Johnson (2007, chap. 15) and Coe and Hall (2010). Yarhouse, Butman, and McRay (2005) have provided a useful and basically positive Christian summary and analysis of mainstream psychopathology, and Flanagan and Hall (2014) have edited a similar volume on mainstream developmental psychopathology. The next step will be a more critical and constructive proposal that will build on the work of those authors and will have to enlist many other psychologists, psychiatrists, theologians, and philosophers. [3]Some might argue that the dramatic nature of such conflicts cannot justify their evil and that we ought not to suggest God makes use of them for his glory or we risk directly implicating God in the evil. However, as we saw in chapter nine, the book of Job shows that God *does* use such conflicts as a theater for his glory,

without justifying their evil or implicating himself in their direct causation. Indeed, excellent novels, plays, and movies, both fiction and nonfiction, demonstrate that there is something intrinsically worthwhile about dramatic conflict, particularly through its arduous resolution.

[4]Some Christians have suggested that original sin is now a part of our genetic code. However, this would mean that sin is directly a part of the created order, and it would imply that salvation from sin could be found through genetic therapy. From a Christian standpoint, sin is better understood to be an ethicospiritual disorder that has deleterious effects on the biopsychosocial orders.

[5]This constitutes the negative side of the "correspondence" or "mental model" hypothesis of the relation between attachment to parents and God (see Kirkpatrick, 1992).

[6]Presumably, according to God's design plan, there is some optimal development of finite creatures in a fallen world that would lead to an ideal ratio of more positive emotion than negative, which would contribute to an attitude that is buoyantly resourceful yet also thoroughly realistic.

[7]Embarrassment, remorse, and contrition are also moral emotions. The last two indicate the recognition, to some extent, of the gravity of one's moral failures and the desire to make things right (Harter, 2012; Narramore, 1984; Roberts, 2003).

[8]*Bôš* is the main word for shame in the Bible, and its primary meaning is "to fall into disgrace, normally through failure, either of self or of an object of trust" (Oswalt, 1980a, p. 98). It occurs 155 times in the Old Testament, mostly in the Prophets and Psalms.

Shame is often a result of things turning out badly, for example, a defeat in battle (e.g., 1 Sam 20:30; Ezek 16:63). God sometimes promised shame as a consequence of personal sin (Jer 22:22). There is an objective shame before God (Ps 89:45; Prov 18:13; Dan 9:8), but the Bible also refers to the subjective experience of shame (Is 26:11; Ezra 9:6), especially because of sin and the calamity it causes, often associated with the awareness of other humans (Ps 40:15; 69:19; Is 20:4; Zeph 3:11) (Stump, 2012). Conversely, *shamelessness*—the lack of feeling shame when it is warranted— was considered evidence of extreme waywardness (Jer 6:15). The New Testament adds little to this understanding.

The primary Hebrew word for guilt is ᵓ*āšām*, which "includes acts of sin, responsibility for them, punishment and its aftermath or, as an alternative, atonement. The word denotes any breach of God's covenant with Israel and any divine act of dealing with it, whether punishment or atonement" (Livingston, 1980, p. 79). As with shame, the Old Testament view of guilt is based in objectivity—"before the Lord" (2 Chron 19:10)—so that people "bear" guilt after they sin (Lev 5:17; Ps 5:10; Hos 10:2) (Stump, 2012). Even unintentional sins accrue guilt, but offenders can afterward recognize it and are encouraged to acknowledge (Hos 5:15) and address it (Lev 4:22; see also Num 5:6). Guilt *feelings*, interestingly, are not referred to. God established a "guilt offering" (*'āšām*; see Lev 5–7; 14) as part of the Israelite cultic system to remove people's guilt (Lev 10:17; "and it will be forgiven him," Lev 5:16). Later we are told that the Messiah would become God's *'āšām* and bear the people's sin (Is 53:10-12).

In the New Testament, the corresponding Greek term *aitia* is rarely used. During his trial, Pilate said in reference to Christ, "I find no guilt (*aitia*) in him" (Jn 19:6)—significantly, in a court-like setting. However, the *concept* of guilt permeates the New Testament, evident in its repeated assertions that sinful humans are deserving of condemnation (e.g., Rom 1–3).

New Testament authors also refer to the "conscience" (*syneidēsis*; see Rom 2:15; 1 Tim 1:5), which mediates the law of God "written on [all humans'] hearts," and bears "witness and their thoughts alternately accusing or else defending them" (Rom 2:12-15), though it can be distorted (1 Cor 8:7-13; 1 Tim 4:2; Titus 1:15). Christians could regard the conscience to be the psychological "module" that is the source of subjective shame and guilt, signifying its objective correlate.

[9]In light of such evidence, most secular researchers regard shame to be a harmful emotion that should generally be avoided. Guilt, by contrast, has come to be considered socially valuable, since it promotes a focus on rule violations, not oneself, and (contrary to shame) actions of reparation to resolve problems with those whom one has offended or hurt. Consequently, researchers recommend child-rearing strategies that promote guilt-proneness, but not shame-proneness. Harter (2012) is generally less critical of shame, however, recognizing that it can also promote humility and deference to others, but she acknowledges it is associated with more problems than guilt. Christians have similarly tended to favor guilt over shame (e.g., McMinn, 2008, p. 46).

[10]Though there is not the space to develop these thoughts adequately, the contemporary distinction between shame and guilt might help theologians with what has been called *original guilt*. Following Augustine, many theologians have believed that original sin necessitated original guilt, that is, all humans are born guilty of eternal condemnation because of Adam's sin, believing this was taught in Romans 5. Different theories have arisen regarding how this guilt is passed on, including Augustine's "realist" theory, which supposes that it occurs through propagation, since descendants are somehow present within the beings of their ancestors. The Reformed community has developed the federal-headship theory, believing that God imputes to Adam's descendants the guilt of his primal sin, because he is a representative of the human race, analogous to Christ being a representative of his people. However, as appreciation for the role of personal responsibility has increased in the West (as a result of the indirect influence of biblical and reformational teaching), such notions have been harder for some to affirm. Edwards (1758/1970), Brunner (1939), and Berkouwer (1971) have raised serious questions about the biblical basis

and plausibility of original guilt. As Blocher (1997) more recently has pointed out, both traditional theories do not seem to do justice to the Bible's emphasis on guilt being a result of one's own deeds, for which one is held responsible. First, note that Deuteronomy 1:39 appears to teach that children do not have the "knowledge of good and evil," a fact that is used to explain why the children of the disobedient Israelites were allowed to enter the promised land when most of the adults were kept from doing so. This suggests that accountability is dependent on having a certain degree of mature understanding. Then consider Ezekiel's repeated proclamation on this score: "The person who sins will die. The son will not bear the punishment for the father's iniquity, nor will the father bear the punishment for the son's iniquity; the righteousness of the righteous will be upon himself, and the wickedness of the wicked will be upon himself" (Ezek 18:20), and "'Therefore I will judge you, O house of Israel, each according to his conduct,' declares the Lord GOD" (Ezek 18:30; but see the entire chapter). Or consider John's remarks regarding those who are not in the heavenly city: "Outside are the dogs and the sorcerers and the immoral persons and the murderers and the idolaters, and everyone who loves and practices lying" (Rev 22:15), where the criteria for exclusion are based entirely on personal deeds and not on the imputation of Adam's guilt. This is the overwhelming testimony of Scripture. Rather than supporting the notion of original guilt, Romans 5 can easily be interpreted as support for an "original shame" doctrine, where Adam's sin spreads to all humanity, resulting in physical death of all the human race, symbolizing their spiritual alienation and deficiency, leading to *inevitable* guilt, and therefore inevitable condemnation, apart from Christ, since those humans who grow up will become personal sinners. In addition there is no mention in Romans 5 of the imputation of personal guilt.

Could some Reformational thinking be called for here? Is it possible to preserve the biblical and Augustinian recognition that all humans are born in sin (and so are born shamefully deficient), as well as the pervasive biblical emphasis that humans are guilty for their own sinful deeds? If this is valid, previous theologians were actually referring to objective shame in their discussions of sin's universal, original consequences, rather than guilt, at that point in time not having the linguistic/conceptual resources we have now to distinguish the two. This would mean that the notion of original guilt was actually a blend of the two concepts. Then, an elaborate theological rationale was developed that seems to go beyond the biblical emphasis on the causal relation between sinful personal deeds and guilt (Romans 5 being sufficiently general in its claims that it could be used to support a variety of theories). To summarize this conjecture: being born in sin, all humans are born with original shame, due to having a profound flaw in their beings, but not original guilt, since guilt refers only to that which is accrued as a result of personal deeds. If they develop into personal agents, they will invariably become guilty by following the tendencies of their indwelling sin and committing personal sins. In all of this, we trust a good God to assess human beings with perfect justice.

[11]Individual human development would seem to recapitulate redemptive history. God gave his law to humanity through the people of Israel, whose full personal agency was formed over centuries precisely through that exposure.

[12]To be clear, God brings good out of these negative features of human life not because they intrinsically promote glory or human well-being but because of their respective opposition to both.

[13]Indeed, in my case, a lack of self-awareness has been particularly marked, given the substantial evidence of my own sinfulness and psychosocial damage in early adulthood.

PART IV: THE DIVINE INTERVENTION

[1]Such an awareness was basic to the apostle Paul's experience, for whom "Christ's presence was a more or less constant factor from within which (he) consciously and subconsciously drew resource and strength for all his activities" (Dunn, 1998, p. 400).

[2]Anticipated by Purves & Achtemeier (1999) and Purves (2004).

CHAPTER 12: THE LIFE OF CHRIST AND THE PERFECTION OF HUMANITY

[1]This passage justifies a family of related words used for psychological and relational activities that are especially associated in Christianity with the crucifixion: *self-denial* (Brunner, 1947b; Calvin, 1559/1960), *self-sacrifice, the renunciation of self* (Okholm, 1995), *cruciformity* (Gorman, 2001), *agape love* or *charity* (Lee, 1973; Lewis, 1960; Nygren, 1953), and even its secularized version *altruism* (Bateson, 1991; Monroe, 1996; Oliner & Oliner, 1988). Both incarnation and crucifixion involve the same movement of self-denying love for the other (the Father and other humans).

[2]"[Christ] descended always lower and deeper and more intimately into our fellowship. The way down into these depths was marked by tiers or steps: conception, birth, the lowly life in Nazareth, baptism and temptation, opposition, disparagement, and persecution, agony in Gethsemane, condemnation before Caiaphas and Pilate, crucifixion, death, and burial. The way led ever farther down from His home with the Father, and it led ever nearer to us in the fellowship of our sin and our death, until finally in the deepest depth of His suffering He gave utterance to the anxious plaint about being forsaken of God" (Bavinck, 1956, p. 337).

[3]"The Son goes forth because going forth is always already who he is as God, because all wealth and all poverty are already encompassed in his eternal life of receiving and pouring out, his infinitely accomplished bliss and love, his *apatheia*; and so he is hidden in being manifest and manifest in being hidden: he is the God

he is in his very divestment and in his glory, both at once, as the same thing, inseparably" (Hart, 2003, p. 322).

[4]No mention is made of Christ experiencing sexual desire either. We cannot make much from silence, but it seems probable that Christ experienced such desire (since he was tempted in all points as we are yet was without sin, Heb 4:15), and if he did, it was well regulated, given his moral perfection, his calling to celibacy and the fervency of his superordinate desire to obey his Father's calling.

[5]"We must think of the work of the cross . . . as beginning immediately with his birth, increasing in his growth into manhood, and deepening in intensity as he entered his public ministry. His whole life is his passion, for his very incarnation as union of God and man is an intervention into the enmity between God and mankind" (Torrance, 2008, p. 110).

[6]Billings (2011) advocates using the terms *conformity* and *participation*, rather than *imitation*, to avoid the common assumption of many people that they can be like Christ under their own power.

[7]Christ's "active obedience" saves us, as well as his death (Edwards, 1994, p. 368). The perfect righteousness and love of Christ realized in his life on earth is that which is given to us upon faith in Christ. The term Reformational theologians have used for this gift is *imputation* (Rom 4:23). The task of believers is not to obtain righteousness by means of their own efforts but to receive the perfect gift of divine salvation and then live their lives on the basis of this reality. Otherwise, we view our efforts at holiness as the ultimate basis for our standing before God and the ground of our confidence. But because of the limitations and sinfulness of humanity, human efforts and actions can never be an adequate foundation of one's confidence. It has to be 100% perfect obedience, and that is exactly what salvation in Christ is. We will return to this theme again and again. Consequently, the imitation of Christ is necessarily preceded by the imputation of Christ's righteousness.

[8]This generalization has to be qualified by the recognition that Christ's life and calling also have unique features that are not held up to the church for emulation (Hauerwas, 1983). He was, after all, the Messiah, and he had a distinct role to play in his day in Israelite culture that his followers are not to follow. For example, his celibacy and lack of a home are not requirements placed on all.

[9]"Jesus is not simply the means to what the triune God wants to give to us out of its fullness; the shape of Jesus' life is the end or goal of that giving, which we are to receive in union with him" (Tanner, 2000, p. 20).

[10]Regarding this identification, Merton (1961b), commenting on the redemptive missions of the triune God, asserted, "My discovery of my identity begins and is perfected in these missions, because it is in them that God Himself, bearing in Himself the secret of who I am, begins to live in me not only as my Creator but as my other and true self (Gal 2:20)" (p. 41). And Sibbes (1635/1967) similarly referred to the Spirit as the believer's "better self" (p. 103).

[11]Such relational dynamics sharply distinguish Christian forms of mindfulness—perhaps better termed meditative prayer—from their secular analogues.

[12]"The one who keeps [God's] commandments abides in Him, and He in him" (1 Jn 3:24), and "the one who says he abides in him ought himself to walk in the same manner as he walked" (1 Jn 2:6). The foregoing may help us to understand Christ's comments after the washing of his disciples' feet. "A new command I give you: love one another. As I have loved you, so you must love one another. By this all men will know that you are my disciples, if you love one another." Love of one's neighbor had been taught in the Torah (Lev 19:18). But this became a new command for two reasons. First, Christ's example transforms it as we see it displayed by the Son of God. Second, it is new because everything has changed in our understanding of ourselves and God in the death of Christ. Before Christ's death, humans, even believers, could deceive themselves that they could in fact obey God and live for God. But in the story of Christ's death we scandalously discover that *out of ourselves* we hated God and put him to death when he came to us in the Son. Everyone's life story has to be read anew after the cross, for now our radical self-determination is seen as the folly it is, and we are led instead to seek help from above.

CHAPTER 13: THE DEATH OF CHRIST AND
THE END OF PSYCHOPATHOLOGY

[1]*Lytron*, used in Mt 20:28; 1 Tim 2:6. See also Rom 3:24; 1 Cor 1:30; Eph 1:7; Col 1:14.

[2]*Agorazō*, "to purchase or set free," found in 1 Cor 6:20; Gal 3:13; 4:6.

[3]The shame, guilt, and deserved punishment of some human beings or all human beings, depending on one's interpretation of the extent of the atonement. Biblical support can be found for both positions, so like many important Christian doctrines, the issue is a theological paradox. See Johnson (2002).

[4]This model of the atonement was strongly influenced by the satisfaction theory of the atonement developed in the Middle Ages by Anselm.

[5]In addition to the above voices of opposition, see also McIntosh (2008) and Tanner (2010). For advocates of penal substitution, see Horton, 2005; 2007; Hill and James (2004), especially the essay by Vanhoozer, which addresses some of its key contemporary opponents. For a mediating position, see Boersma (2004), though without a developmental framework, Boersma's mediation is not quite able to do justice to the role that penal substitution plays in biblical revelation.

[6]A rejection of the principles of retributive justice reflects a remarkable naiveté about human nature. Ethical transgressions have consequences for the self, and it is essential for children to understand this principle in order to grasp more complex ethical matters. Adults who tragically never develop this understanding—e.g., those with antisocial personality disorder—are recognized to be seriously disordered and a danger to themselves as well as to society. The ethically more advanced

notion of forgiveness only makes sense within an ethical universe where there is retribution for one's evil actions. As developmental psychologists are well aware, one does not mature by *rejecting* the accomplishments of earlier developmental stages; one transcends them in a higher order of conceptualization that is able to take more of reality into account (Kegan, 1982). God's revelation of his law and judgment for the law's violations is foundational to human life. Without it, there is no grace, only moral chaos.

Using the perspectival framework of Frame (1987), penal substitution pertains to the perspective he calls the "normative." According to Kierkegaard's developmental stage theory (Evans, 2009), the model fits within the "sphere of life-motivation" that he termed the "ethical." With Kierkegaard, we should recognize that there is a developmental priority of the ethical over later, higher spheres of life-motivation. That helps to make sense of why the ethical is emphasized so strongly in the Old Testament, an emphasis that is assumed in the New Testament—and never repudiated—but then is transformed in Christ.

[7]Ultimately, the problem that some have with the penal substitution model (and the reason others *over*emphasize it) probably has something to do with the limitations of human reasoning (Johnson, 2002). It is difficult to square the framework of retributive justice that underlies it with other moral virtues such as compassion, forgiveness, and self-giving, since they appear to come from contradictory ethical systems. But as with most theological topics, the believer's task is not to take one biblical truth in order to overrule another but to do the best one can to develop a "metasystem" that takes into account all well-substantiated truths of which one is aware—giving each one its due—in order to correspond as fully as possible to God's comprehensive understanding.

[8]The necessity of divine forgiveness is made obvious when we have sinned against people who are now dead; since they cannot forgive us, what are we to do? But our Creator God can still forgive us.

[9]It is this *redemptive realism* that separates classical, orthodox versions of Christian counseling from liberal versions. (See Reno, 2002, for a powerful defense of the objective validity of the atonement. By contrast see Browning, 1966, for a more human-centered, subjectivist approach to the atonement applied to counseling.)

[10]Significantly, no criticism is made of a client's *lack* of guilt over her having an affair with a married man. However, her feeling of guilt over wishing the death of her lover's wife was said to be "understandable in view of the patient's desire to marry her lover" (p. 177). One might expect secular cognitive therapy to discount such feelings of counselees. More surprising is that more explicitly client-centered therapies, such as secular emotion-focused and psychodynamic therapies, abandon their general pattern of trusting the client's experience in the case of their perception of the validity of their deficits or transgressions. This is evident throughout (Dearing & Tangney, 2011).

[11]Murray (1977) called this event "definitive sanctification."

[12]The fatal flaw of liberal ethical systems is the rejection of the lower ethical frameworks.

[13]One can appreciate those orthodox Christians who strongly prefer the cruciform love model over the other models because of its focus on some of the most remarkable features of Christ's moral character, its demonstration of God's solidarity with the oppressed and abused, and the kind of response in humanity it is intended to engender. However, we must be wary of ideological bias, regardless of how well meaning, that embraces one set of data, theory, and assumptions and uses it to justify the rejection of other sets. This is particularly problematic for Christians, whose canon includes the Old Testament. Perhaps one of the greatest dangers in our day is a kind of neo-Marcionism that implicitly ignores vast portions of Scripture, simply because it cannot be easily integrated into what amounts to a hyper-Christian interpretive framework.

[14]A progressive complementarianism appreciates such reminders, no matter the source, for male tyranny over women, even when willingly embraced, exemplifies the curse given to Eve: "your desire will be for your husband, and he will rule over you" (Gen 3:16). Christians are to act so as to undermine that curse, not advance it.

[15]McAdams's (2006) "redemptive self" is a rare example of secular integration of a true Christian psychological concept.

CHAPTER 14: THE RESURRECTION OF CHRIST AND THE BEGINNING OF THE NEW CREATION

[1]"The resurrection is that singular and unique event that inaugurates a new creation" (Vanhoozer, 2005, p. 42).

[2]With likely no awareness of Mahler's work, Fitzmyer (1989, p. 84) suggestively used the term *symbiosis* to describe union with Christ.

[3]Paul's overall teaching, the immediate context, and the aorist passive participle *ktisthenta* in Ephesians 4:24 indicate that the creation of the new self is entirely God's work at conversion (Hoehner, 2002).

[4]"When God adopts men and women into his family he insures that not only may they have the rights and privileges of his sons and daughters but also the nature or disposition consonant with such a status" (Murray, 1955, p. 133).

[5]"Reformation theology does not leave us in the courtroom, but it is the basis for our relocation to the family room" (Horton, 2007, p. 247).

[6]The God-image is one's "complex, subjective emotional experience of God. It is shaped by a person's family history and causes their experience of God to resemble their relationship with their parents" (Moriarity & Hoffman, 2007, p. 2). It should be distinguished from one's God-concept, which is an "abstract, intellectual, mental definition of God" (p. 1).

[7]This is undoubtedly a controversial claim, since so few Americans recognize the falseness of the "myth of neutrality" (Clouser, 2005) that so thoroughly permeates

contemporary American culture in our day. At the same time, some Christians are legitimately employed in soul-care contexts where inquiring into one's relationship with God would be largely inappropriate (e.g., educational evaluations by a school psychologist). Such counseling can be done in the name of the Lord implicitly, without mentioning his name (Tan, 1996). But most psychotherapy and counseling inevitably deal with issues having to do with value, meaning, and significance, so theistic therapists should not have to leave their worldview assumptions at the door when their expertise in such matters may be precisely what is most therapeutic.

[8]The following process of the internalization of the word of God is described from a more theoretical vantage point in Johnson, 2007, chap. 16.

[9]This therapeutic feature of Christian soul care is less important, influential, and necessary for those raised in relatively healthy Christian families, whose story is one of having been raised by Christian parents who more or less adequately portrayed God's sovereignty, righteousness, and love, leading often to an eventual conversion.

[10]"This renewal is a continuing process (Col 3:9), just as the mortification of the old man is a continuing process (Eph 4:22). But it is the redemptive-historical transition, effected in Christ's death and resurrection, that is working itself out in this process" (Ridderbos, 1975, p. 64).

[11]What Torrance (1983) would call "onto-relational."

[12]Secular therapists have long recognized that shame and guilt make therapants defensive and inhibit self-exploration, so without a doctrine of sin, they have worked hard to create an atmosphere of what Rogers called "unconditional positive regard." Christians recognize that secular therapists have simply developed secular analogues of grace, unmediated by God in Christ. Christian therapists have to create an analogous, grace-based atmosphere, but because of their doctrine of sin, their discourse will have to include explicit connections to Christ, since God's grace is intended to be mediated through him and his life, death, resurrection, and ascension.

CHAPTER 15: THE EXALTATION OF CHRIST AND THE SPREAD OF THE NEW CREATION

[1]We should note that in his divine nature the infinite Son of God was still one with the Father "in heaven" when he became incarnate and assumed/added on a finite, human nature (including a finite human consciousness). In the incarnation he did not empty himself of his divine nature but remained who and what he was: the eternal Son of God. But in the ascension, a person now with two natures—divine and human—entered the immediate presence of the Father for the first time, though in his divine nature he had never left. This conclusion follows necessarily from the being of the Son of God, since the divine nature did not become human— only the *person* of the Son of God did (Bavinck, 2006). Here we encounter another of the great mysteries of the Christian faith.

²Christ's second coming is also considered to be a part of his exaltation (Bavinck, 2006, p. 436).

³The mysterious Melchizedek was himself the king of Salem (i.e., a king of *peace* and of righteousness, Heb 7:2), who blessed Abraham (Gen 14:18-20), the father of the Jewish people, in whom all the families of the earth would be blessed (Gen 12:3).

⁴This line is an adaptation of a saying of Men at the Cross (www.crossmg.org) often uttered at their meetings: "You are welcome, and whatever you bring here is welcome." Faith and repentance are qualifications of a sort, but they are best understood as necessary correlates of the gift of Christ announced in the gospel. Rather than being prerequisites or conditions, they are the positive and negative aspects of active receptivity. The corollary of receiving Christ is dying to autonomy, including a Christian version of autonomy.

⁵While we must be careful not to draw unwarranted lessons from word studies, the root of the word used here for blessing, *eulogia*, reminds us that blessings are verbal in nature, and this ties in nicely to the fact that many of the blessings of union with Christ are based in declarative speech-acts that God utters with respect to all who believe in Christ: justification, adoption, and sainthood, to name three. We will discuss this aspect of salvation later in the chapter.

⁶"Calvin saw the Spirit's work as that of transposition: taking what was in the realm of physicality and moving it to the Trinity's domain" (Canlis, 2010, pp. 116-17).

⁷What follows is hopefully relatively more shaped by Scripture and the actual temporal process of salvation than the *ordo salutis* that emerged from Protestant scholasticism, aspects of which were relatively more constrained by logic. As an example of the latter's influence into the twentieth century, see Murray (1955). For a critique of the classical *ordo salutis* from the standpoint of redemptive history, see Gaffin (1978). For a more elaborate discussion of the present model, see Johnson (2011a).

⁸Some Calvinists may conclude that the present model of salvation places too much emphasis on the role of human activity over against divine activity. However, the lengthy discussion on Christian attribution in chapter four should assuage any fears that the author is a proponent of semi-Pelagianism. All believing human activity is ultimately caused by the Holy Spirit (Phil 2:13; and, for that matter, exercised within the providence and outworking of God's decrees). The relations between divine and human activity are a paradox, and perhaps one unresolvable by our reason. Believers simply are to do their best to articulate the coordination of divine and human activity in salvation and the Christian life (and providence, but that's another matter).

⁹The mystery of eternal election is the temporal discovery of faith in Christ. That is why Calvin (1559/1960) rightly noted, "Christ, then, is the mirror wherein we must, and without self-deception may, contemplate our own election" (p. 970). Without such a christocentric framework, the doctrine of election can become a hindrance

to flourishing, as was often the case among the Puritans, rather than a comfort. That is because many post-Reformation Protestants, following a hyper-Calvinist logic more than Scripture, treated election under the heading of the divine decrees, abstracted from Christ. One thing we can do with counselees who struggle with whether or not they are elect is simply encourage them again to believe in Christ.

[10]"Faith is the principal work of the Holy Spirit" (Calvin, 1559/1960, p. 541).

[11]Some might wonder why a speech-act account of salvation is preferred over the more traditional Reformational accounts that concentrate on the terms *justification* and *sanctification*. To begin with, speech-act theory (SAT) enables us to build and expand on the traditional Reformational distinction between justification (what God has said about believers) and sanctification (what God [ultimately] and believers [secondarily] do to make believers holy). One problem in traditional accounts has been the perceived lack of organic connection between justification and sanctification that would seem to allow believers to be justified but not holy. SAT makes much clearer the semiodiscursive nature of all of salvation. Moreover, declarative salvation includes *everything* that God says about believers in Christ (not just justification), and the perlocutionary effects of declarative salvation consists of *all* the ways God's speech-acts in Christ affect believers (not just sanctification) and connects those effects directly to God's word. For further elaboration, see Johnson, 2011a.

[12]Speech-act theorists, however, disagree about whether understanding counts as a perlocutionary effect. For my part, I think that it does.

[13]The Spirit is "the inner teacher by whose effort the promise of salvation penetrates into our minds, a promise that would otherwise only strike the air or beat upon our ears" (Calvin, 1559/1960, p. 541).

[14]"Whereas if we could make this clear to our souls, that God is ours, and then take up our thoughts with the great riches we have in him, laid open in Christ, and in the promises, we need trouble ourselves about nothing, but only get a large vessel of faith, to receive what is offered, nay, enforced upon us" (Sibbes, 1635/1973, p. 272).

[15]This aspect was termed *reformative* salvation in Johnson, 2007, chaps. 6, 8, and 12.

[16]Because explicit use of mental imagery for soul-healing purposes is not directly commanded in the Bible, some Christians have objected to its use, arguing that it has more in common with New Age thought than Christian (e.g., Hunt & McMahon, 1985). This concern is also rooted in what some might call the "regulative principle" of Christian counseling, the belief that only that which is explicitly taught in the Bible should be practiced by Christians. However, such restrictions on the application of biblical teaching infringe on the freedom of new-covenant Christianity and are therapeutically shortsighted. Better to use what we could call the "normative principle of Christian counseling" the belief that Christians are free to use whatever counseling techniques are not forbidden in the Bible, along with the "doxological

principle," that we are free to use whatever contributes to the glory of God. Moreover, the pervasive use of metaphor and imagery in the Bible and the proportion of the Bible composed of historical narrative would seem to promote the use of one's imagination. The human faculty of the imagination is part of God's good creation and like all good gifts can be used for evil. However, it is hard to think of a better use of such a gift than in the service of God's Christiformative and healing glory.

[17]Lincoln (1981) rightly rejects the notion "that the believer has a double which is his or her real self in heaven" (p. 128). Rather, "the force of Paul's statement for the Colossians is that since their life is hidden with Christ in God they need no longer feel any necessity to appease heavenly powers in order to attain the divine presence. Being in God they have completeness and great security" (pp. 128-29). This is true, so far as it goes, but what was Paul saying positively? The real self is not some kind of *ontological* double, a spiritual twin living in a parallel universe. God considers and reckons the individual believer's being to be so woven together with Christ and into all that he is and has done that it constitutes our being there transcending time and space. Therefore, also from an eschatological standpoint, we are already there, though not there yet in a temporal sense.

[18]Christians are also told to "look not at the things which are seen, but at the things which are not seen; for the things which are seen are temporal, but the things which are not seen are eternal" (2 Cor 4:18). In the context of the self, the *actual* self is what is seen and temporal about oneself, while the *real* self is what is unseen and eternal.

[19]In addition to promoting one's ideal self to others (and oneself) as if it were one's actual self, the false self includes the repression of one's current fallenness, alienation from God, and imagined autonomy over oneself, which secular therapeutic and false religious systems cannot resolve but only reinforce.

[20]For example, "Because you are in Christ, picture yourself as royalty, clothed in perfectly white garments," and so on.

[21]Harter (2012), however, calls *this* the real self—"one's actual competencies and adequacies" (p. 64). Rogers (1961) also made passing reference to the real self, suggesting it is "something which is comfortably discovered in one's experiences, not something imposed upon it" (p. 114). Horney, Harter, and Rogers all contrast this entity with one's ideal self.

[22]Though Rogers tended not to use the term *real self* because of a belief that the self is more process than structure (1961, pp. 107-24), similar to Horney, he strongly believed that humans are characterized by a basic, forward-moving "tendency and striving—to actualize, maintain, and enhance" him- or herself (1951, p. 487; see also p. 489).

Masterson (1988), an object relations theorist, blends Horney's actual and real selves in his notion of the real self, which he defines as "the sum of the intrapsychic images of the self and of significant others, as well as the feelings associated with those images, along with the capacities for action in the environment guided by those images" (p. 23). But he also believes it includes the drive toward personal competence and fulfillment in one's life tasks, which encompasses constructive capacities of the individual such as self-awareness, assertiveness, self-affirmation, creativity, intimacy, and healthy autonomy (see chap. 2 on the development of the real self and chap. 3 on the real self in action).

CHAPTER 16: THE HOLY EMBRACE OF THE BODY OF CHRIST

[1]Edwards argued that the Trinity is the eternal archetype of consent. Richard of St. Victor (1979) offers another argument, that the mutual, consensual love of the Father and the Son is delighted in by the third person of the Spirit, who rejoices infinitely in their happiness, and they in turn together lovingly share their love with the Spirit, together forming a perfectly harmonious community that transcends the perfection of a pair.

[2]Luke made a similar link: "the church of God which He purchased with His own blood" (Acts 20:28).

[3]We have noted that Edwards saw the excellence of the Son to consist in a conjunction of opposites (eternal majesty who became a human baby). Extending this aesthetic orientation further, what a conjunction of opposites is seen in a group of broken sinners who are constituted the "body" of Christ indwelt by Holy Spirit. That too is a remarkable form of excellence.

[4]Pascal (1941) agreed, in principle: "We love ourselves, because we are members of Jesus Christ. We love Jesus Christ, because He is the body of which we are members. All is one, one is in the other, like the Three Persons" (p. 159). Over the past few decades, many theologians from a range of orthodox perspectives have suggested that the church offers a social analogy of the Trinity (e.g., Grenz, 2001; Volf, 1998; Zizioulas, 1985). However, this link has come under severe criticism in recent years (see Bidwell, 2011; Holmes, 2012; Tanner, 2010). The critics are right to be cautious about the search for correspondences between the Trinity and specific social proposals, whether in the church or in culture, because of the danger of projection, the fact that opposite proposals are defended with the social analogy, and the preference of biblical authors to point to Christ as the focus of our image bearing rather than the Trinity. However, as suggested in chapter two, such caution does not need to lead to complete agnosticism regarding such correspondences given the biblical evidence that leads in this direction, when combined with plausible arguments based in analogy.

[5]Originally, this chapter was placed after the discussion of the internal division (the next three chapters) to emphasize the importance of individual faith. However, after presenting some lectures on this book at Mid-American Reformed Seminary in 2009, Nelson Kloosterman recommended the current order, which I came to agree with. Christians live within an individual-social dialectic. Believers come to life one at a time but then join the perennial Christian community/tradition in order to grow.

[6]Holy love is the defining feature of the church's resemblance to the triune God and the nature of its growth (Lincoln, 1990).

[7]Along these lines, consider Sibbes's (1635/1973) reflections on the value of spiritual friends: "For besides the presence of a friend, which has some influence of comfort in it: 1. The discovery of his loving affection has a cherishing sweetness in it. 2. The expression of love in real comforts and services, by supplying any outward want of the party troubled, prevails much. Thus Christ made way for his comforts to the souls of men by showing outward kindness to their bodies. Love, with the sensible fruits of it, prepares for any wholesome counsel. 3. After this, wholesome words carry a special cordial virtue with them, especially when the Spirit of God in the affectionate speaker joins with the word of comfort, and thereby closes with the heart of a troubled patient" (p. 193).

[8]There are, of course, many variations of this general pattern. Currently, for example, experiments with satellite campuses and online church are being conducted. Some structures are undoubtedly closer to God's design plan than others—and as a Baptist I have my own opinions—but some variety in the body universal would seem to reflect the variety in the body local.

[9]Believers in eternity should probably be included in the universal church (Heb 12:1; Eph 5:27).

[10]The Greek word for church, *ekklēsia*, means those "called out" to worship God and serve him.

[11]As churches fulfill the passage just quoted, we are told that "then . . . your recovery will speedily spring forth; and . . . the glory of the LORD will be your rear guard" (Is 58:8). Very nice.

[12]According to William K. Frankena, Edwards thought that "loving a Being means, in general, seeking to promote his happiness if it is not yet complete" (Edwards, 1765/1960, foreword, p. x).

[13]For example, when a member is abandoning the Christian faith or abandoning one's spouse or family.

[14]I first heard the phrase "broken and beloved" as a description of the Christian at a Men at the Cross weekend retreat, developed by Bob Hudson. Go to www.crossmg .org for more information.

[15]Some Christians resist using the term *unconscious*, because they assume it is of secular origin. However, it simply refers to that which is "beneath one's consciousness" or "outside one's awareness," and the Bible contains many references to such dynamics (e.g., Ps 19:12; 139:23-24; Jer 17:9; and consider the Pharisees!) without using the term (similar to the concept of the Trinity). Indeed, it is a necessary implication of human finitude and the Christian doctrine of sin.

[16]I know, because this describes me in early adulthood, and I'm not cured.

[17]"Genuine community is not established before confession takes place" (Bonhoeffer, 1985, p. 63).

[18]"The place where [the] recognition of guilt becomes real is the Church" (Bonhoeffer, 1955, p. 111).

[19]In my opinion, the best charismatic churches today are among the most skillful in exploiting the immediate soul-healing potential available in worship services, particularly in the kinds of songs they sing and the way they sing them.

[20]Berger and Neuhaus (1976), and others, have suggested that churches, schools, professional organizations, neighborhoods, and clubs play a significant role in culture as "mediating institutions," that is, voluntary associations that stand between the individual and the state, providing norms, values, support, accountability, meaning, and a sense of belonging.

[21]"Happy is he that in his way to heaven meets with a cheerful and skillful guide and fellow-traveller, that carries cordials with him against all faintings of spirit. It is a part of our wisdom to salvation to make choice of such a one as may further us in our way" (Sibbes, 1635/1973, p. 193).

[22]See, for example, the lack of any mention of church-related resources in Contrada and Baum (2010).

[23]For example, after providing thirty-two pages of biblical counsel for the treatment of mild to moderate melancholia, the Puritan pastor Richard Baxter (1682/1981) wrote, "If other means will not do, neglect not physic (medicine), and though [the person with melancholia] will be averse to it, as believing that the disease is only in the mind, they must be persuaded or forced to it. . . . But choose a physician that is specially skilled in this disease, and have cured many others" (p. 285).

[24]Vineyard churches have generally done a marvelous job at this, and the ministry of Jean Vanier has pointed toward such "welcome as a way of life" (Wall, 2016).

[25]Depending on the presenting problems, this process will usually involve an interview and possibly the completion of one or more assessment instruments.

[26]That would be Faith Baptist Church in Lafayette, Indiana, www.faithlafayette.org.

CHAPTER 17: THE OLD-NEW DIVISION OF THE CHRISTIAN

[1]James also repeatedly alluded to the inner conflict. To his "beloved brethren" (Jas 1:19) he wrote, "Ask in faith without any doubting, for the one who doubts is like the surf of the sea, driven and tossed by the wind. For that man ought not to expect that he will receive anything from the Lord, being a double-minded man [*anēr dipsychos*], unstable in all his ways" (Jas 1:6-8). We find here the fascinating metaphor of a "two-souled" man used to describe a believer with weak faith. James called on his readers to put aside "all filthiness and all that remains of wickedness, [and] in humility receive the word implanted" (Jas 1:21). At one point he addressed them as "adulterers" (Jas 4:4), challenging them to "purify your hearts, you double-minded [*dipsychoi*]" (Jas 4:8). But in spite of his vigorous call to holiness, he was also very realistic: "We all stumble in many ways" (Jas 3:2).

And the apostle John also refers to this conflict. He opens his first epistle with a warning to believers (see 1 Jn 5:13) that they are deceiving themselves if they say they have no sin (1 Jn 1:8), and instructs them to confess their sins (1 Jn 1:9), in the context implying that is part of walking in the light (1 Jn 1:7). Yet, they have an anointing from the Holy One, which abides in them (1 Jn 2:20, 27), and their being born of God enables them to love (1 Jn 4:7).

[2]"It is mercy's wonder, and grace's wonder, that Christ will lend a piece of the lodging, and a back-chamber beside Himself, to our lusts; and that He and such swine should keep house together in our soul. For, suppose they couch and contract themselves into little room when Christ cometh in, and seem to lie as dead under His feet, yet they often break out again; and a foot of the Old Man, or a leg or arm nailed to Christ's cross, looseth the nail, or breaketh out again! And yet Christ, beside this unruly and misnurtured neighbour, can still be making heaven in the saints, one way or other" (Rutherford, 1664/1984, p. 467).

[3]For this reason, Walter Russell (1997), for example, interprets Galatians 5 in terms of Roman 8, arguing that Christians are only "in the Spirit," so they no longer live "in the flesh." This desire for coherence, however, results in a distortion of Galatians 5 (and, indirectly, Romans 7), according to the readings of most commentators, and it sacrifices the richness, comprehensiveness, and complexity of Paul's thought. It is true that believers *have* "crucified the flesh with its passions and desires" (Gal 5:24), but what does it mean that the flesh is "against" the Spirit and the Spirit is "against" the flesh (Gal 5:17)? If believers were no longer in the flesh in any sense, why would they need to be encouraged not to fulfill its desires (Gal 5:16), not to turn their freedom into an "opportunity for the flesh" (Gal 5:13), and not to "sow to his own flesh" (Gal 6:8)? Theologians such as Russell surely want to encourage believers with the radical nature of their salvation. However, in addition to the exegetical problems of this position, it is more likely to discourage believers who continue to struggle with their flesh (and their unredeemed bodies, Rom 8:23).

[4]Why does division so characterize the flesh? As we have seen, because humans are profoundly social, sin is profoundly social as well. Then, sin combines with our having been created for perfection, seeming to justify our divisiveness for "godly" and perfectionistic reasons. In addition, as object relations and Jungian theorists have noticed, early childhood abuse and dissociation lead later in life to a tendency to externalize and project that internal split out onto others, so that some are bad and "we" are good, exacerbating our more fundamental ethicospiritual divisiveness.

[5]Calvin (1559/1960) wrote with reference to Romans 7 that Paul "therefore says that he has a perpetual conflict with the vestiges of his flesh, and that he is held bound in miserable bondage, so that he cannot consecrate himself wholly to obedience to the divine law" (p. 1313).

[6]The problem is that both positions have certain "problematic" expressions that would seem to contradict the respective interpretative stance: if Paul *is* writing as a Christian, how could he say that "I am of flesh, sold into bondage to sin" (Rom 7:14) or that he is a wretched man needing deliverance (Rom 7:24)? And if Paul is *not* writing as a Christian, how could he say that *he* is not the one doing evil but the sin that dwells in him (Rom 7:17) or that he "joyfully [concurs] with the law of God in the inner man" (Rom 7:22)? This twofold dilemma provides good reason not to base the interpretation on Paul's supposed anthropological point of reference. He must have had some other interpretive agenda: general human inability before the law of God.

[7]Nonetheless, Paul's reference to a "war" of the laws [Rom 7:23, *antistrateuomenon*; the "law" in the members of his body makes war against the "law" of his mind) is reminiscent of Galatians 5:17, and his surprising autobiographical language (writing as a "divided I," according to Dunn, 1998, p. 473) suggests that this is a description of his ongoing Christian experience. Moreover, this is how it has been interpreted by most Christians over the centuries, further suggesting that, at the very least, the struggle Paul reported here also resonated with their own Christian experience.

[8]The old self is "the old mode of existence of sin" (Ridderbos, 1975, p. 63).

[9]Most contemporary translations (NIV, NASB, NRSV, and ESV) and commentators (e.g., Moo, 2008; Dunn, 1996) use the term *self* rather than the more literal translation, "man," for *anthrōpos*. This avoids the problem of reading gender bias into the passage, but more importantly, as used in psychology and philosophy, the term *self* probably conveys better to contemporary audiences what Paul was actually communicating. Other commentators, on the other hand, have used the broader term *person* (Best, 1998; Lincoln, 1990; O'Brien, 1999). The goal of translation is to convey the author's original meaning accurately to another language community, and either *person* or *self* seem to accomplish that purpose, given the semantic range of both. The term *self*, however, has particular value for psychological and therapeutic purposes because, according to contemporary psychology, it can refer to multiple aspects of the individual as subject and object (Harter, 2012), which makes it well-suited for referring to Paul's constructs *old man* and *new man*. As a result, *self* will be favored here. We might add that the term *self* is more epistemological in connotation than *person*, which adds to its utility in Christian self-understanding and therapy.

[10]We see in the subtle differences in the verb forms an echo of Paul's paradoxical teaching regarding the Christian life found in Phil 2:12-13, which we looked at in chapter four: "Work out your salvation with fear and trembling; for it is God who is at work in you, both to will and to work for His good pleasure."

[11]Divine causality is reflected in the corresponding verb forms, active or passive, depending on who is the agent or recipient of the action.

[12]As a result, we ought not to expect to find in these two passages a mutually exclusive, dichotomous answer to the question whether Christians have put off the old self and put on the new self, once and for all, at their conversion, or whether these are ongoing activities, practiced throughout one's Christian life. First, because the issue is somewhat obscure, if not contradicted, in the two passages in question, with most commentators persuaded that Colossians teaches the two actions occurred in the past and that Ephesians is more suggestive of their being ongoing imperatives (though not all Ephesians commentators agree; see Hoehner, 2002). But even more determinative, both passages actually teach both truths, at least implicitly; that is, that there is a divinely enabled inception of these two redemptive-orientation activities (called elsewhere a new creation, 2 Cor 5:17; Gal 6:15), as well as an ongoing human activity–based realization of those original actions.

So, in Colossians putting off and putting on seem to provide a reason for not lying, suggesting that the putting on and off occurred previously. Yet the strong imperatival tone throughout the entire Colossians passage implies that the putting off of the old vices (Col 3:5-8) and putting on of the Christians virtues, encouraged later (Col 3:12–4:6), are all ongoing implementations and illustrations of the first acts of putting off and putting on one's old and new selves.

In Ephesians, in slight contrast, the putting off and putting on seem to have been what the disciples were "taught of [Christ]" (Eph 4:21), implying that they are ongoing activities of believers. And here too believers were told to "put away" (Eph 4:25, 31) the old patterns of living (Eph 4:25-31; 5:3-7) that resemble the ways of the Gentiles (Eph 4:17-19) that were their "former manner of life" as well (Eph 4:22). In fact, the old self is still "being corrupted in accordance with the lusts of deceit" (Eph 4:22), the present tense here highlighting the ongoing nature of this corruption that they must still deal with. To resist the deceptive corruption, they are told to no longer practice the old-self ways and replace them with the new-self practices of Christlikeness (Eph 4:32–5:2; 5:8–6:18).

These general teachings the apostle Paul was inspired to write. Our challenge today, as interested therapists, psychologists, theologians, and pastors, is to work out in much greater detail what these brief, occasional remarks entail, biopsychosocially and ethicospiritually in order to develop a comprehensive system of Christian psychotherapy and counseling that corresponds as much as possible to all that God knows and desires.

[13]The implied exhortation throughout the Ephesians passage, for example, "underscores the notion of a continual challenge for the believer" (O'Brien, 1999, p. 329).

[14]See, e.g., Hoehner (2002), Moo (1996; 2008), Murray (1957), Ridderbos (1975), and Russell (1997). To illustrate, Moo (1996) argues that "the assumption that 'old man'

and 'new man' refer to parts, or natures, of a person is incorrect. Rather, they designate the person as a whole, considered in relation to the corporate structure to which he or she belongs. 'Old man' and 'new man' are not, then, ontological, but relational or positional in orientation" (p. 373).

[15]On the other hand, multiplicity can become pathological, as a result of extreme childhood abuse, when the subselves come to be characterized by autonomy and rigidity, and in the worst cases form separate centers of consciousness, most of which are not aware of each other, in what is called dissociative identity disorder.

Secular self-theory, of course, has no interest in the relevance of Christ for self-understanding and for resolving inner conflict. This means, from a Christian perspective, such models are focused exclusively on the internal conflict that exists in all human beings between their created goodness and fallenness, resulting in a divided self (Jas 1:8) that can be integrated in some degree without Christ's redemption, by insight and relational healing with other humans, but they cannot address humanity's fundamental division, our largely unconscious need for and opposition to our Creator, nor the consequent shame and guilt that haunt everyone.

[16]We could also mention here a *hierarchical* perspective, which distinguishes between the heavens/the "above things" and the earth. As discussed in the previous chapter, heaven above is where the Father and Christ especially dwell, for now, and the earth is where all humans live now within the field of human history and where the Spirit has been sent. However, this distinction does not have the marked ethicospiritual division with which we have been concerned in this chapter, since both were created by God. Nonetheless, there is a strong link between the hierarchical and eschatological perspectives, since the age to come will be characterized by some kind of union of heaven and earth (Rev 21).

[17]It should be obvious by now that the terms *old self* or *old-self system* are being used in this book in a way suggested by and encompassing the meaning of Paul's term *palaion anthrōpon*, but elaborating on it by including features that Paul would not have been aware of and considering it to be a particular view of the whole person, as understood in contemporary self psychology (Harter, 2012; Leary & Tangney, 2003), though here from a Christian perspective. Such elaborations are a necessary task of Christian scholarship and part of the church's calling.

[18]This use of "new self" similarly expands on the meaning of Paul's use of *neon anthrōpon* or *kainon anthrōpon*.

[19]Sibbes was one of the greatest Puritan psychologists. "It is the trouble of troubles to have two inhabitants so near in one soul, and these to strive one against another, in every action, and at all times in every part and power in us: the one carrying us upward, higher and higher still, till we come to God; the other pulling us lower and lower, further from him" (1635/1973, p. 237).

[20]"This identification of our person with the new man is, immediately after regeneration, still very slight; while we are so thoroughly bound to the old man, with almost all the fibers of our being, that it seems as though he were still our very self. But by the operation of the Holy Spirit we gradually die to the old man, and at the same time the new man is quickened in us more and more" (Kuyper, 1900, p. 482).

[21]In this chapter we are only touching on a small portion of the kinds of internal conflicts that characterize fallen humanity. In addition to splitting, there are other defenses, the false self (Merton, 1961b), the "drama triangle," "parts" (Schwartz, 1995), and many other models we could look at. For believers, they are all included in the old-self system.

[22]My wife has struggled with this dynamic throughout her life (I share with her permission), and our mutual pathology tragically activated and reinforced each other's for many years, though thankfully we have made some progress in undermining the cycle.

[23]A recent dissertation by Vaden (2015) has begun work on a comprehensive Christian model that results from a synthesis of work of object relations theorists on the psychosocial dynamics of the true self and false self and the work of Merton on their ethicospiritual dynamics.

CHAPTER 18: REDEMPTIVE DIFFERENTIATION

[1]One can also think of these categories developmentally, moving from dependence (in childhood) to independence (in early adulthood) and ideally to interdependence (in middle adulthood), though people may get stuck in one of the two earlier stages, depending on less-than-optimal child experiences and many other factors, including volitional.

[2]There seems to be significant similarity in meaning between Kierkegaard's (1846/1992) term "subjective thinking" or "subjective understanding" (Evans, 2009) and Merton's "interior vision."

[3]We might consider this an existential kind of metacognitive ability or an aspect of intrapersonal intelligence.

[4]"Above all, our life should always be seen in the light of the Cross. The Passion, Death and Resurrection of Christ the Lord have entirely changed the meaning and orientation of man's existence and of all that he does. One who cannot realize this will spend his life building a spider's web that has no substance and no real reason for existence" (Merton, 1960, p. 90).

[5]This phrase, of course, is one of Christ's difficult sayings. Those from dysfunctional family backgrounds may be tempted to see themselves as so fallen and crucified that they cannot also see themselves as made in God's image now united to Christ. Part of maturation and healing involves being able to think differentially and dialectically about oneself: simultaneously fallen and good creatures in Christ.

[6]Though the context in the latter passage does not indisputably reflect a new-self orientation, his language at least reveals the capacity to distance himself from his sinfulness and treat it as an object, and is certainly compatible with it.

[7]Some will rightly recognize a similarity with secular mindfulness concepts. The two main differences between Christian and secular approaches to distanciation are that Christian soul work is (1) fundamentally relational (done with God), whereas mindfulness (following Buddhism and contemporary Western humanism) is fundamentally individualistic; and (2) intrinsically evaluative, reflecting God's assessment, based in the grace of God in Christ, whereas mindfulness explicitly advocates a lack of judgment, since it has no transcendent basis for resolving it. So long as we translate the concept according to these two Christ rules, I have no objection to calling it Christian mindfulness.

[8]The term *emotions* is meant to cover a broad range of emotional experience, including affections, feelings, desires, impulses, appetites, motives, and attitudes, as well as loves and hates—anything that indicates the activation of one's emotion system.

[9]Van der Hart, Nijenhuis, and Steele (2006) suggest that ownership is part of integration, which we will consider in the next chapter. This conclusion shows that differentiation and integration are closely interrelated. As one differentiates, one is engaging in integration.

[10]In confession, the believer's "mouth is now open, and his heart enlarged, and he multiplies one expression upon another to manifest his enlargement" (Owen, 1965, Vol. 6, p. 374).

[11]Pascal made a sound therapeutic observation about confession: "A person told me one day that on coming from confession he felt great joy and confidence. Another told me that he remained in fear. Whereupon I thought that these two together would make one good man, and that each was wanting in that he had not the feeling of the other" (Pascal, 1680/1941, p. 169).

[12]"Our spirit undergoes a conversion, . . . which reorients our whole being after raising it to a new level, and even seems to change our whole nature itself" (Merton, 1961a, p. 125).

[13]Colquhoun differentiated non-Christian repentance (legal) from Christian repentance (evangelical). However, in my experience and observation, legal repentance can also be an earlier, simpler stage of Christian repentance, which leads Christians into closer outward conformity to God's ways, which evangelical repentance takes deeper and makes more authentic (though both stages may use gospel language). But this warrants research. Furthermore, non-Christians can probably practice analogues to both kinds of repentance without redemptive grace (e.g., in AA). This distinction bears some similarity to Worthington's (2009) "decisional forgiveness" and "emotional forgiveness," which research has documented non-Christians can also practice.

[14]Julian of Norwich (1998) understood and practiced cross work: "[God] loves us everlastingly, and we sin habitually and he reveals our sins very gently; and then we sorrow and mourn appropriately, turning to the consideration of his mercy, clinging to his love and goodness, seeing that he is our medicine, knowing that we

do nothing but sin. And so by the humility we gain from seeing our sin, faithfully knowing his everlasting love, thanking and praising him, we please him" (p. 175).

CHAPTER 19: REDEMPTIVE INTEGRATION

[1]Following Pierre Janet (1859–1947), the noted French modern psychologist, Van der Hart, Nijenhuis, and Steele's (2006) model actually divides integration into synthesis and realization. Synthesis involves binding, attentional focus, and differentiation. However, following developmental theory, in this book attentional focus is needed for differentiation, and both would precede binding, so I dealt with them in the previous chapter. Realization entails personification (I think *personalization* better communicates the concept) and presentification (awkward, but I cannot come up with a better noun). Realization was likewise addressed in the previous chapter, using phrases such as "coming to terms with," which seems to be more a process of differentiation than integration. Nevertheless, their model reminds us that differentiation and integration contribute to and reinforce each other.

[2]Some therapy models have not sharply distinguished differentiation from integration, yet their preferred concepts or strategies contribute to both. As a result, they have been cited in both this chapter and the last.

[3]Christianity has its own distinctive kind of "transpirational" integration (Siegel, 2010). But this can be said about every complex worldview community. Siegel himself practices a transpirational integration based on naturalism.

[4]"The Gospel intends us to attain to true simplicity, [which is] the sense of an inward unity of life" (von Hildebrand, 2001, p. 271).

[5]This is the transposition of the ethical order of discourse into the spiritual order (Johnson, 2007). Indeed, we might say that RI is a transposing of one's entire life into the spiritual order of discourse, that is, the order of redemptive grace (Johnson, 2007, chaps. 8-9, 16). A Christian therapy model adds the integration of the ethical and spiritual orders to that of the biological and psychosocial orders, which are the nearly exclusive focus of secular models of therapy, by transposing those lower orders into the higher. That means taking one's created psychosocial dynamic structures (states of mind, moods, emotions, and desires; mental images, memories, and beliefs; action tendencies; self-perceptions, perceptions of others, and one's story, necessarily including their underlying neural architecture) and relating it all to one's ethical awareness, where appropriate, and bringing it all into the spiritual order. But all faithful Christian transposition originates in that great divine transposition of the dead Christ in his resurrection.

[6]"The *simul-iustus-et-peccator* self is secure in the love of another, and at the same time cognizant of its limitations, faults, and insufficiencies—its sins, in other words. . . . This is the place where Christianity becomes a matchless definition of human maturity. It is the key to living, because it lives in hope and belovedness (*iustus*), while at the same time accepting the limitations of a fallen, tripped-up

character (*peccator*). This is integration. *Simul iustus et peccator* integrates the human object" (Zahl, 2007, p. 123). With his radical notion of *simul peccator et justus*, Luther was exploring the implications of Paul's teaching on justification by faith, the eschatological nature of the Christian life, and the already/not-yet tension. *Right now* the new self is the believer as forgiven sinner. Perhaps the growth of Paul's new self helps to explain his increasing humility evident through the course of his letter writing: I am the "the least of the apostles" (1 Cor 15:9), "the very least of all saints" (Eph 3:8), and the "foremost" of sinners (1 Tim 1:15).

[7]Some Christian counselors have used Paul to argue against looking back into one's past: "Forgetting what lies behind and reaching forward to what lies ahead, I press on toward the goal for the prize of the upward call of God in Christ Jesus" (Phil 3:13-14). Paul's point here, however, is to make clear he is not trusting in his pre-Christian accomplishments but is trusting in Christ. He is not arguing against Christians getting healing from their past in Christ.

[8]Some Christians argue against this narrative therapy practice because the Bible nowhere describes and encourages it. In Protestantism this general approach to *worship* has been called the "regulative principle" (held by the Puritans): Christians should only worship in ways directly commanded in the Bible and should not engage in worship practices not so commanded (for example, there should be no musical solos or dancing in public worship). The alternative has been called the "normative principle" (held sometimes by orthodox Anglicans): Christians are free to worship in ways not forbidden in the Bible that are congruent with biblical teaching. The very same positions can be developed regarding counseling techniques and strategies. I obviously favor the latter principle.

One might also argue that the healing of memories is taught implicitly in the physical healing miracles of Jesus. Moreover, practitioners of healing prayer have used such strategies for decades, and many have reported significant soul healing by this means in the name of Christ (see Appleby & Ohlschlager, 2013, for a number of examples). When one of Jesus' disciples complained that some people were casting out demons in his name but were not following him, Jesus replied, "He who is not against us is for us" (Mk 9:40). May we have that attitude toward those who are doing good therapy in his name and following him. However, the Christian community needs psychologists to do well-designed research to document the efficacy of such therapy.

[9]Todd is an amalgam of many different characters, both real and fictional, but I have been gathering from others, formulating, refining, and practicing something like this kind of therapy for twenty years. Kim and Johnson (2013) describes an earlier version that can be found in print.

[10]These claims are based on a good deal of anecdotal evidence (my own and others), combined with published research on evidence-based psychotherapy, both secular

and Christian. My hope is that by presenting many of the therapeutic features of Christianity, this book will lead to many more studies in the growing body of research being done on distinctly Christian models of therapy (Worthington, Johnson, Hook, & Aten, 2012).

CHAPTER 20: LIVING IN THE FUTURE

[1]Indeed, it is a curious and tragic fact that some mentally ill Christians become obsessed with such concerns.

[2]Joel Osteen shows that even Christians can be in the grip of the immanent frame. We might call his teaching anti-eschatological.

[3]The description and explanation of how people live in spite of these realizations is called terror-management theory.

[4]Regarding what happens to believers who die before then, most Christian theologians affirm they will be immediately with Christ and without a body, still in time in an "intermediate state," while some argue they will be ushered immediately into eternity and the final judgment that will determine their eternal destiny.

[5]Though as far as we know there may be no sexual attraction at all (Mt 22:30).

[6]Recall that Stump's (2010) model of love includes joint attentional focus.

[7]Declarative and ongoing forgiveness illustrate what Calvin called "double justification" (Muller, 2001).

[8]Paul's readers were those "upon whom the ends of the ages have come" (1 Cor 10:11).

[9]Some theologians have called this orientation *realized* or *inaugurated eschatology* (Hoekema, 1979), *semi-eschatological* (Vos, 1952), and a focus on the "already accomplished," in contrast to the "not yet finished" (Cullman, 1964).

[10]Because of remaining sin, this unfortunately sometimes includes Christians.

[11]Using concepts developed earlier, we might note that the believer's eschatological self is the union in eternity of their actual self with their real self.

[12]Someday, perhaps, public mental-health facilities will permit counselees to select their therapist based on their own worldview preferences (Johnson & Watson, 2012) and then randomly assign counselors to counselees who have no preference.

References

Aalders, G. C. (1981). *Genesis: Volume 1.* Grand Rapids, MI: Zondervan.

Abramson, L. Y., Seligman, M. E. P., & Teasdale, J. D. (1978). Learned help-lessness in humans: Critique and reformulation. *Journal of Abnormal Psychology, 87,* 49-74.

Adams, J. (1971). *Competent to counsel.* Grand Rapids, MI: Zondervan.

———. (1973). *Christian counselor's manual.* Grand Rapids, MI: Zondervan.

———. (1979). *More than redemption.* Grand Rapids, MI: Zondervan.

Adams, R. M. (1999). *Finite and infinite goods: A framework for ethics.* New York: Oxford University Press.

———. (2006). *A theory of virtue.* New York: Oxford University Press.

Alexander, A. (1978). *Thoughts on religious experience.* Edinburgh: Banner of Truth. (Original work published 1844)

Alexander, F., & French, T. (1946). *Psychoanalytic therapy: Principles and application.* New York: Ronald.

Alicke, M. D., & Govorun, O. (2005). The better-than-average effect. In M. D. Alicke, D. A. Dunning, & J. I. Krueger (Eds.), *The self in social judgment* (pp. 85-108). New York: Psychology Press.

Allender, D. B. (1999). *The healing path.* Colorado Springs: Waterbrook.

Allender, D. B., & Longman, T., III. (1994). *The cry of the soul: How our emotions reveal our deepest questions about God.* Colorado Springs: NavPress.

Allison, G. R. (2012). *Sojourners and strangers: The doctrine of the church.* Wheaton, IL: Crossway.

Alston, W. P. (1988). Divine and human action. In T. V. Morris (Ed.), *Divine and human action: Essays in the metaphysics of theism* (pp. 257-80). Ithaca, NY: Cornell University Press.

American Psychiatric Association. (2013). *Diagnostic and statistical manual of mental disorders* (5th ed.). Washington, DC: Author.

American Psychological Association. (1992, Dec.). *Ethical principles of psychologists and code of conduct.* Washington, DC: Author.

Ames, W. (1997). *The marrow of theology.* Grand Rapids, MI: Baker Books. (Original work published 1629)

Anderson, H. (1997). *Conversation, language, and possibilities: A postmodern approach to therapy.* New York: Basic Books.

Anderson, N. T., Zuehlke, T. E., & Zuehlke, J. S. (2000). *Christ-centered therapy.* Grand Rapids, MI: Zondervan.

Anderson, R. S. (1982). *On being human: Essays in theological anthropology.* Grand Rapids, MI: Eerdmans.

Appleby, D. W., & Ohlschlager, G. (2013). *Transformative encounters: The intervention of God in Christian counseling and pastoral care.* Downers Grove, IL: InterVarsity Press.

Aquinas, T. (1945). *Basic writings of Saint Thomas Aquinas* (A. C. Pegis, Ed.). New York: Random House.

———. (1947). *A compendium of theology* (C. Vollert, Trans.). St. Louis: B. Herder.

Arendt, H. (1958). *The human condition.* Chicago: University of Chicago Press.

Argyle, M. (1999). Causes and correlates of happiness. In D. Kahneman, E. Diner, & N. Schwarz (Eds.), *Well-being: The foundations of hedonic psychology* (pp. 353-73). New York: Russell Sage Foundation.

Arndt, W. F., & Gingrich, F. W. (1957). *Greek-English lexicon of the New Testament.* Chicago: University of Chicago Press.

Arnold, C. E. (2010). *Ephesians: Zondervan exegetical commentary on the New Testament.* Grand Rapids, MI: Zondervan.

Aronson, E. (1988). *The social animal.* New York: W. H. Freeman.

Ashcraft, M. H. (1994). *Human memory and cognition* (2nd ed.). New York: HarperCollins.

Assagioli, R. (1965). *Psychosynthesis.* New York: Hobbs, Dorman.

Audi, R. (1993). *Action, intention, and reason.* Ithaca, NY: Cornell University Press.

Augustine. (1942). *The confessions of St. Augustine.* (F. J. Sheed, Trans.). New York: Sheed & Ward.

———.(1947). *Faith, hope and charity.* (L. A. Arand, Ed.). New York: Newman Press.

———. (1948). On the Trinity. In W. J. Oates (Ed.), *Basic writings of Saint Augustine.* New York: Random House.

———. (1956). Homilies on the First Epistle of John. In P. Schaff (Ed.), *Nicene and post-Nicene fathers of the Christian church: Vol. 7* (pp. 459-529). Grand Rapids, MI: Eerdmans.

———. (1958). *City of God* (G. G. Walsh, S.J., D. B. Zema, S.J., G. Monahan, O.S.U., & D. J. Honan, Trans.). New York: Image.

———. (1997). *On Christian teaching* (R. P. H. Green, Trans.). Oxford: Oxford University Press.

———. (2009). *Confessions* (H. Chadwick, Trans.). New York: Oxford University Press.

Aulen, G. (1931). *Christus Victor* (A. G. Hebert, Trans.). London: SPCK.

Baars, C. W., & Terruwe, A. A. (2002). *Healing the unaffirmed.* New York: St. Paul's.

Bacote, V. E. (2005). *The Spirit in public theology: Appropriating the legacy of Abraham Kuyper.* Grand Rapids, MI: Baker.

Bakan, D. (1966). *The duality of human existence: Isolation and communion in Western man.* Boston: Beacon Press.

Baker, D. L. (1991). *Two testaments, one Bible* (rev. ed.). Downers Grove, IL: InterVarsity Press.

Baldwin, M. W. (1997). Relational schemas as a source of if-then self-inference procedures. *Review of General Psychology, 1,* 326-35.

Balswick, J. O., King, P. E., & Reimer, K. S. (2005). *The reciprocating self: Human development in theological perspective.* Downers Grove, IL: InterVarsity Press.

Baltes, P. B., Glück, J., & Kunzmann, U. (2002). Wisdom: Its structure and function in regulating successful lifespan development. In C. R. Snyder & S. J. Lopez (Eds.), *The handbook of positive psychology* (pp. 327-47). New York: Oxford University Press.

Baltes, P. B., & Staudinger, U. M. (2000). Wisdom: A metaheuristic (pragmatic) to orchestrate mind and virtue toward excellence. *American Psychologist, 55,* 122-36.

Balthasar, H. U. von. (1982–1991). *The glory of the Lord: A theological aesthetics* (Vols. 1-7). San Francisco: Ignatius.

———. (1984). *Christian meditation.* San Francisco: Ignatius.

———. (1988–1998). *Theo-drama: Theological dramatic theory* (Vols. 1-5). San Francisco: Ignatius.

———. (1990). *Mysterium paschale.* San Francisco: Ignatius.

———. (2004). *Love alone is credible.* San Francisco: Ignatius.

Bandura, A. (1977). Self-efficacy: Toward a unifying theory of behavioral change. *Psychological Review, 84,* 191-215.

———. (1986). *Social foundations of thought and action: A social cognitive theory.* Engelwood Cliffs, NJ: Prentice-Hall.

———. (1989). Human agency in social cognitive theory. *American Psychologist, 44,* 1175-84.

———. (1997). *Self-efficacy: The exercise of control.* New York: Freeman.

———. (1999). Social cognitive theory of personality. In L. A. Pervin and O. P. John (Eds.), *Handbook of personality* (2nd ed., pp. 154-96). New York: Guilford.

Bandura, A., & Walters, R. H. (1963). *Social learning and personality development.* New York: Holt, Rinehart, & Winston.

Bargh, J. A., & Chartrand, T. L. (1999). The unbearable automaticity of being. *American Psychologist*, 54, 462-479.

Barlow, D. H., Farchione, T. J., Fairholme, C. P., Ellard, K. K., Boisseau, C. L., Allen, L. B., & Ehrenreich-May, J. (2011). *Unified protocol for transdiagnostic treatment of emotional disorders.* New York: Oxford University Press.

Barrett, J. L. (2012). *Born believers: The science of children's religious belief.* New York: Free Press.

Barth, K. (1936). *Church dogmatics* 1.1 (G. T. Thomson, Trans.). Edinburgh: T&T Clark.

———. (1956a). *Church dogmatics* 3.1 (H. Knight, G. W. Bromiley, J. K. S. Reid, & R. H. Fuller, Trans.). Edinburgh: T&T Clark.

———. (1956b). *Church dogmatics* 4.1 (G. W. Bromiley, Trans.). Edinburgh: T&T Clark.

———. (1957a). *Church dogmatics* 2.1 (T. H. L. Parker, W. B. Johnston, H. Knight, & J. L. M. Hare, Trans.). Edinburgh: T&T Clark.

———. (1957b). *Church dogmatics* 2.2 (G. W. Bromiley, J. C. Campbell, I. Wilson, J. S. McNab, H. Knight, & R. A. Stewart, Trans.). Edinburgh: T&T Clark.

———. (1958). *Church dogmatics* 4.2 (G. W. Bromiley, Trans.). Edinburgh: T&T Clark.

———. (1960a). *Church dogmatics* 3.2 (H. Knight, J. K. S. Reid, & R. H. Fuller, Trans.). Edinburgh: T&T Clark.

———. (1960b). *Church dogmatics* 3.3 (G. W. Bromiley & R. J. Ehrlich, Trans.). Edinburgh: T&T Clark.

———. (1960c). *The humanity of God.* Richmond, VA: John Knox Press.

Bartholomew, C. G., & Goheen, M. W. (2004). *The drama of Scripture: Finding our place in the biblical story.* Grand Rapids, MI: Baker.

Batson, C. D. (1991). *The altruism question: Toward a social-psychological answer.* Hillside, NJ: Lawrence Erlbaum.

Batson, C. D., Ahmad, N., Lishner, D. A., & Tsang, J.-A. (2002). Empathy and altruism. In C. R. Snyder & S. J. Lopez (Eds.), *Handbook of positive psychology* (pp. 485-98). New York: Oxford University Press.

Bauckham, R. (1984). "Only the suffering God can help": Divine possibility in modern theology. *Themelios, 9*(3), 6-12.

———. (2009). Eschatology. In J. B. Webster, K. Tanner, & I. Torrence (Eds.), *Oxford handbook of systematic theology* (pp. 306-22). Oxford: Oxford University Press.

———. (2015). *Gospel of glory: Major themes in Johannine theology.* Grand Rapids, MI: Baker.

Baumeister, R. F. (1991). *Meanings of life.* New York: Guilford.

———. (Ed.). (1993). *Self-esteem: The puzzle of low self-regard.* New York: Plenum.

———. (1997). *Evil: Inside human violence and cruelty.* New York: W. H. Freeman.

———. (1999). *The self in social psychology.* London: Psychology Press.

Baumeister, R. F., & Exline, J. J. (2000). Self-control, morality, and human strength. *Journal of Social and Clinical Psychology, 19,* 29-42.

Baumeister, R. F., & Vohs, K. D. (2002). The pursuit of meaningfulness in life. In C. R. Snyder & S. J. Lopez (Eds.), *Handbook of positive psychology* (pp. 608-18). New York: Oxford University Press.

Baumeister, R. F., Mele, A. R., & Vohs, K. D. (2010). *Free will and consciousness: How might they work?* New York: Oxford University Press.

Baumeister, R., & Tierney, J. (2011). *Willpower: Rediscovering the greatest human strength.* New York: Penguin.

Bavinck, H. (1956). *Our reasonable faith.* (H. Zylstra, Trans.). Grand Rapids, MI: Eerdmans. (Original work published 1909)

———. (2004). *Reformed dogmatics.* Vol. 1, *God and creation.* (J. Vriend, Trans.). Grand Rapids, MI: Baker.

———. (2006). *Reformed dogmatics.* Vol. 2, *Sin and salvation in Christ.* (J. Vriend, Trans.). Grand Rapids, MI: Baker.

———. (2008). *Reformed dogmatics.* Vol. 3, *Holy Spirit, church, and new creation.* (J. Vriend, Trans.). Grand Rapids, MI: Baker.

Baxter, R. (1981). What are the best preservatives against melancholy and overmuch sorrow? In S. Annesley (Ed.), *Puritan sermons: 1659–1689,* Vol. 3 (pp. 253-92). Wheaton, IL: Richard Owen Roberts. (Original work published 1682)

———. (1990). *The practical works of Richard Baxter.* Vol. 1., *A Christian directory.* Ligonier, PA: Soli Deo Gloria.

Bayer, O. (2003). *Living by faith: Justification and sanctification.* Grand Rapids, MI: Eerdmans.

———. (2007). *Theology the Lutheran way.* (J. G. Silcock & M. C. Mattes, Trans.). Grand Rapids, MI: Eerdmans.

———. (2008). *Martin Luther's theology: A contemporary interpretation.* (T. H. Trapp, Trans.). Grand Rapids, MI: Eerdmans.

Beale, G. K. (1999). *The book of Revelation*. Grand Rapids, MI: Eerdmans.

———. (2002). The New Testament and the new creation. In S. J. Hafemann (Ed.), *Biblical theology: Retrospect and Prospect* (pp. 159-73). Downers Grove, IL: InterVarsity Press.

Beck, A. T., Rush, A. J., Shaw, B. F., & Emery, G. (1979). *Cognitive therapy of depression*. New York: Guilford.

Beck, J. A. (2011). *Zondervan dictionary of biblical imagery*. Grand Rapids, MI: Zondervan.

Beck, R., & Taylor, S. (2008). The emotional burden of monotheism: Satan, theodicy, and relationship with God. *Journal of Psychology and Theology, 36*(3), 151-60.

Becker, E. (1973). *The denial of death*. New York: Free Press.

Bellah, R. N., Madsen, R., Sullivan, W. M., Swidler, A., & Tipton, S. M. (1985). *Habits of the heart: Individualism and community in American life*. Berkeley: University of California Press.

Bem, D. (1972). Self-perception theory. In L. Berkowitz (Ed.), *Advances in experimental social psychology* (Vol. 6, pp. 1-62). New York: Academic Press.

Benner, D. G. (1983). The incarnation as a metaphor for psychotherapy. *Journal of Psychology and Theology, 11*, 287-94.

———. (2004). *The gift of being yourself*. Downers Grove, IL: InterVarsity Press.

Bennett, A. (1975). *The valley of vision: A collection of Puritan prayers and devotions*. Edinburgh: Banner of Truth Trust.

Berger, P., & Neuhaus, R. J. (1976). *To empower people: The role of mediating structures in public policy*. Washington, DC: American Enterprise Institute.

Berkhof, H. (1979a). *Christ, the meaning of history*. Grand Rapids, MI: Baker.

———. (1979b). *Christian faith*. (S. Woudstra, Trans.). Grand Rapids, MI: Eerdmans.

Berkhof, L. (1939). *Systematic theology*. Grand Rapids, MI: Eerdmans.

Berkouwer, G. C. (1952a). *Faith and sanctification*. Grand Rapids, MI: Eerdmans.

———. (1952b). *The providence of God*. Grand Rapids, MI: Eerdmans.

———. (1962). *Man: The image of God*. (D. W. Jellema, Trans.). Grand Rapids, MI: Eerdmans.

———. (1971). *Sin*. Grand Rapids, MI: Eerdmans.

Bernard of Clairvaux (1983). *The love of God* (J. Houston, Ed.). Portland, OR: Multnomah.

———. (1987). *Bernard of Clairvaux: Selected works*. (G. R. Evans, Trans.). New York: Paulist Press.

Best, E. (1998). *A critical and exegetical commentary on Ephesians*. Edinburgh: T&T Clark.

Bettenson, H. (Ed.). (1963). *Documents of the Christian church.* New York: Oxford University Press.

Beutler, L. E., & Harwood, T. M. (2000). *Prescriptive psychotherapy: A practical guide to systematic treatment selection.* New York: Oxford University Press.

Bidwell, K. J. (2011). *The church as the image of the Trinity: A critical evaluation of Miroslav Volf's ecclesial model.* Eugene, OR: Wipf & Stock.

Billings, J. T. (2011). *Union with Christ: Reframing theology and ministry for the church.* Grand Rapids, MI: Baker.

Blatt, S. J., Auerbach, J. S., & Levy, K. N. (1997). Mental representations in personality development, psychopathology, and the therapeutic process. *Review of General Psychology, 1,* 351-74.

Blocher, H. (1997). *Original sin: Illuminating the riddle.* Grand Rapids, MI: Eerdmans.

———. (2008). God and the cross. In B. L. McCormack (Ed.), *Engaging the doctrine of God: Contemporary Protestant perspectives* (pp. 125-41). Grand Rapids, MI: Baker.

Block, A. R. (Ed.). (1999). *Handbook of pain syndromes: Biopsychosocial perspectives.* Mahwah, NJ: Lawrence Erlbaum.

Blomberg, C. L., & Kamell, M. A. (2008). *James.* Grand Rapids, MI: Zondervan.

Boa, K. (2001). *Conformed to his image: Biblical and practical approaches to spiritual formation.* Grand Rapids, MI: Zondervan.

Board of Publications of the Christian Reformed Church. (1976). *Doctrinal standards of the Christian Reformed Church: Heidelberg Catechism* in *Psalter Hymnal.* Grand Rapids, MI: Author.

Boersma, H. (2004). *Violence, hospitality, and the cross: Reappropriating the atonement tradition.* Grand Rapids, MI: Baker.

Bolin, E. P., & Goldberg, G. N. (1979). Behavioral psychology and the Bible—general and specific considerations. *Journal of Psychology and Theology, 7,* 167-75.

Bonhoeffer, D. (1954). *Life together.* New York: Harper & Row.

———. (1996). *Life together; Prayer book of the Bible. Dietrich Bonhoeffer Works, Vol. 5.* (J. H. Burtness & G. B. Kelly, Eds.; D. W. Bloesch, Trans.). Minneapolis: Fortress.

———. (1955). *Ethics.* New York: Macmillan.

———. (1959). *Creation and fall; temptation.* New York: Macmillan. (Original work published 1937)

———. (1963). *The cost of discipleship.* New York: Macmillan. (Original work published 1937)

———. (1966). *Christ the center.* New York: Harper & Row.

———. (1985). *Spiritual care.* (J. C. Rochelle, Trans.). Minneapolis: Fortress.

Bonner, G. (2000). Pelagianism. In T. A. Hart (Ed.), *The dictionary of historical theology* (pp. 422-24). Grand Rapids, MI: Eerdmans.

Bowen, M. (1978). *Family therapy in clinical practice.* New York: Aronson.

Bowlby, J. (1988). *A secure base: Parent-child attachment and healthy human development.* New York: Basic Books.

Boyd, G. (1997). *God at war.* Downers Grove, IL: InterVarsity Press.

———. (2003). *Is God to blame?* Downers Grove, IL: InterVarsity Press.

Braaten, C. E. (1984). The person of Christ. In C. E. Braaten & R. W. Jenson (Eds.), *Christian dogmatics* (Vol. 1, pp. 465-569). Philadelphia: Fortress.

Bradshaw, M., & Ellison, C. G. (2008). Do genetic factors influence religious life? Findings from a behavior genetic analysis of twin siblings. *Journal for the Scientific Study of Religion, 47*(4), 529-44.

Braine, D. (1992). *The human person: Animal & spirit.* Notre Dame, IN: University of Notre Dame Press.

Brandtstadter, J. (1998). *Action perspectives on human development.* In W. Damon (Series Ed.) & R. M. Lerner (Vol. Ed.), *Handbook of child psychology.* Vol. 1., *Theoretical models of human development* (5th ed., pp. 807-64). New York: Wiley.

Brickman, P., Rabinowitz, V. C., Karuza, J., Jr., Coates, D., Cohn, E., & Kidder, L. (1982). Models of helping and coping. *American Psychologist, 37,* 368-84.

Brock, B., & Swinton, J. (Eds.). (2012). *Disability in the Christian tradition: A reader.* Grand Rapids, MI: Eerdmans.

Bromiley, G. W. (1979). *Introduction to the theology of Karl Barth.* Grand Rapids, MI: Eerdmans.

Bronfenbrenner, U. (2006). *The ecology of human development: Experiments by nature and design.* Cambridge, MA: Harvard University Press.

Brother Lawrence. (1895). *The practice of the presence of God.* New York: Fleming Revell.

Brown, C. (1978). Redemption. In C. Brown (Ed.), *The new international dictionary of New Testament theology* (Vol. 3, pp. 190-200). Grand Rapids, MI: Zondervan.

Brown, J. (1981). *The sufferings and the glories of the Messiah.* Grand Rapids, MI: Baker. (Original work published 1852)

Browning, D. S. (1966). *Atonement and psychotherapy.* Philadelphia: Westminster Press.

Browning, D. S., & Cooper, T. D. (2004). *Religious thought and the modern psychologies* (2nd ed.). Minneapolis: Fortress.

Bruce, F. F. (1984). *The epistles to the Colossians, to Philemon, and to the Ephesians*. Grand Rapids, MI: Eerdmans.

Brueggemann, W. (2002). *Reverberations of faith: A theological handbook of Old Testament themes*. Louisville, KY: Westminster John Knox.

Brunner, E. (1934). *The mediator*. (O. Wyon, Trans.). London: Lutterworth.

———. (1939). *Man in revolt*. (O. Wyon, Trans.). New York: Charles Scribner's Sons.

———. (1947a). *The divine imperative*. Philadelphia: Westminster Press.

———. (1947b). *The mediator*. Philadelphia: Westminster Press.

Bucci, W. (1997). *Psychoanalysis and cognitive science*. New York: Guilford.

Buchanan, G. M., & Seligman, M. E. P. (Eds.). (1995). *Explanatory style*. Hillsdale, NJ: Lawrence Erlbaum.

Büchsel, H. M. F. (1965). *Thumos*. In G. Kittel (Ed.), *Theological dictionary of the New Testament* (Vol. 3, pp. 167-72). Grand Rapids, MI: Eerdmans.

Bugental, D. B., & Goodnow, J. J. (1998). Socialization processes. In W. Damon (Series Ed.) & N. Eisenberg (Vol. Ed.), *Handbook of child psychology*. Vol. 3. *Social, emotional, and personality development* (5th ed., pp. 389-462). New York: Wiley.

Bugental, J. F. T. (1965). *The search for authenticity*. New York: Holt, Rinehart, & Winston.

Bulgakov, S. (2008). *Churchly joy: Orthodox devotions for the church year*. Grand Rapids, MI: Eerdmans.

Burk, D., & Lambert, H. (2015). *Transforming homosexuality: What the Bible says about sexual orientation and change*. Phillipsburg, NJ: P&R.

Burnaby, J. (1938). *Amor Dei: A study of the religion of St. Augustine*. London: Hodder & Stoughton.

Burrowes, G. (1958). *A commentary on the Song of Solomon*. Edinburgh: Banner of Truth Trust.

Busch, E. (2004). In D. L. Guder & J. J. Guder (Eds.), *The great passion: An introduction to Karl Barth's theology*. (G. Bromiley, Trans.). Grand Rapids, MI: Eerdmans.

Bush, R. (2008). The suffering of God as an aspect of the divine omniscience. *Journal of the Evangelical Theological Society, 51*(4), 769-84.

Buss, A. H. (1966). *Psychopathology*. New York: John Wiley and Sons.

Buss, D. M. (1999). *Evolutionary psychology: The new science of the mind*. Boston: Allyn & Bacon.

———. (2000). The evolution of happiness. *American Psychologist, 55*, 15-23.

Butterfield, R. (2012). *The secret thoughts of an unlikely convert*. Pittsburgh: Crown & Covenant.

———. (2015). *Openness unhindered.* Pittsburgh: Crown & Covenant.

Calhoun, L. G., & Tedeschi, R. G. (Eds.). (2014). *Handbook of posttraumatic growth: Research and practice.* New York: Psychology Press.

Calvin, J. (1960). *Institutes of the Christian religion.* (F. L. Battles, Trans.). Philadelphia: Westminster Press. (Original work published 1559)

———. (1973). *Sermons on the epistle to the Ephesians.* (A. Golding, Trans.). Edinburgh: Banner of Truth. (Original work published 1577)

———. (1979). *Calvin's commentaries.* Grand Rapids, MI: Baker.

Campbell, C. R. (2012). *Paul and union with Christ: An exegetical and theological study.* Grand Rapids, MI: Zondervan.

———. (2015). *Advances in the study of Greek.* Grand Rapids, MI: Zondervan.

Canlis, J. (2010). *Calvin's ladder: A spiritual theology of ascent and ascension.* Grand Rapids, MI: Eerdmans.

Cantor, N., & Banton, H. (1996). Effortful pursuit of personal goals in daily life. In P. M. Gollwitzer & P. A. Bargh (Eds.), *The psychology of action: Linking cognition and motivation to behavior* (pp. 338-60). New York: Guilford.

Capps, D. (1993). *The depleted self: Sin in a narcissistic age.* Minneapolis: Fortress.

Carey, G. (1986). *The gate of glory.* London: Hodder and Stoughton.

Carlton, W. (1988). *Weakness of will: A philosophical introduction.* Oxford: Basil Blackwell.

Carson, D. A. (1990). *How long O Lord? Reflections on suffering and evil.* Grand Rapids, MI: Baker.

———. (1991). *The Gospel according to John.* Grand Rapids, MI: Eerdmans.

———. (2008a). *Christ and culture revisited.* Grand Rapids, MI: Eerdmans.

———. (2008b). The wrath of God. In B. L. McCormack (Ed.), *Engaging the doctrine of God: Contemporary Protestant perspectives* (pp. 37-66). Grand Rapids, MI: Baker.

Carter, J. D., & Moy, A. C. (1980). Assertive behavior in a New Testament perspective. *Journal of Psychology and Theology, 8,* 288-92.

Carter, J. D., Okamoto, T., Barnhurst, L., & Rheinheimer, R. (2003, June). The challenge of new integrated treatments for mood disorder patients. Paper presented at the national conference of the Christian Association for Psychological Studies, Anaheim, CA.

Carver, C. S., & Scheier, M. F. (1981). *Attention and self-regulation: A control-theory approach to human behavior.* New York: Spring-Verlag.

Carver, C. S., & Scheier, M. F. (2002). Optimism. In C. R. Snyder & S. J. Lopez (Eds.), *Handbook of positive psychology* (pp. 231-43). Oxford: Oxford University Press.

Cassian, J. (1985). *Conferences.* New York: Paulist Press.

Cassidy, J., & Shaver, P. R. (Eds.). (2008). *Handbook of attachment* (2nd ed.). New York: Guilford.

Caussade, J. P. de. (1986). *The joy of full surrender.* Brewster, MA: Paraclete. (Original work published 1861)

Chamblin, J. K. (1993a). *Paul and the self: Apostolic teaching for personal wholeness.* Grand Rapids, MI: Baker.

———. (1993b). Psychology. In G. F. Hawthorne, R. P. Martin, & D. G. Reid (Eds.), *Dictionary of Paul and his letters* (pp. 765-75). Downers Grove, IL: InterVarsity Press.

Chang, E. (Ed.). (2003). *Virtue, vice, and personality.* Washington, DC: American Psychological Association.

Charlton, W. (1988). *Weakness of will: A philosophical introduction.* New York: Basil Blackwell.

Charry, E. T. (1997). *By the renewing of your minds: The pastoral function of Christian doctrine.* New York: Oxford University Press.

———. (2001). Theology after psychology. In M. R. McMinn & T. R. Phillips (Eds.), *Care for the soul: Exploring the intersection of psychology & theology* (pp. 118-33). Downers Grove, IL: InterVarsity Press.

———. (2007, February). Reviving Christian psychology. Lecture 1: Psychological theology. Fuller Theological Seminary. Integration of Psychology and Theology Symposium.

———. (2010). *God and the art of happiness.* Grand Rapids, MI: Eerdmans.

Chisholm, R. M. (1986). *Brentano and intrinsic value.* Cambridge: Cambridge University Press.

Cloud, H., & Townsend, J. (1992). *Boundaries.* Grand Rapids, MI: Zondervan.

Clouser, R. A. (2005). *The myth of religious neutrality.* South Bend, IN: University of Notre Dame Press.

Coakley, S. (2005). Palliative or intensification? Pain and Christian contemplation in the spirituality of the sixteenth-century Carmelites. In S. Coakley & K. K. Shelemay (Eds.), *Pain and its transformations: The interface of biology and culture* (pp. 77-100). Cambridge, MA: Harvard University Press.

———. (2013). *God, sexuality, and the self: An essay "On the Trinity."* New York: Cambridge University Press.

Coates, R. (1998). *Christianity in Bakhtin: God and the exiled author.* New York: Cambridge University Press.

Coe, J. (1999). Beyond relationality: Musings toward a pneumadynamic approach to personality and psychopathology. *Journal of Psychology and Christianity, 18,* 109-28.

Coe, J. H., & Hall, T. W. (2010). *Psychology in the Spirit: Contours of a transformational psychology.* Downers Grove, IL: InterVarsity Press.

Cole, B. S., & Pargament, K. I. (1999). Spiritual surrender: A paradoxical path to control. In W. R. Miller (Ed.), *Integrating spirituality into treatment: Resources for practitioners* (pp. 179-98). Washington, DC: American Psychological Association.

Cole, G. A. (2009). *God the peacemaker: How atonement brings shalom.* Downers Grove, IL: InterVarsity Press.

Coleman, E., & Miner, M. (Eds.). (2000). *Sexual offender treatment: Biopsychosocial perspectives.* Binghamton, NY: Haworth.

Coles, R. (1989). *The call of stories: Teaching and the moral imagination.* Boston: Houghton Mifflin.

Colijn, B. B. (2010). *Images of salvation in the New Testament.* Downers Grove, IL: InterVarsity Press.

Collins, G. R. (1980). *Christian counseling.* Waco, TX: Word.

———. (1994). *The biblical basis of Christina counseling.* Colorado Springs: NavPress.

Colquhoun, J. (1965). *Repentence.* Edinburgh: Banner of Truth Trust. (Original work published 1826)

———. (1998). *Spiritual comfort.* Morgan, PA: Soli Deo Gloria. (Original work published 1814)

Combs, J., & Freedman, J. (1996). *Narrative therapy: The social construction of preferred realities.* New York: W. W. Norton.

Comiskey, A. (1992). *Pursuing sexual wholeness: How Jesus heals the homosexual.* Nashville, TN: Thomas Nelson.

Conn, W. E. (1981). *Conscience: Development and self-transcendence.* Birmingham, AL: Religious Education Press.

Contrada, R., & Baum, A. (Eds.). (2010). *The handbook of stress science: Biology, psychology, and health.* New York: Springer.

Cooley, C. H. (1902). *Human nature and the social order.* New York: Charles Scribner's Sons.

Cortez, M. (2010). *Theological anthropology: A guide for the perplexed.* New York: T&T Clark.

———. (2016). *Christological anthropology in historical perspective.* Grand Rapids, MI: Zondervan.

Cox, W. F., Jr., & Wakefield, H. (1984). Spiritual egocentrism: A perspective on spiritual maturity. *Journal of Psychology and Theology, 12,* 40-44.

Cozolino, L. (2010). *The neuroscience of psychotherapy* (2nd ed.). New York: W. W. Norton.

Crabb, L. J., Jr. (1988). *Inside out.* Colorado Springs: NavPress.

———. (1993). *Finding God.* Grand Rapids, MI: Zondervan.

———. (2009). *66 love letters.* Nashville, TN: Thomas Nelson.

Crabb, L. J., Jr., & Allender, D. B. (1984). *Encouragement: The key to caring.* Grand Rapids, MI: Zondervan.

Cramer, P. (1991). *The development of defense mechanisms: Theory, research, and assessment.* New York: Springer-Verlag.

Cranfield, C. E. B. (1985). *The epistle to the Romans.* Edinburgh: T&T Clark.

Crisp, O. D. (2007). *Divinity and humanity.* Cambridge: Cambridge University Press.

Cullman, O. (1964). *Christ and time.* Philadelphia: Westminster.

Cunningham, C. (2010). *Darwin's pious idea: Why the ultra-Darwinists and creationists both get it wrong.* Grand Rapids, MI: Eerdmans.

Cushman, P. (1995). *Constructing the self, constructing America.* Reading, MA: Addison-Wesley.

Daly, R., S.J. (1978). *The origins of the Christian doctrine of sacrifice.* London: Darton, Longman, & Todd.

Damasio, A. R. (1994). *Descartes' error: Emotion, reason, and the human brain.* New York: G. P. Putnam's Sons.

Damon, W. (1988). *The moral child.* New York: Free Press.

Danaher, W. J. (2004). *The trinitarian ethics of Jonathan Edwards.* Louisville, KY: Westminster John Knox.

Daniel, S. H. (1994). *The philosophy of Jonathan Edwards.* Bloomington: Indiana University Press.

Danielou, J. (1969). *God's life in us.* Denville, NJ: Dimension.

———. (1996). *Prayer: The mission of the Church.* (D. L. Schindler Jr., Trans.). Grand Rapids, MI: Eerdmans.

———. (1997). *From glory to glory: Texts from Gregory of Nyssa's mystical writings.* Crestwood, NY: St. Vladimir's Seminary Press.

Dawkins, R. (1989). *The selfish gene* (new ed.). New York: Oxford University Press.

Dawn, M. J. (2001). *Powers, weakness, and the tabernacling of God.* Grand Rapids, MI: Eerdmans.

De Gruchy, J. W. (1986). *Standing by God in his hour of grieving: Human suffering, theological reflection, and Christian solidarity.* Pretoria: C. B. Powell Bible Centre.

Dearing, R. L., Stuewig, J., & Tangney, J. P. (2005). On the importance of distinguishing shame from guilt: Relations to problematic alcohol and drug use. *Addictive Behaviors, 30*(7), 1392-1404.

Dearing, R. L., & Tangney, J. P. (Eds.). (2011). *Shame in the therapy hour.* New York: Guilford.

Deci, E. L., & Ryan, R. M. (Eds.). (2004). *Handbook of self-determination research.* Rochester, NY: University of Rochester Press.

DeCharms, R. (1968). *Personal causation.* New York: Academic Press.

Demarest, B. (1997). *The cross and salvation.* Wheaton, IL: Crossway.

Dembski, W. A. (1999). *Intelligent design.* Downers Grove, IL: InterVarsity Press.

Dempster, S. G. (2003). *Dominion and dynasty: A biblical theology of the Hebrew Bible.* Downers Grove, IL: InterVarsity Press.

Denney, J. (1951). *The death of Christ.* London: Tyndale. (Original work published 1902)

DeYoung, R. K. (2009). *Glittering vices: A new look at the seven deadly sins and their remedies.* Grand Rapids, MI: Brazos.

Diener, E., Lucas, R. E., & Oishi, S. (2002). Subjective well-being: The science of happiness and life satisfaction. In C. R. Snyder & S. J. Lopez (Eds.), *Handbook of positive psychology* (pp. 63-73). Oxford: Oxford University Press.

Dodds, M. J. (2008). *The unchanging God of love: Thomas Aquinas and contemporary theology on divine immutability* (2nd ed.). Washington, DC: Catholic University of America Press.

Dooyeweerd, H. (1960). *In the twilight of Western thought.* Philadelphia: Presbyterian & Reformed.

Doron, G., Sar-El, D., Mikulincer, M., & Kyrios, M. (2012). When moral concerns become a psychological disorder: The case of obsessive-compulsive disorder. In M. Mikulincer & P. R. Shaver (Eds.), *The social psychology of morality: Exploring the causes of good and evil* (pp. 293-310). Washington, DC: American Psychological Association.

Dostoevsky, F. (2009). *Notes from the underground.* Grand Rapids, MI: Eerdmans.

Duarte, J. L., Crawford, J. T., Stern, C., Haidt, J., Jussim, L., & Tetlock, P. E. (2015). Political diversity will improve social psychological science. *Behavioral and Brain Sciences, 38,* 1-58. doi:10.1017/S0140525X14000430,e130

Dueck, A., & Reimer, K. (2009). *A peaceable psychology: Christian therapy in a world of many cultures.* Grand Rapids, MI: Baker.

Dulles, A. (1991). *Models of the church.* New York: Image.

Dunkel-Schetter, C., & Bennett, T. L. (1990). Differentiating the cognitive and behavioral aspects of social support. In B. R. Sarason, I. G. Sarason, & G. R. Pierce (Eds.), *Social support: An interactional view* (pp. 267-96). New York: John Wiley & Sons.

Dunn, J. D. G. (1996). *The epistles to the Colossians and to Philemon: A commentary on the Greek text.* Grand Rapids, MI: Eerdmans.

———. (1998). *The theology of Paul the apostle.* Grand Rapids, MI: Eerdmans.

Dweck, C. S. (2000). *Self-theories: Their role in motivation, personality, and development.* Philadelphia: Taylor & Francis.

Dyer, W. W., Tracy, K., & Siegel, M. (2005). *Incredible you! 10 ways to let your greatness shine through.* Carlsbad, CA: Hay House.

Edwards, J. (1959). *The works of Jonathan Edwards: Vol. 2, Religious affections.* New Haven, CT: Yale University Press. (Original work published 1746)

———. (1960). *The nature of true virtue.* Ann Arbor: University of Michigan Press. (Original work published 1765)

———. (1969). *Charity and its fruits.* Edinburgh: Banner of Truth. (Original work published 1852)

———. (1970). *The works of Jonathan Edwards: Vol. 3, Original sin.* New Haven, CT: Yale University Press. (Original work published 1758)

———. (1971). *Treatise on grace and other posthumously published writings by Jonathan Edwards.* (P. Helms, Ed.). Cambridge: James Clark.

———. (1974). In E. Hickman (Ed.), *The works of Jonathan Edwards.* Edinburgh: Banner of Truth Trust.

———. (1989). *The works of Jonathan Edwards, Vol. 8: Ethical writings.* (P. Ramsey, Ed.). New Haven, CT: Yale University Press. (Original work published 1765)

———. (1993). Images and shadows of divine things. In W. E. Anderson (Ed.), *The works of Jonathan Edwards, Vol. 11: Typological writings.* New Haven, CT: Yale University Press.

———. (1994). *The works of Jonathan Edwards, Vol. 13: The "miscellanies," Nos. a-500.* (T. A. Schafer, Ed.). New Haven, CT: Yale University Press.

———. (1998). A dissertation on the end for which God created the world. In *God's passion for his glory.* Wheaton, IL: Crossway. (Original work published 1765)

———. (2000). *The works of Jonathan Edwards, Vol. 18: The "miscellanies," Nos. 501-832.* (A. Chamberlain, Ed.). New Haven, CT: Yale University Press.

———. (2003). *The works of Jonathan Edwards, Vol. 21. Writings on the Trinity, grace, and faith.* (S. H. Lee, Ed.). New Haven, CT: Yale University Press.

———. (2006). *The works of Jonathan Edwards, Vol. 25: Sermons and writings, 1743-1758.* (W. H. Kimnach, Ed.). New Haven, CT: Yale University Press.

Egan, G. (2002). *The skilled helper* (7th ed.). Belmont, CA: Wadsworth.

Eid, M., & Larson, R. J. (2007). *The science of subjective well-being.* New York: Guilford.

Eisenberg, N. (Ed.). (1998). *Handbook of child psychology: Vol. 3, Social, emotional, and personality development* (5th ed.). New York: John Wiley & Sons.

Eisenberg, N., & Fabes, R. A. (1998). Prosocial development. In W. Damon (Series Ed.) & N. Eisenberg (Vol. Ed.), *Handbook of child psychology: Vol. 3, Social, emotional, and personality development* (5th ed., pp. 701-78). New York: Wiley.

Ellenberger, H. (1970). *The discovery of the unconscious: The history and evolution of dynamic psychiatry.* New York: Basic Books.

Elwell, W. A., & Comfort, P. W. (2001). *Tyndale Bible dictionary.* Tyndale reference library (639). Wheaton, IL: Tyndale House.

Emery, G. (2007). *The trinitarian theology of Saint Thomas Aquinas.* (F. A. Murphy, Trans.). Oxford: Oxford University Press.

———. (2011). *The Trinity: An introduction to Catholic doctrine on the triune God.* Washington, DC: Catholic University of America Press.

Emery, G., & Levering, M. (Eds.). (2011). *The Oxford handbook of the Trinity.* Oxford: Oxford University Press.

Emlet, M. R. (2009). *Crosstalk: Where life & Scripture meet.* Greensboro, NC: New Growth Press.

Emmons, R. A. (1999). *The psychology of ultimate concerns: Motivation and spirituality in personality.* New York: Guilford.

———. (2007). *Thanks! How the new science of gratitude can made you happier.* New York: Houghton Mifflin.

Emmons, R. A., & McCullough, M. E. (2004). *The psychology of gratitude.* New York: Oxford University Press.

Emmons, R. A., & Shelton, C. M. (2002). Gratitude and the science of positive psychology. In C. R. Snyder & S. J. Lopez (Eds.), *Handbook of positive psychology* (pp. 459-71). Oxford: Oxford University Press.

Erickson, M. (1983–1985). *Christian theology.* Grand Rapids, MI: Baker.

Erikson, E. H. (1950). *Childhood and society.* New York: Norton.

———. (1968). *Identity: Youth and crisis.* New York: Norton.

Evagrios. (1979a). On discrimination. In *The Philokalia* (Vol. 1, pp. 38-52). Boston: Faber & Faber.

———. (1979b). Texts on watchfulness. In *The Philokalia* (Vol. 1, pp. 53-54). Boston: Faber & Faber.

Evans, C. S. (1990). *Søren Kierkegaard's Christian psychology.* Grand Rapids, MI: Baker.

———. (2009). *Kierkegaard: An introduction.* New York: Cambridge University Press.

Everly, G. S., Jr., & Lating, J. M. (2002). *A clinical guide to the treatment of the human stress response* (2nd ed.). New York: Kluwer Academic.

Exline, J. J., Hall, T. W., Pargament, K. I., & Harriott, V. A. (2016). Predictors of growth from spiritual struggle among Christian undergraduates: The importance of perceiving a two-way relationship with God. *Journal of Positive Psychology, 12 (5).*

Fairbairn, W. R. D. (1952). *An object-relations theory of the personality.* New York: Basic Books.

Faraone, S. V., & Tsuang, M. T., & Tsuang, D. W. (1999). *Genetics of mental disorders: A guide for students, clinicians, and researchers.* New York: Guilford.

Farrow, D. (1999). *Ascension and ecclesia.* Grand Rapids, MI: Eerdmans.

Fauconnier, G., & Turner, M. (2002). *The way we think: Conceptual blending and the mind's hidden complexities.* New York: Basic Books.

Fava, M. & Kendler, K. S. (2000). Major depressive disorder. *Neuron*, 28 (2), 335-41. doi:http://dx.doi.org/10.1016/S0896-6273(00)00112-4. Fee, G. D. (2014). *The first epistle to the Corinthians* (rev. ed.). Grand Rapids, MI: Eerdmans.

Feinberg, J. S. (Ed.). (1988). *Continuity and discontinuity: Perspectives on the relationship between the Old and New Testaments.* Westchester, IL: Crossway.

Fenichel, O. (1945). *The psychoanalytic theory of neurosis.* New York: Norton.

Ferguson, S. B. (1987). *John Owen on the Christian life.* Edinburgh: Banner of Truth.

———. (1996). *The Holy Spirit.* Downers Grove, IL: InterVarsity Press.

Fiddes, P. S. (1987). *The creative suffering of God.* Oxford: Clarendon.

First, M. B., & Tasman, A. (2004). *DSM-IV-TR mental disorders: Diagnosis, etiology and treatment.* New York: John Wiley & Sons.

Fitzmyer, J. A. (1989). *Paul and his theology: A brief sketch* (2nd ed.). Englewood Cliffs, NJ: Prentice Hall.

Fitzpatrick, E. (2013). *Found in him: The joy of the incarnation and our union with Christ.* Wheaton, IL: Crossway.

Flanagan, K. S., & Hall, S. E. (2014). *Christianity and developmental psychopathology: Foundations and approaches.* Downers Grove, IL: InterVarsity Press.

Flender, O. (1976). Eikon. In C. Brown (Ed.), *The new international dictionary of New Testament theology* (Vol. 2, pp. 286-88). Grand Rapids, MI: Zondervan.

Flett, G. L., & Hewitt, P. L. (2002). *Perfectionism: Theory, research, and treatment.* Washington, DC: American Psychological Association.

Foa, E. B., Huppert, J. D., & Cahill, S. P. (2006). Emotional processing theory: An update. In B. O. Rothbaum (Ed.), *Pathological anxiety: Emotional processing in etiology and treatment* (pp. 3-24). New York: Guilford.

Folkman, S, & Moskowitz, J. T. (2004). Coping: Pitfalls and promise. *Annual Review of Psychology, 55,* 745-75.

Fonagy, P. (2006). The mentalization-focused approach to social development. In J. G. Allen & P. Fonagy (Eds.), *Handbook of mentalization-based treatment* (pp. 53-100). New York: John Wiley & Sons.

Fonagy, P., Gergely, G., Jurist, E., & Target, M. (2002). *Affect regulation, mentalization, and the development of the self*. New York: Other Press.

Ford, D. F. (1999). *Self and salvation: Being transformed*. New York: Cambridge.

Ford, J. M. (1975). *Revelation*. New York: Doubleday.

Forsterling, F. (1986). Attributional conceptions in clinical psychology. *American Psychologist, 41*, 275-85.

Foucault, M. (1965). *Madness and civilization: A history of insanity in the age of reason*. New York: Random House.

———. (1977). *Discipline & punish: The birth of the prison*. New York: Random House.

Fowler, J. W. (1982). *Stages of faith*. New York: Harper & Row.

Fowler, T. B., & Kuebler, D. (2007). *The evolution controversy: A survey of competing theories*. Grand Rapids, MI: Baker Academic.

Frame, J. (1987). *The doctrine of the knowledge of God*. Phillipsburg, NJ: P&R.

———. (1995). *Cornelius Van Til: An analysis of his thought*. Phillipsburg, NJ: P&R.

———. (2002). *The doctrine of God*. Phillipsburg, NJ: P&R.

Francis de Sales. (1955). *Introduction to the devout life*. Garden City, NY: Image. (Original work published 1619)

Franklin, C., & Fong, R. (Eds.). (2011). *The church leader's counseling resource book: A guide to mental health and social problems*. New York: Oxford University Press.

Fredrickson, B. L. (2002). Positive emotions. In C. R. Snyder & S. J. Lopez (Eds.), *Handbook of positive psychology* (pp. 120-34). Oxford: Oxford University Press.

Frei, H. (1980). *The eclipse of the biblical narrative*. New Haven, CT: Yale University Press.

Freud, S. (1935). *A general introduction to psychoanalysis*. (A. A. Brill, Ed., Joan Riviere, Trans.). New York: Liveright.

———. (1959). *Beyond the pleasure principle*. New York: Bantam. (Original work published 1920)

———. (1960). *Group psychology and the analysis of the ego*. New York: Bantam. (Original work published 1921)

Fromm, E. (1956). *The art of loving*. New York: Harper & Row.

Gaffin, R. B., Jr. (1971). Gerhardus Vos and the interpretation of Paul. In E. R. Geehan (Ed.), *Jerusalem and Athens: Critical discussions on the theology and apologetics of Cornelius Van Til* (pp. 228-36). Phillipsburg, NJ: Presbyterian & Reformed.

———. (1978). *Resurrection and redemption: A study in Paul's soteriology*. Grand Rapids, MI: Baker.

———. (2004). Atonement in the Pauline corpus. In C. E. Hill & F. A. James III (Eds.), *The glory of the atonement* (pp. 140-62). Downers Grove, IL: InterVarsity Press.

Garzon, F. (2008). *Pursuing peace: Case studies exploring the effectiveness of theophostic prayer ministry*. Maitland, FL: Xulon.

Gawronski, B., & Payne, B. K. (Eds.). (2010). *Handbook of implicit social cognition*. New York: Guilford.

Gazzaniga, M. S. (Ed.). (2000). *The new cognitive neurosciences*. Cambridge, MA: MIT Press.

———. (2008). *The ethical brain*. New York: Dana Press.

Gentry, P. J., & Wellum, S. J. (2012). *Kingdom through covenant*. Wheaton, IL: Crossway.

Gergen, K. J. (1992). *The saturated self: Dilemmas of identity in contemporary life*. New York: Basic Books.

Gershon, M. (1998). *The second brain*. New York: HarperCollins.

Giddens, A. (1991). *Modernity and self-identity: Self and society in the late modern age*. Palo Alto, CA: Stanford University Press.

Gilbert, P. (2011). Shame in psychotherapy and the role of compassion focused therapy. In R. L. Dearing & J. P. Tangney (Eds.), *Shame in the therapy hour* (pp. 325-54). New York: Guilford.

Gilson, E. (1936). *The spirit of medieval philosophy*. (A. H. C. Downes, Trans.). New York: Charles Scribner's Sons.

Gingrich, H. (2013). *Restoring the shattered self*. Downers Grove, IL: InterVarsity Press.

Girard, R. (1996). *The Girard reader*. J. G. Williams (Ed.). New York: Crossroad.

Goetz, S., & Taliaferro, C. (2008). *Naturalism*. Grand Rapids, MI: Eerdmans.

Goffman, E. (1963). *Stigma: Notes on the management of spoiled identity*. Englewood Cliffs, NJ: Prentice-Hall.

Goldsmith, D. J. (2004). *Communicating social support: Advances in personal relationships*. New York: Cambridge University Press.

Goldsworthy, G. (1991). *According to plan: The unfolding revelation of God in the Bible*. Downers Grove, IL: InterVarsity Press.

———. (2007). *Gospel-centered hermeneutics: Foundations and principles of evangelical biblical interpretation*. Downers Grove, IL: InterVarsity Press.

Goodwin, T. (1996). The trial of a Christian's growth. In *The works of Thomas Goodwin* (Vol. 3, pp. 433-507). Eureka, CA: Tanski Publications. (Original work published 1861–1866)

Gorman, M. J. (2001). *Cruciformity: Paul's narrative spirituality of the cross.* Grand Rapids, MI: Eerdmans.

Gorsuch, R. L., & Miller, W. R. (1999). Assessing spirituality. In W. R. Miller (Ed.), *Integrating spirituality into treatment: Resources for practitioners* (pp. 47-64). Washington, DC: American Psychological Association.

Granqvist, P., & Kirkpatrick, L. A. (2008). Attachment and religious representations and behavior. In J. Cassidy & P. R. Shaver (Eds.), *Handbook of attachment* (2nd ed.) (pp. 906-33). New York: Guilford.

Grauf-Grounds, C., & Steele, L. L. (1982). Language as change-agent: Metaphor in the work of Jay Haley and in the parables of Jesus. *Journal of Psychology and Theology, 10,* 212-20.

Green, J. B. (2006). The kaleidescopic view. In J. Beilby & P. R. Eddy (Eds.), *The nature of the atonement: Four views* (pp. 157-85). Downers Grove, IL: InterVarsity Press.

Greenberg, J., Koole, S. L., & Pyszczynski, T. (Eds.). (2004). *Handbook of experimental existential psychology.* New York: Guilford.

Greenberg, L. S. (2011). *Emotion-focused therapy.* Washington, DC: American Psychological Association.

Greenberg, L. S., & Paivio, S. C. (1997). *Working with emotions in psychotherapy.* New York: Guilford.

Greenberg, L. S., & Van Balen, R. (1998). The theory of experience-centered therapies. In L. S. Greenberg, J. C. Watson, & G. Lietaer (Eds.), *Handbook of experiential therapy* (pp. 28-60). New York: Guilford.

Greenberg, L. S., Watson, J. C., & Lietaer, G. (Eds). (1998). *Handbook of experimental therapy.* New York: Guilford.

Gregory of Nazianzus. (1996). In defense of his flight to Pontus. 2nd oration. *The Nicene and Post-Nicene fathers, Second Series,* Vol. 7 (pp. 398-442). Albany, OR: Sage Digital Library.

———. (2002). *On God and Christ: The five theological orations and two letters to Cledonius.* Crestwood, NY: St. Vladimir's Seminary Press.

Gregory of Nyssa. (1961). *From glory to glory.* New York: Charles Scribner's Sons.

Gregory the Great. (1950). *Pastoral care.* New York: Newman Press.

Grenz, S. J. (2001). *The social God and the relational self: A trinitarian theology of the imago Dei.* Louisville, KY: Westminster John Knox.

Griffin, G. A. E. (1986). Analytical psychology and the dynamics of human evil: A problematic case in the integration of psychology and theology. *Journal of Psychology and Theology, 14,* 269-77.

Groeschel, B. (1993). *Spiritual passages: The psychology of spiritual development.* New York: Crossroad.

Grou, J. N. (1962). *Meditations on the love of God.* Westminster, MD: Newman. (Original work published 1796)

———. (2002). *The spiritual life.* Manchester, NH: Sophia Institute Press.

Grusec, J. E., & Lytton, H. (1988). *Social development: History, theory, and research.* New York: Springer-Verlag.

Gunton, C. E. (1991). Trinity, ontology and anthropology: Towards a renewal of the doctrine of the *imago Dei.* In C. Schwobel (Ed.), *Persons, divine and human* (pp. 47-64). Edinburgh: T&T Clark.

———. (1998). *The triune creator: A historical and systematic study.* Grand Rapids, MI: Eerdmans.

Guntrip, H. (1957). *Psychotherapy and religion.* New York: Harper & Brothers.

———. (1971). *Psychoanalytic theory, therapy, and the self.* New York: Basic Books.

Haidt, J. (2003). Elevation and the positive psychology of morality. In C. L. M. Keyes & J. Haidt (Eds.), *Flourishing: Positive psychology and the life well-lived* (pp. 275-89). Washington, DC: American Psychological Association.

Haidt, J., & Seder, P. (2010). Admiration and awe. In D. Sander & K. Scherer (Eds.), *Oxford companion to emotion and the affective sciences* (pp. 4-5). New York: Oxford University Press.

Haith, M. M., Benson, J. B., Roberts, R. J., Jr., & Pennington, B. F. (Eds.). (1995). *The development of future-oriented processes.* Chicago: University of Chicago Press.

Halder, K. (2003). *Fernkurs—Der Grundlagen Christliche Psychologie, Heft 5a: Der Mensch in Beziehung zu Gott.* Kitzingen, Germany: Akadamie für Christliche Psychologie.

———. (2004). *Fernkurs—Der Grundlagen Christliche Psychologie, Heft 5b: Der Mensch in Beziehung zu Gott. Teil 2: Der complexe Zusammenhang von Sünde, Selbtsherstellung und Störung.* Kitzingen, Germany: Akadamie für Christliche Psychologie.

Hall, M. E. L., & Johnson, E. L. (2001). Theodicy and therapy: Philosophical/theological contributions to the problem of suffering. *Journal of Psychology and Christianity, 20,* 5-17.

Hall, T. W., Fujikawa, A., Halcrow, S. R., Hill, P. C., & Delaney, H. (2009). Attachment to God and implicit spirituality: Clarifying correspondence and compensation models. *Journal of Psychology & Theology, 37,* 227-44.

Halstead, L. B. (1984). Evolution—the fossils say yes! In A. Montagu (Ed.), *Science and creationism* (pp. 240-54). New York: Oxford University Press.

Hamer, D. H. (2002). Genetics of sexual behavior. In J. Benjamin, R. P. Ebstein, & R. H. Belmaker (Eds.), *Molecular genetics and the human personality* (pp. 257-74). New York: American Psychiatric Publishing.

Hamilton, J. H., & Henry, P. J. (2009). *Handbook for therapy for unwanted homosexual attractions: A guide to treatment*. Maitland, FL: Xulon.

Hamilton, N. G. (1988). *Self & others: Object relations theory in practice*. Northvale, NJ: Jason Aronson.

Hamon, S. A., & Houskamp, B. (1977). Beyond self-actualization: Comments on the life and death of Stephen the martyr. *Journal of Psychology and Theology, 5,* 292-99.

Hannaford, C. (2009). *Picking up the pieces handbook*. Nashville, TN: Lifeway.

Harmon-Jones, E., & Winkieleman, P. (Eds.). (2007). *Social neuroscience: Integrating biological and psychological explanations of social behavior*. New York: Guilford.

Harré, R. (1984). *Personal being: A theory for individual psychology*. Cambridge, MA: Harvard University Press.

Harré, R., Clarke, D., & De Carlo, N. (1985). *Motives and mechanisms: An introduction to the psychology of action*. London: Methuen.

Harrison, E. F. (1982). Holiness. In G. W. Bromiley (Ed.), *The international standard Bible encyclopedia* (Vol. 2, pp. 725-29). Grand Rapids, MI: Eerdmans.

Harrisville, R. A. (2006). *Fracture: The cross as irreconcilable in the language and thought of the biblical writers*. Grand Rapids, MI: Eerdmans.

Hart, D. B. (2003). *The beauty of the infinite: The aesthetics of Christian truth*. Grand Rapids, MI: Eerdmans.

———. (2013). *The experience of God: Being, consciousness, bliss*. New York: Oxford University Press.

Harter, S. (2012). *The construction of the self: A developmental perspective* (2nd ed.). New York: Guilford.

Hartley, J. E. (1980). ṣelem. In R. L. Harris, G. L. Archer Jr., & B. K. Waltke (Eds.), *Theological wordbook of the Old Testament* (pp. 767-68). Chicago: Moody Press.

Hauerwas, S. (1981). *A community of character: Toward a constructive, Christian social ethic*. Notre Dame, IN: University of Notre Dame Press.

———. (1983). *The peaceable kingdom*. Notre Dame, IN: University of Notre Dame Press.

———. (1986). *Suffering presence*. Notre Dame, IN: University of Notre Dame Press.

Hauerwas, S., & Jones, L. G. (Eds.). (1997). *Why narrative? Readings in narrative theology*. Grand Rapids, MI: Eerdmans.

Hayes, S. C., Strosahl, K. D., & Wilson, K. G. (2012). *Acceptance and commitment therapy* (2nd ed.). New York: Guilford.

Heckhausen, H. (1991). *Motivation and action*. New York: Springer-Verlag.

Heidegger, M. (1962). *Being and time*. (J. Macquarrie & E. Robinson, Trans.). New York: Harper & Row.

Heider, F. (1958). *The psychology of interpersonal relations*. New York: John Wiley & Sons.

Heims, E. (2011). Person. IV. Dogmatics. In H. D. Betz, D. S. Browning, B. Janowski, & E. Jüngel (Eds.), *Religion past and present: Encyclopedia of theology and religion* (Vol. IX, pp. 732-35). Leiden: Brill.

Helm, P. (1994). *The providence of God*. Downers Grove, IL: InterVarsity Press.

Hendrix, H., Hunt, H. L., Hannah, M. T., & Luquet, W. (Eds.). (2005). *Imago relationship therapy: Perspectives on theory*. San Francisco: Jossey-Bass.

Herbert, G. (1995). *The complete English works*. New York: Alfred A. Knopf.

Hesse, E. (2008). The adult attachment interview: Protocol, method of analysis, and empirical studies. In J. Cassidy & P. R. Shaver (Eds.), *Handbook of attachment* (2nd ed.) (pp. 552-98). New York: Guilford.

Hill, C. E., & James, F. A., III. (2004). *The glory of the atonement*. Downers Grove, IL: InterVarsity Press.

Hill, W. (2015). *Spiritual friendship: Finding love in the church as a celibate gay Christian*. Grand Rapids, MI: Brazos.

Hinshelwood, R. D. (1991). *A dictionary of Kleinian thought* (2nd ed.). New York: Jason Aronson.

Hodge, C. (1993). *Systematic theology*. Grand Rapids, MI: Eerdmans. (Original work published 1872)

Hoehner, H. W. (2002). *Ephesians: An exegetical commentary*. Grand Rapids, MI: Baker.

Hoekema, A. A. (1975). *The Christian's self-image*. Grand Rapids, MI: Eerdmans.

———. (1979). *The Bible and the future*. Grand Rapids, MI: Eerdmans.

———. (1986). *Created in God's image*. Grand Rapids, MI: Eerdmans.

———. (1994). *Saved by grace*. Grand Rapids, MI: Eerdmans.

Hoffman, M. L. (1991). Empathy, social cognition, and moral action. In W. M. Kurtines & J. L. Gerwirtz (Eds.), *Handbook of moral behavior and development:* Vol. 1, *Theory*. (pp. 275-301). Hillsdale, NJ: Erlbaum.

Hoffman, M. T. (2011). *Toward mutual recognition: Relational psychoanalysis and the Christian narrative*. New York: Routledge.

Holifield, E. B. (1983). *A history of pastoral care in America: From salvation to self-realization*. Nashville, TN: Abingdon.

Holmes, S. R. (2001). *God of grace and God of glory: An account of the theology of Jonathan Edwards*. Grand Rapids, MI: Eerdmans.

———. (2012). *The quest for the Trinity: The doctrine of God in Scripture, history and modernity*. Downers Grove, IL: InterVarsity Press.

Hood, R. W., Jr., Hill, P. C., & Spilka, B. (2009). *The psychology of religion: An empirical approach* (4th ed.). New York: Guilford.

Hopkins, G. M. (1985). *Gerard Manley Hopkins: Poems and prose*. New York: Penguin.

Horney, K. (1950). *Neurosis and human growth*. New York: Norton.

Horton, M. S. (2002). *Covenant and eschatology: The divine drama*. Louisville, KY: Westminster John Knox.

———. (2005). *Lord and servant: A covenant Christology*. Louisville, KY: Westminster John Knox.

———. (2007). *Covenant and salvation*. Louisville, KY: Westminster John Knox.

———. (2011). *The Christian faith: A systematic theology for pilgrims on the way*. Grand Rapids, MI: Zondervan.

Howard, G. S. (1992). Behold our creation! What counseling psychology has become and might yet become. *Journal of Counseling Psychology, 39*, 419-42.

Howe, L. T. (1995). *The image of God: A theology for pastoral care and counseling*. Nashville, TN: Abingdon.

Huffman, D. S., & Johnson, E. J. (Eds.). (2002). *God under fire: Modern scholarship reinvents God*. Grand Rapids, MI: Zondervan.

Ickes, W. (1988). Attributional styles and the self-concept. In L. Y. Abramson (Ed.), *Social cognition and clinical psychology: A synthesis* (pp. 66-97). New York: Guilford.

Ingram, R. E., & Price, J. M. (Eds.). (2001). *Vulnerability to psychopathology: Risk across the lifespan*. New York: Guilford.

Irenaeus. (1990). *The scandal of the incarnation: Irenaeus against the heresies*. San Francisco: Ignatius.

Jacobs, A. (2009). *Original sin: A cultural history*. New York: HarperOne.

James, W. (1890). *Principles of psychology*, Vol. 1. New York: Henry Holt.

Jeffrey, S., Ovey, M., & Sach, A. (2007). *Pierced for our transgressions: Rediscovering the glory of penal substitution*. Wheaton, IL: Crossway.

Jenson, R. W. (1984). The triune God. In C. A. Braaten & R. W. Jenson (Eds.), *Christian dogmatics*: Vol. 1 (pp. 83-196). Philadelphia: Fortress.

———. (1988). *America's theologian: A recommendation of Jonathan Edwards.* New York: Oxford University Press.

———. (2003). *On thinking the human: Resolutions of difficult notions.* Grand Rapids, MI: Eerdmans.

John of the Cross. (1935). *The complete works of Saint John of the Cross.* (E. A. Peers, Trans. and Ed.). Westminster, MD: Newman Press.

Johnson, D., & Van Vonderen, J. (2005). *The subtle power of spiritual abuse.* Minneapolis: Bethany.

Johnson, E. A. (1993). *She who is: The mystery of God in feminist theological discourse.* New York: Crossroad.

Johnson, E. L. (1987). Sin, weakness, and psychopathology. *Journal of Psychology and Theology, 15,* 218-26.

———. (1992). A place for the Bible within psychological science. *Journal of Psychology and Theology, 20,* 346-55.

———. (1997a). Christ, the Lord of psychology. *Journal of Psychology and Theology, 25,* 11-27.

———. (1997b). Human agency and its social formation. In R. C. Roberts & M. R. Talbot (Eds.), *Limning the psyche: Explorations in Christian psychology* (pp. 138-64). Grand Rapids, MI: Eerdmans.

———. (2000). Describing the self within redemptive history. *Journal of Psychology and Christianity, 19,* 5-24.

———. (2002). Can God be grasped by our reason? In D. S. Huffman & E. J. Johnson (Eds.), *God under fire: Modern scholarship reinvents God* (pp. 71-104). Grand Rapids, MI: Zondervan.

———. (2007). *Foundations for soul care: A Christian psychology proposal.* Downers Grove, IL: InterVarsity Press.

———. (2010). A brief history of Christians in psychology. In E. L. Johnson (Ed.), *Christianity and psychology: Five views* (pp. 9-47). Downers Grove, IL: InterVarsity Press.

———. (2011a). Re-wording the justification/sanctification relation with some help from speech-act theory. *Journal of the Evangelical Theological Society, 54*(4), 767-86.

———. (2011b). The three faces of integration. *Journal of Psychology and Christianity, 30*(4), 339-55.

———. (2012). Let's talk: Embeddedness, majority-minority relations, and principled pluralism. *Journal of Psychology and Theology, 40*(1), 26-31.

———. (2015a). Dialoging in good form: A response to Rom Harre, Jack Martin, and Mark Freeman's responses to "Form psychology." *New Ideas in Psychology, 38,* 44-53. doi.org/10.1016/j.newideapsych.2014.10.004

———. (2015b). Mapping the field of the whole person: Toward a form psychology. *New Ideas in Psychology, 38,* 4-24. doi.org/10.1016/j.newideapsych.2013.05.005

———. (2015, August). The social dynamics of worldviews in psychology. Presented at the American Psychological Association Convention. Toronto.

———. (2016). One edge of a two-edged sword: The subversive function of Scripture. *Journal of Soul Care and Spiritual Formation, 9,* 54-76.

Johnson, E. L., & Bartholomew, C. G. (unpublished manuscript). Christian transdisciplinarity: A proposal for the renewal of Christian scholarship in the 21st century.

Johnson, E. L., & Burroughs, C. S. (2000). Protecting one's soul: A Christian inquiry into defensive activity. *Journal of Psychology and Theology, 28,* 175-89.

Johnson, E. L., & Sandage, S. J. (1999). A postmodern reconstruction of psychotherapy: Orienteering, religion, and the healing of the soul. *Psychotherapy, 36,* 1-14.

Johnson, E. L., & Watson, P. J. (2012). Worldview communities and the science of psychology. In R. L. Piedmont & A. Village (Eds.), *Research in the Social Scientific Study of Religion,* Vol. 23 (pp. 269-84). Boston: Brill.

Johnson, E. L., Worthington, E. L., Jr., Hook, J. N., & Aten, J. D. (2013). Evidence-based practice in light of the Christian tradition(s): Reflections and future directions. In E. L. Worthington Jr., E. L. Johnson, J. Hook, & J. Aten, *Evidence-based Christian psychotherapy and counseling* (pp. 325-46). Downers Grove, IL: InterVarsity Press.

Jones, R. E., & Lopez, K. H. (2006). *Human reproductive biology.* Amsterdam: Elsevier.

Jones, S. L. (1994). A constructive relationship for religion with the science and profession of psychology: Perhaps the boldest model yet. *American Psychologist, 49,* 184-99.

———. (2001). An apologetic apologia for the integration of psychology & theology. In M. R. McMinn & T. R. Phillips (Eds.), *Care for the soul.* Downers Grove, IL: InterVarsity Press.

Jones, S. L., & Butman, R. E. (Eds.). (2011). *Modern psychotherapies.* Downers Grove, IL: InterVarsity Press.

Jones, S. L., & Wilcox, D. A. (1993). Religious values in secular theories of psychotherapy. In E. L. Worthington Jr. (Ed.). *Psychotherapy and religious values* (pp. 37-61). Grand Rapids, MI: Baker.

Jones, S. L., & Yarhouse, M. A. (2000). *Homosexuality: The use of scientific research in the church's moral debate.* Downers Grove, IL: InterVarsity Press.

Jones, S. L., & Yarhouse, M. (2007). *Ex-gays: A longitudinal study of religiously mediated change in sexual orientation.* Downers Grove, IL: InterVarsity Press.

Julian of Norwich. (1998). *Revelations of divine love.* London: Penguin.

Jung, C. G. (1966). The relations between the ego and the unconscious. In H. Read, M. Fordham, G. Adler, & W. McGuire (Eds.), *The collected works of C. G. Jung* (Vol. 7, pp. 123-244). Princeton, NJ: Princeton University Press. (Original work published 1928)

————. (1983). The shadow. In A. Storr (Ed.), *The essential Jung* (pp. 91-93). Princeton, NJ: Princeton University Press.

Jungel, E. (1983). *God as the mystery of the world.* Grand Rapids, MI: Eerdmans.

Kagan, J. (1984). *The nature of the child.* New York: Basic Books.

Kahneman, D., Diner, E., & Schwarz, N. (Eds.). (1999). *Well-being: The foundations of hedonic psychology* (pp. 353-73). New York: Russell Sage Foundation.

Käsemann, E. (1980). *Commentary on Romans.* Grand Rapids, MI: Eerdmans.

Kegan, R. (1982). *The evolving self: Problem and process in human development.* Cambridge, MA: Harvard University Press.

Kellemen, R. W. (2014). *Gospel-centered counseling.* Grand Rapids, MI: Zondervan.

————. (2016). *Gospel conversations.* Grand Rapids, MI: Zondervan.

Keller, T. (1997). *Ministries of mercy* (2nd ed.). Phillipsburg, NJ: P&R.

————. (2015). *Ministries of mercy: The call of the Jericho road* (3rd ed.). Phillipsburg, NJ: P&R.

Kelsey, D. H. (2009). *Eccentric existence: A theological anthropology.* Louisville, KY: Westminster John Knox.

Kendler, K. S., & Prescott, C. A. (2006). *Genes, environment, and psychopathology: Understanding the causes of psychiatric and substance use disorders.* New York: Guilford.

Kerr, F. (2002). *After Aquinas: Versions of Thomism.* Malden, MA: Blackwell.

Khalil, I. J. (1973). Eastern orthodoxy and psychotherapy. In R. H. Cox (Ed.), *Religious systems and psychotherapy* (pp. 195-223). Springfield, IL: Charles C. Thomas.

Kierkegaard, S. (1938). *Purity of heart is to will one thing.* New York: Harper & Row. (Original work published 1847)

————. (1956). *The prayers of Kierkegaard.* Chicago: University of Chicago Press.

————. (1980). *The sickness unto death.* (H. V. Hong, Trans.). Princeton, NJ: Princeton University Press. (Original work published 1849)

————. (1985). *Philosophical fragments.* (H. V. Hong, Trans.). Princeton, NJ: Princeton University Press. (Original work published 1844)

———. (1990). *For self-examination. Judge for yourselves!* (H. V. Hong & E. H. Hong, Trans.). Princeton, NJ: Princeton University Press.

Kim, L. (2012). The Holy Spirit, common grace, and secular psychotherapy. *Journal of Psychology and Theology, 40,* 229-39.

Kim, L. V., & Johnson, E. L. (2013). Transformation in Christian emotion-focused therapy. In D. W. Appleby & G. Ohlschlager (Eds.), *Transformative encounters: The intervention of God in Christian counseling and pastoral care.* Downers Grove, IL: InterVarsity Press.

Kinghorn, W. (2016). Positive psychology and the end of virtue. *Journal of Positive Psychology, 12 (5).*

Kistemaker, S. J. (2004). Atonement in Hebrews. In C. E. Hill & F. A. James III (Eds.), *The glory of the atonement* (pp. 163-75). Downers Grove, IL: InterVarsity Press.

Kitiyama, S., & Cohen, D. (2010). *Handbook of cultural psychology.* New York: Guilford.

Kittel, G. (1964). δοκέω, δοξα. In G. Kittel (Ed.), *Theological dictionary of the New Testament* (G. Bromiley, Trans.; Vol. 2, pp. 232-55.). Grand Rapids, MI: Eerdmans.

Kline, M. G. (1986). *Images of the Spirit.* Self-published.

———. (2000). *Kingdom prologue: Genesis foundations for a covenantal worldview.* Overland Park, KS: Two Age Press.

Knabb, J. J., & Frederick, T. V. (2017). *Contemplative prayer for Christians with chronic worry: An eight-week program.* New York: Routledge.

Kohut, H. (1971). *The analysis of the self.* New York: International Universities.

———. (1977). *The restoration of the self.* New York: International Universities.

———. (1984). *How does analysis cure?* Chicago: University of Chicago Press.

Kolb, R. (2002). Luther on the theology of the cross. *Lutheran Quarterly, 16,* 443-66.

Koltko-Rivera, M. E. (2004). The psychology of worldviews. *Review of General Psychology, 8*(1), 3-58.

König, A. (1989). *The eclipse of Christ in eschatology: Toward a Christ-centered approach.* Grand Rapids, MI: Eerdmans.

Köstenberger, A. J. (2009). *A theology of John's Gospel and letters.* Grand Rapids, MI: Zondervan.

Kreeft, P. (1992). *Back to virtue.* San Francisco: Ignatius.

Kreeft, P., & Tacelli, R. K. (1994). *Handbook of Christian apologetics.* Downers Grove, IL: InterVarsity Press.

Krummacher, F. W. (1947). *The suffering saviour.* Chicago: Moody Press. (Original work published 1854)

Kruschwitz, R., & Roberts, R. C. (Eds.). (1986). *The virtues: Contemporary essays on moral character*. Belmont, CA: Wadsworth.

Kuyper, A. (1898). *Encyclopedia of sacred theology*. New York: Charles Scribner's Sons.

———. (1900). *The work of the Holy Spirit*. New York: Funk & Wagnalls.

———. (1948). *The practice of godliness*. (M. Schooland, Trans.). Grand Rapids, MI: Eerdmans.

———. (1998). *Abraham Kuyper: A centennial reader*. (J. D. Bratt, Ed.). Grand Rapids, MI: Eerdmans.

LaCugna, C. M. (1991). *God for us: The Trinity and Christian life*. San Francisco: Harper.

Ladd, G. E. (1974). *Theology of the New Testament*. Grand Rapids, MI: Eerdmans.

Lakoff, G., & Johnson, M. (1980). *Metaphors we live by*. Chicago: University of Chicago Press.

Lambert, M. J. (Ed.). (2013). *Bergin and Garfield's handbook of psychotherapy and behavior change* (6th ed.). New York: Wiley.

Lane, T., & Tripp, P. D. (2006). *Relationships: A mess worth making*. Greensboro, NC: New Growth Press.

LaPorte, J.-M. (1997). Kenosis as a key to maturity of personality. In R. C. Roberts & M. R. Talbot (Eds.), *Limning the psyche: Explorations in Christian psychology* (pp. 229-44). Grand Rapids, MI: Eerdmans.

Lasch, C. (1979). *The culture of narcissism*. New York: W. W. Norton.

Lazarus, R. S. (1999). *Stress and emotion: A new synthesis*. New York: Springer.

Leach, J. (2015). *Improving mental health through social support*. London: Jessica Kingsley.

Leary, M. R., & Tangney, J. P. (2003). The self as an organizing construct in the behavioral and social sciences. In M. R. Leary & J. P. Tangney (Eds.), *Handbook of self and identity* (pp. 3-14). New York: Guilford.

Leary, T. (1957). *Inerpersonal diagnosis of personality*. New York: Ronald Press.

Lee, J. A. (1973). *Colors of love*. Toronto: New Press.

Leeman, J. (2010). *The church and the surprising offense of God's love*. Wheaton, IL: Crossway.

Leijssen, M. (1998). Focusing microprocesses. In L. S. Greenberg, J. C. Watson, & G. Lietaer (Eds.), *Handbook of experiential therapy* (pp. 121-54). New York: Guilford.

Leith, J. H. (1963). *Creeds of the churches*. New York: Doubleday.

Lerner, M. J. (1980). *The belief in a just world: A fundamental delusion*. New York: Plenum.

Letham, R. (1993). *The work of Christ*. Downers Grove, IL: InterVarsity Press.

LeVay, S., & Baldwin, J. (2011). *Human sexuality*, 4th ed. Sunderland, MA: Sinauer Associates.

Levering, M. (2008). *Biblical natural law: A theocentric and teleological approach*. New York: Oxford University Press.

Lewis, A. E. (2001). *Between cross and resurrection: A theology of Holy Saturday*. Grand Rapids, MI: Eerdmans.

Lewis, C. S. (1947). *The abolition of man*. New York: Macmillan.

———. (1952). *Mere Christianity*. London: Collins.

———. (1960). *The four loves*. New York: Harcourt, Brace.

Lewis, M., & Brooks-Gunn, J. (1979). *Social cognition and the acquisition of self*. New York: Plenum.

Lewis, P. (2001). *The glory of Christ*. Carlisle, PA: Paternoster.

Lewis, T., Amini, F., & Lannon, R. (2000). *A general theory of love*. New York: Random House.

Lincoln, A. T. (1981). *Paradise now and not yet*. Cambridge: Cambridge University Press.

———. (1990). *Word Biblical Commentary, Volume 42, Ephesians*. Dallas: Word.

Linehan, M. (1993). *Cognitive-behavioral treatment of borderline personality disorder*. New York: Guilford.

Linley, P. A., & Joseph, S. (2004). Positive change following trauma and adversity: A review. *Journal of Traumatic Stress, 17*, 11-21.

Lints, R. (2006). Imaging and idolatry: The sociality of personhood in the canon. In R. Lints, M. S. Horton, & M. R. Talbot (Eds.), *Personal identity in theological perspective* (pp. 204-25). Grand Rapids, MI: Eerdmans.

Livingston. G. H. (1980). ʿāshēm. In R. L. Harris, G. L. Archer, & B. K. Waltke (Eds.), *Theological wordbook of the Old Testament* (p. 79). Chicago: Moody Press.

Lloyd-Jones, D. M. (1968). *Romans, chapter 6: The new man*. Grand Rapids, MI: Baker.

Lombardo, N. E. (2011). *The logic of desire: Aquinas on emotion*. Washington, DC: Catholic University of America Press.

Lopez, A. (2014). *Gift and the unity of being*. Eugene, OR: Cascade.

Lotufo, Z., Jr. (2012). *Cruel God, kind God: How images of God shape belief, attitude and outlook*. Santa Barbara, CA: Praeger.

Louth, A. (1986a). Augustine. In C. Jones, G. Wainwright, & E. Yarnold, S.J. (Eds.), *The study of spirituality* (pp. 134-44). New York: Oxford University Press.

———. (1986b). The Cappadocians. In C. Jones, G. Wainwright, & E. Yarnold (Eds.), *The study of spirituality* (pp. 161-68). New York: Oxford University Press.

Luther, M. (1963). *Luther's works: Vol. 26. Lectures on Galatians: Chapters 1-4*. St. Louis: Concordia Publishing House. (Original work published 1535)

———. (2005). Heidelberg disputation. In T. F. Lull (Ed.), *Martin Luther's basic theological writings* (2nd ed., pp. 47-61). Minneapolis: Fortress. (Original work published 1518)

Lyotard, J.-F. (1979). *The postmodern condition: A report on knowledge*. Minneapolis: University of Minnesota Press.

Maccoby, E. (1980). *Social development: Psychological growth and the parent-child relationship*. New York: Harcourt Brace Jovanovich.

MacDonald, J., Kellemen, B., & Viars, S. (2013). *Christ-centered biblical counseling*. Eugene, OR: Harvest House.

MacIntyre, A. (1984). *After virtue* (2nd ed.). South Bend, IN: University of Notre Dame Press.

———. (1990). *Three rival versions of moral enquiry: Encyclopaedia genealogy and tradition*. Notre Dame, IN: University of Notre Dame Press.

Macmurray, J. (1957). *The self as agent*. London: Faber & Faber.

Maddi, S. R. (1996). *Personality theories: A comparative analysis* (6th ed.). Pacific Grove, CA: Brooks/Cole.

Maddox, D. B. (1994). Union with Christ: The implications for biblical counseling. In J. F. MacArthur Jr. & W. A. Mack (Eds.), *Introduction to biblical counseling* (pp. 116-30). Waco, TX: Word.

Mahler, M. (1968). *On human symbiosis and the vicissitudes of individuation*. New York: International Universities Press.

Mahler, M., Pine, F., & Bergman, A. (1975). *The psychological birth of the human infant: Symbiosis and individuation*. New York: Basic Books.

Mallery, P., Mallery, S., & Gorsuch, R. (2000). A preliminary taxonomy of attributions to God. *The International Journal for the Psychology of Religion, 10*, 135-56.

Malony, H. N. (1981). Integration: The adjoiners. In H. N. Malony (Ed.), *Psychology & theology: Prospects for integration* (pp. 85-124). Nashville, TN: Abingdon.

———. (Ed.). (1983). *Wholeness and holiness: Readings in the psychology/theology of mental health*. Grand Rapids, MI: Baker.

Manning, B. (1994). *Abba's child: The cry of the heart for intimate belonging*. Colorado Springs: NavPress.

Markus, H. (1977). Self-schemata and processing information about the self. *Journal of Personality and Social Psychology, 35*, 63-78.

Markus, H., & Nurius, P. (1986). Possible selves. *American Psychologist, 41,* 954-69.

Marsden, G. M. (1994). *The soul of the American university: From Protestant establishment to established nonbelief.* New York: Oxford University Press.

Marshall, I. H. (1978). *The epistles of John.* Grand Rapids, MI: Eerdmans.

———. (1988). Salvation. In S. B. Ferguson & D. F. Wright (Eds.), *New dictionary of theology* (pp. 610-11). Downers Grove, IL: InterVarsity Press.

———. (2008). The theology of the atonement. In D. Tidball, D. Hilborn, & J. Thacker (Eds.), *The atonement debate* (pp. 69-82). Grand Rapids, MI: Zondervan.

Martin, J. (1994). *The construction and understanding of psychotherapeutic change.* New York: Teachers College Press.

Martin, J., Sugarman, J., & Thompson, J. (2003). *Psychology and the question of agency.* Albany: State University of New York Press.

Maslow, A. H. (1954). *Motivation and personality.* New York: Harper & Row.

———. (1968). *Toward a psychology of being.* New York: D. Van Nostrand.

———. (1970). *Religions, values, and peak-experiences.* New York: Viking.

———. (1971). *The farther reaches of human nature.* New York: Viking.

Mason, D. A., & Frick, J. P. (1994). The heritability of antisocial behavior: A meta-analysis of twin and adoption studies. *Journal of Psychopathology and Behavioral Assessment, 16*(4), 301-23.

Masters, K. S., & Hooker, S. A. (2013). Religion, spirituality, and health. In R. F. Paloutzian & C. L. Park (Eds.), *Handbook of the psychology of religion and spiritual* (2nd ed., pp. 519-39). New York: Guilford.

Masterson, J. F. (1988). *The search for the real self: Unmasking the personality disorders of our age.* New York: Free Press.

Mattes, M. C. (2004). *The role of justification in contemporary theology.* Grand Rapids, MI: Eerdmans.

McAdams, D. P. (1993). *The stories we live by: Personal myths and the making of the self.* New York: Guilford.

———. (2006). *The redemptive self: Stories Americans live by.* Oxford: Oxford University Press.

———. (2008). *The person: An introduction to the science of personality psychology.* New York: Wiley.

McCall, T. H. (2010). *Which Trinity? Whose monotheism? Philosophical and systematic theologians on the metaphysics of trinitarian theology.* Grand Rapids, MI: Eerdmans.

———. (2014). Relational Trinity: Creedal perspective. In J. S. Sexton (Ed.), *Two views on the doctrine of the Trinity* (pp. 113-37). Grand Rapids, MI: Zondervan.

McClymond, M. J., & McDermott, G. R. (2012). *The theology of Jonathan Edwards*. New York: Oxford University Press.

McCormack, B. L. (1998). For us and our salvation: Incarnation and atonement in the Reformed tradition. *The Greek Orthodox Theological Review, 43*(1-4), 281-316.

McCullough, L., Kuhn, N., Andrews, S., Kaplan, A., Wolf, J., & Hurley, C. L. (2003). *Treating affect phobia: A manual for short-term dynamic psychotherapy*. New York: Guilford.

McCullough, M. E., & Larson, D. B. (1999). Prayer. In W. R. Miller (Ed.), *Integrating spirituality into treatment: Resources for practitioners* (pp. 85-110). Washington, DC: American Psychological Association.

McDonald, H. D. (1985). *The atonement of the death of Christ: In faith, revelation, and history*. Grand Rapids, MI: Baker.

McFadyen, A. (2000). *Bound to sin: Abuse, holocaust and the Christian doctrine of sin*. New York: Cambridge University Press.

McGee, R. S. (1990). *The search for significance* (2nd ed.). Houston, TX: Rapha.

McGrath, A. E. (1987). *The enigma of the cross*. London: Hodder and Stoughton.

———. (1994). *Spirituality in an age of change: Rediscovering the spirit of the reformers*. Grand Rapids, MI: Zondervan.

———. (1997). Theology of the cross. In G. F. Hawthorne, R. P. Martin, & D. G. Reid (Eds.), *Dictionary of Paul and his letters* (pp. 192-97). Downers Grove, IL: InterVarsity Press.

———. (2001). *A scientific theology: Vol. 1, nature*. Grand Rapids, MI: Eerdmans.

McIntosh, M. A. (2004). Christology. In E. T. Oakes, S.J., & D. Moss (Eds.), *The Cambridge companion to Hans Urs von Balthasar* (pp. 24-36). New York: Cambridge University Press.

———. (2008). *Divine teaching: An introduction to Christian theology*. New York: Blackwell.

McMinn, M. R. (1996). *Psychology, theology, and spirituality in Christian counseling*. Wheaton, IL: Tyndale.

———. (2001, August). Connection, not logic: Relational cognitive therapy and Christianity. Paper presented at the meeting of the American Association of Christian Counselors, Nashville, TN.

———. (2006). *Christian counseling: Spirituality Video Series*. Washington, DC: American Psychological Association.

———. (2008). *Sin and grace in Christian counseling: An integrative paradigm*. Downers Grove, IL: InterVarsity Press.

McMinn, M. R., & Campbell, C. D. (2007). *Integrative psychotherapy: Toward a comprehensive Christian approach*. Downers Grove, IL: InterVarsity Press.

McMinn, M. R., & Dominquez, A. W. (Eds.). (2005). *Psychology and the church.* New York: Nova Science Publishers.

McMinn, M. R., Vogel, M. J., & Heyne, L. K. (2010). A place for the church within professional psychology. *Journal of Psychology & Theology, 38,* 267-74.

McNamee, S., & Gergen, K. J. (Eds.). (1992). *Therapy as social construction.* London: Sage.

Meissner, W. W. (1996). The pathology of beliefs and the beliefs of pathology. In E. P. Shafranske (Ed.), *Religion and the clinical practice of psychology* (pp. 241-67). Washington, DC: American Psychological Association.

Merriell, D. J. (2005). Trinitarian anthropology. In R. van Nieuwenhove & J. Wawrykow (Eds.), *The theology of Thomas Aquinas* (pp. 123-42). Notre Dame, IN: University of Notre Dame Press.

Merton, T. (1955). *No man is an island.* New York: Harcourt Brace Jovanovich.

———. (1960). *Spiritual direction and meditation.* Collegeville, MN: The Order of St. Benedict.

———. (1961b). *New seeds of contemplation.* New York: New Directions.

———. (1961a). *The new man.* New York: Farrar, Straus and Giroux.

———. (2003). *The inner experience: Notes on contemplation.* New York: HarperCollins.

Meyer, J. C. (2009). *The end of the law: Mosaic covenant in Pauline theology.* Nashville: B&H Academic.

Milbank, J. (2003). *Being reconciled: Ontology and pardon.* New York: Routledge.

Milbank, J., & Pickstock, C. (2001). *Truth in Aquinas.* New York: Routledge.

Miller, A. (1981). *The drama of the gifted child.* New York: Basic Books.

Miller, A. G. (Ed.). (2005). *The social psychology of good and evil.* New York: Guilford.

Miller, W. R. (Ed.). (1999). *Integrating spirituality into treatment: Resources for practitioners.* Washington, DC: American Psychological Association.

Miller, W. R., & Delaney, H. D. (2004). *Judeo-Christian perspectives on psychology: Human nature, motivation, and change.* Washington, DC: American Psychological Association.

Miller, W. R., & Rollnick, S. (2013). *Motivational interviewing* (3rd ed.). New York: Guilford.

Miner, M. H., & McKnight, J. (1999). Religious attributions: Situational factors and effects on coping. *Journal for the Scientific Study of Religion, 38,* 274-86.

Mischel, W. (1974). Processes in delay of gratification. In L. Berkowitz (Ed.), *Advances in experimental social psychology* (Vol. 7, pp. 249-92). New York: Academic Press.

Moltmann, J. (1974). *The crucified God.* London: SCM Press.

———. (1980). *The Trinity and the kingdom of God.* London: SCM Press.

———. (1985). *God in creation: A new theology of creation and the Spirit of God.* San Francisco: Harper & Row.

Monroe, K. R. (1996). *The heart of altruism: Perceptions of a common humanity.* Princeton, NJ: Princeton University Press.

Moo, D. J. (1993). The law of Christ as the fulfillment of the law of Moses: A modified Lutheran approach. In S. N. Gundry (Ed.), *Five views on law and gospel* (pp. 319-76). Grand Rapids, MI: Zondervan.

———. (1996). *The epistle to the Romans.* Grand Rapids, MI: Eerdmans.

———. (2008). *The letters to the Colossians and to Philemon.* Grand Rapids, MI: Eerdmans.

Moore, R. (2009). *Adopted for life.* Wheaton, IL: Crossway.

Moran, G. T., & Foster, J. D. (1985). Piaget and parables: The convergence of secular and scriptural views of learning. *Journal of Psychology and Theology, 13,* 97-103.

Moriarity, G. L., & Hoffman, L. (Eds.). (2007). *God image handbook: For spiritual counseling and psychotherapy.* Binghamton, NY: Haworth.

Moroney, S. (1999). How sin affects Christian scholarship. *Christian Scholar's Review, 28.*

Morris, L. (1971). *The Gospel according to John.* Grand Rapids, MI: Eerdmans.

Morrison, A. P. (2011). The psychodynamics of shame. In R. L. Dearing & J. P. Tangney (Eds.), *Shame in the therapy hour* (pp. 23-44). New York: Guilford.

Moser, P. K. (2013). *The severity of God: Religion and philosophy reconceived.* New York: Cambridge University Press.

Mounce, R. C. (1977). *The book of Revelation.* Grand Rapids, MI: Eerdmans.

Mouw, R. J. (1990). *The God who commands.* South Bend, IN: University of Notre Dame Press.

———. (2001). *He shines in all that's fair.* Grand Rapids, MI: Eerdmans.

Mowrer, O. H. (1961). *The crisis in psychiatry and religion.* Princeton, NJ: D. Van Nostrand.

Muller, R. A. (2001). Justification. In D. K. McKim (Ed.), *The Westminster handbook to Reformed theology* (pp. 127-29). Louisville, KY: Westminster John Knox.

———. (2003). *Post-reformation reformed dogmatics* (4 Vols.). Grand Rapids, MI: Baker.

Mullet, E., & Girard, M. (2000). Developmental and cognitive points of view on forgivenenss. In M. E. McCullough, K. I. Pargament, & C. E. Thoresen (Eds.), *Forgiveness: Theory, research, and practice* (pp. 111-32). New York: Guilford.

Murphy, F. (1995). *Christ the form of beauty: A study in theology and literature.* Edinburgh: T&T Clark.

Murray, H. A. (1938). *Explorations in personality.* New York: Oxford University Press.

Murray, J. (1955). *Redemption: Accomplished and applied.* Grand Rapids, MI: Eerdmans.

———. (1957). *Principles of conduct.* Grand Rapids, MI: Eerdmans.

———. (1959). *The epistle to the Romans.* Grand Rapids, MI: Eerdmans.

———. (1977). *Collected writings of John Murray, Vol. 2.* Edinburgh: Banner of Truth.

———. (1988). Redemption. In G. W. Bromiley (Ed.), *The international Bible encyclopedia* (Vol. 4, pp. 61-63). Grand Rapids, MI: Eerdmans.

Muse, S. (2015). *When hearts become flame: An Eastern approach to the dia-logos of pastoral counseling* (2nd ed.). Waymart, PA: St. Tikhon's Monastery Press.

Myers, D. G. (2000). The funds, friends, and faith of happy people. *American Psychologist, 55,* 56-67.

———. (2012). *Social psychology* (11th ed.). New York: McGraw-Hill.

Nagel, T. (2012). *Mind and cosmos.* New York: Oxford University Press.

Narramore, S. B. (1984). *No condemnation: Rethinking guilt motivation in counseling, preaching, and parenting.* Grand Rapids, MI: Zondervan.

Nash, R. (1988). *Reason and faith.* Grand Rapids, MI: Zondervan.

Naugle, D. K. (2002). *Worldview: The history of a concept.* Grand Rapids, MI: Eerdmans.

Newton, J. (1960). *Letters of John Newton.* Edinburgh: Banner of Truth Trust.

Nicolosi, J. J. (2009). *Shame and attachment loss.* Downers Grove, IL: InterVarsity Press.

Niederhoffer, K. G., & Pennebaker, J. W. (2002). Sharing one's story: On the benefits of writing or talking about emotional experience. In C. R. Snyder & S. J. Lopez (Eds.), *Handbook of positive psychology* (pp. 573-83). Oxford: Oxford University Press.

Norcross, J. C. (Ed.). (2011). *Psychotherapy relationships that work* (2nd ed.). New York: Oxford University Press.

Nouwen, H. J. M. (1986). *Reaching out: The three movements of the spiritual life.* New York: Doubleday.

Nygren, A. (1953). *Agape and eros.* Philadelphia: Westminster.

O'Brien, P. T. (1999). *The letter to the Ephesians.* Grand Rapids, MI: Eerdmans.

———. (2000). *Colossians, Philemon.* Nashville, TN: Thomas Nelson.

Oden, T. (1989). *The Word of life, systematic theology: Vol. II.* New York: HarperCollins.

O'Donovan, O. (1980). *The problem of self-love in St. Augustine.* New Haven, CT: Yale University Press.

———. (1986). *Resurrection and moral order* (2nd ed.). Grand Rapids, MI: Eerdmans.

Okholm, D. L. (1995). Self-denial. In D. J. Atkinson, D. F. Field, A. Holmes, & O. O'Donovan (Eds.), *New dictionary of Christan ethics and pastoral theology* (p. 773). Downers Grove, IL: InterVarsity Press.

Oliner, S. P., & Oliner, P. M. (1988). *The altruistic personality: Rescuers of Jews in Nazi Europe.* New York: Free Press.

Oliphant, K. S. (2012). *God with us: Divine condescension and the attributes of God.* Wheaton, IL: Crossway.

Oliver, S. (2013). Teleology revived? Cooperation and the ends of nature. *Studies in Christian Ethics, 26,* 158-65.

Oswalt, J. N. (1980a). *bôsh.* In R. L. Harris, G. L. Archer, & B. K. Waltke (Eds.), *Theological wordbook of the Old Testament* (pp. 97-98) Chicago: Moody Press.

———. (1980b). *kābēd.* In R. L. Harris, G. L. Archer, & B. K. Waltke (Eds.), *Theological wordbook of the Old Testament* (pp. 426-28). Chicago: Moody Press.

Otterbein, K. F. (1986). *Ultimate coercive sanction: A cross-cultural study of capital punishment.* New Haven, CT: HRAF Press.

Ouellet, M. C. (2006). *Divine likeness: Toward a trinitarian anthropology of the family.* Grand Rapids, MI: Eerdmans.

Owen, J. (1965). *The works of John Owen* (Vols. 1-16). Edinburgh: Banner of Truth Trust. (Original work published 1850–1853)

Packer, J. I. (1973). *Knowing God.* Downers Grove, IL: InterVarsity Press.

———. (1974). What did the cross achieve? The logic of penal substitution. *Tyndale Bulletin, 25,* 3-45.

Page, S. H. T. (2007). Satan: God's servant. *Journal of the Evangelical Theological Society, 50*(3), 49-465.

Pallanti, S., & Quercioli, L. (2000). Shame and psychopathology. *CNS Spectrums, 5*(8), 28-43.

Pannenberg, W. (1985). *Anthropology in theological perspective.* (M. J. O'Connell, Trans.). Philadelphia: Westminster.

Pargament, K. I. (1997). *The psychology of religion and coping.* New York: Guilford.

Pargament, K. I., Falb, M. D., Ano, G. G., & Wachholtz, A. B. (2013). The religious dimension of coping: Advances in theory, research, and practice. In

R. F. Paloutzian & C. L. Park (Eds.), *Handbook of the psychology of religion and spiritual* (2nd ed., pp. 560-79). New York: Guilford.

Pargament, K. I., & Mahoney, A. (2002). Spirituality: Discovering and conserving the sacred. In C. R. Snyder & S. J. Lopez (Eds.), *Handbook of positive psychology* (pp. 646-61). Oxford: Oxford University Press.

Park, C. L., & Slattery, J. M. (2013). Religion, spirituality, and mental health. In R. F. Paloutzian & C. L. Park (Eds.), *Handbook of the psychology of religion and spirituality* (2nd ed., pp. 540-60). New York: Guilford.

Parker, S. T., Mitchell, R. W., & Boccia, M. L. (Eds.). (1994). *Self-awareness in animals and humans: Developmental perspectives*. New York: Cambridge University Press.

Pascal, B. (1941). *Pensees*. New York: Random House. (Original work published 1680)

Paulson, S. D. (2011). *Lutheran theology*. New York: T&T Clark.

Payne, L. (1995). *The healing presence: Curing the soul through union with Christ*. Grand Rapids, MI: Baker.

PDM Task Force. (2006). *Psychodynamic diagnostic manual*. Silver Spring, MD: Alliance of Psychoanalytic Organizations.

Pennebaker, J. W. (1997). *Opening up: The healing power of expressing emotions* (Rev. ed.). New York: Guilford.

Pennington, B. F. (2002). *The development of psychopathology: Nature and nurture*. New York: Guilford.

Pennington, J. T. (2012). *Reading the Gospels wisely*. Grand Rapids, MI: Baker.

———. (2017). *The Sermon on the Mount and human flourishing: A theological commentary*. Grand Rapids, MI: Baker.

Perls, F. S. (1970). Four lectures. In J. Fagan & I. L. Shepherd (Eds.), *Gestalt therapy now* (pp. 14-38). New York: Harper & Row.

Peterson, C., & Seligman, M. E. P. (2004). *Character strengths and virtues: A handbook and classiciation*. New York: Oxford University Press.

Piaget, J. (1977a). The construction of reality in the child. In H. E. Gruber & J. J. Voneche (Eds.), *The essential Piaget* (pp. 250-96). New York: Basic Books.

———. (1977b). Judgment and reasoning in the child. In H. E. Gruber & J. J. Voneche (Eds.), *The essential Piaget* (pp. 89-117). New York: Basic Books.

Pieper, J. (1998). *Happiness and contemplation*. South Bend, IN: St. Augustine's Press.

Pinckaers, S. (2001). *Morality: The Catholic view*. Sound Bend, IN: St. Augustine's Press.

Pineles, S. L., Street, A. E., & Koenen, K. C. (2006). The differential relationships of shame-proneness and guilt-proneness to psychological and somatization symptoms. *Journal of Social & Clinical Psychology, 25*(6), 688-704.

Pink, A. W. (1976). *Spiritual union and communion*. Grand Rapids, MI: Baker.

Pinker, S. (1994). *The language instinct*. New York: William Morrow.

Piper, J. (1991). *The pleasures of God: Meditations on God's delight in being God.* Portland, OR: Multnomah.

———. (1995). *Future grace*. Sisters, OR: Multnomah.

———. (1996). *Desiring God: Meditations of a Christian hedonist* (2nd ed.). Sisters, OR: Multnomah.

———. (1998). *God's passion for his glory: Living the vision of Jonathan Edwards.* Wheaton, IL: Crossway.

Placher, W. (1994). *Narratives of a vulnerable God*. Louisville, KY: Westminster.

Plantinga, A. (1985). Self-profile. In J. E. Tomberlin & P. van Inwagen (Eds.), *Alvin Plantinga*. Dordrecht: Reidel.

———. (1993). *Warrant and proper function*. New York: Oxford University Press.

———. (2000). *Warranted Christian belief*. New York: Oxford University Press.

———. (2011). *Where the conflict really lies*. New York: Oxford University Press.

Plantinga, C. (1995). *Not the way it's supposed to be: A breviary of sin*. Grand Rapids, MI: Eerdmans.

———. (2002). *Engaging God's world: A Christian vision of faith, learning, and living*. Grand Rapids, MI: Eerdmans.

Podmore, S. D. (2009). Kierkegaard as physician of the soul: On self-forgiveness and despair. *Journal of Psychology and Theology, 37,* 174-85.

Poplin, M. (2008). *Finding Calcutta: What Mother Teresa taught me about meaningful work and service*. Downers Grove, IL: InterVarsity Press.

Powlison, D. (1992). Integration or inundation. In M. Horton (Ed.), *Power religion* (pp. 191-218). Chicago: Moody Press.

———. (1995). Idols of the heart and "Vanity Fair." *Journal of Biblical Counseling, 13,* 35-50.

———. (1997). Does biblical counseling really work? In E. Hindson & H. Eyrich (Eds.), *Totally sufficient: The Bible and Christian counseling* (pp. 57-97). Eugene, OR: Harvest House.

———. (2000). Affirmations and denials: A proposed definition of biblical counseling. *Journal of Biblical Counseling, 19*(1), 18-25.

———. (2002). Do you see? In D. Powlison & W. P. Smith (Eds.), *Counsel the Word* (2nd ed., pp. 2-6). Glenside, PA: Christian Counseling & Educational Foundation.

———. (2003). *Seeing with new eyes: Counseling and the human condition through the lens of Scripture*. Phillipsburg, NJ: P&R.

———. (2004). Is the "Adonis complex" in *your* Bible? *Journal of Biblical Counseling, 22*(2), 42-58.

———. (2005). *Speaking truth in love: Counseling in community.* Phillipsburg, NJ: P&R.

Poythress, V. (2001). *Symphonic theology.* Grand Rapids, MI: Zondervan.

Probst, L. R. (1988). *Psychotherapy in a religious framework: Spirituality in the emotional healing process.* New York: Human Sciences Press.

Prochaska, J. O., & Norcross, J. C. (1994). *Systems of psychotherapy: A transtheoretical analysis.* Pacific Grove, CA: Brooks/Cole.

Prochaska, J. O., & Norcross, J. C. (2006). *Systems of psychotherapy: A transtheoretical analysis* (6th ed.). San Diego, CA: Wadsworth.

Pruss, A. (2013). *One body: An essay in Christian sexual ethics.* Notre Dame, IN: University of Notre Dame Press.

Purves, A. (2004). *Reconstructing pastoral theology: A Christianological foundation.* Louisville, KY: Westminster John Knox.

Purves, A., & Achtemeier, M. (1999). *Union in Christ: A declaration for the church.* Louisville, KY: Witherspoon Press.

Quash, B. (2004). The theo-drama. In E. T. Oakes, S.J., & D. Moss (Eds.), *The Cambridge companion to Hans Urs von Balthasar* (pp. 143-57). New York: Cambridge University Press.

Quinn, J. D., & Wacker, W. C. (2000). *The first and second letters to Timothy.* Grand Rapids, MI: Eerdmans.

Rad, G. von (1962). *Old Testament theology.* (D. M. G. Stalker, Trans.). New York: Harper & Row.

———. (1972). *Genesis.* Philadelphia: Westminster Press.

Rahner, K. (1970). *The Trinity.* New York: Herder & Herder.

Reichenbach, B. R. (2006). The healing view. In J. Beilby & P. R. Eddy (Eds.), *The nature of the atonement: Four views* (pp. 117-42). Downers Grove, IL: InterVarsity Press.

Reinders, H. S. (2008). *Receiving the gift of friendship: Profound disability, theological anthropology, and ethics.* Grand Rapids, MI: Eerdmans.

Renfrew, J. W. (1996). *Aggression and its causes: A biopsychosocial approach.* New York: Oxford University Press.

Reno, R. R. (2002). *Redemptive change: Atonement and the Christian cure of the soul.* Harrisburg, PA: Trinity Press International.

Rest, J., Narvaez, D., Bebeau, M. J., & Thoma, S. J. (1999). *Postconventional moral thinking: A neo-Kohlbergian approach.* Mahwah, NJ: Lawrence Erlbaum.

Reynierse, J. H., & Young, C. (1975). Behavior therapy and Job's recovery. *Journal of Psychology and Theology, 3,* 187-94.

Rice, W. R., Friberg, U., & Gavrilets, S. (2012). Homosexuality as a consequence of epigenetically canalized sexual development. *The Quarterly Review of Biology, 87*(4), 343-68. doi:10.1086/668167.

Richard of St. Victor. (1979). Book three of the Trinity. In *Richard of St. Victor*. (G. A. Zinn, Trans.). New York: Paulist.

Richards, P. S., & Bergin, A. E. (1997). *A spiritual strategy for counseling and psychotherapy.* Washington, DC: American Psychological Association.

Richards, P. S., & Bergin, A. E. (2000). *Handbook of psychotherapy and religious diversity.* Washington, DC: American Psychological Association.

Richardson, F. C., Fowers, B. J., & Guignon, C. B. (1999). *Re-envisioning psychology: Moral dimensions of theory and practice.* San Francisco: Jossey-Bass.

Ricoeur, P. (1965). *Fallible man.* (C. Kelbley, Trans.). Chicago: Henry Regnery.

———. (1967). *The symbolism of evil.* (E. Buchanan, Trans.). New York: Harper & Row.

———. (1974). "Original sin": A study in meaning. In D. Ihde (Ed.), *The conflict of interpretations: Essay in hermeneutics* (pp. 269-86). Evanston, IL: Northwestern University Press.

———. (1984). *Time and narrative, Volume 1.* Chicago: University of Chicago Press.

———. (1992). *Oneself as another.* (K. Blamey, Trans.). Chicago: University of Chicago Press.

Ridderbos, H. (1975). *Paul: An outline of his theology.* Grand Rapids, MI: Eerdmans.

Rieff, P. (1966). *The triumph of the therapeutic: Uses of faith after Freud.* New York: Harper & Row.

Ritzema, R. J., & Young, C. (1983). Causal schemata and the attribution of supernatural causality. *Journal of Psychology and Theology, 11,* 36-43.

Rizzuto, A. M. (1979). *The birth of the living God.* Chicago: University of Chicago Press.

Roberts, R. C. (1987). Psychotherapeutic virtues and the grammar of faith. *Journal of Psychology and Theology. 15,* 191-204.

———. (1988). Therapies and the grammar of a virtue. In R. H. Bell (Ed.), *The grammar of the heart: New essays in moral philosophy and theology.* San Francisco: Harper & Row.

———. (1993). *Taking the word to heart: Self and other in an age of therapies.* Grand Rapids, MI: Eerdmans.

———. (1995a). Character. In In D. J. Atkinson, D. F. Field, A. F. Holmes, & O. O'Donovan (Eds.), *New dictionary of Christian ethics & pastoral theology* (pp. 65-71). Downers Grove, IL: InterVarsity Press.

————. (1995b). Virtue, virtues. In D. J. Atkinson, D. F. Field, A. F. Holmes, & O. O'Donovan (Eds.), *New dictionary of Christian ethics and pastoral theology* (p. 881). Downers Grove, IL: InterVarsity Press.

————. (1997a). Attachment: Bowlby and the Bible. In R. C.Roberts & M. R. Talbot (Eds.), *Limning the psyche: Explorations in Christian psychology* (pp. 206-28). Grand Rapids, MI: Eerdmans.

————. (1997b). Parameters of a Christian psychology. In R. C. Roberts & M. R. Talbot (Eds.), *Limning the psyche: Explorations in Christian psychology* (pp. 74-101). Grand Rapids, MI: Eerdmans.

————. (2001). Outline of Pauline psychotherapy. In M. R. McMinn & T. R. Phillips (Eds.), *Care for the soul* (pp. 134-63). Downers Grove, IL: InterVarsity Press.

————. (2003). *Emotions: An essay in aid of moral psychology.* Cambridge: Cambridge University Press.

————. (2007). *Spiritual emotions.* Grand Rapids, MI: Eerdmans.

Robertson, O. P. (1980). *The Christ of the covenants.* Phillipsburg, NJ: Presbyterian & Reformed.

Robins, C. J., & Hayes, A. M. (1995). In G. M. Buchanan & M. E. P. Seligman (Eds.), *Explanatory style* (pp. 71-98). Hillsdale, NJ: Lawrence Erlbaum.

Robins, R. W., Tracy, J. L., & Trzesniewski, K. H. (2008). Naturalizing the self. In O. P. John, R. W. Robins, & L. A. Pervin (Eds.), *Handbook of personality: Theory and research* (3rd ed., pp. 421-47). New York: Guilford.

Rogers, C. R. (1951). *Client-centered therapy.* Boston: Houghton Mifflin.

————. *On becoming a person.* Boston: Houghton Mifflin.

Rogers, J. (2009). *Jesus, the Bible, and homosexuality.* Louisville, KY: Westminster John Knox.

Rogoff, B. (1998). Cognition as a collaborative process. In W. Damon (Ed.), *Handbook of child psychology: Vol. 2. Cognition, perception, and language* (pp. 679-744). New York: John Wiley & Sons.

Rohr, R. (2001). *The enneagram: A Christian perspective.* New York: Crossroad.

Rolnick, P. A. (2007). *Person, grace, and God.* Grand Rapids, MI: Eerdmans.

Rosineau, P. M. (1992). *Post-modernism and the social sciences.* Princeton, NJ: Princeton University Press.

Roth, M. P. (2015). *An eye for an eye: A global history of crime and punishment.* London: Reaktion Books.

Rothbaum, F., Weisz, J. R., & Snyder, S. S. (1982). Changing the world and changing the self: A two-process model of perceived control. *Journal of Personality and Social Psychology, 42*(1), 5-37.

Rotter, J. B. (1966). Generalized expectancies for internal versus external control of reinforcement. *Psychological Monographs, 81,* 1-28.

Rougemont, D. de. (1940). *Love in the Western world.* New York: Pantheon.

Runnels, R. C., & Stauber, M. (2011). Today's best pastoral care: Church-based mental health and social programs. In C. Franklin & R. Fong (Eds.), *The church leader's counseling resource book* (pp. 431-48). New York: Oxford University Press.

Rüsch, N., Lieb, K., Göttler, I., Hermann, C., Schramm, E., Richter, H., Jacob, G. A., Corrigan, P. W., & Bohus, M. (2007). Shame and implicit self-concept in women with borderline personality disorder. *American Journal of Psychiatry, 164*(3), 500-508.

Russell, W. B. (1997). *The flesh/spirit conflict in Galatians.* Lanham, MD: University Press of America.

Rutherford, S. (1984). *Letters of Samuel Rutherford.* Edinburgh: Banner of Truth Trust. (Original work published 1664)

Ryan, R. M., & Deci, E. L. (2000). Self-determination theory and the facilitation of intrinsic motivation, social development, and well-being. *American Psychologist, 55*(1), 68-78.

Rychlak, J. F. (1988). *The psychology of rigorous humanism* (2nd ed.). New York: New York University Press.

Ryff, C. D., & Singer, B. (2002). From social structure to biology: Integrative science in pursuit of human health and well-being. In C. R. Snyder & S. J. Lopez (Eds.), *Handbook of positive psychology* (pp. 541-55). Oxford: Oxford University Press.

Ryken, L., Wilhoit, J. C., & Longman, T., III. (Eds.). (1998). *Dictionary of biblical imagery.* Downers Grove, IL: InterVarsity Press.

Sanford, J. (1981). *Evil: The shadow side of reality.* New York: Crossroad.

———. (1987). *The strange trial of Mr. Hyde: A new look at the nature of human evil.* San Francisco: Harper & Row.

Sarafino, E. R. (1990). *Health psychology: Biopsychosocial interactions.* New York: Wiley.

Sarason, B. R., Pierce, G. R., & Sarason, I. G. (1990). Social support: The sense of acceptance and the role of relationships. In B. R. Sarason, I. G. Sarason, & G. R. Pierce, (Eds.), *Social support: An interactional view* (pp. 267-96). New York: John Wiley & Sons.

Sarbin, T. R. (Ed.). (1986). *Narrative psychology: The storied nature of human conduct.* New York: Praeger.

Sayers, D. L. (1987). *The mind of the maker.* San Francisco: Harper. (Original work published 1941)

Scazzero, P. (2003). *The emotionally healthy church.* Grand Rapids, MI: Zondervan.

Schaefer, F. C. (2014, April). Spiritual pathways to resilient living in traumatic environments. Presentation at the meeting of the Christian Association for Psychological Studies, Atlanta.

Schaefer, F. C., Blazer, D. G., & Koenig, H. G. (2008). Religious and spiritual factors and the consequences of trauma: A review and model of the inter-relationship. *The International Journal of Psychiatry in Medicine, 38*(4), 507-24.

Schafer, R. (1975). *A new language for psychoanalysis.* New Haven, CT: Yale University Press.

Schafer, T. A. (1994). Editor's introduction. In T. A. Schafer (Ed.), *The Works of Jonathan Edwards: Vol. 13. The "miscellanies"* (pp. 1-110). New Haven, CT: Yale University Press.

Scharff, J. S. (1992). *Projective and introjective identification and the use of the therapist's self.* New York: Jason Aronson.

Scheier, M. F., & Carver, C. S. (1992). Effects of optimism on psychological and physical well-being: Theoretical overview and empirical update. *Cognitive Therapy and Research, 16,* 201-28.

Scheier, M. F., Carver, C. S., & Bridges, M. W. (2001). Optimism, pessimism, and psychological well-being. In E. C. Chang (Ed.), *Optimism & pessimism: Implications for theory, research, and practice* (pp. 189-215). Washington, DC: American Psychological Association.

Schilder, K. (1980). *Christ in his suffering.* Minneapolis: Klock & Klock.

Schneider, S. L. (2001). In search of realistic optimism: Meaning, knowledge, and warm fuzziness. *American Psychologist, 56,* 250-63.

Scholl, E. (2009). The light of glory: *Claritas* in Saint Bernard. *Cistercian Studies Quarterly, 44*(2), 161-71.

Schreiner, S. E. (1991). *The theater of his glory: Nature and the natural order in the thought of John Calvin.* Durham, NC: Labyrinth Press.

Schreiner, T. R. (1998). *Romans.* Grand Rapids, MI: Baker.

———. (2001). *Paul: Apostle of God's glory in Christ.* Downers Grove, IL: InterVarsity Press.

———. (2010). *Galatians: Zondervan exegetical commentary on the New Testament.* Grand Rapids, MI: Zondervan.

Schreiner, T. R., & Caneday, A. (2001). *The race set before us.* Downers Grove, IL: InterVarsity Press.

Schwartz, R. C. (1995). *Internal family systems therapy.* New York: Guilford.

Schwarz, H. (2000). *Eschatology.* Grand Rapids, MI: Eerdmans.

Schwobel, C. (1991). Human being as relational being: Twelve theses for a Christian anthropology. In C. Schwobel (Ed.), *Persons, divine and human* (pp. 141-70). Edinburgh: T&T Clark.

Schultz, G. L., Jr. (2014). *A multi-intentioned view of the extent of the atonement.* Eugene, OR: Wipf & Stock.

Scola, A. (1995). *Hans Urs von Balthasar: A theological style.* Grand Rapids, MI: Eerdmans.

Scougal, H. (1976). *The life of God in the soul of man.* Minneapolis: Bethany Press. (Original work published 1677)

Searle, J. R. (1969). *Speech acts: An essay in the philosophy of language.* Cambridge: Cambridge University Press.

———. (1998). *Mind, language and society: Philosophy in the real world.* New York: Basic Books.

Segal, D. L., & Coolidge, F. L. (2001). Diagnosis and classification. In M. Hersen & V. B. Van Hasselt (Eds.), *Advanced abnormal psychology* (2nd ed., pp. 5-22). New York: Kluwer/Plenum.

Seligman, M. E. P. (1991). *Learned optimism.* New York: Alfred A. Knopf.

———. (1992). *Helplessness: On depression, development, and death.* New York: Freeman.

Seligman, M. E. P., & Csikszentmihalyi, M. (2000). Positive psychology: An introduction. *American Psychologist, 55,* 5-14.

Shafranske, E. P. (Ed.). (1996). *Religion and the clinical practice of psychology.* Washington, DC: American Psychological Association.

Shafranske, E. P., & Malony, H. N. (1996). Religion and the clinical practice of psychology: A case for inclusion. In E. P. Shafranske (Ed.), *Religion and the clinical practice of psychology* (pp. 561-86). Washington, DC: American Psychological Association.

Sheldon, K. M., & King, L. K. (2001). Why positive psychology is necessary. *American Psychologist, 56,* 216-17.

Sherwin, M. S. (2005). *By knowledge & by love: Charity and knowledge in the moral theology of St. Thomas Aquinas.* Washington, DC: Catholic University of America Press.

Shiota, M. N., Thrash, T. M., Danvers, A. F., & Dembrowski, J. T. (2014). Transcending the self: Awe, elevation, and inspiration. In M. M. Tugade, M. N. Shiota, & L. D. Kirby (Eds.), *Handbook of positive emotions* (pp. 362-77). New York: Guilford.

Showers, C. J., & Zeigler-Hill, V. (2003). Organization of self-knowledge: Features, functions, and flexibility. In M. R. Leary & J. P. Tangney (Eds.),

Handbook of self and identity (pp. 47-67). New York: Guilford.

Shults, F. L. (2003). *Reforming theological anthropology: After the philosophical turn to relationality.* Grand Rapids, MI: Eerdmans.

Shults, F. L., & Sandage, S. J. (2003). *The faces of forgiveness: Searching for wholeness and salvation.* Grand Rapids, MI: Baker.

Shults, F. L., & Sandage, S. J. (2006). *Transforming spirituality: Integrating theology and psychology.* Grand Rapids, MI: Baker.

Shuster, M. (2004). *The fall and sin: What we have become as sinners.* Grand Rapids, MI: Eerdmans.

Sibbes, R. (1961). *Light from heaven.* Ann Arbor, MI: Sovereign Grace Publishers.

———. (1973). The soul's conflict with itself. In *Works of Richard Sibbes, Vol. 1* (pp. 119-294). Edinburgh: Banner of Truth Trust. (Original work published 1635)

———. (1982). Discouragement's recovery. In *Works of Richard Sibbes, Vol. 7* (pp. 49-64). Edinburgh: Banner of Truth Trust. (Original work published 1629)

———. (1998). *The bruised reed.* Edinburgh: Banner of Truth Trust. (Original work published 1630)

Siegel, D. J. (2010). *Mindsight: The new science of personal transformation.* New York: Bantam.

———. (2012). *The developing mind* (2nd ed.). New York: Guilford.

Singer, E. (1970). *Key concepts in psychotherapy* (2nd ed.). New York: Basic Books.

Sittser, J. (1995). *A grace disguised.* Grand Rapids, MI: Zondervan.

Skillen, J. W. (1994). *Recharging the American experiment: Principled pluralism for genuine civic community.* Grand Rapids, MI: Baker.

Slife, B. D., & Reber, J. S. (2009). Is there a pervasive bias against theism in psychology? *Journal of Theoretical and Philosophical Psychology, 29*(2), 63-79.

Slife, B. D., Reber, J. S., & Richardson, F. C. (2005). *Critical thinking about psychology: Hidden assumptions and plausible alternatives.* Washington, DC: American Psychological Association.

Smith, C. (2003). *The secular revolution: Power, interests, and conflict in the secularization of American public life.* Berkeley: University of California Press.

Smith, C., & Denton, M. L. (2005). *Soul searching: The religious and spiritual lives of American teenagers.* New York: Oxford University Press.

Smith, D. L. (1994). *With willful intent: A theology of sin.* Wheaton, IL: Victor.

Smith, E. M. (2002). *Healing life's deepest hurts.* Ann Arbor, MI: Servant.

Smith, H. W. (1952). *The Christian's secret of a happy life.* Westwood, NJ: Fleming H. Revell. (Original work published 1870)

Smith, J. K. A. (2009). *Desiring the kingdom.* Grand Rapids, MI: Baker.

———. (2012). Reforming public theology: Two kingdoms, or two cities? *Calvin Theological Journal, 47*, 122-37.

———. (2016). *You are what you love: The spiritual power of habit.* Grand Rapids, MI: Brazos.

Smith, T. B., McCullough, M. E., & Poll, J. (2003). Religiousness and depression: Evidence for the main effect and the moderating influence of stressful life events. *Psychological Bulletin, 129*(4), 614-36.

Snell, R. J., & Cone, S. D. (2013). *Authentic cosmopolitan: Love, sin, and grace in the Christian university.* Eugene, OR: Pickwick.

Snyder, C. R. (1994). *The psychology of hope.* New York: Free Press.

———. (Ed.). (2000). *Handbook of hope: Theory, measures, and applications.* San Diego, CA: Academic.

Snyder, C. R., Irving, L., & Anderson, J. R. (1991). Hope and health: Measuring the will and the ways. In C. R. Snyder & D. R. Forsyth (Eds.), *Handbook of social and clinical psychology: The health perspective* (pp. 285-305). Elmsford, NY: Pergamon.

Spero, M. H. (1992). *Religious objects as psychological structures: A critical integration of object relations theory, psychotherapy, and Judaism.* Chicago: University of Chicago Press.

Spiegel, J. S. (2005). *The benefits of providence.* Wheaton, IL: Crossway.

Spilka, B., & Ladd, K. L. (2013). *The psychology of prayer.* New York: Guilford.

Sprague, E. (1999). *Persons and their minds: A philosophical investigation.* Boulder, CO: Westview.

Spring, G. (1982). *The attraction of the cross.* Edinburgh: Banner of Truth Trust. (Original work published 1845)

Spurgeon, C. H. (1971). *Twelve sermons on the passion and death of Christ.* Grand Rapids, MI: Baker.

St. Clair, M. (2000). *Object relations and self psychology: An introduction* (3rd ed.). Belmont, CA: Wadsworth.

St. John of the Cross. (1959). *Dark night of the soul.* New York: Image Books.

Stanford, M. (2010). *The biology of sin: Grace, hope, and healing for those who feel trapped.* Fort Worth, TX: Authentic.

Stanford, M., & Philpott, D. (2011). Baptist senior pastors' knowledge and perceptions of mental illness. *Mental Health, Religion & Culture, 14*(3), 281-90.

Staub, E. (2003). *The psychology of good and evil.* New York: Cambridge University Press.

Steck, C. W., S.J. (2001). *The ethical thought of Hans Urs von Baltasar.* New York: Crossroad.

Stein, M. (1995). *Jung on evil*. Princeton, NJ: Princeton University Press.

Stern, D. (1985). *The interpersonal world of the infant*. New York: Basic Books.

Sternberg, R. J. (Ed.). (1998). *The nature of cognition*. Cambridge, MA: MIT Press.

———. (Ed.). (2000). *Handbook of intelligence*. New York: Cambridge University Press.

Stewart, J. S. (1975). *A man in Christ*. Grand Rapids, MI: Baker.

Stott, J. R. (1986). *The cross of Christ*. Downers Grove, IL: InterVarsity Press.

Strong, A. H. (1907). *Systematic theology*. Westwood, NJ: Revell.

Stump, E. (2010). *Wandering in darkness: Narrative and the problem of suffering*. New York: Oxford University Press.

Swann, W. B., & Pelham, B. W. (2002). The truth about illusions: Authenticity and positivity in social relationships. In C. R. Snyder & S. J. Lopez (Eds.), *Handbook of positive psychology* (pp. 366-81). Oxford: Oxford University Press.

Tamburello, D. E. (1994). *Union with Christ: John Calvin and the mysticism of St. Bernard*. Louisville, KY: Westminster John Knox.

Tan, S.-Y. (1996). Religion in clinical practice: Implicit and explicit integration. In E. Schafranske (Ed.), *Religion and the clinical practice of psychology* (pp. 365-90). Washington, DC: American Psychological Association.

———. (1999). The role of the Holy Spirit in counseling. In D. G. Benner & P. C. Hill (Eds.), *Baker encyclopedia of psychology* (2nd ed., pp. 568-69). Grand Rapids, MI: Baker.

———. (2011). *Counseling and psychotherapy: A Christian perspective*. Grand Rapids, MI: Baker Academic.

———. (2013). Resilience and posttraumatic growth: Empirical evidence and clinical applications from a Christian perspective. *Journal of Psychology and Christianity, 32* (4), 358-64.

Tan, S.-Y., & Gregg, D. H. (1997). *The disciplines of the Holy Spirit*. Grand Rapids, MI: Zondervan.

Tan, S.-Y., & Ortberg, J., Jr. (1995). *Understanding depression*. Grand Rapids, MI: Baker.

Tan, S.-Y., & Scalise, E. T. (2016). *Lay counseling: Equipping Christians for a helping ministry*. Grand Rapids, MI: Zondervan.

Tangney, J. P. (2002). Humility. In C. R. Snyder & S. J. Lopez (Eds.), *Handbook of positive psychology* (pp. 411-22). New York: Oxford University Press.

Tangney, J. P., & Dearing, R. L. (2002). *Shame and guilt*. New York: Guilford.

Tangney, J. P., & Fischer, K. (Eds.). (1995). *Self-conscious emotions*. New York: Guilford.

Tannehill, R. C. (2006). *Dying and rising with Christ: A study in Pauline theology*. Eugene, OR: Wipf & Stock. (Original work published 1967)

Tanner, K. (2000). Creation and providence. *The Cambridge companion to Karl Barth* (pp. 111-26). New York: Cambridge University Press.

———. (2001). *Jesus, humanity and the Trinity: A brief systematic theology.* Minneapolis: Fortress.

———. (2010). *Christ the key.* Cambridge: Cambridge University Press.

Tanquerey, A. (1930). *The spiritual life: A treatise on ascetical and mystical theology.* (H. Branderis, Trans.). Tournai, Belgium: Society of St. John the Evangelist.

Taylor, C. (1985a). The concept of a person. In *Human agency and language: Philosophical papers, 1* (pp. 97-114). Cambridge: Cambridge University Press.

———. (1985b). What is human agency? In *Human agency and language: Philosophical papers, 1* (pp. 15-44). Cambridge: Cambridge University Press.

———. (1989). *Sources of the self: The making of modern identity.* Cambridge, MA: Harvard University Press.

———. (1991). *The ethics of authenticity.* Cambridge, MA: Harvard University Press.

———. (2007). *A secular age.* Cambridge, MA: Harvard University Press.

Taylor, S. E. (1989). *Positive illusions: Creative self-deception and the healthy mind.* New York: Basic Books.

Taylor, S. E., & Brown, J. D. (1988). Illusion and well-being: A social psychological perspective on mental health. *Psychological Bulletin, 116,* 21-27.

Te Velde, R. A. (2011). The divine person(s): Trinity, person, and analogous naming. In G. Emery & M. Levering (Eds.), *The Oxford handbook of the Trinity* (pp. 359-70). Oxford: Oxford University Press.

Teissen, T. (2000). *Providence & prayer: How does God work in the world?* Downers Grove, IL: InterVarsity Press.

Tennen, H., & Affleck, G. (1993). The puzzles of self-esteem: A clinical perspective. In R. F. Baumeister (Ed.), *Self-esteem: The puzzle of low self-regard.* New York: Plenum.

Teresa of Àvila. (1961). *Interior castle.* (E. A. Peers, Trans.). New York: Doubleday. (Original work written 1577)

Teyber, E., McClure, F. H., & Weathers, R. (2011). Shame in families: Transmission across generations. In R. L. Dearing & J. P. Tangney (Eds.), *Shame in the therapy hour* (pp. 137-66). New York: Guilford.

Thielman, F. (2010). *Ephesians: Baker exegetical commentary on the New Testament.* Grand Rapids, MI: Baker Academic.

Thiselton, A. C. (2007). *The hermeneutics of doctrine.* Grand Rapids, MI: Eerdmans.

———. (2013). *The first epistle to the Corinthians.* Grand Rapids, MI: Eerdmans.

Thomas à Kempis. (1864). *On the imitation of Christ.* Boston: E. P. Dutton.

————. (2003). *The imitation of Christ* (reprint ed.). Minneapolis: Dover.

Thomas, G. (2002). *Sacred marriage: What if God designed marriage to make us holy more than to make us happy?* Grand Rapids, MI: Zondervan.

Thomas, R. (2006). *Passing from self to God: A Cistercian retreat.* Kalamazoo, MI: Cistercian.

Thompson, C. (2011). *Anatomy of the soul.* Wheaton, IL: Tyndale.

————. (2015). *The soul of shame.* Downers Grove, IL: InterVarsity Press.

Thompson, J. (1994). *Modern trinitarian perspectives.* Oxford: Oxford University Press.

Thompson, S. C. (2002). The role of personal control in adaptive functioning. In C. R. Snyder & S. J. Lopez (Ed.), *Handbook of positive psychology* (pp. 202-13). Oxford: Oxford University Press.

Thorndike, E. L. (1905). *The elements of psychology.* New York: A. G. Seiler.

Thurston, N. S. (2000). Psychotherapy with evangelical and fundamentalist Protestants. In P. S. Richards & A. E. Bergin (Eds.), *Handbook of psychotherapy and religious diversity* (pp. 131-54). Washington, DC: American Psychological Association.

Tidball, D. (2001). *The message of the cross.* Downers Grove, IL: InterVarsity Press.

Titelman, P. (2015). *Differentiation of self: Bowen family systems theory perspectives.* New York: Routledge.

Tjeltveit, A. C. (1986). The ethics of value conversion in psychotherapy. *Clinical Psychology Review, 6,* 515-37.

————. (1999). *Ethics and values in psychotherapy.* New York: Routledge.

Todd, T. W., Fujikawa, A., Halcrow, S. R., Hill, P. C., & Delaney, H. (2009). Attachment to God and implicit spirituality: Clarifying correspondence and compensation models. *Journal of Psychology and Theology, 37,* 227-44.

Tooby, J., & Cosmides, L. (2000) Toward mapping the evolved functional organization of mind and brain. In M. S. Gazzaniga (Ed.), *The new cognitive neuroscience* (2nd ed., pp. 1167-78). Cambridge, MA: MIT Press.

Toon, P. (1987). *Born again: A biblical and theological study of regeneration.* Grand Rapids, MI: Baker.

Torrance, T. F. (1949). *Calvin's doctrine of man.* London: Lutterworth.

————. (1976). *Space, time and resurrection.* Grand Rapids, MI: Eerdmans.

————. (1983). *The mediation of Christ.* Grand Rapids, MI: Eerdmans.

————. (1992). *The mediation of Christ* (2nd ed.). Colorado Springs: Helmer & Howard.

————. (2008). *Incarnation*. Downers Grove, IL: InterVarsity Press.

————. (2009). *Atonement*. Downers Grove, IL: InterVarsity Press.

Torrell, J.-P. (2003). *Saint Thomas Aquinas: Vol. 2. Spiritual master*. (R. Royal, Trans.). Washington, DC: Catholic University of America Press.

Toulmin, S., & Leary, D. E. (1992). The cult of empiricism in psychology and beyond. In S. Koch & D. E. Leary (Eds.), *A century of psychology as science* (pp. 594-617). Washington, DC: American Psychological Association.

Tournier, P. (1962). *Guilt and grace*. New York: Harper & Row.

Tripp, P. D. (2002). *Instruments in the redeemer's hands*. Phillipsburg, NJ: P&R.

Turiel, E. (1998). The development of morality. In W. Damon (Series Ed.) & N. Eisenberg (Vol. Ed.), *Handbook of child psychology: Vol. 3. Social, emotional, and personality development* (5th ed., pp. 863-932). New York: Wiley.

Turner, D. (2013). *Thomas Aquinas: A portrait*. New Haven, CT: Yale University Press.

Turrettin, F. (1992). *Institutes of elenctic theology*. (G. M. Giger, Trans.). Phillipsburg, NJ: P&R.

Twenge, J. M., & Campbell, W. K. (2010). *The narcissism epidemic: Living in the age of entitlement*. New York: Free Press.

Tyson, P., & Tyson, R. L. (1990). *Psychoanalytic theories of development: An integration*. New Haven, CT: Yale University Press.

Uchino, B. N. (2004). *Social support and physical health*. New Haven, CT: Yale University Press.

Vaden, M. B. (2015). The false self and the true self: A Christian perspective (Doctoral dissertation). Southern Baptist Theological Seminary, Louisville, KY.

Vaillant, G. E. (1977). *Adaptation to life*. Boston, MA: Little, Brown.

————. (1993). *Wisdom of the ego*. New York: Harvard.

Vaillant, L. M. (1997). *Changing character*. New York: Basic Books.

Van der Hart, O., Nijenhuis, E. R. S., & Steele, K. (2006). *The haunted self: Structural dissociation and the treatment of chronic traumatization*. New York: W. W. Norton.

Van Leeuwen, M. S. (1985). *The person in psychology*. Grand Rapids, MI: Eerdmans.

Van Til, C. (1955). *The defense of the faith*. Philadelphia: Presbyterian & Reformed.

————. (1969). *A Christian theory of knowledge*. Phillipsburg, NJ: Presbyterian & Reformed.

————. (1972). *Common grace and the gospel*. Phillipsburg, NJ: Presbyterian & Reformed.

————. (1976). *An introduction to systematic theology*. Philadelphia: Presbyterian & Reformed.

Van Til, H. R. (1959). *The Calvinistic concept of culture*. Grand Rapids, MI: Baker.

Vander Goot, M. (1987). *Healthy emotions: Helping children grow*. Grand Rapids, MI: Baker.

Vanhoozer, K. J. (1998). *Is there a meaning in this text?* Grand Rapids, MI: Zondervan.

———. (2000). The voice and the actor: A dramatic proposal about the ministry and minstrelsy of theology. In J. G. Stackhouse Jr. (Ed.), *Evangelical futures: A conversation on theological method* (pp. 61-106). Grand Rapids, MI: Baker.

———. (2002*). First theology: God, Scripture & hermeneutics*. Downers Grove, IL: InterVarsity Press.

———. (2004). The atonement in postmodernity: Guilt, goats and gifts. In C. E. Hill & F. A. James III (Eds.), *The glory of the atonement* (pp. 367-404). Downers Grove, IL: InterVarsity Press.

———. (2005). *The drama of doctrine*. Louisville, KY: Westminster John Knox.

———. (2010). *Remythologizing theology: Divine action, passion, and authorship*. New York: Cambridge University Press.

———. (2014). *Faith speaking understanding: Performing the drama of doctrine*. Louisville, KY: Westminster John Knox.

Vanier, J. (1971). *Eruption to hope*. Toronto: Griffin House.

Varillon, F. (1983). *The humility and suffering of God*. (N. Marans, Trans.). New York: Alba House.

Venning, R. (1965). *The plague of plagues*. Edinburgh: Banner of Truth. (Originally published in 1669)

Verduin, L. (1970). *Something less than God: The biblical view of man*. Grand Rapids, MI: Eerdmans.

Vining, J. K. (1995). *Spirit-centered counseling: A pneumascriptive approach*. East Rockaway, NY: Cummings and Hathaway.

Vitale, J. E., & Newman, J. P. (2013). Psychopathy as psychopathology: Key developments in assessment, etiology, and treatment. In W. E. Craighead, D. J. Micklowitz, & L. W. Craighead (Eds.), *Psychopathology: History, diagnosis, and empirical foundations* (2nd ed., pp. 583-615). New York: Wiley.

Vitz, P. C. (1988). *Sigmund Freud's Christian unconscious*. New York: Guilford.

———. (1994). *Psychology as religion: The cult of self-worship* (2nd ed.). Grand Rapids, MI: Eerdmans.

———. (1999). *Faith of the fatherless: The psychology of atheism*. New York: Spence.

Voetius, G., & Hoornbeeck, J. (2003). *Spiritual desertion*. Grand Rapids, MI: Baker.

Volf, M. (1998). *After our likeness: The church as the image of the Trinity*. Grand Rapids, MI: Eerdmans.

von Hildebrand, D. (2001). *Transformation in Christ: On the Christian attitude*. San Francisco: Ignatius. (Original work published 1948)

———. (2009). *The nature of love*. South Bend, IN: St. Augustine's Press.

Vos, G. (1948). *Biblical theology*. Grand Rapids, MI: Eerdmans.

———. (1952). *The Pauline eschatology*. Grand Rapids, MI: Eerdmans.

———. (1980). The eschatological aspect of the Pauline conception of the Spirit. In R. B. Gaffin Jr. (Ed.), *Redemptive history and biblical interpretation: The shorter writings of Geerhardus Vos* (pp. 91-125). Phillipsburg, NJ: Presbyterian & Reformed.

Voskamp, A. (2011). *One thousand gifts: A dare to live fully right where you are*. Grand Rapids, MI: Zondervan.

Vygotsky, L. (1978). *Mind in society: The development of higher psychological processes*. Cambridge, MA: Harvard University Press.

Wachholtz, A. B., & Austin, E. T. (2013). Contemporary spiritual meditation: Practices and outcomes. In K. I. Pargament (Ed.), *APA handbook of psychology, religion, and spiritual: Vol. 1. Context, theory, and research* (pp. 311-27). Washington, DC: American Psychological Association.

Wachtel, P. L. (2008). *Relational theory and the practice of psychotherapy*. New York: Guilford.

———. (2011). *Therapeutic communication: Knowing what to say when*. New York: Guilford.

Walker, D. F., Quagliana, H. L., Wilkinson, M., & Frederick, D. (2013). Christian-accommodative trauma-focused cognitive-behavioral therapy for children and adolescents. In E. L. Worthington Jr., E. L. Johnson, J. N. Hook, & J. D. Aten (Eds.), *Evidence-based practices for Christian counseling and psychotherapy* (pp. 101-21). Downers Grove, IL: InterVarsity Press.

Wall, B. S. (2016). *Welcome as a way of life*. Eugene, OR: Cascade.

Wallach, M., & Wallach, L. (1983). *Psychology's sanction for selfishness: The error of egoism in theory and therapy*. San Francisco: Freeman.

Wallerstein, J. S., Lewis, J. M., & Blakeslee, S. (2000). *The unexpected legacy of divorce: The 25-year landmark study*. New York: Hyperion.

Walsh, R., & Shapiro, S. L. (2006). The meeting of meditative disciplines and Western psychology: A mutually enriching dialogue. *American Psychologist, 61*, 227-39.

Wampold, B. E. (2010). *The basics of psychotherapy: An introduction to theory and practice*. Washington, DC: American Psychological Association.

Wardle, T. (2005). *Wounded: How to find wholeness and inner healing in Christ*. Abilene, TX: Leafwood.

Ware, B. (2005). *Father, Son, and Holy Spirit: Relationships, roles, and relevance*. Wheaton, IL: Crossway.

Warfield, B. B. (1956). Calvin's doctrine of the knowledge of God. In S. G. Craig (Ed.), *Calvin and Augustine* (pp. 29-132). Philadelphia: Presbyterian & Reformed.

———. (1970). The emotional life of our Lord. In S. G. Craig (Ed.), *The person and work of Christ* (pp. 93-148). Philadelphia: Presbyterian & Reformed.

Warnock, A. (2010). *Raised with Christ: How the resurrection changes everything.* Wheaton, IL: Crossway.

Watson, D. (2002). Positive affectivity. In C. R. Snyder & S. J. Lopez (Eds.), *Handbook of positive psychology* (pp. 106-19). Oxford: Oxford University Press.

Watson, J. B. (1925). *Behaviorism.* New York: People's Institute.

Watson, P. J. (1993). Apologetics and ethnocentrism: Psychology and religion within an ideological surround. *The International Journal for the Psychology of Religion, 3,* 1-20.

Watson, P. J., Morris, R. J., Loy, T., & Hamrick, M. B. (2007). Beliefs in sin: Adaptive implications in relationships with religious orientation, self-esteem, and measures of the narcissistic, depressed, and anxious self. *Edification, 1*(1), 57-68.

Watson, T. (1986). *All things for good.* Edinburgh: The Banner of Truth Trust. (Original work published 1663)

Weaver, A. J. (1995). Has there been a failure to support parish-based clergy in their role as frontline community mental health workers? A review. *The Journal of Pastoral Care, 49*(2), 129-49.

Weaver, J. D. (2001). *The nonviolent atonement.* Grand Rapids, MI: Eerdmans.

Weber, O. (1981). *Foundations of dogmatics: Vol. I.* (D. L. Guder, Trans.). Grand Rapids, MI: Eerdmans.

Webster, J. (2003). *Holy Scripture: A dogmatic sketch.* New York: Cambridge University Press.

Weeks, M. W., & Lupfer, M. B. (2000). Religious attributions and proximity of influence: An investigation of direct interventions and distal explanations. *Journal for the Scientific Study of Religion, 39,* 348-62.

Wegner, D. M. (2002). *The illusion of conscious will.* Cambridge, MA: MIT Press.

Weil, S. (1951). *Waiting for God.* New York: Harper.

Weinandy, T. G. (2000). *Does God suffer?* South Bend, IN: University of Notre Dame Press.

———. (2011). Trinitarian Christology: The eternal Son. In G. Emery & M. Levering (Eds.), *The Oxford handbook of the Trinity* (pp. 387-99). Oxford: Oxford University Press.

Weiner, B. (1995). *Judgments of responsibility: Foundations for a theory of social behavior.* New York: Guilford.

———. (2006). *Social Motivation, Justice, and the Moral Emotions*. New York: Guilford.

Weiner, B., & Graham, S. (1999). Attribution in personality psychology. In L. A. Pervin & O. P. John (Eds.), *Handbook of personality* (2nd ed., pp. 605-28). New York: Guilford.

Weisberg, R. (1993). *Creativity: Beyond the myth of genius* (2nd ed.). New York: Freeman.

Welch, E. (1998). *When people are big and God is small*. Phillipsburg, NJ: P&R.

———. *Addictions: A banquet in the grave*. Philipsburg, NJ: P&R.

———. *Shame interrupted*. Greensboro, NC: New Growth Press.

Wells, S. (2004). *Improvisation: The drama of Christian ethics*. Grand Rapids, MI: Brazos.

Wells, T., & Zaspel, F. (2002). *New covenant theology*. Frederick, MD: New Covenant Media.

Welton, G. L., Adkins, A. G., Ingle, S. L., & Dixon, W. A. (1996). God control: The fourth dimension. *Journal of Psychology and Theology, 24*, 13-25.

Werner, H. (1957). The concept of development from a comparative and organismic point of view. In D. B. Harris (Ed.), *The concept of development* (pp. 125-48). Minneapolis: University of Minnesota Press.

Wertsch, J. V. (1985). *Vygotsky and the social formation of mind*. Cambridge, MA: Harvard University Press.

Westermann, C. (1984). *Genesis 1-11*. Minneapolis: Augsburg.

White, M., & Epston, D. (1990). *Narrative means to therapeutic ends*. New York: W. W. Norton.

White, R. H. (1959). Motivation reconsidered: The concept of competence. *Psychological Review, 66*, 297-333.

Wilber, K. (2000). *Integral psychology: Consciousness, spirit, psychology, therapy*. Boston: Shambhala.

Wilken, R. L. (2003). *The spirit of early Christian thought*. New Haven, CT: Yale University Press.

Wilkinson, J. (1998). *The Bible and healing: A medical and theological commentary*. Grand Rapids, MI: Eerdmans.

Williams, R. (2004). Balthasar and the Trinity. In E. T. Oakes, S.J., & D. Moss (Eds.), *The Cambridge companion to Hans Urs von Balthasar* (pp. 37-50). New York: Cambridge University Press.

Wilson, S. D. (2002). *Released from shame*. Downers Grove, IL: InterVarsity Press.

Winnicott, D. W. (1965). *The maturational processes and the facilitating environment*. New York: International Universities Press.

Winter, R. (2005). *Perfecting ourselves to death: The pursuit of excellence and the perils of perfectionism.* Downers Grove, IL: InterVarsity Press.

Witherington, B., III. (1994). *Paul's narrative thought world: The tapestry of tragedy and triumph.* Louisville, KY: Westminster John Knox.

———. (2006). *Letters and homilies for Hellenized Christians.* Downers Grove, IL: InterVarsity Press.

Wolff, H. W. (1974). *Anthropology of the Old Testament.* Philadelphia: Fortress.

Wolfinger, N. H. (2005). *Understanding the divorce cycle.* New York: Cambridge University Press.

Wolters, A. M. (2005). *Creation regained: Biblical basics for a reformational worldview.* Grand Rapids, MI: Eerdmans.

Wolterstorff, N. (1983). *Until justice and peace embrace.* Grand Rapids, MI: Eerdmans.

———. (2005). The place of pain in the space of good and evil. In S. Coakley & K. K. Shelemay (Eds.), *Pain and its transformations: The interface of biology and culture* (pp. 406-19). Cambridge, MA: Harvard University Press.

Wong, P. T. P. (2014). From attunement to a meaning-centered good life: Book review of Daniel Haybron's *Happiness: A Very Short Introduction. Internal Journal of Wellbeing, 4*(2), 100-105.

Work, T. (2002). *Living and active: Scripture in the economy of salvation.* Grand Rapids, MI: Eerdmans.

Worthington, E. L., Jr. (2009). *A just forgiveness: Responsible healing without excusing injustice.* Downers Grove, IL: InterVarsity Press.

Worthington, E. L., Jr., Johnson, E. L., Hook, J., & Aten, J. (2013). *Evidence-based Christian psychotherapy and counseling.* Downers Grove, IL: InterVarsity Press.

Wright, J. H., Basco, M. R., & Thase, M. E. (2006). *Learning cognitive-behavior therapy: An illustrated guide.* Washington, DC: American Psychiatric Publishing.

Wright, N. T. (1992). *The climax of the covenant: Christ and the law in Pauline theology.* Minneapolis: Fortress.

Wright, R. (1995). *The moral animal: Why we are the way we are.* New York: Vintage.

Yankelovich, D. (1981). *New rules: Searching for self-fulfillment in a world turned upside-down.* New York: Random House.

Yarhouse, M. A., & Burkett, L. A. (2003). *Sexual identity: A guide to living between the times.* Washington, DC: University Press of America.

Yarhouse, M. A., Butman, R. E., & McRay, B. W. (2005). *Modern psychopathologies: A comprehensive Christian appraisal.* Downers Grove, IL: InterVarsity Press.

Yates, T. P. (1997). The supremacy of God in counseling: A leadership training program in illustrated Bible application. Unpublished doctoral disseration, Westminster Theological Seminary, Glenside, PA.

Yong, A. (2007). *Theology and Down syndrome: Reimagining disability in late modernity*. Waco, TX: Baylor University Press.

Young, F. M. (1990). *Face to face: A narrative essay in the theology of suffering*. Edinburgh: T&T Clark.

Young, J. E., Klosko, J. S., & Weishaar, M. E. (2003). *Schema therapy: A practitioner's guide*. New York: Guilford.

Young, W. A. (1995). *The world's religions: Worldviews and contemporary issues* (2nd ed.). Englewood Cliffs, NJ: Prentice Hall.

Zagzebski, L. T. (2004). *Divine motivation theory*. New York: Cambridge University Press.

Zahl, P. F. M. (2007). *Grace in practice: A theology of everyday life*. Grand Rapids, MI: Eerdmans.

Zizioulas, J. D. (1985). *Being as communion: Studies in personhood and the Church*. Crestwood, NY: St. Vladimir's Seminary Press.

———. (1991). On being a person: Toward an ontology of personhood. In C. Schwobel (Ed.), *Persons, divine and human* (pp. 33-46). Edinburgh: T&T Clark.

Zvolensky, M. J., Bernstein, A., & Vujanovic, A. A. (Eds.). (2011). *Distress tolerance: Theory, research, and clinical applications*. New York: Guilford.

Author Index

Subject Index

Scripture Index

Also by Eric L. Johnson

Foundations for Soul Care
978-0-8308-4054-0

Finding the Textbook You Need

The IVP Academic Textbook Selector
is an online tool for instantly finding the IVP books
suitable for over 250 courses across 24 disciplines.

---

ivpacademic.com
